DIFFUSION OF INNOVATIONS

Fifth Edition

EVERETT M. ROGERS

*f***P**

FREE PRESS

New York   London   Toronto   Sydney

*f*P

FREE PRESS
A Division of Simon & Schuster, Inc.
1230 Avenue of the Americas
New York, NY 10020

This Free Press trade paperback edition 2003

FREE PRESS and colophon are
trademarks of Simon & Schuster, Inc.

The first edition of this book, by Everett M. Rogers, was published as *Diffusion of Innovations;* the second edition, by Everett M. Rogers with F. Floyd Shoemaker, was published as *Communication of Innovations: A Cross-Cultural Approach;* the third edition, by Everett M. Rogers, was published as *Diffusion of Innovations,* as was the fourth edition.

For information regarding special discounts for bulk purchases,
please contact Simon & Schuster Special Sales at
1-800-456-6798 or business@simonandschuster.com

Designed by Nancy Singer Olaguera

Manufactured in the United States of America

10 9 8 7 6

Library of Congress Cataloging-in-Publication Data
Rogers, Everett M.
     Diffusion of innovations / Everett M. Rogers—5th ed.
        p. cm.
     Includes bibliographical references and index.
     1. Diffusion of innovations. 2. Diffusion of innovations—Study and teaching—History. I. Title.

HM621.R57 2003
303.48'4—dc21   2003049022

ISBN 0-7432-2209-1

*Dedicated to Bob Wallace, longtime editor of
Free Press, who had faith in five editions of this book*

Contents

PREFACE

This volume, the fifth edition of my book *Diffusion of Innovations,* builds on its predecessors by retaining the same basic diffusion model that originally appeared in the first edition in 1962. Over the past four decades, this general model of the diffusion of innovations has been modified somewhat and expanded, based on further research and on theoretical developments. What is new in the present edition of *Diffusion of Innovations* is (1) changes in the contributions of various diffusion traditions, with marketing, public health, and communication coming on particularly strong in recent years, (2) many studies of the diffusion of new communication technologies like the Internet and cellular telephones, (3) expanded understanding of diffusion networks through such concepts as the critical mass and individual thresholds, and (4) the use of field experiments (in addition to surveys) to test the effects of such diffusion interventions as using opinion leaders. Many of the case illustrations, and the figures that accompany certain of them, are new to this edition.

My introduction to research on the diffusion of innovations happened in the following manner. I became interested in the diffusion of agricultural innovations by observing farmers in my home community near Carroll, Iowa, who delayed for several years in adopting new ideas that could have been profitable for them. This behavior was puzzling—and frustrating—to me. Why didn't farmers adopt innovations? Factors other than just economic explanations must have been at work.

I had graduated from Iowa State University with a bachelor's degree in agriculture in 1952 and then served as an Air Force officer during the Korean War, when I learned the skills of applied social science research. After my discharge from military service, I returned to Iowa State for graduate work in rural sociology, to study the diffusion of agricultural innovations. At that time, Iowa State was one of the centers of diffusion research as a result of the hybrid seed corn study by Bryce Ryan and Neal C. Gross (1943).

In 1954, Professor George Beal at Iowa State University was initiating a diffusion project in one community, Collins, Iowa, located about twenty miles from Ames. This project was supported by the Iowa Agricultural Experiment Station, the research unit at Iowa State that had funded research to develop hybrid seed corn and other agricultural innovations. I joined Beal's diffusion project in spring, 1954, and within about a week of my discharge from the Air Force, I was participating in a graduate seminar on diffusion, taught by Beal. I read the Ryan and Gross (1943) paper about the diffusion of hybrid seed corn in two Iowa communities. Shortly thereafter, I began interviewing some of the 148 farmers in Collins about their adoption of 2,4-D weed spray and other agricultural innovations. Thus I became a diffusion scholar.

My doctoral dissertation in 1957 was an analysis of the diffusion of several agricultural innovations in the rural community of Collins. While reviewing literature for my dissertation, I encountered studies of the diffusion of kindergartens and of driver training among schools (Mort, 1953), as well as the spread of an antibiotic drug (tetracycline) among medical doctors (Menzel and Katz, 1955). The main findings were strikingly similar to the agricultural diffusion studies in which I was involved: an S-shaped rate of adoption over time, different sources or channels at different stages in the innovation-decision process for an individual, and a tendency for innovators (the first individuals in a system to adopt an innovation) to travel and read widely and to have a cosmopolite orientation. The review of literature chapter in my dissertation argued that diffusion was a *general process,* not bound by the type of innovation studied, who the adopters were, or by place or culture. I was convinced that the diffusion of innovations was a kind of universal process of social change.

Certainly one event that encouraged this type of thinking was a presentation on the diffusion of agricultural innovations by Professors George Beal and Joe Bohlen to the staff of the Iowa Extension Service in December 1954 in Ames. This dramatic presentation had grown out of the graduate seminar on diffusion in which I had enrolled the previous spring at Iowa State and focused (1) on the sources or channels of communication used at stages in the individual-level innovation-decision process, and (2) on characteristics of farmers who adopted relatively earlier and relatively later in the diffusion process. These were important steps toward generalizing a model of diffusion, although the Beal/Bohlen conceptualization was mainly oriented to farm innovations. Soon, however, Beal and Bohlen were being asked to give their presentation to audiences interested in civil defense (where the innovation of interest was building household bomb shelters) and household consumer products. Clearly, a more general diffusion model was being discussed.

After completing graduate work at Iowa State in 1957, I joined the rural sociology faculty at Ohio State University, where I conducted research on the diffusion of agricultural innovations among Ohio farmers. My argument for a generalized diffusion model led me to write the first edition of *Diffusion of Innovations*, which was published in 1962. This book summarized diffusion research findings to date, organized around a general diffusion model, and argued for more standardized ways of adopter categorization and for conceptualizing the diffusion process. In 1963–1964, I taught and conducted research on the diffusion process in peasant communities in Colombia as a Fulbright lecturer. This experience allowed me to test the universality of the diffusion model, such as whether the diffusion of innovations also characterized peasant villages in developing countries, where the mass media were rare and where social change was often just getting under way.

On my return to the United States, I accepted a faculty appointment in the Department of Communication at Michigan State University, then the seed institution for communication study in the United States (Rogers, 2001). This academic change fit with my vision for diffusion research: it would be more generalized, involving various disciplines, but with a firm grounding in communication theory. So my interest in a general diffusion model helped move me out of rural sociology (and the study of agricultural innovations) into the field of communication. I began to study the diffusion of health and family planning innovations in India and the diffusion of educational innovations among government secondary schools in Thailand. Eventually, the study of agricultural innovations by rural sociologists became somewhat passé in the face of farm surpluses (although it has made somewhat of a resurgence in recent years). But the diffusion model spread to many other academic fields.

This book is about regularities in the diffusion of innovations, patterns that have been found across cultures, innovations, and the people who adopt them. The diffusion of innovations explains social change, one of the most fundamental of human processes.

The four editions of my diffusion book (published in 1962, 1971, 1983, and 1995), each about a decade apart, mark turning points in the growth of the diffusion field. At the time the first edition of this book, *Diffusion of Innovations*, was published in 1962, there were 405 publications about this topic. The second edition (and revision), *Communication of Innovations: A Cross-Cultural Approach* (coauthored with F. Floyd Shoemaker), was published in 1971, nine years later. By then the number of diffusion publications had quadrupled, to about 1,500. Twelve years later, in 1983, when the third edition of *Diffusion of Innovations* appeared, the total number of diffusion publications had more than doubled again, to 3,085. The number of diffusion publications approached 4,000 when the fourth edition of *Diffusion of Innovations* was published in 1995. Today I estimate this number to be more than 5,200, and the field of diffusion continues to grow (at about the same rate of 120 diffusion publications per year that characterized the past four decades). No other field of behavior science research represents more effort by more scholars in more disciplines in more nations. The present book is based upon a yet broader foundation of diffusion research than the four earlier editions. I believe that the widespread diffusion of the Internet since about 1990 has changed the nature of the diffusion process in certain important ways, which are discussed in the present volume.

This book is both (1) a revision of the theoretical framework and the research evidence supporting this updated model of diffusion and (2) a new intellectual venture, in that certain new concepts and new theoretical viewpoints are introduced. The stream of diffusion scholarship over the past sixty years represents both similarities and differences, continuities and discontinuities, and so does this book. By no means, however, do I seek only to synthesize the important findings from past research; I also strive to criticize this work (including my own) and to suggest directions for the future that are different from those of the past. I have once again titled this book *Diffusion of Innovations* to identify it with the forty-year sequential tradition of diffusion studies marked by my 1962 book of the same title.

Most diffusion studies prior to 1962 were conducted in the United States and Europe. In the period between the first and second editions of my diffusion book, during the 1960s, an explosion occurred in the number of diffusion investigations that were being conducted in the developing countries of Latin America, Africa, and Asia. The classical diffusion model was usefully applied to the process of development that was a priority for these developing nations. The diffusion approach was a natural framework in which to evaluate the impacts of development programs in agriculture, family planning, public health, and nutrition. In studying the diffusion of innovations in developing nations, I (and others) gradually realized that certain limitations existed in the diffusion framework. In some cases, development programs outran the diffusion model on which they had originally been based. Certain modifications to the classical diffusion model were thus made.

This book reflects a more critical stance than its original ancestor. During the past forty years or so, diffusion research has grown to be widely recognized, applied, and admired, but it has also been subjected to constructive and destructive criticism. This criticism is due in large part to the stereotyped and limited ways in which many diffusion scholars have defined the scope and method of their field of study. Once diffusion researchers formed an "invisible college" (defined as an informal network of researchers who form around an intellectual paradigm to study a common topic), they began to limit unnecessarily the ways in which they went about studying the diffusion of innovations. Such standardization of approaches constrains the intellectual progress of diffusion research.

Social changes and the social problems facing the world, of course, affect the diffusion of innovations. Examples are the Internet, the AIDS epidemic, and world terrorism. The Internet has spread more rapidly than any other technological innovation in the history of humankind. The diffusion of the Internet exemplifies certain concepts, such as that of critical mass. The term *digital divide* indicates those individuals who are advantaged versus those who are relatively disadvantaged by the Internet and helps illuminate our understanding of inequality in the consequences of innovation. We draw on illustrations of Internet diffusion throughout this book. We suggest that such interactive communication technologies may be changing the diffusion process in certain fundamental ways, such as by removing, or at least greatly diminishing, the role of spatial distance in who talks to whom about a new idea.

The AIDS epidemic was first recognized in the United States in 1981, although we now know that it had antecedents going back several decades. The first HIV/AIDS prevention program to successfully halt the spread of the epidemic, STOP AIDS, was organized by gay men in

San Francisco in the mid-1980s and was based directly on the diffusion model. We analyze the STOP AIDS intervention in Chapter 2, along with the thousands of other HIV prevention programs around the world, all based to some degree on the San Francisco model. The AIDS epidemic today is concentrated in the developing world of Latin America, Africa, and Asia, where 95 percent of the 40 million people living with HIV/AIDS are located (Singhal and Rogers, 2003). The epidemic represents one of the world's gravest social problems, and we discuss here how the diffusion model has been, and could be, utilized to slow rates of infection (see Chapter 9).

World terrorism, culminating in the September 11, 2001, attacks on the World Trade Center and Pentagon, poses another challenge to society. This event has focused attention in gaining improved understanding of how Al Qaeda and similar terrorist networks function. We discuss the unique qualities of networks in Chapter 8. In certain important respects, the architects of the United States' antiterrorist efforts have not completely realized that a war on international terrorism is quite different from wars of the past, which were against nations.

The present book makes use of the important concepts of uncertainty and information. *Uncertainty* is the degree to which a number of alternatives are perceived with respect to the occurrence of an event and the relative probabilities of these alternatives. Uncertainty motivates individuals to seek information, as it is an uncomfortable state. *Information* is a difference in matter-energy that affects uncertainty in a situation where a choice exists among a set of alternatives (Rogers and Kincaid, 1981). One kind of uncertainty is generated by an *innovation,* defined as an idea, practice, or object that is perceived as new by an individual or another unit of adoption. An innovation presents an individual or an organization with a new alternative or alternatives, as well as new means of solving problems. However, the probability that the new idea is superior to previous practice is not initially known with certainty by individual problem solvers. Thus, individuals are motivated to seek further information about the innovation in order to cope with the uncertainty that it creates.

Information about an innovation is often sought from peers, especially information about their subjective evaluations of the innovation. This information exchange about a new idea occurs through a convergence process involving interpersonal networks. The diffusion of innovations is essentially a social process in which subjectively perceived information about a new idea is communicated from person to person.

The meaning of an innovation is thus gradually worked out through a process of social construction.

My thinking and writing about the diffusion of innovations have benefited a great deal in recent years from my collaboration with other diffusion scholars. Some are "rookies" in the diffusion field. My daily e-mail messages often contain a query from a young scholar or student asking for advice about a diffusion investigation that he or she is conducting. I learn from these exchanges, as I do from the undergraduate/ graduate course on the diffusion of innovations that I teach at the University of New Mexico. This volume benefits from such fresh questioning of an established framework, which helps advance it.

The help of several old pros in diffusion research and teaching are also acknowledged. Jim Dearing of Michigan State University, Pete Korsching of Iowa State University, Gary Meyer at Marquette University, Todd Shimoda at Colorado State University, Arvind Singhal at Ohio University, and Tom Valente at the University of Southern California. I stay in touch with this network of scholars, exchanging course outlines and publications. I also thank Andrew Rubey of the University of New Mexico for certain of the graphics in this book, and Everett Rogers-King for making the indexes.

Throughout this book, I seek to represent a healthily critical stance. We do not need more-of-the-same diffusion research. The challenge for diffusion scholars of the future is to move beyond the proven methods and models of the past, to recognize their shortcomings and limitations, and to broaden their conceptions of the diffusion of innovations. We offer this fifth edition as one step toward this important goal.

Everett M. Rogers
Albuquerque, New Mexico

DIFFUSION OF INNOVATIONS

Fifth Edition

1

ELEMENTS OF DIFFUSION

> There is nothing more difficult to plan, more doubtful of success, nor more dangerous to manage than the creation of a new order of things. . . . Whenever his enemies have the ability to attack the innovator, they do so with the passion of partisans, while the others defend him sluggishly, so that the innovator and his party alike are vulnerable.
>
> Niccolò Machiavelli, *The Prince* (1513)

Getting a new idea adopted, even when it has obvious advantages, is difficult. Many innovations require a lengthy period of many years from the time when they become available to the time when they are widely adopted. Therefore, a common problem for many individuals and organizations is how to speed up the rate of diffusion of an innovation. The following case illustration provides insight into some common difficulties facing diffusion campaigns.

---

*Water Boiling in a Peruvian Village: Diffusion That Failed**

The public health service in Peru attempts to introduce innovations to villagers to improve their health and lengthen their lives. This change agency encourages people to install latrines, burn garbage daily, control house flies, report cases of infectious diseases, and boil drinking water. These innova-

---

*This case illustration is based on Wellin (1955, pp. 71–103).

1

tions involve major changes in thinking and behavior for Peruvian villagers, who do not understand the relationship of sanitation to illness. Water boiling is an especially important health practice for Peruvian villagers. Unless they boil their drinking water, patients who are cured of an infectious disease in a medical clinic often return within a short time to be treated again for the same disease.

A two-year water-boiling campaign conducted in Los Molinas, a peasant village of two hundred families in the coastal region of Peru, persuaded only eleven housewives to boil water. From the viewpoint of the public health agency, the local health worker, Nelida, had a simple task: to persuade the housewives of Los Molinas to add water boiling to their pattern of daily behavior. Even with the aid of a medical doctor, who gave public talks on water boiling, and fifteen village housewives who were already boiling water, Nelida's diffusion campaign failed. To understand why, we need to take a closer look at the culture, the local environment, and the individuals in Los Molinas.

Most residents of Los Molinas are peasants who work as field hands on local plantations. Water is carried by can, pail, gourd, or cask. The three sources of water in Los Molinas include a seasonal irrigation ditch close to the village, a spring more than a mile away from the village, and a public well whose water most villagers dislike. All three sources are subject to pollution at all times and show contamination whenever tested. Of the three sources, the irrigation ditch is the most commonly used. It is closer to most homes, and the villagers like the taste of its water.

Although it is not feasible for the village to install a sanitary water system, the incidence of typhoid and other waterborne diseases could be greatly reduced by boiling water before it is consumed. During her two-year campaign in Los Molinas, Nelida made several visits to every home in the village and devoted especially intensive efforts to twenty-one families. She visited each of the selected families between fifteen and twenty-five times; eleven of these families now boil their water regularly.

What kinds of people do these numbers represent? We describe three village housewives: one who boils water to obey custom, one who was persuaded to boil water by the health worker, and one of the many who rejected the innovation.

Mrs. A: Custom-Oriented Adopter

Mrs. A is about forty and suffers from a sinus infection. The Los Molinas villagers call her the "sickly one." Each morning, Mrs. A boils a potful of water, which she uses throughout the day. She has no understanding of germ theory, as explained by Nelida. Her motivation for boiling water is a complex local custom of "hot" and "cold" distinctions. The basic principle of this belief system is that all foods, liquids, medicines, and other objects are inherently hot or cold, quite apart from their actual temperature. In essence, the hot-cold distinction serves as a series of avoidances and approaches in such behavior as pregnancy, child rearing, and the health-illness system.

Boiled water and illness are closely linked in the norms of Los Molinas. By custom, only the ill use cooked, or "hot" water. If an individual becomes ill, it is unthinkable to eat pork (very cold) or drink brandy (very hot). Extremes of hot and cold must be avoided by the sick; therefore, raw water, which is perceived to be very cold, must be boiled to make it appropriate.

Villagers learn from early childhood to dislike boiled water. Most can tolerate cooked water only if a flavoring, such as sugar, lemon, or herbs, is added. Mrs. A likes a dash of cinnamon in her drinking water. The village belief system does not involve the notion of bacteriological contamination of water. By tradition, boiling is aimed at eliminating the "cold" quality of unboiled water, not the harmful bacteria. Mrs. A drinks boiled water in obedience to local norms, because she perceives herself as ill. She adopted the innovation, but for the wrong reason.

Mrs. B: Persuaded Adopter

The B family came to Los Molinas a generation ago, but they are still strongly oriented toward their birthplace in the high Andes. Mrs. B worries about lowland diseases that she feels infest the village. It is partly because of this anxiety that the public health worker, Nelida, was able to convince Mrs. B to boil water. To Mrs. B, Nelida is a friendly authority (rather than a "dirt inspector," as she is seen by other housewives) who imparts useful knowledge and brings protection from uncertain threats. Mrs. B not only boils water but has also installed a latrine and sent her youngest child to the health center for a checkup.

Mrs. B is marked as an outsider in the community by her highland hairdo and stumbling Spanish. She will never achieve more than marginal social acceptance in the village. Because the community is not an important reference group to her, Mrs. B can deviate from the village norms on health innovations. With nothing to lose socially, Mrs. B gains in personal security by heeding Nelida's advice. Mrs. B's practice of boiling water has no effect in improving or damaging her marginal status. She is grateful to Nelida for teaching her how to neutralize the danger of contaminated water, which she perceives as a lowland peril.

Mrs. C: Rejector

This housewife represents the majority of Los Molinas families who were not persuaded by the efforts of the change agent during the two-year water-boiling campaign. In spite of Nelida's repeated explanations, Mrs. C does not understand germ theory. How, she argues, can microbes survive in water that would drown people? Are they fish? If germs are so small that they cannot be seen or felt, how can they hurt a grown person? There are enough real threats in the world to worry about—poverty and hunger—without bothering about tiny animals that one cannot see, hear, touch, or smell. Mrs. C's allegiance to traditional village norms is at odds with the boiling of water. A firm believer in the hot-cold superstition, she feels that only the sick should drink boiled water.

Why Did the Diffusion of Water Boiling Fail?

This intensive two-year campaign by a public health worker in a Peruvian village of two hundred families, aimed at persuading housewives to boil drinking water, was largely unsuccessful. Nelida was able to encourage only about 5 percent of the population, eleven families, to adopt the innovation. The diffusion campaign in Los Molinas failed because the innovation was perceived as culturally inappropriate by the villagers. Local tradition links hot foods with illness. Boiling water makes water less "cold" and hence appropriate only for the sick. If a person is not ill, he or she is prohibited by village norms from drinking boiled water. Only individuals who are not integrated into local networks risk defying the community norm on water boiling. An important factor regarding the adoption rate of an innovation is its compatibility with the values, beliefs, and past experiences of individuals in the social system. Nelida and her superiors in the public health agency should have understood the hot-cold belief system, as it is found throughout Peru (and in most nations of Latin America, Africa, and Asia). The indigenous knowledge system caused the failure of the diffusion effort for water boiling in Los Molinas.

Nelida's failure demonstrates the importance of interpersonal networks in the adoption or rejection of an innovation. Socially an outsider, Mrs. B was marginal to the Los Molinas community, although she lived there for several years. Nelida was a more important referent for Mrs. B than were her neighbors, who shunned her. Anxious to win reflected social prestige from the higher-status Nelida, Mrs. B adopted water boiling, not because she understood the correct health reasons but because she wanted to obtain Nelida's approval. Thus we see that the diffusion of innovations is a social process, even more than a technical matter.

Nelida worked with the wrong housewives if she wanted to launch a self-generating diffusion process in Los Molinas. She concentrated her efforts on village women such as Mrs. A and Mrs. B. Unfortunately, they were perceived as a sickly one and a social outsider, respectively, and were not perceived as social models of water-boiling behavior by the other women. The village opinion leaders, who could have activated local networks to spread the innovation, were ignored by Nelida. As a result, the rate of adoption of the innovation did not reach a critical mass, after which the diffusion process would have become self-sustaining.

How potential adopters view a change agent affects their willingness to adopt new ideas. In Los Molinas, Nelida was perceived differently by lower- and middle-status housewives. Most poor families saw the health worker as a "snooper" sent to Los Molinas to pry for dirt and to press already harassed housewives into keeping cleaner homes. Because the lower-status housewives had less free time, they were unlikely to talk with Nelida about water boiling. Their contacts outside the community were limited, and as a result, they saw the technically proficient Nelida with eyes bound by the traditional beliefs of Los Molinas. They distrusted this outsider, whom they perceived as a social stranger. Nelida, who was middle class by Los Molinas standards, was able to secure more positive results from housewives whose socioeconomic status and cultural background were more similar to hers. This tendency for more effective communication to occur with those who are more similar to a change agent occurs in most diffusion campaigns. Unfortunately, those individuals who most need the help provided by the change agent are least likely to accept it.

Nelida was "innovation-oriented" rather than "client-oriented." She was unable to put herself in the role of the village housewives, and thus her attempts at persuasion failed to reach her clients because the message did not suit their needs. Nelida talked to villagers about germ theory, which they could not (and did not need to) understand. These factors produced the diffusion failure in Los Molinas. Once the remainder of the book has been read, it will be easier to understand the water-boiling case.

What Is Diffusion?

Diffusion is the process in which an innovation is communicated through certain channels over time among the members of a social system. It is a special type of communication, in that the messages are concerned with new ideas. *Communication* is a process in which participants create and share information with one another in order to reach a mutual understanding. This definition implies that communication is a process of convergence (or divergence) as two or more individuals exchange information in order to move toward each other (or apart) in the meanings that they give to certain events. We think of communication as a two-way process of convergence, rather than as a one-way, linear act in which one individual seeks to transfer a message to another in order to achieve certain effects (Rogers and Kincaid, 1981). A linear conception of human communication may accurately describe certain communication acts involved in diffusion, such as when a change agent seeks to persuade a client to adopt an innovation. But when we look at what came before such an event and at what followed, we often realize that the event is only one part of a total process in which information is exchanged between the two individuals. For example, a client may go to a change agent with a specific problem, and the innovation may be recommended as a possible solution to this problem. The change agent–client interaction may continue through several cycles, as a process of information exchange.

Diffusion is a special type of communication in which the messages are about a new idea. This newness of the idea in the message content gives diffusion its special character. The newness means that some degree of uncertainty is involved in diffusion. *Uncertainty* is the degree to which a number of alternatives are perceived with respect to the occurrence of an event and the relative probability of these alternatives. Uncertainty implies a lack of predictability, of structure, of information. Information is a means of reducing uncertainty. *Information* is a difference in matter-energy that affects uncertainty in a situation where a choice exists among a set of alternatives (Rogers and Kincaid, 1981). A technological innovation embodies information and thus reduces uncertainty about cause-effect relationships in problem solving.

Diffusion is a kind of *social change,* defined as the process by which alteration occurs in the structure and function of a social system. When new ideas are invented, diffused, and adopted or rejected, leading to certain consequences, social change occurs. Of course, such change can happen in other ways, too; for example, a political revolution, a natural event such as a drought or an earthquake, or a government policy.

Some authors restrict the term "diffusion" to the spontaneous, unplanned spread of new ideas and use the concept of "dissemination" for diffusion that is directed and managed. In this book we use the word "diffusion" to include both the planned and the spontaneous spread of new ideas.

Controlling Scurvy in the British Navy*

Many technologists believe that advantageous innovations will sell themselves, that the obvious benefits of a new idea will be widely realized by potential adopters, and that the innovation will diffuse rapidly. Seldom is this the case. Most innovations, in fact, diffuse at a disappointingly slow rate, at least in the eyes of the inventors and technologists who create the innovations and promote them to others.

Scurvy control illustrates how slowly an obviously beneficial innovation spreads. In the early days of long sea voyages, scurvy killed more sailors than did warfare, accidents, and other causes. For instance, of Vasco da Gama's crew of 160 men who sailed with him around the Cape of Good Hope in 1497, 100 died of scurvy. In 1601, an English sea captain, James Lancaster, conducted an experiment to evaluate the effectiveness of lemon juice in preventing scurvy. Captain Lancaster commanded four ships that sailed from England on a voyage to India. He served three teaspoonfuls of lemon juice every day to the sailors in one of his four ships. These men stayed healthy. The other three ships constituted Lancaster's "control group," as their sailors were not given any lemon juice. On the other three ships, by the halfway point in the journey, 110 out of 278 sailors had died from scurvy. So many of these sailors got scurvy that Lancaster had to transfer men from his "treatment" ship in order to staff the three other ships for the remainder of the voyage.

These results were so clear that one would have expected the British Navy to promptly adopt citrus juice for scurvy prevention on all ships. Not until 1747, about 150 years later, did James Lind, a British Navy physician who knew of Lancaster's results, carry out another experiment on the *HMS Salisbury*. To each scurvy patient on this ship, Lind prescribed either two oranges and one lemon or one of five other supplements: a half pint of sea water, six spoonfuls of vinegar, a quart of cider, nutmeg, or seventy-five drops of vitriol elixir. The scurvy patients who got the citrus fruits were cured in a few days and were able to help Dr. Lind care for the other patients. Unfortunately, the supply of oranges and lemons was exhausted in six days.

Certainly, with this further solid evidence of the ability of citrus fruits to combat scurvy, one would expect the British Navy to have adopted this innovation for all ship's crews on long sea voyages. In fact, it did so, but not until 1795, forty-eight years later, when scurvy was immediately wiped out.

---

*This case illustration is based on Mosteller (1981).

After only seventy more years, in 1865, the British Board of Trade adopted a similar policy and eradicated scurvy in the merchant marine.

Why were the authorities so slow to adopt the idea of citrus for scurvy prevention? Other, competing remedies for scurvy were also being proposed, and each such cure had its champions. For example, Captain Cook's reports from his voyages in the Pacific did not provide support for curing scurvy with citrus fruits. Further, Dr. Lind was not a prominent figure in the field of naval medicine, and so his experimental findings did not get much attention. While scurvy prevention was generally resisted for years by the British Navy, other innovations, such as new ships and new guns, were readily accepted. So the Admiralty did not resist all innovations.

Obviously, more than just the relative advantages of an innovation, even when its benefits are clearly demonstrated, is necessary for its diffusion and adoption. The reader may think that such slow diffusion could only have happened in the distant past, before the contemporary era of scientific, experimental evaluations of innovations. On the contrary, consider the present-day case of the nondiffusion of the Dvorak keyboard.

Nondiffusion of the Dvorak Keyboard*

Most individuals who write on a computer do not realize that their fingers tap out words on a keyboard that is known as "QWERTY," named after the first six keys on the upper row of letters. The QWERTY keyboard is intentionally inefficient and awkward. This keyboard takes twice as long to learn as it should and makes us work about twenty times harder than necessary. But QWERTY has persisted since 1873, and today unsuspecting individuals are taught to use the QWERTY keyboard, unaware that a much more efficient keyboard is available. In recent years of talking about the QWERTY keyboard with hundreds of large audiences, the present author has never encountered *anyone* who uses an alternative.

Where did QWERTY come from? Why does it persist in the face of much more efficient alternative keyboard designs? QWERTY was invented by Christopher Latham Sholes, who designed this keyboard to slow down typists. In his day, the type bars on a typewriter hung down in a sort of bas-

---

*Further details on resistance to the Dvorak keyboard are found in Dvorak et al. (1936), Parkinson (1972), Lessley (1980), and David (1986).

ket and pivoted up to strike the paper; then they fell back into place by gravity. When two adjoining keys were struck rapidly in succession, they jammed. Sholes rearranged the keys on a typewriter keyboard to minimize such jamming; he "anti-engineered" the letter arrangement in order to make the most commonly used letter sequences awkward. By thus making it difficult for a typist to operate the machine and slowing down typing speed, Sholes's QWERTY keyboard allowed early typewriters to operate with a minimum of jamming. His design was then used in the manufacture of all typewriters. Early typewriter salesmen could impress customers by pecking out "TYPEWRITER" as all of the letters necessary to spell this word were found in the top row (QWERTYUIOP) of the machine.

Prior to 1900, most typists used the two-finger, hunt-and-peck system. Later, as touch typing became popular, dissatisfaction with the QWERTY typewriter began to grow. Typewriters became mechanically more efficient, and the QWERTY keyboard design was no longer necessary to prevent jamming. The search for an improved design was led by Professor August Dvorak at the University of Washington, who in 1932 used time-and-motion studies to create a much more efficient keyboard arrangement. Dvorak filmed people while they were typing and spent a decade analyzing which operations slowed them down. The Dvorak keyboard has the letters A,O,E,U,I,D,H,T,N, and S across the home row of the typewriter (Figure 1–1). Less frequently used letters were placed on the upper and lower rows of keys. About 70 percent of typing is done on the home row, 22 percent on the upper row, and 8 percent on the lower row. On the Dvorak keyboard, the amount of work assigned to each finger is proportionate to its skill and strength. Further, Professor Dvorak engineered his keyboard so that successive keystrokes fell on alternative hands; thus, while a finger on one hand is stroking a key, a finger on the other hand can be moving into position to hit the next key. Typing rhythm is thus facilitated; this hand alternation was achieved by putting the vowels (which represent 40 percent of all letters typed) on the left-hand side and the major consonants that usually accompany these vowels on the right-hand side of the keyboard.

Professor Dvorak was thus able to avoid the typing inefficiencies of the QWERTY keyboard. For instance, QWERTY overloads the left hand, which must type 57 percent of ordinary copy. The Dvorak keyboard shifts this emphasis to 56 percent on the stronger right hand and 44 percent on the weaker left hand (for a right-hander, as are 90 percent of the public). Only 32 percent of typing is done on the home row with the QWERTY system, compared to 70 percent with the Dvorak keyboard. The newer arrangement requires less jumping back and forth from row to row. With

Figure 1-1. Layout of the QWERTY and the Dvorak Keyboards.

The Dvorak keyboard is much more efficient for typists than the QWERTY keyboard, which was designed more than a century ago to slow down typists so as to prevent the jamming of keys on early typewriters. Yet almost no one has adopted the Dvorak keyboard. Superior technological innovations do not necessarily diffuse themselves.

the QWERTY keyboard, an efficient typist's fingertips travel more than twelve miles a day, jumping from row to row. These unnecessary, intricate movements cause mental tension and carpal tunnel syndrome and lead to more typographical errors. Typists typing on the Dvorak keyboard have broken all speed records.

One might expect, on the basis of its overwhelming advantages, that the Dvorak keyboard would have completely replaced the inferior QWERTY keyboard. On the contrary, after more than seventy years, almost all typists still use the inefficient QWERTY keyboard. Even though the American National Standards Institute and the Equipment Manufacturers Association have approved the Dvorak keyboard as an alternate design, it is still almost impossible to find a typewriter or a computer keyboard that is arranged in the more efficient layout. Vested interests are involved in hewing to the old design: manufacturers, sales outlets, typing teachers, and typists themselves. Unbeknown to most computer users, their machine that comes equipped with a QWERTY keyboard can easily be switched to a Dvorak keyboard. Nevertheless, a considerable effort, estimated at about a week's training, is required for someone accustomed to the QWERTY design to become proficient on a Dvorak keyboard.

Here we see that technological innovations are not always diffused and adopted rapidly, even when the innovation has obvious advantages. As the reader may have guessed by now, the present book was typed on a QWERTY keyboard.

Four Main Elements in the Diffusion of Innovations

Previously we defined *diffusion* as the process by which (1) an *innovation* (2) is *communicated* through certain *channels* (3) *over time* (4) among the members of a *social system*. The four main elements are the innovation, communication channels, time, and the social system (Figure 1–2). These elements are identifiable in every diffusion research study and in every diffusion campaign or program (such as the attempted diffusion of water boiling in a Peruvian village).

Figure 1-2. The Diffusion Process

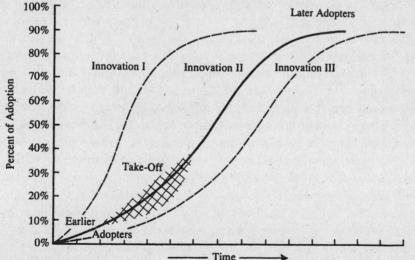

Diffusion is the process by which (1) an *innovation* (2) is *communicated* through certain *channels* (3) over *time* (4) among the members of a *social system*.

The following description of these four elements in diffusion constitutes an overview of the main concepts that will then be detailed in Chapters 2 through 11.

1. The Innovation

An *innovation* is an idea, practice, or object that is perceived as new by an individual or other unit of adoption. It matters little, so far as human behavior is concerned, whether or not an idea is "objectively" new as measured by the lapse of time since its first use or discovery. The perceived newness of the idea for the individual determines his or her reaction to it. If an idea seems new to the individual, it is an innovation.

Newness in an innovation need not just involve new knowledge. Someone may have known about an innovation for some time but not yet developed a favorable or unfavorable attitude toward it, nor have adopted or rejected it. "Newness" of an innovation may be expressed in terms of knowledge, persuasion, or a decision to adopt.

Among the important research questions addressed by diffusion scholars are (1) how earlier adopters differ from later adopters of an innovation (see Chapter 7), (2) how the perceived attributes of an innovation, such as its relative advantage, compatibility, and so on, affect its rate of adoption, whether relatively rapidly or more slowly, as is detailed in Chapter 6, and (3) why the S-shaped diffusion curve "takes off" at about 10 to 20 percent adoption, when interpersonal networks become activated so that a critical mass of adopters begin using an innovation (see Chapter 8). It should not be assumed that the diffusion and adoption of all innovations are necessarily desirable. Some harmful and uneconomical innovations are not desirable for either an individual or the social system. Further, the same innovation may be desirable for one adopter in one situation but undesirable for another potential adopter whose situation differs. For example, mechanical tomato pickers were adopted rapidly by large commercial farmers in California, but these machines were too expensive for small-sized tomato growers, and thousands of farmers were thus forced out of tomato production (see Chapter 4). Similarly, at present about half of U.S. households own a personal computer. The half who do not perceive that they have little use for a computer, or else they use a computer at work or in a cybercafé.

TECHNOLOGICAL INNOVATIONS, INFORMATION, AND UNCERTAINTY
Most of the new ideas whose diffusion has been analyzed are technologi-

cal innovations, and we often use the word "innovation" and "technology" as synonyms. A *technology* is a design for instrumental action that reduces the uncertainty in the cause-effect relationships involved in achieving a desired outcome. A technology usually has two components: (1) a *hardware* aspect, consisting of the tool that embodies the technology as a material or physical object, and (2) a *software* aspect, consisting of the information base for the tool. For example, we often speak of (1) "computer hardware," consisting of semiconductors, transistors, electrical connections, and a frame that protects these electronic components, and (2) "computer software," consisting of the coded commands, instructions, manuals, and other information aspects of this tool that allow us to use it for certain tasks. This example illustrates the close relationship between hardware and software, between a tool and the way it is used.

We often think of technology mainly in terms of hardware. Indeed, sometimes the hardware side of a technology is dominant. But in other cases, a technology may be almost entirely composed of information; examples are a political philosophy such as Marxism, a religious idea such as Christianity, a news event, and a policy such as a municipal no-smoking ordinance. The diffusion of such software innovations has been investigated, although a methodological problem in such studies is that their adoption cannot be so easily traced or observed. Such idea-only innovations have a relatively lower degree of observability and thus a slower rate of adoption.

A number of new products involve both a hardware component and a software component, with the hardware purchased first so that the software component can then be utilized. Examples are VCRs and videotapes, compact disc players and CDs, and personal computers and computer software programs. Often a company will sell a hardware product at a relatively low price in order to capture market share and then sell its software at a relatively high price in order to recover profits. An example is video game players; these are sold at a fairly low price, but the video games to be played on them are sold at a relatively high price. This "shaver-and-blades" strategy is commonly used to speed the diffusion of consumer electronics innovations.

Even though the software component of a technology is often not so apparent, we should not forget that a technology almost always represents a mixture of hardware and software. According to our definition, technology is a means of uncertainty reduction that is made possible by information about the cause-effect relationships on which the technology is based. This information often results from the scientific R&D activities that developed the technology. A technological innovation usually has at least some degree of benefit for its potential adopters, but this advantage is not always clear cut to those intended adopters. They are seldom certain that an innovation represents a superior alternative to the previous practice that it would replace, at least when they initially learn about it.

Knowing of a technological innovation creates uncertainty about its consequences in the mind of potential adopters. Will the innovation solve an individual's perceived problem? The potential advantage of a new idea impels an individual to exert effort to learn more about the innovation. Once such information-seeking activities reduce uncertainty about the innovation's expected consequences to a tolerable level, a decision concerning adoption or rejection can be made. If a new idea is then used, further evaluative information about its effects is obtained. Thus, *the innovation-decision process is essentially an information-seeking and information-processing activity in which an individual is motivated to reduce uncertainty about the advantages and disadvantages of the innovation* (see Chapter 5).

The main questions that an individual typically asks about a new idea include "What is the innovation?" "How does it work?" "Why does it work?" "What are the innovation's consequences?" and "What will its advantages and disadvantages be in my situation?"

TECHNOLOGY CLUSTERS An important conceptual and methodological issue is how to determine the boundaries around a technological innovation. The problem is how to determine where one innovation stops and another begins. If an innovation is defined as an idea that is perceived as new, the boundary question ought to be answered by the potential adopters who do the perceiving. In fact, this approach is used by diffusion scholars and by market researchers in "positioning" studies (described in Chapter 6). For example, some U.S. households that recycle paper also recycle bottles and cans, although many families recycle only paper. Presumably the two recycling behaviors represent two innovations that are part of an interrelated cluster of several recycling ideas. A *technology cluster* consists of one or more distinguishable elements of technology that are perceived as being closely interrelated. Some change agencies promote a "package" of innovations because they find that the innovations are thus adopted more rapidly. An example of a technology cluster was the package of rice- or wheat-growing innovations that led to the Green Revolution in the Third World countries of Latin America, Africa, and Asia. In addition to the so-called miracle varieties of rice or wheat, the cluster included chemical fertilizers, pesticides, and thicker planting of seeds. If the entire cluster were adopted by a farmer, crop yields approximately tripled.

Past diffusion research generally investigated each innovation as if it were independent from other innovations. This oversimplification represents a dubious assumption, in that an adopter's experience with one innovation obviously influences that individual's perception of the next innovation to diffuse through the individual's system. In reality, the innovations diffusing at about the same time in a system are interdependent. While it is much simpler for diffusion scholars to investigate the spread of each innovation as an independent event, this is a distortion of reality. More scholarly attention should be paid to technology clusters.

PERCEIVED ATTRIBUTES OF INNOVATIONS It should not be assumed, as it sometimes has been in the past, that all innovations are equivalent units of analysis. This assumption is a gross oversimplification. While consumer innovations such as cellular telephones and VCR's required only a few years to reach widespread adoption in the United States, other new ideas, such as using the metric system or seat belts in cars, require decades to reach complete use. The characteristics of innovations, as perceived by individuals, help to explain their different rates of adoption.

1. *Relative advantage* is the degree to which an innovation is perceived as better than the idea it supersedes. The degree of relative advantage may be measured in economic terms, but social prestige factors, convenience, and satisfaction are also important factors. It does not matter so much whether an innovation has a great deal of "objective" advantage. What does matter is whether an individual perceives the innovation as advantageous. The greater the perceived relative advantage of an innovation, the more rapid its rate of adoption will be.
2. *Compatibility* is the degree to which an innovation is perceived as being consistent with the existing values, past experiences, and needs of potential adopters. An idea that is incompatible with the values and norms of a social system will not be adopted as rapidly as an innovation that is compatible. The adoption of an incompatible innovation often requires the prior adoption of a new value system, which is a relatively slow process. An example of an incompatible innovation is the use of contraceptive methods in countries where religious beliefs discourage use of family planning, as in certain Muslim and Catholic nations. Previously in this chapter, we saw how

the innovation of water boiling was incompatible with the hot-cold belief system in the Peruvian village of Los Molinas.

3. *Complexity* is the degree to which an innovation is perceived as difficult to understand and use. Some innovations are readily comprehended by most members of a social system; others are more complicated and are adopted more slowly. For example, the villagers in Los Molinas did not understand germ theory, which the health worker tried to explain to them as a reason for boiling their drinking water. New ideas that are simpler to understand are adopted more rapidly than innovations that require the adopter to develop new skills and understandings, such as the Dvorak keyboard.

4. *Trialability* is the degree to which an innovation may be experimented with on a limited basis. New ideas that can be tried on the installment plan will generally be adopted more quickly than innovations that are not divisible. Ryan and Gross (1943) found that every one of their Iowa farmer respondents adopted hybrid seed corn by first trying it on a partial basis. If the new seed could not have been sampled experimentally, its rate of adoption would have been much slower. Even then, many years of trial occurred before the typical Iowa farmer planted 100 percent of his corn acreage in hybrid seed. An innovation that is trialable represents less uncertainty to the individual who is considering it for adoption, as it is possible to learn by doing.

5. *Observability* is the degree to which the results of an innovation are visible to others. The easier it is for individuals to see the results of an innovation, the more likely they are to adopt. Such visibility stimulates peer discussion of a new idea, as the friends and neighbors of an adopter often request innovation evaluation information about it. Solar water-heating adopters, for example, are often found in neighborhood clusters in California, with three or four adopters located on the same block. Many other city blocks have no solar flat-plate collectors. The clustering of visible innovations is one evidence for the importance of observbility (and peer-to-peer networks). Other consumer innovations, such as home computers, are relatively low in observability and thus diffuse more slowly.

Innovations that are perceived by individuals as having greater relative advantage, compatibility, trialability, and observability and less complexity will be adopted more rapidly than other innovations. Past research indicates that these five qualities are the most important characteristics of innovations in explaining the rate of adoption. The first two attributes, relative advantage and compatability, are particularly important in explaining an innovation's rate of adoption.

RE-INVENTION For the first several decades of diffusion research, it was assumed that an innovation was an invariant quality that did not change as it diffused. I remember interviewing an Iowa farmer during my Ph.D. dissertation research at Iowa State University in 1954. I inquired about his adoption of 2,4-D weed spray. The farmer described in some detail the particular and unusual ways in which he used the weed spray on his farm. At the end of his lengthy remarks, I simply checked "adopter" on my interview questionnaire. The concept of re-invention was not yet in my theoretical repertoire, so I condensed the farmer's experience into my existing categories.

In the 1970s, diffusion scholars began to study the concept of *re-invention*, defined as the degree to which an innovation is changed or modified by a user in the process of adoption and implementation. Some researchers measure re-invention as the degree to which an individual's use of a new idea departs from the core or "mainline" version of the innovation promoted by a change agency (Eveland et al., 1977). Once scholars became aware of the concept of re-invention and began to measure it, they began to find that a considerable degree of re-invention had occurred for many innovations. Some innovations are difficult or impossible to re-invent; for example, hybrid seed corn does not allow a farmer much freedom to re-invent, as the hybrid vigor is genetically locked into the seed for only the first generation. Similarly, genetically modified (GM) corn seeds were sold in the early 2000s with a "killer gene" that destroys insects (such as European corn borers, an important pest, but also, unfortunately, many monarch butterfly caterpillars) when they eat the corn leaves. The second generation of this seed will not germinate, forcing the farmer to purchase new GM seed corn each year.

Certain other innovations are more flexible in nature, and they are re-invented by many adopters who implement them in a wide variety of different ways. An innovation is not necessarily invariant during the process of its diffusion. And adopting an innovation is not necessarily a passive role of just implementing a standard template of the new idea. Many adopters want to participate actively in customizing an innovation to fit their unique situation. Later in this book, we show that an innovation diffuses more rapidly when it can be re-invented and that its adoption is more likely to be sustained.

Given that an innovation exists, communication must take place if the innovation is to spread. We now turn our attention to this second element in the diffusion process.

2. Communication Channels

Previously we defined *communication* as the process by which participants create and share information with one another in order to reach a mutual understanding. Diffusion is a particular type of communication in which the message content that is exchanged is concerned with a new idea. The essence of the diffusion process is the information exchange through which one individual communicates a new idea to one or several others. At its most elementary form, the process involves (1) an innovation, (2) an individual or other unit of adoption that has knowledge of, or has experienced using, the innovation, (3) another individual or other unit that does not yet have knowledge of, or experience with, the innovation, and (4) a communication channel connecting the two units. A *communication channel* is the means by which messages get from one individual to another. The nature of the information exchange relationship between a pair of individuals determines the conditions under which a source will or will not transmit the innovation to the receiver and the effect of such a transfer.

Mass media channels are usually the most rapid and efficient means of informing an audience of potential adopters about the existence of an innovation—that is, to create awareness-knowledge. *Mass media channels* are all those means of transmitting messages that involve a mass medium, such as radio, television, newspapers, and so on, which enable one or a few individuals to reach an audience of many. On the other hand, interpersonal channels are more effective in persuading an individual to accept a new idea, especially if the interpersonal channel links two or more individuals who are similar in socioeconomic status, education, or other important ways. *Interpersonal channels* involve a face-to-face exchange between two or more individuals. In addition to mass media and interpersonal communication channels, interactive communication via the Internet has become more important for the diffusion of certain innovations in recent decades.

Diffusion investigations show that most individuals do not evaluate an innovation on the basis of scientific studies of its consequences, although such objective evaluations are not entirely irrelevant, especially to the very first individuals who adopt. Instead, most people depend mainly upon a subjective evaluation of an innovation that is conveyed to them from other individuals like themselves who have already adopted the innovation. This dependence on the experience of near peers suggests that the heart of the diffusion process consists of the modeling and imitation by potential adopters of their network partners who have previously adopted. Diffusion is a very social process that involves interpersonal communication relationships (see Chapter 8).

HETEROPHILY AND DIFFUSION An obvious principle of human communication is that the transfer of ideas occurs most frequently between two individuals who are similar, or homophilous. *Homophily* is the degree to which two or more individuals who interact are similar in certain attributes, such as beliefs, education, socioeconomic status, and the like. In a free-choice situation, when an individual can interact with any one of a number of other individuals, the tendency is to select someone who is very similar. *Heterophily,* the opposite of homophily, is defined as the degree to which two or more individuals who interact are different in certain attributes.

Homophily occurs when similar individuals belong to the same groups, live or work near each other, and share similar interests. Physical and social propinquity makes homophilous communication more likely to occur than heterophilous communication. Such communication is also more likely to be effective and thus to be rewarding to the participants. More effective communication occurs when two or more individuals are homophilous. When they share common meanings and a mutual subcultural language, and are alike in personal and social characteristics, the communication of new ideas is likely to have greater effects in terms of knowledge gain, attitude formation and change, and overt behavior change. When homophily is present, communication is therefore likely to be rewarding to both participants.

One of the most distinctive problems in the diffusion of innovations is that the participants are usually quite heterophilous. A change agent, for instance, is more technically competent than his or her clients. This difference frequently leads to ineffective communication as the two individuals do not speak the same language. However, when two individuals are identical regarding their technical grasp of an innovation, diffusion cannot occur as there is no new information to exchange. The nature of diffusion demands that at least some degree of heterophily be present between the two participants in the communication process. Ideally, the individuals would be homophilous on all other variables (education, socioeconomic status, and the like) even though they are heterophilous regarding the innovation. Usually, however, the two individuals are heterophilous on all of these variables because knowledge of, and experience with, an innovation are highly related to socioeconomic status, education, and so forth.

3. Time

Time is a third element in the diffusion process. Much other behavioral science research is timeless in the sense that the time dimension is simply ignored or does not matter. The inclusion of time as a variable in diffusion research is one of its strengths, but the measurement of the time dimension (often by means of the respondents' recall) can be criticized (see Chapter 3). The time dimension is involved in diffusion in (1) the innovation-decision process by which an individual passes from first knowledge of an innovation through its adoption or rejection, (2) the innovativeness of an individual or other unit of adoption (that is, the relative earliness/lateness with which an innovation is adopted) compared with other members of a system, and (3) an innovation's rate of adoption in a system, usually measured as the number of members of the system who adopt the innovation in a given time period.

THE INNOVATION-DECISION PROCESS The *innovation-decision process* is the process through which an individual (or other decision-making unit) passes from first knowledge of an innovation, to the formation of an attitude toward the innovation, to a decision to adopt or reject, to implementation and use of the new idea, and to confirmation of this decision. We conceptualize five main steps in the innovation-decision process: (1) knowledge, (2) persuasion, (3) decision, (4) implementation, and (5) confirmation.

Knowledge is gained when an individual (or other decision-making unit) learns of the innovation's existence and gains some understanding of how it functions. *Persuasion* takes place when an individual forms a favorable or unfavorable attitude toward the innovation. *Decision* occurs when an individual engages in activities that lead to a choice to adopt or reject the innovation. *Implementation* takes place when an individual puts an innovation into use. Re-invention is especially likely to occur at the implementation stage. *Confirmation* occurs when an individual seeks reinforcement of an innovation-decision that has already been made, but he or she may reverse this previous decision if exposed to conflicting messages about the innovation.

The innovation-decision process is an information-seeking and information-processing activity in which an individual obtains information in order to gradually decrease uncertainty about the innovation. At the knowledge stage, an individual mainly seeks software information that is embodied in the technological innovation, information that reduces uncertainty about the cause-effect relationships that are involved in the innovation's capacity to solve a problem. At this stage the individual wants to know what the innovation is and how and why it works. Mass media channels can effectively transmit such software information.

But increasingly at the persuasion stage, and especially at the decision stage, an individual seeks innovation-evaluation information in order to reduce uncertainty about an innovation's expected consequences. Here an individual wants to know the innovation's advantages and disadvantages for his or her own particular situation. Interpersonal communication networks with near peers are particularly likely to convey such evaluative information about an innovation. Mass media channels are not very important at this stage because their messages are general in nature, and an individual deciding to adopt wants to know specific information: Will the innovation be beneficial to me in my particular situation? Subjective evaluations of a new idea by other individuals are especially likely to influence an individual at the decision stage, and perhaps at the confirmation stage.

The innovation-decision process can lead to either *adoption,* a decision to make full use of an innovation as the best course of action available, or *rejection,* a decision not to adopt an innovation. Such decisions can be reversed at a later point. For example, *discontinuance* is a decision to reject an innovation after it has previously been adopted. Discontinuance may occur because an individual becomes dissatisfied with an innovation or because the innovation is replaced with an improved idea. It is also possible for an individual to adopt an innovation after a previous decision to reject it. Such later adoption and discontinuance occur during the confirmation stage of the innovation-decision process.

The innovation-decision process involves time in the sense that the five steps usually occur in a time-ordered sequence of (1) knowledge, (2) persuasion, (3) decision, (4) implementation, and (5) confirmation. Exceptions to the usual sequence of these five stages may occur for some individuals under some conditions, such as when the decision stage precedes the persuasion stage (perhaps an individual was ordered to adopt by some authority figure).

The *innovation-decision period* is the length of time required to pass through the innovation-decision process. Individuals vary in this innovation-decision period, with some people requiring many years to adopt an innovation, while other people move rapidly from knowledge to implementation.

The present discussion of the innovation-decision process is mainly at the level of a single individual and of individual-optional innovation-decisions. But many innovation-decisions are made by organizations, communities, or other types of adopting units, rather than by individuals. For example, an organization may decide to implement an e-mail system on the basis of a staff decision or an official's authority decision. An individual employee in the organization may have little or no say in this innovation-decision. When an innovation-decision is made by a system, rather than by an individual, the decision process is more complicated because a number of individuals are involved (see Chapter 10).

So time is an important dimension in the innovation-decision process.

INNOVATIVENESS AND ADOPTER CATEGORIES *Innovativeness* is the degree to which an individual or other unit of adoption is relatively earlier in adopting new ideas than the other members of a system. Rather than describing an individual as "less innovative than the average member of a social system," it is more efficient to refer to the individual as being in the "late majority" or in some other adopter category. This shorthand notation saves words and contributes to clearer understanding. Diffusion research shows that members of each of the adopter categories have a great deal in common. If the individual is like most others in the late majority category, he or she is of relatively lower socioeconomic status, makes little use of mass media channels, and learns about most new ideas from peers via interpersonal communication channels. *Adopter categories,* the classifications of members of a social system on the basis of innovativeness, include: (1) innovators, (2) early adopters, (3) early majority, (4) late majority, and (5) laggards.

Innovators are active information seekers about new ideas. They have a high degree of mass media exposure, and their interpersonal networks extend over a wide area, reaching outside their local system. Innovators are able to cope with higher levels of uncertainty about an innovation than are other adopter categories. As the first to adopt a new idea, they cannot depend upon the subjective evaluations of the innovation from other members of their system. We shall present a concise word picture of each of the adopter categories in Chapter 7.

The measure of innovativeness and the classification of a system's members into adopter categories are based upon the relative time at which an innovation is adopted.

RATE OF ADOPTION A third way in which the time dimension is involved in the diffusion of innovations concerns the *rate of adoption*, defined as the relative speed with which an innovation is adopted by members of a social system. When the number of individuals adopting a new idea is plotted on a cumulative frequency basis over time, the resulting distribution is an S-shaped curve. At first, only a few individuals adopt the innovation in each time period (a year or a month, for example); these are the innovators. Soon the diffusion curve begins to climb, as more and more individuals adopt in each succeeding time period. Eventually, the trajectory of the rate of adoption begins to level off, as fewer and fewer individuals remain who have not yet adopted the innovation. Finally, the S-shaped curve reaches its asymptote, and the diffusion process is finished.

Most innovations have an S-shaped rate of adoption. But there is variation in the slope of the "S" from innovation to innovation; some new ideas diffuse relatively rapidly, and the S-curve is quite steep. Other innovations have a slower rate of adoption, and the S-curve is more gradual, with a slope that is relatively lazy. One issue addressed by diffusion research is why some innovations have a rapid rate of adoption, while others are adopted more slowly (see Chapter 6).

The rate of adoption is usually measured by the length of time required for a certain percentage of the members of a system to adopt an innovation. Therefore, we see that the rate of adoption is measured for an innovation in a system, rather than for an individual as the unit of analysis (this variable is innovativeness). The system may be a community, an organization, or some other structure. Innovations that are perceived by individuals as possessing greater relative advantage, compatibility, and the like, have a more rapid rate of adoption, as discussed previously.

There are also differences in the rate of adoption for the same innovation in different social systems. Many aspects of diffusion cannot be explained by just individual behavior. The system has a direct effect on diffusion through its norms and other system-level qualities, as well as an indirect influence through the behavior of its individual members.

4. A Social System

A *social system* is defined as a set of interrelated units that are engaged in joint problem solving to accomplish a common goal. The members or units of a social system may be individuals, informal groups, organizations, and/or subsystems. The system analyzed in a diffusion study may consist of all the peasant families in a Peruvian village, medical doctors in a hospital, or all the consumers in the United States. Each unit in a social system can be distinguished from other units. All members cooperate at least to the extent of seeking to solve a common problem in order to reach a mutual goal. This sharing of a common objective binds the system together.

Diffusion occurs within a social system. The social structure of the system affects the innovation's diffusion in several ways. The social system constitutes a boundary within which an innovation diffuses. Here we deal with how the system's social structure affects diffusion, the effect of norms on diffusion, the roles of opinion leaders and change agents, types of innovation-decisions, and the consequences of innovation. Each of these issues involves relationships between the social system and the diffusion process that occurs within it.

SOCIAL STRUCTURE AND DIFFUSION To the extent that the units in a social system are not all identical in their behavior, structure exists in a system. We define *structure* as the patterned arrangements of the units in a system. This structure gives regularity and stability to human behavior in a system; it allows one to predict behavior with some degree of accuracy. Thus, structure represents a type of information, in that it decreases uncertainty. An illustration of this predictability is provided by structure in a bureaucratic organization such as a government agency. The well-developed social structure in such a system consists of hierarchial positions, giving individuals in higher-ranked positions the right to issue orders to individuals of lower rank. Their orders are expected to be carried out. Such patterned social relationships among the members of a system constitute *social structure*, one type of structure.

In addition to this formal structure among the units in a social system, an informal structure also exists in the interpersonal networks linking a system's members, tracing who interacts with whom and under what circumstances. We define such *communication structure* as the differentiated elements that can be recognized in the patterned communication flows in a system. Previously we defined homophily as the degree to which two or more individuals in a system talk with others who are similar to them. A communication structure is thus often created in a system in which homophilous sets of individuals are grouped together in cliques. A complete lack of communication structure in a system would be represented by a situation in which each individual talked with equal probability to each other member of the system. This situation might occur when complete strangers first come together. However, regular patterns soon begin to occur in the communication network of the system. These aspects of communication structure predict, in part, the behavior of individual members of the social system, including when they adopt an innovation.

The structure of a social system can facilitate or impede the diffusion of innovations. The impact of the social structure on diffusion is of special interest to sociologists and social psychologists, and the way in which the communication structure of a system affects diffusion is a particularly interesting topic for communication scholars. Katz (1961) remarked, "It is as unthinkable to study diffusion without some knowledge of the social structures in which potential adopters are located as it is to study blood circulation without adequate knowledge of the veins and arteries."

Compared to other aspects of diffusion research, however, there have been relatively few studies of how the social or communication structure affects the diffusion and adoption of innovations in a system. It is a rather complicated matter to untangle the effects of a system's structure on diffusion, independent from the effects of the characteristics of individuals that make up the system. Consider an illustration of *system effects,* the influences of the structure and/or composition of a system on the behavior of the members of the system. Rogers and Kincaid (1981) identified two Korean women in their study of the diffusion of family planning in Korea. Both women are illiterate, are married, have two children, and are twenty-nine years of age. The husbands of both women are high school graduates; each operates a farm of five acres. One might expect that both women would be about equally likely, or unlikely, to adopt a new contraceptive method.

But the women are different in one crucial respect: they live in different villages, one in Village A and one in Village B. Family-planning methods have been adopted by 57 percent of the eligible couples in Village A and by only 26 percent in Village B. The social and communication structures of these two villages are quite different regarding the diffusion of contraceptives, even though contraceptives were promoted equally in both villages by the national family-planning program. We predict that the woman in Village A will be more likely to adopt a contraceptive method than her counterpart in Village B because of system effects: Mrs. A's friends and neighbors are more likely to encourage her to adopt since they themselves have adopted, and the village leaders in Village A are especially committed to family planning, while in Village B they are not.

This example shows how a system's structure can affect the diffusion and adoption of innovations, over and above the effect of such variables as the individual characteristics of the members of the system. Individual innovativeness is affected both by an individual's characteristics and by the nature of the social system in which the individual is a member.

SYSTEM NORMS AND DIFFUSION The Korean investigation by Rogers and Kincaid (1981) also illustrates the importance of village norms in affecting the rate of adoption of innovations. For example, their study of twenty-four Korean villages found large differences from village to village, both in the level of adoption of family-planning and in the adoption of particular types of family-planning methods. One village had 51 percent adoption of the intrauterine device (IUD) and only one vasectomy adopter, while another village had 23 percent adoption of vasectomy. Yet another was a "pill village" in which all the adopters of family planning decided to use contraceptive pills. These differences were not due to the nature of the national family-planning program in Korea, which had promoted the same "cafeteria" of contraceptive methods in all villages for ten years prior to our data gathering. The main explanation for the different contraceptive behavior from village to village was these systems' norms.

Norms are the established behavior patterns for the members of a social system. Norms define a range of tolerable behavior and serve as a guide or standard for the behavior of members of a social system. The norms of a system tell individuals what behavior they are expected to perform.

A system's norms can be a barrier to change, as in the previous example of water boiling in a Peruvian community. Such resistance to new ideas is often found in norms on food habits. In India, for example, sacred cows roam the countryside while millions of people are malnourished. Pork is not consumed by Muslims and Jews. Polished white rice is eaten in most of Asia and the United States, even though whole rice is much more nutritious. These are examples of cultural and religious norms. Norms can operate at the level of a nation, a religious community, an organization, or a local system such as a village.

OPINION LEADERS AND CHANGE AGENTS The most innovative member of a system is very often perceived as a deviant from the social system and is accorded a status of low credibility by the average members of the system. This individual's role in diffusion (especially in persuading others to adopt the innovation) is therefore very limited. Certain other members of the system function as opinion leaders. They provide information and advice about innovations to many other individuals in the system.

Opinion leadership is the degree to which an individual is able to influence other individuals' attitudes or overt behavior informally in a desired way with relative frequency. This informal leadership is not a function of the individual's formal position or status in the system. Opinion leadership is earned and maintained by the individual's technical competence, social accessibility, and conformity to the system's norms. When the social system is oriented to change, the opinion leaders are more innovative; but when the system's norms are opposed to change, the behavior of the leaders also reflects this norm. Through their conformity to the system's norms, opinion leaders serve as a model for the innovation behavior of their followers. Opinion leaders thus exemplify and express the system's structure.

Many systems have both innovative opinion leaders and leaders who oppose change. Influential persons can lead in the spread of new ideas, or they can head an active opposition. When opinion leaders are compared with their followers, they (1) are more exposed to all forms of external communication and thus are somewhat more cosmopolite, (2) have somewhat higher socioeconomic status, and (3) are more innovative (although their degree of innovativeness depends, in part, on the system's norms). The most striking characteristic of opinion leaders is their unique and influential position in their system's communication structure: they are at the center of interpersonal communication networks. A *communication network* consists of interconnected individuals who are linked by patterned flows of information. An opinion leader's interpersonal networks allow him or her to serve as a social model whose innovative behavior is imitated by many other members of the system. The respect with which the opinion leader is held can be lost, however, if an opinion leader deviates too far from the norms of the system. Opinion leaders can be "worn out" by change agents who overuse them in diffusion activities. Opinion leaders may begin to be perceived by their peers as too much like professional change agents and therefore lose their credibility with their former followers.

Opinion leaders are members of the social system in which they exert their influence. A different kind of individual with influence in the system is professionals who represent change agencies external to the system. A *change agent* is an individual who influences clients' innovation-decisions in a direction deemed desirable by a change agency. The change agent usually seeks to obtain the adoption of new ideas but may also attempt to slow down diffusion and prevent the adoption of undesirable innovations. Change agents often use opinion leaders in a social system as their lieutenants in diffusion activities.

Change agents are usually professionals with a university degree in a technical field. This professional training, and the social status that goes with it, usually means that change agents are heterophilous from their typical clients, thus posing problems for effective communication about the innovations they are promoting. Many change agencies employ change agent aides. An *aide* is a less than fully professional change agent who intensively contacts clients to influence their innovation-decisions. Aides are usually homophilous with the average client and thus provide one means of bridging the heterophily gap between professional change agents and their client audience.

TYPES OF INNOVATION-DECISIONS The social system has yet another important influence in the diffusion of new ideas. Innovations can be adopted or rejected (1) by an individual member of a system or (2) by the entire social system, which can decide to adopt an innovation by a collective or an authority decision.

1. *Optional innovation-decisions* are choices to adopt or reject an innovation that are made by an individual independent of the decisions of the other members of the system. Even in this case, the individual's decision may be influenced by the norms of the system and by communication through interpersonal networks. The decision of an individual housewife in Los Molinas to adopt or reject boiling water was an optional innovation-decision, although this choice was influenced by community-level factors, such as norms on the hot-cold complex. The distinctive aspect of optional innovation-decisions is that the individual is the main unit of decision making, rather than the social system.

    The classical diffusion model evolved out of early diffusion investigations of optional innovation-decisions: the diffusion of hybrid corn among Iowa farmers, the spread of a new antibiotic drug among medical doctors, and the like. In more recent decades, however, the scope of the diffusion paradigm has included collective and authority innovation-decisions.

2. *Collective innovation-decisions* are choices to adopt or reject an innovation that are made by consensus among the members of a system. All units in the system usually must conform to the system's decision once it is made.

3. *Authority innovation-decisions* are choices to adopt or reject an innovation that are made by a relatively few individuals in a system

who possess power, status, or technical expertise. An individual member of the system has little or no influence in the authority innovation-decision; he or she simply implements the decision once it is made by an authority. For instance, some years ago the president of a large U.S. computer corporation decided that all male employees should wear a white shirt, a conservative necktie, and a dark suit; this authority decision had to be followed by every man who worked for the computer company.

These three types of innovation-decisions range on a continuum from optional decisions (where the adopting individual has almost complete responsibility for the decision), through collective decisions (where the individual has a say in the decision), to authority decisions (where the adopting individual has no influence in the innovation-decision). Collective and authority decisions are more common than optional decisions in most organizations, such as factories, schools, or government organizations, in comparison with other fields such as agriculture and consumer behavior, where most innovation-decisions by farmers and consumers are optional.

Generally, the fastest rate of adoption of innovations stems from authority decisions (depending, of course, on how innovative the authorities are). Optional decisions can usually be made more rapidly than collective decisions. Although made more rapidly, authority decisions may be circumvented by members of a system during their implementation.

The type of innovation-decision for a given idea may change or be changed over time. Automobile seat belts, during the early years of their use, were installed in autos as an option by the car's owner, who had to pay for the cost of installation. Then, in 1966, a federal law was passed requiring that seat belts be included in all new cars in the United States. An optional innovation-decision thus became a collective decision (the law was passed by a consensus of the members of Congress). The decision by a driver or passengers to fasten the belts when in the car was still an optional decision. However, in 1974, a federal law required all new cars to be equipped with a seat belt–ignition interlock system that prevented the driver from starting the engine until the driver and the front-seat passenger had fastened their seat belts. So for one year, the decision to fasten seat belts became a collective authority-decision. The public reaction to this draconian approach was so negative that the U.S. Congress reversed the law, and the fastening of auto seat belts again became an individual-optional decision. Then, during the late 1980s, many states passed laws requiring seat belt use; if the police apprehend someone not using a seat belt, they issue a traffic citation. Thus the seat belt decision again became somewhat more authoritarian.

Smoking cigarettes was completely a matter of individual choice until the late 1980s, when scientific evidence began to accumulate on the health dangers of second-hand smoke. U.S. airlines adopted a policy prohibiting smoking on all domestic flights. The Environmental Protection Agency (EPA) published a report classifying environmental smoke as a carcinogen (that is, as cancer-causing). By 1990, many communities, especially in California, adopted no-smoking ordinances that precluded smoking in such public places as city buildings, restaurants, and bars. Adoption of these no-smoking ordinances diffused rapidly among U.S. municipalities, until by 2002, some 2,400 cities had adopted. Each city made an optional innovation-decision, but once it was made by a city council, everyone in the city was forced to avoid smoking in public places (an authority decision). As a result of municipal no-smoking ordinances, the number of smokers in the United States has continued to decline, until in 2002 only 25 percent of adults were smoking.

This illustration demonstrates a fourth type of innovation-decision that is a sequential combination of two or more of the three types discussed previously. *Contingent innovation-decisions* are choices to adopt or reject that can be made only after a prior innovation-decision. For example, an individual member of a social system may be free to adopt or not adopt a new idea only after (or until) his or her system's innovation-decision. In the seat belt example just discussed, until the 1966 law (a collective innovation-decision by elected legislators representing the public), it was difficult for a vehicle owner to make an optional decision to install seat belts. In the no-smoking illustration, an individual must adopt the innovation of not smoking in public places, once this policy is adopted by the city council.

The distinctive aspect of contingent decision making is that two (or more) tandem decisions are required; either of the decisions may be optional, collective, or authority. The social system is involved directly in collective, authority, and contingent innovation-decisions.

CONSEQUENCES OF INNOVATIONS A social system is involved in an innovation's consequences because certain of these changes occur at the system level, in addition to those that affect the individual (see Chapter 11).

Consequences are the changes that occur to an individual or to a social system as a result of the adoption or rejection of an innovation. Three classifications of consequences are:

1. *Desirable* versus *undesirable* consequences, depending on whether the effects of an innovation in a social system are functional or dysfunctional.
2. *Direct* versus *indirect* consequences, depending on whether the changes to an individual or to a social system occur in immediate response to an innovation or as a second-order result of the direct consequences of an innovation.
3. *Anticipated* versus *unanticipated* consequences, depending on whether or not the changes are recognized and intended by the members of a social system.

Change agents usually introduce innovations into a client system that they expect will have consequences that will be desirable, direct, and anticipated. But often such innovations result in at least some unanticipated consequences that are indirect and undesirable for the system's members. For instance, the steel ax was introduced by missionaries to an Australian aborigine tribe (Sharp, 1952). The change agents intended that the new tool would raise levels of living and material comfort for the tribe. But the new technology also led to a breakdown in family structure, the rise of prostitution, and "misuse" of the innovation itself. Change agents can often anticipate and predict an innovation's *form,* the directly observable physical appearance of the innovation, and perhaps its *function,* the contribution of the idea to the way of life of the system's members. But seldom are change agents able to predict an innovation's *meaning,* the subjective perceptions of the innovation by the clients.

Diffusion of Hybrid Corn in Iowa*

Ryan and Gross's (1943) study of the diffusion of hybrid seed corn in Iowa is the most influential diffusion study of all time, despite the 5,200-plus diffusion investigations conducted since this pioneering study. The hybrid corn investigation includes each of the four main elements of diffusion (an inno-

---

*This case illustration is based on Ryan and Gross (1943), Gross (1942), Ryan and Gross (1951), and Valente and Rogers (1995).

vation, communication channels, time, and the social system) that we have just discussed and serves to illustrate these elements.

Hybrid corn became one of the most important new agricultural technologies after it was released to Iowa farmers in 1928. The new seed ushered in the agricultural innovations in the 1930s through the 1950s that led to an agricultural revolution in farm productivity. Hybrid seed was developed by agricultural scientists at Iowa State University and other state land-grant universities. The diffusion of hybrid seed was heavily promoted by the Iowa Agricultural Extension Service and by salesman from seed corn companies. Hybrid corn yielded an increased harvest of about 20 percent per acre over the open-pollinated varieties that it replaced. It was also more drought-resistant and better suited to harvesting with mechanical corn pickers. The seed lost its hybrid vigor after the first generation, so farmers had to purchase hybrid seed each year. Previously, farmers had saved their own seed, selected from their best-looking corn plants. The adoption of hybrid corn meant that an Iowa farmer had to make important changes in his corn-growing behavior. Hybrid seed corn ushered in a new era of farmers' dependence on agribusiness companies that sold chemical fertilizers, pesticides, and other farm inputs.

When Professor Bryce Ryan, fresh from his Ph.D. studies in sociology at Harvard University, arrived at Iowa State University in 1939, he chose hybrid corn as the innovation of study in his investigation of social factors in economic decisions. This interest drew him to study how Iowa farmers' social relationships with their neighbors influenced them to adopt hybrid corn. Ryan had read anthropological work on diffusion while he was at Harvard, so he cast his Iowa study of hybrid corn in a diffusion framework. But unlike the qualitative methods used in anthropological studies of diffusion, the Iowa investigation mainly utilized qualitative data from survey interviews with Iowa farmers about their adoption of hybrid corn seed.

In the summer of 1941, Neal C. Gross, a new graduate student in rural sociology, was hired as a research assistant on the hybrid corn diffusion project. Ryan and Gross selected two small Iowa communities located some fifty miles west of Ames and conducted personal interviews with all of the farmers living in these two systems. Using a structured questionnaire, Neal Gross, who did most of the data gathering, interviewed each respondent as to when the farmer decided to adopt hybrid corn (the year of adoption was to become the main dependent variable in the data analysis), the communication channels used at each stage in the innovation-decision process, and how much of the farmer's corn acreage was planted in hybrid (rather than open-pollinated seed) each year. In addition to these recall data about the innovation, the two rural sociologists also asked each respondent about his formal education, age, farm size, income, frequency of travel to Des Moines and other cities, readership of farm magazines, and other variables that were later correlated with innovativeness (measured as the year in which each farmer decided to adopt hybrid corn).

Neal Gross was from an urban background in Milwaukee, Wisconsin, and initially felt somewhat uncomfortable interviewing Iowa farmers. Someone in Ames told Gross that farm people got up very early in the morning, so on his first day of data gathering, he arrived at a respondent's home at 6:00 A.M., while it was still half dark. By the end of this first day, Gross had interviewed twenty-one people, and he averaged an incredible fourteen interviews per day for the entire study! Today, a survey interviewer who averages four interviews per day is considered hardworking. During one personal interview, an Iowa farmer, perhaps slyly leading him on, asked Gross for advice about controlling horse nettles. Gross had never heard of horse nettles. He told the farmer that he should call a veterinarian to look at his sick horse (horse nettles are actually a kind of noxious weed).

Neal Gross personally interviewed 345 farmers in the two Iowa communities, but twelve farmers operating less than twenty acres were discarded from the data analysis, as were 74 respondents who had started farming after hybrid corn began to diffuse. Thus, the data analysis was based on 259 respondents.

When all of the data were gathered, Ryan and Gross coded the farmers' interview responses into numbers. The diffusion researchers analyzed the data by hand tabulation and with a desk calculator (computers were not available for data analysis until some years later). Within a year, Gross (1942) completed his master's thesis on the diffusion of hybrid corn, and shortly thereafter Ryan and Gross (1943) published their research findings in the journal *Rural Sociology* (this article is the most widely cited publication from the study, although there are several others). This paper became the founding document for the research specialty of the diffusion of innovations. Several previous studies had been completed on the diffusion of agricultural innovations, but they did not lead to a research tradition because they did not create a research paradigm for the diffusion of innovations (Valente and Rogers, 1995). The Ryan and Gross (1943) study established the customary research methodology to be used by most diffusion investigators: retrospective survey interviews in which adopters of an innovation are asked when they adopted, where or from whom they obtained information about the innovation, and the consequences of adoption. Ryan and Gross (1943) popularized the term "diffusion" (which had previously been used by anthropologists), although they did not use the concept of "innovation." That term would come from later scholars.

All but 2 of the 259 farmers had adopted hybrid corn in the thirteen years between 1928 and 1941. When plotted cumulatively on a year-by-year basis, the adoption rate formed an S-shaped curve over time. After the first five years, by 1933, only 10 percent of the Iowa farmers had adopted. Then the adoption curve "took off," shooting up to 40 percent adoption in the next three years (by 1936). Then the rate of adoption leveled off as fewer and fewer farmers remained to adopt the new idea. The overall shape of the rate of adoption looked like an "S" (see Figure 1–2).

Farmers were assigned to adopter categories on the basis of when they adopted the new seed (Gross, 1942). Compared to later adopters, the innovators had larger-sized farms, higher incomes, and more years of formal education. The innovators were also more cosmopolite, as measured by their number of trips to Des Moines, Iowa's largest city, located about seventy-five miles from the two study communities.

Although hybrid corn was an innovation with a high degree of relative advantage over the open-pollinated seed that it replaced, the typical farmer moved slowly from awareness-knowledge of the innovation to adoption. The innovation-decision period from first knowledge to the adoption decision averaged about nine years for all respondents, an indication that the innovation-decision process involved considerable deliberation, even in the case of an innovation with spectacular results. The average respondent took three or four years after planting his first hybrid seed, usually on a small trial plot of about one acre, before deciding to plant 100 percent of his corn acreage in hybrid varieties.

Communication channels played different roles at various stages in the innovation-decision process. The typical farmer first heard of hybrid seed from a salesman, but neighbors were the most frequently cited channel leading to persuasion. Thus salesmen were more important channels for earlier adopters, and neighbors were more important for later adopters. The Ryan and Gross (1943) findings suggested the important role of interpersonal networks in the diffusion process in a system. The farmer-to-farmer exchanges of their personal experiences with hybrid seed were at the heart of diffusion. When enough such positive experiences were accumulated by the innovators, and especially by early adopters, and exchanged with other farmers in the community, the rate of adoption took off. This threshold for hybrid corn occurred in 1935. After that point, it would have been impossible to halt its further diffusion. The farm community as a social system, including the networks linking the individual farmers within it, was a crucial element in the diffusion process.

In order to understand the role of diffusion networks and opinion leadership, Ryan and Gross (1943) should have asked sociometric questions of their respondents, such as "From which other farmers did you obtain information about hybrid corn?" The sample design, which consisted of a complete enumeration in two communities, would have made the use of such communication network questions appropriate. But "information was simply collected from all community members as if they were unrelated respondents in a random sample" (Katz et al., 1963).

Even without sociometric data about diffusion networks, Ryan and Gross (1943) sensed that hybrid corn had spread in the two Iowa communities as a kind of social snowball: "There is no doubt but that the behavior of one individual in an interacting population affects the behavior of his fellows. Thus, the demonstrated success of hybrid seed on a few farms offers new stimulus to the remaining ones." The two rural sociologists intuitively sensed what later diffusion scholars were to gather more detailed evidence to prove: that the heart of the diffusion process consists of interpersonal network exchanges and social modeling by those individuals who have already adopted an innovation to those individuals who are influenced to follow their lead. Diffusion is fundamentally a social process.

Study of the invisible college of rural sociologists investigating diffusion as of the mid-1960s identified the researchers who first utilized a new concept and/or methodological tool in studying diffusion (Crane, 1972). Ryan and Gross launched fifteen of the eighteen most widely used intellectual innovations in the rural sociology diffusion research tradition. So Bryce Ryan and Neal Gross played key roles in forming the classical diffusion paradigm. The hybrid corn study has left an indelible stamp on the history of all diffusion research.

Summary

Diffusion is the process by which an innovation is communicated through certain channels over time among the members of a social system. Diffusion is a special type of communication concerned with the spread of messages that are perceived as new ideas. *Communication* is a process in which participants create and share information with one another in order to reach a mutual understanding. Diffusion has a special character because of the newness of the idea in the message content. Thus some degree of uncertainty and perceived risk is involved in the diffusion process. An individual can reduce this degree of uncertainty by obtaining information. *Information* is a difference in matter-energy that affects uncertainty in a situation where a choice exists among a set of alternatives.

The main elements in the diffusion of new ideas are: (1) an *innovation* (2) that is *communicated* through certain *channels* (3) *over time* (4) among the members of a *social system*.

1. Innovation

An *innovation* is an idea, practice, or object perceived as new by an individual or other unit of adoption. Most of the new ideas discussed in this book are technological innovations. A *technology* is a design for instrumental action that reduces the uncertainty in the cause-effect relationships involved in achieving a desired outcome. Most technologies have two components: (1) *hardware,* consisting of the tool that embodies the technology as a material or physical object, and (2) *software,* consisting of the knowledge base for the tool.

The characteristics of an innovation, as perceived by the members of a social system, determine its rate of adoption. Five attributes of innovations are: (1) relative advantage, (2) compatibility, (3) complexity, (4) trialability, and (5) observability.

Re-invention is the degree to which an innovation is changed or modified by a user in the process of its adoption and implementation.

2. Communication Channels

A *communication channel* is the means by which messages get from one individual to another. Mass media channels are more effective in creating knowledge of innovations, whereas interpersonal channels are more effective in forming and changing attitudes toward a new idea, and thus in influencing the decision to adopt or reject a new idea. Most individuals evaluate an innovation not on the basis of scientific research by experts but through the subjective evaluations of near peers who have adopted the innovation. These near peers thus serve as role models, whose innovation behavior tends to be imitated by others in their system.

A distinctive aspect of diffusion is that at least some degree of heterophily is usually present in communication about innovations. *Heterophily* is the degree to which two or more individuals who interact are different in certain attributes, such as beliefs, education, social status, and the like. The opposite of heterophily is *homophily,* the degree to which two or more individuals who interact are similar in certain attributes. Most human communication takes place between individuals who are homophilous, a situation that leads to more effective communication. Therefore, the heterophily that is often present in the diffusion of innovations leads to special problems in achieving effective communication.

3. Time

Time is involved in diffusion in (1) the innovation-diffusion process, (2) innovativeness, and (3) an innovation's rate of adoption. The *innovation-decision process* is the process through which an individual (or other decision-making unit) passes from first knowledge of an innovation to forming an attitude toward the innovation, to a decision to adopt or reject, to implementation of the new idea, and to confirmation of this decision. We conceptualize five steps in this process: (1) knowledge, (2) persuasion, (3) decision, (4) implementation, and (5) confirmation. An individual seeks information at various stages in the innovation-decision process in order to decrease uncertainty about an innovation's expected consequences. The decision stage leads (1) to *adoption,* a decision to make full use of an innovation as the best course of action available, or (2) to *rejection,* a decision not to adopt an innovation.

Innovativeness is the degree to which an individual or other unit of adoption is relatively earlier in adopting new ideas than other members of a social system. We specify five *adopter categories,* classifications of the members of a social system on the basis of their innovativeness: (1) innovators, (2) early adopters, (3) early majority, (4) late majority, and (5) laggards. *The rate of adoption* is the relative speed with which an innovation is adopted by members of a social system.

4. Social System

A *social system* is a set of interrelated units that are engaged in joint problem solving to accomplish a common goal. A system has *structure,* defined as the patterned arrangements of the units in a system, which gives stability and regularity to individual behavior in a system. The social and communication structure of a system facilitates or impedes the diffusion of innovations in the system. One aspect of social structure is *norms,* the established behavior patterns for the members of a social system.

Opinion leadership is the degree to which an individual is able to influence informally other individuals' attitudes or overt behavior in a desired way with relative frequency. A *change agent* is an individual who attempts to influence clients' innovation-decisions in a direction that is deemed desirable by a change agency. An *aide* is a less than fully professional change agent who intensively contacts clients to influence their innovation-decisions.

We distinguish among three main types of innovation-decisions: (1) *optional innovation-decisions*, choices to adopt or reject an innovation that are made by an individual independent of the decisions of other members of the system, (2) *collective innovation-decisions*, choices to adopt or reject an innovation that are made by consensus among the members of a system, and (3) *authority innovation-decisions*, choices to adopt or reject an innovation that are made by relatively few individuals in a system who possess power, status, or technical expertise. A fourth category consists of a sequential combination of two or more of these three types of innovation-decisions: *Contingent innovation-decisions* are choices to adopt or reject that are made only after a prior innovation-decision.

A final way in which a social system influences diffusion concerns *consequences*, the changes that occur to an individual or a social system as a result of the adoption or rejection of an innovation.

2

A HISTORY OF DIFFUSION RESEARCH

Diffusion research is thus emerging as a single, integrated body of concepts and generalizations, even though the investigations are conducted by researchers in several scientific disciplines.

Everett M. Rogers with F. Floyd Shoemaker,
*Communications of Innovations: A Cross-Cultural
Approach* (1971), p. 47

Research on the diffusion of innovations started in a series of independent intellectual enclaves during the 1940s and 1950s. Each of these disciplinary cliques of diffusion researchers studied one kind of innovation; for example, rural sociologists investigated the diffusion of agricultural innovations to farmers, while educational researchers studied the spread of new teaching ideas among school personnel. Despite the distinctive nature of these approaches to diffusion research, each invisible college uncovered remarkably similar findings (for example, that the diffusion of an innovation followed an S-shaped curve over time and that innovators had higher socioeconomic status than did later adopters).

My main motivation for writing the first book on this topic, *Diffusion of Innovations* (Rogers, 1962), was to describe a general diffusion model and to argue for greater awareness among the various research traditions. A *research tradition* is a series of investigations on a similar topic in which successive studies are influenced by preceding inquiries. Essentially, each research tradition is an invisible college of researchers, a network of scholars who may be spatially dispersed but who are closely interconnected by exchanging research findings and other scientific information.

By the mid-1960s, the formerly impermeable boundaries between the diffusion research traditions began to break down. Rogers with Shoemaker (1971) computed an index of cross-tradition citations for each diffusion publication in 1968; this index was the number of research traditions (other than the author's) represented in the footnotes and bibliography of each empirical diffusion publication. The average index score (per diffusion publication) hovered at less than 1.0 during the 1940s, 1950s, and early 1960s (this meant that the typical diffusion publication cited one publication from a different diffusion research tradition). But from 1965 to 1968, this average score suddenly doubled. The walls between the diffusion research traditions were breaking down.

This trend toward a more unified cross-disciplinary viewpoint in diffusion research continues today. Every contemporary diffusion scholar is fully aware of the parallel methodologies and findings of other traditions. All of the diffusion research traditions have now merged intellectually to form a single, large invisible college, although scholars in many different disciplines conduct diffusion research. This merger of diffusion approaches has not been an unmixed blessing. Diffusion studies now display a kind of sameness, as they pursue a small number of research issues with somewhat stereotyped approaches. The narrow perspectives of diffusion scholars in an earlier era have been replaced by an unnecessary standardization of diffusion research perspectives

A major theme of this chapter is the story of the merging of the diffusion research traditions and the consequences of this intellectual convergence, both positive and negative. We address such questions as: Where did diffusion research come from? How and why did it grow to its present position of wide recognition by scholars, and its widespread use and application by policy makers? How has the acceptance of the classical diffusion model limited the originality and appropriateness of the work of diffusion researchers?

The Beginnings of Diffusion Research in Europe

The roots of diffusion theory trace to Europe about a century ago, when sociology and anthropology were emerging as new social sciences. Here we discuss three of the important foundations for the diffusion model: the Frenchman Gabriel Tarde, the German Georg Simmel, and the German-Austrian and British diffusionists.

Gabriel Tarde and Imitation

The roots of diffusion research extend back to the European beginnings of social science. Gabriel Tarde, one of the forefathers of sociology and social psychology, was a French lawyer and judge around 1900 who kept an analytical eye on trends in his society as represented by the legal cases that came before his court (Katz, 1999). Tarde observed certain generalizations about the diffusion of innovations that he called "the laws of imitation," and this became the title of his influential book. The purpose of his scholarly observations, Tarde (1903, p. 140) said, was "to learn why, given one hundred different innovations conceived at the same time— innovations in the form of words, in mythological ideas, in industrial processes, etc.—ten will spread abroad while ninety will be forgotten."

Tarde was far ahead of his time in thinking about diffusion. Although he used slightly different concepts from those employed in this book (for example, what Tarde called "imitation" is today called the "adoption" of an innovation), this sociological pioneer was onto several of the main research issues that were pursued by diffusion scholars in later decades, using less intuitive and more quantitative approaches. For example, as the above quotation indicates, Tarde identified the adoption or rejection of innovations as a crucial outcome variable in diffusion research. He observed that the rate of adoption of a new idea usually followed an S-shaped curve over time. Astutely, Tarde recognized that the takeoff in the S-shaped curve of adoption begins to occur when the opinion leaders in a system use a new idea. So diffusion network thinking was involved in Tarde's explanation of the S-curve, even though he did not use such present-day concepts as opinion leaders, networks, homophily, and heterophily. Tarde's key word, "imitation," implies that an individual learns about an innovation by copying someone else's adoption of the innovation, implying that diffusion is a social process of interpersonal communication networks. Tarde (1969, p. 27) proposed as one of his "laws of imitation" that the more similar an innovation is to ideas that have already been accepted, the more likely the innovation will be adopted (today we say that the perceived compatibility of an innovation is positively related to its rapid rate of adoption).

To Tarde, the diffusion of innovations was a basic and fundamental explanation of human behavior change: "Invention and imitation are, as we know, the elementary social acts" (Tarde, 1969, p. 178). Tarde was one of the European forefathers of the diffusion field. But his creative insights were not immediately followed up by empirical studies of diffusion. That was not to happen until after a lapse of forty years, in the Ryan and Gross hybrid corn study. Social scientists of Tarde's day lacked the methodological tools to conduct quantitative diffusion studies. His suggested approach to diffusion research lay low for several decades until an invisible college of American scholars coalesced around Tarde's "laws of imitation." They realized that Gabriel Tarde's theory could be tested by empirical research.

Georg Simmel's Stranger

Another forefather of the discipline of sociology, who lived at about the same time as Tarde, was Georg Simmel, who was trained in philosophy but who taught the first classes in sociology and was the first university professor to be called a sociologist. Simmel was an extremely popular lecturer at the University of Berlin, and his scholarship was creative and productive, but his career went nowhere, perhaps because of anti-Semitism. He studied and wrote about a very wide range of sociological subjects, claiming that he could "Simmelize" any topic. Among his interests were the concept of the *stranger* (*der Fremde* in German), defined as an individual who is a member of a system but who is not strongly attached to the system (Simmel, 1908/1964). In many respects, Simmel was a stranger, and perhaps his own role in society provided him with special insight into the relationships between the individual and the system of which the individual is a member. A relatively disengaged individual, such as a stranger, has a unique view of the system in which he or she is a member (Rogers, 1999).

Later scholars, stimulated by Simmel's concept of the stranger, derived such concepts as social distance, heterophily, cosmopoliteness (see our discussion of innovators in Chapter 7), and the notion that social science research should attempt to be objective (Rogers, 1994). Georg Simmel also pointed social scientists in the direction of studying communication networks, an increasingly useful conceptual tool in understanding how innovations diffuse in a system. Simmel (1922/1955, p. 140) wrote, "The groups with which the individual is affiliated constitute a system of coordinates, as it were, such that each new group with which he becomes affiliated circumscribes him more exactly and less ambiguously." So an individual's network relationships serve to influence, and often to constrain, an individual's actions. The innovator, as a type of stranger, can more easily deviate from the norms of the system by being the first to adopt new ideas.

The British and German-Austrian Diffusionists

Another root of diffusion research was a group of early anthropologists that evolved in England and in Germany-Austria soon after the time of

Gabriel Tarde in France (although they were not influenced by his writings). These anthropologists were called the "British diffusionists" and the "German-Austrian diffusionists." The central viewpoint of each school was rather similar. Diffusionism was the point of view in anthropology that explained social change in a given society as a result of the introduction of innovations spread from one original source, which argued against the existence of parallel invention (today we know that such parallel invention of new ideas has frequently occurred).

The diffusionism viewpoint does not have a following today, owing to the extreme claims of the diffusionists that all social change could be explained by diffusion alone. The dominant viewpoint now is that social change is caused by both *invention* (the process by which a new idea is discovered or created) and diffusion, which usually occur sequentially. The main contribution of the European diffusionists was in calling the importance of diffusion to the attention of other social scientists (Kroeber, 1937). These European diffusionists were some of the first scholars to use the term "diffusion."

The scholars who picked up on the work of the European diffusionists most directly, as one might expect, were anthropologists, especially those in the United States, who, beginning in the 1920s, began to investigate the diffusion of innovations. Indirectly, this anthropological interest in the diffusion of innovations was to influence the Ryan and Gross investigation of hybrid seed corn in Iowa.

The Rise of Diffusion Research Traditions

The anthropological diffusion researchers constitute the oldest of the diffusion research traditions (Table 2-1). In this chapter we trace the intellectual ancestry of the nine main research traditions, as they help us to understand the history of the diffusion research field. Each research tradition consists of an academic discipline (for example, anthropology, marketing, geography) or a subdiscipline (for instance, early sociology and rural sociology). Each tradition usually concentrated on investigating the diffusion of one main type of innovation: for example, rural sociologists specialized in farm innovations. Table 2-1 shows, for each tradition, the main types of innovations studied, methods of data gathering and analysis, and the main findings. This overview and comparison of the diffusion research traditions is complemented by the following narrative description of each tradition.

Table 2.1. The Nine Major Diffusion Research Traditions

Diffusion Research Tradition[a]	Estimated Percentage of All Diffusion Publications	Typical Innovations Studied	Method of Data Gathering and Analysis	Main Unit of Analysis	Major Types of Findings
Anthropology	4%	Technological ideas (steel ax, horse, water boiling)	Participant and non-participant observation and case studies	Tribes or peasant villages	Consequences of innovations; relative success of change agents
Early sociology	—	City manager government, postage stamps, ham radios	Data from secondary sources and statistical analysis	Communities or individuals	S-shaped adopter distribution; characteristics of adopter categories
Rural sociology	20%	Agricultural ideas (weed sprays, hybrid seed, fertilizers)	Survey interviews and statistical analysis	Individual farmers in rural communities	S-shaped adopter distribution; characteristics of adopter categories; perceived attributes of innovations and their rate of adoption; communication channels by stages in the innovation-decision process; characteristics of opinion leaders
Education	8%	Teaching/learning innovations (kindergartens, modern math, programmed instruction, team teaching)	Mailed questionnaires, survey interviews, and statistical analysis	School systems teachers, or administrators	S-shaped adopter distribution; characteristics of adopter categories

Public health and medical sociology	10%	Medical and health ideas (drugs, vaccinations, family-planning methods, AIDS prevention)	Survey interviews and statistical analysis	Individuals or organizations such as hospitals and health departments	Opinion leadership in diffusion; characteristics of adopter categories; communication channels by stages of the innovation-decision process
Communication	15%	News events, technological innovations, new communication technologies	Survey interviews and statistical analysis	Individuals or organizations	Communication channels by stages in the innovation-decision process; characteristics of adopter categories, and of opinion leaders; diffusion networks
Marketing and management	16%	New products (a coffee brand, the touch-tone telephone, clothing fashions; new communication technologies)	Survey interviews and statistical analysis; field experiments	Individual consumers	Characteristics of adopter categories; opinion leadership in diffusion
Geography	4%	Technological innovations	Secondary records and statistical analysis, maps	Individuals and organizations	Role of spatial distance in diffusion
General sociology	9%	A wide variety of ideas	Survey interviews and statistical analysis	Individuals, other units	Characteristics of adopter categories
Other traditions**	14%	—	—	—	—
Total	100%				

*The exact number of major research traditions is arbitrary. We chose these because they represent the relatively greatest number of empirical diffusion publications (an exception is the early sociology tradition, which is included because of its influence on certain of the other traditions that developed later).

**Includes general economics, public administration and political science, agricultural economics, psychology, industrial engineering, statistics, and others/unknown.

Paradigms and Invisible Colleges

Any given field of scientific research is launched with a major break-through or reconceptualization, called a "revolutionary paradigm" by Kuhn (1970) that provides model problems and solutions to a community of scholars (Kuhn, 1970). Recognition of the new paradigm sets off a furious amount of intellectual effort as promising young scientists are attracted to the field, either to advance the new conceptualization with their research or to disprove certain of its aspects. Gradually, a scientific consensus about the field is developed, and, perhaps after some years, the *invisible college* (the informal network of researchers who form around an intellectual paradigm to study a common topic) declines in scientific interest as fewer findings of an exciting nature are discovered. These are the usual stages in the growth of science (Kuhn, 1970; Price, 1963; Crane, 1972). The research process is a very social activity in which crucial decisions are influenced by a network of scientists, organized around one important research idea.

An invisible college centered on an intellectual paradigm provides the typical scientist with the information he or she needs to reduce the uncertainty of the research process. Of the many alternative directions that a research project might pursue, a paradigm structures a researcher into one general approach. Thus, the paradigm, and the invisible college of scientists who follow the paradigm, provide a researcher with security and stability in the uncertain world of an active research front.

Research on the diffusion of innovations followed these rise-and-fall stages rather closely (Crane, 1972), although the final stage of demise does not seem to have begun (except perhaps in certain research traditions, like rural sociology). The hybrid corn diffusion study by Bryce Ryan and Neal Gross (1943), described in Chapter 1, set forth the basic paradigm for studying diffusion; it was soon followed by an increasing number of scholars in many disciplines (Figure 2–1). As a keen observer of diffusion scholarship recently concluded, "It cannot be far wrong to assert that every one of the social sciences and humanities has, at least intermittently, given attention to the question of how things—ideas and practices—get from here to there" (Katz, 1999, p. 145). The amount of scientific activity devoted to investigating the diffusion of innovations has increased at a sharp rate since the revolutionary paradigm appeared sixty years ago, as Kuhn's (1970) theory of the growth of science would predict.

Figure 2-1. Number of Diffusion Publications by Rural Sociologists by Year, for the United States and Europe Versus for Developing Nations

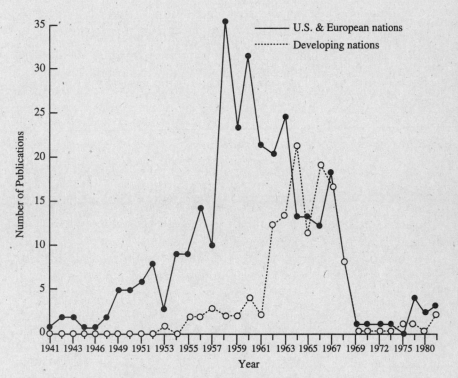

A total of 434 rural sociology publications on diffusion appeared from 1941 to 1981. Of the 331 U.S. and European diffusion publications, 36 (13 percent) were European and one was Australian. A total of 103 publications (24 percent) reported diffusion research in Latin America, Africa, and Asia. The location of each diffusion study is determined by where the data were gathered, not where the research was published.

Source: Valente and Rogers (1995).

Diffusion research is a particular type of communication research, but it began outside of the academic field of communication. The Ryan and Gross (1943) hybrid corn study preceded the establishment of the first university institutes or departments of communication around 1960 (Rogers, 1994). Most diffusion scholars, whatever their discipline, recognize that they are investigating what is essentially a special kind of communication process. The diffusion research approach has been taken up by a variety of disciplinary fields: education, anthropology, public health, marketing, geography, rural sociology, political science, and others. Each of these disciplines initially pursued diffusion research in its own specialized way, without much interchange with the other diffusion research traditions, at least until the mid-1960s, when the boundaries between the traditions began to break down.

Now we turn to the beginnings of the anthropological research tradition, in the 1920s.

The Anthropology Research Tradition

The anthropology tradition is not only the oldest of the research traditions analyzed in this book, it is also the most distinctive in its methodological approach to studying diffusion. Most anthropologists who study diffusion avoid using such quantitative tools as personal interviews, random sample surveys, and computer data analysis.

Anthropologists prefer to gather diffusion data directly from their respondents by means of *participant observation,* an attempt by a researcher to adopt the perspective of respondents by sharing their day-to-day experiences. An anthropologist often goes to live for several years in a system of study, such as a peasant village, seeking to empathize with village respondents. Obviously, such a total immersion approach requires a great deal of patience on the part of the field researcher, who may have to wait a long time for what he or she has come to observe (such as diffusion and adoption behavior). The participant observation method requires that anthropologists are limited to studying diffusion in small systems, such as a single village. Most anthropological research is a one-person operation, and the investigator is therefore limited to what he or she can observe. The results of such inquiry provide valuable insights into the microlevel details of diffusion. However, there is less certainty that the results of anthropological diffusion studies are generalizable. For instance, to what extent can the administrators of the public health service in Peru apply the findings from Wellin's (1955) anthropological investigation of the failure of the water-boiling campaign in Los Molinas to other Peruvian villages? Does Los Molinas have special characteristics that affected the adoption and rejection of water boiling? Do similar diffusion problems occur in other Peruvian villages? We do not know, on the basis of anthropological research.

Anthropological studies of diffusion have several unique advantages. If the anthropologist is successful in empathizing with the respondents under study, the ensuing account of diffusion will tell the story from the respondents' viewpoint, conveying their perceptions of the innovation and the change agency. This perspective helps the anthropologist overcome the pro-innovation bias that is displayed in much other diffusion research. Through total immersion in the respondents' system, the anthropologist gains a holistic perspective of the lifestyles, worldviews, and social relationships of the respondents. This capacity of anthropologists to understand the context and culture of their individuals of study, coupled with their data gathering over time, provides anthropological diffusion scholars with a unique means of understanding the consequences of innovation. Much of the research featured in Chapter 11 on consequences was conducted by anthropologists. An example is Professor Pertti Pelto's (1973) study of the consequences of the snowmobile among the Skolt Lapps of northern Finland.

In addition to their useful contributions to understanding consequences, a good deal of anthropological research has also been conducted on the relationship of culture to an innovation's rate of adoption. Anthropologists often show that the planners and officials in charge of diffusion programs failed to account fully for the cultural values of the expected adopters of an innovation. As a result, the diffusion program often failed or at least led to unanticipated consequences.

Compared to other research traditions, anthropology has been more concerned with the transfer of technological innovations from one society to another (as compared to the diffusion of a new idea within a society or system). This emphasis on intercultural diffusion is consistent with anthropologists' interest in the concept of culture, their favorite intellectual tool. An early illustration of this type of investigation was Wissler's (1914, 1923) study of the diffusion of horses from Spanish explorers to American Indian tribes in the West (see Chapter 5), and the spread of corn growing from the American Indians to European settlers. Contemporary studies of intercultural diffusion evaluate development programs in which Western technologies have been introduced into the developing countries of Latin America, Africa, and Asia. Unlike many development program officials, anthropologists note the importance of indigenous knowledge systems in whether or not technological innovations are accepted.

In part owing to their early appearance on the diffusion research scene, anthropologists influenced the other diffusion research traditions, particularly early sociology and rural sociology. Other traditions have seldom used participant observation as their data-gathering methodology, but they have carried forward into quantitative research certain of the theoretical leads pioneered by anthropology diffusion scholars, such as the importance of perceived compatibility in explaining an innovation's rate of adoption. Anthropology is one of the smaller diffusion research traditions today, representing about 4 percent of all diffusion publications (Table 2-1).

Miracle Rice in Bali: The Goddess and the Computer*

One may have an image of an anthropologist as wearing native dress and a pith helmet and speaking the local dialect fluently. University of Arizona anthropologist Steve Lansing indeed dresses in a traditional Balinese sarong and immerses himself completely in the exotic culture of Bali, the Indonesian island in the South Pacific. Lansing's research in Bali provides understanding of how the indigenous knowledge system influenced the diffusion of technological innovations, a relationship that even Indonesian government officials did not see. Anthropologists' in-depth comprehension comes from studying small systems over a lengthy period of time. Professor Lansing used computer techniques in his research on the introduction and consequences of miracle rice varieties in Bali. In order to understand why miracle rice failed in Bali, one must comprehend the religious meaning of the rice irrigation system.

Rice is central to Balinese life. The steep slopes of volcanic soil, stretching down from mist-covered mountain peaks to the sea, have been ingeniously terraced by Balinese farmers over the past eight centuries so that irrigation water descends from a high crater lake, tumbling from one small rice plot to another, inching its way downward for miles to the sea. For centuries these rice paddies have produced up to a ton of food per acre per year, with little or no added fertilizer. Because of the ample rice yields, the small, densely populated island of Bali supports several million people. The high rice yields are made possible by a complex irrigation system that is coordinated by a hierarchical system of Hindu priests and water temples that regulate water flows. At the top of this indigenous system is the high priest, the Jero Gde (pronounced "Jeero G'day"), at the main water temple at Ulun Danu Batur, the crater lake

*This case illustration is based on Lansing (1987, 1991) and Bardini (1994).

near the peak of Batur volcano. Here offerings are made to Dewi Dano, the water goddess, whom Balinese believe dwells in the crater lake.

The Jero Gde serves as the overall manager of the sacred irrigation system. Below him are a series of major dams, each with a Hindu priest and a water temple responsible for regulating water flows. Lower levels of the irrigation system consist of smaller weirs, each with a minor water temple to regulate water flows. At the local level are 1,300 *subak*s, each a water users' cooperative association of about a hundred farmers. Each *subak* has a water shrine and a priest. Such an elaborate, hierarchically tiered social organization is needed to operate the Balinese irrigation system. Water is a scarce resource, and an efficient system is necessary to distribute the water in an equitable manner.

However, the water temple system of Bali does far more than just deliver water to the rice crops. Each rice terrace is a complex ecosystem, whose variable factors are carefully balanced by the Jero Gde and his cadre of Hindu water priests. For instance, a single farmer cannot control the pests in his small rice plot unless he coordinates with his neighbors. Otherwise, the rats, brown leafhoppers, and other pests simply migrate from field to field. The solution is for hundreds of farmers in several neighboring *subak*s to plant, irrigate, and harvest simultaneously, and then to leave their rice fields to fallow for several weeks. Evidence of such concerted action is easily visible: thousands of rice fields on a mountain slope will either be growing green, harvest yellow, or fallow brown. But until anthropologist Lansing began to investigate, no one understood how the decisions of these hundreds of rice farmers were orchestrated. Rice experts, if they knew of the indigenous irrigation system, dismissed it as unimportant. Lansing (1991) said, "Modern irrigation experts thought the ancient temple system was mere religious nonsense." Throughout the world, technologists often disparage indigenous learning systems (see Chapter 6).

The Balinese ecological system is so complex because the Jero Gde must seek an optimum balance of various competing forces. If all *subak*s were planted at the same time, pests would be reduced; however, water supplies would be inadequate due to peaks in demand. On the other hand, if all *subak*s staggered their rice-planting schedule in a completely random manner, the water demand would be spread out. The water supply would be utilized efficiently, but the pests would flourish and wipe out the rice crop. So the Jero Gde must seek an optimal balance between pest control and water conservation, depending on the amount of rainfall flowing into the crater lake, the levels of the different pest populations in various *subak*s, and so forth. The high priest has considerable influence over the entire irrigation subsystem, and on the rice-growing system of which irrigation is a part. Professor Lansing relates an occasion when a rodent plague was becoming widespread: "Instructions were sent down to all member *subak*s to build a special temporary shrine at all water inlets to every field, and perform a prayer and make an offering. . . . The small shrines duly appeared—on time—by the thousands" (Lansing, 1987). The Jero Gde clearly manages the entire rice-growing ecosystem of Bali, not just the water flows.

Indonesian government officials eagerly introduced the Green Revolution rice varieties in Bali in the 1970s. These innovations had tripled rice yields in other areas, and the agricultural change agents hoped to increase Bali's food production. Balinese farmers were told to grow three, rather than two, crops per year, and to adopt pesticides and chemical fertilizers. The centuries-old indigenous water-and-fallow system, managed by the Hindu priests, was abandoned by many farmers. "As a consequence, the incidence of bacterial and viral [rice] diseases, together with insect and rat populations, began to increase rapidly. Imported organochloride pesticides made some dents in the rising pest populations, but also killed off eels, fish, and, in some cases, farmers in the rice fields" (Lansing, 1987). Instead of increasing, rice yields in Bali dropped precipitously. Balinese rice farmers promptly returned to the water temple system and discontinued the miracle rice varieties (Bardini, 1994). So much for the Green Revolution in Bali.

Lansing made his career studying Balinese culture and was fully aware of how thoroughly Hindu religious thought permeated every aspect of daily life. He first conducted participant observation in one rice-growing village. He traveled with his *subak* on a pilgrimage to the Jero Gde at the High Temple on the crater lake. Gradually, he became fascinated with the rice-growing ecosystem of Bali, triggered by the failure of the miracle rice varieties.

In the late 1980s, Lansing, with the help of an ecological biologist, designed a computer simulation to calculate the effect on rice yields in each *subak* of (1) rainfall, (2) planting schedules, and (3) pest proliferation. He called his simulation model "The Goddess and the Computer." Then he traveled with a Macintosh computer and the simulation model from his U.S. university campus to the Balinese high priest at the temple on the crater lake. The Jero Gde enthusiastically tried out various scenarios on the computer, concluding that the highest rice yields closely resembled the ecological strategies followed by the Balinese rice farmers for the past eight hundred years.

When asked by Professor Lansing what he thought of the computer analysis of this sacred system of water management, the Jero Gde smiled mysteriously and replied, "Certainly you don't think that you came to work on this by coincidence, do you?"

Early Sociology

The intellectual tradition of "early sociology" traces its ancestry to the French sociologist Gabriel Tarde, but most of the research publications in this tradition appeared from the late 1920s to the early 1940s (at approximately the same time period that the anthropology diffusion was getting under way). The importance of the early sociology tradition is not due to its volume of investigations (there are only ten) nor to the sophistication of its research methods, but rather to the considerable influence of these early sociologists upon later diffusion researchers.

Early sociologists typically traced the diffusion of a single innovation over a geographical area like a state or a region. Their objective was to understand the process of social change. Except for Bowers (1937, 1938), who investigated the diffusion of ham radio sets, early sociologists did not emphasize the innovation-decision process, nor did they concentrate on the process by which opinion leaders influenced others in their system to adopt or reject a new idea.

Bowers's (1937, 1938) investigation was probably the first study in the early sociology tradition that used primary data from respondents, in addition to data from secondary sources such as government records. Bowers contacted a sample of 312 ham radio operators in the United States by mailed questionnaire in order to determine the influences that had led to their adoption of the ham radios. Bowers (1938) was the first researcher to find that interpersonal channels are more important than mass media channels for later adopters than for earlier adopters (see Chapter 5). The number of amateur radio operators in the United States had increased sharply from about 3,000 in 1914 to 64,000 in 1935. Bowers found that this adopter distribution followed an S-shaped curve when the number of adopters was plotted by year. Bowers also related such ecological factors as city size and region in the United States to the rate of adoption of ham radios. Like others in the early sociology tradition, Bowers thus correlated ecological variables with innovativeness.

The ten studies in the early sociology diffusion tradition differed from their anthropological counterparts in that they used quantitative data analysis, a methodological approach that would be followed by most other research traditions. But the intellectual paradigm that was to set off widespread research on the diffusion of innovations was not yet available. Creation of the paradigm had to wait for the rural sociology tradition.

Rural Sociology

The research tradition credited with forming the basic paradigm for diffusion research, and that has produced the largest number of diffusion studies, is rural sociology. Dominance of the diffusion field by rural sociology as indexed by the percentage of all diffusion studies completed by rural sociologists, has declined gradually over past decades as other diffusion research traditions have grown more rapidly in size. Up to 1964, 423 of the 950 diffusion publications (45 percent) were in rural sociology. This percentage has declined since then, as only a few rural sociology diffusion publications have appeared each year in the past decade. However, Table 2-1 shows that rural sociology is still very important in its share of all diffusion studies (20 percent), even though it has not grown much in the past decade or two. As Korsching (2001b, p. 106) concluded in his recent review of rural sociological diffusion research, "Research on the diffusion of innovations has declined in rural sociology, but it has not vanished."

Rural sociology is a subfield of sociology that focuses on the social problems of rural life. Many rural sociologists are employed in colleges of agriculture at land-grant universities. These agricultural schools have three main functions: (1) to teach students, (2) to conduct research on agricultural problems, so as to help farmers and agricultural businesses, and (3) to operate a state extension service to diffuse agricultural innovations (coming from research) to potential adopters, particularly farmers. The state colleges of agriculture and their research and extension subunits, the state agricultural experiment stations and the state agricultural extension services, respectively, were dominated for many years by a high value on agricultural production. In an organization where the main value is on raising farm production, diffusion research by rural sociologists was considered very useful. This was certainly true at the time of the Ryan and Gross (1943) study of hybrid seed corn in Iowa and for several decades thereafter.

Diffusion research provided helpful leads to agricultural researchers about how to get their scientific results put into use by farmers. Diffusion research was greatly appreciated by extension service workers, who depend on the diffusion model as the main theory guiding their efforts to transfer new agricultural technologies to farmers. So diffusion research fit in well with the strong value on agricultural production that dominated agricultural colleges. However, in recent decades, when surpluses of food production became a worldwide problem and the farm crisis pushed many American farmers out of agriculture, rural sociologists' interest in diffusion research began to fade. Also, the diffusion model became widely utilized by private agribusiness companies that sell fertilizers, pesticides, and other products to farmers. These commercial interests often misused the diffusion model, to the disgust of rural sociologists (Korsching, 2001b). Today diffusion study is relatively passé among rural sociologists.

THE HYBRID CORN STUDY AND THE RISE OF THE DIFFUSION PARADIGM Although several preparadigmatic diffusion studies had been completed during the 1920s and 1930s, the Ryan and Gross (1943) investigation of the diffusion of hybrid seed corn, more than any other study, influenced the methodology, theoretical framework, and interpretations of later students in the rural sociology tradition, and in other research traditions. As explained in Chapter 1, Dr. Bryce Ryan was a professor of rural sociology at Iowa State University, the state landgrant university in Ames. In 1941, the Iowa Agricultural Experiment Station (the research branch of the college of agriculture) funded his proposed investigation of the spread of hybrid seed to Iowa farmers.

Administrators of the Iowa Agricultural Experiment Station sponsored Professor Ryan's diffusion study to learn lessons that might be applied to the diffusion of other farm innovations. These officials were puzzled as to why such an obviously advantageous innovation as hybrid corn was not adopted more rapidly. Some farmers waited many years to adopt, during which they were surrounded by neighbors who were successfully using the innovation. Such deliberation did not fit with the notion of commercial farmers making rational, economic decisions. Today we understand that the uncertainty and risk associated with hybrid seed was one reason Iowa farmers were deliberate in adopting.

The main findings from the hybrid corn study, described in Chapter 1, will not be repeated here. This classic diffusion study headed later diffusion scholars toward pursuing certain research questions: What variables are related to innovativeness? What is the rate of adoption of an innovation over time, and what factors (such as the perceived attributes of the innovation) explain its speed of adoption? What role do different communication channels play at various stages in the innovation-decision process? These research directions have continued to dominate all diffusion research since 1943. The intellectual influence of the hybrid corn study reached far beyond the study of agricultural innovations and outside the rural sociology tradition of diffusion research. The research paradigm created by the Ryan and Gross investigation became the academic template that would be mimicked first by other rural sociologists in their agricultural diffusion researches and then by almost all other diffusion research traditions (whether they knew it or not).

THE INVISIBLE COLLEGE OF RURAL SOCIOLOGY DIFFUSION RESEARCHERS In the 1950s, a decade after Ryan and Gross set forth the diffusion paradigm in 1943, an explosion occurred in the number of diffusion studies by rural sociologists. Pioneering scholars in this tradition at the University of Wisconsin, the University of Missouri, Iowa State University, and at other land-grant universities carried forward the diffusion work launched by Ryan and Gross. New Ph.D.s in rural sociology, produced at Madison, Columbia, and Ames in the 1950s, then became professors at other state land-grant universities where they, in turn, established diffusion research programs. I was one of these diffusion research missionaries, earning a Ph.D. at Iowa State University in 1957 and then launching diffusion studies at Ohio State University.

The invisible college of diffusion reseachers in the rural sociology tradition was a highly interconnected network of scholars in 1973, when Crane (1972) gathered sociometric data by mailed questionnaire from 221 scholars in this research tradition. Dominating the network were two large cliques (a *clique* is a subsystem whose elements interact with each other relatively more frequently than with other members of the system), one composed of 27 scholars and the other of 32 researchers; each centered on a leading scholar of diffusion whose network links reached out to former Ph.D. students and to the students of these students. Smaller cliques of 13, 12, 7, etc., scholars were highly connected to the two major cliques.

The four largest cliques included all eight of the "high producers" (each of whom had ten or more diffusion publications); most of the clique members were their collaborators or students. All eight high producers were in close communication with one another about current research. As in other invisible colleges that have been studied, the most productive scientists were leaders of cliques, and their contacts with one another linked the cliques into a total network. However, 101 of the 221 researchers were isolates or members of cliques not connected to the rest of the network. Few of these 101 individuals were productive scholars; many completed their master's or Ph.D. theses but produced no further diffusion publications.

This network of rural sociology diffusion researchers provided consensus and coherence to the field. These scholars shared a common
framework for studying diffusion, and they kept abreast of one anoth-
ers' research findings. This invisible college helped the field to progress
toward its research goals in an orderly manner. These research directions
displayed a cumulative nature as each study built upon the accomplish-
ments of previous work. Radical deviations from the diffusion paradigm
were implicitly discouraged. Certain aspects of diffusion behavior were
ignored, because they were not part of the accepted paradigm. For
instance, little or no attention was given to re-invention, which was not
then recognized as a concept.

Another key factor in the growth of the rural sociology diffusion
research tradition in the 1950s, in addition to the interconnectedness of
the invisible college of scholars, was the availability of research funds.
During this period, state agricultural experiment stations, together with
the U.S. Department of Agriculture, which partially funds state agricultural research, were producing an outpouring of farm innovations:
weed sprays, chemical fertilizers, new crop varieties, chemical feeds for
livestock, and new farm machinery. The resulting "agricultural revolution" led to an increase in the number of persons fed and clothed by the
average American farmer from fourteen in 1950 to twenty-six in 1960
to forty-seven in 1970. This rapid increase in agricultural productivity
resulted from the diffusion of innovations to American farmers.

The diffusion studies by rural sociologists helped show agricultural
extension workers how to communicate new technological ideas to
farmers, and thus how to speed up the diffusion process. Thanks to
Ryan and Gross (1943), the rural sociologists had an appropriate paradigm
to guide their diffusion studies. Thanks to the agricultural revolution of
the 1950s, these diffusion scholars were in the right place (colleges of
agriculture at the state universities) at the right time. The result was a
proliferation of diffusion studies by the rural sociology tradition during
the 1960s. Then the volume of diffusion studies by rural sociologists
slowed down considerably (Figure 2–1).*

RURAL SOCIOLOGY DIFFUSION RESEARCH IN DEVELOPING NATIONS In
the early 1960s, American rural sociologists went international. The
decade of the 1960s marked a large-scale attempt to export the land-

---

*Some 185 studies by 1960 and 648 by 1970, but thereafter only 791 by 1981 and 845
by 1994.

grant university/agricultural extension service complex to the developing nations of Latin America, Africa, and Asia. With funding from the U.S. Agency for International Development (USAID) and from private foundations, U.S. land-grant universities created overseas counterparts in which American faculty members taught, conducted agricultural research, and advised extension services and other developmental programs. Rural sociologists were part of this overseas operation, and they (in collaboration with graduate students from these developing nations that they trained) launched diffusion studies in peasant villages. The main thrust of these international activities was agricultural development, so it was natural that the topic of the diffusion of farm innovations was pursued. In addition, rural sociologists investigated the diffusion of nutrition, health, and family-planning innovations to villagers.

The early 1960s marked the beginning of a sharp takeoff in the number of diffusion studies in developing countries (see Figure 2–1). Pioneering investigations by Syed A. Rahim (1961) in Bangladesh, and by Paul J. Deutschmann and Orlando Fals-Borda (1962b) in Colombia, suggested that new ideas spread among peasants in villages in a diffusion pattern generally similar to that in more media-saturated settings, such as the United States and Europe. The diffusion process, and the concepts and models used to analyze it, were cross-culturally valid. In later years, however, the applicability of the diffusion paradigm that was exported from the United States to developing nations began to be questioned (see Chapter 3).

The fast growth of diffusion studies in Third World countries in the 1960s occurred because technology was assumed to be the heart of development, at least as development was then conceptualized. So microlevel investigations of the diffusion of technological innovations among villagers were of direct relevance to development planners and to other government officials in developing nations. About 30 percent of all diffusion studies are conducted in Third World nations. Not all of these studies have been conducted by rural sociologists, but this tradition has played the pioneering role in launching diffusion research in developing nations.

DECLINE OF THE DIFFUSION PARADIGM IN RURAL SOCIOLOGY The number of rural sociology diffusion publications per year in the United States declined dramatically after 1958, and in developing nations after 1967. Thereafter, fewer diffusion publications were authored by rural sociologists each year (see Figure 2–1). The major research problems had been solved, anomalies appeared, and intellectual criticisms arose during the late 1960s and early 1970s. The diffusion paradigm that was developed by rural sociologists in U.S. midwestern universities during the 1940s and 1950s, spread internationally among rural sociologists, as well as to other disciplines. The subfield of rural sociological researchers declined, but not the diffusion paradigm.

The decline of interest in diffusion research by rural sociologists resulted from the very success of the paradigm in answering the major theoretical questions that it addressed. Crane (1972, p. 67) concluded, "In the rural sociology area, a significant proportion of the innovative work in the area had already been done by the time [around 1960] the field began to acquire a significant number of new members." Few interesting intellectual questions remained to be pursued, the number of new scholars attracted to the invisible college declined, and several of the leading diffusion scholars left the field.

Over the twenty-five-year period from 1941 to 1966, the number of research *innovations* (such as the introduction of a new study variable) averaged about 40 for each five-year period. During this twenty-five-year period, the number of diffusion publications increased spectacularly from 6 to 187, with the takeoff occurring over a decade after the publication of the Ryan and Gross (1943) study. Hence the ratio of research innovations in rural sociological diffusion research decreased drastically over the twenty-five-year period, dropping almost to zero in the two final five-year intervals. This decrease meant that the diffusion research front grew stale, as the scholarly literature consisted increasingly of replications. When a paradigm faces such a crisis, the rate of research activity drops (Price, 1963; Kuhn, 1962/1970). In this particular case, the paradigm was not found inadequate in its explanatory power, it became stale as the main research questions had already been answered. Unlike the general case described by Kuhn and others, the Ryan and Gross paradigm was not replaced by an alternate paradigm that offered an improved explanation of the diffusion of innovations.

Further, the mounting food surpluses produced by U.S. farmers led policy makers to question the previous value of raising agricultural production by diffusing farm innovations. Instead, rural sociologists turned their attention to finding solutions to the farm crisis caused by agricultural overproduction. Policy makers in agriculture, and rural sociologists themselves, began to see that the original conditions creating the need for diffusion research in agriculture had changed. After 1975, some rural sociologists turned their scholarly attention to studying the diffusion of conservation and other ecology-related innovations, as a result of growing national concerns with environmental problems. Other rural sociological diffusion studies looked at the role of gender in the diffusion and sustainability of such innovations as hedgerow farming in Africa (David, 1998). Finally, some studies investigated how key decisions made in developing an agricultural innovation led to its failure (Kremer et al., 2001).

During the 1970s, many American rural sociologists began to question whether conducting research on the diffusion of agricultural innovations was indeed their most useful role, as social scientists of rural society. This critical viewpoint was expressed in a radical book written by James Hightower (1972), *Hard Tomatoes and Hard Times: The Failure of America's Land-Grant College Complex*. Mechanized tomato harvesting required that farmers plant varieties so that the tomatoes were still very firm when they ripened. Both the harvesting machine and the hard tomato varieties were developed by agricultural researchers at state colleges of agriculture. These innovations benefited consumers through cheaper tomato prices. Unfortunately, many consumers did not like the hard tomatoes. They wanted ripe, red tomatoes that felt soft. The hard tomatoes also contained fewer vitamins than the older, soft varieties. Further, the mechanized tomato harvesters put thousands of farm laborers out of work and drove thousands of small farmers, who could not afford to buy the expensive harvesting machines, out of tomato production (these consequences of the tomato harvester are detailed in Chapter 4).

Hightower (1972) claimed that the state colleges of agriculture had been responsible for the agricultural revolution in the United States through their development and diffusion of farm innovations but that they had almost totally ignored the consequences of these technological innovations. Hightower said that this technological irresponsibility amounted to a failure on the part of U.S. colleges of agriculture. Most of the professional resources of the publicly supported land-grant colleges went into creating and diffusing agricultural production technology, while social science research on the consequences of innovation was severely short-changed. Currently, this allocation of resources has changed somewhat, due to the influence of the farm crisis in recent decades.

Rural sociologists have questioned the emphasis placed upon agricultural production technology by colleges of agriculture. If the result is increased agricultural production in the United States at the cost of driving many farm families out of agriculture, some rural sociologists wonder if colleges of agriculture are really serving the U.S. farmer.

EDUCATION Although it is an important diffusion research tradition in terms of the number of studies completed, education is less important in terms of its contribution to the theoretical understanding of the diffusion of innovations. An exciting potential contribution could be made by the education research tradition, because organizations are involved, in one way or another, in the adoption of most educational innovations. U.S. farmers and consumers mainly make optional innovation-decisions, but most teachers and school administrators are involved in collective and/or authority innovation-decisions. Teachers, unlike farmers and consumers, work in organizations, and so organizational structures are inevitably involved in educational adoption decisions. The number of educational diffusion studies totaled 23 in 1961 (5 percent of all diffusion research), 71 in 1968 (6 percent), 336 in 1981 (11 percent), and 359 in 1994 (9 percent of all diffusion publications). Since then, the number of new educational diffusion publications has slowed to a trickle.

THE TEACHERS COLLEGE DIFFUSION STUDIES Early educational diffusion studies were almost all completed at one institution, Columbia University's Teachers College, and under the direction of one scholar, Dr. Paul Mort. This tradition traces its roots to research in the 1920s and 1930s by Mort and others on whether local control over school financial decisions (as opposed to federal or state influence on these decisions) led to school innovativeness (Mort, 1957; Ross, 1958). In short, the Columbia University education diffusion studies set out to show that local school control was related to innovativeness, thought to be a desirable characteristic of schools by Professor Mort.

The data in these studies were often gathered by questionnaires mailed to school superintendents or principals. The unit of analysis was the school system. The Columbia University diffusion studies found that the best single predictor of school innovativeness was educational expenditure per student. The wealth factor appeared to be a necessary prerequisite. The stereotype of the rich suburban school in the United States as highly innovative was largely confirmed by the early Teachers College studies. Further, Paul Mort and his colleagues found that a considerable time lag was required for the adoption of educational innovations. "The average American school lags 25 years behind the best practice" (Mort, 1953).

Actually, there is a wide range in the rate of adoption of educational innovations. For instance, it took kindergartens about fifty years (from 1900 to 1950) to be adopted completely by U.S. schools (Mort, 1953).

But driver training needed only eighteen years (from 1935 to 1953) to reach widespread adoption (Allen, 1956), and modern math took only five years, from 1958 to 1963 (Carlson, 1965). Driver training and modern math were heavily promoted by change agencies: insurance companies and auto manufacturers in the case of driver training, and the National Science Foundation and the U.S. Department of Education in the case of modern math.

After Paul Mort's death in 1959, Teachers College at Columbia University lost its dominance in educational diffusion research. More recent studies focused upon (1) teachers as respondents, rather than school administrators, and (2) within-school as well as school-to-school diffusion. Some studies are conducted as a means of evaluating various diffusion initiatives carried out by government agencies (Berman and Pauly, 1975; Berman and McLaughlin, 1974, 1975, 1978; Berman et al., 1975, 1977). Other diffusion studies are carried out by graduate students in education for their doctoral dissertations.

The Diffusion of Modern Math in Pittsburgh*

An outstanding educational diffusion research study is Richard O. Carlson's (1965) analysis of the spread of modern math among school administrators in Pennsylvania and West Virginia. He studied the role of opinion leaders in the diffusion networks for the innovation of modern math among school superintendents, variables related to innovativeness, perceived characteristics of innovations and their rate of adoption, and the consequences of one educational innovation (programmed instruction).

Carlson's study is most impressive for the insight that it provided into the diffusion networks through which modern math spread from school to school in Allegheny County, Pennsylvania (the Pittsburgh metropolitan area). Carlson conducted personal interviews with each of the thirty-eight superintendents who headed these school systems, asking each respondent in what year they had adopted modern math, which other superintendents were their best friends, and certain other questions. Modern math entered the local educational scene of Allegheny County in 1958, when one school superintendent adopted. This cosmopolite innovator traveled outside of the Pittsburgh area, and was a sociometric isolate in the local network. None of

---

*This case illustration is based on Carlson (1965).

the thirty-seven other superintendents talked with him. The S shaped diffusion curve did not take off until 1959–1960, after a clique of six superintendents adopted (see Figure 8–1 for a sociogram of the thirty-eight school administrators). These six included the three most influential opinion leaders in the system. The rate of adoption for modern math then climbed steadily. Only one adoption occurred in 1958 (the innovator), five by the end of 1959, fifteen by 1960, twenty-seven by 1961, thirty-five by 1962, and all thirty-eight by the end of 1963. Thus, modern math spread to 100 percent adoption in about five years, much more quickly than the fifty years required for kindergartens to diffuse (Mort, 1959).

The initial adopter was too innovative to serve as an appropriate role model for the other school superintendents. They waited to adopt until the opinion leaders in the six-member clique favored the innovation. Carlson's focus on interpersonal networks in diffusion represented a step forward from the Ryan and Gross (1943) hybrid seed corn study, which did not gather sociometric data. The school superintendent study reminds one of the diffusion of a new drug among medical doctors, discussed in a following section.

Worldwide Diffusion of the Kindergarten*

Have you ever wondered why you started school in a class with a German name where building blocks, music, and play were more important than learning to read? The idea of a "child's garden" was created by Friedrich Froebel, a German educator, around 1850. His vision was of a special place in which small children were removed from parental influences, to learn to enjoy learning through playful activities. Froebel was labeled an agent of the socialist movement, and he was banned as a revolutionary by the Prussian government of Germany. Some inventors are not honored at home.

Meanwhile, the innovation of kindergartens was spread throughout the world by Froebel's disciples. By the 1870s, the first Froebel-type kindergartens had diffused to Western Europe and the United States. By the time of World War I in the 1910s, kindergartens were everywhere, including Africa and Asia, where colonial powers and missionaries introduced kindergartens to modernize local people. Some diffusion occurred directly from Germany, such as when teachers trained at the Pestalozzi-Froebel Haus in

*This case illustration is based on Wollons (2000a, 2000b).

Berlin and then spread Froebel's vision to other nations. Other diffusion was indirect, through intermediaries, as when Japanese teachers studied kindergartens in St. Louis and at the Froebel Institute in Chicago. China then borrowed Japanese-style kindergartens, which taught a Confucian model of family loyalty and respect for elders and for the emperor.

"In each case, local educators transferred, or recontextualized, the kindergarten" (Wollons, 2000a, p. 3). This re-invention occurred because educators fit the kindergarten to national values. For example, Froebel's original kindergarten emphasized memorization skills and conformity to authority. American kindergartens taught patriotism and folk tales and encouraged individualism, rather than conformity. Japanese kindergartens, although modeled on the American model, were entirely different. In Poland, the kindergarten was used subversively by parents to transmit Polish language and culture during years of foreign rule. In Israel, kindergartens taught Zionist philosophy and Hebrew language. In the United States, women promoted the kindergarten and usually served as the teachers, but in Japan and China, kindergartens were dominated by men.

Thus the miniature world of the kindergarten was connected to national values and to the larger world of politics. Undoubtedly the high degree of re-invention of the kindergarten in each culture greatly aided its widespread diffusion.

Public Health and Medical Sociology

This diffusion tradition began in the 1950s and has continued growing since that time. The innovations of study are (1) new drugs or other new medical ideas that are adopted by doctors or other health professionals or (2) family-planning methods, HIV/AIDS prevention, and other health innovations, where the adopters are patients or members of the public. The number of diffusion studies in the public health/medical tradition increased from 36 in 1961 (7 percent of all diffusion publications), to 76 in 1968 (7 percent), to 226 in 1981 (7 percent), to 227 in 1994 (7 percent), and to about 10 percent in 2002.

Huge improvements in the public's health have occurred in the United States in recent decades: for example, the rate of mammography for breast cancer detection has tripled over the past thirty years, while the rate of cigarette smoking has slowly declined. Much of this health improvement has resulted from intervention programs, such as smoking cessation programs, mammography campaigns, drug abuse interventions, and so forth. Over the past decade, forty-nine national health campaigns costing $1.4 billion have been carried out. A good deal of health improvement has also occurred through spontaneous diffusion of healthy lifestyles. When enough people in an individual's personal network stop smoking, the individual feels uncomfortable when smoking around these friends. Here we see an example of the "tipping point" (Gladwell, 2000), when a small change, such as a few more individuals in a network who cease smoking, triggers a big change in the rate of adoption of smoking cessation in a large system. In the present book, we call this process the critical mass in the diffusion of an innovation.

The diffusion model is centrally involved both in spontaneous diffusion and in planned interventions for health improvement.

The Columbia University Drug Diffusion Study*

The classic study in this tradition was completed by three sociologists, Elihu Katz, Herbert Menzel, and James S. Coleman, at Columbia University's Bureau of Applied Social Research, then America's foremost social science research institute (Rogers, 1994). The drug diffusion investigation is perhaps second only to the Ryan and Gross study of hybrid seed corn diffusion in terms of its contribution to the diffusion paradigm. The most noted impact of the Columbia University drug study was to orient future diffusion research toward investigating the interpersonal networks through which subjective evaluations of an innovation are exchanged among the individuals in a system. The drug study helped illuminate the nature of interpersonal diffusion networks, suggesting the role that opinion leaders play in the takeoff of the S-shaped diffusion curve. The Columbia study established clearly that diffusion was a social process.

The market research department at Charles Pfizer and Company, a large pharmaceutical firm, provided a grant of $40,000 to the three Columbia University sociologists to conduct the drug diffusion study, which began in 1954. Pfizer originally wanted to know if the advertisements it purchased in medical journals were influential in diffusing the company's new drug prod-

---

*This case illustration is based on Burt (1980, 1987), Burt and Janicik (1996), Menzel and others (1959), Menzel and Katz (1955), Coleman and others (1957, 1959, 1966), Katz (1956, 1957, 1961), Katz and others (1963), Menzel (1957, 1959, 1960), Valente (1993, 1995, 1996), and Van den Buelte and Lilien (2001).

ucts. This prosaic market research question was converted by the Columbia University sociologists into an important diffusion study of interpersonal communication networks.

A pilot study of the spread of a new drug was carried out among thirty-three doctors in a New England town (Menzel and Katz, 1955). The main investigation was then conducted in late 1954 in four cities in Illinois: Peoria, Bloomington, Quincy, and Galesburg. The drug study analyzed the diffusion of a new antibiotic, tetracycline, that had appeared in late 1953. This innovation was referred to by the Columbia University researchers in most of their publications by a pseudonym, "gammanym." The drug had been tried at least once by 87 percent of the Illinois doctors under study, who had been using two other closely related "miracle" drugs belonging to the same antibiotic family. The new drug superseded an existing idea, just as hybrid corn had replaced open-pollinated seed. Tetracycline's main advantage over the earlier antibiotics was that it had fewer side effects (Van den Buelte and Lilien, 2001).

Though the medical doctor makes the innovation-decision for a new drug, the patient pays for the prescription. The Columbia University sociologists interviewed 125 general practitioners, internists, and pediatricians in the four Illinois cities. These were 85 percent of the doctors practicing in specialties in which the drug was important. The 125 doctors sociometrically designated 103 additional doctors in other specialties as their network partners, who were also interviewed by the Columbia University research team. The total sample of 228 doctors constituted 64 percent of all medical doctors practicing in the four Illinois cities (Coleman et al., 1957).

An objective measure of each doctor's time of adoption of gammanym was obtained from the record of drugstore prescriptions that were written by the doctors of study. Thus the drug study did not have to depend upon respondents' recall of data about innovativeness (as have most other diffusion studies). Many doctors reported having adopted the drug earlier than their prescription records indicated, although this discepancy might have occurred because only a 10 percent sample of prescription records was gathered by the research team.

The Columbia University investigators were not aware of other research traditions on diffusion at the time that the gammanym data were gathered. They made no secret of their surprise upon discovery of the hybrid seed corn study. Katz (1961) stated "The drug study was completed . . . without any real awareness of its many similarities to the study that had been undertaken by Ryan and Gross almost 15 years before." There were striking parallels between the findings of the hybrid corn study and the drug study, which are all the more impressive given the considerable differences between farmers and physicians. For instance, innovative doctors attended more out-of-town medical meetings than did later adopters, just as innovative Iowa farmers displayed their cosmopoliteness by visiting Des Moines more frequently. Later diffusion studies also reported that innovators have friendship networks that extend outside of their local system. And just as the innovative Iowa farmers had larger farms and higher incomes, the innovative doctors served richer patients and had a more wealthy medical practice. So in both studies, socioeconomic status was positively related to innovativeness. Imagine the present author's excitement when he first compared the drug study's findings with those of the Ryan and Gross (1943) investigation while writing his Ph.D. dissertation in 1956.

The most important findings of the Columbia University drug study dealt with interpersonal diffusion networks. Coleman and his colleagues (1966) found that almost all of the opinion leaders, defined as the doctors who received three or more sociometric choices as social friends, had adopted gammanym by the eighth month (of the seventeen-month diffusion period). At about this point, the S-shaped diffusion curve for the opinion leaders' followers really took off. One reason for the S-shaped curve is that once the opinion leaders in a system adopt, they then convey their subjective evaluations of the innovation to their many network partners, who are thereby influenced to adopt the new idea (Valente, 1995). This point in time at which a critical mass of doctors adopted, and the S-shaped curve took off, is a key factor in the diffusion process (see Chapter 8).

A social system is a kind of collective learning system in which the experiences of the earlier adopters of an innovation, transmitted through interpersonal networks, determine the rate of adoption of their followers. Such learning by doing in a social system can, of course, take a negative turn if the innovation is not efficacious in solving a problem. If the new drug had not been very effective in curing the innovative doctors' patients, they would have quickly passed their dissatisfaction with the new drug along to their peers. Then the S-shaped diffusion curve would have displayed a much slower rate of adoption, or it might have reached a plateau and declined as a result of widespread discontinuance of tetracycline. Thus the social system in which an innovation diffuses acts like a participatory democracy in which the aggregated individual adoption decisions of its members represent a consensus vote on the new idea.

A doctor's position in the communication network of physicians in his community had important consequences for the doctor's innovativeness. Individuals who were *isolates*, defined as doctors not connected to anyone else, required 9.5 months, on the average, to adopt tetracycline, while only 7.9 months from release of the new drug were needed for nonisolates (Valente, 1995). Here, being connected meant being innovative.

The doctors in the Columbia University diffusion study had plentiful information about the new drug. Tetracycline had undergone randomized controlled clinical trials by pharmaceutical firms and by university medical professors prior to its release to the medical community. The results of these scientific evaluations of the new drug were communicated (1) in medical journal articles to physicians and (2) by "detail men" (employees of the drug firms who contacted doctors with information about the new drug, and who gave the doctors reprints of the journal articles and free samples of tetracycline). These promotional activities created awareness-knowledge of the innovation in the medical community, but such scientific evaluations of the new drug were not sufficient to persuade the average doctor to adopt. Subjective evaluations of the new drug based on the personal experiences of each doctor's peers were key in convincing the typical doctor to adopt the drug with his/her own patients. When an office partner said to a colleague, "Look, Doctor, I prescribe tetracycline for my patients, and it cures them more effectively than other antibiotics," such a personal, targeted message often had an effect on persuasion.

The crucial role of interpersonal network communication in the diffusion of gammanym led James Coleman and others (1966) to investigate which doctors talked to whom. Why had a respondent chosen one, two, or three other doctors (out of the several hundred doctors in the community) as his or her best friends? A dyadic network analysis disclosed that religion and age were the main determinants of friendship links, with hometown and the medical school attended also of some importance. But the main reasons for person-to-person links in the medical community were professional affiliations, such as belonging to the same hospital or clinic as another doctor or participating with him or her in an office partnership.

In all, the Columbia University drug study showed the important role of interpersonal networks in the diffusion process. More than anything else, it was the social power of peers talking to peers about the innovation that led to adoption of the new idea.

FAMILY-PLANNING DIFFUSION IN DEVELOPING NATIONS Since the classic investigation of drug diffusion, many other diffusion studies have been completed in the public health diffusion tradition. A few of these studies dealt with the spread of new medical ideas to doctors, but most are investigations of the diffusion of health or family-planning innovations to members of the public, especially in developing countries. Since the early 1980s, many of the public health investigations have dealt with the diffusion of HIV/AIDS prevention (Singhal and Rogers, 2003).

An important initial boost to the internationalization of the diffusion field was the rise of "KAP surveys" in the developing countries of Latin America, Africa, and Asia, beginning in the the 1960s. KAP studies are sample surveys of knowledge (K), attitudes (A), and adoption or practice (P) of family planning innovations. K, A, and P are the main dependent variables in evaluations of family-planning programs (and in many other health interventions). As national family-planning programs were established in recent decades in Latin America, Africa, and Asia to cope with the overpopulation problem, hundreds of KAP-type diffusion researches were carried out.

With the exception of the Taichung experiment in Taiwan (Freedman and Takeshita, 1969), described shortly, the intellectual contribution of these KAP surveys "to scientific understanding of human behavior change has been dismal" (Rogers, 1973, p. 378). Although they may not have advanced the diffusion model, the KAP studies served a practical function by showing that most parents in developing countries wanted fewer children than they actually were having and that the majority of the public desired a government family-planning program. The KAP surveys had an important impact on policy makers in developing nations, initially showing that national family-planning programs were feasible and later providing a means for evaluating the effectiveness of such interventions.

Intellectually speaking, the family-planning diffusion studies were generally disappointing, although several modifications in the classical diffusion model were formulated by family-planning programs: the payment of incentives to promote the diffusion and adoption of contraception, the use of nonprofessional change agent aides, and the use of various communication strategies to help overcome the taboo nature of family-planning methods. Such modifications in the classical diffusion model emerged when family-planning programs in Third World nations found the classical model wanting for purposes of promoting preventive innovations such as contraceptives (Rogers, 1973).

A *preventive* innovation is an idea that an individual adopts at one point in time in order to lower the probability that some future unwanted event may occur (see Chapter 6). The unwanted future event might not have happened anyway, even without adoption of the preventive innovation, so the relative advantage of adoption is not very clear cut to individuals at the time that they are urged to adopt by public health programs. Also, the prevented events, by definition, do not occur, and thus they cannot be observed or counted. For instance, family-planning officials estimate the consequences of contraception in "births averted," a type of behavior that is invisible to individual adopters, which means they have difficulty in perceiving this outcome. For these reasons, preventive innovations such as family planning and HIV/AIDS prevention generally have a relatively slow rate of adoption.

Most national family-planning programs found it much easier to diffuse knowledge about contraceptive methods and to achieve favorable attitudes toward family planning than to secure the widespread adoption of contraception by the intended audience. Thus KAP surveys often find a "KAP-gap," with a relatively high percentage of knowledge increase and favorable attitudes toward family-planning methods (that is, K and A) but a relatively low rate of adoption (P) (this KAP-gap is consistent with the hierarchy-of-effects model, discussed in Chapter 5). In the developing nations of Latin America, Africa, and Asia, government policy makers realized the crucial need to lower the rate of population growth. Otherwise, how could enough food, clothing and schooling be provided for the exploding number of children that are born? So these governments carried out mass media campaigns for family planning, leading to widespread K and A. But most parents did not share their government's desire for a lower rate of population growth. Members of the public wanted to have more children (especially boys) as low-cost farm labor, an eventual source of retirement support, and a means of carrying on the family name. The result was the KAP-gap. Similarly, a KAP-gap has often been found for many other preventive health innovations.

The Taichung Field Experiment*

The Taichung study in Taiwan by Bernard Berelson and Ronald Freedman (1964) was one of the earliest and the most important of the family-planning KAP studies. Unlike the other KAP surveys, the Taichung study was a *field experiment*, that is, an experiment conducted under realistic conditions in

---

*This case illustration is based on Berelson and Freedman (1964) and Freedman and Takeshita (1969).

which preintervention and postintervention measurements are usually obtained by surveys. In a field experiment, data are gathered from a sample of respondents at two points in time by means of a benchmark survey and a follow-up survey. Soon after the benchmark survey, a treatment (or treatments) is implemented in the study area. The effects of the treatment are determined by measuring the change in some dependent variable (for instance, adoption of innovations) between the benchmark survey and the follow-up survey. One advantage of field experimental designs is that they allow the researcher to determine the time order of an independent (treatment) variable on the dependent variable. As such, field experiments are a rather ideal design for evaluating a diffusion intervention. The Berelson and Freedman study in Taiwan was one of the best, as well as one of the biggest: "This effort . . . is one of the most extensive and elaborate social science experiments ever carried out in a natural setting" (Berelson and Freedman, 1964).

The researchers implemented four different communication interventions in approximately 2,400 neighborhoods (each composed of twenty to thirty families) in Taichung, a large city in Taiwan: (1) neighborhood meetings about family planning, (2) neighborhood meetings, plus information about family planning mailed to local adopters, (3) neighborhood meetings, plus a personal visit to the home of likely adopters by a female change agent who sought to persuade women to adopt family planning, and (4) neighborhood meetings, plus personal visits by the change agent to both husband and wife in families likely to adopt. In addition, all of the 2,400 neighborhoods in Taichung were blanketed with family-planning posters as part of a mass communication campaign.

The results of this diffusion field experiment were spectacular: 40 percent of the eligible audience of about 10,000 women adopted some form of family planning. Pregnancy rates immediately decreased by about 20 percent. Seventy-eight percent of the contraceptives adopted were IUDs, a new family-planning method that was promoted by the experiment. The Taichung study showed that home visits by change agents were essential for the success of a family-planning program. Mass media communication (that is, the posters) created awareness-knowledge, but interpersonal communication motivated the adoption of contraceptives. The Taichung researchers were surprised to find that considerable interpersonal diffusion occurred between their 2,400 neighborhoods of study and the rest of the city (which was considered their control group). This unplanned diffusion spoiled their neat experimental design, but it may have been their most important finding. Again, we see that interpersonal networks among near peers energized the diffusion process, in this case even when they were not expected to do so.

The spectacular results of the Taiwan diffusion experiment provided optimism among public officials responsible for national family-planning programs, which were then being initiated in many developing countries, at first in Asia and later in Latin America and Africa. In the decades since the Berelson-Freedman study, however, it has proven impossible to achieve rates of adoption comparable to those achieved in Taiwan. Perhaps the Taiwan experiment led to an unrealistically rosy glow about family-planning diffusion, an optimism that would be dashed during the later 1960s and 1970s, when many other nations launched family-planning programs. In fact, the experience of these programs to date suggests that contraceptives are a particulary difficult type of innovation to diffuse (Rogers, 1973), for reasons discussed in Chapter 6.

A methodological point made by the Taichung family-planning study was that diffusion investigations need not be limited to one-shot surveys of the adopters of an innovation, with data gathering taking place only after a new idea has diffused. A field experimental design allows a diffusion researcher to draw on diffusion theory in order to plan one or more communication interventions that are then evaluated by analyzing differences in K, A, and P variables between benchmark and follow-up surveys. For example, in Chapter 8 we discuss numerous field experiments showing that opinion leaders can speed up the diffusion process. Diffusion field experiments can advance our understanding of diffusion behavior, and help policy makers design and implement more effective diffusion programs. Yet to date only a small percentage of all diffusion studies have been field experiments, for reasons of cost and the number of years required to conduct such experiments.

STOP AIDS in San Francisco

The STOP AIDS experience in San Francisco in the mid-1980s, and the many HIV prevention interventions modeled upon it, show that when the diffusion model is used effectively in public health programs, it can save lives. The STOP AIDS program was organized by and for gay men in San Francisco. This intervention was based on the diffusion model and on social psychologist Kurt Lewin's small group strategy of changing human behavior in groups (Rogers, 1994). STOP AIDS employed outreach workers who were gay, and many of whom were HIV-positive, to recruit individuals to small group meetings of from ten to twelve men. The meetings were held in homes and apartments along Castro Street and in other neighborhoods in San Francisco where gay men lived. Each meeting, led by a gay man, who often was HIV-positive, featured explanation of the means of HIV transmission and of safer sex. Each small group meeting ended with the individuals being asked to raise their hands if they intended to practice safer sex and if they would organize and lead a future small-group meeting (Singhal and Rogers, 2002).

Planners of the STOP AIDS intervention assumed that if they could reach a critical mass of opinion leaders in the gay community of San Francisco, the idea of HIV prevention would then spread spontaneously by interpersonal communication networks to others in the target population. STOP AIDS used the small group approach to recruit leaders to organize further small-group meetings, so that the diffusion process was used to spread the small-group intervention.

STOP AIDS trained 7,000 individuals in the small group meetings, and they reached another 30,000 individuals out of the total gay population in San Francisco of 142,000 individuals (Wolfeiler, 1998). Then, in the late 1980s, attendance at the small-group meetings declined, and STOP AIDS closed down. The number of new HIV infections per year in San Francisco dropped from 8,000 in 1983 to 650 in 1985, a spectacular decrease (not all of which was due to STOP AIDS). The rate of unprotected anal intercourse (one of the main means of HIV transmission in San Francisco) dropped from 71 percent in 1983 to 27 percent in 1987. Accordingly, the number of AIDS-related deaths per year dropped from 1,600 in the mid-1980s to only 250 in recent years (much of the very recent decrease since the mid-1990s is due to the use of anti-retroviral drugs). The applications of diffusion of innovations theory, combined with Lewinian small-group social psychology, helped stem the spread of the epidemic. Unfortunately, this intervention began too late for almost half of the gay population of San Francisco, who were already infected before the STOP AIDS intervention was launched.

The present author studied the STOP AIDS intervention in the early 1990s, and observed replications of this approach being conducted in developing countries (Singhal and Rogers, 2003). One replication in the United States, inspired partially by the San Francisco model, was conducted by Jeffrey A. Kelly and his colleagues (1992, 1997). Opinion leaders were identified by bartenders in gay bars and trained in how to prevent HIV infection among gay men in U.S. cities (the study by Kelly and associates is described later in this chapter). This gay bar/opinion leadership strategy is currently being evaluated in five developing nations.

Communication

The communication tradition of diffusion research today is one of the larger in the number of diffusion publications and one of the fastest-growing in the past decade, representing 15 percent of all diffusion publications (see Table 2-1). At the time of my 1962 book *Diffusion of Innovations,* there were so few diffusion publications by communication scholars (1 percent of the total), and I did not consider communication as a diffusion research tradition. At about that time, however, departments of communication began to spread among U.S. universities. Currently, there are more than 2,000 such departments, with approximately an equal number in other nations. American universities award 50,000 bachelor's degrees in communication each year (approximately 5 percent of the total number of degrees granted), 2,000 master's degrees, and 250 Ph.D. degrees.

Diffusion research began in 1943, before the academic field of communication study got under way around 1960. Human communication as a scientific field of study was not fully appreciated until an influential book, *The Mathematical Theory of Communication* by Claude E. Shannon and Warren Weaver (1949), appeared. Shannon defined the key concept of information and proposed a basic model of communication. Then the field of communication research, initially centered on the effects of the mass media, began to grow. Earlier, in the 1930s and 1940s, established scientists from political science, sociology, and social psychology, such as Harold Lasswell, Paul Lazarsfeld, Kurt Lewin, and Carl Hovland, had conducted communication research. Soon, however, departments of communication were established at many universities, and began producing Ph.D.s in communication. These new scholars then were employed as professors in already existing university departments of journalism and speech, where they injected the new perspective of communication study into the existing curricula (Rogers, 1994). Professors and students of communication naturally look at diffusion as a special kind of human communication in that the messages deal with new ideas.

One early interest of communication scholars was to study the diffusion of news events. More than sixty such studies have now been completed, dealing with such headline news items as Princess Diana's death in 1997, assassination of a head of state, and disasters such as the 1986 Challenger explosion and the September 11, 2001, terrorist attacks on the World Trade Center. Unlike technological innovations, news events are ideas that do not have a material basis. Nevertheless, news events diffuse in a generally similar fashion: the distribution of knowers over time follows an S-shaped curve, interpersonal and mass media channels play comparable roles, and so on. One difference from the diffusion of other innovations is that news events spread much more rapidly. For example, 92 percent of the U.S. adult public was aware of the events in Dallas within one hour of the shot that felled President Kennedy. Similarly, within a few hours of the Challenger disaster, the investment community reacted by dropping the stock market price of Morton Thiokol (the corporation that had made the faulty O-rings on the Challenger's booster rockets) by 20 percent. Within three hours of the September 11 terrorist attacks, almost all of the 127 adults sampled in Albuquerque, New Mexico, had heard the news (Rogers and Siedel, 2002).

This rapidity of news diffusion occurs because the individual only needs to gain awareness-knowledge of the news event, while the adoption of a technological innovation consists of the knowledge, persuasion, decision, and implementation stages in the innovation-decision process. One of the important contributions of news event diffusion studies has been to establish the conditions under which mass media are relatively more important than interpersonal communication channels in spreading a new idea.

DIFFUSION OF NEWS EVENTS Although it was not the first investigation of the diffusion of a major news event, the 1960 study by Paul Deutschmann and Wayne Danielson, more than any other, set the pattern for the many news diffusion researches that were to follow over future decades. The Deutschmann/Danielson (1960) study is the most widely cited of the news event diffusion publications. Deutschmann and Danielson were two of the first individuals to earn Ph.D. degrees in communication study, both from Stanford University under Wilbur Schramm, who pioneered this new field of study (Rogers, 1994). So Deutschmann and Danielson viewed news diffusion as a communication process (both had been newspaper reporters prior to their graduate study), which helped them to formulate the paradigm for news diffusion studies. Although Deutschmann was thoroughly familiar with rural sociological research on diffusion, and this knowledge certainly influenced his research on news diffusion, Deutschmann and Danielson (1960) did not cite diffusion research in any other tradition.

News diffusion investigations focus mainly on tracing the spread of spectacularly important news events such as the assassination of a U.S.

president, or a Norwegian prime minister; the launch of Sputnik or the Challenger disaster; or some other major world news event, such as the September 11 terrorist attacks. At such times, all the mass media virtually crackle with the excitement of the news. People often approach complete strangers on the street to tell them about the news event! As Deutschmann and Danielson (1960) stated, "Every so often a major news story 'breaks'; reporters get the essential facts in a matter of minutes and send them on their way. . . . Radio and television stations break into their programs to broadcast bulletins. Newspapers stop their presses for quick make-overs. In a flood of printed and spoken words, the message leaves the media."

What happens next, as the news reaches the public and spreads from individual to individual, is the main concern of news diffusion scholars. These investigations show how important radio, television, newspaper, and interpersonal channels are in diffusing the news event, and how quickly such diffusion occurs: very rapidly, Deutschmann and Danielson (1960) found. Within half a day of such major news events as President Eisenhower's stroke, launch of the Explorer I satellite, and Alaska's becoming a state, from 70 to 90 percent of the U.S. public knew about these news events. Within thirty minutes of the *Challenger* explosion in 1986, half of a sample of Phoenix residents had heard of the disaster (Mayer et al., 1990).

FIREHOUSE RESEARCH Because news diffusion is so rapid, the process is difficult to study by the usual communication research methods. If a scholar applied for a research grant, designed and pretested a questionnaire, trained survey interviewers, and then contacted a sample of the public, it would be many months or even several years after the news event occurred. Most respondents would by then have forgotten the details of their behavior. Thus a "firehouse research" design was followed by Deutschmann and Danielson. They planned their questionnaire in advance of the three news events that they studied and trained graduate students in how to conduct telephone interviews. The costs of such quick-response data gathering were extremely modest, as samples of several hundred individuals each were contacted in Lansing, Michigan, and Madison, Wisconsin (Deutschmann was a professor at Michigan State University and Danielson was at the University of Wisconsin), and in Palo Alto, California (where the two scholars had previously studied for their Ph.D. degrees). As a result of these quick-response data-gathering methods, Deutschmann and Danielson were able to begin telephone interviewing about twenty-four hours after the news event. A similar firehouse research design has been utilized by most other news diffusion scholars. News events are for communication scholars what Drosophila melanogaster (fruit flies) are for geneticists: a new generation arises very quickly (Rogers, 2000).

Deutschmann and Danielson (1960) found that radio, television, and newspapers were each cited by more respondents as their first source or channel of communication about a news event than were interpersonal networks. The mass media, especially newspapers, were also important in providing further information about a news event. "Two-thirds of our respondents reported being involved in conversations about the news events" (Deutschmann and Danielson, 1960). Then many of these individuals turned to the media, especially television, to confirm the news and to obtain further details.

In general, the two communication scholars documented the lightning-like nature of news diffusion, compared to the more usual diffusion of technological innovations in agriculture, education, and medicine, where months and years, instead of hours, are required for the diffusion process. Relatively earlier knowers about a news event were characterized by more formal education and higher-status occupations, than were later relatively later knowers (see Chapter 5).

Deutschmann and Danielson (1960) concluded that on the basis of the three major news events that they studied in the three university cities, "The diffusion process is far more regular than we suspected." Such common patterns of news event diffusion were later found by other scholars in the news diffusion research tradition (Rogers, 2000).

SALIENCE The rapidity of news diffusion especially characterizes news events of extremely high news value, such as the assassination of President Kennedy in 1963 or the shooting of Pope John Paul II in 1981. The media, especially radio and television, carry the news to many people, and then the news fans out by word of mouth. Less spectacular, everyday news events of the kind that appear on the front page of a daily newspaper, spread mainly via mass media channels. Events of relatively low news value, such as last night's decision by the city council to build a new sewer line, while reported in the media, mainly spread by interpersonal channels among a few people who are really interested in the particular issue (Greenberg, 1964).

Salience is the degree to which a news event is perceived as important by individuals. What determines this salience of a news event? The media convey to their audience strong clues about the degree to which media professionals judge an event to have high news value: whether a news story is given bulletin status (that is, by interrupting regular broadcasts), whether it appears in bold headlines or at the top of a news show, and the length of broadcast time or news space allotted to the news story. Audience individuals evaluate the news story on the basis of whether it concerns someone of celebrity status, such as "Magic" Johnson, the U.S. president, or the pope, whether it affects them directly in some way, and whether it has local implications.

A news story that is perceived by an individual as having high salience leads an audience individual (1) to seek further information and (2) to tell others, often strangers, about the news. When an individual hears the news about Princess Diana's death, John Kennedy, Jr.'s plane crash, or a terrorist attack, this news may be so salient that the individual drops all other concerns. A spontaneous initiation of heterophilous network conversations through talking with strangers explains why high-salience news events spread more rapidly and particularly via interpersonal channels (Rogers, 2000).

The degree of salience is a quality characterizing each news event. The perceived salience of a news event also varies from individual to individual. For example, Catholics would be expected to perceive an attempted assassination of the pope as relatively more salient than would non-Catholics. In India, Hindus learned about statues of Hindu gods drinking milk earlier, talked to more other people about this news event, and were more likely to actually try feeding milk to the gods (Singhal et al., 1999). Princess Diana's death led to overt behavior change by a great many audience individuals. More than a million mourners lined the three-mile funeral route in London, hundreds of millions watched the event on television, people purchased millions of copies of books about Diana in the weeks following her death (several became best-sellers), and Elton John's song "Candle in the Wind," altered slightly to fit the event, became the best-selling single of all time (Brown et al., 1998). What caused this vast outpouring of grief over Princess Diana's death? One explanation is *parasocial interaction,* defined as the degree to which audience individuals perceive that they have a personal relationship with a media personality (Singhal and Rogers, 1999). Younger women tended to have a higher degree of parasocial interaction with Diana, and they were especially likely to watch her funeral service on television (Brown et al., 1998).

SITUATIONAL VARIABLES AND INTERPERSONAL NEWS DIFFUSION In addition to perceived salience, the degree to which an individual learns about a news event from interpersonal communication channels depends on such situational variables as time of day and whether or not he or she is at home or at work. For example, Mayer and colleagues (1990) found that people who were at home were three times as likely to have heard about the *Challenger* disaster (which occurred at 9:40 A.M. local time in Phoenix) from the media than people who were at work. Individuals at home are in a communication situation where the likelihood of being told about the news story by others, and of telling someone else, is more restricted than for individuals who are in a work setting. So women, who were more likely to be at home during the daytime hours on a weekday, were less likely to be exposed to interpersonal communication about the *Challenger* explosion.

Diffusion of News of the September 11 Terrorist Attacks*

"My stepfather was in the World Trade Center and my uncle was in the Pentagon."

"Makes me realize that airport security was a farce."

"Oh my God, we are in war!"

These statements were made by three of the 127 respondents in a survey of the diffusion of news of the September 11, 2001, terrorist attacks on New York City and Washington, D.C. Much more than the news events studied in past research, the September 11 news affected audience members emotionally. The terrorist attacks were intended to create terror, and our survey in Albuquerque, New Mexico, suggested that the terrorists were quite successful. The terrorist attacks also brought forth a high degree of patriotism, with people displaying flags in their homes, at workplaces, and on their vehicles.

The September 11 attacks were a spectacular news event that the American public perceived as highly salient and that diffused very rapidly. The mass media devoted hours of news coverage to them each day, yet the public did not seem to become tired of the news, in part because yet newer

---

*This case illustration is based on Rogers and Siedel (2002).

events continued to occur, such as the bombing of Afghanistan, the threat of anthrax, video speeches by Osama bin Laden, and the landing of special military forces in Afghanistan. Thus the news story was of a continuing nature and received very heavy media coverage for months after September 11.

The first terrorist attacks on the World Trade Center occurred at 6:46 A.M. Albuquerque time (two hours different from New York and Washington time). The percentage of the 127 respondents knowing of the terrorist attacks increased rapidly from 7 percent between 6:00 and 7:00 A.M. to 34 percent between 7:00 and 8:00 A.M., jumped to 70 percent between 8:00 and 9:00 A.M., and then increased to 92 percent between 9:00 and 10:00 A.M. By noon, 99 percent, 120 of the 121 respondents (6 of the 127 did not answer this question) knew about the news event of that morning. The relatively rapid diffusion of this news event was due to its high salience to the respondents and to its complete dominance of the broadcasting media.

After a slow early growth, the diffusion curve took off around 7:00 A.M. People wanted to share information about the terrorist attacks, and person-to-person communication played a major role in the news event's diffusion, especially for individuals who heard later in the morning. The news and photographs of the World Trade Center were so shocking that people felt they had to share this information, and their feelings, with others. Some 88 of the 127 respondents (69 percent) told someone else about the terrorist attacks. These 88 people reached, in total, 418 other people, an average of 4.8 people each. Some 80 percent of the 88 respondents told from one to four people, while two respondents each informed more than fifty people about the terrorist attacks.

The average time of first hearing about the terrorist attacks from mass media channels was 8:38 A.M., while that for first hearing from interpersonal channels was 10:03 A.M., about 1½ hours later. The media created initial awareness for some members of the public, who then told others.

Some 59 percent of the 127 respondents said they had been personally affected by the terrorist attacks of September 11, 2001. They said:

"I am depressed, sad, upset and angry."

"I no longer want to move to New York."

"Reaffirmed my patriotism."

"I am in the military and ready to fly."

"My uncle almost died [in the World Trade Center], but he was late to work."

Some 86 percent of the respondents engaged in some activity as a result of the terrorist attacks. Two thirds prayed for the victims, 21 percent participated in memorial events, 16 percent contributed money, and 8 percent contributed blood (the number would have been greater, but blood collection centers were swamped). More than one third of the respondents displayed a U.S. flag on their home or vehicle. Other people spoke with Muslim friends, volunteered to help in New York, or gave lessons or talks about the terrorist attacks to a class or at a meeting.

CONTRIBUTIONS OF NEWS DIFFUSION RESEARCH The number of news event diffusion publications by decades shows an initial rapid increase following the 1960 Deutschmann and Danielson study and then a leveling off in the 1970s and thereafter, with about one study published each year (Rogers, 2000). One synthesis of the news diffusion studies by Melvin DeFleur (1987) argued that "The tradition has all but run out." After flourishing in the 1960s and 1970s, scholarly interest in news diffusion declined as most of the intriguing research questions were answered, and news event diffusion became stuck in an intellectual rut, perhaps by following the Deutschmann and Danielson (1960) paradigm too closely. The rise-and-fall pattern of a research front is not a historical inevitability, however. A scientific field can reorient its directions so as to pursue new leads. Perhaps one important contribution of this research was to help interest communication scholars in the diffusion paradigm.

The news event studies helped illuminate the broader issue of the inter-media process through which mass media messages stimulate interpersonal communication, which in turn motivates attitude change and overt behavior change. Why do individuals pass on news to others, including total strangers? Some news comes wrapped in a puzzle, which encourages talking it over with peers. For example, Princess Diana's death raised the question of whether the paparazzi pursuing her were responsible for her death; this unknown element of the story encouraged both continuing news coverage and further discussion. In the days following the September 11 terrorist attacks, the public did not know who was responsible for the destruction of the World Trade Center, although bin Laden and his Al Qaeda network were suspected. Perhaps individuals tell others about the news so that friends know that the teller already knows about the news event, a type of boasting and status-seeking behavior. Future news diffusion studies need to explore these issues.

Will the news diffusion research tradition, launched by the Deutschmann and Danielson study in 1960, atrophy and disappear, or will it move in new directions, so as to flourish again?

LATER COMMUNICATION RESEARCH ON DIFFUSION In the early 1960s, communication scholars began to investigate the diffusion of technological ideas, especially agricultural, health, educational, and family planning innovations in developing nations. Deutschmann's study of the diffusion of agricultural innovations in a Colombian village* stands as a landmark, and led other communication scholars to focus upon peasant audiences in the 1960s. During the 1970s, communication scholars began to investigate the diffusion of technological innovations in the United States, sometimes when communities or organizations were the adopting units (see Chapter 10). Since about 1990, the number of diffusion studies by communication scholars has exploded, with many focusing on the rapid spread of the Internet and other new communication technologies (for example, Lin, 1998, 1999, 2001, 2002; Lin and Atkin, 2002; Leung, 1998, 2000; Leung and Wei, 1998, 1999, 2000; Wei, 2001; Wei and Leung, 1998; Lee, Leung, and Soo, 2003; Lievrouw, 2002).

One of the special advantages of the communication research tradition is that it can analyze *any* particular type of innovation. There are no limitations, such as the education tradition's focus on educational innovations, the rural sociologist's main emphasis upon agricultural ideas, or the public health tradition's concern with family-planning methods and HIV/AIDS prevention. This lack of a message content orientation frees the communication researcher to concentrate on the *process* of diffusion. The communication research tradition provided useful concepts and research methods (for example, credibility, parasocial interaction, network analysis, and the semantic differential) for studying diffusion.

Marketing

The marketing/management diffusion tradition came on strong since beginning in the 1960s, with its expansion stimulated in recent years by the diffusion and adoption of new communication technologies in

---

*The publications from this study are Deutschmann (1963), Deutschmann and Fals Borda (1962a, 1962b), and Deutschmann and Havens (1965).

organizations, and by use of the Internet in marketing new products and services to the public. Today, the marketing research tradition represents about 16 percent of all diffusion publications (see Table 2-1).

A particular focus of the marketing tradition in recent years has been on the diffusion of telecommunications services such as mobile telephones. The Bass prediction model, formulated by marketing professor Frank Bass, to estimate the rate of adoption for a new product (Bass, 1969) has attracted and held the research interest of a number of marketing scholars (see Chapter 5). Originally, the Bass model was used to predict the rate of adoption of consumer durables (such as dish washers and air conditioners), but it has since been applied to a very wide range of new goods and services (a review of research on the Bass model is provided by Mahajan, Muller, and Wind, 2001). The Bass model has served as a lightening rod for marketing scholars, leading one marketing scholar, Professor Marnick Dekimpe, to state, "The Bass model is the most popular model in the field of marketing." Various scholars have tested the Bass model's predictions of the rate of adoption of an innovation resulting from advertising and personal selling, often while adding additional variables like the price of the product.

Marketing managers of private firms are centrally concerned with how to launch new products successfully (Rosen, 2000), as many new consumer products end in failure. Only one successful new product survives from the many hundreds of attempts to introduce new consumer items each year. Companies have a vital stake in the diffusion of new products, and a very great number of such researches have undoubtedly been completed. But a large proportion of these diffusion research reports can be found only in the confidential files of the sponsoring companies. The funding of marketing diffusion studies by private sources, who use the results to gain a competitive advantage in the marketplace, restricts scholarly access to the intellectual lessons learned from these diffusion studies in the marketing research tradition. Even so, the number of available diffusion publications in the marketing tradition is impressive.

Marketing diffusion literature emphasizes prediction of the rate of adoption for new products and how the perceived attributes of an innovation, plus the marketing mix of advertising and personal selling, affect its rate of purchase. Marketing scholars are often interested not just in the number of adopters of a new product but also in the amount of *use* of the product over periods of time. For example, the number of new users of mobile telephones is of course important, but much more important, especially to service providers, is the minutes of use of telephone service per month. The providers often give mobile phones free to their new customers and earn their profits from the sale of minutes of telephone use.

In recent years, marketing diffusion scholars have taken the lead in exploring the global diffusion of new products like mobile telephone, in part because the companies marketing these innovations operate in a worldwide market. Marketing scholars seek to understand the role of culture, of national government regulations, and other factors in explaining the global diffusion of new products. For example, mobile telephone service began in Japan in 1979, ten years before this innovation was available in many other nations. Why? And why was the rate of adoption of mobile phones much more rapid in Finland and Scandinavian nations than in Japan? Marketing diffusion scholars seek to answer these questions (for example, Dekimpe, Parker, and Sarvay, 1998, 2000b, 2000c; Grüber and Verboven, 2001a, 2001b; Shermesh and Tellis, 2002).

"Marketing" has a negative connotation in some academic circles because the term is narrowly construed as synonymous with manipulating human purchasing behavior for commercial advantage. Undoubtedly, marketing may sometimes seek to sell products to people who do not really want them, like refrigerators to Eskimos. On the contrary, marketing activities, if they are to be very successful over the long term, must match consumers' needs with commercial products and services. Marketing scholars and practitioners argue that they are providing a useful contribution to society by helping to identify consumer needs and by fulfilling such needs by making commercial products available in a form that is appropriate and at a cost that is affordable.

SOCIAL MARKETING We can *force* people to adopt certain innovations. For example, city and state governments enforce laws requiring motorcycle helmet use, automobile seat belts, and driving under a certain speed limit. Cigarette smoking is not permitted on domestic airlines in the United States, nor in restaurants and other public places in the many cities that have adopted no-smoking ordinances. In these cases, society has imposed its will on individual behavior. Such coercion in forcing behavior change is understandably not popular with certain members of the public. A different approach to effecting the adoption of innovations that can improve health, raise literacy levels, and extend life expectancy is *social marketing*, the application of commercial marketing strategies to the diffusion of nonprofit products and services.

Social marketing was launched more than fifty years ago with the rhetorical question "Why can't you sell brotherhood like you sell soap?" (Wiebe, 1952). In recent decades, the social marketing approach has been applied to energy conservation, smoking cessation, safer driving, decreasing infant mortality, HIV/AIDS prevention, family planning, preventing drug and alcohol abuse, anti-littering campaigns, and improving nutrition. Often social marketing campaigns seek to convince people to do something that may be unpleasant. For instance, many Americans wish to lose weight, stop smoking, exercise, and floss their teeth, but they do not engage in these health behaviors. The main applications of social marketing are to change behaviors in directions desired by individuals whose actions are impeded by inertia or other factors.

An assessment of experiences with social marketing by Fox and Kotler (1980) concluded, "Most social marketing problems will be more formidable than the typical marketing problems facing commercial marketers." One noted success for social marketing has been its use by government family-planning programs to diffuse oral contraceptive pills and condoms in developing countries. For example, a condom campaign in India in the 1970s involved renaming the product "*Nirodh*" (from a Sanskrit word meaning "protection"). Condoms had been known as "French letters" and were considered taboo (*taboo innovations* are defined as new ideas that are perceived as extremely private and personal in nature). A massive advertising campaign helped launch *Nirodh* in India, and the condoms were sold by thousands of tea shops and at cigarette stands on every street corner. The government of India subsidized the product so that each condom cost only two cents. Market research was conducted at every step of the *Nirodh* campaign to provide feedback to the campaign planners: The selection of the name *Nirodh* over various alternatives, the choice of teashops and cigarette stands as distribution outlets that would be accessible and acceptable to the intended audience, and what information was needed by Indian men about how to use condoms. The *Nirodh* campaign showed how commercial marketing expertise could be used in a social marketing campaign for family planning.

What are the essentials of a social marketing campaign?

1. *Audience segmentation* is a communication strategy that consists of identifying certain subaudiences within a total audience, and then conveying a special message to each of these subaudiences. For example, the Stanford Heart Disease Prevention Project, with

which the present author was involved in the 1980s, identified individuals over 45 years of age who smoked cigarettes and who were overweight as a priority subaudience for messages about preventing heart disease. Similarly, the *Nirodh* campaign in India identified young married couples as being particularly receptive to using condoms for spacing their children. Another social marketing campaign, to encourage organ donation, is aimed at young American males who drive motorcycles.

2. *Formative research* is conducted relatively early in a communication campaign in order to create more effective messages. Provisional versions of messages may be pretested with small samples of the intended audience in order to obtain feedback that allows the messages to be redesigned for greater effectiveness. Formative research provides an audience orientation to social marketing campaigns. For example, a Healthy Highways Project in India in the mid-1990s was designed to reach long-distance truck drivers with safer sex messages at truck stops, where intercourse with commercial sex workers often took place. This HIV prevention intervention failed until formative research showed the public health professionals how to think like a lower-class truck driver (Singhal and Rogers, 2003). Then effective messages could be created.

3. The innovation is *positioned* relative to the intended audience's meanings so as to emphasize certain desired aspects. Sometimes this positioning can be facilitated by the name that is chosen for the innovation. Examples of trademarks for condoms are *Nirodh* in India, as mentioned previously, "Panther" in Jamaica (a name that conveys an image of masculine vitality), *"Preethi"* ("beautiful") in Sri Lanka, and "Catapult" in St. Lucia. Often a logo is chosen to symbolize the innovation, particularly if the innovation is too sensitive or embarrassing to talk about. For instance, in Sri Lanka, the logo for *Preethi* condoms was a circle made with the thumb and index finger (a nonverbal gesture meaning "okay" in the United States). An individual could enter a drugstore in Sri Lanka and silently indicate in a symbolic way that he or she wished to purchase a *Preethi*. The logo is prominently displayed on the *Preethi* package, which is in an eye-catching, pleasing color that was chosen through pretesting. Sometimes, symbolism is used to position an innovation; an example was the U.S. television ad of an egg frying in a skillet, accompanied by the caption "This is your brain on drugs."

4. The *price* of the innovation is kept very low, as the purpose of social marketing is to change behavior, not to earn profits. The conventional wisdom in social marketing campaigns is to charge a low price for a product or service, even though it could be given away free. Further, distribution of the innovation should be convenient for its adopters. Free condoms are distributed by policemen in Bangkok's red light district, as part of a social marketing campaign jokingly referred to as "Cops and Rubbers" (Singhal and Rogers, 2003). Humor helps Thai people deal with the tabooness of condoms.
5. Finally, a social marketing campaign should utilize communication channels (for instance, paid advertising) over which the campaign planners have control (rather than public service announcements, for example, which are often broadcast at inappropriate times).

An example of a very successful social marketing campaign for ORT (oral rehydration therapy) in Egypt is discussed in Chapter 9. This social marketing effort saved the lives of hundreds of thousands of Egyptian babies.

Opinion Leaders and Mavens in the Diffusion of Electric Cars

In the early 1990s, the California and Arizona state governments mandated that at least 10 percent of the total sales of automobile companies would have to be nonpolluting, which meant that they would have to be electric vehicles or some combination of electric/gasoline vehicles. The purpose was to decrease smog levels in cities such as Los Angeles and Phoenix. General Motors (GM) dedicated $2 billion to designing, manufacturing, and marketing electric vehicles. One purpose of this initiative was to reposition GM as an innovative company in the minds of the U.S. public.

Auto engineers in GM's R&D unit in Detroit created a sleek, powerful auto that operated entirely on battery power. Due to the battery technology of the time, the IMPACT (as the prototype vehicle was first called) was limited to a range of 100 miles. Then the vehicle had to be plugged into a 220-volt electrical outlet for three or four hours to recharge the batteries. The IMPACT was lightweight (with many of its parts made of aluminum) and silent (the electric motor was very quiet). In almost every respect, the IMPACT was a very different kind of automobile than had ever been seen on U.S. highways. It was aerodynamically styled and had powerful pickup.

When 150 protoype IMPACTs became available, GM marketing executives, aided by expert diffusion scholars, rolled out a marketing campaign in each of eighteen California and Arizona cities. The local electrical utility, in conjunction with GM, placed ads in each local newspaper, inviting interested individuals to apply for an opportunity to test-drive the new vehicle. The immediate response was overwhelming. In Sacramento, with a population of close to half a million, seven thousand individuals applied! Each applicant was sent a lengthy questionnaire to complete that measured their degree of opinion leadership and innovativeness. From the responses, several hundred individuals who combined opinion leadership with innovativeness were selected in each city and invited for a thirty-minute test drive of the IMPACT.

These individuals were what most people call "car nuts" but marketing experts term *mavens,* individuals who possess a high degree of interest and expertise about some type of product. Because mavens know so much about certain products, they are often sought as opinion leaders by other consumers. The test drivers wanted to know every detail of the IMPACT's performance (How many seconds to reach ninety miles per hour? How much did the IMPACT weigh? How long was the wheelbase? How powerful was the electric motor? How much would the IMPACT cost? Would the batteries perform satisfactorily in winter weather?). After the test drive, each maven was allowed up to thirty minutes of questions and answers with a GM automobile engineer. The mavens universally complained that 30 minutes was not nearly enough time for them to ask all of their questions!

They were then debriefed by GM market researchers and given an eight-by-ten-inch color photograph of a bright red IMPACT, which they were urged to post on a bulletin board at their place of work or in some other public place. Each test driver also received fifty two-by-three-inch "baseball cards" with a color photo of the red IMPACT on one side and detailed performance data about the electric car on the other side. The mavens were told to hand these wallet-sized cards to their friends. Each card had a distinctive identification number, and a toll-free telephone number that the individual could call to register for a test drive of the IMPACT. Some mavens handed out their initial fifty cards, and asked for more, and then yet more. A word-of-mouth diffusion process, stimulated by the test drivers, was under way in each of the eighteen cities. The marketing campaign was creating a "buzz" about the electric vehicle.

One of the first lessons learned from the test marketing campaign was that "IMPACT" was a terrible name for the new car. The mavens worried about the light weight of the electric vehicle and the consequences of a crash with a heavier vehicle. So the GM car was renamed the "EV-1," for the corporation's first electric vehicle (it was evident that the new vehicle would go through at least several models before it was perfected, so there would be an EV-2, an EV-3, and so on). One of the main drawbacks of the electric vehicle was its driving range of only 100 miles, which limited its use mainly to soccer moms and commuters. Until 220-volt outlets were installed at gas stations, drive-in restaurants, offices, and shopping malls, the usefulness of the EV-1 would be quite restricted.

Nevertheless, many of the mavens who had test-driven the electric vehicle were crazy to buy one. The environmental friendliness of a non-polluting vehicle, the low cost of electricity (compared to gas), and the streamlined appearance of the new car, as well as the status-conferring advantage of driving the slickest car on the road, were strong consumer draws. In late fall, 1997, the EV-1 went on sale at dozens of Saturn dealerships in Los Angeles, San Diego, and Phoenix. Sales were modest, and within a year the two state governments postponed adherence to their original mandates. Interest in electric vehicles on the part of consumers and automobile manufacturers faded until 2000, when several auto companies began marketing "hybrid" gas-and-electric-powered vehicles.

At a rather high cost, General Motors gained important lessons about how diffusion scholars would stimulate interpersonal communication about a new vehicle. Some of these lessons were immediately put to work in marketing another GM innovation, on-board global positioning systems (GPS) that allowed an automobile driver to always know his/her exact location.

ADVANTAGES AND DISADVANTAGES OF THE MARKETING TRADITION
The marketing tradition of diffusion research has certain advantages and some attendant disadvantages, compared with other research traditions. Because marketing scholars often conduct diffusion studies with the sponsorship, or at least the collaboration, of the sellers of a new product, the researchers are able to conduct experimental interventions (often an especially useful type of diffusion research design). Other than in marketing, diffusion scholars have seldom been in a position to control the intervention strategies through which an innovation is introduced, so it has not been possible to conduct field experiments (such as the Taichung family planning experiement, mentioned previously, and the Tanzania Project, discussed in Chapter 5).

Such close siding with the sources of an innovation in diffusion research can also lead to certain intellectual and ethical problems. For example, the needs of marketers are usually given priority over those of consumers. Sources often wish to know how they can influence consumers' adoption behavior. In contrast, consumers may wish to know how to insulate themselves from such influence attempts or, more generally, how they can evaluate new products. The source bias in marketing diffusion studies may lead to highly applied research that, although methodologically sophisticated, deals with trivial diffusion problems in a theoretical sense.

As a result, we may know more about consumer preferences for deodorant scents and the taste of beer than about how to best advance the theory of diffusion.

Geography

Although one of the smaller-sized diffusion research traditions (with 4 percent of all diffusion publications), the geography tradition is unique in its emphasis upon space as a factor affecting the diffusion of innovations. In 1961, there were only three diffusion publications in geography, all by Dr. Torsten Hägerstrand at the University of Lund in Sweden (Rogers, 1962). In 1995, there were 160 diffusion studies by geographers, representing about 4 percent of the total number of diffusion publications, but little further research in this tradition has been completed since then.

Maps are one of the geographers' favorite tools. Space is the crucial variable for geographers, and they specialize in investigating how spatial distance affects other aspects of human behavior. Professor Hägerstrand (1952, 1953) pioneered a simulation approach to investigating how spatial distance affects diffusion. First, Hägerstrand constructed a mathematical model of the diffusion process as it should theoretically occur over time and through space. For instance, Hägerstrand's model contained, as one of its elements, the "neighborhood effect," which expressed the greater likelihood that an innovation would spread from one adopter to another adopter (in the following unit of time) who was close by, rather than far away. This neighborhood effect was built into Hägerstrand's computer model of diffusion by means of mathematical probabilities of adoption that decreased with distance away from the previous adopter. Hägerstrand then entered a map of the Swedish countryside in his computer, and, beginning with the location of the first adopter of an agricultural innovation, he simulated the ensuing diffusion process. He then compared the resulting simulation of the diffusion process with data (1) on the innovation's actual rate of adoption and (2) on the geographical spread of the farm innovation of study.

A diffusion simulation is an attempt to mimic the reality of diffusion. If the simulated process does not correspond to the reality data, then the researcher adjusts the theoretical model of diffusion to more fully take reality into account. The eventual result is a series of abstracted rules about the diffusion process, a model. The geography research tradition shows clearly that space is important in determining the adoption of an innovation. Diffusion scholars in general sociology, marketing, and political science are currently carrying on research investigating spatial factors in the diffusion process.

General Sociology

The general sociology tradition of diffusion research is a residual category, consisting of other diffusion studies by sociologists not included in early sociology, rural sociology, and public health/medical sociology. After the 1960s, diffusion studies by general sociologists proliferated; in 2002, this research tradition represented approximately 9 percent of the total (see Table 2-1). The rise of general sociology as a research tradition indicates that the diffusion approach has caught on among many sociologists today, in addition to those concerned with agricultural, medical, or public health innovations. Sociologists have studied a very wide range of new ideas, from the establishment of shantytowns on university campuses as a means of student protest (Soule, 1999), the spread of hate crime laws throughout the fifty states (Grattet, Jenness, and Curry, 1998), the contagiousness of airplane hijackings (Holden, 1986), the ordination of women as religious leaders in various religions (Chaves, 1996), and the development of recruitment networks for Freedom Summer (McAdam, 1986, 1988; McAdam and Paulson, 1993). The main emphasis in sociological investigations of diffusion is on the social relationships involved in the person-to-person spread of a new idea.

Networks in Recruitment to Freedom Summer*

Mahatma Gandhi led the successful struggle to drive the British out of India, their former colony, by using strategies of peaceful social change. The British

---

*This case illustration is based on McAdam (1986, 1988), McAdam and Rucht (1993), and McAdam and Paulson (1993).

colonialists had a powerful army on their side, while all Gandhi could muster were the many millions of unarmed Indians who wanted independence. Shrewdly, he utilized such strategies as the Salt March to gain world sympathy and to make the British feel guilty for their treatment of the Indian masses. Reverend Martin Luther King, Jr., assiduously studied Gandhi's strategies and applied them to the racial inequalities of the American South. For instance, King organized marches and other demonstrations to create news events, which were covered on evening television news, showing the American public the brutality with which African Americans were prevented from exercising their legal rights. Southerners saw on U.S. television how they appeared to the rest of the world, and they did not like what they saw.

Joining a protest, demonstration, social movement, or some other form of activism amounts to adopting an innovation, although in this case the new idea is an ideology rather than a technology (McAdam and Rucht, 1993). An illustration is provided by Professor Doug McAdam's (1986) study of university students who joined the 1964 Mississippi Freedom Summer Project. Hundreds of young people volunteered to travel to Mississippi to register black voters and dramatize their denial of civil rights. The students gave up their opportunity of summer jobs in order to carry forward the civil rights movement in the South. They lived with black families, enduring their poverty and fear. Three of the Freedom Summer activists were killed by segregationists that included Mississippi law enforcement officers. The volunteers endured arrests, beatings, and bombings, often at the hands of police and legal authorities. A high percentage of the students who went to Mississippi were severely intimidated, had arms or legs broken, and suffered various indignities. Certainly volunteering for the 1964 Freedom Summer was a major decision. Recruitment of the volunteers typically resulted from a speech by a civil rights activist at a meeting on a university campus. Then the recruit filled out a five-page application form and was personally interviewed by a recruiter for Freedom Summer.

Twenty years later, sociologist Doug McAdam, while conducting historical research in an archive, obtained access to the applications of 720 volunteers and 239 other students who were selected but who then withdrew prior to departing for Mississippi in 1964. McAdam also conducted indepth personal interviews with 80 of the participants and withdrawals from the Freedom Summer Project. Importantly, the application form asked each student to list the names of ten people whom they wished to be kept informed of their summer activities. These data allowed McAdam to measure each student's network links with (1) others who went on the Mississippi Freedom Summer and (2) students who withdrew. Further, indirect network links were measured, such as with a student who was not named directly but who was named by someone else a respondent named. These indirect network ties were "weak ties" (see Chapter 8).

Weak ties did not explain whether a student volunteer went to Mississippi or withdrew. Neither did such other variables as prior activism, race, distance from Mississippi, college major, or other personal characteristics. Being male, of older age, and active in campus organizations were variables somewhat related to participation in Freedom Summer. But by far the best predictor of going to Mississippi was having strong network relationships with other participants or with a Freedom Summer activist. Having a close friend who withdrew from the project influenced others to withdraw. Some of the withdrawals resulted from the opposition of parents or other adults. One example was a freshman woman who said, "I heard a SNCC [Student Non-violent Coordinating Committee] person speak. . . . at [the university] and was absolutely mesmerized. It was like I now had a mission in life. I remember filling out the application and racing back to my dorm to call my parents, thinking, of course, that they would be as thrilled with my 'mission' as I was." But her mother started crying, and her father threatened to stop paying her tuition. Faced with these strong negative influences, the student withdrew from Freedom Summer.

As in the adoption of technological innovations, the diffusion of an ideological innovation is a social process. Interpersonal network links, more than any other single factor, explained whether or not university students risked their lives by participating in the 1964 Mississippi Freedom Summer. Perhaps because an ideological innovation does not have a material referent (that is, hardware) to the extent that a technological innovation does, its social construction through interpersonal communication with others is especially crucial.

Experience in Freedom Summer, which was a very radicalizing experience, had important consequences for later events. The founders and initial leaders of the anti–Vietnam War movement, the feminist movement, and the environmental movement were all veterans of Freedom Summer. So spending the summer of 1964 in Mississippi served as an informal school for learning about protesting and organizing techniques.

Trends in Diffusion Research Traditions

Table 2-1 shows that all of the behavioral science disciplines are involved in research on the diffusion of innovations. Diffusion research began to increase after formation of the diffusion paradigm by Ryan and Gross (1943). In each succeeding decade, the number of diffusion publications has increased, with the rate of increase slowing somewhat since 1980. Over the years, the scope of diffusion research has broadened, as more and more disciplines became involved, and as the paradigm was applied to studying a much broader range of innovations. Some research traditions, like rural sociology, made important early contributions to diffusion study, but then scholarly interest tailed off somewhat. In the geography tradition, interest in diffusion study waxed but then, after the mid-1990s, waned. In other research traditions such as communication, marketing, and public health, scholarly interest in diffusion continues to be strong, stimulated by the Internet, the HIV/AIDS epidemic, and other factors. World events, to a certain extent, determine what types of innovations are most important, and thus which disciplinary fields are involved in studying their diffusion.

A Typology of Diffusion Research

Here we present an overview of the various types of diffusion research, which are detailed in later chapters. Our present concern differs from the previous discussion of the history of diffusion research in that we now look at the diverse *types* of diffusion research, rather than at the various *research traditions*.

Table 2-2 shows eight different types of diffusion analysis and the approximate amount of research attention paid to each. By far the most popular diffusion research topic has been to study variables related to individual innovativeness (Type 3 in Table 2-2). Almost two thirds of all the empirical generalizations reported in diffusion publications deal with innovativeness. We illustrate each of the eight types of diffusion research with one or two studies, in order to convey the nature of such diffusion investigations.

1. *Earliness of knowing about innovations.* Michael E. Mayer and others (1990) determined what, when, and how people first had learned about news of the 1986 *Challenger* disaster. Data were gathered by telephone interviews with adults in Phoenix, Arizona. These respondents were categorizd as "early knowers" versus "late knowers." This news event diffused very rapidly; half of the respondents heard in the first thirty minutes after the spacecraft exploded just after takeoff. Most early knowers reported that they

had heard of the event by radio or television, while most of the late knowers had first learned of the disaster by interpersonal communication channels (a common finding in other news event diffusion studies). Most individuals who first learned about the *Challenger* disaster from a mass medium then told other individuals about the message. Most individuals who first heard the news through an interpersonal network then turned to a mass media channel for further information and to obtain confirmation of the news event.

2. *Rate of adoption of different innovations in a social system.* Frederich Fliegel and Joseph Kivlin (1966b) conducted personal interviews with 229 Pennsylvania dairy farmers. The investigation used farmers' perceptions of fifteen attributes of each of thirty-three dairy innovations to explain their rate of adoption for the sample of Pennsylvania farmers. Innovations perceived as having most relative advantage (measured as most economically rewarding and least risky) were adopted more rapidly. The complexity, observability, and trialability of the innovations were less highly related to the innovations' rate of adoption, but innovations that were most compatible with farmers' values were adopted more rapidly (see Chapter 6).

3. *Innovativeness.* Paul J. Deutschmann and Orlando Fals Borda (1962b) conducted a diffusion survey in a Colombian village to test the cross-cultural validity of correlates of innovativeness derived from prior U.S. diffusion research. A striking similarity was found between the results obtained in the Colombian study and those reported for Ohio farmers by Rogers (1961): innovators were characterized by greater cosmopoliteness, higher education, and larger-sized farms, both in the Colombian village of Saucío and in Ohio (see Chapter 7).

Another correlates-of-innovativeness study is Lawrence Mohr's (1969) survey of the directors of county departments of public health in Michigan, Ohio, and Ontario, Canada. An innovativeness score was computed for each of the 120 health departments of study, indicating the degree to which each organization had adopted various new ideas in public health (such as new programs and new procedures). The most innovative health departments were characterized by greater financial resources, a director who was more highly committed to innovation, and larger size (see Chapter 10).

Table 2-2. Eight Types of Diffusion Research

Type	Main Dependent Variable	Independent Variables	Units of Analysis	Approximate Percentage of Generalizations of This Type in Available Diffusion Publications	Chapter in This Book Dealing with This Type of Research	Representative Diffusion Research Study
1	Earliness of knowing about an innovation by members of a social system	Characteristics of members (e.g., cosmopoliteness, communication channel behavior)	Members of a social system (usually individuals)	5%	Chapter 5, "The Innovation-Decision Process"	Greenberg (1964)
2	Rate of adoption of different innovations in a social system	Attributes of innovations (e.g., complexity, compatibility, etc.) as perceived by members of a system	Innovations	1%	Chapter 6 "Perceived Attributes of Innovations and Their Rate of Adoption"	Fliegel and Kivlin (1966b)
3	Innovativeness of members of a social system (the members may be individuals or organizations)	Characteristics of members (e.g., cosmopoliteness, communication channel behavior, resources, social status, contact with change agents); system-level variables	Members of a social system (individuals or organizations)	58%	Chapter 7, "Adopter Categories," and Chapter 10, "Innovation in Organizations"	Deutschmann and Fals Borda (1962b); Mohr (1969)

4	Opinion leadership in diffusing innovations	Characteristics of members (e.g., cosmopoliteness); system norms and other system variables; communication channel behavior	Members of a social system (usually individuals)	3%	Chapter 8, "Diffusion Networks"	Kelly et al. (1991, 1997)
5	Diffusion networks	Patterns in the network links between two or more members of a system	Dyadic network links connecting pairs of individuals (or organizations) in a system	Less than 1%	Chapter 8, "Diffusion Networks"	Coleman et al. (1966)
6	Rate of adoption of innovations in different social systems	System norms; characteristics of the social system (e.g., concentration of opinion leadership); change agent variables (e.g., their strategies of change); types of innovation-decisions	Social systems	2%	Some attention is given in Chapter 9, "The Change Agent," and Chapter 10, "Innovation in Organizations"	Rogers and Kinkaid (1981)

Table 2-2. Eight Types of Diffusion Research (*continued*)

Type	Main Dependent Variable	Independent Variables	Units of Analysis	Approximate Percentage of Generalizations of This Type in Available Diffusion Publications	Chapter in This Book Dealing with This Type of Research	Representative Diffusion Research Study
7	Communication channel use (e.g., whether mass media or interpersonal)	Innovativeness and other characteristics of members of a social system (e.g., cosmopoliteness); system norms; attributes of innovations	Members of systems (or the innovation-decision)	7%	Chapter 9, "The Change Agent," and Chapter 5, "The Innovation-Decision Process"	Ryan and Gross (1943)
8	Consequences of an innovation	Characteristics of members; the nature of the social system; the nature and use of the innovation	Members or social systems or innovations	0.2%	Chapter 11, "Consequences of Innovations"	Sharp (1952)
	Others			22%		
	Total			100%		

4. *Opinion leadership.* The success or failure of diffusion programs rests in part on the role of opinion leaders. Jeffrey Kelly and his associates in the Center for AIDS Intervention Research at the Medical College of Wisconsin, in Milwaukee, tested the opinion leadership strategy, first in a series of field experiments in gay bars in U.S. cities and then in five developing nations. Bartenders were enlisted to help identify opinion leaders from among their customers. These influential individuals were then trained in the means of HIV transmission, methods of practicing safer sex, and how to communicate such information to their followers in the gay community. Free condoms were also made available in the gay bars. The results of these opinion leader interventions were a decrease in HIV infection rates in the intervention cities, compared to a set of control cities (Kelly et al., 1991, 1997). Kelly and a set of international collaborators are currently testing the opinion leadership strategy in thirty poor neighborhoods in Chennai, India; market centers in Fujan, China; large apartment buildings in St. Petersburg, Russia; thirty-two villages in Zimbabwe; and several cities in Peru (see Chapter 8).

5. *Diffusion networks.* In the drug diffusion study by James S. Coleman and colleagues (1966), mentioned earlier, each respondent was asked to name the other medical doctors who were his best friends. Coleman and his colleagues then determined the main variables that explained who talked to whom in network links. Similarity in age, religion, hometown, and the medical school attended were important factors structuring who talked to whom. But the most important variable determining network links in the medical community were such professional affiliations as practicing in the same clinic, hospital, or office partnership. Doctors were more likely to discuss the new drug if they worked together.

6. *Rate of adoption in different social systems.* Everett M. Rogers and D. Lawrence Kincaid (1981) sought to explain the rate of adoption of family planning innovations in twenty-four Korean villages. Unlike diffusion research Type 2, which seeks to explain why some *innovations* have a faster rate of adoption than others, Type 6 research studies why the same innovation is adopted more rapidly in certain *systems* than it is in others. The Korean villages with the fastest rates of contraceptive adoption were made up of families with higher mass media exposure, had leaders with more highly connected networks in their village, and had more change

agent contact. The economic resources of the villages were less important in explaining the village rate of adoption of family planning.

7. *Communication channel usage.* Bryce Ryan and Neal C. Gross's (1943) investigation of the diffusion of hybrid seed corn in Iowa found that the typical Iowa farmer first heard of hybrid seed from a commercial salesman, but that neighbors were the most influential channel in persuading a farmer to adopt the innovation (later research generally showed that salesmen are not the most important channel at the knowledge stage for most innovations). Ryan and Gross were the first researchers to suggest that an individual passes through different stages (knowledge and persuasion, for example) in the process of adopting a new idea, although the notion of stages in an individual's decision process has a long intellectual history (see Chapter 5). Different communication channels play different roles at various stages in the innovation-decision process. Salesmen were more important communication channels about the innovation for earlier adopters, and neighbors were more important for later adopters. This finding suggests that communication channel behavior is different for various adopter categories, a proposition supported by later diffusion researches.

8. *Consequences of innovation.* As mentioned in Chapter 1, the consequences of the use of the steel ax by a tribe of aborigines were studied by the anthropologist Lauriston Sharp (1952). The Yir Yoront were relatively unaffected by modern civilization, owing to their isolation in the Australian bush, until some well-meaning missionaries moved nearby. They distributed steel axes among the Yir Yoront as gifts and as pay for work performed. Before the introduction of the steel ax, the stone ax had served as the Yir Yoront's principal tool and as a symbol of masculinity and respect. Only men could own stone axes, so the women and children, who were the main users of these tools, borrowed them according to a system prescribed by custom. But the missionaries gave axes to anyone, which caused a major disruption of Yir Yoront culture, and a revolutionary confusion of age and sex roles. Elders, once highly respected, now became dependent upon women and younger men for steel axes. The consequences of the steel ax were unanticipated, far-reaching, and disruptive (see Chapter 11).

Summary

This chapter showed that although diffusion research began as a series of scientific enclaves, it has emerged as a single, integrated body of concepts and generalizations, even though the investigations are conducted by researchers in different scientific disciplines. A *research tradition* is a series of investigations on a similar topic in which successive studies are influenced by preceding inquiries. The major diffusion traditions described are anthropology, early sociology, rural sociology, education, public health/medical sociology, communication, marketing, geography, and general sociology.

Eight main types of diffusion research were identified:

1. Earliness of knowing about innovations.
2. Rate of adoption of different innovations in a social system.
3. Innovativeness.
4. Opinion leadership.
5. Diffusion networks.
6. Rate of adoption in different social systems.
7. Communication channel usage.
8. Consequences of innovation.

When scholars follow an intellectual paradigm in a research field, it enables them to pursue a coherent set of research directions. The paradigm also imposes and standardizes a set of assumptions and conceptual biases that, once begun, are difficult to recognize and overcome. That is the challenge for the next generation of diffusion scholars. In my first book on diffusion (Rogers, 1962, p. x), I stated, "This book suggests that students of diffusion have been working where the ground was soft. . . . The challenge for future research is to expand the area of digging and to search for different objectives than those of the past. Perhaps there is a need to dig deeper, in directions that theory suggests."

3

CONTRIBUTIONS AND CRITICISMS OF DIFFUSION RESEARCH

Innovation has emerged over the last decade as possibly the
most fashionable of social science areas.
George W. Downs and Lawrence B. Mohr, "Conceptual
Issues in the Study of Innovations" (1976), p. 700.

This chapter reviews the main critiques of diffusion research and points
out directions for possible amelioration of current weaknesses. What are
the assumptions and biases of diffusion research? How has acceptance
of the classical diffusion model limited the originality and appropriateness of diffusion researches? Starting in the 1970s, certain observers
began to raise criticisms of diffusion theory. These criticisms should be
taken seriously, for they offer directions for future improvement of this
well-established field. Despite these criticisms, we should not forget
that diffusion research has reached a point at which its contributions are
highly regarded, both in providing theoretical understanding of human
behavior change and in bringing about more effective programs of social
change around the world.

The Status of Diffusion Research Today

The contributions of diffusion research today are impressive. For recent
decades the results of diffusion research have been incorporated into
basic textbooks in social psychology, communication, public relations,

advertising, marketing, consumer behavior, public health, rural sociology, and other fields. Articles reporting diffusion research have appeared in the top journals of every discipline. Both practitioners (like change agents) and theoreticians regard the diffusion of innovations as a useful field of social science knowledge. Several U.S. government agencies have a division devoted to diffusing technological innovations to the public or to local governments. These federal agencies also sponsor research on diffusion, as do private foundations. Federal R&D laboratories in the United States are required by law to transfer their technologies to private companies, which commercialize these technological innovations into new products that are then sold in the marketplace. Most commercial companies have a marketing department that is responsible for diffusing new products and a market research arm that conducts diffusion investigations to aid the company's marketing efforts. Because innovation occurs so frequently in modern society, the applications of diffusion theory and research are found on all sides.

Diffusion research has achieved a prominent position today. But such was not always the case. Almost four decades in the past, two members of the diffusion research fraternity, Frederick Fliegel and Joseph Kivlin (1966b), complained that "Diffusion of innovation has the status of a bastard child with respect to the parent interests in social and cultural change: Too big to ignore but unlikely to be given full recognition." The status of diffusion research has improved considerably in the eyes of academic scholars since the Fliegel and Kivlin assessment. "Innovation has emerged over the last decade as possibly the most fashionable of social science areas," said Downs and Mohr (1976), as quoted at the beginning of this chapter. They continued, "This popularity is not surprising. The investigations by innovation research of the salient behavior of individuals, organizations, and political parties can have significant social consequences. [These studies] imbue even the most obscure piece of research with generalizability that has become rare as social science becomes increasingly specialized."

What is the appeal of diffusion research to scholars, to sponsors of such research, and to students, practitioners, and policy makers who use the results of diffusion research? Why has so much diffusion literature been produced?

1. The diffusion model is a conceptual paradigm with relevance for many disciplines. The multidisciplinary nature of diffusion research cuts across various scientific fields. A diffusion approach

provides a common conceptual ground that bridges these divergent disciplines and methodologies. There are few disciplinary limits as to who studies innovation, as we saw in Chapter 2. Most social scientists are interested in social change, and diffusion research offers a particularly useful means of gaining an understanding of change because innovations are a type of communication message whose effects are relatively easy to isolate. Diffusion study thus is something like the use of radioactive tracers in studying the process of plant growth: it helps illuminate processes.

One can understand social change processes more accurately if the spread of a new idea is followed over time as it courses through the structure of a social system. Because of their salience, innovations usually leave deep etchings in individuals' minds, thus aiding their recall. The process of behavior change is identified in a distinctive way by the diffusion research approach, especially in terms of concepts such as information and uncertainty (see Chapter 1). The focus of diffusion research on tracing the spread of an innovation through a system over time and/or across space has the unique quality of giving "life" to a behavioral change process. Conceptual and analytical strength is gained by incorporating time as an essential element in the analysis of human behavior change.

Diffusion research offers something of value to each of the social science disciplines. Economists are centrally interested in growth, and technological innovation is an important variable for increasing the rate of economic growth in a society. Students of organization are concerned with processes of change within formal institutions, and in how an organizational structure is altered by the introduction of a new technology. Social psychologists try to understand the process of human behavior change, especially as such individual change is influenced by groups and networks to which the individual belongs. Sociologists and anthropologists share an academic interest in social change, although they use different methodological tools. Political scientists study policy changes, such as how no-smoking ordinances or other policies are accepted and implemented by city councils. The exchange of information in order to reduce uncertainty is central to communication study. So the diffusion of innovations is of note to each of the social sciences.

2. Diffusion research has a pragmatic appeal in getting research results utilized. The diffusion approach promises a means to pro-

vide solutions (1) to individuals and/or organizations who have invested in research on some topic and seek to get the scientific findings utilized and/or (2) those who desire to use the research results of others to solve a particular social problem or to fulfill a need. The diffusion approach helps connect research-based innovations with the potential users of such innovations in a knowledge-utilization process (Rogers et al., in press).

3. The diffusion paradigm allows scholars to repackage their empirical findings in the form of higher-level generalizations of a more theoretical nature, as Downs and Mohr (1976), quoted previously, implied. Such an orderly procedure in the growth of the diffusion research field allowed it to gradually accumulate empirical evidence. Were it not for the general directions for research provided by the diffusion paradigm, the impressive amount of research attention given to studying diffusion would amount to much less by way of distilled understandings. Without the diffusion model, this huge body of completed research might just be "a mile wide and an inch deep." The diffusion paradigm provided a basis for creating a coherent body of generalizations, which can be applied to specific cases. In fact, numerous studies were completed prior to the Ryan and Gross (1943) hybrid seed corn study, but they did not add up to much, due to lack of a paradigm.

4. The research methodology implied by the classical diffusion model is clear cut and relatively facile. The data are not especially difficult to gather, and the methods of data analysis are well laid out. Diffusion scholars have focused especially on characteristics related to individual innovativeness through cross-sectional analysis of survey data. Although the methodological straighforwardness of such diffusion studies encouraged many scholars to undertake such investigation, it may also have restricted their theoretical advance.

Criticisms of Diffusion Research

Although diffusion research has made numerous important contributions to our understanding of human behavior change, its potential would be even greater were it not for certain shortcomings and biases. If the 1940s marked the original formulation of the diffusion paradigm, the 1950s were a time of proliferation of diffusion studies in the United States, the 1960s involved the expansion of such research into developing nations (see Chapter 2), and the 1970s were the beginnings of introspective criticism of diffusion research. Until the 1970s, almost nothing of a critical nature was written about the diffusion field. Such absence of critical viewpoints may have indeed been the greatest weakness of diffusion research.

Every scientific field makes certain simplifying assumptions about the complex reality that it studies. Such assumptions are built into the intellectual paradigm that guides a scientific field. Often these assumptions are not recognized, even though they affect such important matters as what is studied and what ignored, and which research methods are favored and which rejected. So when a scientist follows a theoretical paradigm, a set of intellectual blinders prevents him or her from seeing certain aspects of reality. "The prejudice of [research] training is always a certain 'trained incapacity': The more we know about how to do something, the harder it is to learn how to do it differently" (Kaplan, 1964, p. 31). Such trained incapacity is, to a certain extent, necessary. Without it, a scientist could not cope with the vast uncertainties of the research process in a chosen field of study. Every research worker, and every field of science, has blind spots. They necessarily accompany a dominant paradigm.

The growth and development of a research field are a gradual puzzle-solving process by which important research questions are identified and eventually answered. The progress of a scientific field is helped by realization of its own assumptions, biases, and weaknesses. Such self-assessment is greatly assisted by intellectual criticism. That is why it is a healthy matter for the diffusion field to face the criticisms that have been raised.

The Pro-Innovation Bias of Diffusion Research

One of the most serious shortcomings of diffusion research is its pro-innovation bias. This problem was one of the first biases to be recognized (Rogers with Shoemaker, 1971), but not enough has been done to remedy the problem. What is the pro-innovation bias? Why does it exist in diffusion research? What could be done about it?

The *pro-innovation bias* is the implication in diffusion research that an innovation should be diffused and adopted by all members of a social system, that it should be diffused more rapidly, and that the innovation should be neither re-invented nor rejected. Seldom is the pro-innovation bias straightforwardly stated in diffusion publications; rather, the bias is assumed and implied. This lack of recognition of the pro-innovation bias makes it especially troublesome and potentially dangerous in an intellectual sense. The bias leads diffusion researchers to ignore the study of ignorance about innovations, to underemphasize the rejection or discontinuance of innovations, to overlook re-invention (although much research on the subject has been done in recent years), and to fail to study antidiffusion programs designed to prevent the spread of "bad" innovations (crack cocaine or cigarettes, for example). The result of the pro-innovation bias in diffusion research is a failure to learn about certain very important aspects of diffusion. As a result, what we do know about diffusion is unnecessarily limited.

Pure Drinking Water in Egyptian Villages*

When villagers in Third World countries are asked in surveys, "What is the most important problem in your daily life?" they consistently respond, "Water." The water problem is particularly severe for Egyptian villagers living in the Nile River delta. Here, water is conveniently available in the small canals that bisect this densely populated farming area. But the stagnant canal water is a serious health threat because the canals are used by villagers for washing clothes and dishes and for urinating and defecating, as well as a source of drinking water. A green scum of algae often covers the stagnant canals, especially in the hot summer months.

The canals are also breeding grounds for the snails that are hosts for the tiny parasites that cause schistosomiasis, a terrible disease endemic in the Nile delta. Village children infested with schistosomiasis act like "walking zombies," sapped of their energy by the parasites in their liver, lungs, brain, and other vital organs. Many children die of schistosomiasis (also called "snail fever" or "bilharzia"). The canal water is also loaded with bacteria that cause infectious diarrhea among village babies, who can die within hours due to dehydration and the loss of body liquids (see Chapter 9).

Given these unhealthy conditions associated with consuming canal water, it might seem surprising that the canals are the main source of drinking water for villagers in the Egyptian delta. A diffusion scholar, David Belasco (1989), sought to find out why. On one occasion, he observed a village woman gathering water for her family's consumption from a stagnant canal. Someone was urinating nearby. A dead donkey, its body bloated by the hot sun, floated in the canal. Why would anyone drink such obviously polluted water?

---

*This present case illustration is based on Belasco (1989).

In an effort to improve the public health conditions of villages, the government ministry of health, with funding from the U.S. Agency for International Development (USAID), constructed a system of pumps and pipes that deliver pure, chlorinated water to public spigots in many villages in the Nile delta. But more than half of the villagers served by this piped water system preferred the unhealthy canal water, and almost no one drank *only* the pure water. Even though most villagers knew from a government health campaign on television and radio that canal water was contaminated with "microbes" that caused disease and death, they still drank the canal water.

Belasco conducted survey interviews with female water gatherers in three villages; he supplemented these data with observations and ethnographic analysis of water-related behavior (this investigation is unique among diffusion studies in using both quantitative and qualitative data). Belasco found that the technological innovation of piped, chlorinated water was actually not such an appropriate technology for Egyptian villagers as health experts and sanitation engineers had claimed. *Thus he overcame the pro-innovation bias that characterizes many diffusion studies.*

Egyptian politicians had promised pure water to all villagers in the Nile delta. This popular goal severely overextended the water system that could be constructed with available resources. Further, much pure water was wasted. Each spigot was originally equipped with a spring-loaded shut-off valve, so that the flow of water would stop when the valve was not held open. However, the constant use of this valve often broke the spring. Many of the springs were intentionally broken by villagers, who preferred constantly running water. So pure water ran out of the spigot day and night, creating a filthy mudhole around the spigot. The water pressure throughout the piped water system was lowered.

Obviously, the technology for providing pure water supplies in villages of the Nile delta was poorly planned, without an adequate consideration of human behavior and of Egyptian village culture. As in many technological systems, the context of users' behavior was not fully taken into account by the hydraulic engineers who planned the pure water system. So the technological innovation did not match villagers' needs. The innovation lacked compatability.

Belasco's respondents preferred canal water because they perceived that the chlorinated water from the spigot tasted "chemical" or "medicinal." Many believed that it weakened their sex drive. A rumor circulated that the government's unpopular family-planning program had added chemicals to the piped water in order to decrease the rate of population growth in Egypt. Most village water gatherers stored the canal water in a *zir,* an earthen vase whose evaporation cooled the water. The dirt and other solids in the canal water settled to the bottom of the *zir*, so that the resulting clear water appeared to be pure. The bacteria were still present, as were the microscopic schistosomiasis parasites. But villagers *perceived* that the *zir* purified their drinking water. Most *zirs* do not have lids, so the dust and flies in the air further contaminated the water.

Social reasons also explain why canal water was preferred by most female water gatherers. The women congregated on the canal banks to wash their clothes and dishes and to gather water, providing a social setting for the exchange of news and gossip. In comparison, standing in line at a water spigot was unpleasant. The long lines of female water gatherers congregated at each spigot in the very early morning, and these queues lengthened as the day wore on. Only a tiny stream of water emerged from the spigot. Pushing frequently occurred and fighting often broke out, sometimes spreading to the male relatives of the water gatherers. Worse, during the hot summer, when demand for the piped water was greatest, the government-installed water system was totally inadequate. The water supply was shut off completely for several hours each day, and often for days at a time. These highly unreliable conditions forced even those individuals who preferred piped water to drink canal water. Some women poured their inadequate supply of pure water into their *zir* of polluted canal water, thus negating the health effects of the piped water.

Belasco's respondents, who were devout Muslims, washed their hands and feet prior to praying five times each day at the village mosque. Islamic belief calls for washing with pure water. Incredibly, Belasco found that villagers often cleaned their hands and feet with pure tap water from a spigot but then drank the polluted canal water. Village religious leaders, who are highly respected opinion leaders, could have played an important role in promoting pure drinking water, but this strategy was not pursued by government change agents.

The Egyptian villagers who reject the chlorinated, piped water and who drink polluted canal water are not actually as irrational as they might at first appear to be. One of the important contributions of diffusion studies such as David Belasco's study in Egypt is to illuminate the complex nature of individuals' perceptions of an innovation. Understanding such perceptions can provides useful lessons to technological experts. After all, perceptions count. Taking into account the people's perceptions of an innovation, rather than the technologists', is essential in overcoming the pro-innovation bias.

REASONS FOR THE PRO-INNOVATION BIAS How did the pro-innovation bias become part of diffusion research? One reason is historical: hybrid corn was very profitable for each of the Iowa farmers in the Ryan and Gross (1943) study. Most other innovations that have been studied do not have this extremely high degree of relative advantage. Many individuals, for their own good, should *not* adopt many of the innovations that are diffused to them. Perhaps if the field of diffusion research had not begun with a highly profitable agricultural innovation in the 1940s, the pro-innovation bias would have been avoided or at least recognized and dealt with properly.

During the 1970s, several critics of diffusion research recognized the pro-innovation bias. For example, Downs and Mohr (1976) stated: "The act of innovating is still heavily laden with positive value. Innovativeness, like efficiency, is a characteristic we want organisms to possess. Unlike the ideas of progress and growth, which have long since been casualties of a new consciousness, innovation, especially when seen as more than purely technological change, is still associated with improvement." So innovation is a good word in modern society, similar to "motherhood" and "patriotism."

What causes the pro-innovation bias in diffusion research?

1. Much diffusion research is funded by change agencies: *They* have a pro-innovation bias (understandably so, since their very purpose is to promote innovations), and this viewpoint has often been accepted by the diffusion researchers whose work they sponsor, whom they call upon for consultation about their diffusion problems, and whose students they hire as employees.

2. "Successful" diffusion leaves a rate of adoption that can be retrospectively investigated by diffusion researchers, while an unsuccessful diffusion effort does not leave visible traces that can easily be reconstructed. A rejected and/or a discontinued innovation is thus less likely to be investigated by a diffusion researcher. For somewhat similar reasons, the variety of forms taken by the reinvention of an innovation makes it more difficult to study, posing methodological problems of classifying just what "adoption" means (see Chapter 5). The conventional methodologies used by diffusion researchers led to a focus on investigating successful diffusion. Thus, a pro-innovation bias came into diffusion research.

One of the important ways in which the pro-innovation bias creeps into much diffusion research is through the selection of the innovations that are studied. This aspect of the pro-innovation bias may be especially dangerous because it is implicit, latent, and largely unintentional. How are innovations of study usually selected in diffusion research?

First, the sponsor of an investigation may approach a diffusion researcher with a particular innovation (or class of innovations) already in mind. For example, a manufacturer of cellular telephones or hand-held personal digital assistants may request a diffusion researcher to study how this product is diffusing and, on the basis of the ensuing research findings, make recommendations for speeding up the diffusion process. Or a federal government agency may provide funds to a university-based diffusion researcher for a research project on the diffusion of a technological innovation to the public, a new idea that government experts feel the public should adopt. For example, federal government agencies have funded research by the present author on "five-a-day" (eating five servings of fruits and vegetables per day) nutrition for cancer prevention, the Internet and World Wide Web, and no-smoking ordinances enacted by cities. These innovations would seem to be of unquestionable benefit, although closer analysis might identify certain disadvantages that accompany the advantages for some adopters. For instance, once people adopt the Internet, they may have to deal with their children's access to pornographic material.

In many other cases, a diffusion researcher selects an innovation of study (with little influence from a research sponsor) on the basis of which new ideas look intellectually interesting to the investigator. The researcher often chooses to study an innovation with a relatively rapid rate of adoption. Such innovations are often perceived as particularly noteworthy and dynamic. They are more likely to have policy implications. But one unintended result is that a pro-innovation bias is again injected into the diffusion study.

Because of the pro-innovation bias, we know much more about (1) the diffusion of rapidly spreading innovations than about the diffusion of slowly diffusing innovations, (2) adoption than about rejection, and (3) continued use rather than about discontinuance. The pro-innovation bias in diffusion research is understandable from the viewpoint of financial, logistical, methodological, and policy considerations. The problem is that we know too much about innovation successes and not enough about innovation failures. The later might be more valuable in an intellectual sense.

In the future, we need a different kind of diffusion study from those of the past, so that we shed the pro-innovation bias. For balance, we need a number of diffusion researches with an "anti-innovation bias" in order to correct past tendencies.

OVERCOMING THE PRO-INNOVATION BIAS How might the pro-innovation bias be overcome?

1. Alternative research approaches to post hoc data gathering about how an innovation has diffused should be explored. Diffusion research does not necessarily have to be conducted *after* an innovation has diffused completely to the members of a system (Figure 3–1). Such a rearward orientation to most diffusion studies leads them to concentrate on successful innovations.

    It is possible to investigate the diffusion of an innovation while the diffusion process is still under way (Figure 3–2). Data can be gathered at two or more points during the diffusion process, rather than only after the diffusion process is completed (as is the usual case). This type of research design might be a field experiment in which data are gathered before and after an intervention, as in the Berleson and Freedman (1964) study of family planning

Figure 3-1. Methods of Gathering Data

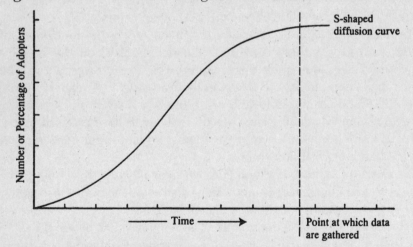

The usual diffusion study gathers data from adopters after the innovation has diffused widely by asking respondents to look backward in time. Because cases of successful diffusion are usually selected for study, a pro-innovation bias is introduced into much diffusion research.

Figure 3-2. Alternative Research Design

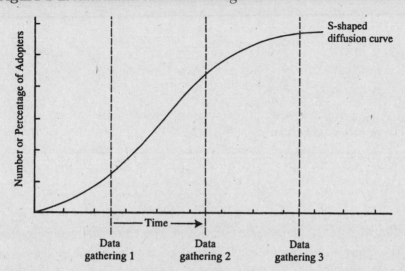

An alternative research design for a diffusion study is to gather data from adopters at several points in time during the diffusion process. When data are gathered from respondents at several points in the diffusion process, they do not have to recall information about their date of adoption of the innovation over such a long time period.

diffusion in Taiwan (see Chapter 2) and the Tanzania Project on family planning and HIV prevention (Rogers et al., 1999; Vaughan and Rogers, 2000), discussed in Chapter 5. Also possible are experiments in which the opinion leadership strategy is evaluated (see Chapter 8). An experiment or some other type of in-process diffusion research design allows a scholar to investigate less successful, as well as more successful, cases of innovation diffusion, and therefore to avoid the pro-innovation bias.

2. Diffusion researchers should become much more questioning of, and careful about, how they select their innovations of study. Even if a successful innovation is selected for investigation, a diffusion scholar might also investigate an unsuccessful innovation that failed to diffuse widely among members of the same system during the same time frame. Such a comparative analysis would help illuminate the seriousness of the pro-innovation bias. In general, a much wider range of innovations should be studied in diffusion research to overcome the pro-innovation bias.

Figure 3-3. Avoiding the Pro-Innovation Bias

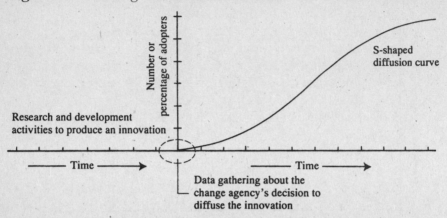

One means of avoiding the pro-innovation bias might be to investigate the broader context of diffusion, such as the decision by a change agency to diffuse the innovation. A diffusion scholar might also study how the decision was made to begin R&D work to create the innovation, and how the innovation was shaped into its final form.

3. It should be acknowledged that rejection, discontinuance, and re-invention frequently occur during the diffusion of an innovation and that such behavior may be rational and appropriate from the individual's point of view, if only the diffusion scholar could adequately understand the individual's perceptions of the innovation and of the individual's situation. For instance, adopters often feel that they know relevant information about their local situation that a professional change agent may not know or understand. Indigenous knowledge systems, like the hot-cold complex in the Peruvian village of Los Molinas (see Chapter 1), may affect the diffusion of a new idea. Until recent years, agricultural change agents in Mexico recommended that *campesinos* cease interplanting corn and beans in the same field, which was the traditional method of farming. Later, agricultural research showed that such interplanting actually led to higher crop yields and to other benefits (such as when either the corn or the bean crop failed). In this case, Mexican villagers knew more about farming than did Ph.D. agronomists.

Re-invention is an important way in which an innovation is changed to fit the adopting unit's situation. For the first several decades of diffusion research, we did not recognize that re-invention existed. An innovation was regarded by diffusion scholars as an invariant during its diffusion process. Now it is realized, belatedly, that an innovation may be perceived somewhat differently by each adopter and modified to suit the individual's particular situation. Thus, diffusion scholars no longer assume that an innovation is "perfect" for all potential adopters in solving their problems and meeting their needs.

4. Researchers should investigate the broader context in which an innovation diffuses, such as how the initial policy decision is made that the innovation should be diffused to members of a system, how the innovation of study is related to other innovations and to the existing practice(s) that it replaces, and how it was decided to conduct the R&D that led to the innovation in the first place (Figure 3–3). This wider scope of diffusion studies helps illuminate the broader system in which the diffusion process occurs, and aids in illuminating possible pro-innovation biases.

5. We should increase our understanding of motivations for adopting an innovation. Such "why" questions about adoption have seldom been probed effectively by diffusion researchers. Undoubtedly, motivations for adoption are a difficult topic to investigate. Some adopters may not be able to tell a researcher why they decided to use a new idea, and other adopters may be unwilling to do so. Seldom are simple, direct questions in a survey interview adequate to uncover an adopter's reasons for using an innovation. But we should not give up on trying to find out the "why" of adoption just because valid data about adoption motivations are difficult to obtain by the usual methods of survey data gathering. We should also study why individuals reject or discontinue a new idea, as in David Belasco's investigation of why Egyptian villagers did not drink piped water.

An economic motivation is often assumed to be the main thrust for an individual's adoption of an innovation, especially if the new idea is expensive. Economic factors are undoubtedly very important for certain types of innovations. But the prestige from adopting an innovation prior to most of one's peers may also be important. For instance, Becker (1970a; 1970b) found that prestige motives were very important for city and county health departments in deciding to adopt new health programs. Mohr (1969) explained: "A great deal of innovation in [health] organizations, especially large or successful ones, is 'slack' innovation. After solution of immediate problems, the quest for prestige rather than the quest for organizational effectiveness or corporate profit motivates the adoption of most new programs and technologies." Perhaps prestige motivations are less important and profit considerations paramount in private organizations, unlike in the public organizations studied by Becker and Mohr. The desire for prestige is probably very important in decisions to adopt certain innovations, such as new clothing fashions, new-model cars (such as "hybrid" autos), and very thin laptop computers. We do not really know because so few diffusion researchers have tried to assess motivations for adoption.

If diffusion scholars could more adequately see an innovation through the eyes of their respondents, including why the innovation was adopted or rejected, diffusion research would be in a better position to shed the pro-innovation bias of the past. A pro-innovation tilt is dangerous in that it may cloud adopters' perceptions of an innovation.

An astute observer of diffusion research, J. D. Eveland (1979), stated: "There is nothing inherently wrong with . . . a pro-innovation value system. Many innovations currently on the market are good ideas in terms of almost any value system, and encouraging their spread can be viewed as virtually a public duty." But even in the case of an overwhelmingly advantageous innovation, potential adopters may perceive it very differently than change agents or researchers. Simply to regard the adoption of the innovation as *rational* (defined as use of the most effective means to reach a given end) and to classify rejection as stupid is to fail to understand that individual innovation-decisions are idiosyncratic. They are based on an *individual's* perceptions of the innovation. Whether considered right or wrong by a scientific expert who seeks to evaluate an innovation objectively, adoption or rejection is always "right" in the eyes of the individual who made the innovation-decision (at least at the time the decision is made). Diffusion scholars would do well to remember that individuals' own perceptions count in determining their innovation behavior.

In the past, we diffusion researchers placed an overreliance upon models of diffusion that are too rationalistic. The unfortunate consequence is that we often assumed that all adopters perceive an innovation in a positive light, as we ourselves may perceive it. We need to question this assumption of the innovation's advantage for all adopters and to gather data about how individuals actually perceive the innovation, much as David Belasco (1989) did in his study of the rejection of piped water in Egypt.

Certainly the first and most important step in shedding a pro-innovation bias in diffusion research is to recognize that it may exist.

Preference for Sons in India and China*

Most diffusion activities in *most* countries have beneficial consequences for *most* people who adopt the innovations that are promoted. Thus the pro-innovation bias of past diffusion research is at least partially justified. But in some cases, an innovation that is *generally* beneficial can be disastrous for *certain* adopters and for society. And in a few cases, a widely diffused innovation has disastrous consequences for society.

One example is the diffusion of sex determination medical technology, especially ultrasound tests, to rural areas in India and China. Parents in both nations have a strong preference for sons, which in the past was expressed in terms of various folk theories to explain the sex of an unborn fetus (such as that if the unborn baby hangs low on the mother's body, it will be a boy), female infanticide, and neglect of girl children through inadequate nutrition (Luthra, 1984). Boy children carry on the family name, and sons, not daughters, care for the parents when they grow old. There is no government social security system in India or China. Furthermore, a family must pay a dowry when a daughter marries. As one advertisement for ultrasound tests in India proclaimed, "Better to pay the cost of sex determination plus abortion now, than to pay a dowry later" (Luthra, 1984, p. 265). The preference for boys is so strong in India that when parents are asked how many children they have, they often mention only the number of their sons.

Sex determination equipment became available in Indian cities in the 1980s and was outlawed in 1984, but this law has not been enforced. Compact ultrasound machines soon diffused to small towns and rural villages in India, where preference for sons is strongest. The results of an ultrasound test in a rural clinic may be conveyed subtly, such as by a doctor frowning to indicate a girl fetus and signifying a boy fetus with a smile. The test costs about $11 (U.S.), and the demand is greatest in the better-off north Indian states such as the Punjab. Here the ratio of the number of boy children to girl children at birth changed from 114 boys to 100 girls in 1991 to 126 to 100 in 2001. In the United States and throughout most of the world, the sex

---

*This case illustration is based on various sources, including Luthra (1994), Dugger (2001), and Wiseman (2002).

ratio at birth has remained for years at 105 to 107 boys to 100 girls (Dugger, 2001).

In China, where the government's one-child family policy since 1979 has inadvertently served to emphasize preference for sons, the sex ratio at birth changed from 108 to 100 in 1982, to 113 to 100 in 1990, to 117 to 100 in 2000 (Wiseman, 2002). The highest ratio in China is found in Hubei Province: 130 boys to 100 girls. It is estimated that by 2020, due to the lower number of girls being born, 30 to 40 million young Chinese men will not be able to marry. There simply will not be enough wives to go around. In China, unmarried males are called *guang guan* ("bare branches"). They are the losers in a societal competition for increasingly scarce females. Rural, uneducated young men without a stable job are least likely to find a wife.

Professor Rashmi Luthra (1984), who helped call the problems of ultrasound diffusion and the resulting lopsided sex ratios to public attention, concludes that it is important to study the diffusion of harmful technologies, as well as to investigate the diffusion of beneficial innovations.

The Individual-Blame Bias in Diffusion Research

A source bias is a tendency for diffusion research to side with the change agencies that promote innovations rather than with the individuals who are potential adopters. This source bias is perhaps suggested by the words that we use to describe this field of research: "diffusion" research might have been called something like "problem solving," "innovation seeking," or "evaluation of innovations" had the audience originally been a stronger influence on this research. One cannot help but wonder how the diffusion research approach might have been different if the Ryan and Gross (1943) hybrid corn study had been sponsored by the Iowa Farm Bureau Federation (a farmers' organization) rather than by the Iowa Agricultural Experiment Station. What if the Columbia University drug study had been sponsored by the American Medical Association rather than by the Pfizer Drug Company? The source sponsorship of early diffusion studies may have given these investigations not only a pro-innovation bias but also structured the nature of diffusion research in other important ways.

INDIVIDUAL-BLAME VERSUS SYSTEM-BLAME As a result of who sponsors diffusion research, along with other pro-source factors, one can detect individual-blame, rather than system-blame, in diffusion research. *Individual-blame* is the tendency to hold an individual responsible for his or her problems, rather than the system of which the individual is a part. An individual-blame orientation implies that "If the shoe doesn't fit, there's something wrong with your foot." An opposite point of view would blame the system, not the individual. It might imply that the shoe manufacturer or the marketing system could be at fault for a shoe that does not fit.

Some factors underlying a particular social problem may indeed be individual in nature, and any effective solution to the problem may have to change these individual factors. In many other cases the causes of a social problem lie in the larger context or system of which the individual is a part. Ameliorative social policies that are limited to individual interventions cannot be very effective in solving system-level problems. How a social problem is defined is an important determinant of how we go about solving it, and ultimately of the effectiveness of the attempted solution. A frequent error is to overstress individual-blame in defining a social problem, and to underestimate system-blame. *System-blame* is the tendency to hold a system responsible for the problems of individual members of the system.

Consider the following cases, in which a social problem was defined initially in terms of individual blame.

1. Posters were captioned: "LEAD PAINT CAN KILL!" Such posters placed the blame on low-income parents for allowing their children to eat paint peeling off the walls of older housing. The posters blamed the parents, not the paint manufacturers or the landlords. In the mid-1990s, federal legislation was enacted to require homeowners to disclose that a residence is lead-free when a housing unit is rented or sold.
2. Motor vehicle accidents are the leading cause of death of individuals in the United States under thirty-five years of age. Until the mid-1960s, highway safety problems were defined in terms of speeding, reckless driving, and drunk drinking (see Chapter 4). Public communication campaigns were aimed at the individual driver, urging "Don't drink and drive," "Buckle up for safety," and "Slow down and live." Unfortunately, the highway accident rate continued to climb. Ralph Nader's (1965) book *Unsafe at Any Speed* helped to redefine the problem from mainly one of blaming "the nut behind the wheel" to a system-blame of unsafely designed automobiles and highways. Once the problem was redefined as one of system-blame as well as individual-blame, federal legislative mandates for safer cars and highways

followed, and the traffic fatality rate decreased (Walker, 1976, 1977). For instance, safety laws required more padding on auto dashboards and stronger car bumpers, as well as impact absorbers placed in front of the concrete columns supporting highway viaducts. This redefinition of the traffic safety problem did not deny that individual drivers' behavior could also contribute to safer driving. MADD (Mothers Against Drunk Driving) helped secure tougher penalties for drunk driving in the 1980s and 1990s, leading to decreased highway deaths.

3. A large training program in Chicago sought to improve the employability of black inner-city men. The training course stressed the importance of punctuality in holding a job. But such an individual-blame approach did not achieve much results. An investigation found that only one fourth of the trainees had alarm clocks or wristwatches, so most had to rely on someone else to wake them up in the morning. Furthermore, the retrained workers had to depend upon unreliable means of public transportation and to cope with traffic congestion in traveling from their inner-city homes to suburban workplaces (Caplan and Nelson, 1974). However, the training program refused to spend even a few dollars for alarm clocks.

In each of these illustrations, a social problem was initially defined in terms of individual-blame. The resulting diffusion program to change human behavior was not successful until system-blame factors were also recognized.

INDIVIDUAL-BLAME AND THE DIFFUSION OF INNOVATIONS "The variables used in diffusion models [to predict innovativeness], then, are conceptualized so as to indicate the success or failure of the individual *within the system* rather than as indications of success or failure *of the system*" (Havens, 1975, p. 107, emphasis in original). Examples of such individual-blame variables that have been correlated with individual innovativeness in past diffusion investigations include formal education, size of operation, income, cosmopoliteness, and mass media exposure (see Chapter 7). In addition, these past studies of individual innovativeness included predictor variables that might be considered system-blame factors, such as change agent contact with clients and the degree to which a change agency provides financial assistance (such as in the form of credit to purchase an innovation). But seldom is it implied in diffusion research publications that the source or the channel of innovations might be at fault for not providing more adequate information, for promoting inappropriate innovations, or for failing to contact less educated members of the audience who may especially need a change agent's help.

Late adopters and laggards are often individually blamed for not adopting an innovation and/or for being much later in adopting than the other members of their system. Change agents feel that such later adopters are not dutifully following the experts' recommendations to use an innovation. These individuals are considered "traditionally resistant to change" and/or "irrational." A more careful analysis might show that the innovation is not as appropriate for these later adopters, perhaps because of their smaller-sized operations and more limited resources. In fact, for them, *not* adopting may be extremely rational. A system-blame approach might question whether the R&D source of innovations was properly tuned to the actual needs of the later adopters in the system and whether the change agency, in recommending the innovation, was fully informed about the actual life situation of the later adopters. One thinks of the piped water program in Egypt, as described earlier in this chapter, and whether it was really designed with the needs of the intended users in mind.

A stereotype of later adopters by change agents and others as traditional, uneducated, and/or resistant to change can become a self-fulfilling prophecy. Change agents do not contact the later adopters in their system because they feel, on the basis of their stereotypic image, that such contact will not be fruitful in leading to adoption. Without information inputs and other assistance from change agents, later adopters are even less likely to adopt. Thus, the individual-blame image of later adopters thus fulfills itself. Individual-blame interpretations are often in everybody's interest—except those who are subjected to individual blame.

Evidence of how an individual-blame bias can limit understanding of the diffusion process is provided by a study of recycling behavior in Edmonton and Calgary, Canada. In the early 1990s, when the data were gathered, the environmental issue was very high on the public agenda. Yet Derksen and Gartell (1993) found that individual attitudes toward the environment were related to the recycling of cans, bottles, and newspapers *only* for people who had access to a curbside recycling program. Edmonton, a city with a recycling program, had much more widespread adoption of recycling than did Calgary, which did not have a city program of curbside pickup. "Recycling has been conceptualized as an issue of individual behavior" (Derksen and Gartell, 1993). Such an individual-blame perception on the part of city officials was a mistake. Before individual attitudes toward the environment could be crystal-lized into recycling actions, a community-level decision had to made to provide a recycling program. Diffusion research on recycling should have focused on how cities such as Calgary and Edmonton had adopted recycling programs, rather than how individuals in these cities had adopted recycling. Here we see how a system-blame perspective would have shifted the unit of analysis from the individual to the city (or at least the city and the individuals in cities, with recycling adoption seen as a contingent innovation-decision).

REASONS FOR ASSIGNING INDIVIDUAL-BLAME It may be understandable (although regrettable) that professional change agents fall into individual-blame thinking about why their clients do not adopt an innovation. But why and how does diffusion research also reflect such an individual-blame orientation?

1. As implied previously, diffusion researchers sometimes accept a definition of the problem that they are to study from the sponsors of their research. If the research sponsor is a change agency with an individual-blame bias, the diffusion scholar may accept an individual-blame orientation. Ensuing research may then contribute, in turn, toward change agency policies of an individual-blame nature. "Such research frequently plays an integral role in a chain of events that results in *blaming people in difficult situations for their own predicament*" (Caplan and Nelson, 1973, emphasis in original).

    The essential error on the part of some diffusion researchers in the past is that they may have inadvertently equated the *cause* of an event or a condition, a matter to be theoretically and empirically ascertained, with the *blame* for an event or condition, which may be a matter of opinion and interpretation, based upon an observer's values and beliefs (Caplan and Nelson, 1973). Cause and blame are two different matters. The individual-blame bias in past diffusion research sometimes occurred when researchers uncritically accepted others' definitions of blame as a scientific cause. The investigators should have attributed cause among their variables of study only on the basis of empirical evidence, not on the basis of others' beliefs and judgments. Social scientists are not value-free when choosing or framing a research problem, although the conduct of the research should be objective.

    Defining a problem correctly and understanding individuals' perceptions of the problem are important first steps in planning an intervention. For example, accident prevention experts produced a training video on home gun safety for children, which emphasized not playing with handguns. In a pretest evaluation of the video in an inner-city school in Chicago, the researchers showed the video and then asked schoolchildren to react to a drawing of an open dresser drawer containing a revolver. The children, in unison, said, "Don't pick up the gun." "Why?" asked the evaluators. "Fingerprints," said the children. This surprising response sent the researchers back to the drawing board to rethink how they had initially defined the problem of gun safety.

A health communication scholar from Johns Hopkins University traveled to the Ivory Coast in West Africa as a consultant to a diffusion campaign intended to decrease the high rate of teenage pregnancy. Prior research had suggested that teenagers did not possess adequate knowledge about contraceptives and had difficulty in obtaining condoms from drugstores and health clinics. The intervention campaign was centered on drama plays created by high school students and their teachers. At a theater workshop in drama production, teenagers told the Johns Hopkins University consultant that the *real* cause of teenage pregnancy in the Ivory Coast was "sugar daddies" (older, powerful men who rewarded teenage girls with food, money, or jewelry in exchange for sexual favors). The sugar daddies included schoolteachers and principals, as well as Ministry of Education officials who visited the schools. The university consultant then encouraged the Ivorian students to include this redefinition of the teenage sexuality problem in the plays they were designing. The resulting play about sugar daddies won the national theater contest and was broadcast on national television in the Ivory Coast and throughout Africa. In this case, a redefinition of the problem as one of system-blame led to an effective diffusion intervention.

A similar point is made by the redesign of a Swedish tractor. The manufacturer was troubled by falling sales of the tractor and engaged market researchers to conduct research on what farmers wanted in a tractor. Design engineers were thinking about revving up the tractor's horsepower or reconfiguring the controls for operating the tractor. Instead, the formative evaluation showed that most farmers wanted an improved sound system (most tractors today have a radio). Accordingly, the tractor's cab was sound-proofed and a relatively expensive CD player was installed. When the new model went on the market, sales shot up. Once the prob-

lem was defined (or redefined) by the potential adopters, the tractor designers gained a whole new vision of why their product was
not being purchased. The farmers were saying, "You are not selling just traction power, you are selling operator comfort."

2. Another possible reason for the individual-blame bias in some diffusion research is that the researcher may feel that while it is difficult
or impossible to change system-blame factors, individual-blame
variables may be more amenable to change. System-level variables,
especially if they involve changing the social structure of a system,
may indeed be difficult to alter. But a first step toward system change
is to define (or redefine) a social problem more accurately. Then an
effective means of changing the system can usually be identified,
as several of the previous examples suggest.

3. Individuals are often more accessible to diffusion researchers as
objects of study than are systems, and the research tools of most diffusion investigators lead them to focus on individuals as units of
analysis. The diffusion paradigm headed diffusion scholars in the
direction of conducting surveys of individual adopters. For example.
Ryan and Gross (1943) studied individual Iowa farmers. Gathering
data from the change agencies diffusing the innovations (such as the
seed corn salespeople and extension service agents) and/or the R&D
organizations that produced the innovations (such as the Iowa Agricultural Experiment Station) was not part of this diffusion study.
Officials in such systems may be at least equally as much to "blame"
for certain diffusion problems as the potential adopters (who are the
usual objects of diffusion study). In a later chapter, we describe how
a tomato-harvesting machine in California was designed to be large
and expensive. Not surprisingly, the farmers who adopted the
machine were large operators, and the small farmers were forced
out of tomato growing.

Most social scientists who conduct diffusion research are specialists in gathering data from potential adopters by means of surveys. This particular research skill helps channel the researchers
into an individual-blame definition of diffusion problems and
away from a system-blame viewpoint. The anthropological diffusion research tradition, which conducts qualitative research
instead of surveys, has been least accepting of an individual-blame
point of view and most likely to point to system-blame aspects of
diffusion problems (see Chapter 11).

The overwhelming focus on the individual as the unit of analysis in diffusion research, while largely ignoring the importance of the individual's network relationships, is often due to the assumption that if the individual is the unit of *response,* he or she must consequently be the unit of *analysis.* The use of survey methods in diffusion research tends to "destructure" human behavior: "Using random sampling of individuals, the survey is a sociological meat-grinder, tearing the individual from his social context and guaranteeing that nobody in the study interacts with anyone else in it. It is a little like a biologist putting his experimental animals through a hamburger machine and looking at every hundredth cell through a microscope; anatomy and physiology get lost; structure and function disappear, and one is left with cell biology" (Barton, 1968).

Even when the individual is the unit of response in a diffusion study, network relationships can be the unit of analysis in some type of network analysis. *Communication network analysis* is defined as a method of research for identifying the communication structure in a system, in which relational data about communication flows are analyzed by using some type of interpersonal relationship as the unit of analysis (see Chapter 8). Network analysis permits understanding communication structure as it channels the process of an innovation's diffusion.

The influential Ryan and Gross (1943) study did not obtain data about diffusion networks. The refocusing of diffusion researches had to wait for later investigations, especially the drug study of medical doctors by Coleman and colleagues (1966). Today, diffusion scholars commonly ask their respondents sociometric questions such as: "From whom in this system did you obtain information that led you to adopt this innovation?" Now the network link, rather than the individual, becomes the unit of analysis, and the diffusion scholar may have taken a first step away from assigning individual-blame.

OVERCOMING THE INDIVIDUAL-BLAME BIAS How can the individual-blame bias, where inappropriate in diffusion research, be overcome?

1. Diffusion scholars should seek alternatives to using individuals as their sole units of analysis, as discussed above.
2. Researchers should keep an open mind about the causes of a social problem, at least until exploratory data are gathered, and they should guard against accepting change agencies' definitions of diffusion problems, which tend to be in terms of individual-blame.

3. All the participants, including potential adopters and rejectors, should be involved in the definition of the diffusion problem, rather than just those persons who are seeking amelioration of a problem (such as change agents).
4. Social and communication structural variables, as well as intra-individual variables, should be incorporated in diffusion research. Past diffusion studies largely consisted of audience research, while seriously neglecting source research. The broader issues of (1) who owns and controls the R&D system that produces the innovations, (2) which change agency diffuses them, and (3) for whose benefit, also need attention in future diffusion investigations.

As in the case of the pro-innovation bias in diffusion research, perhaps one of the first and most important ways to guard against the individual-blame bias is to be aware that it may exist. An individual-blame orientation is not always inappropriate. Perhaps individual-level variables *are* the most appropriate to investigate in a particular diffusion study. But in almost all cases such a psychological approach, centering on individual-level variables, is not a complete explanation of the diffusion behavior being investigated.

The Recall Problem in Diffusion Research

Time is an important methodological enemy in studying a process such as diffusion. By definition, an innovation diffuses in a process through time. It might seem a simple enough matter to obtain data from respondents about the time at which they decided to adopt an innovation, but this is not always so.

PROBLEMS IN MEASURING THE TIME OF ADOPTION Diffusion differs from most other social science research in the fact that the time variable is not ignored. Time is one of the four essential elements of diffusion (see Chapter 1). Diffusion is a process that occurs over time, so there is no way to avoid including time when one studies diffusion. Although there are blessings that accrue from the inclusion of the time variable in diffusion studies (for example, the tracerlike qualities of innovations), there are also methodological curses.

One weakness of diffusion research is a dependence upon self-reported *recall data* from respondents as to their date of adoption of a new idea. Essentially, respondents are asked to look back in time in order to reconstruct their past history of innovation experiences. But hindsight is not completely accurate, with the degree of accuracy varying on the basis of the innovation's salience to the individual, the length of time over which recall is requested, and on the basis of individual differences in education, memory, and the like. In Chapter 2, we discussed the firehouse nature of research on news event diffusion in which data are obtained from members of the public about the news event within a few days of its occurrence. Scholars are concerned that unless they move quickly to gather the data, respondents will forget how they first learned about the news event, how they gathered further information, and what they did as a result. To the contrary, Mayer and colleagues (1990) found that individuals could accurately recall data about the *Challenger* disaster for at least several weeks after the event. This finding is reassuring, although the general problem of the accuracy of respondents' recall remains a concern of diffusion scholars.

Diffusion research designs consist mainly of correlational analyses of cross-sectional data gathered in one-shot surveys of respondents (usually the adopters and/or potential adopters of an innovation), thus following the methods pioneered by Ryan and Gross (1943) in their hybrid corn study. Diffusion studies ideally should rely on "moving pictures" of behavior, rather than "snapshots," because of the need to trace the sequential flow of an innovation as it spreads through a social system. Diffusion researchers have mainly relied, however, upon one-shot surveys of their respondents, a methodology that amounts to making the diffusion process almost "timeless" through its stop-action effect of freezing a continuous process over time. Survey research on the diffusion process is a convenient methodology for the researcher, but it is intellectually destructive of the "process" aspects of the diffusion of innovations. If data about a diffusion process are only gathered at one point in time, the investigator can only measure time through respondents' recall, a possibly weak reed on which to base the measurement of such an important variable.

Alternative research designs for gathering data about the time dimension in diffusion are (1) field experiments, (2) longitudinal panel studies, (3) use of archival records, and (4) case studies of the innovation process with data from multiple respondents (each of whom provides a validity check on the others' data). These methodologies can reflect the time dimension of the diffusion process more accurately. Unfortunately, alternatives to the one-shot survey have not been widely used in past diffusion research (although greater use of experiments and case studies has occurred in recent years). The research designs predominantly used in diffusion research do not tell us much about the process of diffusion over time, other than what can be reconstituted from respondents' recall data.

PROBLEMS IN DETERMINING CAUSALITY   Cross-sectional survey data are unable to answer many of the "why" questions about diffusion. "Such factors [as wealth, size, cosmopoliteness, etc.] may be causes of innovations, or effects of innovativeness, or they may be involved with innovation in cycles of reciprocal causality through time, or both they and the adoption of new ideas may be caused by an outside factor not considered in a given study" (Mohr, 1966, p. 20). One-shot surveys cannot tell us much about time order, or about the broader issue of causality.

The pro-innovation bias in diffusion research, and the overwhelming reliance on correlational analysis of survey data, often led in the past to avoiding or ignoring the issue of causality among the variables of study. We often speak of "independent" and "dependent" variables in diffusion research. A dependent variable is the main variable in which the investigator is interested. In about 60 percent of all diffusion research, this dependent variable is innovativeness (see Table 2–2). Diffusion research usually implies that the independent variables "lead to" innovativeness, although it is often unstated or unclear whether this really means that an independent variable *causes* innovativeness. In order for variable X to be the *cause* of variable Y, (1) X must precede Y in time-order, (2) the two variables must be related, or co-vary, and (3) X must have a "forcing quality" on Y (meaning that X must have a theoretical basis for affecting Y).

Again, we see the importance of research designs that allow clearer understanding of the aspects of diffusion over time. Field experiments are ideally suited for assessing the effect of various independent variables (the interventions or treatments) on a dependent variable (like the adoption of innovations). A *field experiment* is an experiment conducted under realistic conditions in which preintervention and postintervention measurements are usually obtained by surveys. In a typical diffusion field experiment, the intervention is some communication strategy to speed up the diffusion of an innovation. For example, the diffusion intervention may be an entertainment-education soap opera about family planning or HIV/AIDS prevention that is broadcast in one area and not in another (Rogers et al., 1999). Or the diffusion strategy being tested might be using opinion leaders to introduce an innovation in one set of systems, while opinion leaders are not used in another set of systems (see Chapter 8). We recommend that *much greater use should be made of field experiments in diffusion research so as to help avoid the respondent recall problem and to evaluate alternative diffusion strategies.*

ALTERNATIVES TO DIFFUSION SURVEYS Social science data-gathering techniques such as personal interviews do not work very well when the researcher is asking the respondent to recall his or her previous mind states over a long time period. For example, consider questioning a respondent as to his or her sources or channels of communication for an innovation that he or she adopted ten years or more ago. Obviously, one could not put complete faith in such recall data, even if they were provided by a cooperative respondent who was sincerely trying to offer valid data.

In addition to field experiments, another solution to the respondent recall problem in diffusion studies is to gather data at multiple points in the diffusion process. Instead of waiting until the innovation is widely diffused to gather data via respondents' recall, a diffusion researcher might gather data at several points during the diffusion process (Figure 3–2). At each data point, respondents are asked whether or not they have adopted, and for the details about their innovation-decision. In essence, establishing multiple data points amounts to dividing the total length of the recall period into smaller segments for the average respondent. Thus, more accurate recall is facilitated.

Another alternative solution to the respondent recall problem is a "point of adoption" study in which respondents are asked to provide details about their adoption of an innovation at the time that they adopt, such as when they go to a clinic (in the case of adopting a family-planning innovation or AIDS prevention), a dealer or a warehouse (such as for an agricultural innovation), or a store (to purchase a consumer innovation, for example). This data-gathering strategy solves the recall problem by gathering data at the time of adoption. For example, data about family planning adoption were gathered at seventy-nine health clinics in Tanzania as a check on the recall data obtained from respondents in survey interviews about the role of an entertainment-education radio soap opera in convincing them to adopt (Rogers et al., 1999).

Various research strategies may be used to minimize the seriousness of the respondent recall problem in diffusion surveys:

1. Innovations for study that have recently diffused rapidly and that are salient to the adopters (unfortunately, this strategy may increase the possibility of a pro-innovation bias) can be selected.

2. Data about respondents' recall of their time of adoption can be gathered from alternative sources, such as at point of adoption or from archival records. An example is the Coleman and others (1966) drug study in which doctors' recall data were checked against drugstore prescription records (in this case, the two sets of data generally agreed, although medical doctors tended to report adopting tetracycline slightly earlier than the prescription records indicated).
3. Careful pretesting of the survey questions and high-quality interviewing by well-trained interviewers should be emphasized, so as to maximize the likelihood of obtaining recall data that are as valid as possible.
4. Certain innovative products and services are now marketed through the Internet, and computer records may provide an indication of the time of individuals' adoption.

The Issue of Equality in the Diffusion of Innovations

As will be detailed in Chapter 11, diffusion researchers have not paid much attention to the consequences of innovation. More specifically, they have been particularly inattentive to the issue of how the socioeconomic benefits of innovation are distributed among individuals in a social system. When the issue of equality has been investigated, it has been shown that the diffusion of innovations often widens the socioeconomic gap between the higher- and lower-socioeconomic status segments in a system. This tendency for the diffusion of innovations to increase socioeconomic inequality can occur in any system, but it has especially been noted in developing nations. We therefore begin our discussion of equality issues with an examination of diffusion research in Latin America, Africa, and Asia.

DEVELOPMENT As shown in Chapter 2, research on the diffusion of innovations began in the United States. Then, during the 1960s, diffusion research caught on in the developing nations of Latin America, Africa, and Asia. The diffusion paradigm was followed closely. Many of these diffusion studies were conducted by sojourning scholars from the United States or Europe, or else by Latin American, African, or Asian scholars who had learned the diffusion approach during graduate study in the United States. A strong stamp of "made in America" characterized these diffusion researches. At first, during the 1960s, it seemed that most diffusion research methods and theoretical generalizations were cross-culturally valid; that is, the diffusion process in developing nations seemed to be generally similar to that in the richer, industrialized nations of Euro-America (Rogers with Shoemaker, 1971). Even though a peasant village was characterized by very limited financial resources, lower levels of formal education, and a paucity of mass media, innovations seemed to diffuse in approximately the same way as in the United States. For example, the rate of adoption followed the familiar S-shaped curve over time. As in the United States, innovators were characterized by higher social status, greater cosmopoliteness, and greater tolerance for uncertainty than were other adopter categories in villages in Colombia (Deutschmann and Fals Borda, 1962a, 1962b) and Bangladesh (Rahim, 1961).

But during the 1970s, questions were raised about the cultural importation of the diffusion paradigm to developing nations. Some critics were Americans or Europeans who had conducted diffusion studies in developing nations. Other critics were local social scientists (especially in Latin America) who raised troubling questions about the conduct and the results of diffusion research as it was carried out in their nations. The key intellectual issue here is the cultural appropriateness of social science research as it originally grew to strength in the United States, and was then applied under very different sociocultural conditions in developing nations. One reason that diffusion research is particularly subject to criticism in developing nations is because, compared to any other field of behavioral science, it received so much more attention in Latin America, Africa, and Asia. Approximately 16 percent of all diffusion studies have been conducted in Latin America, Africa, and Asia.

During the 1970s, an intellectual shift occurred in the basic conception of development. Four main elements in the dominant paradigm of development (Rogers, 1976) were:

1. *Economic growth* through industrialization and urbanization.
2. Capital-intensive, laborsaving *technology,* mainly transferred from industrialized nations.
3. *Centralized planning,* mainly by government economists and bankers, in order to speed up the process of development.
4. *The causes of underdevelopment,* which lay mainly within the developing nation, rather than in their trade or other external relationships with industrialized countries (this perspective was an example of individual-nation blame, rather than world-system blame).

The classical diffusion model fit this dominant paradigm of development. The paradigm of development implied that the transfer of technological innovations from development agencies to their clients lay at the heart of the development process. Diffusion studies proliferated in Latin America, Africa, and Asia in the 1960s and early 1970s. Then a major shift occurred in the conceptualization of development. Today, *development* is defined as a widely participatory process of social change in a society intended to bring about both social and material advancement (including greater equality, freedom, and other valued qualities) for the majority of people through their gaining greater control over their environment (Singhal and Rogers, 2001).

A greater concern with equality of the benefits of development after the 1970s pointed toward the priority of villagers, urban poor, and women as the main target audiences for development programs in developing nations. The empowerment of women gained attention, as it was realized that they were often subordinated to men in patriarchal societies and that the technological innovations being introduced made them more so (Davis, 1998; Shefner-Rogers et al., 1998).

APPROPRIATENESS OF THE DIFFUSION PARADIGM TO DEVELOPING NATIONS An eminent Latin American communication scholar who conducted diffusion research on his continent, Juan Diaz Bordenave (1976), argued that the diffusion research questions asked by Latin American researchers do not really get to the main issues affecting development. The typical research issues in past diffusion studies have been:

1. How are technological innovations diffused in a social system?
2. What are the characteristics of innovators, early adopters, and other adopter categories?
3. What is the role of opinion leaders in the interpersonal networks through which a new idea diffuses in a system like a peasant village?

Bordenave (1976) suggested that the following research questions would be more appropriate if one were planning for a more just social structure as the result of development programs:

1. What criteria guide the choice of innovations that are to be diffused: (1) promoting the public welfare, (2) increasing production of goods for export, (3) maintaining low prices for urban consumers, or (4) increasing profits for society's elites, such as large landowners and industrialists?

2. What influence does society's social structure have on individual innovation-decisions?
3. Are the technological innovations that are being diffused appropriate, well proven, and adequate for the stage of socioeconomic development of the nation?
4. What are the likely consequences of the technological innovation in terms of employment and unemployment, migration of rural people to already overcrowded cities, and a more equitable distribution of individual incomes?
5. Will the innovation widen or narrow socioeconomic gaps?

Considering these important issues will help diffusion research to overcome its pro-innovation bias and individual-blame assumptions. The most important single way in which diffusion research in developing nations should be different from the past is in regard to the equity issue. In Latin America, Africa, and Asia, the social structure of a nation or of a local community is often in sharp contrast to that in Euro-America. For example, the author studied the diffusion of innovations in a Colombian village in which one landowner possessed half of all the land in the village. He was also the most innovative farmer (Rogers with Svenning, 1969). Power, economic wealth, and information are highly concentrated in a few hands in most developing nations, and this aspect of social structure affects not only the nature of an innovation's diffusion but also who reaps the main advantages and disadvantages of such technological change. The classical diffusion model was conceived in sociocultural conditions that were substantially different from those in Latin America, Africa, and Asia. Bordenave (1976) argued that when the diffusion model was used uncritically, it did not touch such basic issues as changing the social structure in developing countries.

SOCIOECONOMIC GAPS AND DIFFUSION The social structure in developing nations is a powerful determinant of individuals' access to technological innovations. Development agencies tend to provide assistance especially to their more innovative, wealthier, more highly educated, information-seeking clients. Following this diffusion strategy leads to a lower degree of equality in the consequences of technological innovations. For example, more progressive farmers are eager to adopt new ideas and have the economic means to do so. They can also more easily obtain credit if they need it to adopt the innovation. Because they have larger-sized farms, the direct effect of their adoption on total agricultural production is relatively important. Change agents cannot contact all of their clients, so they concentrate on their most responsive clients, with whom they are most homophilous. The result is a widening of the socioeconomic benefits gap among the change agent's client audience.

Does the diffusion of innovations necessarily have to widen socio-economic gaps in a social system? Some reason for optimism about this issue was provided by two field experiments in developing nations. Shingi and Mody (1976) in India and Röling and colleagues (1976) in Kenya designed and evaluated diffusion approaches that narrowed, rather than widened, socioeconomic gaps. Essentially, these approaches sought, with some success, to overcome the inequity bias of the usual diffusion program. They introduced appropriate innovations to lower-socioeconomic clients through a special development program. These studies (discussed in Chapter 11) suggest that if communication strategies are used effectively in narrowing the socioeconomic benefits gap, then the socioeconomic structure is no longer a major barrier to the diffusion of innovations to the most disadvantaged segment of the population. Thus it may be possible to bring about *greater* equality through appropriate diffusion strategies.

Summary

We reviewed four major shortcomings of diffusion research in this chapter. We conclude that the beginnings of diffusion research left an indelible stamp on the approaches, concepts, methods, and assumptions of the field. The biases that we inherited from our research ancestors have been inappropriate for certain important diffusion research tasks of today. It is ironic that the study of innovation has itself been so traditional.

The four major criticisms of diffusion research discussed in this chapter are:

1. The *pro-innovation bias,* the implication of most diffusion research that an innovation should be diffused to and adopted by all members of a social system, that it should be diffused rapidly, and that the innovation should be neither re-invented nor rejected.
2. The *individual-blame bias,* the tendency to hold an individual responsible for his or her problems, rather than the system of which the individual is a part.
3. The *recall problem* in diffusion research, which may lead to inaccu-

racies when respondents are asked to remember the time at which they adopted a new idea.

4. The *issue of equality* in the diffusion of innovations, as socioeconomic gaps among the members of a social system are often widened as a result of the spread of new ideas.

Alternatives to the usual diffusion research approaches were proposed for overcoming each of these four criticisms of diffusion research.

4

THE GENERATION OF INNOVATIONS

The fundamental impulse that sets and keeps the capitalist engine in motion comes from the consumer's goods, the new methods of production or transportation, the new markets, the new forms of industrial organization that capitalist enterprise creates.

Joseph A. Schumpeter, *Capitalism, Socialism, and Democracy* (1950), p. 117.

Build a better mousetrap, and the world will beat a path to your door.

Ralph Waldo Emerson

Where do innovations come from? How do their origins later influence their diffusion and consequences? As pointed out in the previous chapter, past diffusion studies typically began with the point at the left-hand tail of the S-shaped diffusion curve, that is, with the very first adopters of an innovation. However, decisions and events occurring previous to this point often have a strong influence on the diffusion process. In this wider view of the innovation-development process, diffusion is but a later phase of the larger sequence through which an innovation goes from the decision to begin research on a recognized problem to the consequences of the innovation.

Past diffusion investigations overlooked the fact that relevant activities and decisions usually occurred long before the diffusion process

136

began: a perceived problem, funding decisions about R&D activities that led to research work, invention of the innovation and then its development and commercialization, a decision that it should be diffused, transfer of the innovation to a diffusion agency, and its communication to an audience of potential adopters. *Then* the first adoption of the innovation occurs, and the diffusion process begins. This entire pre-diffusion series of activities and decisions is an important part of the innovation-development process, of which the diffusion phase is one component.

In this chapter we review researches completed on pre-diffusion aspects of the technology-development process.

The Innovation-Development Process

In Chapter 1, we defined an *innovation* as an idea, practice, or object that is perceived as new to an individual or another unit of adoption. The *innovation-development process* consists of all the decisions, activities, and their impacts that occur from recognition of a need or a problem, through research, development, and commercialization of an innovation, through diffusion and adoption of the innovation by users, to its consequences. Now we take up each of these main steps in the innovation-development process.

1. Recognizing a Problem or Need

The innovation-development process often begins with recognition of a problem or need, which stimulates research and development activities designed to create an innovation to solve the problem or need (Figure 4–1). In certain cases, scientists may perceive a future problem and launch research to find a solution. An example was an agricultural scientist at the University of California at Davis who foresaw a severe labor shortage for California tomato farmers when the *bracero* (Mexican farmworker) program ended and initiated an R&D program to breed hard tomato varieties that could be machine-picked (details about this case appear in a later section).

In other cases, a problem or need may rise to high priority on a system's agenda of social problems through an agenda-setting process. An illustration is the issue of automobile safety in the United States. Research and development to manufacture safer cars and design safer highways had been conducted for several years, but the results were not

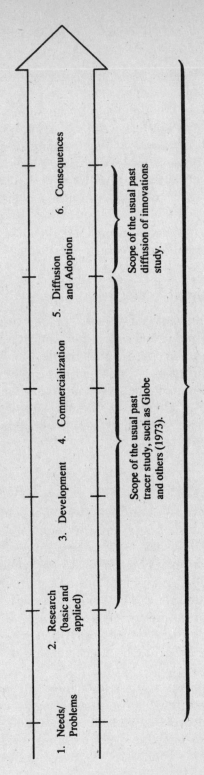

Figure 4-1. Six Main Stages in the Innovation-Decision Process, Showing the Limited Scope of Past Tracer Studies and of Past Diffusion Studies

1. Needs/ Problems
2. Research (basic and applied)
3. Development
4. Commercialization
5. Diffusion and Adoption
6. Consequences

Scope of the usual past tracer study, such as Globe and others (1973).

Scope of the usual past diffusion of innovations study.

These six stages are somewhat arbitrary in that they do not always occur in exactly the order shown here, and certain stages may be skipped in the case of certain innovations.

put into practice until the mid-1960s, when a series of highly publicized congressional hearings and Ralph Nader's (1965) book *Unsafe at Any Speed* called national attention to the high rate of traffic fatalities. The social problem of auto safety was boosted to a high national priority when the annual vehicle death rate reached 50,000 in the early 1960s. The agenda-setting process through which this dangerous trend became a political issue required several years (Dearing and Rogers, 1996).

Havelock (1972) surveyed (1) several hundred researchers specializing in auto safety, and (2) several hundred decision-makers in the most prominent national highway safety organizations. The decision makers generally shared the public's view of the traffic safety problem: that it was due to "the nut behind the wheel" (an individual-blame perspective). On the other hand, the research community rejected this view, and felt that solutions had to come from redesigning autos and highways (a system-blame view). The invisible college of safety researchers, mainly university professors, was led by a cadre of opinion leaders/professors whom their peer researchers regarded as conducting the most important research. These leaders had a high degree of contact with government officials and insurance company executives. As a result, the perception of the traffic safety problem as due to the nut behind the wheel gradually gave way to a system-blame perspective. Safety research was thus redirected, and new public policies were formed to effectuate safer cars and roads. Eventually, a federal law was passed that (1) required automakers to design safer cars (such as with padded dashboards and stronger bumpers) and (2) forced the highway construction industry to build safer roads, such as by placing impact attenuators in front of viaduct pillars.

In this case, existing research results were put into use as public policies that redefined the traffic safety problem from one of individual-blame to system-blame. The social construction of this problem involved both scientific expertise and political forces as the agenda-setting process of determining innovation-needs evolved over time.

2. Basic and Applied Research

Most innovations that have been investigated in diffusion research have been technological innovations, and so the term "technology" is often used as a synonym for innovation. What is technology? *Technology* is a design for instrumental action that reduces the uncertainty in the cause-effect relationships involved in achieving a desired outcome (see Chapter 1). This definition implies a need or problem that a tool can help to solve. The tool has (1) a hardware aspect, consisting of the material equipment, products, and so on, and (2) a software aspect, consisting of knowledge, skills, procedures, and/or principles that provide the information base for the tool. Almost every technology embodies software aspects, although they are less visible than the hardware aspects.

Most technological innovations are created by scientific research, although they often result from the interplay between scientific methods and practical problems. The knowledge base for a technology usually derives from *basic research,* defined as original investigations for the advancement of scientific knowledge and that do not have a specific objective of applying this knowledge to practical problems. In contrast, *applied research* consists of scientific investigations that are intended to solve practical problems. Scientific knowledge is put into practice as an innovation that will solve a perceived need or problem. Applied researchers are the main users of basic research. Thus, an *invention* (defined as the process by which a new idea is discovered or created) may result from a sequence of (1) basic research, followed by (2) applied research, leading to (3) development.

One measure of the success of research is whether or not it leads to a patent, through which the government protects the rights of the inventor for a period of years. A U.S. patent guards the rights of the inventor during the period in which the new idea is being commercialized (that is, converted into a new product for sale). In order to be awarded a patent, an inventor must prove to the U.S. Patent Office that his or her new idea is genuinely original, that it does not overlap with existing knowledge. Ordinarily, an inventor will sell a license to use the new idea for an initial fee plus a royalty (which is usually a percentage of sales from a product that is based on the patented idea).

R&D workers occasionally chance upon an invention while pursuing research to find a very different invention. *Serendipity* is the accidental discovery of a new idea. A case of serendipity occurred in the R&D laboratories of 3M, a company best known for Scotch tape. Several decades ago, 3M researchers found a new bonding agent, but decided it was worthless because it did not stick paper very tightly to a surface. This failure was converted into a successful product when a 3M researcher used the new bonding agent to create "Post-its," the little stick-on squares of colored paper that can be used to attach a note to a letter or other document. The researcher gave some Post-it pads to the 3M president's executive secretary, who found them very useful. A box of Post-it pads was then mailed to the executive secretary of the president of each *Fortune 500* company, and the new product was on its way to becoming a big marketing success. Today Post-its are one of 3M's most profitable products, earning the company millions of dollars each year.

Another example of serendipity is Rogaine, a hair restorer for balding individuals created by the Upjohn Company. In the mid-1990s, Upjohn's R&D workers discovered minoxidil, a drug that dilates the body's arteries and thus reduces blood pressure. To their great surprise, the R&D workers on the Minoxidil Project discovered that their own hair had begun to sprout luxuriantly. As an experiment, they applied minoxidil on their forearms. A resulting swatch of hair grew thickly. The minoxidil dilated the blood vessels, bringing more blood to the hair roots, and thus stimulated hair growth. Initially, the company's top officials did not think that a hair restorer fit in with Upjohn's product line and reputation. But the R&D workers eventually persuaded the company's president to market Rogaine, the name given to Upjohn's hair growth stimulant after Food and Drug Administration (FDA) approval. Once an individual stops applying the product to a bald spot, the balding process proceeds rapidly, a feature that discourages discontinuance of the innovation.

Many other technologies resulted from serendipity. A well-known example is penicillin, which was discovered by accident by Sir Alexander Fleming. He was puzzled by the fact that the biological materials he was studying in petri dishes were occasionally dying unexpectedly. Upon investigation, the cause turned out to be the first antibiotic to be discovered, penicillin. Sir Alexander was awarded the Nobel Prize for his discovery. Similarly, DDT was discovered in the 1930s, when a Swiss chemist, Paul Müller, was searching for a means of protecting wool clothes against moths (see Chapter 11). During World War II, DDT became widely used as a mosquito killer.

The serendipitous discovery of new ideas can occur to members of the public, as well as to scientists and inventors. For example, SMS (short message service), which transmits short text messages by cellular phones, is thought to have been discovered by Japanese teenagers in the mid-1990s. Currently, most manufacturers of cell phones provide equipment on which short messages can be sent and received. And billions of short messages are sent each day.

LEAD USERS An implicit assumption of the innovation-development process is that innovations are developed by manufacturers, who then produce and sell them. Research by Professor Eric von Hippel (1988) at MIT found that this basic assumption is often wrong. In some fields, *lead users* develop innovations and then convince a manufacturing company to produce and sell the innovation, often after a lead user has created a prototype of the innovation (Figure 4–2). Obviously, lead users have a need for a new product that are well ahead of the market. Typically, a lead user develops the innovation before the beginning of the S-shaped diffusion

Figure 4-2. The Role of Lead Users in the Diffusion Process

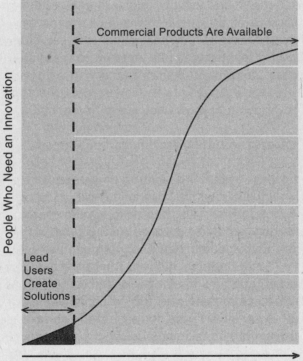

Lead users have needs for innovations that are well ahead of those of the general market, and play an important role in the innovation-decision process. A *lead user* develops an innovation and then convinces a manufacturing company to produce and sell the innovation, after the lead user has created a prototype of the new product.

Source: Based on Von Hippel and others (1999).

curve. He or she encounters a problem, thinks of a solution, and often creates a prototype of the innovation. Then he or she may lobby a manufacturing company to take over the new idea and market it to customers. Von Hippel (1988) found that lead users had developed 77 per cent of the innovations in the scientific instruments field and 67 per cent of the innovations in semiconductors and printed circuit boards.

One example of a lead user is Arnold Beckman, a chemistry professor at the California Institute of Technology who created new laboratory equipment for chemical research. Beckman was often asked by his chemistry colleagues to build copies of his electronic measurement devices for them, so often that their requests were preventing Beckman from accomplishing his own chemistry research. Accordingly, some decades ago, Beckman spun off a new company to design and manufacture laboratory devices, while he continued his career as a chemistry professor at Caltech. This company, Beckman Instruments, grew into a large enterprise, making him very wealthy. In this case, Beckman was a lead user.

Companies that supply components and materials for a product may develop a technological innovation, which a manufacturer then takes over to produce and sell. Conversely, a manufacturing company may express a need for a technology to one of its suppliers and offer to collaborate to develop the innovation. This process occurred in the late 1960s, when Busicom, a Japanese consumer electronics company, contacted Intel Corporation in California's Silicon Valley about its need for a complicated set of twelve semiconductor chips for a new calculator. Dr. Masatoshi Shima of Busicom traveled from Tokyo to California to discuss his company's needs with Dr. Ted Hoff, an R&D employee at Intel. Hoff had the idea of combining all twelve chips onto a single semiconductor chip, which led him to think about putting the central processing unit for a computer on a single semiconductor chip. Thus was born the microprocessor, which made possible the mirocomputer (also called a personal computer). Shima and Hoff collaborated at Intel for several months on development of the microprocessor, which was used in the new Busicom calculator and thereafter became Intel's main product line (Noyce and Hoff, 1981). In this case, the innovation grew out of close contact between a manufacturer (Busicom, who acted as the lead user) and a supplier.

In certain fields, such as tractor shovels, engineering plastics, and plastic additives, much of the innovation-development is by the manufacturing company, which then markets these new products (von Hippel, 1988). Here, lead users do not play an important role.

Innovation-development occurs as people talk, when information is exchanged about needs and wants and possible technological solutions to them. Often, users have important information to contribute to such discussions of innovation-development. Sometimes the initial impetus for an innovation comes from a lead user; under other conditions, a manufacturer may initiate an innovation's development. The lead user concept is so important that some large corporations, such as 3M, utilize the lead user strategy as a means of coming up with new product ideas (von Hippel et al., 1999). 3M identifies potential lead users in a technology field by asking sociometric questions of leading practitioners and then invites lead users to a two-day workshop in which possible technological solutions are discussed. Some companies use the Internet to contact lead users. For example, in the late 1990s Sony set up a Web site to contact hackers who were developing new video games for Sony's PlayStation (von Hippel et al., 1999). Amazingly, ten thousand hackers responded!

The Birth of the Laptop Computer at Toshiba

In the first years of their existence, all personal computers were desktops. Then, in 1986, Toshiba, a Japanese electronics company, manufactured the first laptop computer, an innovation that received an enthusiastic reception from consumers. The laptop made particular sense in Japan, due to crowded offices and small homes. Several employees may be assigned to the same small desk in an office crowded with a dozen workers and their boss. There is simply no space for desktop computers. Furthermore, Japanese professionals are compelled to take their work home, but few have a personal computer at home.

Despite these factors favoring the laptop computer, the Toshiba Corporation was dragged into developing this important innovation against its top executives' wishes. Twice corporate headquarters vetoed the laptop project, which succeeded only thanks to the persistence of an ingenious champion, Tetsuya Mizoguchi. "A brilliant engineer, he was full of new ideas, not afraid of upsetting others, a hard driver of his team, and he never missed an opportunity. At the time, he appeared to be highly admired, but not loved, by his subordinates" (Abetti, 1997). Mizoguchi had traveled frequently to the United States, and in 1983, while visiting the United States with an R&D team from Toshiba, he envisioned a portable personal computer. It would have to be compatible with the desktop made by IBM, which at the time had dominant market share in personal computers.

Convincing the corporate leaders at Toshiba that Mizoguchi's vision for a laptop computer made sense turned out to be extremely difficult. The company had just failed in the marketplace with its personal computer, taking huge losses, and corporate leaders had decided to get out of the computer business. They denied Mizoguchi's request for development funds and refused to assign him any experienced engineers for a laptop R&D team. Not discouraged, Mizoguchi went "underground" with the laptop project at the company's Ome factory, located some twenty-five miles from Toshiba's Tokyo headquarters. He diverted funds and shifted ten engineers from military projects to design the laptop. A prototype was created in twenty-four months, but the process was very stressful to those involved. For example, one Friday afternoon, the exhausted engineers were unable to find space to pack one more device into the already jam-packed prototype (Abetti, 1997). Mizoguchi ripped the cover off of the laptop and poured a glass of water inside (thus ruining all the electrical circuits). He turned the laptop upside down, and a few drops of water came out. Turning to his stunned engineers, Mizoguchi exclaimed, "See, there *is* some space left! Work smarter!"

Finally, in 1985, Mizoguchi triumphantly presented his laptop at Toshiba headquarters. To his disappointment, corporate executives argued that the new product was just a fad that would fill only a small market niche. He was ordered not to sell the laptop in Japan, where Toshiba had recently taken a beating with its desktop computer. At this point, Mizoguchi found an ally in Atsutoshi Nishida, senior vice president of Toshiba Europe, who was enthusiastic about the new product. He said, "Make me seven prototypes that I can show around Europe and I will commit to sell 10,000 units the first year" (quoted in Abetti, 1997). The seven were built in a few days, and Nishida, the marketing champion, went to work. In fourteen months, the first ten thousand laptops had indeed been sold! Nishida then offered his resulting profits to test the innovation in the United States. By 1988, Toshiba commanded a 38 percent market share for laptops in Europe and 21 percent in the United States; a year later, it commanded 46 percent market share in Japan, despite the quick reactions of its competitors. Production of laptops at the Ome factory increased from 5,000 units per month in 1986 to 100,000 in 1989 (Abetti, 1997). Mizoguchi was promoted to the Toshiba board of directors in 1996, and Nishida was moved into a top corporate position.

Toshiba's top brass resisted the laptop because it was a radically different innovation at the time. So its development was relegated to a "skunkworks" (the factory at Ome) in order to escape corporate displeasure. The laptop skunkworks was all the more unusual because it had to be hidden from corporate view. The usual skunkworks has the blessing of a company's leaders, and may even be headed by the company president, as when Steven Jobs led the Macintosh skunkworks at Apple Computer (see below). Tetsuya Mizoguchi was a highly unusual Japanese technologist, disobeying orders and risking his career for the sake of innovation-development. A general principle about innovation champions is that the lower they are in the organizational hierarchy, the more innovative their new product (Day, 1994). Only later, after the laptop's success in the marketplace, was Mizoguchi rewarded by Toshiba and became a company hero.

3. Development

The acronym "R&D" corresponds closely to the concept that it represents: "R" always precedes "D." As is implied, development is based closely on research. In fact, it is usually difficult or impossible to separate development from research, which is why the term "R&D" is so often used. But here we argue that research and development can be considered as distinct phases, at least conceptually, in the innovation-development process.

Development of an innovation is the process of putting a new idea in a form that is expected to meet the needs of an audience of potential adopters. This phase customarily occurs after research, as part of the creation of an innovation that stems from research. In the case illustration of the mechanized tomato harvester (discussed later), the innovation was developed by agricultural researchers at the University of California at Davis. They designed a tomato-harvesting machine, built a prototype model, and then contracted with a farm machinery company to manufacture the mechanized harvester. This later phase, called "commercialization," is discussed in a following section.

THE ROLE OF UNCERTAINTY IN R&D The inventor-developer of a new idea must anticipate the problems of other individuals and/or organizations that will be the ultimate adopters of an innovation. In addition, the behavior of others in his or her own R&D organization, his or her competitors, government policy makers, and a host of other factors may all affect the success of an inventor's new idea. Information-exchange about a technological innovation is thus a crucial component affecting the innovation-development process. R&D workers devote much effort to obtaining and using information: data about the performance of the

innovation they are creating and marketing and the materials and com
ponents they are fabricating into the innovation, as well as information
about competitors' innovations, the nature of existing patents related to
their proposed innovation, government policies affecting their proposed
innovation, and the problems faced by expected consumers and how the
proposed innovation might help solve certain of these problems.

So the innovation-development process is, most of all, driven by the
exchange of technical information in the face of a high degree of uncertainty.

How the Refrigerator Got Its Hum*

Every household refrigerator has a motor that drives a compressor that
condenses a liquid, releasing heat into the surrounding environment that the
liquid had previously absorbed inside the refrigerator when the liquid vaporized. A superior alternative is the gas refrigerator, in which the ammonia
refrigerant is vaporized by heating it with a gas flame. Later, the refrigerant
dissolves in water, thus cooling the refrigerator box. The gas refrigerator has
no moving parts and hence is unlikely to break down. It also does not make
any noise. By about 1930, prototype refrigerators of both types were developed, and one might expect that the gas refrigerator, because of its overwhelming advantages, would have captured the consumer market. It didn't.

The main reason was the extensive R&D investment in the electric
refrigerator by General Electric, General Motors, Kelvinator, and Westinghouse. These corporations decided that larger profits could be made from
the electric refrigerator, so they poured huge amounts of R&D funding into
the electric refrigerator, and also aggressively promoted this product. Several
smaller companies that marketed the gas refrigerator could not compete
with their larger opponents. So the technology available to the consumer
was shaped by considerations of corporate profitability, determined mainly
by General Electric and other companies during the R&D phase, rather
than by consumer choice in the marketplace. As a result, the product that
diffused was the refrigerator with a hum.

---

*This case illustration is based on Cowan (1985).

THE SOCIAL CONSTRUCTION OF TECHNOLOGY *Technological determinism* is the belief that technology causes changes in society. This

viewpoint implies that technology is somehow autonomous (that is, outside of society). Obviously, it is not. An opposite viewpoint, called social determinism or the *social construction of technology*, argues that technology is shaped by social factors. Technology is a product of society, and is influenced by the norms and values of the social system. For example, the previous case illustration, "How the Refrigerator Got Its Hum," shows that the technology selected was one that offered the greatest profits to the corporate manufacturers, not the technology that had the most advantages for consumers. So in this case economic factors such as potential profitability shaped the technological innovation that was diffused to the public. Many important technologies are shaped by military demands. Examples are nuclear power, jet aircraft, and the Internet. Yet other technologies are influenced by government regulations on health and safety, environmental pollution, and antitrust.

Classifying the Segway*

Dean Kamen is a fifty-year-old college dropout who has invented a portable insulin pump for people with diabetes and a wheelchair that climbs stairs. In late 2001, Kamen launched a radical new product called the Segway, a scooterlike device controlled by computer chip–driven gyroscopes and sensors that mimic the movements of its rider. The rider stands, gripping a handlebar. When the rider leans forward or backward, the Segway responds accordingly. The device has no brakes or accelerator, as the Segway stops when the rider stands up straight. Weighing sixty-five pounds and standing about four feet high, the Segway moves at up to twelve miles per hour. The Segway was introduced in late 2001 on television shows such as *Good Morning America, Fraser,* and Jay Leno's *Tonight* show. Kamen estimated that 50,000 to 100,000 Segways, priced at $3,000, would be sold during 2002.

Then the question of how to classify the Segway reared its head. Was the transporter a motorized scooter or a motor vehicle? If the latter, the Segway would be barred from being driven on sidewalks. If it were limited to roads, most people would fear having accidents with cars and trucks. Suddenly the federal government became an important player in determining the future rate of adoption of the Segway. Dean Kamen began spending much of his time in Washington, lobbying government agencies. The National Highway

---

*This case illustration is based on Armstrong and Guidera (2002).

Traffic Safety Administration ruled that the Segway was similar to a motorized wheelchair and thus not subject to vehicle regulations. Kamen convinced police and postal workers in various cities to test drive his people mover. Governors and U.S. congressmen were also given highly publicized rides on the Segway. The Consumer Product Safety Commission classified the Segway as a "consumer product." However, safety experts demanded that the federal government require lights and reflectors, specify age restrictions, and license Segway drivers.

A key issue was how the Segway should be classified, a matter ultimately to be decided by policy makers through a social construction process that will determine the future rate of adoption of this innovation.

SKUNKWORKS Evidence that the usual bureaucratic structure of an organization is not very conducive to creating technological innovation is provided by the important role of skunkworks, the small and often subversive units within a larger organization that are created in order to pioneer the development of a technological innovation. A *skunkworks* is an especially enriched environment that is intended to help a small group of individuals design a new idea by escaping routine organizational procedures. The R&D workers in a skunkworks are usually highly selected, given special resources, and work on a crash basis to create an innovation.

The distinctive name "skunkworks" originated during World War II, when the P-80 Shooting Star was designed by Lockheed's Advanced Development Projects Division in Burbank, California. A closely guarded incubator was set up in a circus tent next to a plastics factory in Burbank. The strong smells that wafted into the tent made the Lockheed R&D workers think of the foul-smelling "Skunk Works" factory in Al Capp's *Li'l Abner* comic strip. The name stuck and came to be generalized to similar high-priority R&D units that have been created by various companies since.

As mentioned previously, a particularly famous skunkworks was established by Steve Jobs, president of Apple Computer, in the early 1980s to design the Macintosh computer. This secret lab was located behind the Good Earth Restaurant in Cupertino (in northern California's Silicon Valley). About fifty highly-dedicated young computer designers labored day and night, under Job's aggressive and abusive leadership. In this case, the company president personally led the skunkworks. After the Macintosh was announced—and then disappointingly postponed several times—the revolutionary new computer was finally displayed at Apple's annual stockholders' meeting in January 1984. The Macintosh received rave notices (several million American consumers visited computer stores the next day to look at the new machine). The fifty young designers who had toiled so long in the Apple Skunkworks suddenly found themselves celebrities. Several became millionaires overnight.

Why are skunkworks needed in order to develop technological innovations such as Lockheed's P-80 Shooting Star, the Toshiba laptop, and the Apple Macintosh? Most R&D organizations are bureaucracies, structured to provide stability and continuity but not flexible enough to nurture innovation. Here we see an illustration of the inherent conflict between organizational structure and technological innovation. A skunkworks provides a means getting the best of both.

TECHNOLOGY TRANSFER *Technology transfer* is the application of information to use (Rogers, 2002b). The conventional conception of technology transfer is that it is a process through which the results of basic and applied research are put into use by receptors. This viewpoint implies that technology transfer is a one-way process, usually from university-connected basic researchers to individuals in private companies who develop and commercialize a technological innovation. Further, in this traditional and limited view of technology transfer, the technology is seen mainly as hardware.

Clearly, if one understands that a technology usually consists of software as well as hardware and thus that a technology is essentially composed of information (matter-energy that affects an individual's choice of alternatives in a decision-making situation), technology transfer is a communication process (Eveland, 1986). Most scholars realize that technology transfer is really a two-way exchange. Even when technology moves mainly in one direction, such as from a university or a federal R&D lab to a private company, the two or more parties participate in a series of communication exchanges as they seek to establish a mutual understanding about the meaning of the technology. Problems flow from potential users to researchers, and technological innovations flow to users, who ask many questions about them. Thus technology transfer is usually a two-way, back-and-forth process of communication.

In past decades, technology transfer has become a very important policy issue for the U.S. government. In industry after industry, from cars to VCRs to semiconductor memory chips, Japanese high-technology companies have conquered market share from their American counterparts. The result has been a growing trade deficit with Japan. Even though U.S. R&D led Japan in creating technological innovations, Japanese firms were much more effective in transferring this technology into commercial products that were manufactured with higher quality and at a lower price. American firms had to learn to do a better job of technology transfer.

The VCR is an illustration of the inadequacies of American-style technology transfer. The VCR was invented in the late 1950s by the Ampex Corporation, headquartered in Redwood City, California, just south of San Francisco. Ampex initially sold VCRs to television stations, which replaced their film with videotape. These VCRs used one-inch-wide tape, were about the size of a refrigerator, and cost $50,000. Sales boomed, and the Ampex company flourished. R&D workers at Ampex suggested to management that they should sell a miniaturized version of their VCR for consumers to use in their homes. But the company management insisted they were not in that market and instead sold the rights to the technology to Sony Corporation of Japan, which then commercialized the idea into a home VCR.

Sony and other Japanese electronics manufacturers have earned billions of dollars from VCRs each year. No American company manufactures the product. American inventiveness was thus converted into commercial advantage by Japanese companies through more adroit commercialization, manufacturing, and marketing.

Following the end of the Cold War in 1989, federal R&D laboratories, especially weapons labs such as those at Los Alamos, Sandia, and Oak Ridge, sought to transfer their military technologies to private companies to produce peacetime products. This type of technology transfer is extremely difficult. For more than fifty years, the federal weapons labs were secret, closed systems, enclosed in wire fences and tightly guarded. Their organizational culture emphasized the prevention of technology leakage. Suddenly, after the end of the Cold War in 1989, the mission of these R&D labs was redirected by the federal government to technology transfer. But the organizational culture of these federal R&D labs did not change as quickly as world events. Several years passed before Federal R&D labs learned how to transfer technological innovations to private firms.

The international competitiveness of the United States was threatened by its shortcomings in technology transfer. Several laws and policies were put in place to encourage technology transfer, including the Bayh-Dole

Act of 1980, which encouraged U.S. research universities to transfer the technologies resulting from their research. Over the ensuing years, most American research universities have established an office of technology transfer, and many universities earn several million dollars per year from technology royalties (Rogers, Yin, and Hoffman, 2000).

What is so difficult about technology transfer? One problem is to understand correctly what it is, and how to measure it. Three possible levels (or degrees) of technology transfer (Gibson and Rogers, 1994) are:

1. *Knowledge.* Here the receptor knows about the technological innovation.
2. *Use.* Here the receptor has put the technology into use in his or her organization. This level of technology transfer is much more complex than just knowing about the technology. The difference is equivalent to the knowledge stage in the innovation-decision process versus the implementation stage (see Chapter 5).
3. *Commercialization.* Here the receptor has commercialized the technology into a product that is sold in the marketplace. For such commercialization to occur, a great deal of time and resources must be invested by the technology receptor. Commercialization requires interpersonal communication exchanges about the technology over an extended period of time.

These three levels of technology transfer often have been confused in thinking and writing about technology transfer. One result is that technology transfer often fails. Technology transfer is difficult, in part, because we have underestimated just how much effort is required for such transfer to occur effectively.

4. Commercialization

Many innovations result from research activities (other new ideas may come from practitioners). Thus innovations are scientific results packaged in a form ready to be adopted by users. The packaging of research results is usually done by private companies, so this stage in the technology-development process is called "commercialization." *Commercialization* is the production, manufacturing, packaging, marketing, and distribution of a product that embodies an innovation. Commercialization is the conversion of an idea from research into a product or service for sale in the marketplace.

Not all innovations come from research and development. They may instead arise from practice as certain practitioners seek new solutions to their needs or problems. As mentioned previously, an example is the innovations created by "lead users" (Von Hippel, 1988).

Two or more innovations are often packaged together to facilitate their diffusion because they have a functional interrelatedness, or at least they are so perceived by potential adopters. A *technology cluster* (also called an "innovation package" in Chapter 5) consists of one or more distinguishable elements of technology that are perceived as being interrelated closely. The basic argument in favor of clustering innovations in a package is that more rapid diffusion results.

Fumbling the Future at Xerox PARC

One of the most famous examples of the failure of technology transfer is the case of the personal computer, which was developed at Xerox PARC (Palo Alto Research Center), located in a research park on the Stanford University campus. PARC was founded in 1970 and within five years had developed an incredible set of important computer technologies:

1. The world's first personal computer (a computer designed for an individual), called the "Alto"
2. The mouse, a means for an individual to interact with a computer
3. Icons and pull-down menus
4. Laser printing
5. Local area networks of computers

The Xerox Corporation, then the world's leading document copier manufacturer, invested $150 million in Xerox PARC during its first fourteen years (Uttal, 1983). Unfortunately for Xerox, none of the personal computing technologies coming out of PARC, except for laser printing, were commercialized by the Xerox Corporation into useful products. The book about the failure of technology transfer from Xerox PARC to the Xerox Corporation is entitled *Fumbling the Future: How Xerox Invented, and Then Ignored, the First Personal Computer* (Smith and Alexander, 1988).

Xerox PARC was founded in 1970 to create "the office of the future." The president of the Xerox Corporation gave PARC the vague mission of developing "the architecture of information." No one knew quite what that meant.

PARC attracted a set of very talented young computer R&D workers. "In the mid-1970s, close to half of the top 100 computer scientists in the world were working at PARC" (Perry and Wallich, 1985). PARC was a spectacular success in developing technological innovations, particularly during its Camelot era from 1970 to 1975. What led to the amazing performance of Xerox PARC in developing important personal computing innovations?

1. Outstanding R&D personnel. Several key R&D employees moved to PARC from nearby SRI International, where they had been working for a visionary computer scientist, Douglas C. Engelbart, who had invented the mouse as an alternative to the keyboard for interfacing with a computer. During the 1960s, Englebart experimented with the mouse as a means of controlling terminals connected to a mainframe computer. Several of his staff moved to Xerox PARC. They took the mouse with them (Bardini, 2001).

2. Dr. Robert Taylor, who led the computer scientists at PARC, believed in a management style that was conducive to creating technological innovation. He encouraged the free exchange of technical information among the research workers at PARC. Their regular meeting room was equipped with beanbag chairs, and the walls were lined with China boards. Long hair, sandals, T-shirts, and jeans symbolized the personal freedom of the researchers. There was little hierarchy in PARC, and resources were plentiful.

3. R&D employees at Xerox PARC used the innovations that they created in their daily work: the Alto computer, computer languages, the mouse, and icons.

4. In the early 1970s, the time was ripe for technological innovation in personal computing. A crucial prior innovation, the microprocessor, had been invented at nearby Intel Corporation (Noyce and Hoff, 1981). The microprocessor, a single computer chip, is a computer's central processing unit. Invention of the microprocessor made possible the personal computer, as discussed previously in this chapter. Rapid advances in miniaturizing semiconductor functions, with a corresponding decrease in price per unit of computer memory, occurred in the early 1970s. The lower price of semiconductor memory meant that personal computers could be sold to the mass consumer market. By 2002, one half of all U.S. households owned a personal computer.

Why did Xerox PARC fail to transfer the mouse and other important personal computing technologies to the marketplace?

1. The Xerox Corporation was the leading company in the paper copier business in the 1970s, and it perceived itself as *only* in the office copier business, not in the microcomputer business. The one PARC technology that was commercialized effectively by the Xerox Corporation, laser printing, was incorporated into a Xerox copier.

   Steve Jobs of Apple Computer visited Xerox PARC in November, 1979, and was very impressed by the personal computing technologies that he saw there. Shortly, Jobs hired several key PARC employees and established a skunkworks to develop the widely sold Macintosh, announced in 1984. Apple Computer was in the personal computer business from the beginning, so the people at Apple Computer understood the marketing of personal computers.

2. No effective mechanisms were created for technology transfer from Xerox PARC to the manufacturing and marketing/sales divisions of the Xerox Corporation. PARC was located in Palo Alto, California, an ideal location for conducting R&D in personal computing but unfortunately a long distance from the corporation's headquarters in Stamford, Connecticut. Geographical distance diminishes the opportunities for frequent personal contact, and thus makes technology transfer more difficult (Gibson and Rogers 1994).

3. The button-down organizational culture at the Xerox Corporation headquarters clashed with PARC's freewheeling hippie culture. When East Coast corporate leaders traveled to PARC, they noted disapprovingly the beanbag chairs, the endless volleyball games, and the laid-back management style of Bob Taylor. Unfortunately, Xerox executives rejected the promising personal computer technologies at PARC, as well as the work styles and lifestyles they observed there.

   Technology transfer of the mouse from SRI to PARC, and the transfer of personal computer technologies from PARC to Apple Computer, occurred rapidly. But the conversion of these technologies into a commercialized product (the Macintosh) in the Apple skunkworks required five years, from 1979 to 1984. The Xerox Corporation failed to take the final step in commercializing the personal computer technologies developed at PARC.

5. Diffusion and Adoption

Gatekeeping is controlling the flow of messages through a communication channel. One of the most crucial choices in the entire innovation-development process is the decision to begin diffusing an innovation to potential adopters. On the one hand, there is usually pressure to approve an innovation for diffusion as soon as possible, especially when the social problem or need that it seeks to solve has a high priority. On the other hand, a change agency's reputation and credibility in the eyes of its clients rests on only recommending innovations that will have beneficial consequences for adopters. Scientists become very cautious when it comes time to translate their scientific findings into practice.

Innovation gatekeeping—controlling whether or not an innovation is diffused to an audience of potential adopters—can occur in a variety of ways. Agricultural experiment stations in each of the fifty states develop farm innovations, and then they are diffused by their corresponding state agricultural extension services. After an innovation is judged ready for diffusion, it is recommended to farmers for their adoption by agricultural extension agents. The innovation may be given blanket approval, or it may be recommended for certain climatic or soil conditions. An organizational interface is thus involved at the point of deciding to begin diffusing an innovation, as the new idea passes from R&D workers in an agricultural experiment station to a diffusion agency (the agricultural extension service). A similar organizational interface between an R&D unit and a diffusion agency is involved in many other fields, and this decision point is managed in a variety of ways.

In medical diffusion there is a strong concern with exerting "quality control" over new technologies that spread to practitioners. This concern is understandable, given the possible threat to human life that might be involved in diffusing an unsafe medical innovation to practitioners. The National Institutes of Health (NIH) conducts *consensus development,* a process that brings together scientists, practitioners, consumers, and others in an effort to reach general agreement on whether or not a given innovation is both safe and effective (Lowe, 1980; Asch and Lowe, 1984; Larsen and Rogers, 1984). The medical innovation may be a device, a drug, or a medical or surgical procedure. An NIH consensus conference typically ends with preparation of a brief consensus statement, which is then published by the U.S. government and widely disseminated to physicians in medical journals and by other means.

Before consensus development conferences were begun, the medical field lacked a formal gatekeeping process to ensure that medical research discoveries were identified and scientifically evaluated to determine if they were ready to be used by doctors and other health providers. It was feared that some new technologies might have diffused without an adequate scientific evaluation, while other well-validated medical technologies might be diffusing too slowly. Consensus development panels have also been used by other federal agencies, by the American Medical Association, and by private companies such as pharmaceutical houses. In fact, currently there are so many practice guidelines being disseminated that medical practitioners are swamped by information overload (Shaneyfette, Mayer, and Rothwang, 1999; Grilli et al., 2000).

Clinical trials are scientific experiments designed to determine prospectively the effects of an innovation (such as a new drug) in terms of its efficacy, safety, and other factors. The purpose of clinical trials is to evaluate the effects of an innovation under real-life (rather than laboratory) conditions, as a basis for making a go/no-go decision as to the diffusion of the innovation. Evidence from extensive clinical trials is required before the Federal Drug Administration (FDA) approves a new drug. Once several clinical trials of a medical innovation have been conducted, perhaps with funding provided by the NIH, the results are pulled together in a consensus development conference.

The consensus development process serves the important function of gatekeeping the flow of medical innovations from research into practice.

6. Consequences

The final phase in the innovation-development process is the *consequences* of an innovation, defined as the changes that occur to an individual or to a social system as a result of the adoption or rejection of an innovation (see Chapter 11).

We have implied in this section that the six stages in the innovation-development process occur in the linear sequence in which they were discussed. In many cases, certain of these phases do not occur, or the exact time order of the phases may be changed. Nevertheless, the notion of stages in the innovation-development process is useful for understanding where innovations come from.

Serendipity in the Discovery of Warfarin*

The story of warfarin, the most widely used rat poison in the world, helps illustrate how scientific research aimed at solving one problem led to a technologi-

---

*This case illustration is based on Lowe (1981) and on personal interviews with WARF officials.

cal innovation that is tremendously effective at solving a quite different problem. Serendipity, the chance discovery of a new idea, often plays an important role in the innovation-development process, and in the consequences of R&D.

Research by Professor K. P. Link and his associates at the University of Wisconsin in 1934 was designed to find the chemical in spoiled sweet clover hay that led to cattle hemorrhage. In the 1930s, many farmers fed their cattle sweet clover hay in part because agronomists recommended planting sweet clover to "sweeten" acidic soils and to minimize soil erosion. But when the sweet clover hay was fed to cattle, they sometimes died from internal bleeding. Farmers called this mysterious illness "sweet clover disease."

One day a Wisconsin farmer barged into Link's laboratory to give him a tubful of blood from the stomach of one of his dairy cows. He demanded that Link find the cause of sweet clover disease. Professor Link isolated the hemorrhaging agent, an anticoagulant called coumarin, in spoiled sweet clover hay. The stick-like hay stems punctured the cows' stomach walls, and the coumarin caused them to bleed to death. Biomedical researchers soon began to test the usefulness of coumarin in certain types of surgery and on some heart conditions. But the most important application of Link's findings from research on sweet clover disease occurred a dozen years later, when Link experimented with coumarin as a rodenticide. He found to his surprise that the anticoagulant was a very effective rat killer.

Link applied to the Wisconsin Alumni Research Foundation (WARF), the technology transfer office at the University of Wisconsin, for assistance in patenting coumarin as a rat killer. A chemical derivative of coumarin called warfarin (after WARF) was licensed by WARF to commercial manufacturers. The licensing royalties from warfarin today support Madison professors' research projects, provide research assistantships for doctoral students, and pay for other research expenses.

Warfarin is highly lethal to rats; it causes internal bleeding, and the stricken rodents seek water and thus do not usually die in their burrows. Farmers and homeowners can thus readily observe its effectiveness in eradicating rats, and the innovation's observability enhances its rate of adoption (see Chapter 6). Warfarin is not dangerous to dogs, cats, or humans who might happen to consume it. Today, more than 3.5 million tons of warfarin are sold each year.

Professor Link began the research eventually leading to the rat killer by investigating sweet clover disease. The innovation-development process for warfarin was uncertain and unpredictable, with serendipity playing a major role. So our present model of the six-phase process of innovation-development should be considered only a general guide to the process from which many innovations may deviate.

Socioeconomic Status, Equality, and Innovation-Development

A consistent finding from past diffusion researches is that individuals' socioeconomic status is highly related to their degree of change agent contact. Status and change agent contact are in turn highly related to their degree of innovativeness (see Chapter 9). Thus, change agencies often cause increased socioeconomic inequality among their audience through their diffusion activities (see Chapter 1).

Further, the socioeconomic status of individual adopters is connected with the innovation-development process. For example, whether a new automobile such as the hybrid gas/electric car is designed as a low-priced sedan or as a high-end model determines whether middle-income or wealthy consumers will purchase it. Whether a research topic will benefit larger or smaller farmers largely determines who will eventually adopt the results of such research and the consequences of the research-based technological innovations (Hightower, 1972).

Can technologies be developed and diffused in a way that leads to greater equality (rather than inequality) in their socioeconomic consequences? The answer lies in how socioeconomic status factors affect each stage in the innovation-development process. An example is provided by the following study of tomato harvesting.

Hard Tomatoes in California*

The nature of an innovation's diffusion and its consequences are often determined in part during the R&D stage to create the innovation. How the consequences of the diffusion process are predetermined by decisions that occurred prior to the first adoption is illustrated by the case of the mechanized tomato harvester in California.

California is the number one agricultural state in America, and tomatoes are one of California's most important farm products. Prior to the introduction of the mechanized harvester in 1962 about 4,000 farmers produced tomatoes in California. Nine years later, only 600 of these growers were still in business. Before the new machine, 50,000 farmworkers, mostly immigrant Mexican men, were employed as tomato pickers in California. They

---

*This case illustration is based on Friedland and Barton (1975).

were replaced by 1,152 machines (each costing about $65,000), plus about 18,000 workers, who rode the harvesters to sort out the damaged and immature tomatoes. About 80 percent of these sorters were women, and only a few were Mexican Americans.

The mechanized harvesters moved tomato growing out of California's San Joaquin County into Yolo and Fresno Counties, where the soil and weather conditions were more ideally suited to growing tomatoes for mechanized picking. To enable machine picking, agricultural scientists bred hard tomatoes that would not bruise easily, even though American consumers preferred soft tomatoes. The hard tomatoes tasted the same, but they contained somewhat fewer vitamins.

So the development of the mechanized tomato picker had far-reaching consequences on labor, location, and consumer behavior. Had the effects been anticipated by the R&D workers who developed the mechanized pickers at the University of California at Davis? Not at all, say Friedland and Barton (1975, p. 28), who labeled these agricultural scientists "social sleepwalkers." The creators of the mechanical harvesters were motivated to save the tomato industry for California when it was threatened by the termination of the Mexican *bracero* program in 1964 (which meant the end of cheap labor). The scientists showed little concern for how the social consequences of this new technology would adversely affect human lives, leading James Hightower (1972) to title his book about the land-grant university system *Hard Tomatoes, Hard Times.*

Research to develop the tomato-picking technology was carried out by agricultural professors at the University of California at Davis, using more than $1 million of public funds (Schmitz and Seckler, 1970). The chief researcher was G. C. "Jack" Hanna, a professor of vegetable crops. He bred a hard tomato variety that could be machine-harvested, despite the vigorous opposition of his colleagues and administrators who believed that his idea of mechanical picking was ridiculous. Hanna teamed with an agricultural engineer at UC Davis named Coby Lorenzen to design a tomato-harvesting machine that would cut off the tomato plant at soil level, pluck the fruits from the vine, and elevate them past a crew of tomato sorters into a gondola truck for transportation to market. The harvester, designed by Lorenzen, was then produced by Hanna's friend Ernest Blackwelder, a farm machinery manufacturer who contracted with the University of California.*

In 1964, 224 tomato-picking machines harvested 25 percent of all toma-

*By 1969, Blackwelder paid $225,000 in technology royalties to the University of California for the intellectual property rights to manufacture the tomato harvester (Schmitz and Seckler, 1970).

toes grown. This sudden increase in adoption occurred because the U.S. Congress ended the *bracero* program through which Mexican farmers had been brought to California. The tomato industry honored Hanna as the individual who "saved the tomato for California." Six years later, in 1970, 1,521 of the machines harvested 99.9 percent of the tomato crop and 32,000 former hand pickers were out of work.

In retrospect, one might wonder how differently the diffusion and adoption of this innovation might have been had the R&D workers designed a smaller machine, one that more of the 4,000 tomato farmers (as of 1962) could have adopted. What if the impending threat of a severe labor shortage in 1964 had not forced Hanna, Lorenzen, and Blackwelder to rush their prototype machine into production? What if the University of California at Davis had conducted social and economic research on the impacts of farm mechanization before 1962, so that the destructive consequences of the new technology on employment, and the unhappiness of tomato consumers, might have been anticipated, and perhaps mitigated?

The decisions and activities occurring in the R&D stage of the technology development process directly affect the later diffusion stage. A similar experience to that of the tomato harvester in California has occurred in more recent years with precision farming in the United States. Precision farming uses expensive equipment, consisting of a global positioning system (GPS) and an onboard computer, to improve the efficiency of seeding rates, chemical fertilizer, and pesticide and weedicide applications. This technology is attached to a farmer's seeding and harvesting equipment, so that as the farmer rides across a field, the application rates of seeds and other inputs are adjusted specifically for each small plot of the field, typically about a yard square. Much greater efficiency can be achieved with precision farming than with the usual farm management techniques of planning for an eighty-acre field.

Unfortunately, the precision farming equipment is relatively expensive, from $50,000 to $70,000, and only large commercial farmers can justify the cost. Could the precision farming equipment also have been designed by farm machinery companies for smaller farmers?

Tracing the Innovation-Development Process

Considerable research has been devoted to tracing the research, development, and commercialization phases of the innovation-development process (see Figure 4–1). Such retrospective tracer studies reconstruct the sequence of main events and decisions in the innovation-development process. The sources of data are usually personal interviews with key investigators and other participants, research publications, and archival records of research grants, patents, and change agency records.

One of the first and best-known retrospective tracer studies of the research and development phase of the innovation-development process is Project Hindsight (Isenson, 1969). This massive tracer study investigated the R&D process leading to twenty different military weapons systems, such as the Minuteman missile, the Polaris submarine, and the M-61 nuclear warhead. The key events and decisions in the process of creating each of the twenty technological innovations were identified, an average of about thirty-five events per innovation. Project Hindsight concluded that most of the research that had contributed to the creation of the twenty innovations was highly applied and had been funded to produce the particular weapons system that eventually resulted. The findings of Project Hindsight are usually interpreted to mean that applied research contributes more directly to the creation of a technological innovation than does basic research (hardly a surprising conclusion).

Project Hindsight led to further innovation tracer studies. Project TRACES (Technology in Retrospect and Critical Events in Science) was conducted by the Illinois Institute of Technology in 1968 and later carried on by Batelle-Columbus Laboratories in what were termed TRACES II (Globe et al., 1973) and TRACES III (Batelle-Columbus Laboratories, 1976). These investigations, along with Project Sappho in England (Achilladelis et al., 1971), were further improvements in the methodology of retrospective tracer studies and a broadening of the technological innovations studied, from military weapons to a variety of biomedical, agricultural, consumer, and other innovations. The Minnesota Innovation Project was a more recent tracer study, investigating such technologies as oral contraceptives, hybrid grain seeds, and 3M's Post-Its (Van de Ven, Angle, and Poole, 1989).

These tracer studies generally show that a major technological advance in such fields as military weapons, medicine, or agriculture requires not just one innovation but a cluster of innovations, often as many as a dozen. For example, the heart pacemaker was an innovation cluster that depended upon the prior invention of transistors, compact batteries, and other developments (Globe et al., 1973). This functional interdependence of innovation clusters is often overlooked by diffusion scholars who investigate single innovations as if they were completely independent (see Chapter 6).

Further, the innovation tracer studies show that a lengthy period, often as much as twenty years, occurs between an invention in basic research, and its application in a weaponry or medical innovation. It seems that basic research results have to "age" before they can be packaged into a useful innovation. For example, the length of time from first conception of a technological innovation to its first realization was nine years (from 1951 to 1960) for oral contraceptives (Globe et al., 1973). The comparable period for two agricultural innovations was much longer: twenty-five years for hybrid corn (1908 to 1933) and thirteen years for insecticides (1934 to 1947). The ten innovations studied in the TRACES II study required an average of nineteen years from first conception to first realization (Globe et al., 1973).

Finally, the tracer studies show that research is often conducted without a practical application to a social problem in mind. This point is made by Comroe (1977), who traced the innovation-development process for the ten most important technologies in cardiopulmonary medicine. Of the five hundred or so key research articles leading to these innovations, 41 percent reported research that, at the time it had been conducted, had had no relationship whatsoever to the disease it eventually helped treat. So the innovation-development process does not always begin with a perceived problem or need. A considerable degree of serendipity may occur.

Several of the case illustrations in this chapter, such as "Fumbling the Future of the Personal Computer," "Serendipity in the Discovery of Warfarin," and "Hard Tomatoes in California," are tracer studies.

The Shortcomings of Tracer Studies

Several weaknesses of the innovation tracer studies need improvement in future research. These tracer studies are *retrospective,* looking backward in time at the innovation-development process. Much could also be learned from conducting *prospective* studies of the innovation-development process. Further, past tracer studies focused upon very important technological innovations like the heart pacemaker, oral contraceptives, and the Minuteman missile. We do not know if similar results would obtain for less socially significant innovations.

Further, the data sources for tracer studies are rather limited due to the following factors:

1. These tracer studies depended almost entirely upon the availability of research publications about the technology, in order to reconstruct a

partial view of the R&D phases of the innovation-development process.

2. Because of these limited data sources, tracer studies generally describe the research and development phases of the innovation-development process but do not tell much about the diffusion/adoption phase, and almost nothing about the consequences of the innovation. Investigations of the *entire* innovation-development process are needed.

3. Tracer studies imply that the research and development phases are relatively rational and planned. Serendipitous and accidental aspects of the innovation-development process are unlikely to be fully reported in research publications written by the inventors and researchers.

Future Research on the Innovation-Development Process

What research questions should be studied in the future so as to improve our understanding of the innovation-development process?

1. How is the agenda of research priorities in a scientific field set? How are users' needs and problems communicated to R&D workers? What role does a change agency play in translating users' needs to R&D decision makers?

2. What is the impact on users' credibility in a change agency when it reverses its policy concerning an innovation, for example, by recommending the discontinuance of an innovation that was previously recommended? An example is 2,4-D weed spray, whose diffusion the present author investigated during his Ph.D. dissertation research in 1954, when this innovation was widely adopted by Iowa farmers. Some years later, 2,4-D was found to be a carcinogen and was banned for use on food crops. The Iowa Extension Service, who had recommended the weed spray to farmers, now explained to them that it was banned. Will Iowa farmers be less likely to regard the Extension Service as credible when it makes its next recommendation?

3. To what extent are technological innovations developed by "lead" users, rather than by R&D experts? Is the creation of innovations by end users, as Von Hippel (1988) found, a general pattern?

4. What are the consequences of a technological innovation on socioeconomic equality, and how is this impact of an innovation affected

by its size and cost, which were determined at the development and commercialization phases?

5. What are the key linkages and interrelationships among the various organizations involved in the innovation-development process? Particularly, how do researchers interface with change agents in making the decision to launch the diffusion of an innovation?

The Agricultural Extension Model

The government agency that has been by far the most successful in securing users' adoption of its research results is the agricultural extension services. Although this system is commonly called "the agricultural extension model," it actually consists of three main components: (1) a research subsystem, consisting of professors of agriculture supported by the fifty state agricultural experiment stations and the U.S. Department of Agriculture, (2) county extension agents, who work as change agents with farmers and rural people at the local level, and (3) state extension specialists who link agricultural researchers to the county agents. Both the researchers and the extension specialists are located in state agricultural universities and have similar levels of expertise (both are usually Ph.D.s in agriculture). So the agricultural extension model is an integrated system for the innovation-development process (Rogers, 1988a).

The agricultural university teaching component of the agricultural extension model was established in 1862 as land-grant universities, one in each state. Examples are Ohio State University, New Mexico State University, and the University of Nebraska. A college of agriculture was one unit (along with a college of education, a college of medicine, and so on), so many students today refer to the land-grant universities as "cow colleges." It is not intended to be a compliment, but from the viewpoint of transferring agricultural research into practice, the cow colleges have been exemplars.

Originally, the land-grant universities mainly engaged in teaching agriculture and engineering, but in 1887 a federal law, the Hatch Act, provided funding for agricultural research. Now the professors of agriculture began to conduct experiments on crops and livestock. The agricultural experiments were applied research and the professors wanted their findings to be utilized by farmers. In 1914, state agricultural extension services were established by the Smith-Lever Act, whose purpose was "To aid in diffusing among the people of the United States useful and practical information on subjects relating to agriculture and home economics, and to encourage application of the same." The extension service is probably the oldest diffusion system in the United States. Certainly, by reputation it is the most successful.

The budget for the extension services comes from federal, state, and county governments, and is approximately equal to the annual public investment in agricultural research. This fifty-fifty level of funding for diffusion activities in agriculture is one reason for the success of the agricultural extension service. No other federal mission agency spends more than a few percent of its research program on diffusion activities (see Chapter 9).

Several other government agencies have tried to copy the agricultural extension model, but with little success. These attempts to extend the agricultural extension model often ignored one or more of the main elements in the model (Rogers et al., 1982). Some federal agencies established a diffusion system with the equivalent of extension specialists but failed to establish local-level change agents to contact clients directly (the counterpart of county extension agents). Other federal agencies forgot that the agricultural extension service required many years to establish its reputation for success. Agricultural research projects are highly applied, conducted to be put into use to solve farmers' problems.

The attempts to copy the agricultural extension model in such fields as education, public transportation, vocational rehabilitation, energy conservation, and family planning have therefore not been very successful.

Summary

Past diffusion researches usually began with the first adopter of an innovation, that is, with the left-hand tail of the S-shaped diffusion curve. Events and decisions occurring previous to this point have a considerable influence upon the diffusion process. The scope of future diffusion research should be broadened to include study of the entire process through which an innovation is generated.

The *innovation-development process* consists of all the decisions, activities, and their impacts that occur from recognition of a need or problem, through research, development, and commercialization of an innovation, through diffusion and adoption of the innovation by users, to its consequences. Recognition of a problem or need may occur when a social problem rises to a high priority on the agenda of topics which deserve research.

Many, but not all, technological innovations come out of research. *Basic research* is defined as original investigations for the advancement of scientific knowledge and that do not have the specific objective of applying this knowledge to practical problems. The results of basic research may be used in *applied research,* which consists of scientific investigations that are intended to solve practical problems. *Lead users* develop innovations and then convince a manufacturing company to produce and sell the innovation, often after the lead user has created a prototype of the innovation. The usual next stage in the innovation-development process is *development,* defined as the process of putting a new idea into a form that is expected to meet the needs of an audience of potential adopters. *Technological* determinism is the belief that technology causes changes in society. An opposite viewpoint is *social constructionism,* which states that social factors shape a technology. A next stage, *commercialization,* is defined as the production, manufacturing, packaging, marketing, and distribution of a product that embodies an innovation. Commercialization is carried out mainly by private firms.

A particularly crucial point in the innovation-development process is the decision to begin diffusing an innovation to potential adopters. How are innovations evaluated for their efficacy, safety, and other factors?

Finally, an innovation may diffuse, be adopted, and, eventually, cause consequences, the final stage in the innovation-development process. The six stages described here may not always occur in a linear sequence, the time order of the stages may be different, and certain stages may not occur at all.

5

THE INNOVATION-DECISION PROCESS

One must learn by doing the thing, for though you think you
know it, you have no certainty until you try.

Sophocles, 400 B.C.

The *innovation-decision process* is the process through which an individual (or other decision-making unit) passes from gaining initial knowledge of an innovation, to forming an attitude toward the innovation, to making a decision to adopt or reject, to implementation of the new idea, and to confirmation of this decision. This process consists of a series of choices and actions over time through which an individual or a system evaluates a new idea and decides whether or not to incorporate the innovation into ongoing practice. This behavior consists essentially of dealing with the uncertainty that is inherently involved in deciding about a new alternative to an idea previously in existence. The perceived newness of an innovation, and the uncertainty associated with this newness, is a distinctive aspect of innovation decision making (compared to other types of decision making).

This chapter describes a model of the innovation-decision process and the five stages in this process, and summarizes evidence about these stages. Our main concern here is with optional innovation-decisions that are made by individuals, although much of what is said contributes a basis for our later discussion of the innovation-decision process in organizations (see Chapter 10) or in other systems.

A Model of the Innovation-Decision Process

Diffusion scholars have long recognized that an individual's decision about an innovation is not an instantaneous act. Rather, it is a *process* that occurs over time and consists of a series of different actions. The notion of stages in an innovation-decision process was conceptualized by Ryan and Gross (1943) in the Iowa seed corn study, although their stages were not exactly the same as the five stages used by most diffusion scholars today. The rural sociologists understood, however, that an Iowa farmer did not make an impulse decision to adopt the new seed corn. Instead, the typical farmer learned about the existence of the new idea from certain sources or channels of communication, then sought further information (often from different sources or channels), tried out the new seed on a few acres of corn, and finally, several years later, adopted the innovation completely. Most diffusion researchers who have probed the innovation-decision process for their respondents have arrived at a somewhat similar set of stages.

What is the nature of these sequential stages in the process of innovation decision making? Our present model of the innovation-decision process, depicted in Figure 5–1, consists of five stages:

1. *Knowledge* occurs when an individual (or other decision-making unit) is exposed to an innovation's existence and gains an understanding of how it functions.
2. *Persuasion* occurs when an individual (or other decision-making unit) forms a favorable or an unfavorable attitude towards the innovation.
3. *Decision* takes place when an individual (or other decision-making unit) engages in activities that lead to a choice to adopt or reject the innovation.
4. *Implementation* occurs when an individual (or other decision-making unit) puts a new idea into use.
5. *Confirmation* takes place when an individual seeks reinforcement of an innovation-decision already made, but he or she may reverse this previous decision if exposed to conflicting messages about the innovation.

Now we describe the behavior that occurs at each of the five stages in the innovation-decision process.

Figure 5-1. A Model of Five Stages in the Innovation-Decision Process

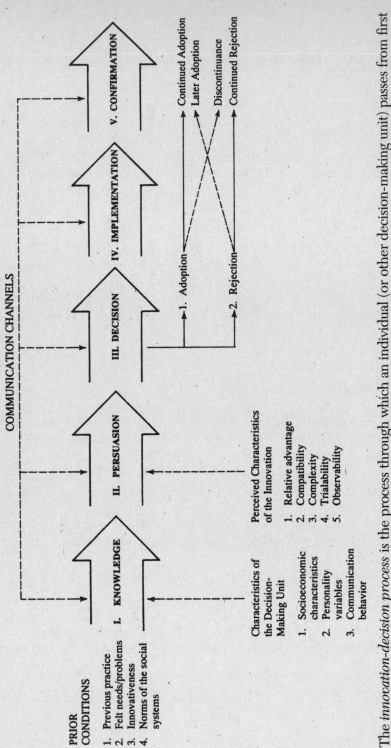

COMMUNICATION CHANNELS

I. KNOWLEDGE   II. PERSUASION   III. DECISION   IV. IMPLEMENTATION   V. CONFIRMATION

1. Adoption

2. Rejection

Continued Adoption
Later Adoption
Discontinuance
Continued Rejection

PRIOR
CONDITIONS

1. Previous practice
2. Felt needs/problems
3. Innovativeness
4. Norms of the social
   systems

Characteristics of
the Decision-
Making Unit

1. Socioeconomic
   characteristics
2. Personality
   variables
3. Communication
   behavior

Perceived Characteristics
of the Innovation

1. Relative advantage
2. Compatibility
3. Complexity
4. Trialability
5. Observability

The *innovation-decision process* is the process through which an individual (or other decision-making unit) passes from first knowledge of an innovation, to forming an attitude toward the innovation, to a decision to adopt or reject, to implementation of the new idea, and to confirmation of this decision.

The Knowledge Stage

The innovation-decision process begins with the knowledge stage, which commences when an individual (or other decision-making unit) is exposed to an innovation's existence and gains an understanding of how it functions.

Which Comes First, Needs or Awareness of an Innovation?

Some observers claim that an individual plays a relatively passive role when being exposed to awareness-knowledge about an innovation. If an individual becomes aware of an innovation by accident, the individual could not actively seek the innovation. For example, Coleman and colleagues (1966) concluded that initial knowledge about a new medical drug occurred mainly through communication channels and messages (such as salespersons and advertising in medical journals) that physicians did not seek. At later stages in the innovation-decision process, however, the medical doctors became active information seekers, usually from their peers in communication networks.

Other individuals may gain awareness-knowledge about an innovation through behavior that they initiate, so their awareness-knowledge is not a passive activity. Then the predispositions of individuals influence their behavior toward communication messages about an innovation and the effects that such messages are likely to have. Individuals tend to expose themselves to ideas that are in accordance with their interests, needs, and existing attitudes. Individuals consciously or unconsciously avoid messages that are in conflict with their existing predispositions. This tendency is called *selective exposure,* defined as the tendency to attend to communication messages that are consistent with the individual's existing attitudes and beliefs.

Hassinger (1959) argued that individuals seldom expose themselves to messages about an innovation unless they first feel a need for the innovation, and that even if individuals are exposed to innovation messages, such exposure will have little effect unless the innovation is perceived as relevant to the individual's needs and is consistent with the individual's attitudes and beliefs. This process is *selective perception,* defined as the tendency to interpret communication messages in terms of the individual's existing attitudes and beliefs. For example, a farmer could drive past a hundred miles of hybrid corn in Iowa and never "see" the innovation. A Californian could walk past a house with a satellite dish on the rooftop and not perceive this innovation. Selective exposure and selective perception act as particularly tight shutters on the windows of our minds in the case of innovation messages, because such ideas are new. We cannot have consistent and favorable ideas about ideas that we have not previously encountered. There is much in the ideas of selective exposure and selective perception to support Hassinger's viewpoint that the need for an innovation usually precedes awareness-knowledge of the innovation.

How are needs created? A *need* is a state of dissatisfaction or frustration that occurs when an individual's desires outweigh the individual's actualities. An individual may develop a need when he or she learns that an innovation exists. Therefore, innovations *can* lead to needs, as well as vice versa. Change agents may create needs among their clients by pointing out the existence of desirable new ideas. Thus knowledge of the existence of an innovation can create a motivation to learn more about it and, ultimately, to adopt it.

Perceived needs or problems are not a very complete explanation of why individuals begin the innovation-decision process. Individuals do not always recognize when they have a problem, and the individuals' perceived needs may not agree with what experts think the individuals need. The late Edgar Dale of Ohio State University was fond of saying, "We may want food and not need it. And we may need vitamins and minerals and fail to want them."

Does a need precede awareness-knowledge of a new idea, or does such knowledge of an innovation create a need for the new idea? Research does not provide a clear answer to this question as to which comes first. The need for certain innovations, such as a pesticide to treat a new bug that is destroying an individual's garden, probably comes first. But for many other new ideas, an innovation may create a need for it. This sequence may be especially likely for consumer innovations such as clothing fashions and electronic products such as compact discs, DVDs, and cellular telephones. We become aware of a consumer product, are attracted by it, and then decide that we must have it.

Three Types of Knowledge About an Innovation

The innovation-decision process is essentially an information-seeking and information-processing activity in which an individual is motivated to reduce uncertainty about the advantages and disadvantages of an innovation. An innovation typically comes with such questions as "What is the innovation?" "How does it work?" and "Why does it work?" The first question represents one of three types of knowledge about an innovation, *awareness-knowledge,* information that an innovation exists. Awareness-knowledge may motivate an individual to seek a second and a third type of knowledge: "how-to" knowledge and principles knowledge. Such information seeking is concentrated at the knowledge stage of the innovation-decision process, but it may also occur at the persuasion and decision stages.

How-to knowledge consists of information necessary to use an innovation properly. The adopter must understand what quantity of an innovation to secure, how to use it correctly, and so on. In the case of innovations that are relatively complex, the amount of how-to knowledge needed for adoption is much greater than in the case of less complex ideas (see Chapter 6). And when an adequate level of how-to knowledge is not obtained prior to the trial and adoption of an innovation, rejection and discontinuance are likely to result. To date, few diffusion investigations deal with how-to knowledge, although it must be a fundamental variable in the innovation-decision process.

Principles-knowledge consists of information dealing with the functioning principles underlying how an innovation works. Examples of principles knowledge include the notion of germ theory, which underlies the functioning of water boiling, vaccinations, and latrines in village sanitation and health campaigns; the fundamentals of human reproduction, which form a basis for family-planning innovations; the biology of plant growth, which underlies the adoption of fertilizers by farmers; and microelectronics, which underlies the functioning of computers, the Internet, and consumer electronics. It is usually possible to adopt an innovation without principles-knowledge, but the danger of misusing a new idea is greater and discontinuance may result. Certainly, the competence of individuals to judge the effectiveness of an innovation is facilitated by their understanding of principles know-how.

What is the role of change agents in bringing about each of the three types of knowledge? Most change agents concentrate their efforts in creating awareness-knowledge (although this goal could often be achieved more efficiently by mass media channels). Change agents could perhaps play their most distinctive and important role in the innovation-decision process if they concentrated on how-to knowledge, which is probably most essential to clients in their trial of an innovation at the decision stage in the innovation-decision process. Most change agents perceive that creation of principles-knowledge is outside the purview of their responsibilities and is a more appropriate task for formal education. But when such understanding of the principles underlying an innovation is lacking, the change agent's long-run task is more difficult.

Early Versus Late Knowers of Innovations

The following generalizations summarize the results of findings regarding early knowing about an innovation:

Generalization 5-1: *Earlier knowers of an innovation have more education than do later knowers.*

Generalization 5-2: *Earlier knowers of an innovation have higher social status than do late knowers.*

Generalization 5-3: *Earlier knowers of an innovation have more exposure to mass media channels of communication that do later knowers.*

Generalization 5-4: *Earlier knowers of an innovation have more exposure to interpersonal channels than do later knowers.*

Generalization 5-5: *Earlier knowers of an innovation have more contact with change agents than do later knowers.*

Generalization 5-6: *Earlier knowers of an innovation have more social participation than do later knowers.*

Generalization 5-7: *Earlier knowers of an innovation are more cosmopolite than are later knowers.*

The characteristics of earlier knowers of an innovation are generally similar to the characteristics of innovators and early adopters: more education, higher social status, and the like. But earlier knowers are not necessarily earlier in adopting new ideas. Knowing about an innovation is quite different from using it. Most individuals know about many innovations that they have not adopted. An individual may know about a new idea but not regard it as relevant to his or her situation or as potentially useful. Attitudes toward an innovation, therefore, frequently intervene between the knowledge and decision functions in the innovation-decision process. In other words, the individual's attitudes or beliefs about an innovation have much to say about his or her passage through the stages of the innovation-decision process. Consideration of a new idea does not go beyond the knowledge function if an individual does not define the information as relevant to his or her situation, or if sufficient knowledge is not obtained to become adequately informed, so that persuasion can then take place.

The Persuasion Stage

At the *persuasion* stage in the innovation-decision process, the individual forms a favorable or unfavorable attitude toward the innovation. *Attitude* is a relatively enduring organization of an individual's beliefs about an object that predisposes his or her actions. Whereas the mental activity at the knowledge stage was mainly cognitive (or knowing), the main type of thinking at the persuasion stage is affective (or feeling). Until an individual knows about a new idea, of course, he or she cannot begin to form an attitude toward it.

We do not define persuasion in exactly the same way as some other scholars, who use the term to imply a source's communication with the intent to induce attitude change in a desired direction on the part of a receiver. Our meaning of persuasion is equivalent to attitude formation and change on the part of an individual, but not necessarily in the direction intended by some particular source, such as a change agent.

At the persuasion stage the individual becomes more psychologically involved with the innovation. He or she actively seeks information about the new idea, decides *what* messages he or she regards as credible, and decides *how* he or she interprets the information that is received. Thus, selective perception is important in determining the individual's behavior at the persuasion stage, for it is at the persuasion stage that a general perception of the innovation is developed. Such perceived attributes of an innovation as its relative advantage, compatibility, and complexity are especially important at this stage (see Figure 5–1).

In developing a favorable or unfavorable attitude toward an innovation, an individual may mentally apply the new idea to his or her present or anticipated future situation before deciding whether or not to try it. This vicarious trial involves the ability to think hypothetically and counterfactually and to project into the future: What if I adopt this innovation? Forward planning is involved at the persuasion stage.

All innovations carry some degree of uncertainty for an individual, who is typically unsure of the new idea's functioning and thus seeks social reinforcement from others of his or her attitude toward the innovation. The individual wants to know whether his or her thinking is on the right track in the opinion of peers. Mass media messages are too general to provide the specific kind of reinforcement that the individual needs to confirm his or her initial beliefs about the innovation.

At the persuasion stage and at the decision stage, an individual seeks innovation evaluation information, messages that reduce uncertainty about an innovation's expected consequences. Here an individual usually wants to know the answer to the question "What are the innovation's advantages and disadvantages in my situation?" This type of information, while often available from scientific evaluations of an innovation, is instead sought by most individuals from their near peers, whose subjective opinions of the innovation (based on their personal experience with adoption of the new idea) are more accessible and convincing to them.

The main outcome of the persuasion stage in the innovation-decision process is a favorable or unfavorable attitude toward the innovation. It is assumed that such persuasion will lead to a subsequent change in overt behavior (that is, adoption or rejection) consistent with the individual's attitude. But in many cases attitudes and actions may be disparate. For example, such a discrepancy between favorable attitudes and actual adoption is frequently found for preventive health innovations such as contraceptives in developing nations. For instance, surveys of people of childbearing age show that almost all are informed about family-planning methods and have a favorable attitude toward using them. But perhaps only 15 or 20 percent of fertile-aged parents use contraceptives (Rogers et al., 1999). This attitude-use discrepancy is commonly called the "KAP-gap" (KAP refers to "knowledge, attitudes, practice"). So the formation of a favorable or unfavorable attitude toward an innovation does not always lead directly or indirectly to an adoption or rejection decision.

A *preventive innovation* is a new idea that an individual adopts in order to avoid the possible occurrence of some unwanted event in the future. The undesired event may or may not occur if the innovation is not adopted. So the desired consequences of a preventive innovation are uncertain. Under such circumstances, the individual's motivation to adopt the preventive innovation is relatively weak. So the rate of adoption of preventive innovations is relatively slower than for nonpreventive innovations. For example, a sexually active man living in a nation such as South Africa, in which more than 22 percent of adults are HIV-positive, has only one chance of being infected in every 1,000 unprotected heterosexual contacts (Singhal and Rogers, 2003). Given this probability, is it likely that this individual will adopt safer sex practices, such as using condoms?

The persuasion-adoption discrepancy for preventive innovations (that is, the KAP-gap) can sometimes be closed by a *cue-to-action* an event occurring at a time that crystallizes a favorable attitude into overt behavioral change. Some cues-to-action may occur naturally. For instance, many women begin to use a contraceptive after they experience a pregnancy scare or have an abortion (Rogers, 1973). In other cases, a cue-to-action may be created by a change agency. For instance, some national family-planning programs pay incentives to create a cue-to action for potential adopters. Perhaps the positive experience of a peer with the innovation serves as a cue-to-action for an individual. Many Americans are triggered to stop smoking cigarettes after a brother or sister dies from lung cancer. So cues-to-action can take a variety of forms.

The Decision Stage

The *decision* stage in the innovation-decision process takes place when an individual (or other decision-making unit) engages in activities that lead to a choice to adopt or reject an innovation (see Figure 5–1). *Adoption* is a decision to make full use of an innovation as the best course of action available. *Rejection* is a decision not to adopt an innovation.

One way to cope with the inherent uncertainty about an innovation's consequences is to try out the new idea on a partial basis. Most individuals do not adopt an innovation without first trying it on a probationary basis to determine its usefulness in their own situation. This small-scale trial is often an important part of the decision to adopt. Some innovations cannot be divided for trial and so they must be adopted or rejected in toto. Innovations that can be divided for trial are generally adopted more rapidly (see Chapter 6). Most individuals who try an innovation then move to an adoption decision, if the innovation proves to have at least a certain degree of relative advantage. Methods to facilitate the trial of innovations, such as the distribution to clients of free samples of a new idea, usually will speed up the rate of adoption. For example, seed corn salesmen in Iowa in the 1930s gave a small bag of the new seed to Iowa farmers entering the decision stage. The free seed was enough to plant about an acre of corn, a large enough trial to convince the farmer to adopt the new idea on all of his corn acreage in the next few years.

The trial of a new idea by a peer can substitute, at least in part, for the individual's trial of an innovation, at least for some individuals and for some innovations. This "trial by others" provides a vicarious trial for an individual. Change agents often seek to speed up the innovation-decision process for individuals by sponsoring demonstrations of a new idea in a social system. A demonstration can be quite effective in speeding up the diffusion process, especially if the demonstrator is an opinion leader (see Chapter 9).

The innovation-decision process can just as logically lead to a rejection decision as to adoption. In fact, each stage in the innovation-decision process is a potential rejection point. For instance, it is possible to reject an innovation at the knowledge stage by simply forgetting about it after gaining the initial awareness-knowledge. Rejection can occur even after a prior decision to adopt. *Discontinuance* is defined as a decision to reject an innovation after having previously adopted. Two different types of rejection are:

1. *Active rejection,* which consists of considering adoption of the innovation (including its trial) but then deciding not to adopt it.
2. *Passive rejection* (also called nonadoption), which consists of never really considering the use of the innovation.

These two types of rejection represent quite different types of behavior. Unfortunately, they have seldom been distinguished in past diffusion research. Perhaps owing to the pro-innovation bias that pervades much diffusion inquiry (see Chapter 3), investigation of rejection behavior has not received much scholarly attention.

Furthermore, there is usually an implicit assumption in diffusion studies of a linear sequence of the first three stages in the innovation-decision process: knowledge, persuasion, and decision. In some cases, the actual sequence of stages might be knowledge, decision, persuasion. For example, in a Korean village that the present author once studied, a meeting of married women was called, and, after a presentation by a government change agent about the intrauterine device (IUD), a show of hands indicated that eighteen women wanted to adopt (Rogers and Kincaid, 1981). They all promptly marched off to a nearby clinic to have IUDs inserted. In this case, a presumably optional innovation-decision became almost a collective innovation-decision as a result of group pressure. A similar group-oriented strategy for family planning was called the "group planning of births" in the People's Republic of China (Rogers and Chen, 1980). A community would decide who should have babies each year, and then married people were influenced to follow these birth plans. A somewhat similar strategy of utilizing group influence to secure the adoption of family-planning methods in Indonesian villages suggests that while the rate of adoption increases, the quality of such adoption decisions is dubious and demands a high degree of change agent contact (Tuladhar et al., 1998).

Such strong group pressure for adoption of an innovation is abhorrent to the value placed on individual freedom in individualistic cultures but might be more acceptable in collectivistic cultures such as Korea, China, and Indonesia. *Individualistic culture* are those in which the individual's goal takes precedence over the collectivity's goals. *Collectivistic cultures* are those in which the collectivity's goals take precedence over those of the individual (Rogers and Steinfatt, 1999).

So the knowledge-persuasion-decision sequence proposed in our model of the innovation-decision process may be somewhat culture-bound. In some sociocultural settings, the knowledge-decision-persuasion sequence may occur frequently, at least for certain innovations.

The Implementation Stage

Implementation occurs when an individual (or other decision-making unit) puts an innovation to use. Until the implementation stage, the innovation-decision process has been a strictly mental exercise of thinking and deciding. But implementation involves overt behavior change as the new idea is actually put into practice. It is one thing for an individual to decide to adopt a new idea, quite a different thing to put the innovation to use, as problems in exactly how to use the innovation crop up at the implementation stage. Implementation usually follows the decision stage rather directly, unless it is held up by some logistical problem, such as temporary unavailability of the innovation. For example, in 2001, purchase of a hybrid automobile in the United States by a consumer entailed a waiting period of up to six months, due to an inadequate supply of the innovative autos.

A certain degree of uncertainty about the expected consequences of the innovation still exists for the typical individual at the implementation stage, even though the decision to adopt has been made previously. An individual particularly wants to know the answers to such questions as "Where can I obtain the innovation?" "How do I use it?" and "What operational problems am I likely to encounter, and how can I solve them?" So active information seeking usually takes place at the implementation stage in order to answer these questions. Here the role of change agents is mainly to provide technical assistance to the client as he or she begins to use the innovation.

Problems of implementation are usually more serious when the adopter is an organization rather than an individual. In an organizational setting, a number of individuals are usually involved in the innovation-decision process, and the implementers are often a different set of people from the decision makers. Also, the organizational structure that gives stability and continuity to an organization may resist the implementation of an innovation (see Chapter 10).

The implementation stage may continue for a lengthy period of time, depending on the nature of the innovation. Eventually a point is reached at which the new idea becomes institutionalized as a regularized part of an adopter's ongoing operations. The innovation loses its distinctive quality as the separate identity of the new idea disappears. This point is considered the end of the implementation stage. It may also represent the termination of the innovation-decision process, at least for many individuals. But for others, a fifth stage of confirmation may occur (as will be explained below). First, we discuss the concept of re-invention, which is often important in the implementation stage.

Re-Invention

In the early years of diffusion study, adoption of an innovation meant the exact copying or imitation of how the innovation had been used previously by earlier adopters. Sometimes the adoption of an innovation does indeed represent identical behavior; for example, the California Fair Trade Law of 1931, the first law of its kind, was adopted by ten other states, complete with three major typographical errors that had appeared in the California bill (Walker, 1971). In many other cases, however, an innovation is not invariant as it diffuses. The new idea changes and evolves during the diffusion process as it moves from adopter to adopter.

Diffusion scholars now recognize the concept of *re-invention*, defined as the degree to which an innovation is changed or modified by a user in the process of its adoption and implementation. Until about the 1970s, re-invention was not thought to occur or was considered a very infrequent behavior. When a respondent in a diffusion survey told about his or her re-invention of a new idea, it was considered a very unusual kind of behavior and was treated as "noise" in diffusion research. Adopters were thus considered to be rather passive acceptors of an innovation, rather than active modifiers of a new idea. Once diffusion scholars made the mental breakthrough of recognizing that re-invention could happen, they began to find that quite a lot of it occurred. Re-invention could not really be investigated until diffusion researchers began to gather data about implementation, for most re-invention occurs at the implementation stage of the innovation-decision process. In the past decade, a large number of studies of re-invention have been completed. These investigations have found that a great deal of re-invention occurs for many innovations. Previous diffusion research, by measuring adoption as a stated intention to adopt (at the decision stage), may have erred by measuring innovation as the individual expected it would happen, rather than how it actually occurred. The fact that re-invention may happen is a strong argument for measuring adoption at the implementation stage, as change that has really happened.

Most scholars in the past made a distinction between invention and innovation. *Invention* is the process by which a new idea is discovered or created, while the adoption of an innovation is a decision to make full use of an innovation as the best course of action available. Thus the adoption of an innovation is the process of using an existing idea. This difference between invention and innovation, however, is not so clear cut when we acknowledge that an innovation is not necessarily a fixed entity as it diffuses within a social system. For this reason, "re-invention" is an appropriate word to describe the degree to which an innovation is changed or modified by the user in the process of its adoption and implementation, although other terms for re-invention are also used, such as its opposite, "fidelity" (Emshoff and Blakely, 1987; Lewis and Seibold, 1996; Backer, 2000; Kelly et al., 2000; Emshoff et al., 2002).

How Much Re-Invention Occurs?

Charters and Pellegrin (1972) were the first scholars to recognize the occurrence of re-invention (although they did not use the term per se). These researchers traced the adoption and implementation of the educational innovation of "differentiated staffing" in four schools over a one-year period. They concluded that "differentiated staffing was little more than a word for most [teachers and administrators], lacking concrete parameters with respect to the role performance of participants. . . . The word could (and did) mean widely differing things to the staff, and nothing to some. . . . The innovation was to be invented on the inside, not implemented from the outside." These scholars noted the degree to which the innovation was shaped differently in each of the four organizations they studied. One main reason why these diffusion scholars were able to detect re-invention, while most previous scholars had ignored it, was that they investigated the implementation stage.

Re-invention can be encouraged if inventions are designed with the possibility of re-invention in mind. For instance, previous research on innovation in organizations assumed that a new technological idea enters a system from external sources and is then adopted (with relatively little adaptation of the innovation) and implemented as part of the organization's ongoing operations. Thus it was assumed that adoption of an innovation by individual A or organization A will look much like adoption of this same innovation by individual B or by organization B. Recent investigations show that this assumption should be seriously questioned.

1. A national survey of schools adopting educational innovations promoted by the National Diffusion Network, a decentralized diffusion system, found that 56 percent of the adopters implemented only selected aspects of an innovation. Much such re-invention was relatively minor, but in 20 percent of the adoptions important changes were made in the innovations (Emrick et al., 1977).

2. An investigation of 111 innovations in scientific instruments by von Hippel (1976) found that in about 80 percent of the cases, the innovation process was dominated by the lead user (that is, an especially early customer). The user typically built a prototype model of the new product and then turned it over to a manufacturer. So the "adopters" played a very important role in designing and redesigning these industrial innovations.

3. Of the 104 adoptions of innovations by mental health agencies that were studied in California, re-invention occurred somewhat more often (in 55 cases) that did unchanged adoption (in 49 cases) (Larsen and Agarwala-Rogers, 1977).

4. A study of the adoption by fifty-three local government agencies of a computer-based planning tool called GBF/DIME, which was promoted to them by a federal agency, found that about half of the "adoptions" represented at least some degree of re-invention (Eveland et al., 1977).

5. Research on the rapid diffusion of a school-based drug abuse prevention program called DARE (Drug Abuse Resistance Education) disclosed a high degree of re-invention by local schools. DARE began in 1983 in Los Angeles, and ten years later, more than 5 million fifth- and sixth-graders were taught the nineteen-lesson DARE curriculum in their classroom by a uniformed policeman. This speedy rate of adoption occurred because the drug problem was high on the public agenda in the late 1980s (Dearing and Rogers, 1996), and also because a good deal of re-invention took place (Rogers, 1993a). For instance, one of the nineteen DARE lessons encouraged children not to join gangs. Many schools, perceiving that they did not have a gang problem,

did not teach the DARE material on that topic. However, the basic idea of DARE (having a uniformed policeman teach the material) was used by all adopters. Evaluations of the DARE program in U.S. schools showed little lasting effects in decreasing drug use by students (Ennett et al., 1994; Lyman et al., 1999), and many U.S. schools have discontinued the program in recent years. Some schools rather completely re-invented DARE by having a uniformed school policeman teach certain of the DARE anti-drug lessons, while discarding all other elements of the program.

Generalization 5-8 states: *Re-invention occurs at the implementation stage for many innovations and for many adopters.* Once the concept of re-invention was recognized, a great deal of re-invention was found in most diffusion programs. Diffusion scholars began to give much more attention to re-invention, and a growing research literature on this topic has accumulated in the past decade.

Generalization 5-9: *A higher degree of re-invention leads to a faster rate of adoption of an innovation.* The logic behind this generalization is that innovations that are more flexible and that can be more easily re-invented can be fit to a wider range of adopters' conditions. Thus the rate of adoption for these innovations is more rapid (Backer, 2000).

Generalization 5-10: *A higher degree of re-invention leads to a higher degree of sustainability of an innovation.* The concept of *sustainability* is defined as the degree to which an innovation continues to be used over time after a diffusion program ends. Most diffusion studies ended with the decision to adopt or with implementation of the new idea. However, many innovations are important only if they continue to be used. For example, adopting condom use has little impact in preventing HIV infection unless condoms continue to be utilized by an individual. So for many innovations, sustainability is a kind of bottom line.

Goodman and Steckler (1989) investigated the degree of sustainability (which they called "institutionalization") of ten new health programs in Virginia. A key factor was the degree to which the innovation fit with the objectives and other characteristics of a local health program (this is compatibility). A similar study of the sustainability of eight health innovations in New Mexico arrived at a similar conclusion: Re-invention led to greater sustainability (Rogers et al., in press). Other studies also support Generalization 5-10.

Another study of re-invention, and how it can lead to a more rapid rate of adoption and to greater sustainability, is reported by Ray-

Couquand and colleagues (1997), who investigated the spread of practice guidelines for breast and colon cancer among eighty medical doctors in a French cancer center. In a two-year period, an increase from 19 percent to 54 percent occurred in the breast cancer treatment recommended by the guidelines, accompanied by an increase from 50 percent to 70 percent in adhering to the colon cancer guidelines. These behavior changes are rather phenomenal, given that most other studies of the effects of practice guidelines have found that they have few results (Larsen and Rogers, 1984; Shaneyfette, Mayer, and Rothway, 1999; Einsiedel and Eastlick, 2000; Grilli et al., 2000). One explanation is that considerable re-invention of the guidelines occurred by the health providers. Also, the medical doctors in the cancer center participated in writing the guidelines, so presumably the guidelines fit their situation.

Re-Invention Is Not Necessarily Bad

Whether re-invention is considered good or bad depends on one's point of view. Re-invention is generally not regarded favorably by research and development agencies, which may consider re-invention to be a distortion of their research findings. Some designers of an innovation structure a new idea so that it is particularly difficult to re-invent. They feel that "re-invention proofing" is a means of maintaining quality control of their innovation. Diffusion agencies may also be unfavorable toward re-invention, feeling that they know best as to the form of the innovation that users should adopt. Change agents find it difficult to measure their performance if a specific innovation changes over time and across different adopters. Their usual measure, the rate of adoption of an innovation, can become an ambiguous index when a high degree of re-invention occurs. In extreme cases of re-invention, the original innovation might even lose its identity.

One method of measuring the degree of re-invention is to identify the number of elements in each implementation of an innovation that are similar to, or different from, the "main-line" or "core" version of the innovation, such as that promoted by the change agency (Eveland et al., 1977). Most innovations can be broken down into their constituent elements, which can then be used to measure the degree of re-invention from a core configuration. The *core elements* of an innovation consist of the features that are responsible for its effectiveness (Kelly et al., 2000).

For example, a study of the diffusion of clean indoor air ordinances found that while all such city regulations prevented smoking cigarettes in public places, each city's no-smoking ordinance differed in important ways. Some city ordinances were very comprehensive in that they precluded smoking in government buildings, restaurants, bars, bowling alleys, and bingo parlors. Other clean indoor air ordinances prevented smoking only in one or more of these sites (these ordinances were easier to get adopted by city councils). Still other no-smoking ordinances prevented smoking inside public places *and* within fifty feet of the door of any such buildings. While the core element of preventing second-hand smoke was included in all of these ordinances, the details of where smoking was prohibited varied widely (Rogers, Peterson, and McOwiti, 2002). Generally, later-adopting cities in the southwestern United States adopted more comprehensive no-smoking ordinances.

Adopters generally think that re-invention is a very desirable quality. They tend to emphasize or even overemphasize the amount of re-invention that they have accomplished (Rice and Rogers, 1980). The choices available to a potential adopter are not just adoption or rejection. Modification of the innovation or selective rejection of some components of the innovation may also be options (as in the case of DARE and the no-smoking ordinances). At least some implementation problems are likely to be created by individuals or organizations, so adopters of an innovation almost always attempt to make changes in the original innovation to fit their situation better.

Re-invention can be beneficial to adopters of an innovation. Flexibility in the process of adopting an innovation may reduce mistakes and encourage customization of the innovation to fit it more appropriately to local and/or changing conditions. As a result of re-invention, an innovation may be more appropriate in matching an adopter's preexisting problems and more responsive to new problems that arise during the innovation-decision process. A national survey of innovation in public schools found that when an educational innovation was re-invented by a school, its adoption was more likely to be continued and less likely to be discontinued (Berman and Pauly, 1975). Discontinuance happened less often because the re-invented innovations better fit a school's circumstances, leading to sustainability. This investigation disclosed that a rather high degree of re-invention occurred: the innovations and the schools engaged in a kind of mutually influencing interaction as the new idea and the school adapted to each other (Berman and McLaughlin, 1974, 1975, 1978; Berman et al., 1975, 1977). Usually, the school changed very little and the innovations substantially.

Why Does Re-Invention Occur?

Some reasons for re-invention lie in the innovation itself, while others involve the individual or organization adopting the new idea.

1. Innovations that are relatively more complex and difficult to understand are more likely to be re-invented (Larsen and Agarwala-Rogers, 1977). Re-invention in such cases may be a simplification of the innovation, or even represent a misunderstanding of it.
2. Re-invention can occur owing to an adopter's lack of detailed knowledge about the innovation, such as when there is relatively little direct contact between the adopter and change agents or previous adopters (Eveland et al., 1977; Larsen and Agarwala-Rogers, 1977a; Kelly et al., 2000). For example, re-invention of a geographically based computer system occurred more frequently when change agents created only awareness-knowledge of the innovation than when consultation was provided to the adopting organization at the implementation stage. Re-invention sometimes happens due to ignorance and inadequate learning.
3. An innovation that is a general concept or a tool with many possible applications (such as a computer or the Internet) is more likely to be re-invented. The elements making up an innovation may be tightly or loosely bundled or packaged. A tightly bundled innovation is a collection of highly interdependent components. It is difficult to adopt one element without adopting the other elements. A loosely bundled innovation consists of elements that are not highly interrelated; such an innovation can be flexibly suited by adopters to their conditions. So the designer or manufacturer of an innovation can affect the degree of re-invention by making the innovation easy or difficult to re-invent.
4. When an innovation is implemented in order to solve a wide range of users' problems, re-invention is more likely to occur. A basic reason for re-invention is that each individual or organization matches the innovation with a different problem than does another. The problem that originally motivates an individual to search for an innovation determines in part how the innovation will be used. The degree of re-invention of an innovation is greater when greater heterogeneity exists in the individuals and the organizational problems with which the innovation is matched.
5. Local pride of ownership of an innovation may also be a cause of

re-invention. Here the innovation is modified in certain rather cosmetic or minor ways so that it appears to be a local product. In some cases of such "pseudo-re-invention," the innovation may just be given a new name, without any fundamental changes being made in the innovation itself. Such localization may be motivated by a desire for status or recognition on the part of the adopter, or by a desire to make the innovation more acceptable to the local system. Often, when they are asked, "Locals say that the innovation is local," as Havelock (1974) found in a survey of 353 U.S. school superintendents. Perhaps, as one observer suggested, innovations may be somewhat like a toothbrush in that people do not like to borrow them from one another. At least they want to put their own "bells and whistles" on the basic innovation so that it looks different from others'.

6. Re-invention may occur because a change agency influences its clients to modify or adapt an innovation. While most change agencies generally oppose re-invention, decentralized diffusion systems may encourage their clients to re-invent new ideas (see Chapter 9). For example, the diffusion of DARE was not managed or orchestrated by a federal agency, so each school was left to do its own thing with the curriculum.

7. Re-invention occurs when an innovation must be adapted to the structure of the organization that is adopting it (Westphal, Gulati, and Shortell, 1997; Majchrzak et al., 2000).

8. Re-invention may be more frequent later in the diffusion process for an innovation, as later adopters profit from the experiences gained by earlier adopters (Hays, 1996a). For instance, a state law may become more comprehensive as it diffuses to other states, with loopholes gradually being closed (Hays, 1996b).

Recognition of the existence of re-invention brings into focus a different view of adoption behavior than that originally held by diffusion scholars. Instead of simply accepting or rejecting an innovation, potential adopters are on many occasions active participants in the adoption and diffusion process, struggling to give meaning to the new idea as the innovation is applied to their local context. This conception of adoption behavior, involving re-invention, is in line with what certain respondents in diffusion research have been trying to tell researchers for many years.

The general picture that emerges from studies of re-invention is that an innovation is not a fixed entity. Instead, people who use an innovation shape it by giving it meaning as they learn by using the new idea. "Artifacts are not only constructed by their designers, they are also reconstructed by their users" (Boczhowski, 1999). For example, the telephone was originally conceived as a business tool, but early telephone callers, especially females, embedded sociability in the telephone calling process (Fischer, 1992). Similarly, the French Minitel, a videotext system, was designed as a one-to-many messaging system but was soon transformed into a many-to-many messaging system. In Chapter 8, we mention the creation of SMS (short message service) by cell phone users, probably Japanese teenagers. So an innovation, or at least many innovations, are coconstructed by users into dynamic, flexible ideas.

Re-Invention of Horse Culture by the Plains Indians

When European colonists encountered the Plains Indians in the vast grasslands west of the Mississippi River, the horse was the central element of Indian culture. The Indians killed buffalo from horseback, fought other tribes while mounted on their ponies, and utilized their horses to move their wigwams from place to place. But the horse was not indigenous to the Plains Indians. Rather, it had been introduced to these Indian tribes by Spanish explorers prior to 1650. Within a decade or two, French fur traders found that men, women, and children in the Plains Indian tribes were riding horses. The Indians had copied saddles, stirrups, the crupper, and the lariat from the Spanish explorers, who in turn had borrowed these innovations from the Moors (Arabic people from North Africa, who had previously occupied Spain for seven hundred years). In short, the Plains Indians "copied the whole [horse] culture from a to z" (Wissler, 1923, p. 119). Extensive contact occurred with the Spanish, and the horse culture spread quickly throughout the American grasslands, from Iowa to Idaho and from Montana to Texas.

But one aspect of horse culture was re-invented: the travois. Previous to the coming of the horse, the Plains Indians used dogs as beasts of burden. Tents and baggage were transported on the travois, a kind of triangular drag frame. So when the Plains Indians first saw the horse, they called it a dog. Many Indian tribes in the United States still speak of the horse by a name meaning "dog." They enlarged the travois and harnessed the horse to it. Only later did they begin to ride on horseback.

The Confirmation Stage

Empirical evidence supplied by several researchers indicates that a decision to adopt or reject a new idea is often not the terminal stage in the innovation-decision process. For example, Mason (1962) found that the Oregon farmers he studied sought information *after* they had decided to adopt, as well as before. At the *confirmation* stage the individual (or other decision-making unit) seeks reinforcement for the innovation-decision already made, and may reverse this decision if exposed to conflicting messages about the innovation.

At the confirmation stage, the individual seeks to avoid a state of dissonance or to reduce it if it occurs.

Dissonance

Human behavior change is often motivated in part by a state of internal disequilibrium or dissonance, an uncomfortable state of mind that an individual seeks to reduce or eliminate. A dissonant individual is motivated to reduce this condition by changing his or her knowledge, attitudes, or actions (Festinger, 1957). In the case of innovative behavior, this dissonance reduction may occur:

1. When the individual becomes aware of a need and seeks information about an innovation to meet this need. Here, a receiver's knowledge of a need for innovation can motivate the individual's information-seeking activity about the innovation. This behavior occurs at the knowledge stage in the innovation-decision process.
2. When the individual knows about a new idea and has a favorable attitude toward it but has not adopted (this is the KAP-gap). Then the individual is motivated to adopt the innovation by dissonance between what he or she believes versus what he or she is actually doing. This behavior occurs at the decision and implementation stages in the innovation-decision process.
3. After the innovation-decision to implement an innovation, when the individual secures further information that persuades him or her that he or she should *not* have adopted. This type of dissonance may be reduced by discontinuing the innovation. If he or she originally decided to reject the innovation, the individual may become exposed to pro-innovation messages, causing a state of dissonance that can be reduced by adoption of the new idea. Dis-

continuance or later adoption occur during the confirmation function in the innovation-decision process (see Figure 5–1).

These three types of dissonance reduction consist of changing behavior so that attitudes and actions are more closely in line. But it is often difficult for the individual to change a prior decision to adopt or reject. Activities may have been set into motion that stabilize the original decision. Perhaps a considerable cash outlay was involved in adopting the innovation. Therefore, individuals frequently try to avoid becoming dissonant by seeking only information that they expect will support or confirm a decision already made (this behavior is an example of selective exposure). During the confirmation stage, the individual wants supportive messages that will prevent dissonance from occurring. Nevertheless, some information reaches the individual that leads to questioning the adoption versus rejection decision previously made during the innovation-decision process.

Discontinuance

Discontinuance is a decision to reject an innovation after having previously adopted it. A rather surprising high rate of discontinuance has been found for certain innovations. Leuthold (1967) concluded from his study of a statewide sample of Wisconsin farmers that the rate of discontinuance was just as important as the rate of adoption in determining the level of adoption of an innovation at any particular time. In any given year, there were about as many discontinuers of an innovation as there were first-time adopters.

Two types of discontinuance are: (1) replacement and (2) disenchantment. A *replacement discontinuance* is a decision to reject an idea in order to adopt a better idea that supersedes it. Constant waves of innovations may occur in which each new idea replaces an existing practice that was an innovation in its day. For example, the adoption of tetracycline led to the discontinuance of two other antibiotic drugs (Coleman et al., 1966). Hand calculators replaced slide rules. CDs (compact disks) replaced vinyl records. E-mail has replaced much postal mail. Many replacement discontinuances occur in everyday life.

A *disenchantment discontinuance* is a decision to reject an idea as a result of dissatisfaction with its performance. Such dissatisfaction may come about because the innovation is inappropriate for the individual and does not result in a perceived relative advantage over alternatives. Perhaps a government agency has decreed that the innovation is not safe and/or that it has side effects that are dangerous to health. Discontinuance may result from the misuse of an innovation that might have functioned advantageously for the individual. This later type of disenchantment seems to be more common among later adopters than among earlier adopters, who have more formal education and perhaps more understanding of the scientific method, so they know how to generalize more carefully the results of an innovation's trial to its full-scale use. Later adopters also have fewer resources, which may either prevent adoption or cause discontinuance because the innovations do not fit their limited financial position. We thus suggest Generalization 5-11: *Later adopters are more likely to discontinue innovations than are earlier adopters.*

Researchers previously assumed that later adopters are relatively less innovative because they did not adopt or were slower to adopt. But the evidence about discontinuances suggests that many laggards adopt but then discontinue, usually owing to disenchantment. For instance, Bishop and Coughenor (1964) reported that the percentage of discontinuance for Ohio farmers ranged from 14 percent for innovators and early adopters, to 27 percent for early majority, to 34 percent for late majority, to 40 percent for laggards. Leuthold (1965) reported comparable figures of 18 percent, 24 percent, 26 percent, and 37 percent, respectively, for Canadian farmers.

High discontinuers are characterized by less formal education, lower socioeconomic status, and less change agent contact, which are the opposites of the characteristics of innovators (see Chapter 7). Discontinuers share the same characteristics as laggards, who indeed have a higher rate of discontinuance.

The discontinuance of an innovation is one indication that the new idea may not have been fully routinized into the ongoing operations of the adopter at the implementation stage of the innovation-decision process. Such sustainability is less likely (and discontinuance more frequent) when the innovation is less compatible with the individual's beliefs and past experiences. Perhaps (1) there are innovation-to-innovation differences in rates of discontinuance, just as there are such differences in rates of adoption and (2) the perceived attributes of innovations (for example, relative advantage and compatibility) are negatively related to the rate of discontinuance. For instance, we would expect an innovation with low relative advantage to have a slow rate of adoption and a fast rate of discontinuance. Innovations that have a high rate of adoption should have a low rate of discontinuance.

Organizations, as well as individuals, can discontinue innovations. One illustration is provided by Greve's (1995) study of how U.S. radio stations discontinued their "easy listening" format. At one time, around 1984, this radio format was very popular, with almost every city having at least one station that broadcast this type of music. But over the following decade, this format's cohort of listeners aged and hence were of less interest to advertisers. By 1993, 90 percent of the radio stations with an easy listening format had discontinued this style of music and switched to a different format. Abandonment of easy listening was influenced by corporate contacts with other radio stations. So "jumping ship" from the earlier format was itself a diffusion process.

As an eminent diffusion scholar, Ronald S. Burt, stated: "As much as change is about adapting to the new, it is about detaching from the old." Adoption of a new idea almost always means discontinuing a previous idea.

The Discontinuance of Smoking

An illustration that adopting an innovation means discontinuing a previously adopted idea is provided by smoking-cessation behavior. A lifestyle revolution has occurred in the United States in the past several decades as half of all individuals who ever smoked regularly (and who are still alive) have stopped smoking. Smoking cigarettes is an addictive behavior, one that is extremely difficult to change. So smoking is not fully under the control of the individual once he or she begins smoking.

How did the U.S. smoking cessation revolution take place? Such widespread discontinuance did not happen mainly as the result of economic factors. A California referendum in 1989 added a 25-cent-per-pack tax that is used to provide cigarette cessation advertising and training programs for individuals who want to stop smoking. The U.S. tobacco industry settlement in 2000 meant that the price per pack jumped. But 25 percent of the U.S. population continued smoking.

The thrust for cigarette cessation in America dates from the 1964 Surgeon General's report that smoking was dangerous to health. This report was based on scientific studies of the effects of smoking cigarettes. Warnings were placed on cigarette packs and on cigarette advertising. In 1971, tobacco companies stopped their radio and television advertising. City governments and private companies began to restrict places in which it was acceptable to smoke. For example, until the mid-1960s, airline flight attendants distributed free packets of cigarettes with the after-meal coffee. In the late 1980s, U.S. airlines banned smoking from all domestic flights. Scientific evidence accumulated about the health effects of "second-hand smoke." Many restaurants now provide no-smoking eating areas, and most workplaces have banned smoking. Gradually, the perception of smoking changed from that of being a "cool" act to being a very negative behavior ("Only losers smoke").

In 1995, Las Cruces, a small university town in southern New Mexico, adopted a city ordinance that banned smoking in all public places. At that time, Las Cruces was one of the first cities in the southwestern United States with such a clean indoor air ordinance. Soon this no-smoking act spread from Las Cruces to other New Mexico town and cities (Santa Fe, Mesilla, Carlsbad, Deming, and Silver City), to El Paso and Lubbock, Texas, and even to Anchorage, Alaska. So a city-to-city diffusion process for the city no-smoking ordinance occurred from 1995 to 2002. Increasingly, the issue of no-smoking ordinances was framed as a *health* issue based on biomedical research showing the hazards of second-hand smoke, and not as an *economic* issue (that restaurants and bars would lose business if they did not allow a smoking area). However some individuals framed the no-smoking issue as a matter of *individual rights*. As an irate restaurant owner in New Mexico said to the author in 2002, "What right does the government have to come in here, a property that I own, and tell me what I and my customers can do?" In places where enough people framed no-smoking as an individual rights issue, the decision to adopt a city no-smoking ordinance failed. An example is Alamagordo, New Mexico, whose population includes many conservative thinkers who highly value individual rights, and where a Las Cruces–type ordinance was rejected in 2002.

Many years were necessary to change American smoking norms. The widespread discontinuance of cigarette smoking happened in part due to price increases and, more so, to changes in the media's depiction of smoking, and to city restrictions on where individuals can smoke.

Forced Discontinuance and the Rise of Organic Farming

In my 1954 Ph.D. dissertation research, I gathered data from 148 farmers in an Iowa farm community about their adoption of such agricultural innovations as 2,4-D weed spray, antibiotic swine feeding supplements, and chemical fertilizers. These chemical innovations were recommended to farmers by agricultural scientists at Iowa State University and by the Iowa Agricultural Extension Service. I accepted the recommendations of these agricultural experts about the chemical innovations as valid. So did most of the Iowa farmers that I interviewed in my diffusion study. One farmer, however, rejected all of these agricultural chemicals because, he claimed, they killed the earthworms and songbirds in his fields. At the time, I personally regarded his attitude as irrational. He was classified as a laggard on my innovativeness scale (because he had not adopted any of the dozen agricultural innovations recommended by agricultural experts).

But the rise of the environmental movement in the United States in the 1960s and research on the long-term effects of agricultural chemicals began to make me wonder. In 1972, the U.S. Environmental Protection Agency banned the use of DDT as an insecticide because of its threats to human health. Then DES (diethylstilbestrol) was banned in cattle feed, as were antibiotic swine feed supplements and 2,4-D weed spray. Biomagnification of the concentration of such chemicals in the food chain was found to be dangerous to human health.

More and more U.S. consumers were willing to pay a premium price for organically grown products at health food stores. "Organic" farmers achieve somewhat lower crop yields than "chemical farmers," but their costs of production were lower and they secured a higher price for their organic products from natural food stores. In 1980, the U.S. Department of Agriculture reversed its policy of opposing organic farming and gardening, and began to advise U.S. farmers and gardeners to consider alternative production methods using fewer chemicals. The USDA also began a research program to develop appropriate seed varieties for organic farming and gardening. Surveys of organic farmers indicated that most were not "hippies," nor were they less educated traditional farmers. Most organic farmers are commercial, progressive farmers with above-average education, larger farms, and so on. These are the characteristics of innovators.

The USDA realized that chemical pesticides were being overused by many farmers and launched a program called "integrated pest management" (IPM). A key factor in diffusing the IPM program was the fact that many types of insects developed resistance to existing pesticides. Integrated pest management consists of carefully scouting a farmer's fields, usually by trained scouts, who advise the farmer when a pest problem has increased above an economic threshold so that spraying with a chemical pesticide is justified. Farmers who adopt IPM typically report important savings from decreased use of pesticides, with some farmers saving thousands of dollars.

Today, looking back five decades to my Iowa diffusion study, the organic farmer I interviewed in the Collins study has had the last laugh over agricultural experts. My 1954 research classified him as a laggard. By present-day standards he was a superinnovator of the then-radical idea of organic farming.

Are There Stages in the Innovation-Decision Process?

What empirical evidence is available that the stages posited in our model of the innovation-decision process (see Figure 5–1) exist in reality? A definitive answer is impossible to provide, as it is difficult for a researcher to probe the intrapersonal mental processes of individual respondents. Stages may be useful as a means of simplifying a complex reality, so as to provide a basis for understanding human behavior change and for introducing an innovation. Perhaps we should think of stages as a social construction, a mental framework that we have created and generally agreed to. But it is quite a different matter to obtain empirical evidence that a specified series of stages exists. Individuals passing through the stages may or may not recognize when one stage ends and another stage begins. Certainly the degree and nature of involvement with an innovation change as an individual (or an organization) passes through the stages in the innovation-decision process. But we should not expect sharp distinctions between each stage.

There is a long intellectual tradition of the basic notion of stages or steps in the process of human behavior change. Wilhelm Wundt, a pioneering German psychologist at the University of Leipzig, conceptualized the gesture as a basic human act. John Dewey at the University of Chicago then drew on Wundt's conceptualization in his famous article "The Reflex Arc Concept in Psychology" (Dewey, 1896). Individualistic stimulus-response (S-R) theorizing predominated at this time, prior to Dewey's notion of stages in human action. S-R explanations had argued that an external stimulus was perceived by an individual; it then followed a nerve path to the proper muscles, whose action was the response, which ended the process. S-R might indeed describe certain behaviors, such as a knee-jerk reflex, but it was an incomplete model of human action.

Dewey, George Herbert Mead, and their colleagues at the Chicago School argued that the reflex arc and stimulus-response were oversimplifications, in that an individual's interpretation of the stimulus was also involved in the response (Rogers, 1994). Stimulus-response thus became a stimulus-interpretation-response model, with meanings derived from interaction with others. The notion of stages in a decision process gradually became apparent. Further, Dewey argued that the reflex arc concept was fallacious because it conceptualized a stimulus as external and a response as internal to the individual. But what an individual defined as a stimulus depends on the person's previous experience. For instance, once an individual has learned of the existence of an innovation, he/she encounters this new idea with surprising frequency.

The thinking of John Dewey and George Herbert Mead had a direct bearing on the rural sociologists who first posited the idea of stages in the innovation-decision process (Beal, Rogers, and Bohlen, 1957).

Process Versus Variance Research

Research designed to answer the question of whether stages exist in the innovation-decision process needs to be quite different from the study of various independent variables associated with dependent variables like innovativeness. *Process research* is defined as a type of data gathering and analysis that seeks to determine the sequence of a set of events over time (Mohr, 1978, 1982). Usually such process research is conducted using qualitative research methods, which seek to gain insight and understanding of human behavior. *Variance research* is a type of data gathering and analysis that consists of determining the covariances (or correlations) among a set of variables, but not their time order. Such variance research usually is conducted using quantitative research methods, which measure variables by assigning numerical values to behaviors.

Most diffusion research (and most social science research) is variance-type investigation. It consists of highly structured quantitative gathering and analysis of cross-sectional data, such as from one-shot surveys of the diffusion and adoption of an innovation. Because behavior is represented at only one point in time, the process dimension of the data cannot be measured (except by asking individuals to recall when they adopted an innovation). Variance research is appropriate for investigating variables related to innovativeness, for example. But it cannot probe backward in time to understand what happened first, next, and so on, and how each of these events influenced the next event in an individual's innovation-decision process.

In order to explore the nature of a process, one needs a dynamic perspective to explain the causes and sequences of a series of events over time. Data-gathering methods for process research are less structured and might entail using in-depth personal interviews. The data are typically more qualitative in nature than in variance research. Seldom are statistical methods used to analyze the data in process research. Diffusion scholars have frequently failed to recognize the important distinction between variance and process research in the past (Mohr, 1978). Research on a topic such as the innovation-decision process should be quite different from the variance research that has predominated in the diffusion field. The scarcity of process research on the innovation-decision process is a basic reason why we lack definitive understanding of the degree to which stages exist. Nevertheless, there is tentative evidence from several studies supporting the concept of stages in the innovation-decision process.

Evidence of Stages

Empirical evidence of the validity of stages in the innovation-decision process comes from an Iowa study (Beal and Rogers, 1960) which shows that most respondents recognized that they went through a series of stages as they moved from awareness-knowledge to a decision to adopt. Specifically, they realized that they had received information about an innovation from different channels and sources at different stages in the process. It is possible for an individual to use the same sources or channels at each stage, but the reported different sources or channels by stage indicate differentiation of the stages. None of Beal and Rogers's 148 respondents reported adopting immediately after becoming aware of a new weed spray. And 63 percent of the adopters of a new livestock feed reported a different year at which they acquired knowledge from the year in which they decided to adopt. Most individuals seemed to require a period of time that could be measured in years to pass through the innovation-decision process. So adoption behavior is a process that contains stages, and these stages occur over time.

Yet another type of evidence provided by Beal and Rogers (1960) deals with skipped stages. If most respondents report not having passed through a stage in the innovation-decision process for a given innovation, some question would thus be raised as to whether that stage should be included in the model. Beal and Rogers found that most farmers described their behavior at each of the first three stages in the innovation-decision process: knowledge, persuasion, and decision. None reported skipping the knowledge or decision stages, but a few farmers did not report a trial stage prior to adoption (perhaps because of the nature of the innovation under study, a chemical weed spray).

Coleman and others (1966) found that most physicians reported different communication channels about a new drug at the knowledge stage versus the channels reported at the persuasion stage. LaMar (1966) studied the innovation-decision process for 262 teachers in twenty California schools. The teachers went through the stages in the innovation-decision process much as had the farmers in the earlier studies. Kohl (1966) found that all 58 Oregon school superintendents in his sample reported that they passed through all of the stages for such innovations as team teaching, language laboratories, and flexible scheduling.

We thus suggest Generalization 5-12: *Stages exist in the innovation-decision process.* The evidence is clearest cut for the knowledge and decision stages, and somewhat less so for the persuasion stage. Only limited data are available on the distinctiveness of the implementation and confirmation stages.

The Hierarchy-of-Effects

The basic notion of a hierarchy of communication effects is that an individual usually must pass from knowledge change to overt behavior change in a cumulative sequence of stages that are generally parallel to the stages in the innovation-decision process (Table 5-1). Social psychologist William McGuire (1989) originally posited this hierarchy-of-effects model, which has been widely used in communication research.

Communication effects thus occur in a hierarchy for most individuals who pass through stages in the innovation-decision process, with different communication channels playing a different role in causing different effects. For example, mass media communication channels are generally more effective in leading to knowledge effects, while interpersonal channels are more likely to cause persuasion effects. An intervention such as a communication campaign will have greater effects near the top of the hierarchy, as knowledge is easier to change than is bringing about behavior change, at least in the relatively short term (Vaughan and Rogers, 2000). Thus a six-month communication intervention might increase knowledge of an innovation on the part of 35 percent of the audience while influencing only 2 or 3 percent of the individuals to adopt the new idea.

Stages-of-Change

A somewhat similar model of stages in the innovation-decision process was proposed by Professor James O. Prochaska, a preventive health researcher at the University of Rhode Island. Prochaska's five-stage

Table 5-1. Stages in the Innovation-Decision Process The Hierarchy-of-Effects and the Stages-of-Change Correspond to Stages in the Innovation-Decision Process

Stages in the Innovation-Decision Process	Hierarchy-of-Effects	Porchaska's Stages-of-Change
I. *Knowledge Stage*		I. Precontemplation
1. Recall of information		
2. Comprehension of messages		
3. Knowledge or skill for effective adoption of the innovation		
II. *Persuasion Stage*		II. Contemplation
4. Liking the innovation		
5. Discussion of the new behavior with others		
6. Acceptance of the message about the innovation		
7. Formation of a positive image of the message and the innovation		
8. Support for the innovative behavior from the system		
III. *Decision Stage*		III. Preparation
9. Intention to seek additional information about the innovation		
10. Intention to try the innovation		
IV. *Implementation Stage*		IV. Action
11. Acquisition of additional information about the innovation		
12. Use of the innovation on a regular basis		
13. Continued use of the innovation		
V. *Confirmation Stage*		V. Maintenance
14. Recognition of the benefits of using the innovation		
15. Integration of the innovation into one's ongoing routine		
16. Promotion of the innovation to others		

Source: Based on McGuire's (1989, p. 45) hierarchy-of-effects, as modified by Population Communication Services at Johns Hopkins University, and with the addition of Prochaska's stages-of-change (Prochaska, DiClemente, and Norcross, 1992).

model of how individuals change an addictive behavior is widely utilized in the public health field to explain the adoption of preventive
health innovations, such as safer sex to prevent HIV/AIDS, contraception, seeking a mammogram for the early detection of breast cancer,
and cigarette smoking cessation. Prochaska, DiClemente, and Norcross
(1992) defined the five stages-of-change (S-O-C) as follows:

1. *Precontemplation,* when an individual is aware that a problem exists
   and begins to think about overcoming it.
2. *Contemplation,* when an individual is aware that a problem exists
   and is seriously thinking about overcoming it but has not yet made a
   commitment to take action.
3. *Preparation,* the stage at which an individual intends to take action
   in the immediate future but has not yet done so.
4. *Action,* when an individual changes behavior in order to overcome
   the problem.
5. *Maintenance,* the stage at which an individual consolidates and continues the behavior change that was made previously.

Like the hierarchy-of-effects model, Prochaska's stages-of-change
model implies a cascading progression of an individual's behavior through
the stages. A changing decisional balance of expected costs and benefits of
an innovation moves an individual through the stages-of-change. Individuals increase the number of "pros" and decrease the number of "cons"
regarding an innovation as they move through the S-O-C model. For
example, when an individual becomes aware of the health benefits of
stopping smoking and learns how easy it is to enroll in a cessation class, he
or she is likely to make this change. An individual's self-efficacy (the belief
that he or she can control the future) increases at each successive stage in
the stages-of-change (Galavotti et al., 1995).

Prochaska found that the vast majority of smoking-addicted individuals were not in the action stage when they enrolled in smoking cessation
courses. He estimated that 10 to 15 percent of smokers were prepared
for action, 30 to 40 percent were in the contemplation stage, and 50 to
60 percent were in the precontemplation stage. A smoking cessation
program will fail if all three categories are assumed to be equally ready
to break their addiction. This mistake is one reason why so many individuals drop out of smoking cessation programs, drug abuse treatment,
and dieting for weight control, or else relapse to their addiction after

completing the training program. The stages-of-change can thus serve to classify individuals into segments on the basis of their readiness for behavior change, with a different program tailored to each individual (see Chapter 9). Communities, as well as individuals, can be classified into readiness for change (Edwards et al., 2000).

One use of the stages-of-change model by communication scholars is to measure the effects of a diffusion intervention by how far it moves individuals through the stages. Thus the stages-of-change become a variable on which each individual can be measured. Two recent experimental studies using this approach are Vaughan and Rogers (2000), who studied the effects of a diffusion intervention in Tanzania, and Polacsek and colleagues (2001), who evaluated the effects of Mothers Against Drunk Driving (MADD) Victim Impact Panels on drunk driving in New Mexico.

The Tanzania Project concerned the effects of broadcasting an entertainment-education radio soap opera, *Twende na Wakati* (Let's Go with the Times), on the adoption of family planning, from 1993 to 1997. This radio program was very popular and featured positive and negative role models for contraception. Data were gathered in annual surveys of about three thousand households in Tanzania, so as to calculate individuals' movement through the stages-of-change from precontemplation through contemplation, preparation, and action, to maintenance of contraception. From 1993 to 1995, the radio program was broadcast throughout the nation except for the Dodoma area, which acted as a control or comparison. Exposure to the broadcasts had a certain degree of direct effect on listeners, but the main impacts were in stimulating peer communication about the adoption of family-planning methods (Vaughan and Rogers, 2000). Entertainment-education may be unique in its ability to stimulate interpersonal communication about an innovation (Singhal and Rogers, 1999). Approximately 23 percent of the listeners to the radio soap opera adopted a family-planning method (Rogers et al., 1999). These effects were measured in the treatment (broadcasting) areas from 1993 to 1995 and thereafter throughout the nation, when the radio program was also broadcast in the Dodoma area.

Polacsek and others (2001) utilized the stages-of-change to measure the effects of MADD's Victim Impact Panels (VIPs) on 813 driving while intoxicated (DWI) offenders in New Mexico. The VIPs consisted of presentations by the mothers of children killed or injured by drunk drivers. They often broke down in tears while addressing an auditorium of recently convicted drunk drivers. DWI offenders were randomly assigned to participate in a VIP or not, and all attended a DWI school (required by state law) that represented a more informational approach to preventing continued drunk driving. No difference was found between drunk drivers who were exposed to a VIP versus those who were not so exposed, either (1) in movement through the stages-of-change or (2) in drunk driving recidivism over the following two years (measured from state driving records).

The Tanzania Project and the New Mexico DWI project illustrate how experiments can be designed and conducted in order to measure the effects of various communication interventions on movement through the stages in the innovation-decision process. This variance type research helps illuminate the nature of the process by intervening in it.

The present discussion of the hierarchy-of-effects, the stages-of-change, and the innovation-decision process suggests the basic similarity of these process models, and implies that yet further conceptualizations of the stages might be fruitful. For instance, Wenstein and Sandman (2002) created a special version of the innovation-decision process for preventive innovations.

Communication Channels in the Innovation-Decision Process for Tetracycline

The five stages in the innovation-decision process help our understanding of the role of different communication channels, as is illustrated in the diffusion of tetracycline (called "gammanym" by the researchers) among medical doctors in Illinois. Gammanym was a new antibiotic "wonder drug" that spread rapidly among the doctors in the medical community, mainly due to its lesser side effects (Coleman et al., 1966). This innovation had spectacular results, and it was adopted very rapidly by doctors. Within two months of its release, 15 percent of the physicians had tried it; this figure reached 50 percent four months later, and at the end of seventeen months, gammanym dominated doctors' antibiotic prescriptions. Gammanym had such a striking relative advantage over previous antibiotic drugs that most of a doctor's peer networks conveyed very positive messages about the innovation. One of the most important contributions of the drug study was to establish the importance of interpersonal networks as a communication channel in the innovation-decision process (see Chapter 2).

Information that creates awareness-knowledge of an innovation seldom comes to individuals from a source or channel of communication that they actively seek, as information about a new idea can be actively sought by individuals only after (1) they are aware that the new idea exists and (2) they know which sources or channels can provide information about the innovation. Further, the relative importance of different sources or channels of communication about an innovation depends in part on what is available to the audience of potential adopters. For example, if a new idea is initially promoted only by commercial firms that sell it, it is unlikely that other sources or channels will be very important, at least at the knowledge stage of the innovation-decision process. Coleman and colleagues (1966) found that 80 percent of the medical doctors in their drug study reported first learning about gammanym from drug companies (57 percent from pharmaceutical detail men, 18 percent from drug house mailings, 4 percent from drug house magazines, and 1 percent from drug ads in medical journals).

Later in the innovation-decision process, at the persuasion and decision stages, near peer networks became more important sources or channels of communication about the new drug, and the commercial role became somewhat less important (Van den Bulte and Lilien, 2001). Awareness-knowledge that a new drug existed could be communicated by commercial sources or channels, but doctors tended to rely on the experiences of their peers for evaluative information about the innovation. The pharmaceutical firms that sold tetracycline were regarded as less credible by medical doctors at the persuasion stage than were peers, when they were deciding whether or not to adopt the innovation.

Scientific evaluations of tetracycline were communicated to the doctors, but such information did not convince them to adopt the innovation. Coleman and colleagues (1966, pp. 31–32) concluded that "The extensive trials and tests by manufacturer, medical schools, and teaching hospitals—tests that a new drug must pass before it is released—are not enough for the average doctor." They found that "teaching at the expert level cannot substitute for the doctor's own testing of the new drug; but testing through the everyday experiences of colleagues on the doctor's own level can substitute, at least in part." Individuals depend on their near peers for innovation evaluation information, which decreases their uncertainty about the innovation's expected consequences.

Evidence that the interpersonally communicated experience of near peers can substitute, in part, for the individual's personal experience with an innovation is provided by analyses of the degree to which earlier versus later adopters of an innovation adopt the new idea completely at the time of their first trial. The first medical doctors to adopt gammanym did so on a very partial basis; the nineteen physicians who adopted the new drug in the first and second months of its use wrote prescriptions for an average of only 1.5 patients each.

The twenty-two doctors who adopted the innovation in the third or fourth months wrote 2.0 prescriptions each, while the twenty-three doctors who adopted in the fifth through eighth months wrote an average of 2.7 prescriptions each (Coleman et al., 1966). Other studies have also found that innovators and early adopters start using a new idea on a more tentative basis than do laggards, who move almost immediately to full-scale adoption. For example, Ryan and Gross found that Iowa farmers adopting hybrid seed corn prior to 1939 initially planted only 15 percent of their corn acreage in hybrids, but those who adopted in 1939 and 1940 planted 60 percent of their acreage in hybrid seed in their first year of adoption. Farmers adopting in 1941–1942 (the laggards) planted 90 percent of their corn acreage in hybrid seed.

Why are the first individuals in a system to adopt an innovation usually most tentative in their degree of trial of the new idea? The basic reason is the role of uncertainty in the diffusion process. Even though most innovative adopters of gammanym and hybrid corn were fully informed of the scientific evaluations that had been made of these new ideas, this information did not reduce their uncertainty about how the innovation would work out for *them*. The innovators had to conduct their own personal experimentation with the new idea in order to assure themselves that it was indeed advantageous under their conditions. They could not depend on the experience of peers with the innovation, because no one else had adopted the innovation at the time that the innovators adopted (at least in their system). Later adopters profit from their peers' accumulated personal experiences with the innovation. Thus, much of the uncertainty of the innovation is removed by the time later adopters first use a new idea, making a personal trial of the new idea less necessary for them.

Communication Channels by Stages of the Innovation-Decision Process

Different communication channels play different roles at each stage in the innovation-decision process.

Categorizing Communication Channels

It is often difficult for individuals to distinguish between the source of a message and the channel that carries the message. A *source* is an individual or an institution that originates a message. A *channel* is the means by which a message gets from the source to the receiver. Here we speak mainly of "channels," but "source or channel" might be more accurate. We categorize communication channels as (1) interpersonal versus mass media and (2) localite versus cosmopolite. These channels play different roles in creating knowledge versus persuading individuals to change their attitude toward an innovation. Communication channels also differ for earlier adopters versus later adopters.

Mass media channels are means of transmitting messages that involve a mass medium, such as radio, television, newspapers, and so on, which enables a source of one or a few individuals to reach an audience of many. The mass media can:

1. Reach a large audience rapidly.
2. Create knowledge and spread information.
3. Change weakly held attitudes.

The formation and change of strongly held attitudes, however, is accomplished mainly by interpersonal channels. *Interpersonal channels* involve a face-to-face exchange between two or more individuals. These channels are more effective in dealing with resistance or apathy on the part of an individual, which is one reason why peer communication is so important for later adopters and laggards. What can interpersonal communication channels do best?

1. Provide a two-way exchange of information. One individual can secure clarification or additional information about an innovation from another individual. This characteristic of interpersonal networks often allows them to overcome the social-psychological barriers of selective exposure, selective perception, and selective retention (forgetting).
2. Persuade an individual to form or to change a strongly held attitude. This role of interpersonal channels is especially important in persuading an individual to adopt a new idea.

Mass Media Versus Interpersonal Channels

Generalization 5-13: *Mass media channels are relatively more important at the knowledge stage, and interpersonal channels are relatively more important at the persuasion stage in the innovation-decision process.* The importance of interpersonal and mass media channels in the innovation-decision process was first investigated in a series of researches with farmers, and then largely confirmed in studies with other types of respondents. For example, Sill (1958) found that if the probability of adoption were to be maximized, communication channels must be used in an ideal time sequence, progressing from mass media to interpersonal channels. Copp and colleagues (1958, p. 70) found that "A temporal sequence is involved in agricultural communication in that messages are sent out through mass media directed to awareness, then to groups, and finally to individuals. A farmer upsetting this sequence in any way prejudices progress at some point in the adoption process." The greatest thrust out from the knowledge stage was provided by the use of the mass media, while interpersonal channels were salient in moving individuals out of the persuasion stage. Using a communication channel that was inappropriate to a given stage in the innovation-decision process (such as an interpersonal channel at the knowledge stage) was associated with later adoption of the new idea by an individual because such channel use delayed progress through the innovation-decision process.

Data on the relative importance of interpersonal and mass media channels at each stage in the adoption of 2,4-D weed spray were obtained by Beal and Rogers (1960) from 148 Iowa farmers. Mass media channels, such as farm magazines, bulletins, and container labels, were more important than interpersonal channels at the knowledge stage for this innovation. The percentage of respondents mentioning an interpersonal channel increased from 37 percent at the knowledge function to 63 percent at the persuasion function.

The evidence above came from diffusion research conducted in the United States, where the mass media are widely available. The mass media, however, are not so widely available in developing countries. For example, Deutschmann and Fals Borda (1962b) found that interpersonal channels were heavily used even at the knowledge stage by Colombian villagers. In Bangladeshi villages, Rahim (1961, 1965) found that mass media channels were seldom mentioned as channels for agricultural innovations, whereas cosmopolite interpersonal channels were very important and in some ways seemed to perform a similar role to that played by mass media channels in more developed countries. An example of a cosmopolite interpersonal channel is an Iowa farmer attending a farm machinery show in Des Moines or a medical doctor traveling to an out-of-town medical specialty meeting in Chicago.

Rogers with Shoemaker (1971) made a comparative analysis of the role played by the mass media and cosmopolite interpersonal channels by stages in the innovation-decision process for twenty-three different innovations (mostly agricultural) in the United States, Canada, India, Bangladesh, and Colombia. Mass media channels were of relatively greater importance at the knowledge stage in both developing and developed countries, although there was a higher *level* of mass media channel usage in the developed nations, as we would expect. Mass media channels were used by 52 percent of the respondents at the persuasion stage, and 18 percent at the decision stage. The comparable figures for respondents in developing nations were 29 percent and 8 percent. This meta-research showed that cosmopolite interpersonal channels were especially important at the knowledge stage in developing nations.

A recent investigation in Bolivia suggests that under certain conditions, mass media communication may substitute for interpersonal communication in motivating the adoption of innovations. Valente and Saba (1998) found that for individuals whose personal networks (that is, the other people with whom he or she interacts) included relatively few contraceptive adopters, a media campaign promoting family planning could move them to adoption.

The exact importance of mass media versus interpersonal channels for any particular innovation rests in part on the degree to which media advertising is used to promote the new product. For example, End-Note, a computer software product to help scholars and students keep track of their bibliographic references, diffused very widely in the United States via peer networks, in part because the high-tech company marketing EndNote did not purchase advertising. This fascinating story began in 1988 when the creators of EndNote demonstrated their brand new product at the University of California at Berkeley Faculty Club. Shortly thereafter, the company received its first order, from Princeton, New Jersey. How had this innovation spread across the country? By interpersonal networks. Today, more than two hundred thousand copies of EndNote have been sold (Rosen, 2001). A diffusion study of EndNote would show, of course, that this new product spread almost entirely via interpersonal channels.

Cosmopolite Versus Localite Channels

Generalization 5-14: *Cosmopolite channels are relatively more important at the knowledge stage, and localite channels are relatively more important at the persuasion stage in the innovation-decision process.* Cosmopolite communication channels are those linking an individual with sources outside the social system under study. Interpersonal channels may be either local or cosmopolite, while mass media channels are almost entirely cosmopolite.

The meta-research on twenty-three different innovations in ten nations (mentioned previously) showed that if cosmopolite interpersonal and mass media channels are combined to form a category of cosmopolite channels, in the developing nations the percentage of such channels was 81 percent at the knowledge stage and 58 percent at the persuasion stage. In developed nations, the percentages were 74 percent at the knowledge function and 34 percent at the persuasion function. In both developed and developing nations, cosmopolite channels are more important at the knowledge stage and less important at the persuasion stage (as Generalization 5-14 indicates). These meta-research data suggest that the role played by mass media channels in developed countries (creating awareness-knowledge) is perhaps partly replaced by cosmopolite-interpersonal channels in developing countries (where the mass media are less pervasive). These cosmopolite interpersonal channels include change agents, visits outside the local community, and visitors to the local system by outsiders.

The Bass Forecasting Model

A tremendous expansion has occurred in the marketing literature on diffusion since the 1970s. The most important single impetus to this scholarly explosion is a model for forecasting the diffusion of new consumer products proposed by Frank Bass in 1969, then a marketing professor at Purdue University, and presently at the University of Texas at Dallas. The Bass forecasting model became so important in the marketing field because it offers some plausible answers to the uncertainty associated with the introduction of a new product in the marketplace. Some of the largest U.S. corporations have used the Bass model, including Kodak, IBM, RCA, Sears, and AT&T. Much of the scholarly research inspired by the Bass forecasting model has been carried out by U.S. business school professors, but it has also been conducted in other nations and in other academic fields. For instance, Lawton and Lawton (1979) used the Bass model to predict the diffusion of educational ideas, and Akinola (1986) analyzed the diffusion of coco-spray chemicals among Nigerian farmers. As mentioned in Chapter 2, Professor Monick Dekimpe, a leading marketing scholar in Europe, states that the Bass diffusion model is the most widely utilized theoretical model in marketing today.

What is the Bass model? It assumes that potential adopters of an innovation are influenced by two types of communication channels: Mass media and interpersonal channels. Individuals adopting a new product because of a mass media message occur continually throughout the diffusion process but are concentrated in the relatively early time periods (see Figure 5–2). Individuals adopting as a result of interpersonal messages about the new product expand in numbers during the first half of the diffusion process and thereafter decline in numbers per ensuing time periods, creating a bell-shaped diffusion curve (which is the familiar S-shaped curve when plotted on a cumulative basis). The Bass model assumes that the rate of adoption during the first half of the diffusion process is symmetrical with that in the second half, as would necessarily occur for an S-shaped curve.

All of these elements in the Bass model are soundly based on the results of diffusion research. What is the unique contribution of the Bass model? It is a predictive model that seeks to forecast how many adoptions of a new product will occur at future time periods, or on the basis of pilot launches of a new product, or from managerial judgments made on the basis of the diffusion history of analogous products. The Bass model addresses the market in an aggregate way in that it forecasts the total number of adopters who purchase in each time period, rather than the adoption or nonadoption by individual customers.

A second important contribution of the Bass model is to provide a mathematical formula for predicting rate of adoption. The three parameters of the Bass model, explained in Figure 5–2, give much greater weighting to interpersonal communication, which is consistent with the results of past diffusion research. Expressing the diffusion process in a mathematical formula greatly simplifies and codifies our understanding of the diffusion process. Essentially, Bass repackaged diffusion understandings in a form that were more usable by the business community and marketing scholars. Bass's (1969) original forecasts were for consumer durables such as television sets, clothes dryers, and air conditioners. The invisible college of marketing professors following his model has added various "bells and whistles." Some thirteen publications dealing with the Bass model appeared in the 1970s, eighty-two during the 1980s, and the field continues to grow, with at least thirty-five further tests of the Bass model published since 1990.

Despite the large and growing number of scholarly publications dealing with the Bass diffusion model, most of these investigations have been carried out in North America and Europe, rather than in the developing nations of Latin America, Africa, and Asia, where the coefficients in the model for media communication might be quite different (Talukdar, Sudhir, and Ainslie, 2002). The majority of studies of the Bass model have been

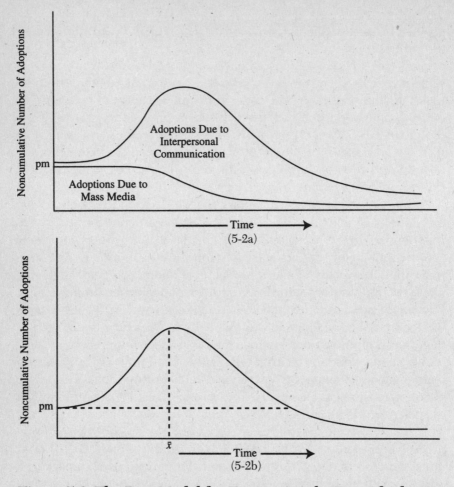

Figure 5-2. The Bass Model for Forecasting the Rate of Adoption of a New Product Key elements in Frank Bass's forecasting model are (1) adopters due to media messages (p), (2) adopters due to interpersonal communication channels (q), and (3) an index of market potential (m) for the new product. Figure 5-2a shows the number of new adopters per time unit is due to mass media channels and to interpersonal communication, with the later much more important. Figure 5-2b shows that the crucial variable to predict is the number of adopters from the time of the prediction to the mean time of adoption, when a point of inflection occurs in the diffusion curve. The cumulative number of adopters can then be estimated (Figure 5-2c) because the S-shaped diffusion curve is symmetrical around the mean year of adoption.

Source: Based on Mahajan, Muller, and Bass (1990).

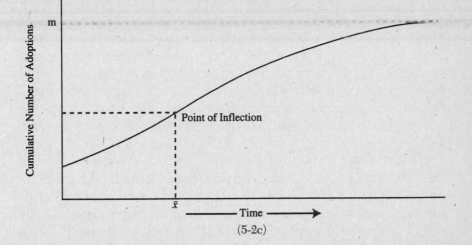

(5-2c)

conducted of consumer durables, although in recent years the Bass model has been tested with the diffusion of telecommunications innovations like cellular telephones (Dekimpe, Parker, and Sarvay, 1998, 2000b, 2000c; Grüber and Verboven, 2001a, 2001b; Shermesh and Tellis, 2002). Finally, most studies of the Bass diffusion model are conducted with data from a single nation, although today many innovations diffuse globally. Current marketing research seeks to test the Bass model with global diffusion data (for a comprehensive summary of recent work on the Bass model, see Mahajan, Muller, and Wind, 2000a).

Frank Bass created a diffusion model to suit the conditions of a particular diffusion research tradition—marketing—and thus greatly boosted diffusion study in that tradition. The two main predictor variables in the Bass model deal with communication channels.

Communication Channels by Adopter Categories

The preceding discussion of communication channels by stages in the innovation-decision process ignored the effects of a respondent's adopter category, a topic explored in several diffusion studies.

Generalization 5-15: *Mass media channels are relatively more important than interpersonal channels for earlier adopters than for later adopters.* At the time innovators adopt a new idea, there is almost no one else in their system who is experienced with the innovation. Later adopters do not need to rely so much on mass media channels because an ample storehouse of interpersonal, local experience has accumu-

lated in their system by the time they decide to adopt. Perhaps interpersonal influence is not so necessary to motivate earlier adopters to
decide favorably on an innovation. They possess a more venturesome
orientation, and the mass media message stimulus is enough to move
them over the mental threshold to adoption. But the less change-
oriented later adopters require a stronger and more immediate influence, such as that from interpersonal networks and especially from
peers.

There is strong support for Generalization 5-15 from researches in
both developed and developing nations. Data illustrating this proposition are shown in Figure 5–3 for the adoption of a chemical weed spray
by Iowa farmers. Interpersonal channels are more important for all
adopter categories (except innovators) at the persuasion stage than at
the knowledge stage.

Figure 5-3. Importance of Interpersonal Channels

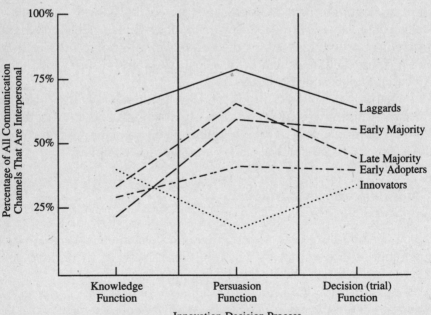

Interpersonal channels are relatively less important for earlier adopters
than for later adopters of 2, 4-D weed spray in Iowa.

Source: Beal and Rogers (1960, p. 19).

Reasoning similar to that just presented leads to Generalization 5-16: *Cosmopolite channels are relatively more important than localite channels for earlier adopters than for later adopters.** Innovations enter a system from external sources, and those who adopt first are more likely to depend upon cosmopolite channels. These earlier adopters, in turn, act as interpersonal and localite channels for their later-adopting peers.

The Innovation-Decision Period

The *innovation-decision period* is the length of time required for an individual or organization to pass through the innovation-decision process. The length of the innovation-decision period is usually measured from first knowledge to the decision to adopt or reject, although in a strict sense it should be measured to the time of confirmation. Such meaurement is often impractical or impossible because the confirmation stage may continue over an indefinite period. The time elapsing between awareness-knowledge of an innovation and decision for an individual is measured in days, months, or years. The period is thus a gestation period during which a new idea ferments in an individual's mind.

The Rate of Awareness-Knowledge and Rate of Adoption

Most change agents wish to speed up the process by which innovations are adopted. One method of doing so is to communicate information about new ideas more rapidly or more adequately so that knowledge is created at an earlier date. Another method is to shorten the amount of time required for the innovation-decision after an individual is aware of a new idea. At any given point in time, many potential adopters are aware of a new idea, but are not yet motivated to try it. For example, almost all of the Iowa farmers in the hybrid corn study heard about the innovation before more than a handful were planting it. "It is evident that . . . isolation from knowledge was not a determining factor in late adoption for many operators" (Ryan and Gross, 1950, p. 679). Shortening the innovation-decision period is one of the main methods of speeding the diffusion of an innovation for most individuals.

---

*Generalization 5-16 bears a resemblance to Generalization 7-25, which states that earlier adopters are more cosmopolite than later adopters, but the present proposition deals with cosmopolite channel usage, not cosmopoliteness.

Knowledge proceeds at a more rapid rate than does adoption, which suggests that relatively later adopters have a longer average innovation-decision period than do earlier adopters. For example, a study of the diffusion of a new weed spray among Iowa farmers by Beal and Rogers (1960) found 1.7 years between 10 percent awareness-knowledge and 10 percent adoption but 3.1 years between 92 percent awareness-knowledge and 92 percent adoption. The slope of the rate-of-awareness curve is steeper than that for the rate of adoption. These data, along with evidence from other studies, suggest Generalization 5-17: *The rate of awareness-knowledge for an innovation is more rapid than its rate of adoption.*

Innovations vary in their average length of the innovation-decision period. For instance, the average period for hybrid corn in Iowa was 9.0 years (Gross, 1942), while 2.1 years was the average for the weed spray studied by Beal and Rogers (1960). What explains these differences? Innovations with certain characteristics (like a high relative advantage and compatibility) are adopted more rapidly (see Chapter 6), and these innovations have a shorter innovation-decision period.

The Length of the Innovation-Decision Period by Adopter Category

The data discussed above for the new weed spray showed a longer innovation-decision period for later adopters. This relationship is detailed in Figure 5–4, where the average length of the period is shown for the five adopter categories. These data and those from other studies support Generalization 5-18: *Earlier adopters have a shorter innovation-decision period than do later adopters.* Thus, the first individuals to adopt a new idea (the innovators) are the first to adopt not only because they become aware of the innovation somewhat sooner than others in their system, but also because they require fewer months or years to move from the knowledge stage to the decision stage. Innovators perhaps gain part of their innovative position (relative to late adopters) by learning about innovations at an earlier time, but the present data suggest that the main reason innovators are the first to adopt is because they require a shorter innovation-decision period.

Why do innovators require a shorter innovation-decision period? Innovators have more favorable attitudes toward new ideas (this is venturesomeness) and so communication messages about innovations face less resistance. Innovators may also have a shorter innovation-decision period because (1) they utilize more technically accurate sources and

Figure 5-1. Innovators Have Shorter Innovation-Decision Periods than Laggards in Adopting 2, 4-D Weed Spray

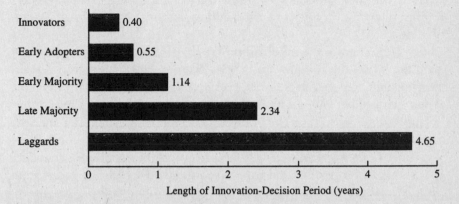

Length of Innovation-Decision Period (years)

One reason why innovators are earlier than others in their system in adopting new deas is because they have much shorter innovation-adoption periods.

Source: Based on data from 148 Iowa farmers gathered by Beal and Rogers (1960).

channels about innovations, such as direct contact with scientists, and (2) they place higher credibility in these sources than does the average individual. Innovators may also possess a type of mental ability that better enables them to cope with uncertainty and to deal with abstractions. An innovator must be able to conceptualize relatively abstract information about innovations and apply this new information to his or her own situation. Later adopters can observe the results of innovations by earlier adopters and may not require this type of abstract mental ability.

How the Internet Is Changing the Innovation-Decision Process

How is the Internet changing the nature of the innovation-decsision process? Is communication via the Internet more like mass media communication or interpersonal communication? Can Internet messages serve a role in the innovation-decision process similar to that performed by interpersonal channels?

The Internet allows people to reach many other people in a one-to-many process (similar to that of the mass media), but e-mail messages are like interpersonal communication in that they can be personalized to the individual. We know that the Internet can largely remove the cost of communicating across space. An e-mail message usually goes around the world in the same time and at the same cost as to someone next door.

For certain innovations, diffusion via the Internet greatly speeds up an innovation's rate of adoption. For example, Hotmail, a free e-mail service launched on July 4, 1996, had spread to 12 million users eighteen months later, when it was sold to Microsoft for $400 million (Singhal and Rogers, 2001). The founder of Hotmail, an Indian named Sabeer Bhatia working in Silicon Valley, was only thirty-one years old at the time! How was Hotmail's phenomenal rate of adoption achieved? When one receives an e-mail from someone with a Hotmail account, a promotional message appears at the bottom of one's computer screen: "Get your free e-mail at Hotmail.com." Thus a message promoting Hotmail is included in every e-mail message sent by means of Hotmail, creating an S-shaped curve of cumulatively increasing promotional messages. Importantly, these promotional messages came from the person who sent one an e-mail message, so the ad was highly personalized. Hotmail purchased almost no mass media advertising but created "word-of-mouth advertising at Internet speed" (Rosen, 2001, p. 21).

The rate at which the Internet speeds up the diffusion process in some cases is illustrated by Internet viruses, which can travel worldwide in a day or two. Clearly, the world in which we live today is a different one than that of sixty years ago, when study of the diffusion process began.

Summary

The *innovation-decision process* is the process through which an individual (or other decision-making unit) passes from first knowledge of an innovation, to forming an attitude toward the innovation, to a decision to adopt or reject, to implementation of the new idea, and to confirmation of this decision. This process consists of five stages: (1) *knowledge,* when the individual is exposed to the innovation's existence and gains an understanding of how it functions; (2) *persuasion,* when the individual forms a favorable or unfavorable attitude toward the innovation; (3) *decision,* when the individual engages in activities that lead to a choice to adopt or reject the innovation; (4) *implementation,* when the individual puts an innovation into use; and (5) *confirmation,* when the individual seeks reinforcement for an innovation-decision already made but may reverse the decision if exposed to conflicting messages about it.

Earlier knowers of an innovation, when compared to later knowers, are characterized by more formal education, higher social status, greater exposure to mass media channels of communication, greater exposure to interpersonal channels of communication, greater change agent contact, greater social participation, and greater cosmopoliteness (Generalizations 5-1 to 5-7).

Re-invention is the degree to which an innovation is changed or modified by a user in the process of its adoption and implementation. Re-invention occurs at the implementation stage for many innovations and for many adopters (Generalization 5-8). A higher degree of re-invention leads to (1) a faster rate of adoption of an innovation and (2) a greater degree of sustainability of an innovation (Generalizations 5-9 and 5-10). *Sustainability* is the degree to which an innovation is continued over time after a diffusion program ends.

Discontinuance is a decision to reject an innovation after having previously adopted it. Discontinuance can be of two types: (1) *replacement discontinuance*, in which an idea is rejected in order to adopt a better idea which superseded it, and (2) *disenchantment discontinuance*, in which an idea is rejected as a result of dissatisfaction with its performance. Later adopters are more likely to discontinue innovations than are earlier adopters (Generalization 5-11).

We conclude that stages exist in the innovation-decision process (Generalization 5-12), although further study of this issue is needed.

A *communication channel* is the means by which a message gets from a source to a receiver. We categorize communication channels (1) as either interpersonal or mass media in nature and (2) as originating from either localite or cosmopolite sources. *Mass media channels* are means of transmitting messages that involve a mass medium such as radio, television, newspapers, and so on, that enable a source of one or a few individuals to reach an audience of many. *Interpersonal channels* involve a face-to-face exchange between two or more individuals.

Mass media channels are relatively more important at the knowledge stage, and interpersonal channels are relatively more important at the persuasion stage in the innovation-decision process (Generalization 5-13). Cosmopolite channels are relatively more important at the knowledge stage, and localite channels are relatively more important at the persuasion stage in the innovation-decision process (Generalization 5-14). Mass media channels are relatively more important than interpersonal channels for earlier adopters than for later adopters (Generalization 5-15). Cosmopolite channels are relatively more important than localite channels for earlier adopters than for later adopters (Generalization 5-16).

The *innovation-decision period* is the length of time required for an individual or organization to pass through the innovation-decision process. The rate of awareness-knowledge for an innovation is more rapid than its rate of adoption (Generalization 5-17). Earlier adopters have a shorter innovation-decision period than do later adopters (Generalization 5-18).

6

ATTRIBUTES OF INNOVATIONS AND THEIR RATE OF ADOPTION

If men perceive situations as real, they are real in their consequences.

W. I. Thomas and Florian Znaniecki (1927), p. 81.

Some innovations diffuse from first introduction to widespread use in a few years; for example, in a dozen years, from 1989 to 2002, some 71 percent of adult Americans adopted the Internet. Another consumer innovation may level out at less than 20 percent use. What characteristics of innovations affect the rate at which they are adopted? This chapter identifies five characteristics of innovations and shows how individuals' perceptions of these characteristics predict the rate of adoption of innovations.

Much diffusion research has studied "people" differences in innovativeness (that is, in determining the characteristics of the different adopter categories). Much less effort has been devoted to analyzing "innovation" differences (that is, in investigating how the perceived properties of innovations affect their rate of adoption), although the imbalance between people versus innovation differences in diffusion research may be disappearing in recent years. The latter type of research can be valuable in predicting the reactions of people to an innovation. These reactions can be modified by the way in which an innovation is named and positioned, and how it is related to the existing beliefs and past experiences of potential adopters. Diffusion researchers in the past tended to regard all innovations as equivalent units from the viewpoint of their analysis. This oversimplification is dangerously incorrect.

Black Music in White America: Rap

If one were to write a scenario for an innovation that would *not* diffuse in America, it might be a new musical form originating with lower-income black men from distressed urban areas who used its lyrical content to draw attention to their feelings of anger, frustration, and violence. The African rhythmic quality of the new music is in stark contrast to the European notions of melody that dominate American music. In other words, rap music is a radical innovation, or was so at the time of its introduction. When rap first emerged in the United States around 1980, most radio stations refused to play the new music, mainly because its fans were not an important audience for commercial advertisers. Most popular music climbs the popularity charts in the U.S. because of airplay, so the radio embargo on the new music pushed it to the fringes of society and practically guaranteed its failure, at least in its initial years.

But rap music, despite these resistances and limitations, has become enormously popular in white America, and throughout the world. It is *the* contemporary musical form, ranking with such earlier types of black-originated music as jazz, blues, ragtime, and the cakewalk. Rap has been called "musical graffiti" (vandalism to some, art to others). How does one explain its popularity? Steve Greenberg, an authority on the diffusion of music in America, reasons that rap, because of its underclass origins, appealed to middle- and upper-class youths who wished to rebel against the status quo establishment of their parents and society. Suburban white teenagers, who one might expect would object to rap's radical tone, became its biggest fans.

Many of the teenagers' parents regard rap as ugly noise. The parental generation of suburban whites is attracted to European classical music, which "expresses feelings of class and worth that speak to a certain segment of society—one which possesses the power and wealth to maintain the institutions necessary to the perpetuation of the classical music world" (Greenberg, 1992). These upper-class aspects of classical music include concert halls, expensive opera costumes and stage sets, and high-priced tickets to concerts and operas.

Rap music initially flourished without access to the music establishment. Most rap was originally performed by artists in their own homes, using inexpensive equipment, in contrast to the sound studios and sophisticated recording equipment of other musical genres. Rap music was initially disseminated on homemade cassette tapes and by locally owned independent record companies. For a decade, the major recording companies resisted rap, and even in the mid-1990s only a small portion of the music on the *Billboard* rap singles chart was produced by the major labels. Gradually, radio stations specializing in rap music arose in every U.S. city. Rap artists such as the late Tupac Shakur, Snoop Doggy Dog, and Eminem continued the antiestablishment tradition of rap, with lyrics that called for killing policemen and that rebelled against parents, the government, and society.

Nevertheless, rap music gained in popularity with U.S. teenagers each year, especially upper-middle-class suburban white adolescents. Rap music is perceived by these youths as compatible with the values they want to express: Opposition to adult values and to parental control.

Rate of Adoption

Rate of adoption is the relative speed with which an innovation is adopted by members of a social system. It is generally measured as the number of individuals who adopt a new idea in a specified period, such as a year. So the rate of adoption is a numerical indicator of the steepness of the adoption curve for an innovation.

The perceived attributes of an innovation are one important explanation of the rate of adoption of an innovation. Most of the variance in the rate of adoption of innovations, from 49 to 87 percent, is explained by five attributes: relative advantage, compatibility, complexity, trialability, and observability (Rogers, 1995). In addition to these five perceived attributes of an innovation, such other variables as (1) the type of innovation-decision, (2) the nature of communication channels diffusing the innovation at various states in the innovation-decision process, (3) the nature of the social system in which the innovation is diffusing, and (4) the extent of change agents' promotion efforts in diffusing the innovation, affect an innovation's rate of adoption (Figure 6–1).

Innovations requiring an individual-optional innovation-decision are generally adopted more rapidly than when an innovation is adopted by an organization (see Chapter 10). The more persons involved in making an innovation-decision, the slower the rate of adoption. One means of speeding the rate of adoption of an innovation is to attempt to alter the unit of decision so that fewer individuals are involved.

Figure 6-1. Variables Determining the Rate of Adoption of Innovations

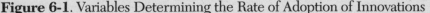
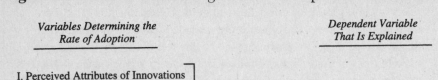

Variables Determining the *Rate of Adoption*	*Dependent Variable* *That Is Explained*

I. Perceived Attributes of Innovations

    1. Relative advantage
    2. Compatibility
    3. Complexity
    4. Trialability
    5. Observability

II. Type of Innovation-Decision

    1. Optional
    2. Collective
    3. Authority

III. Communication Channels (e.g., mass
    media or interpersonal)

IV. Nature of the Social System
    (e.g., its norms, degree of network
    interconnectedness, etc.)

V. Extent of Change Agents' Promotion Efforts

RATE OF ADOPTION
OF INNOVATIONS

The five types of variables that determine an innovation's rate of adoption have not received equal attention from diffusion scholars. The five perceived attributes of innovations have been most extensively investigated and have been found to explain about half of the variance in innovations' rates of adoption.

The communication channels used to diffuse an innovation also may influence the innovation's rate of adoption (see Figure 6–1). For example, if interpersonal channels (rather than mass media channels) create awareness-knowledge, as often happens for later adopters, the rate of adoption is slowed. The nature of a social system, such as its norms, and the degree to which the communication network structure is highly interconnected, also affect an innovation's rate of adoption. An innovation's rate of adoption is also affected by the extent of change agents' promotion efforts. The relationship between the rate of adoption and change agents' efforts, however, may not be direct and linear. A greater payoff from a given amount of change agent activity occurs at certain stages in an innovation's diffusion. The greatest response to change agent effort occurs when opinion leaders adopt, which usually occurs at somewhere between 3 and 16 percent adoption in most systems. The innovation will then continue to spread with little promotional effort by change agents, after a critical mass of adopters is reached.

Little diffusion research has been carried out to determine the relative contribution of each of the five types of variables shown in Figure 6–1. In this chapter we concentrate on the perceived attributes of innovations in explaining an innovation's rate of adoption. Subjective evaluations of an innovation, derived from individuals' personal experiences and perceptions and conveyed by interpersonal networks, drives the diffusion process and thus determines an innovation's rate of adoption.

Research on the Attributes of Innovations

We need a standard classification scheme so that the perceived attributes of innovations can be described in universal terms. We could say, for example, that innovation A is more like innovation B (in the eyes of its adopters) than it is like innovation C. Such a general classification system is an eventual objective of diffusion research on innovation attributes. While this goal has not been reached, the present section discusses one approach that has been widely used for the past fifty years or so. Five different attributes of innovations are described. Each is somewhat interrelated empirically with the other four, but they are conceptually distinct. Selection of these five characteristics is based on past writing and research, as well as on a desire for maximum generality and succinctness. These five attributes of innovations are (1) relative advantage, (2) compatibility, (3) complexity, (4) trialability, and (5) observability.

The crucial importance of perceptions in explaining human behavior was emphasized by an early dictum of the Chicago School of Sociology, quoted at the beginning of this chapter. In other words, perceptions count. The individuals' perceptions of the attributes of an innovation, not the attributes as classified objectively by experts or change agents, affect its rate of adoption.

Measuring the Attributes of Innovations

The first research on attributes of innovations and their rate of adoption was conducted with farmers, but studies of teachers and school administrators suggested that similar attributes predict the rate of adoption for educational innovations. Holloway (1977) designed his research with a hundred high school principals around the five attributes described in this chapter. He factor-analyzed Likert-type scale items measuring his respondents' perceptions of new educational ideas to derive a set of attributes and found general support for the present framework, although the distinction between relative advantage and compatibility was not very clear cut and the status-conferring aspects of educational innovations emerged as a sixth dimension predicting rate of adoption (status conferral is considered a sub-dimension of relative advantage in most conceptualizations).

A number of investigations of the perceived attributes and the rate of adoption of innovations have been conducted with various types of respondents in the past decade or so. Gary C. Moore and Izak Benbasat (1991) developed fifteen scale items to measure the five main attributes (plus three other attributes) of an information technology, personal work-stations (high-powered personal computers). With proper adaptation, these fifteen scale items can be applied to any particular innovation that is adopted by any set of individuals. Several diffusion scholars have done so, for such respondents as college students adopting computer-based delivery of a university course, alcohol treatment counselors adopting a computer-assisted counseling innovation, and so forth.

Moore and Benbasat (1991) pooled a set of existing and newly created scale items and then subjected the resulting seventy-five items to four rounds of sorting by expert judges. Moore and Benbasat included scale items to measure the ten attributes of innovations identified by Tornatzky and Klein (1982) as studied most frequently in 105 diffusion publications. Finally, the scale items were administered to 540 employees in seven companies, and these data were factor analyzed. In addition to the five attributes discussed in this chapter, three additional attributes were measured: (1) *voluntariness,* the degree to which use of personal work stations is perceived as being an optional innovation-decision, (2) *image,* the degree to which use of a personal work station enhanced an individual's status in the organization, and (3) *result demonstrability,* the degree to which a personal workstation is easy to communicate to others (similar to the concept of observability).

A typical scale item to measure relative advantage was: "Using a personal workstation improves the quality of work I do." Compatibility was measured by scale items such as "I think that using a personal workstation fits well with the way I like to work." A typical scale item to tap complexity was "Learning to use a personal workstation is easy for me" (this item actually measured simplicity, the opposite of complexity). Trialability was measured by scale items such as "I've had a great deal of opportunity to try various personal workstation applications." Observability was measured by items such as "In my organization, one sees personal workstations on many desks." The outcome of Moore and Benbasat's (1991) study was a set of twenty-eight scale items to measure the five attributes, and a short form of this scale with fifteen scale items. Validity of these scale items was gauged by comparing the scores of adopters of personal work stations with non-adopters. As expected, adopters scored higher on relative advantage, compatibility, trialability, and observability, and lower on complexity.

Some diffusion scholars want to utilize exisiting scale items already developed by other investigators, but the present author generally discourages this approach in favor of creating new scale items for each set of innovations to be adopted by a particular set of individuals. The specific ways in which the five attributes are expressed differs in each study, and so the measures of these attributes should be uniquely created afresh in each investigation. Nevertheless, the Moore and Benbasat (1991) scale items, and the sophisticated and careful methodology they utilized to develop their measures of the perceived attributes of innovations, may suggest other techniques to future investigators.

Organizations as the Units of Adoption

Most research on the attributes of innovations and their rate of adoption utilized individuals as the units of analysis, but this need not be the case. For instance, why not use organizations, communities, or some other systems as the unit of analysis? Goldman (1992) investigated the perceived attributes of a Campaign for Healthier Babies that was promoted by a national organization, the March of Dimes, to its local chapters for their implementation. Some 116 directors of local chapters reported their perceptions of the campaign five months after it was launched. Four attributes (each measured with a scale composed of several items), perceived compatibility with the local chapter's needs, simplicity (the opposite of complexity), relative advantage, and observability, were related to the degree of adoption and implementation of the Campaign for Healthier Babies. In this investigation, each local chapter of the March of Dimes was the unit of adoption, with the director of each chapter reporting his or her perceived attributes of the campaign.

One possible problem with measuring the five attributes of innovations is that they may not always be the five most important perceived characteristics for a particular set of respondents. The solution, of course, is to first elicit the main attributes of innovations from the respondents as a prior step to measuring these attributes as predictors of the rate of adoption.

This formative research procedure was followed by Kearns (1992) in a study of the adoption of eight computer innovations among the 127 suburban municipalities of Pittsburgh, Pennsylvania. The eight innovations were identified by contacting computer consultants and city officials in the Pittsburgh metropolitan area. The name of each of the eight innovations of study was written on a 3-by-5 inch card, together with a one-sentence description of each innovation. Each of the 127 respondents was handed three of the innovation cards and asked, "Can you think of any way in which two of these innovations are alike, and different from the third?" A respondent might say, for example, that two of the innovations were technologically complex, while the third was costly. Then the same respondent was handed another triplet of innovation cards and asked the same question. Kearns (1992) utilized this procedure to elicit twenty-five attributes of the eight innovations. Note that the twenty-five attributes came from the respondents, not from the investigator.

These twenty-five attributes included the five main attributes discussed in this chapter (relative advantage, compatibility, etc.), along with several additional attributes, such as flexibility in the way an innovation is implemented, the need for approval of the innovation by some authority (like a city council), and so forth. Note that the additional attributes were specific to the eight computer innovations and to the city officials who were the respondents, while the five main attributes came from the diffusion model (and from previous research). The respondents were asked to rank the eight innovations on each of the twenty-five attributes. For example, each respondent ranked the eight innovations from most costly to least costly. Then these perceived attribute ratings were correlated with the rate of adoption of the eight innovations. The twenty-five perceived attributes explained 27 percent of the variance in the rate of adoption of the eight innovations. The five main attributes (relative advantages, compatibility, etc.) explained 26 percent of the variance, only slightly less than that explained by all twenty-five attributes. The measurement approach used by Kearns (1992) guaranteed that the twenty-five attributes were grounded in the respondents' own frames of reference. Nevertheless, the five attributes discussed in the present chapter explained most of the innovation's rate of adoption.

We conclude that the main attributes of innovations for most respondents can be described by the five attributes in the general framework described in this chapter. However, diffusion scholars should keep an open mind toward other possible attributes that may be important in a specific situation for a particular set of individuals adopting a unique set of innovations.

Postdiction Versus Prediction

Generalizations about such attributes as relative advantage or compatibility to explain the rate of adoption are derived from *past* research, but these generalizations can be used to predict the rate of adoption of innovations in the future. Such forward-looking investigations are sometimes called "acceptability" research because their purpose is to identify a basis for positioning an innovation so that it will be more acceptable (that is, have a more rapid rate of adoption). Acceptability research is discussed in a later section of this chapter.

An ideal research design would measure the attributes of innovations at t_1 in order to predict the rate of adoption for these innovations at some future time, t_2 (Tornatzky and Klein, 1981). Several approaches are useful for helping predict the rate of adoption into the future:

1. Extrapolation from the rate of adoption of past innovations into the future for other similar innovations.
2. Describing a hypothetical innovation to its potential adopters, and determining its perceived attributes, so as to predict its forthcoming rate of adoption.
3. Investigating the acceptability of an innovation in its prediffusion stages, such as when it is being test-marketed and evaluated in trials.

None of these methods of studying the attributes of innovations is an ideal means for predicting the future rate of adoption of innovations. Research on predicting an innovation's rate of adoption would be more valuable if data on the attributes of the innovation were gathered prior to, or concurrently with, individuals' decisions to adopt the innovation.

An Agricultural Innovation That Failed[*]

Most past research on the perceived attributes of innovations as predictors of innovations' rates of adoption has been completed on new ideas that have already diffused successfully. What about an innovation that fails to diffuse? Can the perceived attributes of an innovation explain such failure?

An unusual investigation by Professor Peter Korsching, one of the leading diffusion scholars in rural sociology, and his colleagues at Iowa State Univer-

---

[*]This case illustration is based on Kremez et al. (2001).

sity suggests that the attributes of an innovation can also explain its failure (Kremer et al., 2001). These investigators studied the diffusion of the N-Trak soil nitrogen test to Iowa farmers during the decade of the 1990s. Prior to this innovation, farmers took soil samples in their fields every few years, mailed them to distant soil-testing labs, and then waited several weeks for the results, which provided a basis for deciding how much chemical fertilizer to apply. Most farmers used too much nitrogen fertilizer, which was wastefully expensive and caused problems when rainfall runoff carried the excess nitrogen into streams and rivers, causing environmental problems.

The N-Trak soil testing kit, sold by the Hach Company for $125, allowed the farmer to run his own tests and to see the results immediately. Thus farmers could apply a minimum of fertilizer at the time of planting their corn and then, when the corn was six inches or so high, in the late spring, test the fertility level of each ten-acre plot by taking sixteen to twenty-four core samples of soil in each plot, then apply the needed nitrogen fertilizer on each side of the rows of corn (a technique called side-dressing). The purpose of the N-Trak system was to reduce the overapplication of nitrogen fertilizer in cornfields, saving money for the farmer and reducing nitrogen runoff and the resulting environmental problems.

The N-Trak test was developed with the collaboration of agronomy professors at Iowa State University, who had conducted research on late-spring nitrogen testing. Such a test had been successfully developed in Vermont, Connecticut, and Pennsylvania, and there were high hopes for its rapid diffusion in Iowa. The Hach Company distributed 127,000 catalogs describing the innovation. When the new product was introduced in 1990, a promising 1,700 kits were sold. Then disaster set in, and in 1999 only 17 kits were sold. Kremer and colleagues (2001) concluded, "Today the sales level of the N-Trak kit is insignificant." What went wrong?

1. Under practical farming conditions, the innovation had little relative advantage. It was labor-intensive and time-consuming for the farmer, and this just at the time of the crop season (July), when farmers were particularly busy. As one Iowa farmer explained, "The kit added more work to what I had to do at a time of year when I was already busy" (quoted in Kremer et al., 2001). During the decade of the 1990s, Iowa farms were getting much larger, making the problem of time especially severe. As one respondent who rejected the innovation stated, "Back when I used N-Trak, we had 135 to 150 acres of corn, now we're up to 500 to 600 acres, with additional cattle as well. The issue with the use

of side-dressing is time" (quoted in Kremer et al., 2001). A farmer with five hundred acres of corn had to take about a thousand soil samples, which was a major task.

   During the diffusion process for the N-Trak soil test in Iowa, soil testing laboratories reduced the cost of their tests and improved the turnaround time required to get results back to the farmer. This change meant that the comparative relative advantage of the N-Trak innovation was reduced. A former adopter of the N-Trak test explained, "After a couple of years of using N-Trak, I knew I didn't need a second side-dressing [in July], so really N-Trak helped me confirm what I already thought. So now every year I just take the samples and send them off to the lab. It's just less hassle" (quoted in Kremer et al., 2001).

2. Use of the late spring N-Trak soil test was incompatible with the use of anhydrous ammonia as nitrogen fertilizer, which most farmers preferred as a method of fertilizing their cornfields. This fertilizer had to be applied prior to planting the corn, rather than as a side-dressing of nitrogen fertilizer in July.

3. Observability of the N-Trak test was low, as an entire crop season was required before seeing the results. Further, there was little opportunity for neighbors to observe the results of the N-Trak testing system or to understand its possible advantages.

   The innovation *could* have been designed to overcome these difficulties, but farmers were not involved in developing the N-Trak soil test. Instead, Ph.D. scientists in soil fertility created the new idea, with the expectation that farmers would enthusiastically perceive the N-Trak test as a major advantage. Thus local knowledge was not considered important. So the innovation failed.

Relative Advantage

Relative advantage is the degree to which an innovation is perceived as being better than the idea it supersedes. The degree of relative advantage is often expressed as economic profitability, as conveying social prestige, or in other ways. The nature of the innovation determines what specific type of relative advantage (economic, social, and the like) is important to adopters, although the characteristics of the potential adopters may also affect which specific subdimensions of relative advantage are most important.

Economic Factors and Rate of Adoption

The initial cost of an innovation may affect its rate of adoption. For example, when PalmPilots began to diffuse in the United States in the late 1990s, their selling price of only a few hundred dollars seemed like a real bargain to many consumers, given the computer power and the range of applications (for storing addresses and telephone numbers, as a date book, as a notebook, etc.) of the handheld device. As one buyer stated, the cost of a Palm organizer was "a price you could hide on an expense account" (quoted in Rosen, 2000, p. 5). Some 65 percent of customers who purchased a PalmPilot said they had heard about it from another person. What they often heard was the reasonable price of the handheld device.

A new product may be based on a technological advance that results in a reduced cost of production for the product, leading to a lower selling price to consumers. An example is the video cassette recorder (VCR), which sold for more than $1,200 in 1980, when it was introduced in the United States. Several years later, thanks to technological improvements, volume production, and to increasing competition, a VCR sold for less than $50.

When the price of a new product decreases so dramatically during its diffusion process, a rapid rate of adoption is encouraged. In fact, one might even question whether an innovation like the VCR is really the same object in 2002, when it cost $50, as in 1980, when it cost twenty-four times as much. Certainly, its absolute relative advantage increased tremendously. Here we see that a characteristic of the innovation changed as its rate of adoption progressed. Thus, measuring the perceived characteristics of an innovation cross-sectionally at one point in time may provide only a partial picture of the relationship of such characteristics to an innovation's rate of adoption.

Status Aspects of Innovations

One motivation for many individuals to adopt an innovation is the desire to gain social status. Gabriel Tarde (1903) observed that status seeking was a main reason for imitating the innovation behavior of others. For certain innovations, such as new clothing fashions, the social prestige that the innovation conveys to its adopter is almost the sole benefit the adopter receives. In fact, when many other members of a system have also adopted the same fashion, an innovation such as shorter skirts or a bare midriff may lose its prestige value to earlier adopters. This gradual loss of status conferral on the part of a particular clothing innovation provides pressure for yet newer fashions. Many clothing fashions are *fads,* innovations that represent a relatively unimportant aspect of culture, which diffuse very rapidly, mainly for status reasons, and then are rapidly discontinued.

Clothing fashions are by no means the only class of innovations for which status-conferring considerations are a primary reason for adoption, and upper-class women are by no means the only members of a population who are attracted to status-giving innovations. The adoption of other highly visible innovations, such as new cars and hairstyles, is especially likely to be status-conferring. A spectacular example of the status-providing capacity of certain farm innovations is provided by the diffusion of "Harvestore" silos in the rural United States (see Chapter 8). These navy blue silos are constructed of steel and glass and prominently display the manufacturer's name. Their height dominates a farm's skyline, so they are easily visible from nearby roads. Because Harvestores are extremely expensive (from $50,000 on up, depending on the size), agricultural experts recommend that U.S. farmers buy a much cheaper type of silo for storing their corn and hay silage. But the status-conferring quality of the Harvestores appeals to many farmers. In fact, some American farmers own, and prominently display, two or three Harvestores, perhaps the rural equivalent of the three-car garage in a suburban home.

Certain individuals who adopt an innovation at a certain time are more highly motivated by status seeking than are other individuals. For example, most lower-income individuals could not care less about clothing fashions. Status motivations for adoption seem to be more important for innovators, early adopters, and early majority, and less important for the late majority and laggards. The status motivations for adopting innovations have been understudied in past diffusion research. Respondents may be reluctance to admit that they adopted a new idea for status conferral. Direct questioning of adopters about status motivations is likely to underestimate its real importance in adoption decisions, but other research methods can be used.

Overadoption

Even though every innovation is judged on economic grounds, at least to some degree, by its potential adopters, every innovation also has at least some degree of status conferral. Overadoption is one result of the prestige-conferring aspects of adopting an innovation. *Overadoption* is the adoption of an innovation by an individual when experts feel that he or she should reject. Overadoption may occur because of insufficient knowledge about the new idea on the part of the adopter, an inability to predict the innovation's consequences, and/or the status-conferring aspect of a new idea. Certain individuals have such a penchant for anything new that they occasionally appear to be suckers for change. They adopt even when they should not.

Rationality, defined as the use of the most effective means to reach a given goal, is not easily measured in the case of many innovations. The classification as to whether or not adoption is rational or not can sometimes be made by expert on the innovation under study. Through lack of knowledge or inaccurate perceptions, an individual's evaluation of an innovation may not agree with the expert's. Most individuals perceive, or at least report, their actions as rational. Our main concern is with objective rationality in the present case, rather than with subjective rationality as perceived by the individual.

The notion of overadoption implies that one role of the change agent is to prevent "too much" adoption of an innovation, as well as to try to speed up the diffusion process. Overadoption is a major problem in some fields. We mentioned previously the adoption of Harvestore silos by American farmers, an innovation not recommended by agricultural experts. In the field of medicine, expensive hospital equipment such as CAT scanners is sometimes purchased when its use cannot be justified. Many consumers adopt high-speed computers that they then use only for word processing or for other tasks for which much less computer power would be adequate. (Often, it is almost impossible for a consumer to buy a lower-power new computer.)

Overadoption sometimes happens when some attribute, or subattribute, of an innovation is perceived as so attractive to an individual that it overrules all other considerations. For example, the status-conferring aspect of a consumer innovation may be so important to an individual that adoption occurs, even though other perceptions of the new idea would lead the innovation to be rejected. The author remembers the first time that he saw a hand calculator in the 1970s. He immediately felt a strong need to own such a device and soon purchased one, even though he seldom did much calculating.

Relative Advantage and Rate of Adoption

Throughout this book we have emphasized that the diffusion of an innovation is an uncertainty reduction process. As individuals (or an organization) pass through the innovation-decision process, they are motivated to seek information in order to decrease uncertainty about the relative advantage of an innovation. Potential adopters want to know the degree to which a new idea is better than an existing practice. So relative advantage is often an important part of message content about an innovation. The exchange of such innovation information among peers lies at the heart of the diffusion process.

Diffusion scholars have found relative advantage to be one of the strongest predictors of an innovation's rate of adoption. "Relative advantage" is a ratio of the expected benefits and the costs of adoption of an innovation. Subdimensions of relative advantage include economic profitability, low initial cost, a decrease in discomfort, social prestige, a saving of time and effort, and immediacy of reward. This latter factor explains in part why preventive innovations generally have an especially slow rate of adoption, as discussed in the following section. A *preventive innovation* is a new idea that an individual adopts now in order to lower the probability of some unwanted future event. Examples are stopping smoking, using auto seat belts, adopting soil conservation practices, being screened for breast cancer, getting inoculations against a disease, flossing one's teeth, preventing HIV/AIDS, and adopting contraceptive methods. The relative advantage of preventive innovations is difficult for change agents to demonstrate to their clients, because the advantages occur at some future and unknown time, and may not happen at all. Thus the relative advantage of a preventive innovation is highly uncertain.

Past investigations of the perceived attributes of innovations almost universally report a positive relationship between relative advantage and rate of adoption. We summarize these research findings on relative advantage in Generalization 6-1: *The relative advantage of an innovation, as perceived by members of a social system, is positively related to its rate of adoption.* The respondents in many of the early studies of relative advantage were U.S. commercial farmers, and their motivation for adoption of these innovations centered on the economic aspects of relative advantage. As Frederick Fliegel and Joseph Kivlin (1966a), the deans of such research, pointed out, "Since we are dealing here with innovations having direct economic significance for the acceptor, it is not surprising that innovations perceived as most rewarding and involving least risk and uncertainty should be accepted most rapidly." A study by Kivlin and Fliegel (1966a) that included U.S. small-scale farmers (who were oriented less to profit considerations) found that a decrease in discomfort, one subdimension of relative advantage, but *not* economic profitability, was positively related to rate of adoption.

Economic aspects of relative advantage may be even less important for peasant farmers in developing nations. Fliegel and others (1968) found that Indian farmers behaved more like small-scale Pennsylvania farmers than like large-scale U.S. farmers, regarding their perceptions of innovations: "Much more than financial incentives will be necessary to obtain a widespread and rapid adoption of improved practices. . . . Unlike the Pennsylvania dairy farmers, the Punjabi [Indian] respondents apparently attach greater importance to social approval and less to financial return" (Fliegel et al., 1968).

Preventive Innovations

One type of innovation has a particularly slow rate of adoption because individuals have difficulties in perceiving its relative advantage. A *preventive innovation* is a new idea that an individual adopts now in order to lower the probability of some unwanted future event. The desired consequence is distant in time, and so the relative advantage of a preventive innovation is a delayed reward. In contrast, an incremental (that is, non-preventive) innovation provides a desired outcome in the near-term future. An example is an Iowa farmer who planted hybrid seed corn so as to obtain a 20 percent increase in crop yield. Compare this behavior with a preventive innovation such as practicing "safer sex" to avoid contracting HIV/AIDS. Adoption by an individual at present may prevent getting AIDS at some future time. But the individual might not have contracted AIDS even without adopting the idea of safer sex. So not only are the rewards of adoption delayed in time, but it is uncertain as to whether they actually are essential (Figure 6–2).

Further, the unwanted event that is avoided by adopting a preventive innovation is difficult to perceive because it is a nonevent, the absence of something that otherwise might have happened. For example, the fact that an individual has *not* contracted HIV/AIDS is invisible and unobservable, and hence difficult or impossible to comprehend (Singhal and Rogers, 2003). Family-planning experts, in calculating the effects of contraceptive campaigns, estimate the number of "births averted" by calculating the pregnancies that would have occurred if various contraceptives had not been adopted. Obviously, the concept of births averted is not very meaningful to a peasant family in a developing country that is being urged to adopt a preventive innovation such as family planning.

One of the most important preventive innovations in America, which, if completely adopted, could save 9,238 lives per year, is fastening automo-

Figure 6-2. Rate of Adoption of Incremental and Preventive Innovations

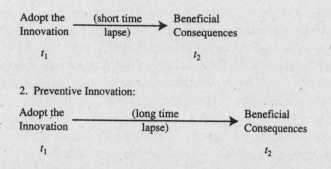

Preventive innovations are more difficult to diffuse than are incremental innovations. A *preventive innovation* is a new idea that an individual adopts in order to lower the probability of some unwanted future event.

bile seat belts. In 2002, after decades of public safety campaigns and federally mandated efforts, 73 percent of Americans buckled up. This rate of adoption is the highest yet attained in the United States, but is still the lowest among industrialized countries in the world. Of the thirty thousand people killed in auto crashes each year, 60 percent are not belted. Why do approximately one fourth of American drivers not fasten their seat belts? Some are teenagers or drunk drivers who are risk takers. Others insist that it is their individual right not to use seat belts. Nonadopters argue that using a seat belt wrinkles their clothes or that fastening their seat belt takes too much time. In a general sense, these people are saying that the cost and effort required to use seat belts is greater than the possible benefits (they feel their probability of being in an accident is negligible).

Given these complex difficulties in perceiving the relative advantage of preventive innovations, it may be understandable why individuals do not adopt. However, in recent decades several preventive health campaigns have been carried out, with successful results. One noted example is the Stanford Heart Disease Prevention Program conducted in the 1970s and 1980 in several California communities. Large numbers of individuals at risk for heart disease changed their personal lifestyles regarding (1) cigarette and alcohol use, (2) jogging, aerobics, and other forms of physical exercise, (3) nutritional habits, such as eating less red meat and using less salt, and (4) reducing stress. How was this revolution in healthy lifestyles brought about?

The Stanford Program consisted of a series of communication sub-campaigns, each aimed at a preventive innovation such as smoking-cessation or weight reduction. A *communication campaign* (1) intends to generate specific effects (2) on the part of a relatively large number of individuals (3) within a specified period of time and (4) through an organized set of communication activities (Rogers and Storey, 1988). The word "campaign" derives from the Latin word for "field," as when Julius Caesar went to the field with a military campaign. The Stanford Heart Disease Prevention Program carefully planned the use of mass media communication to recruit at-risk individuals to small group training classes, such as for aerobic exercise and smoking cessation. The health promotion messages were aimed at especially high-risk individuals in California communities, such as older men who were overweight and who had high-cholesterol diets. The Stanford campaigns used *formative research,* conducted while an activity is ongoing in order to improve its effectiveness. Health promotion messages were pretested with their intended audience so as to be sure that they were understood and had the intended effects. Campaign messages showed positive role models for healthy living, such as highly credible individuals who had lost weight by jogging and eating more nutritious foods.

The results of the Stanford Heart Disease Prevention Program showed an important reduction in the risk of heart disease in the California communities. The success of the Stanford Program encouraged numerous other health communication campaigns, aimed at drug abuse prevention and smoking prevention among schoolchildren, family planning, and HIV/AIDS prevention. The Stanford Heart Disease Prevention Program and its many intellectual spin-offs show that the adoption of preventive health innovations can be facilitated effectively but that special efforts are needed, particularly to emphasize the relative advantage of preventive innovations.

The Effects of Incentives

Many change agencies award incentives or subsidies to clients in order to speed up the rate of adoption of innovations. The main function of an incentive for adopters is to increase the degree of relative advantage of the new idea. *Incentives* are direct or indirect payments of cash or in kind that are given to an individual or a system in order to encourage behavioral change. Often the change entails the adoption of a new idea.

Incentives have been paid in order to speed up the diffusion of innovations in a variety of fields: agriculture, health, medicine, and family planning. In recent decades more research has been conducted on family planning incentives than on any other type. Incentives can take a variety of different forms:

1. *Adopter versus diffuser incentives.* Incentives may be paid either directly to an adopter or to another individual to persuade an adopter. An illustration of a diffuser incentive is a finder's fee that is paid to someone for recruiting a new adopter.
2. *Individual versus system incentives.* Payments may be made to individuals or to the system to which they belong. For example, the government family-planning agency in Indonesia paid a community incentive to villages that achieved a high rate of adoption of contraceptives. Such an incentive policy increases the relative advantage of family planning and encourages word-of-mouth communication about adoption among villagers.
3. *Positive versus negative incentives.* Most incentives are positive in that they reward a desired behavior change (such as adoption of a new idea), but it is also possible to penalize an individual by imposing an unwanted penalty or by withdrawing some desiderata for not adopting an innovation. For example, the government of Singapore decreed that the mother in any family with a third (or further) child would not be eligible to receive maternity leave and that the parents would have to pay all hospital and delivery costs (which are otherwise free to all citizens). Government-owned apartments in Singapore are quite small, so that a three-child family is very crowded.
4. *Monetary versus nonmonetary incentives.* While incentives are often financial payments, they may also take the form of some commodity or object that is desired by the recipient.
5. *Immediate versus delayed incentives.* Most incentives are paid at the time of adoption, but others can be awarded only at a later time (such as when the adoption of contraceptives has an effect on fertility).

Any combination of these five types of incentive policies can be awarded in a given situation, depending on which particular combination of incentives has the desired influence on the diffusion and adoption of innovations. Offering incentives is one diffusion strategy that affects the perceived attributes of innovations, especially relative advantage, and thus an innovation's rate of adoption. Some incentive policies are designed only to encourage trial of a new idea. An illustration is the free samples of a new product that many commercial companies offer to their customers. The strategy here is that by facilitating trial use, full-scale adoption usually follows (if the innovation possesses a potential relative advantage that can be perceived by the receiver).

Other incentive policies are designed only to secure adoption of a new idea by the earlier adopters. Once a level of, say, 20 percent adoption is reached in a social system, the economic incentive is discontinued. For example, in the 1970s the U.S. government and several state governments offered tax rebates for the adoption of residential solar heating. The cost of such incentives became too large to be affordable, and the incentive payments were halted once a level of 5 or 10 percent adoption was reached. These pump-priming incentives were utilized to launch the diffusion process in the expectation that further diffusion would then become a self-generating process.

On the basis of research and experience with family planning innovations, Rogers (1973) drew the following conclusions:

1. *Incentives increase the rate of adoption of an innovation.* Adopter incentives increase relative advantage, and diffuser incentives increase the observability with which an innovation is perceived. Further, an adopter incentive can act as a *cue-to-action* (an event occurring at a point in time that crystallizes an individual's favorable attitude into overt behavior change) in triggering the adoption of an innovation (see Chapter 5).

2. *Adopter incentives lead to adoption of an innovation by individuals different from those who would otherwise adopt.* Innovators and early adopters usually have higher socioeconomic status and other characteristics that set them off from later adopters (see Chapter 7). When a relatively large adopter incentive is paid to family-planning adopters, for example, individuals of the *lowest* socioeconomic status adopt. Paying an adopter incentive may change the characteristics of the earlier adopters of an innovation. Such a change has important implications for socioeconomic equality in the diffusion process.

3. *Although incentives increase the quantity of adopters of an innovation, the quality of such adoption decisions may be relatively low, thus limiting the intended consequences of adoption.* If individuals adopt an innovation partly in order to obtain an incentive,

there is relatively less motivation to continue using the innovation (if it can be discontinued), and so the innovation's sustainability may be lessened.

Paying incentives often involves serious ethical issues, which deserve to be explored in future studies. Also, the effectiveness of incentive policies can be improved by conducting empirical studies to evaluate the effects of incentives on the rate of adoption, continuation, and consequences of innovations.

Mandates for Adoption

Providing incentives is one means through which a higher level of social organization, such as a government, community, or a commercial company, can exert its influence on the behavior of individual members of the system. Certain types of behavior change may be desired or demanded by a government, for example, but not by individual citizens. For instance, a national government may wish to slow its rate of population growth so that it can better provide schools and jobs for the next generation. But individual parents may wish to have large-size families in order to carry on the family name, to obtain cheap labor, or for purposes of security in old age. Under these conditions, a national government must often provide strong incentives to parents to persuade them to have fewer children (as occurred in Singapore). Where there is strong public resistance to voluntary incentives, a government may mandate adoption of family-planning innovations or the desired consequences of such adoption (a small family).

Since the early 1980s, in desperation, the government of the People's Republic of China has mandated the one-child family. China has the largest national population in the world, more than 1.3 billion people. During the 1970s, the Chinese government began to encourage Chinese parents to adopt contraceptives and have only two children each. This policy was inadequate to stem the rate of population increase. So the one-child ideal was strongly encouraged by the government. Factory work groups, urban neighborhoods, and rural villages began the "group planning of births." Group discussions were held each year to decide which parents could have their one child. After the birth of the first child, a couple was strongly encouraged to be sterilized. If a couple did not follow the group plan or if a second pregnancy occurred, the mother faced group pressure to have an abortion. Such draconian mandates for adoption of the one-child family norm led to a sharp decrease in the population growth rate of China, but also to other, unwanted behavior (see Chapter 3).

Environmental behavior may also involve a conflict between what is best for the system, say a city or a nation, and what an individual would prefer to do. For example, smog and traffic congestion have become worse each year in many large cities such as Los Angeles. The cost of building additional freeways is prohibitive, and the existing thorough-fares have become so clogged with vehicles that they have increasingly become "parking lots," with stop-and-go traffic moving at a snail's pace. Each year the number of vehicles in southern California increased by 3 percent. Something had to be done. In the 1990s a new city regulation called Article XV went into effect, requiring that every organization employing 100 or more people had to increase the average number of employees coming to work in each vehicle over a five-year period until an average of 1.5 was reached. A variety of positive and negative incentives were utilized to reach this goal: higher charges for employee parking, free bus passes, the organization of ride pools, and the provision of free commuter van service. If an employer organization did not make year-by-year progress toward the goal of 1.5 employees per vehicle, it faced stiff fines under Article XV. The main purpose of this regulation was to cause a major reduction in commuter traffic and a corresponding improvement in air quality through less smog.

Similarly, the California and Arizona mandates for nonpolluting vehicles, such as electric cars, were requirements (see Chapter 2). Mandates for adoption are a mechanism through which the system exerts pressure on an individual to recognize the relative advantage of an innovation, particularly a preventive innovation.

Compatibility

Compatibility is the degree to which an innovation is perceived as consistent with the existing values, past experiences, and needs of potential adopters. An idea that is more compatible is less uncertain to the potential adopter and fits more closely with the individual's situation. Such compatibility helps the individual give meaning to the new idea so that it is regarded as more familiar. An innovation can be compatible or incompatible with (1) sociocultural values and beliefs, (2) previously introduced ideas, and/or (3) client needs for the innovation.

Compatibility with Values and Beliefs

An innovation's incompatibility with cultural values can block its adoption. Chapter 1 showed how the residents of the Peruvian village of Los Molinos perceived water boiling as incompatible with their culturally defined hot-cold classification. American farmers place a strong value on increasing farm production. Soil conservation innovations (such as contour farming) are perceived as conflicting with this production value and have generally been adopted very slowly.

In modern urban India there is a strong norm against eating food with the left hand, which is believed to be unclean. This habit began centuries ago, when Indian villagers used their left hand for certain functions associated with defecation. At that time there were inadequate washing and sanitary facilities, and the left-hand-as-unclean complex was functional. But today it is easy for urban, middle-class Indians to wash their hands before meals. Nevertheless, the unclean-hand belief persists as a strongly held cultural element in urban India. How would you like to be the change agent responsible for persuading 1 billion Indians to eat with their left hand? Many change agents face equally difficult assignments in promoting innovations that run counter to strongly held cultural values.

One important agricultural innovation was the so-called "miracle" varieties of rice bred at the International Rice Research Institute (IRRI) in the Philippines. These improved rice varieties, when accompanied by heavy applications of chemical fertilizers, the use of pesticides, thicker planting, and other management practices, often *tripled* a farmer's rice yields. The IRRI miracle rice varieties spread rapidly throughout Asia, causing the so-called Green Revolution. But the agronomists and plant breeders at IRRI had bred only the miracle rice varieties for high yields and resistance to pests. No attention had been given to the taste of the rice. The author's diffusion studies of miracle rice in south India found that the new varieties did not taste "right" to the villagers who adopted the new seed. They sold the harvest from the IRRI rice varieties in the marketplace, while continuing to plant some of the traditional rice seed for their family's consumption. The author informed the rice breeders at IRRI about the taste incompatibility problem, but in the 1960s they scoffed at this recommendation, saying "We triple rice yields. People will soon learn to like the taste of our IRRI rice!"

Forty years later, south Indian farmers, like their counterparts in many other Asian nations, were still planting small amounts of traditional rice varieties for their own consumption while growing the IRRI rice for sale. The "miracle rice" sells for a price about 20 percent lower than the local varieties. In recent years, the International Rice Research Institute finally began breeding its new rice varieties for consumer taste, as well as high yield.

Other examples of the cultural incompatibility of an innovation sometimes occur when an idea is designed for use in one culture but then spreads to a different culture with different cultural values. An illustration is a bar-code reader that IBM designed in the 1970s for checkout counters in U.S. supermarkets. This equipment could sum a series of product prices to a six-digit total, for example, $9,999.99. This total was more than adequate at the time, when the food bill for most customers was less than $100. Unfortunately, designers of the bar-code readers did not think globally. In Italy, which was experiencing an exorbitant rate of inflation, 10,000 lire would hardly buy a loaf of bread. Similarly, Lotus 1–2–3, the popular computer spreadsheet program, encountered incompatibility problems in India, where lakhs (10,000) and crores (10,000,000) are used instead of thousands, millions, and billions and where the meanings of a comma and a period (a decimal point) are reversed, so that $9,999.99 is written $9.999,99.

A particularly strongly held, and extremely sensitive, cultural belief in most of Africa, and in parts of the Middle East and Asia, is female clitoridectomy. The World Health Organization estimates that 130 million women and girls have been subjected to clitoridectomy, often as part of a coming-of-age ceremony to celebrate a girl's transition to womanhood. The clitoris is usually removed by village midwives or barbers with primitive instruments under unsanitary conditions. Medical and health experts object to clitoridectomy because of the resulting infection rates. Feminists object because they say the practice is an expression of patriarchal culture to control women's bodies, behaviors, and lives. Defenders of clitoridectomy claim that the practice helps ensure chastity and increases a girl's marriage potential. Many efforts are under way to halt the practice of clitoridectomy in various countries, but resistance is strong.

Some understanding of why it is so difficult to change this cultural practice is provided by a study in a poor, rural area of northern Ghana (Mensch et al., 1999). Traditionally, if a girl was found not to be a virgin at the time of clitoridectomy, she was regarded with great shame by members of her community. Thus clitoridectomy strongly discouraged adolescent sexual intercourse. Following the ceremony, the age cohort of newly circumcised girls was instructed by village elders in how to act like women. They were then considered eligible for marriage. So this coming-of-age ritual marked a clear transition between being a girl and being a woman.

In 1994, the Ghanaian government outlawed female circumcision, and a diffusion campaign was mounted to encourage discontinuance of clitoridectomy. Public pledges were made by the excisors when they relinquished their knives. Alternative ceremonies to mark the coming-of-age (which did not include cutting) were encouraged. The traditional belief was difficult to change, but in 1998 only one fourth of the females aged fifteen to nineteen in the area of Ghana studied by Mensch and others (1999) had undergone clitoridectomy. This change, accompanied by increasing female education, growing freedom from parental control, and development of a money economy, led to an increase in adolescent childbirths to unmarried mothers, abortion, and maternal mortality in first births (especially to young mothers). So the end of a tradition led to a new set of social problems.

Compatibility with Previously Introduced Ideas

An innovation may be compatible not only with deeply embedded cultural values but also with previously adopted ideas. Compatibility of an innovation with a preceding idea can either speed up or retard its rate of adoption. Old ideas are the main mental tools that individuals utilize to assess new ideas and give them meaning. Individuals cannot deal with an innovation except on the basis of the familiar. Previous practice provides a standard against which an innovation can be interpreted, thus decreasing its uncertainty.

Examples of the use of past experience to judge new ideas come from an early diffusion study in a Colombian peasant community (Fals Borda, 1960). At first, farmers applied chemical fertilizers on top of their potato seed (as they had done with cattle manure), thereby damaging the seed and causing a lower yield. Other peasants excessively sprayed their potatoes with insecticides, transferring to the new idea their old methods of watering their plants. Given their lack of understanding of how chemical fertilizer and insecticides affected potato yields, the Colombian farmers gave meaning to these innovations in terms with which they were familiar.

Another example of the importance of compatibility comes from a study by Brandner and Straus (1959). They found that hybrid sorghum was planted on 28 percent of the sorghum acreage in northeastern Kansas the first year the new seed was available, despite the fact that this innovation was not yet recommended by the Kansas Agricultural Experiment Station or the Extension Service. This rapid adoption resulted from the compatibility of hybrid sorghum with hybrid corn, an innovation previously adopted. However, in western Kansas, where climatic conditions were too dry for corn growing, hybrid sorghum was adopted slowly.

In these cases, the perceived compatibility of the new idea with previous experience led the adopters to utilize the innovations incorrectly. Here, compatibility led to adoption of a new idea, but also to incorrect use of the innovation. Compatibility with a previously introduced idea can cause overadoption or misadoption. An illustration comes from the introduction of tractors in the Punjab, a prosperous farming area in northern India (Carter, 1994). Tractors gave social prestige to the owner, much as had the bullocks that the tractor replaced as a means of farm power and as transportation to market towns. Punjabi farmers, however, did not carry out the basic maintenance of their tractors, such as cleaning the air filters and replacing the oil filter. As a result, a new tractor typically broke down after a year or two of use, with the farmer often failing to repair it. A foreign consultant was invited to investigate the problem of tractor sustainability. The consultant made up a tractor maintenance chart and had it translated into Punjabi. The chart was printed in five colors, and distributed by agricultural extension workers to all farmers who had tractors. Still the tractors broke down due to lack of proper maintenance.

Then a salesman who had previously sold blankets to farmers for covering their bullocks in cold weather came to the Punjab. Within a few days tractors were observed with a blanket covering the hood. The foreign expert warned farmers that the blanket could cause the tractor engine to overheat. Nevertheless, within ten days, virtually every tractor had a blanket covering its hood. To Punjabi farmers, it made sense to keep their source of farm power warm during winter weather. But cleaning the air filters and the oil filter on their tractor was not compatible with their previous experience with caring for their bullocks. In this case, past experience had negative consequences.

Hawley (1946) sought to determine why the Roman Catholic religion, promoted by proselytizing Spanish priests, was readily accepted by eastern Pueblo Indians in Arizona and New Mexico, whereas the western Pueblos, "after a brief taste of Catholicism, rejected it forcefully, killed the priests, burned the missions, and even annihilated the village of Awatobi when its inhabitants showed a tendency to accept the acculturation so ardently proffered." Hawley concluded that the eastern Pueblos, whose family structure was heavily patrilineal and father-oriented, were attracted by the new religion, in which the deity was a male figure. Catholicism, however, was incompatible with the mother-centered beliefs of the western Pueblos. Perhaps if the change agents had been able to emphasize the female aspects of Catholicism (such as the Virgin Mary), they would have achieved greater success among the western Pueblo tribes.

The rate of adoption of a new idea is affected by the old idea that it supersedes. Obviously, however, if a new idea were completely congruent with existing practice, there would be no innovation, at least in the minds of the potential adopters. In other words, the more compatible an innovation is, the less of a change in behavior it represents. How useful, then, is the introduction of a very highly compatible innovation? Quite useful, perhaps, if the compatible innovation is seen as the first step in a cluster of innovations that are to be introduced sequentially. The compatible innovation can pave the way for later, less compatible innovations.

An interesting example of how *low* compatibility of an innovation can be related to a rapid rate of adoption comes from an investigation of the diffusion of art. Lievrouw and Pope (1994) investigated the popularity of new art and new artists. Such aesthetic innovations seem to display some unique qualities regarding their diffusion. For example, while most innovations that are higher in perceived compatibility have a more rapid rate of adoption, the reverse may be true for artworks. If aesthetic innovations are too closely derivative of older works, they are unlikely to meet much critical or economic success. Artworks must be somewhat radical if they are to diffuse rapidly.

A negative experience with one innovation can damn the adoption of future innovations. Such innovation negativism (Arensberg and Niehoff, 1964) can be an undesirable aspect of compatibility. *Innovation negativism* is the degree to which an innovation's failure conditions a potential adopter to reject future innovations. When one idea fails, potential adopters are conditioned to view all future innovations with apprehension. For this reason, change agents should begin their efforts with an innovation that has a high degree of relative advantage, so that they can then build on this initial success with innovations that are compatible with the pioneering new idea. The national family-planning program in India began with promotion of the IUD, a method that was widely discontinued in the 1960s (Rogers, 1973). Family planning in north India has never been able to recover from this disastrous failure.

Compatibility with Needs

One indication of the compatibility of an innovation is the degree to which it meets a felt need. Change agents seek to determine the needs of their clients and then to recommend innovations that fulfill these needs. Determining felt needs is not a simple matter, however. Change agents must have a high degree of empathy and rapport with their clients in order to assess their needs accurately. Informal probing in interpersonal contacts with individual clients, client advisory committees to change agencies, and surveys of clients are sometimes used to determine needs for innovations.

Potential adopters may not recognize that they have a need for an innovation until they become aware of the new idea or its consequences. Change agents may seek to generate needs among their clients, but this must be done carefully or else the felt needs upon which a diffusion campaign is based may be a reflection only of the change agent's needs, rather than those of clients. Thus one dimension of compatibility is the degree to which an innovation is perceived as meeting the needs of the client system. When felt needs are met, a faster rate of adoption usually occurs.

Photovoltaics on a Million Roofs

Photovoltaic-generated electrical power has been strongly encouraged by the U.S. government in recent years, with a recent U.S. president unveiling a Million Roofs Initiative, seeking to populate one million rooftops across the nation with solar power by 2010. Clearly, if photovoltaics (PVs) are to play an important role in freeing America from dependence on Middle Eastern oil imports, utility companies must promote their diffusion. However, a national survey of these companies by Kaplan (1999) found that only 2.5 percent had adopted photovoltaic technology, even though most power company managers possessed a high level of technical knowledge about PVs. One reason for this KAP-gap is that photovoltaics are a misfit: "PVs are decentralized, modular, and easily disconnected from the utility grid" (Kaplan, 1999, p. 177). Power company managers *should* adopt photovoltaics, but they don't. These potential adopters have knowledge, but not experience, with this disruptive technology ("disruptive" in the sense that it is radically different from the usual operations of power companies). The more radical and disruptive an innovation and the less its compatibility with existing practice, the slower its rate of adoption (Walsh and Linton, 2000; Bower and Christensen, 1995).

Most individuals do not evaluate an innovation solely or perhaps at all on the basis of its performance as judged by scientific research. Rather, they decide whether or not to adopt on the basis of the subjective evaluations of the innovations conveyed to them by others like themselves (peers). Fortunately, a few power utilities have pioneered in adopting photovoltaic technology themselves or in promoting it for adoption by their customers. The Gainesville, Florida, power company raised funding by voluntary contributions from its customers and purchased a large PV system. The Sacramento city utility assists households to install photovoltaic panels on their rooftops. Many of the Hopi people in Arizona have installed PVs. A small trailer, provided by the Hopi Foundation, is equipped with photovoltaic equipment and is parked at the home of a potential adopter for a week to encourage adoption through increasing the trialability of PVs. Adoption of PVs is being pioneered in certain bright spots in the United States. Perhaps eventually these experiences will spread to other power utility companies and their customers (Kaplan, 1999), and PV adoption will become widespread.

The Daughter-in-Law Who Doesn't Speak*

"Thump-thump-thump" is the usual sound heard in an African village as women pound grains and nuts with heavy wooden pestles. But recently this sound changed to "chug-chug-chug" in one West African village, Sanankoroni, in Mali. A woman brings a sack of peanuts into a small mud-brick shed that houses a diesel engine and a variety of contraptions that it powers. She pours her load into a funnel that leads to a grinder and blender, pays 25 cents, and, ten minutes later, scoops thick peanut butter into a dozen jars. The woman says that previously it would have taken her all day to pound and grind the sack of peanuts. Now she can sell the jars of peanut butter in the village market and then take a nap.

---

*This case illustration is based on Thurow (2002).

The United Nations Development Programme (UNDP) calls this Rube Goldberg machine a "multifunctional platform." The women of Sanankoroni, who own and operate the durable, uncomplaining machine, refer to it as "The Daughter-in-Law Who Doesn't Speak." It was invented ten years ago by a UNDP development worker in Mali to ease the domestic labor of African women. The Daughter-in-Law Who Doesn't Speak centers on a ten-horse-power diesel motor, connected by rubber belts to various tools: a rice husker, a wood saw, a water pump, a grinder/blender, and a generator used to recharge batteries. This industrial-size Cuisinart cost about $4,000, of which the Sanankoroni Women's association raised half, and the United Nations and other donor agencies contributed the rest. A large blackboard on the wall of the mud-brick building that houses the machine lists that day's earnings of $12. One third of this amount goes to pay the several women who operate The Daughter-in-Law Who Doesn't Speak and the maintenance man hired by the Women's Association. Other expenditures are for diesel fuel and repairs. The first nine months of operation yielded $380 for the association, a sizeable sum by the standards of Mali, where the per capita annual income is only $300.

Some three hundred Malian villages now have their own diesel-powered platforms, each owned by a women's association. One effect of the innovation has been to free women from the time-consuming work of pounding grain and nuts. A forty-five-kilogram sack of corn that required three days of pounding is now ground in fifteen minutes. Girls who previously had to stay home to do domestic work can now go to school. Mothers now have free time to enroll in literacy classes or start a small business. The men of Sanankoroni approve of the women's progress. One said, "Our wives aren't so tired anymore. And their hands are smoother. We like that."

The Daughter-in-Law Who Doesn't Speak empowers village women, unleashing their entrepreneurial zeal. The Sanankoroni Women's Association plans to use its savings to branch out into other businesses, such as dyeing clothing and making soap. A neighboring village connected its diesel power source to a large generator, which provides electricity for 1,580 electric lights.

The new machine is too expensive for any single person in the village to afford it, but the Sanankoroni Women's Association, once formed, served to foster collective efficacy among the village women. The notion of collaborative associations of women to accomplish some action that they could not achieve individually is compatible with West African village values and with past experiences. So the innovation of The Daughter-in-Law Who Doesn't Speak was highly compatible with West African village life, as well as having considerable relative advantage.

Compatibility and Rate of Adoption

Generalization 6-2: *The compatibility of an innovation, as perceived by members of a social system, is positively related to its rate of adoption.* Past diffusion research suggests that compatibility may be somewhat less important in predicting rate of adoption than is relative advantage. In certain diffusion studies, reviewed previously in this chapter, relative advantage and compatibility were found not to be empirically distinct, although they are conceptually distinct.

Any new idea is evaluated in comparison to existing practice. Thus compatibility is, not surprisingly, related to the rate of adoption of an innovation.

Technology Clusters

Innovations often are not viewed singularly by individuals. Instead, they may be perceived as an interrelated bundle of new ideas. The adoption of one new idea may trigger the adoption of others. A *technology cluster* consists of one or more distinguishable elements of technology that are perceived as being interrelated. The boundaries around any given innovation are often not clear cut or distinct. In the minds of potential adopters, one innovation may be perceived as closely related to another new idea. A change agency may find it useful to promote a cluster or package of innovations to clients, rather than to treat each new idea separately.

For instance, in India and in other Asian nations, a package of agricultural innovations, including the IRRI rice varieties, chemical fertilizers, and other agricultural chemicals, was recommended *in toto* to farmers. Villagers adopted the package more rapidly than they would have adopted if each of the innovations had been diffused independently. More important, by adopting all at once, farmers achieved the total yield effects of all the innovations, plus the synergistic effects of each new idea on the others. The result was often a tripling of rice yields and the virtual end of food grain shortages in Asia.

Unfortunately, the effects of using a package approach have seldom been investigated in diffusion research, although it makes sense intuitively. Naturally, the packaging should be based on the user's *perceptions* of the compatibility of the interrelated innovations, but this has seldom been done.

One of the few investigations of a complex of new ideas is Silverman and Bailey's (1961) analysis of the adoption of three corn-growing innovations by 107 Mississippi farmers. The three ideas (chemical fertilizer, hybrid seed, and thicker planting) were functionally interrelated in such a way that adoption of the last innovation without concurrent use of the other two ideas actually resulted in *lower* corn yields than if none of the three new ideas was used. Most farmers adopted either all three of the corn-growing ideas or none of them, but 8 percent used unsuccessful combinations. Silverman and Bailey suggested the need for agricultural change agents to show farmers the interrelationships among the three corn-growing innovations.

Some merchandisers offer tie-ins, which recognize the compatibility of several new products. A new clothes washer may be offered to housewives in a package deal along with a dryer, for example. Some marketing schemes "hook on" an unwanted product to a compatible innovation that possesses a high degree of relative advantage.

LaRose and Atkin (1992) investigated the degree of clustering among eighteen consumer telecommunications innovations by a national sample of 1,400 U.S. adults. They found narrow, specific clusters of these innovations, rather than a general cluster of communication technology composed of all 18 new ideas representing a high-tech lifestyle. For example, using ATMs and toll-free telephone numbers and having a telephone credit card were interrelated in a cluster, as were the adoption of speaker phones, automatic dialers, and using 900 (polling) numbers. Using e-mail and having a personal computer constituted yet another cluster. Owning a VCR was separate from the other innovation clusters.

Future research needs to analyze complexes of innovations, to study new ideas in an evolutionary sequence, and to determine the degree of compatibility perceived by individuals among interrelated ideas. Such study would provide a sounder basis for assembling innovations in easier-to-adopt packages.

Naming an Innovation

The name given to an innovation often affects its perceived compatibility, and therefore its rate of adoption. Inadequate attention has been paid to what innovations are called by potential adopters, and as a result many serious mistakes have been made. For instance, a major U.S. soap company introduced a product called "Cue" into French-speaking nations, where the word has an obscene connotation. Another well-known example is a certain model of U.S. automobile, the Nova, which means "no-go" *(no va)* in Spanish. Such egregious errors have shown commercial companies the importance of market research to pretest the name for a new product prior to its release. Public change agencies generally have not realized the importance of what an innovation is called, at least until social marketing began to gain attention in recent years (see Chapter 2).

The perception of an innovation is colored by the word symbols used for it. The selection of an innovation's name is a delicate and important matter. Words are the thought units that structure perceptions. And of course it is the potential adopter's perceptions of an innovation's name that affects its rate of adoption. Sometimes a medical, chemical, or technical name is used for an innovation during its research and development stage in the innovation-development process. Unfortunately, such names are not very meaningful to potential adopters, unless they are physicians, chemists, or technicians. Examples are "2,4-D weed spray," "IR-20 rice variety," "human immunodeficiency virus," and "intrauterine device," terms that were often confusing and misunderstood by potential adopters. In comparison, notice how the women in the Mali village were encouraged to call their innovation "The Daughter-in-Law Who Doesn't Speak," rather than the technical name used by the change agency. A new intrauterine device, the "Copper-T," was introduced in South Korea some years ago without careful consideration of an appropriate Korean name. The letter "T" does not exist in the Korean alphabet, and copper is considered a very base metal with a very unfavorable connotation. A worse name could hardly have been chosen (Harding et al., 1973).

We recommend a receiver-oriented, empirical approach to naming an innovation, so that the word symbol for a new idea has the desired meaning for the intended audience. Too often in the past, the importance of what an innovation is called has been ignored.

Positioning an Innovation

A basic assumption of the positioning strategy, based on market research, formative evaluation, and on social marketing, is that an individual will behave toward a new idea in a similar manner to the way the individual behaves toward other ideas that are perceived as similar to the new idea. For instance, consider a set of existing ideas, A, B, and C.

If a new idea, X, is introduced to the audience for these ideas, and if they perceive X as similar to B but unlike A and C, the consumers who purchased B will be as likely to buy X as B. If other factors (such as price and accessability) are equal, X should attain about one half of the former B consumers, but the introduction of X should not affect the sale of ideas A and C. Further, if we can learn why consumers perceive B and X as similar but as different from A and C, X can be positioned (through its name, color, packaging, taste, and the like) so as to maximize its distance from A, B, and C in the minds of the consumers and thus gain a unique niche for this new idea. Obviously, the positioning of an innovation rests on accurately measuring its compatibility with previous ideas.

Positioning research can help identify the ideal niche for an innovation relative to perceptions of existing ideas in the same category. This ideal niche is determined by the new idea's perceived position relative (1) to previous ideas and (2) to the characteristics of the new idea that make it similar to, and different from, existing ideas. Tetracycline, the new antibiotic drug whose diffusion among medical doctors was studied by Coleman and others (1996), was similar to two previously introduced antibiotics that it partially replaced but superior to them in its lack of unpleasant side effects. The positioning approach views an innovation's perceived characteristics (at least some of them) as dynamic and changeable. Positioning research puts the diffusion researcher in the role of designer (or at least a codesigner) of the innovation. An example is provided by research on the Copper-T in Korea.

As mentioned previously, Harding and others (1973) used positioning methods to introduce the Copper-T, then a new intrauterine contraceptive device, in Korea. First, they asked a small sample of potential adopters to identify twenty-nine perceived attributes of eighteen contraceptive methods in a relatively open-ended, unstructured approach. Then a different sample of Korean respondents was asked to rate each of the eighteen family-planning methods (including the Copper-T, the only new method) on these twenty-nine attributes (which included numerous subdimensions of the five main attributes of innovations discussed in this chapter). The results led to recommendations about which attributes of the Copper-T to stress in its diffusion campaign in order to maximize its rate of adoption. For instance, Harding and others (1973) recommended stressing the Copper-T's long lifetime, its reliability in preventing unwanted pregnancies, its lack of interference with sexual intercourse, and its newness. The researchers also recommended a change in the physical nature of the innovation: "Certain features of the Copper-T, such as the string [a plastic thread that can be used to remove the intrauterine device], perhaps should be altered since the string is associated with causing bacteria to enter the womb and with causing an inflammation of the womb" (Harding et al., 1973, p. 11).

Acceptability Research

A special kind of positioning research, acceptability research, can be conducted to guide R&D activities on what kind of innovations to create. *Acceptability research* is defined as investigation of the perceived attributes of an ideal innovation in order to guide R&D so as to create such an innovation. If innovations of type X will not be accepted by potential adopters but innovations of type Y will be accepted, obviously R&D workers should direct their efforts toward developing type Y innovations.

An example of acceptability research was provided in the 1970s by the World Health Organization's (WHO) research program on contraceptives for use in developing nations. Most past contraceptive methods at that time faced difficult problems of acceptability. So WHO conducted a special type of diffusion studies to determine what types of contraceptives would be most acceptable. These recommendations gave directions to WHO biomedical researchers who sought to create a new contraceptive with an "ideal" set of attributes for its acceptability.

Acceptability studies of contraceptive behavior showed that men and women in developing nations were very averse to using a family-planning method that required manipulation of the human genitals. Unfortunately, the main contraceptives promoted by government family-planning programs in developing nations required genital manipulation: the IUD (intrauterine device), condoms, and the diaphragm, for instance. The incompatibility of these contraceptive methods with aversion to genital handling was one reason why their rate of adoption was discouraging. WHO biomedical research was directed, in part, toward developing contraceptives that did not require genital handling (Rogers and Pareek, 1982). Examples include an injectable contraceptive such as Depo-Provera and an implant such as Norplant.

A major health problem in developing nations today is the acquired immunodeficiency syndrome (AIDS) epidemic. Since the first AIDS cases were detected in the United States in 1981 among gay men, the human immunodeficiency virus (HIV) spread to 40 million people worldwide, and another 20 million have died. Within a few years after contracting HIV, the typical individual is diagnosed with the symptoms of AIDS and, a few years later, dies. Intravenous drug users, commercial sex workers, truck drivers, and rural-to-urban migrants are key high-risk groups during the early stages of the epidemic in most nations. Then, if the epidemic is unchecked, it breaks out of these special populations into the general population as husbands infect wives and mothers infect their babies at birth (Singhal and Rogers, 2003).

How can the HIV/AIDS epidemic be contained? Prevention campaigns urge individuals to have "safer sex," which means using a condom and being monogamous or celibate. But condoms are often perceived as incompatible with sexual pleasure, messy, and requiring genital handling. So even in nations in which the AIDS epidemic is widespread, health officials have been able to convince only 10 percent or so of sexually active individuals to adopt safer sex practices (Singhal and Rogers, 2003). Until more effective technologies of AIDS prevention or cure are found through biomedical research, the only way to combat the AIDS epidemic is through more effective prevention campaigns to diffuse condom use. Is it possible to position condoms so that they are perceived as relatively more acceptable? Perhaps acceptability research could help find the answer.

Indigenous Knowledge Systems

The basic notion of the compatibility attribute is that a new idea is perceived in relationship to existing practices that are already familiar to the individual. Change agents and others who introduce an innovation often commit an "empty vessels fallacy" by assuming that potential adopters are blank slates who lack any relevant experience with which to associate the new idea. The empty vessels fallacy denies that compatibility is important. In the past decade the empty vessels fallacy has been overcome in agriculture, health, and family planning by analysis of indigenous knowledge systems. Scholars, often anthropologists, probe the traditional experiences of individuals in developing nations in order to understand how these indigenous knowledge systems can serve as a mental bridge when introducing innovations. For example, Dr. Juan Flavier, a health expert in the rural Philippines, found that villagers understood that when chicken hens ate the seeds of the iping-iping tree, they stopped laying eggs. Flavier explained to villagers that oral contraceptive pills for humans acted in a similar way to the iping-iping seeds. Thus he built on the compatibility of the new idea with existing knowledge.

Steve Lansing, an anthropologist at the University of Arizona, studied the irrigation system of the island of Bali in Indonesia (Lansing, 1991). As explained in Chapter 2, he found that the seasonal flow of water among the rice fields was controlled by a series of Hindu water temples and their priests. This indigenous system of irrigation control fallowed a large area of several square miles, so that rice pests would die. Then the water would be released for planting the next crop of rice. When Indonesian agricultural extension workers introduced the IRRI miracle rice varieties, they ignored the indigenous irrigation system. What did religion have to do with rice growing? they asked. The miracle rice had a shorter growing session than the existing rice varieties on Bali and hence was incompatible with the Hindu priests' irrigation schedule. The eventual result was lower, instead of higher, yields from the new rice, which was quickly discontinued by Balinese farmers (Bardini, 1994). This problem could have been avoided, Lansing (1991) pointed out, if the extension workers had not ignored the indigenous knowledge system for rice irrigation.

Why are indigenous knowledge systems often ignored or denigrated by change agents who introduce innovations? A strong belief in the relative advantage of a new idea often leads technocrats to assume that existing practices are so inferior that they can be completely dismissed. This superior attitude often leads to the empty vessels fallacy and to the introduction of an innovation that is perceived as incompatible with the ideas that it seeks to replace.

Change agents frequently overlook the fact that every innovation is evaluated by clients in terms of their prior experience with something similar. The innovation may be "new wine," but it is poured into "old bottles" (the clients' existing perceptions). The solution to the empty vessels fallacy is for a change agent to understand clients' prior experiences with the practice that the innovation will replace. An effective change agent must comprehend clients' indigenous knowledge systems.

A great deal of useful knowledge is often contained in indigenous knowledge systems. For example, Squanto and other Native Americans taught the Pilgrims in colonial Massachusetts to fertilize their corn by dropping a small fish into the ground along with each seed kernel when planting corn. Similarly, a large number of "modern" drugs come from traditional herbal medications: morphine, quinine, and codeine, for example. The active ingredient in oral contraceptive pills was originally obtained from a tropical yam that grew in the mountains of Mexico. Many HIV-positive individuals in developing countries are turning to the use of traditional herbs that may have anti-retroviral qualities (Singhal and Rogers, 2003). Since 1996, anti-retroviral drugs have been available that can lower the viral load in the body of an HIV-positive individual and thus prolong life. Unfortunately, these drugs are relatively expensive, costing much more than the typical individual in a developing country (where 95 percent of the 40 million HIV-positive people live today) can afford.

Indigenous knowledge systems are represented by a cadre of practitioners of the traditional knowledge system. The practitioner specialists of indigenous knowledge systems, such as the Hindu priests in Bali, traditional birth attendants (midwives) in many nations, and *curanderos* of Latin America are considered "quacks" by their more modern counterparts. A majority of babies in Third World countries today are delivered by traditional midwives, who are usually older, uneducated, low-income women who were taught to deliver babies by their mother or another older relative. These traditional midwives in Latin America, Africa, and Asia are perceived as highly credible by the rural and urban poor women who have the highest fertility rates. Thus, national family-planning programs in several countries have provided traditional midwives with special training courses on antiseptic methods of infant delivery, in which each trainee is given a delivery kit containing disinfectant, bandages, etc. Trained traditional midwives may be paid a small incentive for each family planning adopter they recruit and are urged to refer difficult birth cases to a government health clinic.

However, most professional change agents regard traditional practitioners as "quacks" and either ignore them or attack them. This antagonism is an outcropping of the empty vessels fallacy. In many nations, in addition to traditional birth attendants, every peasant village includes a traditional veterinarian, a masseuse, and a traditional medical doctor. *Curanderos* (traditional practitioners of mental health) are widely found throughout Latin America and the American Southwest. For a change agent to ignore these traditional practitioners and the indigenous knowledge systems they represent is to court disaster when introducing innovations. For example, when traditional midwives were ignored or attacked by government family-planning programs, the traditional birth attendants planted rumors about the contraceptive methods that were being introduced by the national family-planning program, and a high rate of discontinuance resulted (Rogers, 1973). In India, *dais* (traditional midwives) spread a rumor that the husband of a wife who had adopted an IUD could not become disengaged. The rate of adoption of

IUDs plateaued, and then plummeted as discontinuance became widespread.

In recent years, the government of Indonesia has trained 54,000 young women as para-professional health workers (*bidans*), and placed each one in a village, where they were expected to replace traditional birth attendants (*dukuns*). However, the *dukuns* were older, highly respected women who were well connected in village networks. They also charged a smaller fee for a delivery than did the *bidans*. As a result, most of the *bidans* could not support themselves from their fees earned from deliveries, and dropped out of health work. Again we see the strength of indigenous knowledge systems.

Complexity

Complexity is the degree to which an innovation is perceived as relatively difficult to understand and use. Any new idea may be classified on the complexity-simplicity continuum. Some innovations are clear in their meaning to potential adopters while others are not. Although the research evidence is not entirely conclusive, we suggest Generalization 6-3: *The complexity of an innovation, as perceived by members of a social system, is negatively related to its rate of adoption.*

Complexity may not be as important as relative advantage or compatibility for many innovations, but for some new ideas complexity is a very important barrier to adoption. The very first adopters of home computers in the United States were hobbyists, individuals who simply loved technological gadgets. Many were engineers, scientists, or other individuals who had had extensive experience with mainframe and/or minicomputers before home computers became available around 1980. These hobbyist adopters of home computers did not perceive the innovation as complex. To them it wasn't. But the individuals who adopted home computers thereafter did not have such a high level of technical expertise, and they typically went through a period of intense frustration during the several weeks after they acquired a personal computer. They were baffled by how to connect the various components, how to get word-processing and other software programs to run, and so on. The frustrated adopter was puzzled by the computer manual and got little help from salespeople, who talked a confusing technical jargon. Eventually, however, most individuals joined a computer users' club, obtained help from friends, or found other means to cope with the complexity of their home computer. But the perceived complexity of home computers was an important negative force in their rate of adoption in the 1980s. Eventually, home computers became more user-friendly, and their rate of adoption gradually rose to about 50 percent of all U.S. households by 2002.

Trialability

Trialability is the degree to which an innovation may be experimented with on a limited basis. New ideas that can be tried on the installment plan are generally adopted more rapidly than innovations that are not divisible. Some innovations are more difficult to divide for trial than are others. The personal trying out of an innovation is one way for an individual to give meaning to an innovation and to find out how it works under one's own conditions. A personal trial can dispel uncertainty about a new idea. We suggest Generalization 6-4: *The trialability of an innovation, as perceived by the members of a social system, is positively related to its rate of adoption.* If an innovation can be designed so as to be tried more easily, it will have a more rapid rate of adoption. Trying a new idea may involve re-inventing it so as to customize it more closely to the individual's conditions. So an innovation may actually be changed during its trial.

Relatively earlier adopters of an innovation perceive trialability as more important than do later adopters (Gross, 1942; Ryan, 1948). More innovative individuals have no precedent available to follow when they adopt, while later adopters are surrounded by peers who have already adopted the innovation. These peers act as a kind of vicarious trial for later adopters, and hence their own personal trial of the new idea is less crucial. Laggards move from initial trial to full-scale use more rapidly than do innovators and early adopters (see Chapter 5).

Observability

Observability is the degree to which the results of an innovation are visible to others. Some ideas are easily observed and communicated to other people, whereas other innovations are difficult to observe or to describe to others. We suggest Generalization 6-5: *The observability of an innovation, as perceived by members of a social system, is positively related to its rate of adoption.*

Most of the innovations studied in past diffusion research are technological ideas. As explained in Chapter 1, a technology has two components: (1) a *hardware* aspect that consists of the tool that embodies the technology in the form of a material or physical object and (2) a *software* aspect that consists of the information base for the tool. Computer hardware consists of electronic equipment, while software is the computer programs for a computer system. The software component of a technological innovation is not so apparent to observation, so innovations in which the software aspect is dominant possess less observability, and usually have a relatively slower rate of adoption. One example is "safer sex," the preventive approach recommended to individuals by health experts to avoid contracting HIV/AIDS. Safer sex is a rather ambiguous idea, including abstinence and sexual monogamy as well as the specific behavior of using condoms. As a result, the preventive innovation of safer sex has spread slowly and to a relatively small percentage of all individuals at risk for HIV/AIDS (Singhal and Rogers, 2002).

Cellular Telephones and the Lifestyle Revolution

The innovation of cellular telephones (also called mobile telephones) was first offered to American consumers in 1983, and an amazing 130 million phones were sold in the following decade. During the next decade, the diffusion of cellular telephones really took off, with 1.1 billion sold worldwide. Nations such as Finland, Denmark, Sweden, and Korea have the highest rates of adoption, with the United States lagging somewhat behind. Finland has certain age groups, such as people aged eighteen to thirty-four, with 104 percent adoption (this quirk is due to the many people who have two or more mobile phones). Some 25 percent of Finnish households have *only* a mobile phone and do not have a fixed-line telephone.

A cellular telephone operates with a built-in rechargeable battery, so that it is portable or mobile. It is called "cellular" because each geographical area is divided into cells, each from one to twenty-five miles in radius. When an individual travels from one cell to another, the telephone system automatically switches a call from one cell to another without interrupting service. The usual charges for a cellular telephone are a onetime activation fee, a flat rate per month, plus an air charge per minute (depending on the time of day and the day of the week) for both incoming and outgoing calls.

The first U.S. adopters of mobile phones in 1983 were male executives whose companies provided the phone as an office perk. At that time, a cellular phone cost about $3,000 and was a large rectangular object about the size of a brick. Actually, these early mobile phones were not very mobile, as most were car-mounted (Grüber and Verboven, 2001). They allowed the user to talk on a telephone during dead time, such as when stalled in traffic. Among the innovative businessmen who adopted mobile phones were building contractors; the cell phone fit well with the highly mobile nature of their work.

Soon the quality of cellular service improved, the price of a cellular phone dropped steeply (to $200 or less), and the product became so small that it could fit into a shirt pocket or even into tight jeans. Rather quickly, cellular telephones became a very popular consumer product, with non-business use predominating. Cell phones became a fashion statement, with Nokia, the Finnish company, first capitalizing on this new perception of mobile telephony. Color and shape became increasingly important, as Nokia gained dominant market share worldwide. Currently, more than one third of all cell phones sold worldwide are made by Nokia (Specter, 2001). During the 1990s, the mobile phone became a fashion accessory like a watch or pen. The *meaning* of a telephone was transformed into a quite different object, causing a lifestyle change for many people in the process. This social change happened very quickly, and Nokia was the driving force.

The story of how color and style initially came to Nokia's attention begins in a seedy bar, Rikala, in Salo, a company town located about sixty-five miles west of Helsinki. In 1993, Nokia engineers would pile into the Rikala on a Friday night after work, remove their big black mobile phones from their belts, and slap them down on the bar. Then they would drink beer and eat peanuts and talk about cell phones until 4:00 A.M. When someone decided to go home, he would say, "Oh, my God, which is my phone?" All were the same color and had the same ring. So the Nokia engineers took car paint and painted their phones various colors. A Nokia employee says, "That's where the route to color and fashion phones begins . . . in a bar in Salo" (Specter, 2001, p. 67). Nokia promptly went on to design *lots* of perfect phones, one for each market segment. Cell phones in Asia were smaller and had a strap attached, to which each user could fasten various objects (little teddy bear dolls, for example) to personalize his or her instrument. Mobile phones in the United States generally have an extendable aerial. Some customers prefer larger-size phones with a full computer keyboard.

The Phone Guy

The "phone guy" who designed not only the heavy black cell phones that the Nokia engineers wore on their belts into the bar in Salo but all of the brightly colored tiny phones with removable faceplates for personalized equipment that Nokia has sold since then, is Frank Nuovo. He is vice president for design at Nokia, a forty-year-old American who graduated from Pasadena's Art Center College of Design. Instead of working in Nokia's headquarters in Espoo, a suburb of Helsinki, Nuovo insists on locating his design center somewhere in southern California (Nokia will not identify the exact city, nor does Nuovo's office have a Nokia sign on the door, out of concern for industrial spies), where he feels the environment contains more stimulus for stylish phone design. He favors bubbles and elliptical shapes in his aerodynamic phone designs. As a Nokia executive, rubbing his thumb slowly across the lines and contours of one of Nuovo's early designs, the Nokia 101, explained, "Look at the earpiece. It has three holes. But what shape are the holes? Three *ovals*. Look at the microphone. It's a little *oval*. It cost money to make those holes into oval shapes. A circle would have been cheaper. You don't notice it—but you see it, you feel it" (quoted in Specter, 2001, p. 65).

What Nuovo gives Nokia's cell phones is a feeling of coherence, and the customer feels a subconscious pleasure when hefting the tiny instrument. Nokia phones may be the best-selling products on earth today. So Nuovo is the Henry Ford, or the Calvin Klein, of cellular phones.

After the businessmen segment had adopted mobile phones, the fastest-growing target audience in adopting cell phones became teenagers. This innovation was an important step toward freedom from parental control. Once young people had their own cell phone, they could call anyone they wanted to without fear of a parent overhearing their conversation (many parents still maintain some degree of control over the amount of cell phone use by putting a cap on their children's monthly telephone bills). Now the customer for telephone service was an individual, not a household. Younger and younger people began to adopt. In Finland today, many second-graders, aged eight, have mobile phones. The basic nature of parent/child relationships has been changed by the cell phone.

During the 1990s Frank Nuovo designed smaller and smaller cell phones, appropriate for the hands that held them: children, Asians, women. Then, when cell phones started to become all-purpose communication devices, Nuovo began to create larger phones. An example is Nokia's Communicator, a six-inch-long gizmo with a flip-up lid that allows access to a full keyboard and to fax, the Internet, and other computer functions.

Perceived Attributes of Cell Phones

Cellular phones have an almost ideal set of perceived attributes, which is one reason for this innovation's very rapid rate of adoption (see Figure 6-3).

Figure 6-3. Rate of Adoption of Mobile Telephones in Finland

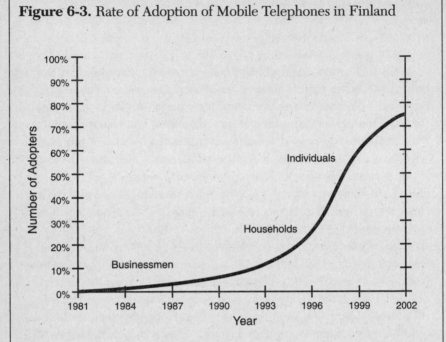

By 2002, 75 percent of Finland's population of 5.2 million people had adopted mobile telephones. The first major segment to adopt consisted mainly of businessmen, who purchased cell phones as timesaving devices. The next segment adopted after the critical mass in 1994 and consisted mainly of households who used mobile phones for reasons of sociability, to stay in touch with relatives and family members. Thereafter, mobile phone adopters were mainly individuals who adopted the innovation to seek a new type of lifestyle. Mobile telephones are constantly being re-invented, thanks to a constant stream of new services, such as SMS (short message service) after 1994, individualized ringing tones after 1998, and the ability to buy soft drinks from a machine or to pay for a meal at a restaurant by means of an infrared transmission from a cell phone.

1. *Relative advantage:* One of the main benefits of the cellular telephone for businessmen was that it saved an estimated two hours per week by allowing them to avoid missed appointments and cope with delayed schedules. These time savings are especially important for individuals living in urban areas, who are frequently trapped in congested traffic. The portable nature of cellular phones frees users from being in any fixed place. Individuals can talk on their cell phone hands free while

driving (to avoid distraction and accidents). One special advantage of a cellular phone is that it can be used when a vehicle is disabled or during medical emergencies, and many men give cell phones to their wives and daughters for this reason.

Cellular phones are an important status symbol, which is one reason why they are used in restaurants and other public places. The prestige of the innovation was suggested by the widespread sale of replicas of cellular phones in the 1980s. More than forty thousand "Cellular Phoneys," a $16 nonworking model manufactured by a California company, were sold. Such phony phones today seem almost unbelievable, as cell phones have become so commonplace.

The falling cost of a cellular phone and its smaller size spurred its rate of adoption. Gradually, cellular came out of the automobile and into people's pockets and purses.

2. *Compatibility:* A cellular phone connects its user with the existing telephone system and allows a user to talk with anyone who has a regular telephone. Thus formation of a critical mass of cellular phone users was not necessary in the early stages of this innovation's diffusion. Further, the names commonly used for cellular telephones were nontechnical and conveyed a positive image in most nations (for example, a cell phone is called a "handy" in Germany). A range of colors, styles, and sizes of cell phones were available, and a user could personalize their instrument by choosing from a variety of call signals.

3. *Complexity:* From the user's perspective, a cellular telephone operates exactly the same way as a regular phone, and so it was unnecessary to learn any new skills. When short message service (SMS) became popular as a means of transmitting text messages, first among young people in Japan in the late 1990s, the needed skills were quickly learned. Today, about 1 billion SMS messages are sent every day! Telephone manufacturers were initially surprised by SMS, which represents a kind of re-invention by users. SMS is very popular in Finland, where the dour Finns (who hate to talk) send short text messages instead; therefore the SMS function makes cell phones highly compatible in Finland.

4. *Trialability:* A friend's cellular phone can be borrowed for trial use. In the early 1990s, rental cars often came equipped with a cellular telephone, which provided a trial of the innovation for many individuals. Further, companies providing cellular telephone service commonly offer an initial month of free service to encourage adoption. A variety of other incentives (such as free cell phones) have also promoted initial trial of mobile telephones.

5. *Observability:* The use of cellular phones in automobiles, restaurants, and other public places helped emphasize their conferral of status on potential buyers. This innovation is highly observable, both visually and in an auditory sense (such as when a cell phone rings in a public place).

A Visit to Espoo

In order to understand the rapid rate of diffusion of mobile telephones, one needs to visit the Nokia company headquarters, Nokia House, in Espoo. Thanks to Nokia's explosive growth, Espoo has become Finland's second largest city. Perhaps Espoo is the European equivalent of Bellvue, Washington, home of several thousand Microsoft millionaires. Some twenty thousand Nokia employees get stock options, including many self-made millionaires (although fewer than in the glory days of the galloping stock market in the 1990s). Nokia is a very secretive organization (for example, Nokia employees are not allowed to send e-mail attachments, out of fear that they may not be secure). Our visit was arranged as a special favor to a vice president of Sonera, the dominant Finnish telephone service provider and an important Nokia customer.

The stylish headquarters building in Espoo is constructed of steel and glass, very open and naturally lit, with wooden floors and furniture. The name "Nokia" derives from that of a small city near Tampere, Finland, where the company began 137 years ago. It produced rubber galoshes, electrical cables, and paper products and then grew a thriving personal computer business. But in 1988, Nokia faced a financial crisis and almost went under. The president of the company committed suicide, and Jorma Ollila, Nokia's present CEO, was brought in to save the company. He sold off all the existing business units and concentrated the company on mobile telephones and the telecommunications networks to support them. Ollila was confident that the rate of adoption of mobile phones was ready to take off worldwide. He was right. The first-ever call using GSM (Global System for Mobile Communications) was placed on a Nokia telephone in 1991. This technology allowed cell phones to roam throughout the world. By pioneering GSM, Nokia grabbed a big chunk of market share. Nokia has annual sales of $7 billion and accounts for more than half of the total capitalization of all companies listed on the Finnish stock exchange. Nokia alone accounts for more than 60 percent of all activity in Finalnd's stock market.

Nokia leads the world in the global cell phone business because it devotes 9.6 percent of its sales to R&D (the usual rate of investment in R&D for most large corporations is only 2 or 3 percent of sales). Nokia estimates that one third of its 58,000 employees are in R&D, charged with developing a constant stream of new cell phones. Due to Nokia's global position, its fifty-four R&D centers are scattered over the world, with only two in Finland. Some forty nationalities are represented among the 120 R&D employees at Espoo. Out of Nokia's R&D labs come innovative products so that the company can continue to dominate the world marketplace for cell phones. During 2002, Nokia launched twenty new models, each to fit a particular market segment. The Nokia 7210, for example, comes with a stereo radio and a screen with 4,095 colors. The Nokia 5210, designed for extreme sportspeople, has a tough outer shell to protect against splashes, bumps, and dust, and features a stopwatch and a thermometer. The Nokia 7650 has a digital camera and photo album. At the high end, the Nokia Vertu, with a starting price of $20,000, has a shell of gold, platinum, or covered with diamonds!

Summary

This chapter suggested five attributes of innovations by which an innovation can be described. Individuals' perceptions of these attributes predict an innovation's rate of adoption. We recommend that measures of the five perceived attributes should be developed in each diffusion study, rather than utilizing existing scales borrowed from previous investigations.

Rate of adoption is the relative speed with which an innovation is adopted by members of a social system. In addition to the perceived attributes of an innovation, such other variables affect its rate of adoption as (1) the type of innovation-decision, (2) the nature of communication channels diffusing the innovation at various stages in the innovation-decision process, (3) the nature of the social system, and (4) the extent of change agents' efforts in diffusing the innovation. Most past research, however, concentrated on predicting the rate of adoption by the five perceived attributes of innovations.

Relative advantage is the degree to which an innovation is perceived as better than the idea it supersedes. The relative advantage of an innovation, as perceived by members of a social system, is positively related to its rate of adoption (Generalization 6-1). *Overadoption* is the adoption of an innovation when experts feel that it should be rejected. *Preventive innovations,* defined as new ideas that an individual adopts now in order to lower the probability of some unwanted future event, diffuse more slowly than incremental (nonpreventive) innovations.

Compatibility is the degree to which an innovation is perceived as consistent with the existing values, past experiences, and needs of potential adopters. The compatibility of an innovation, as perceived by members of a social system, is positively related to its rate of adoption (Generalization 6-2). Naming an innovation and positioning it relative to previous ideas are important means of making an innovation more compatible. Change agents often ignore indigenous knowledge systems, which provide one means by which individuals give meaning to an innovation.

Complexity is the degree to which an innovation is perceived as relatively difficult to understand and to use. The complexity of an innovation, as perceived by members of a social system, is negatively related to its rate of adoption (Generalization 6-3).

Trailability is the degree to which an innovation may be experimented with on a limited basis. The trialability of an innovation, as perceived by members of a social system, is positively related to its rate of adoption (Generalization 6-4).

Observability is the degree to which the results of an innovation are visible to others. The observability of an innovation, as perceived by members of a social system, is positively related to its rate of adoption (Generalization 6-5).

A basic theme of this chapter is that change agents and diffusion scholars must understand how potential adopters perceive new ideas. Such perceptions count in determining the nature of the diffusion process.

7

INNOVATIVENESS AND ADOPTER CATEGORIES

Be not the first by whom the new is tried, nor the last to lay
the old aside.

Alexander Pope, *An Essay on Criticism* (1711)

A slow advance in the beginning, followed by rapid and uni-
formly accelerated progress, followed again by progress that
continues to slacken until it finally stops: These are the three
ages of . . . invention. . . . If taken as a guide by the statistician
and by the sociologists, [they] would save many illusions.

Gabriel Tarde, *The Laws of Imitation* (1903), p.127.

The individuals in a social system do not all adopt an innovation at the
same time. Rather, they adopt in an over-time sequence, so that individuals can be classified into adopter categories on the basis of when
they first begin using a new idea. We could describe each individual
adopter in a system in terms of his or her time of adoption, but this
would be very tedious. It is much more efficient to use *adopter categories,* the classifications of members of a system on the basis of their
innovativeness. Each adopter category consists of individuals with a
similar degree of innovativeness. So adopter categories are a means of
convenience in describing the members of a system.

We know more about *innovativeness,* the degree to which an individual (or other unit of adoption) is relatively earlier in adopting new ideas
than other members of a system, than about any other concept in diffu-

sion research. Because increased innovativeness is a main objective of many change agencies, it became the main dependent variable in diffusion research. Innovativeness indicates overt behavioral change, the ultimate goal of most diffusion programs, rather than just cognitive or attitudinal change. Innovativeness is the bottom-line behavior in the diffusion process.

This chapter suggests a standard method for categorizing adopters and demonstrates the usefulness of this technique with research findings about the characteristics of adopter categories.

Diffusion of Farm Innovations in a Colombian Village in the Andes[*]

The Saucío study in the early 1960s was a turning point for diffusion research in several important respects. This investigation in Colombia was the first diffusion study in a peasant village in Latin America, Africa, or Asia (although a diffusion study by Syed Rahim was under way in Bangladesh at about the same time). All of the five hundred or so diffusion researches completed by 1960 were conducted in North America and Europe, despite the fact that 80 percent of the world's population lived in developing countries. At the time that the Saucío study was carried out in 1962, it was not known whether the diffusion model would apply to peasant villages. These systems were characterized by widespread illiteracy and poverty, and by very little mass media exposure.

The Saucío study was conducted by the late Paul J. Deutschmann, a professor of communication at Michigan State University, and Orlando Fals Borda, an American-trained Ph.D. who founded the field of sociology in Colombia. Professor Fals Borda had been carrying out research in Saucío for a decade, and had introduced various new ideas in the village as experiments in social change: a new school building, a sewing cooperative, a cooperative store, and two important agricultural innovations: the vaccination of chickens against cholera and a new potato variety, Papas Monserrate. The seventy-one farmers of Saucío depended on potatoes as their main crop, and also raised poultry, livestock, and wheat.

Professor Deutschmann had studied the diffusion of news events in the United States (Deutschmann and Danielson, 1960), and was well

---

[*]This case illustration is based on Deutschmann and Fals Borda (1962b).

acquainted with research on the diffusion of agricultural innovations. Fals Borda had become familiar with agricultural diffusion research when he was earning his doctorate in the United States. In 1961, Deutschmann moved from East Lansing to San José, Costa Rica, where he directed a program on communication research in Latin America. He obtained funds for the collaborative restudy of Saucío, with Fals Borda and his students at the National University of Colombia (in Bogotá), using a diffusion approach.

Saucío was a small village located more than two miles high in the steep volcanic soils of the Andes Mountains. The residents of Saucío had originally been Indians and were conquered by Spanish explorers five hundred years ago. By 1962 most aspects of Indian culture had disappeared. The Saucíans were poor, with half of the farms less than four acres in size. Forty-two percent of the farmers were illiterate, and only two of the seventy-one farmers had more than four years of formal education. Illiteracy and poverty limited their mass media exposure. Only 14 percent of the households owned a radio. Compared to a media-saturated nation such as the United States, Saucío appeared to be an unlikely setting in which innovations would diffuse.

However, two of the six innovations of study, chemical fertilizers and spray guns for insecticides and fungicides, had diffused in Saucío over the previous thirty years, reaching almost 100 percent adoption. The rate of adoption for these two innovations was similar to that for hybrid seed corn in Iowa (Ryan and Gross, 1943). Two other innovations, a concentrated poultry and livestock feed and a potato fungicide, had diffused in the ten years prior to the 1962 diffusion study, with both reaching 75 percent adoption. All six innovations of study (including the two introduced by Fals Borda) followed an S-shaped curve over time. During the first years of the introduction of an innovation in the village, only a few farmers adopted each year. Then a critical mass of adopters was reached, and the cumulative rate of adoption speeded up as many farmers adopted each year. Finally, the rate of adoption gradually leveled off as fewer and fewer farmers remained to adopt the innovation.

Deutschmann and Fals Borda combined all six innovations into a composite measure of innovativeness, the general tendency for individuals to adopt new ideas. Four farmers in Saucío had adopted all six innovations, while one farmer had not adopted any of the innovations. Each villager who had adopted an innovation was asked when such adoption had taken place, and greater weight was given in each individual's innovativeness scores for relatively earlier adoption. The cumulative distribution of the innovativeness scores for the seventy-one farmers was S-shaped and approached normality. Thus the respondents were classified into five adopter categories:

1. *Innovators:* The two farmers with the highest innovativeness scores.
2. *Early adopters:* The ten farmers with the next highest innovativeness scores.
3. *Early majority:* The twenty-three farmers with the next highest innovativeness scores.
4. *Late majority:* The twenty-three farmers with the next highest innovativeness scores.
5. *Laggards:* The 13 farmers with the lowest innovativeness scores.

Deutschmann and Fals Borda (1962b) then proceeded to determine the characteristics of the five adopter categories, and to compare these results with the present author's study of Ohio farmers (Rogers, 1961). In *both* Saucío and in Ohio, farm size, formal education, exposure to mass media, and opinion leadership (measured as the degree to which a farmer was sought by others for information and advice about agricultural innovations) were the variables most highly related to innovativeness. That is, innovators differed most sharply from laggards on these socioeconomic and communication variables in both Saucío and Ohio. The diffusion of agricultural innovations seemed to display striking similarities in the two quite different settings. The diffusion process represented a general model of human behavior, rather than being limited to the United States and Western Europe.

However, there were certain sharp differences between the two systems of study regarding the diffusion of innovations. For example, the range in average farm size from innovators to laggards in Ohio was 339 to 128 acres (Rogers, 1961). In Saucío, the most innovative farmer had one hundred times the amount of farmland of the least innovative farmer! Such extremes in socioeconomic status are often characteristic of peasant villages in Third World nations. As in most other diffusion researches, the innovators in Saucío were much more cosmopolite than the laggards, traveling outside of the village to market towns and cities, and learning about new ideas from the mass media.

The diffusion process in Saucío was mainly via interpersonal communication channels within the village. In previous farm diffusion research in the United States, the mass media were most important at the knowledge stage in the innovation-decision process. However, in Saucío 43 percent of the sources or channels reported by farmers at the knowledge stage for innovations involved face-to-face communication with other farmers in the village. Only five farmers reported using mass media sources or channels at the knowledge stage in adopting an innovation. This heavy dependence on interpersonal communication in Saucío seemed to slow the diffusion process, especially that of the first two innovations, a process that began during the 1930s. Their S-curves had a long "tail" to the left, in which five to ten years were required before the rate of adoption took off. So word of mouth was particularly important in the diffusion process in the peasant village of Saucío.

The Ryan and Gross (1943) hybrid seed corn study found that most farmers did not adopt an innovation until they had tried it on an experimental basis on their own farm. The typical Iowa farmer adopted the new seed only after several years of trial planting. In contrast, most Saucío villagers went directly to full-scale use of the six innovations without first trying them out. Perhaps such impulsive behavior occurred because the Colombian villagers, due to their low level of formal education, did not have a "scientific" learning-from-experience attitude. Deutschmann and Fals Borda (1962b) suggested that such plunge-type decisions may have been due to the conditioning of Colombian peasants to respond immediately to authoritarian sources. The more recently introduced innovations in Saucío, however, were more likely to be adopted on a trial basis, suggesting that the peasant farmers were learning to evaluate agricultural innovations on the basis of their own experimental experience.

Although exposure to mass media in Saucío was very limited, innovators had much higher exposure than did laggards, averaging a mass media exposure score (composed of radio, newspapers, and books) of 26, while laggards averaged only 4. Innovators were more likely than laggards to utilize mass media sources or channels at the knowledge stage, 11 percent to 2 percent. Innovators were also more cosmopolite at the knowledge stage, using sources or channels from outside the village, 33 percent to 17 percent. The innovators played an important role in launching the diffusion of each innovation in the village, as they utilized communication channels that brought new ideas into the system. Once an innovation was introduced from cosmopolite and mass media sources, the diffusion process could take off in a self-sustaining nature by means of interpersonal communication channels within the village.

The Saucío study became a diffusion classic, opening the way for hundreds of diffusion investigations to be conducted in developing countries in the years that followed. The Deutschmann and Fals Borda (1962b) study particularly demonstrated the usefulness of the conceptual tools of innovativeness and adopter categories.

Classifying Adopter Categories on the Basis of Innovativeness

Titles of adopter categories were once about as numerous as diffusion researchers themselves. The inability of researchers in the early days of diffusion research to agree on common semantic ground in assigning terminology led to this plethora of adopter descriptions. The most innovative individuals were termed "progressists," "high-triers," "experimentals," "lighthouses," "advance scouts," and "ultraadopters." The least innovative individuals were called "drones," "parochials," and "diehards." This disarray of adopter categories and methods of categorization emphasized the need for standardization. How could a reader compare research findings about adopter categories from one study to another until there was standardization of both the nomenclature and the classification system? Fortunately, one method of adopter categorization, based upon the S-shaped curve of adoption, gained a dominant position in the early 1960s (Rogers, 1962).

The S-Shaped Curve of Adoption and Normality

The time element of the diffusion process allows us to classify adopter categories and to draw diffusion curves. The adoption of an innovation usually follows a normal, bell-shaped curve when plotted over time on a frequency basis. If the cumulative number of adopters is plotted, the result is an S-shaped curve. Figure 7–1 utilizes data from the Iowa hybrid corn study to show that the rate of adoption for an innovation can be represented by either a bell-shaped (frequency) curve or an S-shaped (cumulative) curve. These are just two different ways to display the same data.

The S-shaped adopter distribution rises slowly at first, when there are only a few adopters in each time period. The curve then accelerates to a maximum until half of the individuals in the system have adopted. Then it increases at a gradually slower rate as fewer and fewer remaining individuals adopt the innovation. This S-shaped curve is normal. Why?

Many human traits are normally distributed, whether the trait is a physical characteristic, such as weight or height, or a behavioral trait, such as intelligence or the learning of new information. Hence, a variable such as the degree of innovativeness is also expected to be normally distributed. If a social system is substituted for the individual in the learning curve, it seems reasonable to expect that experience with the innovation is gained as each successive member in the social system

Figure 7-1. The Number of New Adopters Each Year, and the Cumulative Number of Adopters, of Hybrid Seed Corn in Two Iowa Communities

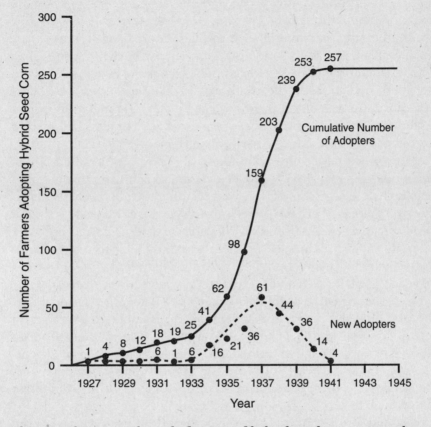

The cumulative number of adopters of hybrid seed corn approaches an S-shaped curve over time, while the frequency distribution of the number of mean adopters per year approaches a normal, bell-shaped curve. Early in the diffusion process, relatively few individuals adopt in each time period. Gradually, however, the rate of adoption speeds up until all (or almost all) members of the system adopt the innovation.

Source: Based on Ryan and Gross (1943).

adopts it. Each adoption in the social system is in a sense equivalent to a learning trial by an individual (in fact, if the individual tries the innovation prior to adoption, each adoption is indeed a learning trial).

We expect a normal adopter distribution for an innovation because of the cumulatively increasing influences upon an individual to adopt or reject an innovation, resulting from the activation of peer networks about the innovation in a system (see Chapter 8). This influence results from the increasing rate of knowledge and adoption (or rejection) of the innovation in the system. We know that the adoption of a new idea results from information exchange through interpersonal networks. If the first adopter of an innovation discusses it with two other members of the system, each of these two adopters passes the new idea along to two peers, and so forth, the resulting distribution follows a binomial expansion, a mathematical function that follows a normal shape when plotted over a series of successive generations. The process is similar to that of an unchecked infectious epidemic (Bailey, 1957/1975).

Of course, several assumptions underlying this hypothetical example are seldom found in real life. For instance, members of a system do not have completely free access to interact with all other members. Status differences, geographical barriers, and other variables affect who talks to whom about an innovation. The S-shaped diffusion curve begins to level off after half of the individuals in a social system have adopted, because each new adopter finds it increasingly difficult to tell the new idea to a peer who has not yet adopted, for such nonknowers become increasingly scarce.

The S-shaped curve of diffusion "takes off" once interpersonal networks become activated in spreading individuals' subjective evaluations of an innovation from peer to peer in a system (see Figure 7–1). The part of the diffusion curve from about 10 percent adoption to 20 percent adoption is the heart of the diffusion process. After that point, it is often impossible to stop the further diffusion of a new idea, even if one wished to do so.

Ryan and Gross (1943) tested the S-shaped diffusion curve for the adoption of hybrid seed corn in Iowa, using the chi square goodness-of-fit test to determine whether or not the rate of adoption deviated significantly from a cumulative normal curve. It did in the years 1935 and 1936, just prior to the average year of adoption in 1937, as fewer Iowa farmers adopted the innovation in these years than were expected to do so on the basis of the normal curve (see Figure 7–1). Then, in the immediately following period, during 1937, more farmers adopted the new seed than predicted by a normal curve. There seemed to be rather strong resistance to the new idea in the early part of the diffusion process, which was then overcome, perhaps after a critical mass of satisfied adopters was achieved. Nevertheless, the overall rate of adoption over time generally approached a normal S curve, with year-to-year deviations from normality (noted above) tending to cancel one another out over the total diffusion process.

Generalization 7-1 states that: *Adopter distributions follow a bell-shaped curve over time and approach normality.* Evidence supporting this statement comes from investigations of many agricultural, consumer, and other innovations in a variety of systems, in the United States and in other nations (see e.g., Ryan, 1948; Dimit, 1954; Rogers, 1958; Beal and Rogers, 1960; Bose, 1964; Hamblin et al., 1973). A variety of different mathematical formulae have been proposed to fit the shape of adopter distributions. This research shows that S-shaped diffusion curves are essentially normal, a conclusion that is very useful for classifying adopter categories.

The S-curve, it must be remembered, is innovation-specific and system-specific, describing the diffusion of a particular new idea among the member units of a specific system. The S-shaped curve describes only cases of successful innovation, in which an innovation spreads to almost all of the potential adopters in a social system. Many innovations are not successful. For example, thousands of new consumer products appear on store shelves and in media advertisements each year. Most fail (Goldsmith and Flynn, 1992). After being adopted by only a few people in a system, the innovation may ultimately be rejected, so that its rate of adoption levels off and, through discontinuance, nose-dives.

Measuring Organizational Innovativeness

When *organizations'* time of adoption of an innovation is plotted over time, the cumulative distribution of adopters usually forms an S-shaped curve. An example is the diffusion of hate crime laws in the United States (Grattet, Jenness, and Curry, 1998). Since the 1970s, in response to a perceived escalation of racial, religious, and ethnic group conflict, hate-motivated intimidation, and violence, many states passed legislation that criminalized such behavior. California passed the first hate crime law in 1978, and then, after a three-year period, Oregon and Washington, two other West Coast states, adopted. In the following two years, seven other states, scattered across the continent, adopted. By 1995, seventeen years after California's initial adoption, only seventeen of the fifty states had not adopted hate crime laws. The cumulative rate of adoption formed the usual S-shaped curve (Figure 7–2).

Figure 7-2. Year in Which Each U.S. State Adopted a Hate Crime Law

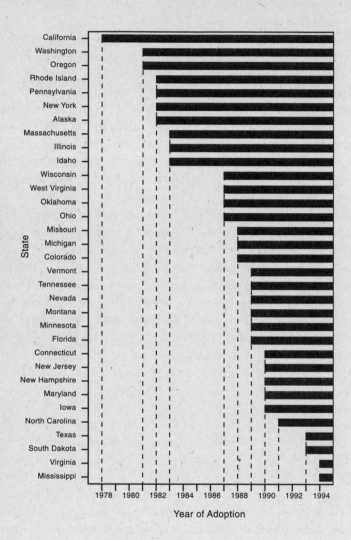

Here the date of adoption of an innovation is shown in a bar graph rather than in the customary S-shaped curve, which plots the cumulative number of adopters over time. At the time the data were gathered on hate crime laws, seventeen American states had not yet adopted. The more innovative states were larger and richer and had a more liberal and progressive tradition. They also tended to have neighboring states that had previously adopted a hate crime law.

Source: Adapted from Grattet, Jenness, and Curry (1998).

So organizations, like individuals, adopt an innovation in a manner that suggests various degrees of resistance to the new idea. More innovative states, such as California, possess a political culture that is progressive and liberal and have a reputation for being innovative in adopting new laws and programs (Walker, 1969). Innovative states also bordered on other states that had adopted previously. Oregon and Washington are also progressive states and seem to have followed the lead of California (see Figure 7–2). So communication networks, based in part on spatial propinquity, explain a certain degree of a state's innovativeness in adopting hate crime laws. As these laws spread among the American states, considerable re-invention occurred, as the exact details of each state's law varied. For example, some state laws prohibited hate crimes on the basis of gender or sexual orientation in addition to race, religion, and ethnic group.

The S-curve of diffusion is so ubiquitous that students of diffusion often expect every innovation to be adopted over time in an S-shaped pattern. However, certain innovations do not display an S-shaped rate of adoption, perhaps for some idiosyncratic reason. Perhaps the innovation is taboo in nature, so that individuals cannot discuss it freely. Perhaps the new idea is applicable only to certain unique population groups within the total population. For example, adopting "safe sex" may be most appropriate for individuals who are at high risk for contracting HIV/AIDS, such as users of injected drugs, gay men, and sexually promiscuous individuals with many partners. In this case, the diffusion curve for the idea of safe sex will not be S-shaped for the entire population, although it may be for a specific population segment. Also, HIV prevention is a preventive innovation and hence likely to diffuse slowly (see Chapter 6).

The main point here is not to assume that an S-shaped rate of adoption is an inevitability. Rather, the shape of the adopter distribution for a particular innovation ought to be regarded as an open question, to be determined empirically. In most cases when this has been done in past research, an adopter distribution is found to follow a bell-shaped, normal curve or is S-shaped on a cumulative basis.

Who Adopts?

The early diffusion studies of Iowa farmers and Illinois doctors headed diffusion scholars into assuming that individuals should usually be their units of analysis. Later, when studying organizational innovativeness, diffusion scholars initially gathered data from the top official in the organizations about its innovativeness (see Chapter 10). Then, a few decades back, serious attention began to be given to the issue of who makes the innovation-decisions in a system. For example, although a school principal may provide data about a school's adoption of innovations, that individual's personal and social characteristics may prove to have little relationship to the school's innovativeness. Perhaps someone else, or a set of other individuals, in the school's organizational structure actually initiated or implemented the innovations of study. This realization led to investigation of the innovation process in organizations, rather than assuming that the top official was necessarily responsible for an organization's innovativeness.

Similarly, in very recent years, other diffusion scholars have pointed out how important it is to identify exactly who makes the innovation-decisions of study in other systems. For instance, in an agricultural diffusion study conducted in eastern Nigeria, the author and his research team initially assumed that the male head of a farm household would be interviewed in their survey (as had been the case in previous diffusion studies in the United States, Colombia, Bangladesh, Brazil, and India). During a pretest interview in a Nigerian village, we learned otherwise. The male head of the first household that we contacted actually proved to know very little about the agricultural innovations that had been adopted on his farm. He told us that we would have to talk to his various wives, each of whom was responsible for operating a plot of farmland, about their innovation adoptions, as they, not he, made such decisions. We found that some of his wives had adopted an innovation such as chemical fertilizer on their farm, while other wives had not. We came to see that the *farm,* and whoever made the innovation-decisions for it, should be our unit of analysis in Nigeria. Only occasionally would the decision maker be the male head of household. Just what constituted a farm in Nigeria was not easily apparent. Was it the household, consisting of a male head and multiple wives, or was it the land that each wife operated?

An illustration of the complexities sometimes encountered in determining who adopts is provided by Soniia David's (1998) study of the diffusion of hedgerow intercropping in Africa. This innovation (also called "alley cropping") involves planting fast-growing, nitrogen-fixing trees in hedges along fencerows so as to provide firewood, with the foliage used for livestock feed and as a mulch and green manure on the crops planted between the hedges. This innovation was introduced to African farmers as a replacement for the traditional slash-and-burn fallow system that had been followed in the past. Hedgerow intercropping was diffused to farmers by international agricultural agencies, who sought to evaluate their development program by measuring the rate of adoption of the innovation.

Deciding who adopts hedgerow intercropping did not turn out to be an easy question to answer. For instance, as in the author's Nigerian study, mentioned above, gender roles varied from place to place. In eastern Nigeria, Igbo men traditionally made decisions about tree planting, while women decided when to plant crops in the alley plots and they cut fodder for their livestock. These gender roles led to conflict when the women excessively pruned the nitrogen-fixing trees during the dry season to feed their goats, which killed many of the trees. In western Kenya, among the Luo and Luhya, many males have emigrated to find off-farm work, so that almost half of the farms are headed by females. They do not have enough strength to trim tree branches, which requires a single upward slash with a machete. In any case, they define this work as a male task; by custom Luhya women are not allowed to cut trees planted by their husband. However, when the trees are not trimmed regularly, they shade the crops, which are the women's responsibility, and decrease yields.

So who is the adopter of the innovation of hedgerow intercropping in Africa?

Adopter Categorization

The dominant method of adopter categorization was developed when the author was a doctoral student at Iowa State University. I was discouraged by the confusing disarray of terms used for adopter categories and the looseness of methods of categorization. I was studying for a minor in statistics, so of course I knew about the mean and standard deviation and how these statistics could be utilized to lay off categories containing standard portions of a normal distribution. Further, I knew of standard classifications used in other fields, such as the selection of candidates for Air Force pilot training. I first published the method of adopter categorization described here in a 1958 journal article (Rogers, 1958), and in the first edition of *Diffusion of Innovations* (Rogers, 1962).

Anyone seeking to standardize adopter categories must decide on (1) the number of adopter categories, (2) the portion of the members of a system to include in each category, and (3) the method, statistical or otherwise, of defining the adopter categories.

The criterion for adopter categorization is *innovativeness*, the degree to which an individual or other unit of adoption is relatively earlier in adopting new ideas than other members of a social system. Innovativeness is a relative dimension, in that an individual has more or less of this variable than others in a system. Innovativeness is a continuous variable, and partitioning it into discrete categories is a conceptual device, much like dividing the continuum of social status into upper, middle, and lower classes. Such classification is a simplification that aids the understanding of human behavior, although it loses some information as a result of grouping individuals.

Ideally, a set of categories should be (1) *exhaustive,* including all the units of study, (2) *mutually exclusive,* by excluding a unit of study that appears in one category from also appearing in any other category, and (3) derived from a single *classificatory principle.*

We have previously demonstrated that S-shaped adopter distributions closely approach normality. The normal frequency distribution has several characteristics that are useful in classifying adopters. One characteristic or parameter is the mean ($\bar{x}$), or average, of the individuals in the system. Another parameter of a distribution is its standard deviation (sd), a measure of dispersion or variation about the mean. The standard deviation indicates the average amount of variance from the mean for a sample individuals.

These two statistics, the mean ($\bar{x}$) and the standard deviation (sd), are used to divide a normal adopter distribution into five categories. Vertical lines are drawn to mark off the standard deviations on either side of the mean so that the normal curve is divided into categories with a standardized percentage of respondents in each category. Figure 7–3 shows the normal frequency distribution divided into five adopter categories: (1) innovators, (2) early adopters, (3) early majority, (4) later majority, and (5) laggards. These five adopter categories and the approximate percentage of individuals included in each are located on the normal adopter distribution in the figure.

The area lying to the left of the mean time of adoption (of an innovation) minus two standard deviations includes the first 2.5 percent of the individuals in a system to adopt an innovation, the *innovators.* The next 13.5 percent to adopt the new idea are included in the area between the mean minus one standard deviation and the mean minus two standard deviations; they are labeled *early adopters.* The next 34 percent of the adopters, called the *early majority,* are included in the area between the mean date of adoption and the mean minus one standard

Figure 7-3. Adopter Categorization on the Basis of Innovativeness

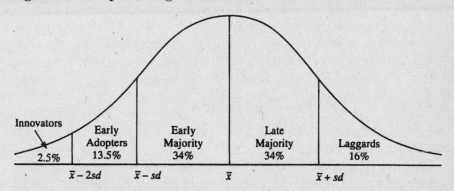

The innovativeness dimension, as measured by the time at which an individual adopts an innovation or innovations, is continuous. The innovativeness variable is partitioned into five adopter categories by laying off standard deviations (sd) from the average time of adoption ($\bar{x}$).

deviation. Between the mean and one standard deviation to the right of the mean are the next 34 percent to adopt the new idea, the *late majority*. The last 16 percent to adopt are called *laggards*.

This adopter classification system is not symmetrical, in that there are three adopter categories to the left of the mean and only two to the right. One solution would be to break laggards into two categories, such as early and late laggards, but laggards seem to form a fairly homogeneous category. Similarly, innovators and early adopters could be combined into a single category to achieve symmetry, but their quite different characteristics suggest that they are two distinct adopter categories.

One difficulty with this method of adopter classification is incomplete adoption, which occurs for innovations that have not reached 100 percent use. For example, two of the 259 Iowa farmers in Ryan and Gross's (1943) hybrid seed corn study had not adopted the innovation at the time of the 1941 diffusion survey. Such incomplete adoption means that the fivefold classification scheme is not exhaustive. The problem of incomplete adoption or nonadoption can be avoided when a series of innovations are combined into a composite innovativeness scale (as in Deutschmann and Fals Borda's Saucío study, described previously).

Innovativeness as a criterion for adopter categorization fulfills each of the three principles of categorization suggested previously. The five adopter categories are exhaustive (except for nonadopters), mutually exclusive, and derived from one classification principle. The method of adopter categorization just described is the most widely used in diffusion research today. It is essentially the only method of adopter categorization. Terms such as "innovators" and "early adopters" are widely used and understood by the public.

Adopter Categories as Ideal Types

The five adopter categories set forth in this chapter are *ideal types*, concepts based on observations of reality that are designed to make comparisons possible. Ideal types are not simply an average of all observations about an adopter category. Exceptions to the ideal types can be found. If no exceptions or deviations existed, ideal types would not be necessary. Ideal types are based on abstractions from empirical investigations. Pronounced breaks in the innovativeness continuum do not occur between each of the five categories, although some scholars claimed that a discontinuity exists between the innovators and early adopters versus the early majority, late majority, and laggards (Moore, 1991). Past research shows no support for this claim of a "chasm" between certain adopter categories. On the contrary, innovativeness, if measured properly, is a continuous variable and there are no sharp breaks or discontinuities between adjacent adopter categories (although there are important differences between them).

We now present an overview of the main characteristics and values of each adopter category, which will be followed by more detailed generalizations.

Innovators: Venturesome

Venturesomeness is almost an obsession with innovators. Their interest in new ideas leads them out of a local circle of peer networks and into more cosmopolite social relationships. Communication patterns and friendships among a clique of innovators are common, even though these individuals may be quite geographically distanced. Being an innovator has several prerequisites. Control of substantial financial resources is helpful in absorbing the possible losses from an unprofitable innovation. The ability to understand and apply complex technical knowledge is also needed. The innovator must be able to cope with a high degree of uncertainty about an innovation at the time he or she adopts.

The salient value of the innovator is venturesomeness, due to a desire for the rash, the daring, and the risky. The innovator must also be willing to accept an occasional setback when a new idea proves unsuccessful, as inevitably happens. While an innovator may not be respected by other members of a local system, the innovator plays an important role in the diffusion process: that of launching the new idea in the system by importing the innovation from outside of the system's boundaries. Thus, the innovator plays a gatekeeping role in the flow of new ideas into a system.

Early Adopters: Respect

Early adopters are a more integrated part of the local social system than are innovators. Whereas innovators are cosmopolites, early adopters are localites. This adopter category, more than any other, has the highest degree of opinion leadership in most systems. Potential adopters look to early adopters for advice and information about an innovation. The early adopter is considered by many to be "the individual to check with" before adopting a new idea. This adopter category is generally sought by change agents as a local missionary for speeding the diffusion process. Because early adopters are not too far ahead of the average individual in innovativeness, they serve as a role model for many other members of a social system. Early adopters help trigger the critical mass when they adopt an innovation.

The early adopter is respected by his or her peers, and is the embodiment of successful, discrete use of new ideas. The early adopter knows that to continue to earn this esteem of colleagues and to maintain a central position in the communication networks of the system, he or she must make judicious innovation-decisions. The early adopter decreases uncertainty about a new idea by adopting it, and then conveying a subjective evaluation of the innovation to near peers through interpersonal networks. In one sense, early adopters put their stamp of approval on a new idea by adopting it.

Early Majority: Deliberate

The early majority adopt new ideas just before the average member of a system. The early majority interact frequently with their peers but seldom hold positions of opinion leadership in a system. The early majority's unique location between the very early and the relatively late to adopt makes them an important link in the diffusion process. They provide interconnectedness in the system's interpersonal networks. The early majority are one of the most numerous adopter categories, making up one third of all members of a system.

The early majority may deliberate for some time before completely adopting a new idea. Their innovation-decision period is relatively longer than that of the innovators and the early adopters (see Chapter 5). "Be not the first by which the new is tried, nor the last to lay the old aside," quoted at the beginning of this chapter, particularly fits the thinking of the early majority. They follow with deliberate willingness in adopting innovations but seldom lead.

Late Majority: Skeptical

The late majority adopt new ideas just after the average member of a system. Like the early majority, the late majority make up one third of the members of a system. Adoption may be both an economic necessity for the late majority and the result of increasing peer pressures. Innovations are approached with a skeptical and cautious air, and the late majority do not adopt until most others in their system have already done so. The weight of system norms must definitely favor an innovation before the late majority are convinced to adopt. The pressure of peers is necessary to motivate adoption. Their relatively scarce resources mean that most of the uncertainty about a new idea must be removed before the late majority feel that it is safe to adopt.

Laggards: Traditional

Laggards are the last in a social system to adopt an innovation. They possess almost no opinion leadership. Laggards are the most localite of all adopter categories in their outlook. Many are near isolates in the social networks of their system. The point of reference for the laggard is the past. Decisions are often made in terms of what has been done previously, and these individuals interact primarily with others who also have relatively traditional values. Laggards tend to be suspicious of innovations and of change agents. Their innovation-decision process is relatively lengthy, with adoption and use lagging far behind awareness-knowledge of a new idea. Resistance to innovations on the part of laggards may be entirely rational from the laggards' viewpoint, as their resources are limited and they must be certain that a new idea will not fail before they can adopt. The laggard's precarious economic position forces the individual to be extremely cautious in adopting innovations.

"Laggard" might sound like a bad name. This title of the adopter category carries an invidious distinction (in much the same way that "lower class" is a negative nomenclature). Laggard is a bad name because most nonlaggards have a strong pro-innovation bias (see Chapter 3). Diffusion scholars who use adopter categories in their research do not mean any particular disrespect by the term "laggard." Indeed, if they used any other term instead of laggards, such as "late adopters," it would soon have a similar negative connotation. But it is a mistake to imply that laggards are somehow at fault for being relatively late to adopt. System-blame may more accurately describe the reality of the laggards' situation (see Chapter 3).

People Who Said No to Innovation: The Old Order Amish*

If you were an Old Order Amish person living in the United States today, you would not believe in using buttons (instead you would fasten your clothing with hooks and eyes), tractors, automobiles (which are considered "worldly"), family planning, wallpaper, cigarettes, wristwatches, or neckties; you would not engage in dating, military service, or voting; and you would not be educated beyond the eighth grade. You would believe that large families are good (the average Amish family has seven to nine children), that the only proper occupation is farming, and that you should marry an Amish partner.

The Amish are a religious sect that began in Switzerland during the 1690s when the followers of Jakob Ammann (hence the name "Amish") split off from existing Christian religions. The Amish were persecuted in Europe, and began migrating to Pennsylvania prior to the Revolutionary War of 1775. About five hundred Amish came during this initial wave; later, three thousand more Amish came after the War of 1812.

Today an estimated 100,000 Old Order Amish live in rural communities in the United States. In recent decades, the number of Amish in America has increased manifold. Ohio has the largest Amish population, followed by Pennsylvania and Indiana, and Amish communities are also located in Michigan, Iowa, Kansas, Kentucky, Florida, and other states.

---

*This case illustration is based on Hostetler (1980, 1987).

It is impossible to remain Amish without marriage to an Amish mate, so inbreeding is a problem. Only eight family names account for nearly 80 percent of all Amish people in Ohio, Pennsylvania, and Indiana. Virtually all of the several thousand Amish people in Lancaster County, Pennsylvania, for instance, are descendants of Christian Fisher, who was born in 1757. The selection of marriage partners among the Amish is limited by their horse-and-buggy transportation, as they seldom marry an individual living outside their local community.

When an Amish person deviates from church teachings, he or she is punished by a form of excommunication known as shunning (*Meidung*). When a person is shunned, no other Amish person may speak to the individual. As the Old Order Amish know only others of the same faith, shunning means that the individual may not have a friend in the world. Even the member's children, brothers, sisters, and spouse must refuse to speak to the individual and even to eat at the same table. Marital relations are forbidden. Only upon public repentance by the sinner is the excommunication lifted. For example, a young Amishman in Ohio was shunned for driving a car. After a week of shunning, he went before the local congregation and repented symbolically by tearing up his driver's license.

Despite the social pressure exerted by Amish parents on their youth, an estimated 20 percent defect. The high birthrates of the Amish, however, more than make up for this attrition. Many who leave the Amish faith join the Mennonite church, which is closely related in its lifestyle but is less strict in rejecting change.

Amish children have almost no contact with the non-Amish world around them. Television, radio, magazines, and non-Amish schooling are forbidden. Friendships with non-Amish children are banned. Amish teenagers are forbidden to attend public high schools, where their parents fear they will be lost to popular music, cars, and dating. A distinctive language is also important in maintaining socialization of the young into the Old Order Amish culture. The Amish speak a special German dialect, which also sets them apart from the non-Amish.

Religious persecution of the Amish during their European beginnings several centuries ago led to a strong value on separation from the society in which they live. The Amish stress this history of persecution in socializing their children; each schoolchild reads about the Amish martyrs who were tortured, raped, and killed by Christians in Europe.

One key ingredient in Amish survival is rich soil, which the Amish farm in a labor-intensive manner, growing tobacco, vegetables, fruit, and specialty crops. They operate such intensive livestock enterprises as dairying and raising chickens. The Amish family seeks to set up each of its offspring in farming. Tractors are rejected in order to maintain labor opportunities for Amish children. Hard work and high fertility go hand in hand for the Amish, as they seek to balance their rapidly increasing population with their local environment. In recent years, escalating land prices have threatened the Amish way of life. Today about half of the adult Amish people in Lancaster County work in such nonfarm employment as carpentry, blacksmithing, crafts, or cheese making, or in restaurants. One Amish business converts tractor-drawn farm implements to horse-drawn equipment, replacing pneumatic tires with metal rims.

While the Amish say "no" to most consumer innovations and to many agricultural innovations, they are very innovative in adopting new ideas that fit with their religious and family values. For example, Sommers and Napier (1993) gathered personal interview data from a sample of 366 Amish and non-Amish farmers living in three Ohio counties. The Amish farmers were greatly concerned with the problem of groundwater pollution due to agricultural chemicals. Such protection of soil and water resources is believed by the Amish to have a religious significance. Living in harmony with nature is highly valued, understandably so because the Amish way of life is dependent on high agricultural productivity. Community norms among the Amish reflect this value on conservation, so the same interpersonal pressures that oppose adoption of farm machinery, automobiles, and tractors encourage farmers to apply less fertilizer and pesticides.

Amish families are culturally forbidden to use modern technologies such as household water filtering systems or to purchase bottled water (Sommers and Napier, 1993). Accordingly, the adoption of such farm conservation innovations such as lower chemical applications to their crops is the most appropriate means for Amish farm families to avoid groundwater pollution.

So while the Amish are relatively uninnovative in a general sense, they are very innovative in adopting innovations that are consistent with Amish cultural values.

Characteristics of Adopter Categories

A voluminous research literature has accumulated about variables related to innovativeness. Here we summarize this diffusion research in a series of generalizations under three headings: (1) socioeconomic status, (2) personality values, and (3) communication behavior.

Socioeconomic Characteristics

Generalization 7-2: *Earlier adopters are no different from later adopters in age.* There is inconsistent evidence about the relationship of age and innovativeness. About half of the many diffusion studies on this subject show no relationship, a few found that earlier adopters are younger, and some indicate they are older.

Generalization 7-3: *Earlier adopters have more years of formal education than do later adopters.*

Generalization 7-4: *Earlier adopters are more likely to be literate than are later adopters.*

Generalization 7-5: *Earlier adopters have higher social status than do later adopters.* Status is indicated by such variables as income, level of living, possession of wealth, occupational prestige, self-perceived identification with a social class, and the like. However measured, social status is usually positively related with innovativeness.

Generalization 7-6: *Earlier adopters have a greater degree of upward social mobility than do later adopters.* Evidence suggests that earlier adopters are not only of higher status but are on the move in the direction of still higher levels of social status. In fact, they may be using the adoption of innovations as one means of getting there.

Generalization 7-7: *Earlier adopters have larger-sized units (farms, schools, companies, and so on) than do later adopters.* The social characteristics of earlier adopters mark them as more educated, of higher social status, and the like. They are wealthier and have large-sized units. Socioeconomic status and innovativeness appear to go hand in hand. Do innovators innovate because they are richer, or are they richer because they innovate? This cause-and-effect question cannot be answered solely on the basis of available cross-sectional data. But there are understandable reasons why social status and innovativeness vary together. Some new ideas are costly to adopt and require large initial outlays of capital. Only the wealthy units in a system may be able to adopt these innovations. Greatest profits usually go to the first to adopt; therefore, the innovator gains a financial advantage through relatively early adoption of the innovation. The innovators become richer and the laggards become relatively poorer as a result of this process.

Because the innovator is the first to adopt, risks must be taken that can be avoided by later adopters who do not wish to cope with the high degree of uncertainty concerning the innovation when it is first introduced into a system. Certain of the innovator's new ideas inevitably are likely to fail. He or she must be wealthy enough to absorb the loss from these occasional failures. Although wealth and innovativeness are highly related, economic factors do not offer a complete explanation of innovative behavior (or even approach doing so). For example, although agricultural innovators tend to be wealthy, there are many rich farmers who are *not* innovators.

Personality Variables

Personality variables associated with innovativeness have not yet received much research attention, in part because of difficulties in measuring personality dimensions in diffusion surveys.

Generalization 7-8: *Earlier adopters have greater empathy than do later adopters. Empathy* is the ability of an individual to project himself or herself into the role of another person. This ability is an important quality for an innovator, who must be able to think counterfactually, to be particularly imaginative, and to take the roles of heterophilous other individuals in order to exchange information effectively with them. To a certain extent, the innovator must be able to project into the role of individuals outside of his or her local system (as the innovator is the first to adopt in the local system): innovators in other systems, change agents, and scientists and R&D workers.

Generalization 7-9: *Earlier adopters may be less dogmatic than are later adopters. Dogmatism* is the degree to which an individual has a relatively closed belief system, that is, a set of beliefs which are strongly held. A highly dogmatic person would not welcome new ideas. Such an individual would instead prefer to hew to the past. Evidence in support of this generalization is not very strong, consisting of only several research studies.

Generalization 7-10: *Earlier adopters have a greater ability to deal with abstractions than do later adopters.* Innovators must be able to adopt a new idea largely on the basis of rather abstract stimuli, such as are received from the mass media. Later adopters can observe the innovation in the here-and-now of a peer's operation. They need less ability to deal with abstractions.

Generalization 7-11: *Earlier adopters have greater rationality than do later adopters. Rationality* is use of the most effective means to reach a given end.

Generalization 7-12: *Earlier adopters have more intelligence than do later adopters.*

Generalization 7-13: *Earlier adopters have a more favorable attitude toward change than do later adopters.*

Generalization 7-14: *Earlier adopters are better able to cope with uncertainty and risk than are later adopters.*

Generalization 7-15: *Earlier adopters have a more favorable attitude toward science than do later adopters.* Because innovations are often the product of scientific research, it is logical that innovators are more favorably inclined toward science.

Generalization 7-16: *Earlier adopters are less fatalistic than are later adopters. Fatalism* is the degree to which an individual perceives a lack of ability to control his or her future. An individual is more likely to adopt an innovation if he or she has more self-efficacy and believes that he or she is in control, rather than thinking that the future is determined by fate (Bandura, 1997).

Generalization 7-17: *Earlier adopters have higher aspirations (for formal education, higher status, occupations, and so on) than do later adopters.*

Communication Behavior

Generalization 7-18: *Earlier adopters have more social participation than do later adopters.*

Generalization 7-19: *Earlier adopters are more highly interconnected through interpersonal networks in their social system than are later adopters. Connectedness* is the degree to which an individual is linked to others.

Generalization 7-20: *Earlier adopters are more cosmopolite than are later adopters.* Innovators' interpersonal networks are more likely to be outside, rather than within, their system. They travel widely and are involved in matters beyond the boundaries of their local system. For instance, Iowa hybrid corn innovators traveled to urban centers such as Des Moines more often than did the average farmer (Ryan and Gross, 1943). Medical doctors who innovated in adopting a new drug attended more out-of-town professional meetings than did noninnovators (Coleman et al., 1966). *Cosmopoliteness* is the degree to which an individual is oriented outside a social system.

Innovators act like the early German sociologist Georg Simmel's (1908/1964, pp. 404–405) "stranger," whose special perspective stems from a lack of integration into the local system: "He is not radically committed to the unique ingredients and peculiar tendencies of the group, and . . . is bound by no commitments which could prejudice his perception, understanding, and evaluation of the given." The stranger's orientation outside of the group allows him or her to import information from the wider society (Rogers, 1999). The *stranger* was defined by Simmel (1908/1969) as an individual who is a member of a system but who is not strongly attached to the system (see Chapter 2).

The model for Simmel's stranger was the itinerant trader, who was often a Jew. Simmel was the son of Jewish parents who converted to Christianity, and he experienced anti-Semitism during his academic career in Germany. Perhaps the stranger is a recent immigrant into the system who retains the freedom of coming and going. Because the stranger is socially distant from others in the system, the stranger is relatively free from the system's norms. Further, the stranger sees the system in a different light than do others, and with greater objectivity. In fact, the Chicago School, which flourished at the University of Chicago from 1915 to 1935, applied Simmel's concept of the stranger to the empirical study of social problems, thus emphasizing the objectivity with which social scientists should view their respondents. Social scientists were trained to adopt the perspective of strangers. The concept of the stranger stimulated such intellectual offspring as the concepts of social distance (see Chapter 8), heterophily, and cosmopoliteness.

Obviously, our present conceptualization of the innovator has much in common with Georg Simmel's stranger. The innovator is a member of a system but is a cosmopolite, oriented outside of the system. The innovator has weak ties to other members of the system. This orientation frees the innovator from the constraints of the local system and allows him or her the personal freedom to try out previously untried new ideas.

Generalization 7-21: *Earlier adopters have more contact with change agents than do later adopters.*

Generalization 7-22: *Earlier adopters have greater exposure to mass media communication channels than do later adopters.*

Generalization 7-23: *Earlier adopters have greater exposure to interpersonal communication channels than do later adopters.*

Generalization 7-24: *Earlier adopters seek information about innovations more actively than do later adopters.*

Generalization 7-25: *Earlier adopters have greater knowledge of innovations than do later adopters.*

Generalization 7-26: *Earlier adopters have a higher degree of opinion leadership than do later adopters.* Although innovativeness and opinion leadership are positively related, the degree to which these two variables are related depends in part on the norms of the social system. In a system with norms favorable to change, opinion leaders are more innovative (see Chapter 8).

A fairly typical mini–case study of opinion leadership and adopter categories is shown in Figure 7–4. These data come from a neighborhood composed of fourteen farmers in Collins, Iowa, the community studied by the author for his doctoral dissertation. The innovator in this neighborhood, who adopted a new weed spray in 1948, the first year this innovation was available, received only one sociometric vote as an opinion leader (this vote came from an early adopter). The next individual to adopt (in 1950), an early adopter, was named by eight of the other thirteen farmers as their source or channel of communication for the new weed spray. When this early adopter began using the weed spray, many of his neighbors soon followed. In one sense, however, the innovator was *indirectly* very influential in that he influenced the opinion leader, who in turn influenced eight other farmers to adopt.

Audience Segmentation and Adopter Categories

In most of the generalizations above, an independent variable is positively related to innovativeness. This relationship means that innovators score higher on these independent variables than do laggards. For instance, Rogers with Svenning (1969) found that in traditional Colombian villages the innovators averaged thirty trips a year to cities, whereas the laggards averaged only 0.3 trips. A few variables, such as dogmatism and fatalism, are negatively related to innovativeness, and opinion leadership is greatest for early adopters, at least in most systems.

These characteristics of each adopter category have emerged from diffusion research. The important differences among these adopter categories suggest that change agents should use a different approach with each adopter category, or audience segmentation. *Audience segmentation* is a strategy in which different communication channels or messages are used to reach each subaudience. This strategy breaks down a heterophilous audience into a series of relatively more homophilous subaudiences. Thus, one might appeal to innovators who adopted an innovation because it was soundly tested and developed by credible scientists, but this approach would not be effective with the

Figure 7-4. The Diffusion of a New Weed Spray in an Iowa Farm Neighborhood

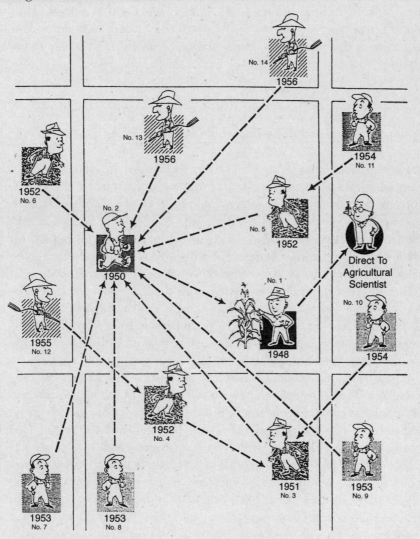

The fourteen Iowa farmers in this neighborhood network were asked by the author, "Where or from whom did you obtain information that convinced you to adopt 2,4-D weed spray?" The innovator, who adopted in 1948, said that he had learned about the innovation from an agricultural scientist. The early adopter served as an opinion leader for eight of the thirteen other farmers in this small system.

Source: Bohlen and others (1958).

late majority and laggards, who have a less favorable attitude toward science. They will not adopt a new idea until they feel that most uncertainty about the innovation's performance has been removed. These later adopters place greatest credibility in their peers' subjective experiences with the innovation, conveyed to them through interpersonal networks.

Cell Phone Laggards in Hong Kong*

Perhaps because change agencies are more interested in innovators and early adopters, relatively few diffusion studies are conducted of laggards, although interesting understandings could be derived from such research. A series of pioneering studies by Professors Ran Wei and Louis Leong at the Chinese University of Hong Kong of cell phone laggards proves this point. Hong Kong has one of the highest rates of cell phone adoption in the world (77 percent in late 2000, when the study was conducted). Data were gathered by telephone interviews from large samples of Hong Kong households in 1998 and 2000. These samples were large enough that 388 cell phone have-nots were included in 1998, and 202 in 2000. The characteristics of these 590 cell phone laggards were compared with the adopters at each of the two points in time.

As in many other countries, the first adopters of cell phones in Hong Kong were businesspeople, who were well educated, with higher incomes, and of higher socioeconomic status. For these relative elites, the cell phone was a technology that allowed business to be conducted on the run. Cell phones were advertised as a prestige consumer item, and fancy phone kits came with tailor-made leather covers and custom-designed ringing signals. Cell phones, along with other communication technologies such as karaoke, DVDs, and cable television, contributed to the increasingly popular self-centered lifestyle in Hong Kong, in which owning these technologies was considered part of enjoying life.

Then cell phones became much cheaper in cost. They diffused to later adopter categories and lower-status individuals such as blue-collar workers, homemakers, and students. The socioeconomic differences between adopters versus nonadopters began to diminish, suggesting that as the diffusion of a

*This case illustration is based on Wei (2001), Wei and Leung (1998), and Leung and Wei (2000).

new communication technology takes place, socioeconomic factors become less important (Dutton et al., 1987). Later adopters of cell phones mainly used them for emotional rather than business functions, such as to talk with their family members and to convey affection. Laggards, who had not adopted at the time of the 1998 and 2000 surveys in Hong Kong, said they did not have a cell phone because of (1) its complexity ("The cell phone services are confusing"), (2) incompatibility with their values ("Public phones are everywhere and are inexpensive"), and (3) relative disadvantage ("I have no need for a cell phone, and it usually has poor transmission").

The Hong Kong diffusion studies of laggards help us understand the diffusion process from their perspective. An innovation that almost everyone is adopting looks quite different when seen from the perspective of laggards.

The Innovativeness/Needs Paradox and the Strategy of Least Resistance

The individuals or other units in a system who most need the benefits of a new idea (the less educated, less wealthy, and the like) are generally the last to adopt an innovation. The units in a system who adopt first generally least need the benefits of the innovation. This paradoxical relationship between innovativeness and need for the benefits of an innovation tends to widen socioeconomic gaps between the higher- and lower-socioeconomic individuals in a system (see Chapter 11).

One illustration of the innovativeness/needs paradox is the adoption of contraceptive innovations in Third World nations. Elite families in these societies are already relatively small-sized, even though these families could well afford to raise many children. When a national family-planning program is launched by the national government, these elite families are the first to adopt contraceptives (Rogers, 1973). While socioeconomically elite families average only two or three children each, lower-status families average five or six children, which they often cannot afford to feed, clothe, or educate. The poorer families generally do not adopt contraceptives, even though one might think that they would feel a stronger need for family planning and for smaller-sized families. But they do not. And they wonder suspiciously why their government claims that it is providing free contraceptives for their benefit. Thus, the paradox occurs in which those individuals who might need an innovation most are the last to adopt.

What creates this paradox? In the case of family planning, poor families believe that having many children (especially sons) is an economic asset, in that the sons provide labor. Poor parents do not believe the government officials who tell them that a small family is a happy family. A second reason for the paradoxical tendency of those who most need an innovation to adopt it last, is that change agents often follow a segmentation strategy of *least resistance,* in that they especially contact socioeconomic elites, who are most receptive to innovations. The adoption of most contraceptive methods requires some degree of resources, skills, and/or training, which the nonelite members of a system are less likely to possess. For example, family-planning innovations are used more easily and more effectively by elites, as these contraceptive technologies require planning behavior, understanding the human reproductive function, and other knowledge and skills. So even when family-planning methods are provided to individuals at no cost by a government program, in most countries the socioeconomic elites adopt first.

The innovativeness/needs paradox need not occur. Change agents could pursue a segmentation strategy of *greatest resistance,* in which communication efforts are concentrated on the subaudiences who are lowest in socioeconomic status, who feel the least need for the innovation, and who would ordinarily be the last to adopt. An unfortunate consequence of the tendency of change agents to concentrate their efforts on elite clients, while largely ignoring the hard-to-reach subaudience of late majority and laggards, is widening gaps between the information-rich and the information-poor in a social system (see Chapter 11).

Today, the Internet may offer a new means of overcoming the innovativeness/needs paradox. Later adopters can now be reached with highly targeted, individualized messages about an innovation, delivered via the Internet. Such Internet targeting has been widely utilized to reach lower-income, less-educated individuals (who have access to computers) with health messages.

Network Influences on Innovativeness

Much past diffusion research focused on individual characteristics related to innovativeness, such as formal education, socioeconomic status, and other factors. In recent years, several diffusion scholars also investigated the role of an individual's network partners in explaining the focal individual's innovativeness. For example, Foster and Rozenzweig (1995) analyzed data from a nationwide sample of Indian farmers to show that neighbors' experience with agricultural innovations contributed to a farmer's innovativeness (and profitability), especially as the diffusion process for an innovation continued. In the following chapter, we discuss Shaheed Mohammed's (2001) study of how an individual's personal network variables influenced that individual's adoption of family planning innovations in Tanzania. For example, individuals with more adopters of family planning among their network partners were more likely to adopt family-planning methods themselves.

Similar results have been reported by diffusion scholars (mainly general sociologists and political scientists) studying the spread of such innovations as hate crime laws (Grattet, Jenness, and Curry, 1998), state lotteries (Berry and Berry, 1990), and so forth through the American states. Having a previously adopting neighbor state can facilitate a state's adoption of these innovations, as we saw earlier for California's influence on Oregon and Washington's adoption of hate crime laws. Not surprisingly, in the face of a high level of uncertainty about an innovative policy, a state's politicians and officials turn to other states who already have experience with the innovation they are considering for adoption. Here again we see that diffusion is a social process, with an innovation moving through interpersonal networks.

A similar kind of research has been conducted with regions in Italy as the units of analysis. Putnam (1993) computed an innovativeness score, composed of twelve new laws, for each of the twenty-one regional governments in Italy. The new laws included strip-mining regulation, fisheries promotion, and air and water pollution control. Adoption or rejection of each of the twelve laws was determined, and more points were awarded in the innovativeness score to regional governments that adopted a new law relatively earlier (this is a similar procedure to that used in the Saucío community study, discussed earlier in this chapter). The most innovative regional governments tended to influence their neighbors.

Further research is needed on network influences on individual's (and organizations') innovativeness.

Summary

Adopter categories are the classifications of the members of a social system on the basis of *innovativeness*, the degree to which an individual or other unit of adoption is relatively earlier in adopting new ideas than other members of a system. A variety of categorization systems and titles for adopters have been used in past studies. This chapter described the standard five adopter categories that are widely followed today in diffusion research, and their applications.

Adopter distributions tend to follow an S-shaped curve over time and to approach normality (Generalization 7-1). The continuum of innovativeness can be partitioned into five adopter categories (innovators, early adopters, early majority, late majority, and laggards) on the basis of two characteristics of a normal distribution, the mean and the standard deviation. The dominant attributes of each category are: Innovators—venturesome; early adopters—respect; early majority—deliberate; late majority—skeptical; and laggards—traditional. The relatively earlier adopters in a social system are no different from later adopters in age (Generalization 7-2), but they have more years of formal education (Generalization 7-3), are more likely to be literate (Generalization 7-4), and have higher social status (Generalization 7-5), a greater degree of upward social mobility (Generalization 7-6), and larger-sized units, such as farms, companies, schools, and so on (Generalization 7-7). These characteristics of adopter categories indicate that earlier adopters have generally higher socioeconomic status than do later adopters.

Earlier adopters in a system also differ from later adopters in personality variables. Earlier adopters have greater empathy (Generalization 7-8), less dogmatism (Generalization 7-9), a greater ability to deal with abstractions (Generalization 7-10), greater rationality (Generalization 7-11), greater intelligence (Generalization 7-12), a more favorable attitude toward change (Generalization 7-13), a greater ability to cope with uncertainty and risk (Generalization 7-14), a more favorable attitude toward science (Generalization 7-15), less fatalism and greater self-efficacy (Generalization 7-16), and higher aspirations for formal education, higher-status occupations, and so on (Generalization 7-17).

Finally, the adopter categories have different communication behavior. Earlier adopters have more social participation (Generalization 7-18), are more highly interconnected in the interpersonal networks of their system (Generalization 7-19), are more cosmopolite (Generalization 7-20), have more contact with change agents (Generalization 7-21), greater exposure to mass media channels (Generalization 7-22), and greater exposure to interpersonal communication channels (Generalization 7-23), engage in more active information seeking (Generalization 7-24), and have greater knowledge of innovations (Generalization 7-25) and a higher degree of opinion leadership (Generalization 7-26).

Past research thus shows many important differences between earlier and later adopters of innovations in (1) socioeconomic status, (2) personality variables, and (3) communication behavior. The distinctive characteristics of the five adopter categories mean that these adopter categories can be used for *audience segmentation,* a strategy in which different communication channels and/or messages are used to reach each subaudience.

8

DIFFUSION NETWORKS

Every herd of wild cattle has its leaders, its influential heads.
Gabriel Tarde, *The Laws of Imitation* (1903), p. 4.

In previous chapters of this book, we emphasized the importance of interpersonal network influences on individuals in convincing them to adopt innovations. Here we summarize what is known about such diffusion networks and how they convey innovation evaluation information to an individual in order to decrease uncertainty about a new idea. We begin with a discussion of *opinion leadership,* the degree to which an individual is able informally to influence other individuals' attitudes or overt behavior in a desired way with relative frequency. Opinion leaders are individuals who lead in influencing others' opinions. The behavior of opinion leaders is important in determining the rate of adoption of an innovation in a system. In fact, the diffusion curve is S-shaped because once opinion leaders adopt and begin telling others about an innovation, the number of adopters per unit of time takes off in an exponential curve.

The central idea of this chapter is how interpersonal communication drives the diffusion process by creating a critical mass of adopters.

Opinion Leadership in the Diffusion of Modern Math *

Understanding of opinion leadership is provided by a classic study of the spread of an important educational innovation, modern math, among the

---

*This case illustration is based on Richard O. Carlson (1965, pp. 17–21) and builds on the brief description of the modern math study in Chapter 2.

thirty-eight school superintendents in Allegheny County, Pennsylvania, which is essentially the city of Pittsburgh. The innovation of modern math began in the early 1950s, when top mathematicians in the United States completely overhauled the mathematics curriculum of public schools. Out of their efforts came "modern math," a radically new approach to teaching mathematics that was packaged to include textbooks, audiovisual aides designed for teaching the new concepts, and summer institutes to retrain school teachers in the new subject matter. The innovation spread relatively quickly because of powerful federal sponsorship by the National Science Foundation and the U.S. Department of Education. Modern math was widely hailed by educators as a major improvement. It was quite different from the "old" math in that it used set theory, Venn diagrams, and an emphasis upon probability. Math teachers had to learn an entirely new approach to their subject.

Modern math entered the schools of Allegheny County through one school superintendent, shown in Figure 8-1 as "I," who adopted in 1958. This innovator was a sociometric isolate in that he had no interpersonal network links with any of the thirty-seven other school superintendents in the Pittsburgh area. Innovators like "I" are frequently disdained by their fellow members in a local system. Innovators interact primarily with cosmopolite friends located outside of the system.

Figure 8-1 is a sociogram, or communication network map, which traces the interpersonal links in the diffusion of an innovation. The arrows show the patterns of communication flows among the superintendents. The shaded area encircles six friends, who constitute a clique, or informal friendship group. The superintendents in this clique interact more with one another than they do with outsiders. In Pittsburgh, these clique members often got together to play golf or poker.

This clique played a central role in the diffusion of modern math among Pittsburgh's schools. Once the clique members (especially the three main opinion leaders who decided to use the innovation in 1959 and 1960) adopted, the rate of adoption of modern math began to climb rapidly. Figure 8-1 shows that there was only one adopter in 1958 (the innovator), five by the end of 1959, fifteen by 1960, twenty-seven by 1961, thirty-five by 1962, and all thirty-eight by the end of 1963. The rapid spurt in 1959, 1960, and 1961 appeared to occur as a direct result of the opinion leaders' adoption.

Opinion leaders conform highly to the norms of their system. The cosmopolite innovator was *too* innovative to serve as an appropriate role model for the other thirty-seven superintendents. They waited to adopt until after the three opinion leaders in the six-member clique favored the innovation.

Figure 8-1. Opinion Leadership in the Diffusion Network for Modern Math among School Superintendents in Allegheny County, Pennsylvania

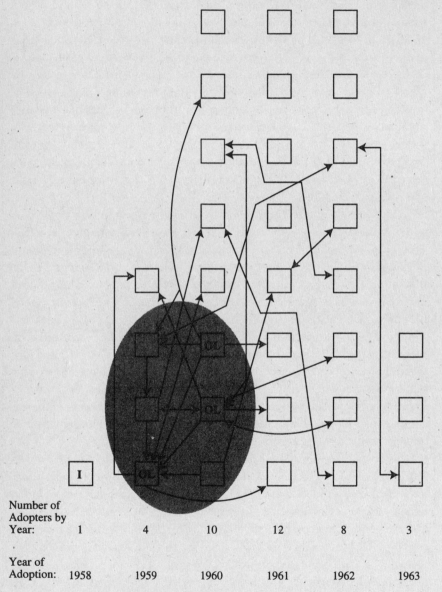

Number of Adopters by Year:	1	4	10	12	8	3
Year of Adoption:	1958	1959	1960	1961	1962	1963

Source: Constructed from data provided by Carlson (1965, p. 19). For the sake of simplicity, only thirty-two of the thirty-eight superintendents who adopted modern math are shown.

A change agent responsible for diffusing modern math in Allegheny County should concentrate promotional efforts on these opinion leaders, as they would then leverage such promotional efforts.

Figure 8-1 shows a rather high degree of homophily in the time of adoption of modern math by the thirty-eight superintendents. Many friendship arrows are between superintendents who adopted in the same year or within one year of each other. When two superintendents in a dyadic relationship adopted in different years, the difference was usually slight, suggesting that the source was different enough from the receiver to be perceived as competent but not so different as to be thought of as an inappropriate role model.

Models of Communication Flows

Understanding opinion leadership and diffusion networks is aided by several models of communication flows, which are discussed in the temporal sequence of their entrance on the stage of communication study.

The Hypodermic Needle Model

The *hypodermic needle model* postulated that the mass media had direct, immediate, and powerful effects on a mass audience. The mass media in the 1940s and 1950s were perceived as a strong influence on behavior change. The omnipotent media were pictured as conveying messages to atomized masses of individuals (Katz and Lazarsfeld, 1955). Conclusions about the power of the mass media were drawn from such historical events as (1) the role of the Hearst newspapers in arousing public support for the Spanish-American War, (2) the power of Nazi leader Joseph Goebbel's propaganda apparatus during World War II in Europe, and (3) the influence of Madison Avenue advertising on consumer and voting behavior in the United States.

Eventually, when more sophisticated research methods were used in communication research, doubt was cast on the hypodermic needle model. This survey research was directed by Paul F. Lazarsfeld of Columbia University, a pioneering mass communication scholar (Rogers, 1994). The hypodermic needle model was based primarily on intuitive theorizing from unique historical events and was too simple, too mechanistic, and too gross to give an accurate account of media effects. It ignored the role of opinion leaders.

The Two-Step Flow Model

The decisive end of the hypodermic needle model resulted serendipitously from a classic study of the 1940 presidential election in Erie County, Ohio (Lazarsfeld et al., 1944). This investigation was designed with the hypodermic needle model in mind and was aimed at analyzing the role of the media in changing political decisions. A panel study was conducted with a sample of six hundred voters over each of the six months prior to the November election and found, to the researchers' surprise, that very few voting decisions were directly influenced by the media. "This study went to great lengths to determine how the mass media brought about such changes. To our surprise we found the effect to be rather small. . . . People appeared to be much more influenced in their political decisions by face-to-face contact with other people. . . . than by the mass media directly" (Lazarsfeld and Menzel, 1963).

Instead the data suggested "that ideas often *flow* from radio and print *to* opinion leaders and *from* these to the less active sections of the population" (Lazarsfeld et al., 1944, p. 151). The first step, from media sources to opinion leaders, is mainly a transfer of *information*, whereas the second step, from opinion leaders to their followers, also involves the spread of interpersonal *influence*. This *two-step flow hypothesis* suggested that communication messages flow from a source, via mass media channels, to opinion leaders, who in turn pass them on to followers. This model has been widely tested in diffusion of innovations studies, and found generally to provide useful understandings of the flow of communication. Although important notions have been borrowed from the two-step model and amplified by later research, the oversimplified idea of a two-step flow is scarcely mentioned by scholars today.

The two-step flow model helped focus attention upon the interface between mass communication channels and interpersonal communication channels. The model implied that the mass media were neither as powerful nor as directly influential as had previously been thought. Of course, an individual can be exposed to a new idea through either mass media or interpersonal channels and then engage in communication exchanges about the innovation with peers. The communication process does not necessarily consist of just two steps. In some instances there may be only one step, as when the media have direct impact on an individual. In other instances a multistage communication process may occur.

Different communication sources or channels function at different stages in an individual's innovation-decision process (see Chapter 5).

The original two-step flow model did not recognize the role of different communication sources or channels at various stages in the innovation-decision process. We know that individuals pass from (1) *knowledge* of an innovation (2) to *persuasion* (3) to a *decision* to adopt or reject (4) to *implementation,* and then (5) to *confirmation* of this decision. Mass communication channels are primarily knowledge creators, whereas interpersonal networks are more important in persuading individuals to adopt or reject. This notion was masked in the original statement of the two-step model because the time sequence involved in an individual's innovation decision-making process was ignored. Such source/channel differences at the knowledge versus the persuasion stages usually exist for *both* opinion leaders and followers. Thus, opinion leaders are not the only individuals to use mass communication channels, as the original statement of the two-step flow model suggested.

The two-step flow model did not tell us enough. The flow of communication in an audience is far more complicated than just two steps. What is known about the communication process is too detailed to be expressed in one sentence or two steps. Nevertheless, the two-step flow hypothesis focussed communication study upon the study of opinion leadership.

Homophily and Heterophily in Communication Networks

Understanding of the nature of communication flows through interpersonal networks is enhanced by the concepts of homophily and heterophily. The structure of *who* relays messages to *whom* is brought out in such network analysis.

Homophily and Heterophily

A fundamental principle of human communication is that the exchange of ideas occurs most frequently between individuals who are alike, or homophilous. *Homophily* is the degree to which a pair of individuals who communicate are similar. Such similarity may be in certain attributes, such as beliefs, education, socioeconomic status, and the like. The conceptual label of "homophily" was given to this phenomenon several decades ago by Paul F. Lazarsfeld and Robert K. Merton (1964, p. 23), but the general idea of homophilous behavior was noted a century ago by the French sociologist Gabriel Tarde (1903, p. 64): "Social relations,

I repeat, are much closer between individuals who resemble each other in occupation and education."

Heterophily is the degree to which pairs of individuals who interact are different in certain attributes. Heterophily is the opposite of homophily. Homophily occurs frequently because communication is more effective when source and receiver are homophilous. When two individuals share common meanings, beliefs, and mutual understandings, communication between them is more likely to be effective. Individuals enjoy the comfort of interacting with others who are similar. Talking with those who are markedly different requires more effort to make communication effective. Heterophilous communication between dissimilar individuals may cause cognitive dissonance because an individual is exposed to messages that are inconsistent with existing beliefs, an uncomfortable psychological state.

Homophily and effective communication breed each other. The more communication there is between individuals in a dyad, the more likely they are to become homophilous. The more homophilous that two individuals are, the more likely that their communication will be effective. Individuals who depart from the homophily principle and attempt to communicate with others who are different often face the frustration of ineffective communication. Differences in technical competence, socioeconomic status, beliefs, and language often lead to mistaken interpretations, thereby causing messages to go unheeded.

But heterophilous communication has a special informational potential, even though it may occur only rarely. Heterophilous network links often connect two cliques, thus spanning two sets of socially dissimilar individuals in a system. These heterophilous interpersonal links in a system, called "bridges," are especially important in conveying information about innovations, as is implied in Granovetter's (1973) theory of "the-strength-of-weak-ties." So homophilous communication may be frequent and easy, but may not be as crucial as less frequent heterophilous communication in diffusing innovations. Homophily accelerates the diffusion process, but limits the spread of an innovation to those individuals connected in a close-knit network. Ultimately, the diffusion process can occur only through communication links that are at least somewhat heterophilous.

Homophily as a Barrier to Diffusion

Homophily can act as an invisible barrier to the flow of innovations within a system. New ideas usually enter a system through higher status and more innovative members. A high degree of homophily would mean that these elite individuals interact mainly with one another, and thus the innovation would not trickle down to nonelites. Homophilous diffusion patterns cause new ideas to spread horizontally, rather than vertically, within a system. Homophily can therefore act to slow down the rate of diffusion in a system. If homophily is a barrier to diffusion, change agents should work with several different sets of opinion leaders in a system. If the interpersonal networks in a system are characterized by a high degree of heterophily, a change agent could concentrate attention on only a few opinion leaders near the top in socioeconomic status and innovativeness (however, this is seldom the case).

Available evidence suggests Generalization 8-1: *Interpersonal diffusion networks are mostly homophilous.* For instance, individuals of highest status in a system seldom interact directly with those of lowest status. Likewise, innovators seldom converse with laggards. Although this homophily pattern in interpersonal networks acts to slow the diffusion of innovations within a system, it also has certain benefits. For example, a high-status opinion leader might be an inappropriate role model for someone of lower status, so interaction between them might not be beneficial to the latter. An illustration of this point comes from an investigation by Van den Ban (1963) in a Netherlands agricultural community. He found that only 3 percent of the opinion leaders had farms smaller than fifty acres in size, but 38 percent of all farms in the community were smaller than fifty acres. The wisest farm management decision for the large farmers was to purchase mechanized farm equipment, such as tractors and milking machines, as a substitute for hired labor, which was expensive. The best economic choice for the smaller farmers, however, was to ignore the expensive equipment and concentrate on intensive horticultural farming that required a great deal of labor per acre. As might be expected, however, the small farmers followed the example of the opinion leaders with large farms, even though their example was inappropriate for the small farmers' economic situation.

An illustration of homophilous and heterophilous diffusion networks is provided by a study of two Indian villages (Rao, Rogers, and Singh, 1980). One village was very innovative, while the other village had more traditional norms. Diffusion networks for a new rice variety were more homophilous in the traditional village. The opinion leaders here were elderly and had little formal education. In comparison, the opinion leaders in the innovative village were younger, highly educated, and of a high social caste. In the more traditional village, diffusion network links were highly homophilous on the basis of caste: Brahmins talked to Brahmins and Harijans talked to Harijans. But in the progressive vil-lage, the new rice variety started at the top of the social structure and then spread rapidly downward across the caste lines through het-erophilous network links. These heterophilous network links aided rapid diffusion.

Following is a generalization about characteristics of leaders versus followers when network links are heterophilous.

Generalization 8-2: *When interpersonal diffusion networks are het-erophilous, followers seek opinion leaders of higher socioeconomic sta-tus, with more formal education, with a greater degree of mass media exposure, who are more cosmopolite, have greater contact with change agents, and are more innovative.*

This generalization indicates a general tendency for followers to seek information and advice about innovations from opinion leaders per-ceived as more technically competent. When heterophily occurs, it is usually in the direction of individuals seeking a greater degree of com-petency, but not *too* much greater. We should not forget that the gen-eral pattern of interpersonal networks in the diffusion process is one of homophily. Such homophily means that the dyadic followers of opinion leaders usually learn appropriate lessons about an innovation through their ties with near peer opinion leaders. But these homophilous diffu-sion networks also slow the percolation of an innovation through the structure of a social system.

Measuring Opinion Leadership and Network Links

Four main methods of measuring opinion leadership and diffusion net-work links have been used in the past: (1) sociometric techniques, (2) informants' ratings, (3) self-designating techniques, and (4) observation (Table 8-1).

1. The *sociometric* method consists of asking respondents whom they sought (or hypothetically might seek) for information or advice about a given topic, such as a particular innovation. Opin-ion leaders are those members of a system who receive the great-est number of sociometric choices (and thus who are involved in the largest number of network links). Undoubtedly, the sociomet-ric technique is a highly valid measure of opinion leadership, as it

Table 8-1. Advantages and Limitations of Four Methods of Measuring Opinion Leadership and Diffusion Networks

Measurement Method	Description	Questions Asked	Advantages	Limitations
Sociometric method	Ask system members to whom they go for advice and information about an idea	Who is your leader?	Sociometric questions are easy to administer and are adaptable to different types of settings and issues; highest validity	Analysis of sociometric data can be complex. Requires a large number of respondents to locate a small number of opinion leaders. Not applicable to sample designs where only a portion of the social system is interviewed.
Informants' ratings	Ask subjectively selected key informants in a system to designate opinion leaders	Who are leaders in this system?	A cost-saving and timesaving method as compared to the sociometric method	Each informant must be thoroughly familiar with the system.
Self-designating method	Ask each respondent a series of questions to determine the degree to which he/she perceives himself/herself to be an opinion leader	Are you a leader in this system?	Measures the individual's perceptions of her/his opinion leadership, which influence her/his behavior	Dependent upon the accuracy with which respondents can identify and report their self-images.
Observation	Identify and record communication network links as they occur	None	High validity	Obtrusive; works best in a very small system and may require much patience by the observer.

is measured through the perceptions of followers. It necessitates, however, interrogating a large number of respondents in order to locate a small number of opinion leaders. The sociometric method is most applicable when all (or most) members of a social system provide network data, rather than when a small sample of the total population is contacted.

It is usual to specify the number of sociometric network partners to be named by a respondent: "Who are the three (or four or five) other women in this village with whom you have discussed family-planning methods?" Such limited-choice questioning leads a respondent to name only the strongest network partners. It is, however, possible that others with whom a respondent converses less often may exchange information with the respondent that is more crucial in the diffusion process. Perhaps sociometric questions should allow an unlimited number of choices, letting the respondent name any number of network partners with whom a topic is discussed. Another approach is to conduct a "roster study," in which each respondent is presented with a list of all the other members of the system and asked whether he or she talks with each of them and how often. The roster technique has the advantage of measuring "weak" as well as "strong" links.

2. An alternative to using sociometry to identify opinion leaders is to ask *key informants* who are especially knowledgeable about the networks in a system. Often a handful of informants can identify the opinion leaders in a system with a precision that is almost as accurate as sociometric techniques, particularly when the system is small and the informants are well informed. The key informants technique was utilized in Taos County, New Mexico, where Buller and others (2001) sought to bridge the digital divide by recruiting opinion leaders to learn how to use computers and the Internet. The opinion leaders then recruited other people to learn these skills. The opinion leaders were identified by asking key informants (religious leaders, town officials, school administrators, and other long-time residents) to nominate individuals whom other people sought out for information and advice. The opinion leaders were individuals nominated by two or more of the key informants.

3. The *self-designating* technique asks respondents to indicate the degree to which others in the system regard them as influential. "Individuals select themselves to be peer leaders" (Valente and Davis, 1999). A typical self-designating question is "Do you think

people come to you for information or advice more often than to others?" The self-designating method depends upon the accuracy with which respondents can identify and report their images. This measure of opinion leadership is especially appropriate when interrogating a random sample of respondents in a system, a sampling design that precludes effective use of sociometric methods.

4. Opinion leadership can be measured by *observation,* in which an investigator identifies and records the communication behavior in a system. One advantage of observation is that the data usually have a high degree of validity. If network links are appropriately observed, there is no doubt about whether or not they occur. Observation works best in a very small system, where the observer can actually see and record interpersonal interactions as they occur. Unfortunately, in such small systems observation may be a very obtrusive data-gathering technique. Because the members of a system know they are being observed, they may act differently. Further, an observer may need to be very patient if the diffusion network behavior that he or she wants to observe occurs only rarely.

In practice, observation has been used infrequently to measure diffusion networks and opinion leadership. One well-known example was a randomized controlled trial of an intervention for HIV prevention in gay bars in four U.S. cities (Kelly et al., 1997). Bartenders were trained in how to observe opinion leadership among their customers for ten days and to record the names of individuals who were most popular with other men. The criteria suggested were which men were most often greeted, greeted others, and seemed well liked. Each gay bar had several bartenders, who made independent observations. Men whose names were on several bartenders' lists were then recruited to serve as opinion leaders (they constituted about 8 percent of a bar's customers). These opinion leaders were trained in HIV prevention and safer sex and given badges (a logo of a traffic light) to wear, in order to stimulate questions from their acquaintances. A sample of gay men in the four intervention bars was surveyed about their safe sex behavior before and after the one-year opinion leader intervention.

Kelly and his collaborators (1997) found a 45 percent increase in condom-protected anal intercourse (unprotected anal intercourse is one of the main means of HIV transmission for gay men) by customers in the gay bars in the four intervention cities, as compared to four control cities. Similar results have been found in similar experiments in the United States (Kelly et al., 1991, 1992; Kegeles et al., 1996; Sikkema et al., 2000) but not in five gyms in London (Elford et al., 2001, 2002) or in gay bars in Glasgow and Edinburgh, Scotland (Flowers et al., 2002), although these later studies did not select and train as opinion leaders the minimum of 15 percent of the target audience that Jeff Kelly feels is necessary. "Kelly's work underscored that the distinctive nature of urban gay male bar networks provides a particularly powerful place in which diffusion might occur" (Miller et al., 1998, p. 99). The gay bar approach did not assume that all members of a system must have direct contact with an opinion leader, because the opinion leader's message (safer sex) spreads naturally through the communication networks in which the opinion leader is embedded. In this sense, the gay bar opinion leadership strategy of Kelly and others (1991, 1992, 1997) is similar to the STOP AIDS intervention in the early years of the AIDS epidemic in San Francisco (see Chapter 2).

When two or three types of opinion leadership measurement have been utilized with the same respondents, positive correlations among the measures have been obtained, although these relationships show far from complete agreement. The choice of any one of the four methods (sociometric, key informants, self-designating, and observation) can be based on convenience, as all four are about equally valid.

Further, studies of the opinion leaders in a system generally find a high degree of stability over time. For example, O'Brien and others (1998) reported that the leaders in five rural communities in Missouri and their communication networks remained stable over the six-year period from 1989 to 1995, despite the social disruptions caused by flooding of two communities and the introduction of corporate hog production into two communities. Of course, over a period of decades the opinion leaders in a system must inevitably change, even in a relatively stable community or organization. In general, however, opinion leadership structures are stable in the relatively short term.

In a typical distribution of opinion leadership in a social system, a few individuals receive a great deal of opinion leadership, while most individuals have none or very little. Opinion leadership is a matter of degree. The most influential opinion leaders are key targets for the efforts of change agents in diffusion campaigns.

The Role of Alpha Pups in the Viral Marketing of a Cool Electronics Game*

A market research company asked thousands of boys aged eight to thirteen in Chicago, "Who's the coolest kid you know?" Then they interviewed the kid who was so named, asking him the same question. The researchers ascended the hierarchy of coolness until someone finally answered, "Me." Using this combination of sociometric and self-designating methods, the research teams identified 1,600 opinion leader kids, whom they called "alpha pups." In April 2001, when eight of the alpha pups were invited to a focus group interview in a building near the downtown Loop, a narrator asked them to raise their hand if they were cool. Every hand shot up.

Then the narrator passed out a Pox unit, each somewhat larger than a cellular phone, to each kid. This new game, sold by Hasbro, the giant toy maker, appeals to kids to fight off an invasion by deadly extraterrestrials called Pox, who have escaped from a laboratory. Each Pox unit allows the player to assemble a warrior from available body parts. A radio transmitter allows a kid to battle any other player within thirty feet. The focus group narrator in the Chicago meeting explained to the eight alpha pups that once they had assembled their warrior, they could put their unit into Battle mode and attack someone else's Pox in the next room. The alpha pups pumped their fists and shouted with enthusiasm.

In order to excel at the game, a player must learn hundreds and hundreds of permutations, as each body part has particular strengths and weaknesses when matched against another warrior. The battle is something like the old game of rock-paper-scissors but is much more complicated. The distinctive aspect of Pox is that a single kid cannot have much fun alone. The game demands play against other kids who are also armed with Pox units. When one Pox player wipes out another player, the winner gets the body parts of the slain warrior.

At the end of the focus group interview, each alpha pup was paid $30 and given a day pack containing ten Pox units to hand out to friends. This marketing approach is what Hasbro calls "viral marketing," so called because they are seeding the Pox units through opinion leaders to their friends in a process resembling an epidemic. The company decided to launch the new toy in one place, Chicago. Hasbro identified 1,600 alpha pups and used them to infect nine hundred of the 1,400 schools in the Chicago area. Then Pox went on sale at about $25 per unit. No attempt was made to interest girls in the new game (this marketing strategy is one of targeting).

Why does Hasbro call the opinion leader kids "alpha pups"? When Tom

---

*This case illustration is based on Tierney (2001).

Schneider, president of the market research company that conducted the opinion leader identification for Hasbro, purchased an English spaniel, the breeder warned him not to select the alpha (leader) dog of the litter, because it would ruin his life. Schneider said, "It seemed to me that was just the kind of kid we were looking for."

Monomorphic and Polymorphic Opinion Leadership

Is there one set of all-purpose opinion leaders in a system, or are there different opinion leaders for different issues? *Polymorphism* is the degree to which an individual acts as an opinion leader for a variety of topics. The opposite, *monomorphism,* is the degree to which an individual acts as an opinion leader for only a single topic. The degree of polymorphic opinion leadership in a given social system seems to vary with such factors as the diversity of the topics on which opinion leadership is measured, whether system norms are innovative or not, and so on. An analysis of opinion leadership among housewives in Decatur, Illinois, for four different topics (fashions, movies, public affairs, and consumer products) by Katz and Lazarsfeld (1955) found that one third of the opinion leaders exerted their influence in more than one of the four areas. Other studies report more, or less, polymorphism. For instance, village leaders in developing countries are frequently opinion leaders for health, agricultural, and educational ideas, as well as political and moral issues.

Paul Revere's Ride*

Every American school child knows the famous poem by Henry Wadsworth Longfellow that begins "Listen, my children, and you shall hear of the midnight ride of Paul Revere." The poem tells how a Boston silversmith rode through the night of April 18–19, 1775 to warn the citizens of Massachusetts that British troops were marching from Boston in order to seize the colonial leaders, John Hancock and Samuel Adams, and to capture stores of guns and ammunition. Patriotic Americans met the invaders the next day at the towns of Lexington and Concord, soundly beating them. The resulting conflict launched the American Revolutionary War.

By 1:00 A.M. on the morning following the British march out of Boston,

---

*This case illustration is based on Fischer (1994).

April 19, thanks to Revere's nocturnal ride, news that the British were coming reached Lincoln, Massachusetts; the warning was in Sudbury by 3:00 A.M., and it reached Andover, twenty-five miles northwest of Boston, by 5:00 A.M. (Figure 8-2). By 9:00 A.M., Revere's alarm had spread as far as Ashby, Massachusetts, some forty-five miles from Boston, and had aroused people over a 750-square-mile area! Thousands of American militia were thus organized to meet the British troops at Lexington and Concord later on the morning of April 19, and to attack them that afternoon on their retreat to Boston. Had reinforcements not reached the British regulars during their return trip, the entire expedition would have been wiped out.

Figure 8-2. Diffusion of the Alarm that the British Were Coming on April 18–19, 1775

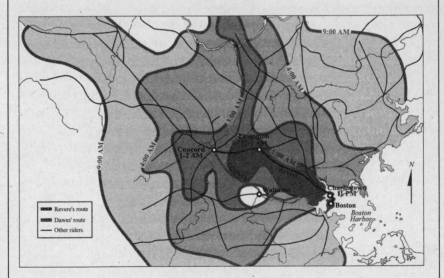

Paul Revere rode from Boston during the night of April 18–19 to warn the American colonists that a British army was marching to capture their revolutionary leaders and arms. So many American militia were gathered at Lexington and Concord the next day that they soundly defeated the British. Not so well known is that a second nocturnal rider, William Dawes, also raised the alarm, but he did not know the opinion leaders in the small Massachusetts towns. Notice that Waltham, a town on Dawes's route, never received an effective alarm, and its militia did not join the fighting at nearby Lexington.

Source: Based on Fischer (1994, p. 146).

What is not well known is that another American horseman, William Dawes, also rode from Boston that night to spread the alarm. But Dawes's ride had relatively little effect in raising American militia, as he did not know the network structure of the anti-British opinion leaders in Massachusetts's small towns and villages. William Dawes started from Boston at 11:00 P.M., the same time as Paul Revere, on an equally fast horse and with the same objective, although he took a different route. Why was Dawes so ineffective in raising the alarm? Revere had played a key role in the earlier Boston Tea Party and belonged to many of the clubs of revolutionaries that plotted to throw off British rule. Revere knew exactly which doors to pound on during his ride on Brown Beauty that April night. As a result, he awakened key individuals, who then rallied their neighbors to take up arms against the British. They sounded the alarm, for instance by firing a gun three times in quick succession, in order to turn out the neighboring militia. Some village leaders sent riders off to spread the alarm to other communities. During his night ride, Revere encountered young men on horseback who were returning from courting missions. Revere convinced these individuals to further spread the alarm, setting into motion an S-shaped diffusion curve as the news fanned out to a huge number of New Englanders. In fact, the news spread so far that the word-of-mouth transmission eventually looped back around and returned to Boston (see Figure 8-2).

In comparison, Dawes did not know the territory as well as Revere. As he rode through rural Massachusetts on the night of April 18–19, he simply knocked on random doors. The occupants in most cases simply turned over and went back to sleep.

Characteristics of Opinion Leaders

How do opinion leaders differ from their followers? The following seven generalizations summarize empirical studies designed to answer this question. In each proposition we refer to "opinion leaders" and "followers" as if opinion leadership were a dichotomy and as if all nonleaders were followers (these oversimplifications are necessary for the sake of clarity).

External Communication

Generalization 8-3: *Opinion leaders have greater exposure to mass media than their followers*. The original conception of the two-step flow hypothesis stated that opinion leaders have greater exposure to mass communication channels (Lazarsfield et al., 1944). Opinion leaders gain their perceived competency by serving as an avenue for the entrance of new ideas into their system. The external linkage may be provided via mass media channels, by an opinion leader's cosmopoliteness, or by an opinion leader's greater contact with change agents.

Generalization 8-4: *Opinion leaders are more cosmopolite than their followers.* An eminent sociologist of communication networks, Professor Ron Burt, described opinion leaders as "people on the edge": opinion leaders have a certain degree of cosmopoliteness in that they bring new ideas from outside their social group to its members. They "carry information across the boundaries between groups. They are not people at the top of things so much as people at the edge of things, not leaders within groups so much as brokers between groups" (Burt, 1999, p. 37). Opinion leaders gain part of their perceived expertise regarding innovations by their greater contact across their system's boundaries.

Generalization 8-5: *Opinion leaders have greater contact with change agents than their followers.* As explained previously, change agents try to utilize opinion leaders to leverage diffusion activities; thus, not surprisingly, opinion leaders often have greater contact with change agents than do their followers.

Accessibility

In order for opinion leaders to spread messages about an innovation, they must have extensive interpersonal network links with their followers. Opinion leaders must be socially accessible. One indicator of such accessibility is social participation. Face-to-face communication about new ideas may occur at meetings of formal organizations and through informal discussions. One reason that Paul Revere was in such a key social position to spread the alarm in Massachusetts was that he belonged to many men's clubs in the Boston area, such as the London Enemies List, North Caucus, and Long Room Club. Revere was also connected to two important taverns, Cromwell's Head and Bunch of Grapes, that were gatherings of revolutionaries. The membership of these clubs and taverns included the political leaders who started the American Revolutionary War in 1775 (Fischer, 1994).

Generalization 8-6: *Opinion leaders have greater social participation than their followers.*

Socioeconomic Status

We expect that a follower typically seeks an opinion leader of somewhat higher socioeconomic status, as suggested in Generalization 8-2. So opinion leaders, on the average, are of higher status than their followers. This point was stated by Gabriel Tarde (1903, p. 221): "Invention can start from the lowest ranks of the people, but its extension depends upon the existence of some lofty social elevation." Generalization 8-7: *Opinion leaders have higher socioeconomic status than their followers.*

Innovativeness

If opinion leaders are to be recognized by their peers as competent and trustworthy experts about innovations, the opinion leaders should adopt new ideas before their followers. There is strong empirical support for Generalization 8-8: *Opinion leaders are more innovative than their followers.* However, opinion leaders are not necessarily innovators. Sometimes they are, but usually they are not. What explains this apparently contradictory finding? We must consider the effect of system norms on the innovativeness of opinion leaders, because the degree to which opinion leaders are innovative depends in large part on their followers.

Innovativeness, Opinion Leadership, and System Norms

How can opinion leaders conform to system norms and at the same time lead in the adoption of new ideas? The answer is expressed as Generalization 8-9: *When a social system's norms favor change, opinion leaders are more innovative, but when the system's norms do not favor change, opinion leaders are not especially innovative.* In systems with more traditional norms, the opinion leaders are usually a separate set of individuals from the innovators. The innovators are perceived with suspicion and often with disrespect by the members of such systems, who do not trust the innovators' sense of judgment about new ideas. For instance, in a study of Colombian farmers in traditional villages, Rogers with Svenning (1969) found that opinion leaders were only slightly more innovative than their followers and were older and less cosmopolite. So the system's norms determine whether or not opinion leaders are innovators.

Data from inquiries in various nations support the notion of opinion leaders as highly conforming to system norms. For instance, Herzog and others (1968, p. 72) concluded from their study of Brazilian villages that

"In most traditional communities, neither the leaders nor their followers are innovative, and as a result, the community remains traditional. In the most modern communities, community norms favor innovativeness and both the leaders and followers are innovative. In the middle-range communities, where modernization is just getting under way, divisions occur and the community opinion leaders lead the way toward modernization, by trying new ideas before the other farmers in the community."

A common error made by change agents is that they select as opinion leaders individuals who are *too* innovative. Change agents work through opinion leaders in order to close the heterophily gap between themselves and their clients (see Chapter 9). But if opinion leaders are very much more innovative than the average client, the heterophily that formerly existed between the change agent and his or her clients now exists between opinion leaders and followers. Innovators are inappropriate opinion leaders in systems with traditional norms: they are too elite and too change-oriented. The innovator is an unrealistic model for the average individual. The norms of the system determine the adopter category in which opinion leaders in a system are found.

Sometimes change agents identify potentially effective opinion leaders among their clients, but then they concentrate their contacts on these leaders to such a degree that they become innovators and lose their former followers. The interpersonal relationships between opinion leaders and their followers hang in a delicate balance. If an opinion leader becomes too innovative, or adopts a new idea too quickly, followers may begin to doubt his or her judgment. One role of the opinion leader in a social system is to help reduce uncertainty about an innovation for his or her followers. To fulfill this role, an opinion leader must demonstrate prudent judgment in decisions about adopting new ideas. So the opinion leader must continually look over his or her shoulder and consider where the rest of the system is at regarding new ideas.

Opinion Leader Organizations

Are there opinion leaders among organizations? A study by Jack Walker (1966) suggested that innovations can diffuse from organization to organization through interorganizational networks, in a process parallel to that among individuals in a social system.* The organizations studied by Pro-

---

*Publications bearing on the Walker study of innovativeness among the U.S. states include Walker (1966, 1971, 1973, 1976, 1977) and Gray (1973a, 1973b).

fessor Walker were the fifty state governments in the United States. Each state was scored on its innovativeness in adopting eighty-eight statewide programs in welfare, health, education, conservation, highways, civil rights, police, and the like. Each adoption by a state amounted to offering a new service, establishing a new regulation, or creating a new state agency. Examples were having a gasoline tax, enacting a civil rights bill, providing for slaughterhouse inspection, and having a state health board. The five most innovative states, Walker (1971) found, were New York, Massachusetts, California, New Jersey, and Michigan. These pioneering states, which Professor Walker called "the national league," have large populations and are urbanized and industrialized. Perhaps they faced a social problem several years before the more rural and smaller states and enacted a new law to cope with it. They are also richer states, so they had the resources to adopt innovations.

Within each region of the United States, certain states emerged as opinion leaders; once they adopted a new program, other states in their region followed their lead. If an innovation was first adopted by other than one of these opinion leader states, it then spread to the other states slowly or not at all. Thus, a communication network structure existed for innovation diffusion among the American states.

In a further analysis, Walker (1971) gathered network data from personal interviews with state officials in ten of the states in order to determine the diffusion networks linking the fifty states. State officials looked to their immediate neighbors when searching for information about innovations: "State administrators communicate most readily with their counterparts in states that they believe have similar resources, social problems, and administrative styles" (Walker, 1971, p. 381). For instance, Iowa officials followed Michigan's and California's lead in certain innovations, although they were much more influenced by Wisconsin, a state bordering Iowa that was considered a more appropriate model. Wisconsin was an opinion leader for other midwestern states. Wisconsin ranked tenth on Walker's index of innovativeness among the fifty states while Iowa ranked twenty-ninth. Walker found that the follower states in his study often copied the exact wording of a law previously adopted by an opinion leader state, including, in several cases, a major typographical error!

In summary, one can think of the diffusion process among the fifty American states as beginning with a new law that is adopted by one or more of the five "national league" states. After a few years, the new law may be adopted by an opinion leader state in each region. Then the innovative law spreads rapidly among the several states in that region. The opinion leader states mediated between the five innovators and the other forty-five states. They provided connectedness to the nationwide diffusion network.

Further evidence that opinion leadership patterns exist among organizations, as well as individuals, comes from research on an important policy innovation diffusing among U.S. cities in recent decades: a city ordinance preventing smoking in public places, such as city buildings, restaurants, bars, and so forth (Rogers, Peterson, and McOwiti, 2002). One of the first cities in the southwestern United States to adopt such a clean indoor air ordinance was Las Cruces, New Mexico, in part because this small university town had a no-smoking champion on the city council as well as a respected biomedical researcher who had conducted investigations of the harmful effects of second-hand smoke (Hays et al., 2000). Within a few years, the Las Cruces no-smoking ordinance had spread to a dozen other cities in the Southwest (including El Paso, Texas), in part through the activities of a local coalition of community health leaders. Las Cruces thus served as an opinion leader city in the diffusion of this policy innovation in its region.

Do Opinion Leaders Matter?

"A network . . . can be used, rather than ignored, when creating [diffusion] programs" (Valente and Davis, 1999, p. 56). The most common way to use a network is to identify and utilize opinion leaders. Numerous experiments have been conducted in recent years in order to determine whether working through opinion leaders in a system speeds up the diffusion process. Some of these studies involve lay opinion leaders in health interventions, while one investigation deals with how an innovation spread among medical doctors. A well-known study by Jonathan Lomas and colleagues (1991) compared two interventions designed to gain the adoption of practice guidelines recommending vaginal birth delivery, in order to decrease the risk associated with Cesarean delivery of babies. One intervention involved selecting opinion leaders among the seventy-six medical doctors in sixteen community hospitals, who encouraged adoption of the vaginal birth guidelines. The comparative intervention that was evaluated in an experiment involved an audit of charts and feedback to the doctors. After two years, the audit intervention had no measurable results, while the opinion leader approach led to an 85 percent increase in adoption of vaginal birth delivery.

Notice here that the experiment compared using an opinion leader versus an alternative approach.

Table 8-2 shows that all eight of the completed experiments on the effects of opinion leadership reported that the opinion leadership intervention was effective in bringing about behavior change, whether the intervention entailed HIV prevention, the adoption of mammography for breast cancer screening, or the prevention of heart disease. Importantly, most of these health intervention studies were randomized controlled trials, considered the "gold standard" for testing the efficacy of a new drug, new medical procedure, or some other means of intervening in a system to improve the health of its members. What is a randomized controlled trial (RCT)? Data are gathered before and after (and perhaps more often) an intervention is randomly assigned to individuals or systems in a treatment condition, but not in a control (or comparison) condition. The effects occurring in the latter condition are subtracted from the effects in the treatment condition in order to remove the effects of contemporaneous changes. Thus the evidence from the ten experiments summarized in Table 8-2 is particularly convincing regarding the importance of opinion leaders in diffusing innovations. This conclusion is hardly surprising, and it builds upon previous studies of opinion leadership that were not experimental in nature. As explained in Chapter 2, most diffusion researches are surveys, rather than experiments. So the experiments on opinion leadership in recent years may be particularly important, perhaps marking a growing trend toward using experimental designs to answer research questions about the diffusion of innovations.

Why did individuals identified as opinion leaders in these ten experiments agree to exert their network influence on other people for the behalf of the intervention program? A common reason was a personal experience with the health problem being remedied by the intervention program. For example, many of the 170 opinion leaders in Earp and colleagues' (2002) North Carolina mammography promotion program had themselves been successful in recovering from breast cancer due to early detection. Thus they served as positive role models for mammography screening. As mentioned previously, a few decades ago, North Karelia had the highest rates of heart disease in Finland, which had the highest rate of any nation at the time. Many of the 805 opinion leaders in the North Karelia Heart Disease Prevention Project had had a heart attack or had lost a father, brother, or husband to cardiovascular disease (Puska et al., 1986). In addition to such personal involvement with a health problem, most opinion leaders dis-

Table 8-2. Effects of Opinion Leaders
Experiments show that the effects of opinion leaders in diffusion programs are robust.

Investigators, Research Design	Method of Identifying Opinion Leaders	Objectives of the Diffusion Program	Effects of the Opinion Leader Intervention
Castro et al. (1995), Randomized controlled trial over 3 years.	Key informants (priests/ministers in seven churches in Phoenix, Arizona)	Opinion leaders in each church who had successfully battled breast cancer encouraged church members in cancer prevention (cancer screening, nutrition, etc.)	None reported, as the project was still under way
Celentano et al. (2000), randomized controlled trial over 21 months.	Key informants and sociometric (Thai Royal Army draftees)	To decrease the high rate of STD and HIV infection among 450 men in the Thai Army	Robust effects on STD and HIV prevention
Earp et al. (2002), randomized controlled trial over 3 years.	Key informants (170 opinion leaders in 5 North Carolina counties)	To promote mammography breast cancer screening among African American women through presentations at beauty parlors, churches, etc.	Mammography rates increased by 7 percent over 5 comparison counties
Kelly et al. (1992), randomized controlled trial over 6 months.	Observation and key informants in gay bars (bartenders in 3 cities identified 43 opinion leaders)	To decrease rates of HIV infection among customers of gay bars by decreasing high-risk behaviors	15 to 29 percent reduction of unprotected anal intercourse
Kelly et al. (1997), randomized controlled trial over 1 year.	Observation and key informants (bartenders in gay bars in 4 cities)	To decrease rates of HIV infection among 1,126 customers of gay bars by decreasing high-risk behaviors	Decrease in unprotected anal intercourse and increased use of condoms
Lomas et al. (1991), randomized controlled trial over 2 years.	Sociometric nomination of 4 opinion leaders by doctors in 4 Ontario hospitals	To decrease birth by cesarean delivery for 3,552 pregnant women	A major reduction in the rate of cesarean birth deliveries only in the hospitals with opinion leader doctors

Table 8-2. Effects of Opinion Leaders (*continued*)
Experiments show that the effects of opinion leaders in diffusion programs are robust.

Investigators, Research Design	*Method of Identifying Opinion Leaders*	*Objectives of the Diffusion Program*	*Effects of the Opinion Leader Intervention*
Miller et al. (1998), randomized controlled trial with data collected at 5 points in time over 8 months.	Observation and key informants (bartenders in hustler bars in New York City)	To decrease the risk of HIV infection among 1,862 male prostitutes and other patrons in hustler bars	Twenty trained opinion leaders influenced men to decrease high-risk behaviors by 3 to 25 percent
Puska et al. (1986), field experiment over 4 years.	805 opinion leaders, 2 in each village identified by key informants in North Karelia County, Finland	To reduce heart disease risk factors in a system characterized by very high cardiovascular disease	A reduction in smoking and an increase in healthy nutrition
Tessaro et al. (2000), field experiment over 18 months.	Key informants in 4 worksites recruited 104 female opinion leaders	To improve health behavior of all employees in the 4 work organizations	Opinion leaders distributed printed health materials, conducted health meetings, diffused health information through informal networks
Valente et al. (2002), randomized controlled trial over 3 months.	Key informants (teachers), sociometric methods (survey) and network methods (1,960 sixth-graders in 16 California schools)	To compare rates of smoking prevention resulting from training by teachers, opinion leaders, or by network partners	None reported, as the project is still under way

played a high degree of altruism. Female opinion leaders in the four work organizations studied by Tessaro and others (2000) were motivated to serve as opinion leaders in a worksite health program because of their concern for the health of their fellow employees.

The exact procedure through which opinion leaders are identified and the care taken in this process undoubtedly determine, at least to a certain extent, the impacts of the opinion leadership approach in changing their followers' behavior. Opinion leaders must be constantly retrained and encouraged in order for them to keep up their influence activities with their followers. At the end of four years, half of the 805 opinion leaders in the North Karelia Project had become inactive (Puska et al., 1986). Further, the nature of the diffusion responsibilities that opinion leaders were trained to carry out in a diffusion intervention varied widely from experiment to experiment. In the gay bars experiment, mentioned earlier, opinion leaders were trained to be positive role models for safer sex and HIV prevention (Kelly et al., 1992, 1997; Miller et al, 1998). The trained opinion leaders in the gay bars were approached by bar patrons frequently, mainly in response to the small traffic light logo buttons that the opinion leaders wore on their clothing (Kelly et al., 1991). In contrast, the 170 opinion leaders in a North Carolina experiment were expected to contact women about mammography for breast cancer screening in churches, beauty parlors, and other appropriate places to discuss this sensitive topic (Earp et al., 2002).

Just how and where opinion leaders and followers come into contact with each other varies from experiment to experiment (Table 8-2). Some opinion leaders, as in the gay bars, were simply available to talk with their followers. In other studies, opinion leaders were trained to actively seek out and contact members of their system, to organize meetings, and to distribute printed messages (Tessaro et al., 2000). The experiment in California schools by Valente and colleagues (2002) compared the smoking prevention performance of opinion leaders identified by key informants (teachers), by sociometric methods (nominations by fellow sixth-graders), and by a network partner (in which each student was assigned to the opinion leader that she or he nominated). The network method was more effective than the teacher method, which was more effective than the sociometric method in changing attitudes toward smoking and intention not to smoke.

Perhaps the most important conclusion from these ten experiments is that no matter how opinion leaders are identified or trained, or precisely how they influence the behavior of others, the opinion leadership strategy generally has robust effects in health improvement.

*Networks in the Diffusion of a Medical Drug**

Early diffusion scholars simply counted the number of network links reported for each individual in a system to measure the individuals' degree of opinion leadership and then determined the characteristics of opinion leaders and followers. In this type of investigation, individuals were the units of analysis, even though the variable of opinion leadership was measured for individuals as the number of interpersonal network choices they received. The next step was to begin using diffusion network *links* as units of analysis (rather than the individual). This shift represented a profound change in the nature of diffusion research. Network analysis allowed deeper understanding of the previously hidden interpersonal mechanisms of the diffusion process.

The first diffusion investigation to explore the nature of diffusion networks was the study of a new drug's spread among medical doctors by sociologist James S. Coleman and colleagues (1966) (see Chapter 2). Like previous diffusion scholars, Coleman and others first studied various independent variables related to individual innovativeness (the month in which a medical doctor adopted the new drug, tetracycline). Unlike most previous scholars, however, Coleman and his coresearchers included various indicators of network communication behavior among their independent variables of study. They found these network variables to be the most important predictors of innovativeness (more important than such individual characteristics as age, cosmopoliteness, and socioeconomic status).

But Coleman and others (1966) did not stop there, as previous diffusion researchers had done. They studied the way in which interpersonal networks explained the nature of the diffusion process. In this way, they departed from the previous reliance of diffusion scholars on the individual as the unit of analysis. Instead they used diffusion network links as their units of data analysis. This methodological advance provided an important understanding of the interpersonal mechanisms creating the S-shaped diffusion curve.

Tetracycline was a useful antibiotic drug, with potential for daily use by a physician in general practice. Tetracycline's effectiveness in any particular case could be determined quickly and easily. It was also accompanied by fewer side effects than the antibiotics it replaced (Van den Bulte and Lilien, 2001). The new drug seemed to be the approximate equivalent for doctors of what hybrid corn meant to Iowa farmers: a change in previous behavior,

---

*This case illustration is based on Coleman et al. (1960).

whose results (in terms of relative advantage) were strikingly evident. Unlike the Iowa farmers, who adopted hybrid corn for themselves, the medical doctors were making adoption decisions for their patients. Similarly to the Iowa farmers, the physicians were making a decision about adoption of an innovation in the face of high uncertainty. They dealt with this uncertainty by relying on the opinions and actions of others around them.

Only two months after the new drug became available, 15 percent of the doctors tried it; four months later this figure had reached 50 percent (Coleman et al., 1966). Undoubtedly, the perceived attributes of tetracycline, such as relative advantage, affected its rapid rate of adoption (it reached almost complete adoption by the doctors in the Illinois cities under study in only seventeen months). The results of using the new drug were strikingly positive, and almost all of the interpersonal network messages about the innovation encouraged doctors to adopt. Practically no discontinuance of tetracycline occurred during the seventeen-month period of its diffusion. Coleman and colleagues (1966) found that innovativeness in adopting the new drug was associated with seven measures of network *interconnectedness* (defined as the degree to which the units in a social system are linked by interpersonal networks) for their medical doctor respondents:

1. Affiliation with a hospital as a regular staff member
2. More frequent attendance at hospital staff meetings
3. Sharing an office practice with one or more other doctors
4. Being named sociometrically as a source of information and advice by other doctors
5. Being named by other doctors as someone with whom they discussed their patients' cases
6. Being named sociometrically as a best friend by other doctors
7. Reciprocating the sociometric network links reported by other doctors who chose a respondent as a discussion partner

For each of these seven network variables, doctors with more network links were more innovative in adopting tetracycline, while doctors who were isolates (that is, who received no sociometric choices from their peers) were later in adopting the new drug (see Figure 8-3). The degree of network interconnectedness of a physician was a better predictor of innovativeness than any of the other independent variables investigated by Coleman and others (1966), such as a doctor's personal characteristics, exposure to communication channels, patients' average incomes, and the like. "Between-doctor" (network) variables were more important than "within-doctor" (personal characteristics) variables. Among the various network connectedness measures, the best predictor of innovativeness was the friendship variable (variable 6 in the list above). More than half of the forty-six isolate doctors (who received only one or no friendship sociometric choices and who practiced medicine alone rather than in an office partnership) had still not adopted the new drug ten months after it began to diffuse in the medical community (Coleman et al., 1966). In comparison, at this same ten-month point, almost all of the interconnected doctors (who received two or more network choices) had adopted tetracycline.

Coleman and others (1966) explained the greater innovativeness of the

Figure 8-3. Rate of Adoption of Tetracycline

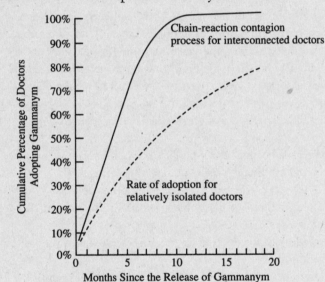

The rate of adoption for interconnected doctors "took off" in a snowballing contagion process, while the rate of adoption for relatively isolated doctors approached a straight line. The rates of adoption shown are a somewhat stylized version of the actual rates of adoption of tetracycline reported by Coleman and others (1966) for interconnected versus isolated doctors, for each of seven network measures of interconnectedness. The chain-reaction contagion process occurs for interconnected doctors because they are closely linked by interpersonal networks.

Source: Based upon Coleman and others (1966, p. 89).

interconnected doctors on the basis of a chain-reaction contagion process
that seemed to take place during the early months of the diffusion process
for tetracycline. Figure 8-3 shows that the S-curve for the interconnected
doctors took off rapidly in a kind of snowballing process: an early adopter
conveyed his or her personal experience with the innovation to two or more
of his or her peers, who each might then adopt and, in the next time period,
interpersonally convey their subjective experiences with the new idea to
two or more other doctors, and so on. Within several months, almost all of
the interconnected doctors had adopted, and their rate of adoption necessarily began to level off. This contagion process occurred because of the
interpersonal networks that linked the medical doctors, thus providing
communication avenues for the exchange of subjective evaluations of the
innovation.

The chain-reaction snowballing of adoption did not happen, however, for
the relatively isolated individuals, who lacked peer-network contacts from
which to learn about others' subjective evaluations of the innovation. So the
isolated individuals' rate of adoption is almost a straight line, though curving
slightly because the number of new adopters in each period remained a
constant percentage of those who had not already adopted the innovation
(see Figure 8-3). There is no sudden takeoff in the rate of adoption for the
isolated individuals. However, eventually most or all of these isolated individuals adopted. Interconnected doctors were more innovative in adopting
the new drug because of their interpersonal networks: "The impact [of net-
works] upon the integrated doctors was quick and strong; the impact upon
isolated doctors was slower and weaker, but not absent" (Coleman et al.,
1966, p. 126). A reanalysis of the drug study data by Valente (1995) found
that the average time of adoption by isolates was 9.5 months after the diffusion process began, compared to 7.9 months for the connected doctors.

When the doctors were confronted with making a decision about the
new drug in an uncertain situation that did not speak for itself, they turned
to one another for information that would help them make sense of the new
idea. Thus, the meaning of the new drug was socially constructed. Doctors
closely linked in networks tended to interpret the innovation similarly. In
the case of tetracycline, the medical community studied by Coleman and
others (1966) gradually arrived at a positive perception of the innovation.
This shared opinion led the interconnected doctors to adopt the new drug
more rapidly, but eventually the medical community's favorable perceptions
of the innovation trickled out to even the relatively isolated doctors on the
social margins of the network. Three important opinion leaders in the
physician community influenced their followers to adopt the new drug, and

this spurt in adoption seems to have occurred relatively early in the diffusion process.

We conclude this discussion with Generalization 8-10, which states: *The network interconnectedness of an individual in a social system is positively related to the individual's innovativeness.* If individuals are convinced to adopt new ideas by the experience of near peers with an innovation, then the more interpersonal communication that an individual has with such near peers, the more innovative the individual will be in adopting the new idea.

In recent years, several scholars have reanalyzed Coleman and colleagues' (1966) drug diffusion data to question and extend several of the original conclusions about the role of social networks in the diffusion process. Ronald S. Burt (1980, 1987) concluded that the similarity in the time of adoption of tetracycline of two doctors was not due mainly to a network link but rather to "structural equivalence," which occurs when two individuals occupy the same social space in the structure of a network. Peter V. Marsden and Joel Podolny (1990) also reanalyzed Coleman and colleagues' (1966) data using the technique of event history analysis. They concluded that network variables had little influence on doctors' innovativeness in adopting tetracycline. Thomas W. Valente (1993, 1995) reanalyzed Coleman and colleagues' drug data using a threshold model, in which each doctor had an individual threshold of resistance to the medical innovation, which was gradually overcome by network influences about the innovation from near peers. Valente (1995) found that a combination of external influences from cosmopolite sources (particularly medical journals) and the network interconnectedness of the medical doctors best explained their innovativeness in adopting tetracycline. Innovativeness in adopting the new drug was correlated .23 with opinion leadership (Valente, 1995). Finally, Van den Bulte and Lilien (2001) showed that aggressive marketing efforts by drug companies, rather than diffusion through the physicians' interpersonal networks, may explain why tetracycline spread so rapidly.

These reanalyses of the drug diffusion data illustrate how several scholars, each with a unique theoretical model and distinctive methodological tools, came to somewhat different conclusions about the way in which network influences explain the adoption of an innovation.

Diffusion Networks

We argued that the heart of the diffusion process is the modeling and imitation by potential adopters of their near peers' experiences with the

new idea. In deciding whether or not to adopt an innovation, individu
als depend mainly on the communicated experience of others much
like themselves who have already adopted a new idea. These subjective
evaluations of an innovation flow mainly through interpersonal networks. So we must understand the nature of networks in order to
understand the diffusion process.

Building a Network for the Diffusion of Photovoltaics in the Dominican Republic*

In 1984, Peggy Lesnick, on an exploratory visit to the Caribbean area,
installed a photovoltaic facility at a school in Jamaica to provide a solar-pow-
ered pump so that the schoolchildren could drink pure water. At about the
same time, Richard Hansen walked past customs officials in the Dominican
Republic with a photovoltaic panel under his arm, which he then installed
on his residence so that he could enjoy electric lights and operate his television
set. Photovoltaic is a renewable energy technology that uses semiconductor
chips laced with conducting wires to convert electromagnetic radiation
from sunlight into electricity. For example, many handheld calculators use
photovoltaic power.

Some fifteen years later, in 1999, when gathering data for her Ph.D. dissertation on the diffusion of photovoltaics, Peggy Lesnick returned to
Jamaica. The principal, an enthusiast for photovoltaics, had left the school.
The panel had been vandalized and the wiring ripped out. The schoolchildren had no clean water. But to Lesnick's surprise, in the nearby Dominican
Republic, there were more than eight thousand photovoltaic adopters! The
residents were among the poorest segment of the nation's population, living
on the rural, remote North Coast. What factors explain this very different
experience with photovoltaic diffusion in these two Caribbean nations?

Richard Hansen, with an engineering degree from MIT and an MBA,
quit his job at the Westinghouse Corporation to move to the Dominican
Republic in 1984. His use of photovoltaic technology aroused the curiosity
of his neighbors, whose homes were lit with kerosene lamps and whose
radios and television sets operated off car batteries, an inconvenient power
source (as they did not have vehicles). Hansen installed photovoltaic panels
for three of his neighbors, lending them the money needed to adopt (about

---

*This case illustration is based on Lesnick (2000).

$600 each) from his personal funds. The first adopter installed a photovoltaic panel on his rooftop as a surprise gift to his wife while she was away. When she came home that evening, she could not believe their brightly lit house. One of the early adopters said: "Where once there was total darkness, there is now light and opportunity" (quoted in Lesnick, 2000, p. 20). A twelve-by-forty-eight-inch photovoltaic panel on the rooftop of a village home in the Dominican Republic provided enough electrical power for five lights, a radio, a television set, and perhaps a blender and a fan. Hansen trained each of the first three adopters to become photovoltaic installers, and they soon diffused the innovation to twenty-seven other households, all within a fifteen-mile radius and most living along one main road.

These early adopters formed the Association for the Expansion of Solar Energy, which trained 150 installers, provided loans to adopters, and lobbied the national government to lower the 100 percent import tax on photovoltaic panels to 18 percent. A new adopter would make a down payment of $65 to the association and then pay off the rest of the loan over four or five years. The association fought off the national government's electrical power utility, which began to offer central station electricity at a cheap price to adopters of photovoltaics. People soon learned that photovoltaic electricity was better, once they experienced blackouts and other problems with the power utility. As one photovoltaic adopter stated, "PV [photovoltaic] never goes out. Plus, we own it" (quoted in Lesnick, 2000, p. 127). The empowering aspects of the photovoltaic technology were very important to the poor Dominicans who adopted this innovation.

Their enthusiasm for the innovation helped spread it over the impoverished North Coast of the island nation, with the association playing a key role in funding and providing technical support. Through their association, the Dominicans felt that they were in charge of the diffusion process, especially after Richard Hansen returned to live in the United States (he is a board member of the association and flies back to the Dominican Republic twice a month for board meetings). With his help, the association decided to go international. In 1999, the association launched a diffusion program for photovoltaics in the Central American nation of Honduras, and within a year there were more than one thousand adopters.

What explains the successful diffusion of photovoltaics in the Dominican Republic? One main reason was that the adopters organized a network (the Association for the Expansion of Solar Energy), which facilitated the spread of the innovation.

Cluster Studies

Strong evidence for the importance of network influences on individuals in the diffusion of innovations comes from investigations of family-planning adoption in villages in developing countries. For example, Rogers and Kincaid (1981) studied the diffusion of several different family-planning innovations in twenty-five Korean villages. They found that certain of the villages were "pill villages," others were "IUD villages," and one was a "vasectomy village." In one "pill village," *all* of the adopters of family-planning methods were using oral contraceptive pills. Similarly, in other villages of study, all (or almost all) contraceptive adopters were using the same family-planning method. Certainly such amazing homogeneity in the choice of contraceptives could hardly have occurred by chance. Each of the Korean villages had been the target of the same national family-planning program, in which a standard "cafeteria" of several contraceptive methods were promoted throughout the country. In the "IUD village," for example, certain opinion leaders first adopted a particular family-planning method, the IUD, and their experiences were then shared with fellow villagers via interpersonal networks. At one point, a dozen women in this village decided to adopt the IUD and all traveled together to a health clinic to get IUDs inserted. The result, after several years of further diffusion in the village, was a tendency for every adopter in that village to use the same method of family planning. These findings suggest that in Korea, the diffusion of family planning occurs mainly within villages, even though the government program was aimed at the national population.

Evidence similar to that provided by the Rogers and Kincaid (1981) Korean study comes (1) from a reanalysis of their data by Kohler (1997), (2) an investigation of Egyptian villages by Entwisle, Casterline, and Sayed (1989), (3) a study of Thai villages by Entwisle and colleagues (1996), and (4) research by Montgomery and Casterline (1993) in Taiwanese townships. For example, Entwisle and colleagues (1996) found "pill villages," "IUD villages," and so forth in rural Thailand.

Further evidence of the importance of networks in the diffusion of family planning was provided by the wide range in the rate of adoption by Korean village, measured as the percentage of married, fertile-aged couples adopting family planning (Rogers and Kincaid, 1981). In some Korean villages, more than 50 percent of the target audience had adopted. In other villages, the rate of adoption was only 10 or 15 percent. Such differences trace to the nature of intravillage communication networks. So an individual's network links were one important predictor of the individual's adoption of an innovation.

In fact, the average Korean woman knew the family-planning method being used by seven other women in her village, who tended to be her best friends (Kohler, 1997). Contraceptive use is not observable, so interpersonal communication must be the main means by which a woman knew of the family-planning methods used by others. Of women using the IUD, 4.3 of their network partners also adopted the IUD, 2 adopted the pill, and 1.7 adopted condoms or vasectomy. A similar tendency was found for women using the oral contraceptive pill, whose network partners mainly used the same contraceptive method. Valente and others (1997) found a strong association between the contraceptive methods used by a woman in Cameroon and the method used by her network partner. This tendency for homogeneity of contraceptive used, when aggregated at the village level, creates such seeming oddities as "pill villages," "IUD villages," etc. Here is strong evidence of the effects of communication networks in the diffusion and adoption of innovations. There is also one worrisome aspect of this phenomenon: some Korean women undoubtedly used a contraceptive inappropriate to their personal situation, just because their network partners were using that method (Kohler, 1997).

Similar clustering of adopters of an innovation has been observed in other settings. For example, William H. Whyte (1954) noted that window air conditioners were adopted by clusters of neighboring houses in a Philadelphia suburb. These clusters of air conditioning adopters were easily identifiable in the aerial photographs that Whyte took, as the air-conditioners protruded out of the windows of Philadelphia row houses in the suburb he studied. When Whyte followed up with personal interviews on the ground with the adopters of window air conditioners, he found that neighboring adopters seldom purchased the identical brand of the cooling equipment. Satisfied adopters told their network partners about the pleasures of air-conditioning, but they did not push the particular brand of equipment that they had adopted. Instead, they said that all brands of air conditioners were pretty much alike.

Each household in a hilltop village, San Gimignano, in northern Italy, near Florence, has constructed a three- or four-story stone tower. The towers serve no known function, other than as status symbols. Initially, one family built a stone tower. Then a neighbor, not to be outdone, constructed a yet taller tower. Eventually, every household built a tower. No other Italian villages have such towers.

The fact that certain innovations are adopted by clusters of individuals suggests that interpersonal networks among neighbors are powerful influences on individual decisions to adopt. Similar evidence of this important point about network influences in the diffusion process comes from studies of "copycat" crimes. The massacre at Columbine High School in Littleton, Colorado, happened on April 20, 1999. Within the next twenty-two months, nineteen similar incidents of school violence occurred in the United States. Several were strikingly similar to the Columbine crime and certainly were inspired by the earlier event. For instance, a seventh-grader in Fort Gibson, Oklahoma, obsessed with the Columbine shootings, fired fifteen rounds from a semiautomatic handgun into a group of classmates in December 1999. Three boys were arrested in Kansas and police found guns and bomb-making materials in their homes, along with three black trench coats like those worn by the Columbine gunmen (Gladwell, 2000, Afterword).

In the case of copycat crimes, network influences on criminal behavior occur via the mass media rather than through face-to-face channels. Aircraft hijacking is a contagious behavior that occurs by means of media news coverage of hijacking incidents. Holden (1986) analyzed the diffusion of aircraft hijackings that occurred between 1968 and 1972 in the United States. During this period, 137 hijacking attempts took place, one every two weeks! Many of the hijackings were for purposes of freeing prisoners or extorting money. Each successful extortion hijacking in the United States generated two additional attempts within forty-five days. This contagion effect explained 85 percent of all U.S. extortion hijackings. Further, many of the unique details of a hijacking were replicated in later hijackings. In this case, hijacking was an innovation that diffused to other criminals.

Dr. John Snow and the Cholera Epidemic in London*

The diffusion of an innovation and the spread of an epidemic have much in common, and similar mathematical models have been used to understand these processes (Bailey, 1975). One of the important fathers of epidemiology (the study of epidemics, how a disease is distributed in a population and factors that influence this distribution) was Dr. John Snow, a medical doctor in London in 1854. A cholera epidemic was under way in the city, and some five-hundred people had died of the mysterious disease. Some believed that

---

*This case illustration is based on McLeod (2000).

the disease was carried by miasmata ("bad airs"), while others blamed Jews for the illness (a form of anti-Semitism).

John Snow set out to find the cause of cholera through "shoe-leather epidemiology." He plotted the number of cholera deaths in each house on a dot-map (Figure 8-4) for a neighborhood in London, Golden Square (a subdistrict of Soho), in which the epidemic was especially severe. Snow found that many of the cholera deaths were concentrated around a water pump on

Figure 8-4. Dot-Map of Cholera Deaths Around the Broad Street Pump in London in 1854

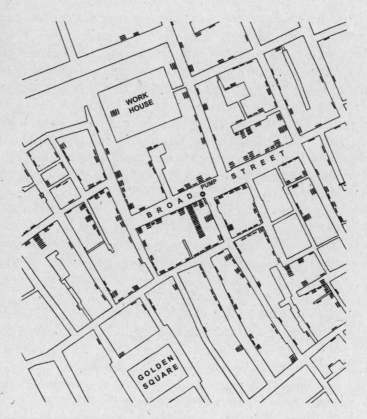

Dr. John Snow's dot-map of cholera deaths supported his conclusion that cholera was a waterborne disease and that the Broad Street pump (near the center of the map) was the cause. Snow removed the pump handle, and the cholera epidemic was halted.

Source: Based on McLeod (2000).

Broad Street. Of the eighty-three cholera victims in the area, all but ten were located closer to the Broad Street pump than to any other public water pump. He talked to the affected families, who admitted that they always fetched their water from the Broad Street pump. Snow concluded that cholera was carried by water polluted by sewage.

On September 8, 1854, he removed the pump handle, and the cholera deaths soon stopped. Snow became a hero of public health for his theory of waterborne disease transmission. Today, a replica of a handleless pump stands on Broadwick Street (the current name for Broad Street), kitty corner to the pump's original location. A plaque is affixed to a building on Frith Street where Snow had his first medical practice, commemorating him as a pioneer of epidemiology. His dot-maps of the cholera cases in London remind one of the "pill village" in Korea, the clusters of Harvestores on North American farms, and the stone towers in San Gimignano. Perhaps Snow should also be honored for detecting the effects of network behavior.

Communication Network Analysis

A *communication network* consists of interconnected individuals who are linked by patterned flows of information. Networks have a certain degree of structure or stability. This patterned aspect of networks provides predictability to human behavior. The study of networks helps illuminate *communication structure*, the differentiated elements that can be recognized in the patterned communication flows in a system. This communication structure is so complex that in any but a very small system even the members of the system may not understand the communication structure of which they are part. There are so many possible network links in a system, that a problem of information overload is caused for the individual who tries to detect the system's communication structure. For instance, in a social system with 100 members, 4,950 network links are possible (computed by the formula $\frac{N(N-1)}{2}$ where N is the number of individuals in the system). In a system of 200 members, 19,900 network links are possible. A system with 1,000 members can have almost a half-million links. A computer is necessary to analyze the patterns among these myriad of network links. *Communication network analysis* is a method of research for identifying the communication structure in a system, in which network data about communication flows are analyzed by using interpersonal communication relationships as the units of analysis.

Methods of network analysis identify individuals in cliques on the basis of their communication proximity in network links, so that individuals who are less socially distant are assigned to the same clique. The pioneering German sociologist Georg Simmel regarded *social distance* (defined as the degree to which an individual perceives a lack of intimacy with individuals who differ in socioeconomic status, ethnicity, and other variables) as a fundamental concept in understanding human behavior (Simmel, 1908/1964). Simmel's concept of social distance is equivalent to the network concept of communication proximity. An example of proximity is provided by "Erdős numbers," which indicate the closeness of any given mathematician to Paul Erdős, the famous, eccentric Hungarian-born mathematician who published 1,475 scientific papers, more than any other mathematician, and who coauthored very widely (Hoffman, 1998). The 485 scholars who coauthored a scientific paper with Erdős all have an Erdős number of 1; if a scholar coauthored a paper with another mathematican who in turn coauthored with Erdős, his or her number is 2; and so on. Albert Einstein had an Erdős number of 2. The Erdős numbers are a measure of interpersonal proximity that is similar to the "degrees of separation" from a movie actor, computed as 1 if another actor or actress performed in a movie with him, and so forth.

Communication proximity is the degree to which two linked individuals in a network have personal communication networks that overlap. A *personal communication network* consists of the individuals who are linked by patterned communication flows to a given individual. Each individual possesses a personal network, consisting of the set of other individuals to whom the focal individual is linked in network relationships. The focal individual's behavior is determined, in part, by information and influence that are communicated from the members of the individual's personal network.

Some personal networks consist of a set of individuals, all of whom interact with one another; these are *interlocking personal networks*. In contrast, a *radial personal network* consists of a set of individuals who are linked to a focal individual but do not interact with one another. Radial personal networks are less dense and more open (*openness* is the degree to which a unit exchanges information with its environment), and thus allow the focal individual to exchange information with a wider environment. Such radial networks are particularly important in the diffusion of innovations because the links reach out into the entire system, while an interlocking network is more ingrown in nature.

Valente (1995) reanalyzed three diffusion data sets (medical doctors in Illinois, Brazilian farmers, and Korean women). He found that personal network radiality was positively related to innovativeness (Valente and Foreman, 1998).

The Strength-of-Weak-Ties Theory

The general notion of classifying network links on the basis of the degree to which they convey information began with Mark S. Granovetter's (1973) theory of "the strength-of-weak-ties." This network scholar sought to determine how people living in the Boston suburb of Newton got jobs. Granovetter gathered data from a sample of 282 respondents who had taken a new job within the past year. To his surprise, most of these individuals said that they heard about their positions from heterophilous individuals who were not very close friends. These "weak ties" occurred with individuals "only marginally included in the current network of contacts, such as an old college friend or a former workmate or employer, with whom sporadic contact had been maintained" (Granovetter, 1973). Chance meetings with such acquaintances sometimes reactivated these weak ties, leading to the exchange of job information with the individual. Sometimes the network leading to a new job came from a complete stranger.

An example of successful job seeking through weak network links was an accountant who flew to Boston to attend a convention. The accountant shared a taxi at Logan Airport with a Bostonian businessman. They began a conversation, and the businessman disclosed that his company was seeking to hire an accountant. Perhaps you can imagine what happened next. The accountant, who resided in Newton at the time of Granovetter's survey, was one of his respondents.

Only 17 percent of Granovetter's Newton respondents said they found their new job through close friends or relatives. Why were weak ties so much more important than strong network links? Because an individual's close friends seldom know much that the individual did not also know. One's intimate friends are usually friends of each other's, forming a close-knit clique (an interlocking personal network). Such an ingrown system is an extremely poor net in which to catch new information from one's environment. Much more useful as a channel for gaining such information are an individual's more distant (weaker) acquaintances, the people in one's radial network. They are more likely to possess information that the focal individual does not already possess, such as about a new job or about an innovation. Weak ties connect an individual's small clique of intimate friends with another, distant clique. Thus, weak ties are often *bridge links* (defined as an individual who links two or more cliques in a system from his or her position as a member of one of the cliques), connecting two or more cliques. If these weak ties were somehow removed from a system, the result would be an unconnected set of separate cliques. Even though weak ties are not a frequent path for the flow of communication messages, the information flowing through them can play a crucial role for individuals and for the system. This importance of weak ties in conveying new information is why Granovetter (1973) called his theory "the-[informational]-strength-of-weak [network]-ties."

This weak-versus-strong-ties dimension is *communication proximity,* defined previously as the degree to which two individuals in a network have personal communication networks that overlap. Weak ties are low in communication proximity because they connect two individuals who do not share network links with a common set of other individuals. At least some degree of heterophily must be present in network links in order for the diffusion of innovations to occur. Low-proximity weak ties are often heterophilous, which is why they are so important in the diffusion process. For example, Liu and Duff (1972) and Duff and Liu (1975) found that a family-planning innovation spread rather quickly among the members of small cliques of Filipino housewives. But this new idea did not diffuse throughout the total community until information about the contraceptive was conveyed by weak ties from one tight-knit clique to another. The weak ties were usually heterophilous in socioeconomic status, linking, for example, a higher-status clique with a lower-status one.

We summarize this discussion with Generalization 8-11: *The information-exchange potential of communication network links is negatively related to their degree of (1) communication proximity and (2) homophily.* Heterophilous links of low proximity (Granovetter's "weak ties"), while rare, play a crucial role in the flow of *information* about an innovation. This information may also be *influential* if it consists of a personal evaluation of an innovation by an individual who has already adopted. Perhaps there is a strength-of-weak-ties in networks that convey information about an innovation and a "strength-of-*strong*-ties" in networks that convey interpersonal influence. Certainly the influence potential of network ties with an individual's intimate friends is stronger than the opportunity for influence with an individual's "weak ties"

(seldom-contacted acquaintances). Closely linked peers in an interlock
ing network seldom exert their potential influence because this type of
homophilous, high-proximity personal network is seldom activated by
information about an innovation. An individual's intimate friends rarely
possess much information that the individual does not already know.
Information must flow into such an interlocking network from outside
to provide energy for further information exchange.

Who Is Linked to Whom in Networks?

Generalization 8-12 states: *Individuals tend to be linked to others who
are close to them in physical distance and who are relatively
homophilous in social characteristics.* Individuals form the network
links that require the least effort and are most rewarding. Both spatial
and social proximity can be indicators of least effort. Communication
network links with neighboring and homophilous partners are relatively
easy and require little effort. But we have just shown that such low-
effort network links are usually of limited value for obtaining information about innovations. In contrast, heterophilous links with socially and
spatially distant others are usually stronger in carrying information
about new ideas to an individual. Easy network links are thus of less
value informationally.

The implication for individuals in managing their personal networks,
if they wish to receive information effectively, is to break out of the
comfortable nature of close links and to form more heterophilous and
spatially distant network links. The choice of weak ties has been made
much easier for most individuals in recent years with the availability of
the Internet (Rosen, 2000).

Social Learning Theory

A social psychological theory with direct applicability to diffusion networks is social learning theory. Most psychological approaches to
human learning look within the individual in order to understand how
learning occurs. But the social learning approach looks outside of the
individual at a specific type of information exchange with others in
order to explain how human behavior changes. The intellectual leader
of social learning theory is Professor Albert Bandura (1977, 1986), a
social psychologist at Stanford University.

The central ideal of social learning theory is that one individual learns from another by means of observational modeling. That is, one observes another person's behavior and then does something similar. The observer's behavior is not exactly the same as the model's, which would be simple imitation or blind mimicry. Rather, in social modeling the observer extracts the essential elements from an observed behavior pattern in order to perform a similar behavior. Modeling allows the learner to adapt the observed behavior (much like the re-invention of an innovation).

The basic perspective of social learning theory is that the individual can learn from observation of other people's activities, so the individual does not necessarily have to experience a verbal exchange of information in order for the individual's behavior to be influenced by the model (although of course interpersonal communication accompanies the nonverbal modeling in many cases). Thus, nonverbal communication (as well as verbal communication) is important in behavior change. Because social learning theory recognizes external factors to the individual as important in behavior change, it is essentially "social" as it views communication as a cause of behavior change. The individual can learn a new behavior by observing another individual in person or via the mass media (especially visual media such as television and film). Social modeling often occurs through interpersonal networks, but it can also occur through a public display by someone with whom one is unacquainted (such as in a television program). Ideally, an individual learns more from a social model if the model is positively rewarded, rather than punished, for the behavior that is displayed.

Social learning and the diffusion of innovations have much in common: Both theories seek to explain how individuals change their overt behavior as a result of communication with other individuals. Both theories stress information exchange as essential to behavior change and view network links as a main explanation of how individuals alter their behavior.

Sociologists at the University of Arizona (Hamblin et al., 1973, 1979; Kunkel, 1977; Pitcher et al., 1978) applied social learning theory to the diffusion of innovations to explain the rate of airplane hijackings. Their viewpoint is that "Diffusion models portray society as a huge learning system where individuals are continually behaving and making decisions through time but not independently of one another. . . . Everyone makes his own decisions, not just on the basis of his own individual experiences, but to a large extent on the basis of the observed or talked about experiences of others" (Hamblin et al., 1979). This perspective reflects the main idea of diffusion theory: that interpersonal communication with near peers about an innovation drives the diffusion process.

The Critical Mass in the Diffusion of Interactive Innovations

A crucial concept in understanding the social nature of the diffusion process is the "critical mass," the point after which further diffusion becomes self-sustaining. The notion of the critical mass originally came from scholars of social movements, and in recent years has been advanced by communication scholars. The rate of adoption of interactive media such as e-mail, telephones, fax, and teleconferencing often displays a distinctive quality that we here call the critical mass. The *critical mass* occurs at the point at which enough individuals in a system have adopted an innovation so that the innovation's further rate of adoption becomes self-sustaining.

The interactive quality of new communication technologies creates interdependence among the adopters in a system. An interactive innovation is of little use to an adopting individual unless other individuals with whom the adopter wishes to communicate also adopt. Thus, a critical mass of individuals must adopt an interactive communication technology before it has much utility for the average individual in the system. With each additional adopter, the utility of an interactive communication technology increases for all adopters. An illustration is provided by the very first individual to adopt a telephone in the 1870s. This interactive technology had no utility until a second individual adopted. Until a critical mass occurs at a relatively early stage in the diffusion process, the rate of adoption is very slow (Fischer, 1992). After critical mass is achieved, the rate of adoption accelerates (see Figure 8-5).

What is an interactive communication technology? *Interactivity* is the degree to which participants in a communication process can exchange roles in, and have control over, their mutual discourse (Williams, Rice, and Rogers, 1988). "Mutual discourse" is the degree to which a given communication act is based on a prior series of communication acts. Thus, each message in a sequence of exchanges affects the following messages in a cumulative process. "Exchange of roles" means the empathic ability of individual A to take the position of individual B (and thus to perform B's communication acts) and vice versa. "Control" is the extent to which an individual can choose the timing, content, and sequence of a communication act, search out alternative choices, enter the content into storage for other uses, and perhaps create new communication capabilities (Williams, Rice, and Rogers, 1988). In the case of interactive communication, such control of the communication process is broadly shared.

Figure 8-5. The Rate of Adoption for an Interactive Innovation, Showing the Critical Mass

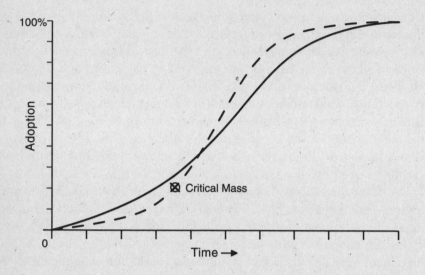

The *critical mass* occurs at the point at which enough individuals in a system have adopted an innovation so that the innovation's further rate of adoption becomes self-sustaining.

Earlier adopters of noninteractive innovations have a *sequential* interdependence effect on later adopters. As more and more individuals in a system adopt, the noninteractive innovation is perceived as increasingly beneficial to future adopters (and this encourages them to adopt). But in the case of interactive innovations, not only do earlier adopters influence later adopters, but *later* adopters also influence *earlier* adopters in a process of *reciprocal* interdependence (Markus, 1990). The benefits from each additional adoption of an interactive innovation increase not only for all future adopters, but also for each previous adopter. The distinctive aspect of interactive communication technologies, in a diffusion sense, is "reciprocal interdependence, in which later adopters influence earlier adopters as well as the other way around" (Markus, 1990, p. 214). For instance, with each additional adopter of the Internet, e-mail became slightly more valuable to everyone, as a larger number of other people could be reached by e-mail. So the benefits of an interactive innovation flow backward in time to previous adopters, as well as forward in time to future adopters.

The Critical Mass in the Diffusion of Fax

A rapid diffusion of fax occurred in the United States from 1983 to 1989, although after a wait of 150 years while the technology was shaped into its present form, the appropriate telephone infrastructure to support fax was put in place, and until a critical mass of users slowly accumulated. Fax was invented in 1843 by Alexander Bain, a Scotch clockmaker, who called it a "recording telegraph" because the message was transmitted over telegraph lines. There were no adopters. A century later, in 1948, RCA announced a fax machine that transmitted messages via radio waves; it was called "ultra-fax." During the 1960s, Xerox manufactured a fax machine called a "tele-copier" that was sold to the Associated Press, UPI, and Reuters news agencies to send photographs and documents over telephone lines to media newsrooms. At this point, accessing telephone lines still required operator assistance, telecopiers were slow (it took eight minutes to transmit a single page), and the machines emitted a very unpleasant smell.

Next, automatic telephone dialing and direct connection of a fax machine to regular telephone lines was allowed. Faster transmission was demanded by users. A fax machine scans a page and converts the material on it into electrical signals, which are sent over telephone lines. The time required for telephone transmission limited the speed of sending a fax. Fax equipment was relatively expensive, about $8,000 per machine. The price began to fall, and the trans-mission speed increased, when Japanese companies entered the market in 1980. Sharp introduced the first low-priced machine ($2,000) in 1984, and large U.S. companies began to purchase fax machines. Soon the price of a fax machine dropped further, to $500 in 1980 and to $250 in 1993. A single page could be faxed from Los Angeles to Washington, D.C., for as little as a dime, whereas a first-class stamp then cost 29 cents.

Although the fax boom began in the United States around 1983, the rate of adoption remained quite slow until 1987, the year in which a critical mass of users occurred. Starting that year, Americans began to assume that "everybody else" had a fax machine (Holmlöv and Warneyd, 1990). "What's your fax number?" became a common query among American businesspeo-ple. Fax numbers were included on individuals' business cards. Dating ser-vices used fax messages, and many take-out restaurants, such as pizza shops, began to encourage customers to fax in their orders.

So it took 150 years for fax to become an overnight success. During the 1990s, as the Internet diffused to millions of users, the main advantage of fax (faster speed and lower cost) became less important, and fax began to fade, although it remains part of the modern business office.

Diffusion of the Internet

The growth of computer networks has increased at an exponential rate since about 1990, when the critical mass for this innovation occurred. The main impetus for this expansion was the formation of the Internet, a computer network that linked over twenty thousand existing computer networks. The origins of the Internet go back to ARPANET, which was created in 1969 to allow thirty U.S. Department of Defense contractors to share computer software and databases. E-mail was added as an afterthought, but soon came to be the dominant function for this computer network's users. ARPANET was designed in the Cold War era to survive a nuclear attack, so there was no single headquarters or control point.

When the Internet was born of ARPANET in 1983, it continued this many-to-many, decentralized network structure. Millions and millions of computers are linked by telephone lines through billions of possible network paths. A particular message may course its way toward its intended destination, passed along from computer to computer by the telephone lines that link them.

By 1995, the Internet connected approximately 20 million computers, a number that began to double annually. In 1996, there were 50 million Internet users; in 1997, 100 million; in 1998, 150 million; in 1999, 200 million; in 2000, some 410 million; and in 2001, 520 million (Kwon, 2002). By early 2002, Internet users numbered 544 million people worldwide, or 9 percent of the world's population (Figure 8-6). This is an amazingly rapid rate of adoption, perhaps one of the fastest in the history of humankind (possible reasons for this speed of diffusion were discussed in Chapter 6). This rapid diffusion of the Internet presented a unique opportunity for scholars to investigate various aspects of the diffusion model, especially the role of the critical mass. For instance, a high proportion of all users in North America access the Internet through personal accounts maintained for them by their employers or by educational institutions with which they are affiliated (LaRose and Hoag, 1997). Relatively few users of the Internet access it directly from their homes. So the Internet is, in certain respects, an organizational innovation, or at least an idea influenced strongly by organizational factors.

What do people use the Internet for? Authors collaborate in writing books on the Internet. Some Internet users arrange dates and may fall in love on the network. Other individuals utilize bulletin boards to post and seek information, including jokes. A computer company offers free use of its new computer to those who wish to try it out by linking to the new com-

Figure 8.6. Cumulative Rate of Adoption of the Internet Worldwide

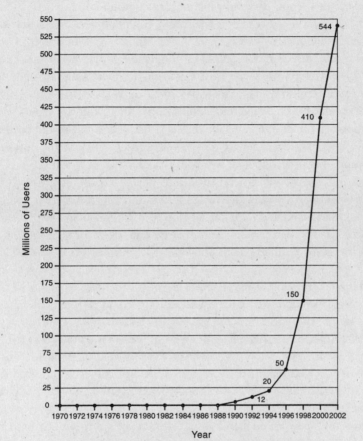

After 1969, when the first computer network, ARPANET, was created to connect U.S. Department of Defense contractors in computer science, the rate of adoption was very slow, almost approaching a straight line. Finally, in the late 1980s, ARPANET and many other existing computer networks merged to form the Internet. The critical mass occurred about 1990. Then, aided by technological advances such as browsers and by the addition of commercial applications of the World Wide Web in the mid-1990s, the rate of adoption sky-rocketed, until in 2002, 9 percent of the world's population (544 million people) were Internet users.

Source: Kwon (2002), based on estimates by NVA Ltd. Online Population Survey (www.nva.com/surveys).

puter via the Internet. Patients with pancreatic cancer and their family members exchange messages with others stricken with this cancer on an Internet listserv. They seek information and emotional support, discuss their participation in cancer drug trials, and complain about their doctors (Ginossar, 2002). A homeless man in Santa Monica, California, expresses his opinion about a community issue through the Public Electronic Network (PEN), which he accesses for free through a local library. Computer networks can empower the underdogs of society (Rogers et al., 1994; Schmitz et al., 1995). Some individuals (including young people) seek pornographic Web sites, a behavior that is difficult for parents or governments to limit or prevent, given the decentralized nature of the Internet ("sex" is one of the most popular words in World Wide Web searches).

In the mid-1990s, the U.S. government permitted the Internet to be used for business purposes. The Internet is utilized for marketing and for buying, and has facilitated the globalization of world business (Singhal and Rogers, 2001). The first product sold in large quantities through the Internet was books, and Amazon.com and other e-commerce businesses have changed the nature of commerce through credit card purchases and overnight delivery. Now e-mail connects you both to the person in the neighboring office and to a virtual employee or friend who may be on the opposite side of the world.

By 2002, there were 313 billion Web pages on 37 million Web sites on the World Wide Web, with 68 percent of this material in English (Kwon, 2002). This vast and rapidly increasing information resource added to the perceived value of the Internet, thus boosting the rate of adoption of computer networking.

The Internet has created increased interest in the study of diffusion, and particularly in the role of communication networks in the diffusion process. In the pre-Internet era, interpersonal networks were ethereal and thus difficult to understand. Now people communicate over hard wires that link computers, which capture a record of human message exchange and thus can illuminate the nature of networks (Rogers, 1987). Each individual participant in a network knows who he or she is connected to but seldom knows to whom these individuals are linked. As a top official at Hewlett-Packard stated, "We don't know what we know, or, often, who knows it." Computer network analyses can aid such understanding, by showing individuals in a system the total network structure of their system.

The Concept of Critical Mass

The notion of critical mass originated in physics, where it was defined as the amount of radioactive material necessary to produce a nuclear reaction. "An atomic pile 'goes critical' when a chain reaction of nuclear fission becomes self-sustaining" (Schelling, 1978, p. 89). Various illustrations of critical mass situations, in which a process becomes self-sustaining after some threshold point has been reached, abound in everyday life. A single log in a fireplace, for example, will not continue to burn by itself. A second log must be present so that each log reflects its heat onto the other. When the ignition point is reached, the fire takes off, and the two logs burn to ashes.

The critical mass bears on the relationship between the behavior of individuals and the larger system of which they are part. It thus centers on a crucial cross-level analysis that is "characteristic of a large part of the social sciences, especially the more theoretical part" (Schelling, 1978, p. 13). "The principle of 'critical mass' is so simple that it is no wonder that it shows up in epidemiology, fashion, survival and extinction of species, language systems, racial integration, jaywalking, panic behavior, and political movements" (Schelling, 1978, p. 89).

The concept of the critical mass is fundamental to understanding a wide range of human behavior because an individual's actions often depend on a perception of how many other individuals are behaving in a particular way (Schelling, 1978). Much of the theory and research concerning the critical mass in recent decades has been inspired by Mancur Olson's (1965) logic of collective action: "Even if all the individuals in a large group are rational and self-interested, and would gain if, as a group, they acted to achieve their common interest or objective, they would still not voluntarily act to achieve that common or group interest." This seeming irrationality of individuals in a social system attracted scholarly attention to the study of collective action by communication scholars, sociologists, social psychologists, economists, and scholars of public opinion. Why is individual behavior in a system so seemingly illogical? The basic reason is that each individual acts in ways that are rational in pursuing *individual* goals without fully considering that he or she might be disadvantaging the system at the *collective* level.

Garrett Hardin's (1968) "tragedy of the commons" occurs when each individual pursues a rational course of behavior that ironically drives the entire system (that is, the "commons") to disaster. Hardin's concept takes its name from the commons pasture in Medieval European villages, which was filled to its grazing capacity. Say that each of a hundred farmers in a village calculated that the addition of one more animal (to their average of ten cows each) would not exceed the capacity of the commons (one thousand cattle). It each of the one hundred herdsmen makes a similar calculation, however, the commons has 1,100 cattle. The result is overgrazing, erosion, and destruction of the commons pasture. This tragedy of the commons eventually led to fencing commons pastures into individual farm plots.

The use of air conditioners by urban dwellers during a heat wave illustrates the tragedy of the commons: "Each individual is most comfortable using his or her air conditioner at full power; yet if everyone does so, the result is a power overload that leaves everyone with no cooling at all" (Brewer, 1985). Other examples of the tragedy of the commons include air and water pollution, city traffic jams, and litter on streets and sidewalks. One means of combating the tragedy of the commons is for a central authority (such as a government) to impose restrictive rules or laws (Ostrom, 1990).

Yet another concept related to the critical mass is *network externalities,* defined as a quality of certain goods and services such that they become more valuable to a user as the number of users increases (Mahler and Rogers, 1999). Thus the utility of an innovation with externalities is *external* to the individual, such as in the size of the user community for a new interactive telecommunications service. A lack of network externalities slows the rate of adoption of an interactive innovation such as the Internet in the early stages of its diffusion. When enough adoptions have occurred that many individuals in a system perceive that "everybody's doing it," the rate of adoption speeds up (for the Internet, this point happened around 1990 in North America) and the critical mass occurs.

The diffusion of cellular telephones did not have to overcome the externality problem of interactive telecommunications services because mobile phone adopters are connected to the existing base of *all* telephone users. Had cellular telephones been designed so that each adopter could talk only with other cell phone users, a critical mass would have been important in the diffusion of this innovation (Mahler and Rogers, 1999). Fax, e-mail, and videoconferencing were characterized by a critical mass in their rate of adoption, while voice mail was not (because voice mail was utilized with the existing base of all telephone users). Factors which act to slow the rate of adoption of an interactive innovation before the critical mass is reached (like network externalities), then serve to speed up the adoption rate after the critical mass is attained (Wieber, 1992, 1995).

The effects of network externalities on the rate of adoption of telecommunications innovations depend on compatibility standards. For example, two standards for VCR equipment (Beta versus VHS) were supported by opposing camps of Japanese electronics manufacturers during the first decade of VCR diffusion in the 1980s. The lack of a single standard slowed down the rate of VCR adoption by consumers. A critical mass of adopters had to be achieved for *each* of the standards. A critical mass was reached for only one of the standards, and the other standard failed in the marketplace in the United States.

Here we see that the critical mass concept is closely related to several social science theories: the logic of collective action, the tragedy of the commons, and network externalities. These related concepts help us understand the role of the critical mass in the diffusion of interactive communication innovations.

The concept of critical mass in the diffusion process has important implications for businesses marketing a new product. Marketing diffusion scholars have pioneered in identifying a new dependent variable for their analyses, the amount of time required to reach critical mass for a new product in a nation (this variable is called "time-to-take-off"). For example, Shermesh and Tellis (2002) gathered data on the rate of sale of ten products in each of sixteen European countries. They found that a distinct takeoff (or critical mass) occurred for each of the new products in each country, averaging six years from introduction of the new product to its critical mass. Shermesh and Tellis (2002) determined the year in which the critical mass occurred by inspecting their data on the annual rate of adoption for each new product. The average time-to-take-off for kitchen and laundry products was 7.5 years, compared to only 2 years from introduction to takeoff for information and entertainment products. The likelihood of a relatively short time-to-take-off for a new product in a nation was higher if that product had already reached critical mass in neighboring countries.

The study by Shermesh and Tellis (2002) suggests the potential of a comparative analysis of the time-to-take-off for an innovation in different systems, such as European nations or the United States. Such an investigation by Lauri Frank (2001) in Finland looked at the rate of mobile telephone diffusion in the fifteen countries of the European Union. Frank found that the nations of northern Europe (for instance, Sweden, Denmark, and Finland) led in this diffusion process, with southern European countries lagging in mobile telephone adoption. The northern European nations gained part of their advantage by introducing mobile phones relatively earlier (for instance, Sweden introduced mobile telephones in 1981 and Finland and Denmark the following year; Greece did not launch mobile telephony until twelve years after Sweden, in 1993). Greece had the slowest rate of adoption of mobile phones, in part because it was relatively unconnected to the nations with more rapid diffusion. Frank drew on the spatial diffusion theory of Torsten Hägerstrand (1952), the pioneering Swedish geographer (see Chapter 2). But Frank improved on previous research by calculating not just the influence of the number of neighboring adopters on a focal nation but also the rate of adoption of mobile phones by each neighbor at each time period.

Here we see how the concept of the critical mass can not only help us understand the diffusion process in an intuitive way, but how it also suggests new dependent variables for study and new theory-driven analyses.

Watching While Being Watched

Think about when a new e-mail system is introduced in an organization. E-mail has greater and greater utility for all users as additional individuals adopt. If the first adopters were to think only of their own *immediate* benefits, rather than about how they might *eventually* benefit or how their organization might benefit, no one would adopt and the S-shaped diffusion process for the innovation would not get under way. Until there is a critical mass of adopters, an interactive innovation has little advantage (and considerable disadvantage) for individual adopters. Here is another illustration of individual/system relationships, as in the previous case of the logic of collective action, the tragedy of the commons, and network externalities. When a critical number of individuals have adopted an interactive innovation, a further rate of diffusion becomes self-sustaining as reciprocal interdependence increases the relative advantage of the interactive innovation for both past and future adopters. The critical mass is thus a kind of "tipping point" (Gladwell, 2000) or social threshold in the diffusion process. After the critical mass is reached, the norms of the social system encourage further adoption by individual members of the system. As the tipping point is approached, just a few more adopters of the innovation suddenly make a big difference, as the rate of adoption rapidly escalates (see Figure 8-6).

Individuals adopt an innovation, in part, on the basis of their expectations of others' future adoption, as suggested by Allen (1983): "It seems likely that individuals base their choice on what they expect the others to decide. Thus, the individual's effort to decide hinges upon 'watching the group'—the other members in the community of actual/potential subscribers—to discern what the group choice may be. . . . The outcome for the group then turns literally upon everybody watching while being watched." A contagion effect occurs when an individual sees his or her peers adopting an interactive communication technology like e-mail. So watching while being watched plays an especially important role in the diffusion of interactive innovations.

The critical mass can also affect *discontinuance* of an interactive innovation. As noted previously, diffusion theory ordinarily assumes a certain degree of one-directional influence in individuals' decisions to adopt: later adopters are influenced by earlier adopters but not vice versa. For noninteractive innovations, this one-way-influence relationship is one of sequential interdependence. A critical mass implies that reciprocal interdependence also occurs, in which early adopters are influenced by later adopters (and discontinuers and rejecters), as well as vice versa: "As users defect, the benefits to the remaining users will decrease and the costs increase, thus stimulating further defection" (Markus, 1987). Just as the critical mass affects the rate of adoption of an interactive innovation, it may also speed up the rate of discontinuance.

For example, consider an individual in an organization who stops responding to e-mail messages. This discontinuance soon becomes evident to other individuals, who send electronic messages to the discontinuer but do not receive a response. They then conclude that e-mail is no longer an effective way to reach that person. A dropout in a communication network affects many others in the network, and everyone else becomes slightly more likely to discontinue the use of e-mail. Discontinuance of an interactive innovation by one individual may lead eventually to a critical mass of discontinuers, and then perhaps to complete rejection of a new idea such as e-mail by the entire system. Although this rejection of e-mail would be unlikely today (due to the widespread adoption of e-mail), it did occur in some organization in the early 1990s.

Until this point in our discussion of the critical mass, we treated all adopters as equivalent in their potential influence on others. Obviously they are not all equal. A small number of highly influential individuals who adopt a new idea may represent a much stronger critical mass than an equally sized number of individual adopters who have little influence. The critical mass typically involves the opinion leaders in a system, so that the communication network structure of the system contributes to the power of the critical mass in the diffusion process for interactive innovations. This phenomenon explains, in part, how new books, movies, music, and other "taste products" can sometimes become overnight sensations.

The Sleeper*

Many books by big-name authors such as Danielle Steel and Tom Clancy receive heavy promotion and almost immediately become blockbusters, shooting to the top of the best-seller list with hundreds of thousand of copies sold in the first weeks after the book's release. These books are known quantities, and a ready market preexists for them.

A very different kind of book is what the publishing industry calls a "sleeper," whose sales take off very slowly, mainly through an invisible and often mysterious process of word of mouth until a critical mass is reached. An example is a 1992 book by an unknown writer named Rebecca Wells, *Little Altars Everywhere*, published by a small, now-defunct press in Seattle. Wells had a friend who spent the 1992 Thanksgiving with a producer of National Public Radio (NPR). This individual liked Wells's book and passed it on to Linda Wertheimer, host of the show. She liked the book too, and interviewed Wells on NPR. A man in Blytheville, Arkansas, heard the radio interview. He purchased a copy and gave it to his wife, Mary Gay Shipley, who owns the town's bookstore, That Bookstore in Blytheville. She decided that people ought to be reading *Little Altars Everywhere*, and she ordered dozens of copies during 1993. She placed copies of Wells's book in a special rack at the front of her store and wrote about it in her newsletter. Soon the Wells book was number two in sales at That Bookstore in Blytheville.

Similar pockets of enthusiasm for Wells's book sprang up around the country, and the increasing sales figures eventually came to the attention of a New York editor, Diane Reverand, who in 1996 offered a contract to Rebecca Wells for her next book, *Divine Secrets of the Ya-Ya Sisterhood*. Mary Gay Shipley was ready. She ordered a hundred copies, which was unknown for her small bookstore (she usually orders one or two copies of a book). Shipley told the sales representative from the publisher that she would love to have

---

*This case illustration is based on Gladwell (1999).

Wells visit Blytheville. When Wells read from *Ya-Ya Sisterhood* in That Bookstore, the place was packed. Women in the front row wore placards saying "Ya-Ya."

Soon the book had sold some tens of thousands of copies, and Diane Reverand purchased an ad in *The New Yorker*, the first media advertising the book received. In a month, sales doubled to 60,000 copies. By February 1998, two years after publication, *Ya-Ya Sisterhood* reached the best seller list, and soon there were 3 million copies in print. Clearly, the Mary Kay Shipleys of the world play a crucial role for sleepers such as Wells's book. Shipley has lived in Blytheville all her life and has run That Bookstore for twenty-five years. She knows her customers and is often able to match the right book with a certain customer. Her recommendations are highly respected.

Such recommendations of taste products are now available through collaborative filtering systems, provided through the Internet, which predict books or music that you may like on the basis of your previous purchases and preferences. For example, Amazon.com tells you that many people who have purchased Rogers's *Diffusion of Innovations* also bought Thomas W. Valente's (1995) *Network Models of the Diffusion of Innovations* and Emanuel Rosen's (2000) *The Anatomy of Buzz: How to Create Word of Mouth Marketing*. This clustering of purchases is hardly surprising, given that these three books have much in common. Collaborative filtering systems go further. They ask you about the last ten books you have purchased and for your tastes in books (such as military history, alternative medicine, and so forth). Such preference data help collaborative filtering systems make very specific recommendations about taste products. Then the problem is avoided of Amazon.com sending you prompts for children's books because you purchased *Little Women* for your niece last Christmas. But will collaborative filtering systems ever be able to replace the Mary Kay Shipleys of the world in creating sleepers?

Individual Thresholds for Adoption

A *threshold* is the number of other individuals who must be engaged in an activity before a given individual will join that activity (Granovetter, 1978; Markus, 1987). In the case of the diffusion of an innovation, a threshold is reached when an individual is convinced to adopt as the result of knowing that some minimum number of other individuals in the individual's personal communication network have adopted and are satisfied with the innovation. Notice that a threshold occurs at the *indi-*

vidual level of analysis, whereas the critical mass operates at the *system* level. Individuals have adoption thresholds, while systems such as communities and organizations and publics have a critical mass.

Individual thresholds explain the microlevel process through which aggregated individual decisions make up the critical mass in a system. Granovetter (1978) provided an illustration of how the two-level phenomenon of individual thresholds and the system-level critical mass are interrelated:

> Imagine 100 people milling around in a square—a potential riot situation. Suppose their riot thresholds are distributed as follows: There is one individual with threshold 0, one with threshold 1, one with threshold 2, and so on up to the last individual with threshold 99. This is a distribution of thresholds. The outcome is clear and could be described as a "bandwagon" or "domino" effect: The person with threshold 0, the "instigator," engages in riot behavior—breaks a window, say. This activates the person with threshold 1. The activity of these two people then activates the person with threshold 2, and so on, until all 100 people have joined.

If we remove the individual with threshold 1 and replace that individual by someone with threshold 2, the riot would end with just one rioter. Only one window would be broken with a rock, let's say. No critical mass would be reached.

Threshold models assume that an individual decision to adopt an innovation depends on the number of other individuals in the system who have already made the behavior change. In the window-breaking illustration above, each individual could easily observe the number of other window breakers. Many innovations, such as the adoption of contraceptives or HIV prevention, are much less observable. Only an individual's sexual partner may know whether or not the individual has adopted. For such less observable innovations, a high degree of *pluralistic ignorance* (defined as the degree to which individuals in a system do not know about the extent of the behavior of other members' behavior in their system) occurs. In this situation, individual thresholds are less important in influencing when an individual adopts a new idea.

Although the conceptual notion of a distribution of individual thresholds facilitates our understanding of the diffusion process (especially for interactive innovations), relatively few empirical studies of this topic have been conducted. One problem, as Professor Thomas Valente (1993, 1995) pointed out, is that very few studies are available in which diffusion network data were gathered along with the date of adoption of an innovation of all individuals in a system. Advancing our understanding of thresholds and the critical mass in the diffusion of innovations is thus constrained by lack of empirical data. In fact, Valente (1995) was forced to test his hypotheses about network models of diffusion by reanalyzing the several existing data sets currently available.

Why Do Individuals Adopt Prior to the Critical Mass?

A key question in understanding the role of the critical mass in the diffusion process is why an individual adopts an interactive technology *prior to* the point at which a critical mass is reached (see Figure 8-5). At any earlier point, the perceived cost of adopting the innovation outweighs its perceived relative advantage. An early adopting individual may decide to adopt in anticipation that the innovation's rate of adoption will take off in the near future (when others adopt), although past diffusion research suggests that most individuals do not adopt an innovation until after learning of their peers' successful experiences.

Figure 8-7 shows the threshold behavior of medical doctor number 3 in Peoria, a respondent in the Coleman and colleagues (1966) study of tetracycline diffusion. This doctor has a personal network of five other doctors in his community. As the diffusion process begins, none of these doctors have adopted the new drug. Three months later, two of the focal individual's network partners have adopted (40 percent of the five individuals in the doctor's personal network). As an increasing percentage of his personal network adopted the new drug, he was gradually influenced to adopt also. The percentage of network partners who had adopted rose from 40 percent at three months, to 80 percent at five months and to 100 percent at eight months into the seventeen-month diffusion process, when a "tipping point" (the respondent's individual threshold) was reached. Then the respondent adopted. The medical community in Peoria was a system in which, in Allen's (1983) words, everybody was watching while being watched in the process of the drug's diffusion.

The threshold for adoption varies for different individuals in a system, which is one explanation for the occurrence of the S-shaped diffusion curve. The innovators who rush to adopt an innovation first have a very low threshold for adoption, due to their high degree of venturesomeness. Later adopters have higher thresholds (that is, stronger resistance to the innovation), which are reached only when many other individuals in their personal network have adopted (such as the medical doctor in Figure 8-7). Individual thresholds for adoption are normally distributed, thus creating the S-curve of diffusion.

Figure 8-7. An Individual's Threshold for Adoption (Indexed as the Percentage of Adopters in the Individual's Personal Communication Network) for a New Drug by Medical Doctor No. 3 in Peoria

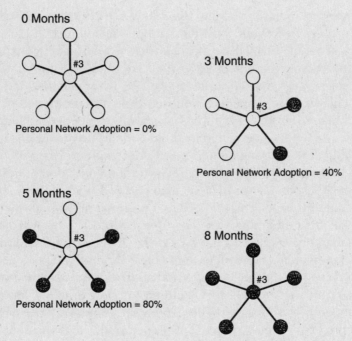

This doctor is the focal individual in his personal communication network of five doctors, as they adopted tetracycline over the first eight months of the diffusion process. This doctor had a relatively high threshold of resistance to the new drug, which had to be overcome by extensive network influences from near peers who had adopted previously.

Source: Based on Valente's (1995) reanalysis of the Coleman and others (1966) drug diffusion data.

Valente (1995) showed that network thresholds can be used to classify individuals according to (1) their innovativeness with respect to their system and (2) their innovativeness with respect to their personal network partners. This type of analysis can locate individuals who have adopted early in the diffusion process, but late relative to their personal network partners. Similarly, Valente's (1995) analysis showed that some individuals were late adopters who were exposed to the innovation through their network partners, but who still did not adopt (not all individuals adopt immediately when their threshold is reached; a threshold lag may occur). Other individuals were late adopters due to a lack of exposure to the innovation through their personal networks. Here we see the analytical advantages of exploring an individual's innovativeness as a function of his or her network partners' innovativeness in adopting an innovation.

Generalization 8-13 states: *An individual is more likely to adopt an innovation if more of the other individuals in his or her personal network have adopted previously* (Rogers and Kincaid, 1981; Valente, 1995). Diffusion is highly social in nature: an individual's threshold for adoption is reached when a certain number of the individual's peers have adopted. Innovators, having a very low threshold, adopt an innovation relatively early and thus launch the diffusion process for an innovation in a system. By adopting early, the innovators help other, later-adopting individuals reach their adoption threshold. When the critical mass in the rate of adoption of an interactive innovation is reached, the percentage of all individuals' network partners takes a sudden jump, triggering a much more rapid rate of adoption thereafter. This process explains how the critical mass occurs in terms of different individual thresholds.

In order to explain the effect of the critical mass on the adoption behavior of a system's members it is useful to think about microlevel personal communication networks. Many key questions about the critical mass can only be answered by investigating the networks through which the critical mass occurs and how it exerts its effects. For example, in our discussion of the medical doctor's adoption of tetracycline (see Figure 8-7), we measured his adoption threshold as the percentage of his personal communication network partners who adopted prior to him. We did not measure his adoption threshold as the percentage of all of the other doctors in Peoria, as he communicated directly about the innovation with only five of these fellow doctors. Measures of individuals' adoption thresholds are of course more precise in predicting an individual's adoption when measured at the personal network level than at the system level.

The notion of a critical mass calls for important modifications in diffusion theory, particularly in the case of interactive communication innovations (which have become very important in recent decades). The critical mass may also occur for certain noninteractive innovations. For example, a new article of clothing becomes fashionable when a critical mass of social elites begins wearing it (Grindereng, 1967; Crane, 1999). Fashionable dressers are watching while being watched (a woman wearing a new fashion becomes furious when she meets another woman at a party wearing the same dress). Other individuals then rapidly adopt the new fashion, until it is eventually supplanted by a yet newer clothing fashion. Such is the fashion diffusion process for lower or higher hemlines, bare midriffs, and square-toed shoes.

A good deal of interdependence occurs among the adopters of any innovation in the sense that adopters influence their peers to adopt by providing them with a positive (or negative) evaluation of the innovation. Such peer influence usually makes the diffusion curve take off somewhere between 5 and 20 percent of cumulative adoption (the exact percentage varies from innovation to innovation, and with the network structure of the system). Once this takeoff is achieved, little additional promotion of the innovation is needed, as further diffusion is self-generated by the innovation's own social momentum. This explanation for the S-shaped curve of adoption for a noninteractive innovation sounds much like the critical mass. What is different in the special case of interactive innovations is that there is a built-in "forcing quality" in the adopter-to-decider relationship, which stems from the reciprocal interdependence of interactive innovations. "It takes two to tango," as Katz (1962) pointed out. At least two.

Networks and the Turbocharger Effect

Taking personal network variables into account can help a diffusion scholar explain more of the variance in a dependent variable like innovativeness. The *turbocharger effect* is the additional variance in a dependent variable explained by network variables beyond the direct effects of the individual-level variables (Wellman, 1983). Dr. Shaheed Mohammed (2001) investigated the turbocharger effect for his 3,020 Tanzanian respondents in a study of family-planning diffusion. Each respondent was asked to identify the four other individuals with whom they discussed important matters. A high degree of homophily was found, with respondents talking to others of the same gender, religion, and tribe. Listeners to a radio soap opera promoting family planning and HIV prevention talked to other listeners.

Mohammed (2001) found that adding network variables to such individual-level variables as education and socioeconomic status explained additional variance in the dependent variable of adopting family-planning methods, although the increase was modest. Further study of network turbocharger effects on individual innovativeness are needed.

Strategies for Getting to Critical Mass

What strategies can be used to reach critical mass for an interactive innovation in a system?

1. Highly-respected individuals in a system's hierarchy for initial adoption of the interactive innovation should be targeted. For example, when the president of an organization champions an interactive technology such as e-mail and is the first to utilize the new technology to send messages to other individuals in the organization, an obvious meta-communication message is implied: That other individuals should adopt the new technology to respond to the president's electronic messages.

    The system's context for the critical mass can be important in providing pressures to adopt an interactive innovation. A system's hierarchy, reward system, and regulations can encourage, or discourage, the adoption of a new idea. A system can provide special resources (incentives) for the first adopters of an innovation and thus lower individuals' perceived efforts to adopt.

2. Individuals' perceptions of the innovation can be shaped, for instance, by implying that adoption of it is inevitable, that it is very desirable, or that the critical mass has already occurred or will occur soon.

3. The innovation should be introduced to intact groups in the system whose members are likely to be relatively more innovative. For example, e-mail systems were often introduced in the R&D division of a corporation. R&D units usually represent an especially enriched environment for this innovation. Then, after e-mail reached critical mass in the R&D unit of an organization, it was introduced on a companywide basis.

4. Incentives for early adoption of the interactive innovation should be provided, at least until a critical mass is reached. "The most

direct approach [to reaching critical mass] is to give the service free to a selected group of people for a limited time" (Rholfs, 1974). An auto company marketing the new hybrid vehicles (powered by both a gasoline engine and electric batteries) in the United States in 2001, set the selling price at about two thirds of the actual cost of production (a saving for the consumer of $10,000) and provided free maintenance and service for three years as incentives to encourage innovators to adopt. After two years, eighteen thousand vehicles had been sold, and critical mass was being approached. Soon the special incentives to reach critical mass for hybrid cars will be reached, and the incentives will be ended.

Summary

This chapter dealt with opinion leadership, communication networks, and the critical mass. *Opinion leadership* is the degree to which an individual is able to influence informally other individuals' attitudes or overt behavior in a desired way with relative frequency. Opinion leaders play an important role in diffusion networks, and are often identified and utilized in diffusion programs.

Homophily is the degree to which individuals who communicate are similar. *Heterophily* is the degree to which individuals who interact are different in certain attributes. Interpersonal diffusion networks are mostly homophilous (Generalization 8-1). Homophily can act as an invisible barrier to the rapid flow of innovations within a social system, as similar people interact in socially horizontal patterns, thus preventing a new idea from trickling down from those of higher socioeconomic status, more education, and greater technical expertise.

When interpersonal diffusion networks are heterophilous, followers generally seek opinion leaders of higher socioeconomic status, with more formal education, greater mass media exposure, more cosmopoliteness, greater contact with change agents, and more innovativeness (Generalization 8-2). Compared to followers, opinion leaders have greater mass media exposure, more cosmopoliteness, greater contact with change agents, greater social participation, higher social status, and more innovativeness (Generalizations 8-3 through 8-8). Opinion leaders conform more closely to a system's norms than do their followers. When a social system's norms favor change, opinion leaders are especially innovative (Generalization 8-9).

A *communication network* consists of interconnected individuals who are linked by patterned flows of information. An individual's network links are important determinants of his or her adoption of innovations. The network interconnectedness of an individual in a social system is positively related to the individual's innovativeness (Generalization 8-10). *Interconnectedness* is the degree to which the units in a social system are linked by interpersonal networks.

Networks provide a certain degree of structure and stability in the predictability of human behavior. *Communication structure* is the differentiated elements that can be recognized in the patterned communication flows in a system. This structure consists of the cliques within a system and the network interconnections among them that are provided by bridges and liaisons. Individuals are identified as belonging to cliques on the basis of *communication proximity*, the degree to which two linked individuals in a network have personal communication networks that overlap. A *personal network* consists of those interconnected individuals who are linked by patterned communication flows to a given individual. Personal networks that are radial (rather than interlocking) are more open to an individual's environment, and hence play a more important role in the diffusion of innovations. The information exchange potential of communication network links is negatively related to their degree of (1) communication proximity and (2) homophily. This generalization (8–11) expresses Mark Granovetter's theory of "the strength-of-weak-ties." Individuals tend to be linked to others who are close to them in physical distance and who are relatively homophilous in social characteristics (Generalization 8-12).

The *critical mass* occurs at the point at which enough individuals in a system have adopted an innovation so that the innovation's further rate of adoption becomes self-sustaining. The critical mass is particularly important in the diffusion of interactive innovations such as e-mail, where each additional adopter increases the utility of adopting the innovation for all adopters. *Interactivity* is the degree to which participants in a communication process can exchange roles in, and have control over, their mutual discourse. As more individuals in a system adopt a noninteractive innovation, it is perceived as increasingly beneficial to future adopters (this is a *sequential* interdependence effect on later adopters). However, in the case of an interactive innovation, the benefits from each additional adoption increase not only for all future adopters, but also for each previous adopter (this is *reciprocal* interdependence).

A *threshold* is the number of other individuals who must be engaged in an activity before a given individual will join that activity. An innovator has a low threshold of resistance to adopting a new idea, and so few (or no) interpersonal network influences are needed for adoption. In contrast, a late majority individual has a much higher threshold that must be overcome by near-peer network influences in order to overcome resistance to the innovation. Thresholds act for individuals in a somewhat parallel way to the critical mass at the system level. An individual is more likely to adopt an innovation if more of the other individuals in his or her personal network adopted previously (Generalization 8-13).

9

THE CHANGE AGENT

One of the greatest pains to human nature is the pain of a new idea. It . . . makes you think that after all, your favorite notions may be wrong, your firmest beliefs ill-founded. . . . Naturally, therefore, common men hate a new idea, and are disposed more or less to ill-treat the original man who brings it.
Walter Bagehot, *Physics and Politics* (1873), p.169.

The effect of targeting interventions by change agents is illustrated by an HIV prevention program for about one thousand commercial sex workers (CSWs) in Pumwari, a low-income area of Nairobi, Kenya. Some 80 percent of the CSWs were already HIV-positive in 1985, when the intervention program started. Change agents provided free condoms, and a free health clinic was established that treated sexually transmitted diseases (STDs), provided counseling, and gave medical checkups to CSWs every six months. Outreach efforts by peer educators were carried out through one-on-one contacts and through *barazas* (group meetings) with CSWs. The average CSW in Pumwari had four clients per day. The intervention prevented an estimated six thousand to ten thousand HIV infections per year, at a cost of approximately $10 per case of HIV infection prevented (Moses et al., 1991).

If instead of targeting the thousand CSWs in Pumwari, one thousand men had been randomly chosen from Nairobi to receive similar health services, and if they had achieved the same rates of condom use, only eighty HIV infections would have been averted annually (Altman, 1997). Here we see the advantages of change agents intervening upstream in a problem such as an epidemic. The Pumwari program provided additional health services, other than just condoms, that the CSWs wanted (such as the health clinic and STD treatment), which also contributed indirectly to HIV prevention, as STDs are a co-factor for HIV infection. Here we see how much cheaper (and more humane) HIV *prevention* can be, compared to the *treatment* of infected individuals.

This chapter is about the role of the change agent, relationships with clients, and various strategies for human behavior change. A *change agent* is an individual who influences clients' innovation-decisions in a direction deemed desirable by a change agency. A change agent usually seeks to secure the adoption of new ideas, but he or she may also attempt to slow the diffusion process and prevent the adoption of certain innovations with undesirable effects.

Targeting

Much has been learned in the past decade or two about the role of change agents in HIV/AIDS prevention. In 1993, the author and several colleagues began investigating the relative effectiveness of HIV/AIDS prevention programs in San Francisco, where there were an amazing 212 such programs (this in a city of three fourths of a million people). These HIV prevention programs had proliferated because each was highly targeted to a specific population. At this point, the AIDS epidemic had broken out of the initial high-risk population of gay and bisexual men and had spread to other high-risk groups. For example, one of the prevention programs of study was targeted to young Thai girls who worked in massage parlors and were also commercial sex workers. Another program was aimed at Deadheads (followers of the Grateful Dead rock musicians), who numbered only about 150 individuals in San Francisco. Importantly, each such prevention program was typically organized and operated by members of the target audience. Thus, Filipino male commercial sex workers conducted a prevention program aimed at young Filipino men who hung out in "rice bars" in the city. Each of the 212 programs in San Francisco was an *intervention*, defined as actions with a coherent objective to bring about behavioral change in order to produce identifiable outcomes.

Funding for many of the 212 prevention programs was provided, at least in part, by the Centers for Disease Control and Prevention (CDC) with funds channeled through the city's public health agency (Rogers et al., 1995; Dearing et al., 1996). One might wonder whether such a proliferation of prevention programs in San Francisco was an efficient use of public funds. Undoubtedly there was some unnecessary duplication of efforts, and resources were wasted through competition between programs aimed at similar audiences. On the other hand, the high degree of targeting meant that the prevention programs were culturally sensitive to the target audiences.

Targeting is the process of customizing the design and delivery of a communication program based on the characteristics of an intended audience (Dearing et al., 1996). A targeting strategy can emphasize cultural sensitivity, especially if the target audience is involved in the intervention program through formative research, as peer educators, and/or through advising on the program's implementation. Examples of such involvement in an HIV/AIDS intervention occurred in the STOP AIDS program in San Francisco, which was culturally sensitive because the prevention activities were designed and carried out *by* gay men *for* gay men and were based on a detailed understanding of how gay men perceived the epidemic (see Chapter 2).

The ultimate targeting strategy is *tailoring*, in which a communication message is directed to an individual, who represents a very homogeneous audience indeed. Tailoring is made possible, in most cases, by use of a computer (and perhaps the Internet) to store a large number of alternative messages on a topic such as HIV prevention and then to send one message to an individual so that the message fits precisely with that individual's situation, such as his or her stage-of-change in the innovation-decision process (see Chapter 5).

Effectiveness is the degree to which an intervention program fulfills its objectives. If a peer outreach program with CSWs, such as that in Punwari, is intended to prevent HIV infection, its effectiveness is measured as the degree to which this objective is achieved. Cost-effectiveness is calculated as the cost of each unit of behavior change achieved. For instance, the cost per HIV infection prevented is estimated at $8 to $12 for peer educator intervention programs with commercial sex workers in various developing countries (Jha et al., 2001).

Uniqueness is the degree to which an audience of relatively homophilous individuals differs from the larger population of which it is part (Dearing et al., 1996). High-risk groups targeted for HIV prevention intervention are examples of unique populations. Society perceives them as unique and may stigmatize them. For example, in India, such high-risk groups as CSWs, truck drivers, and injecting drug users are all looked down upon by society. Partly as a result, the personal lives of high-risk audience segments for HIV prevention in many countries are colored by "hopelessness, despair, and bitterness" (Dearing et al.,

1996). The stigma associated with being HIV-positive is so strong in some nations, such as India, that lynchings of HIV-positive individuals have occurred. Outreach workers like peer educators are homophilous with their high-risk audience members and do not stigmatize them. Being nonjudgmental is an essential quality of effective outreach workers for HIV/AIDS prevention.

Change Agents as Linkers

Many different occupations fit our definition of change agent: teachers, consultants, public health workers, agricultural extension agents, development workers, and salespeople. All of these change agents provide a communication link between a resource system with some kind of expertise and a client system. One main role of the change agent is to facilitate the flow of innovations from a change agency to an audience of clients. For this type of communication to be effective, the innovations must be selected to match clients' needs. Feedback from the client system must flow through the change agent to the change agency so that it appropriately adjusts its intervention programs to fit the changing needs to clients.

Change agents would not be needed in the diffusion of innovations if there were no social and technical chasms between the change agency and the client system. Change agents usually possess a high degree of expertise regarding the innovations that are being diffused. Change agency personnel may have a Ph.D. in agriculture or an M.D. degree or possess other technical training. Most change agents are university graduates in some technical field. Their superior know-how actually poses a barrier, making it difficult for them to communicate directly with clients. Their heterophily in technical competence usually is accompanied by heterophily in subcultural language differences, socioeconomic status, and beliefs and attitudes. Change agents, even though they link their clients with technical experts in the change agency, may be relatively heterophilous from either system. This heterophily gap on both sides of the change agent creates role conflicts and certain problems in communication. As a bridge between two differing systems, the change agent is a marginal figure with one foot in each of two worlds.

In addition to facing this problem of social marginality, change agents also must deal with problems of *information overload*, the state of an individual or a system in which excessive communication inputs cannot be processed and utilized, leading to breakdown. The large volume of information about innovations flowing from the change agency may overcome the change agent's capacity to select the most relevant messages for the client system. By understanding the needs of the clients, a change agent can selectively transmit to them only information that is relevant.

The Sequence of Change Agent Roles

Seven roles can be identified for the change agent in the process of introducing an innovation in a client system.

1. *To develop a need for change.* A change agent often initially helps clients become aware of the need to alter their behavior. In order to initiate the innovation-decision process, the change agent points out new alternatives to existing problems, dramatizes the importance of these problems, and may assure clients that they are capable of confronting these problems. The change agent assesses clients' needs at this stage and also may help to create needs.

2. *To establish an information exchange relationship.* Once a need for change is created, a change agent must develop rapport with his or her clients. The change agent can enhance these relationships with clients by being perceived as credible, competent, and trustworthy, and by empathizing with the clients' needs and problems. Clients often must accept the change agent before they will accept the innovations that he or she is promoting. The innovations are judged, in part, on the basis of how the change agent is perceived.

   The standard instruction for the peer outreach workers in HIV prevention interventions is to first develop a personal relationship with an audience individual (say a commercial sex worker), to learn from the individual what his or her problems are, and to understand and accept the individual's situation. The peer educators must be nonjudgmental, or interpersonal relationships with their client will be ruptured. An HIV prevention change agent may need several weeks or months to get acquainted with a commercial sex worker. Only then can the outreach worker effectively intervene with a social change communication message like practicing safer sex. Repeated contacts (perhaps a dozen or more) with a target individual are usually necessary to change that individual's behavior. The innovation-decision process for safer sex seldom involves an impulse decision (Singhal and Rogers, 2003).

3. *To diagnose problems.* The change agent is responsible for analyzing clients' problems in order to determine why existing alternatives do not meet their needs. In arriving at such diagnostic conclusions, the change agent must view the situation emphatically from the clients' perspective.

4. *To create an intent to change in the client.* After a change agent explores various avenues of action that clients might take to achieve their goals, the change agent seeks to motivate their interests in the innovation.

5. *To translate an intent into action.* A change agent seeks to influence clients' behavior change in accordance with recommendations based on the clients' needs. Interpersonal network influences from near peers are most important at the persuasion and decision stages in the innovation-decision process (see Chapter 5). The change agent usually can operate only indirectly here, by working with opinion leaders to activate near-peer networks. Or perhaps the change agent is a peer-educator/opinion leader and can thus encourage interpersonal communication from near peers.

6. *To stabilize adoption and prevent discontinuance.* Change agents may effectively stabilize new behavior through reinforcing messages to clients who have adopted, thus helping to "freeze" the new behavior. This assistance is given when a client is at the implementation or confirmation stage in the innovation-decision process (see Chapter 5).

7. *To achieve a terminal relationship.* The end goal for a change agent is to develop self-renewing behavior on the part of clients. The change agent should seek to put himself or herself out of business by developing the clients' ability to be their own change agents. In other words, the change agent seeks to shift the clients from a position of reliance on the change agent to one of self-reliance.

This seven-step sequence of change agent roles is an ideal, and the reality of change agent–client relationships may be quite different. The agent/client investigation of such real/ideal differences can provide understanding of why many diffusion interventions are ineffective, as the following case study suggests.

Coercion in Norplant Diffusion Safaris in Indonesia[*]

The main criterion for judging the relative success of diffusion interventions is usually the rate of adoption of an innovation that they achieve. In some cases, however, this measure of change agency effectiveness needs to be seriously questioned. The *quality* of adoption decisions resulting from a diffusion campaign may be more important than just the number of adoptions achieved. An example of this crucial point is provided by the introduction of a new contraceptive, Norplant, in Indonesia. By the usual criterion of effectiveness, Norplant diffusion was a huge success. Indonesia in 1998 had 3.6 million Norplant adopters, more than any other country in the world. Officials from some eighty-six other nations visited Indonesia, and utilized its family-planning program as a model for their own approaches.

But a careful look at the microlevel process of how Norplant adoption was achieved in Indonesia discloses a rather different story. A certain degree of coercion was used to achieve the high rate of adoption, the change agents who provided this contraceptive gave little explanation or counseling to women at their time of their adoption, and discontinuance of the contraceptive by women who experienced side effects was actively discouraged. As a result, the quality of the Norplant innovation-decisions in Indonesia was far from perfect by any standard, raising ethical and moral questions about the Norplant diffusion campaign and posing threats to its long-term sustainability.

When Norplant initially became available in the mid-1980s, it was the first important advance in contraceptive technology since the intrauterine device (IUD) and the oral contraceptive pill in the early 1960s. The international family planning community was enthusiastic about Norplant, hailing it as the perfect contraceptive for women in developing countries. A woman adopts Norplant by having six small plastic tubelets inserted with a needle on the underside of one forearm. The tubelets, each about one inch long, slowly leak progestin, a sex hormone, into the woman's bloodstream. Pregnancy is thus prevented for a five-year period. The Norplant tubelets can be removed by health providers any time that the woman wishes to discontinue. The Food and Drug Administration (FDA) approved Norplant for use in the United States in 1991 on the basis of extensive clinical trials showing that the contraceptive was safe and efficacious.

This rather ideal picture of Norplant contrasts with the reality of its diffusion and adoption in Indonesia. First, Norplant was diffused through

---

[*]This case illustration is based on Tuladhar, Donaldson, and Noble (1998).

intensive local campaigns called *safaris* in which policemen, local political leaders, and military forces participated in an all-out effort to gain adopters of the new contraceptive in each community in Indonesia. The *safaris* were based on the Indonesian minister of population's concept of "guided democracy," in which certain women were encouraged by providers to adopt a particular contraceptive, although a full cafeteria of family-planning methods were made available. Surveys showed that 73 percent of the Norplant adopters in West Java adopted during a *safari*. Justification for the *safari* approach by change agents was based on the notion that health providers knew more about the different contraceptives than did potential adopters. This top-down, coercive approach contradicts several of the recommended change agent rules described in the previous section.

Because Norplant was provided to a large number of women in a community in a relatively short period of time during a *safari* (which usually lasted for six weeks or so), individual counseling and provision of how-to knowledge and principles knowledge was shortchanged. Norplant adopters were not adequately informed about the possible side effects of the contraceptive, such as prolonged bleeding, that might accompany adoption. Many women were not told that the Norplant tubelets could be removed if they wished to discontinue. In fact, Norplant discontinuation rates were only one fourth those for IUDs and oral contraceptive pills in Indonesia. A diffusion survey showed that discontinuance was much lower for women who did not know that discontinuance was possible. Women could not discontinue without the assistance of health providers, and many requests for discontinuance were denied. Of the women who were able to discontinue, many had to demand removal of their Norplant tubelets two or three times.

Clearly, the Indonesian family-planning program officials were superenthusiasts for Norplant adoption, rather than showing concern for improving the quality of contraceptive services for their clients. These overzealous innovation champions were not counterbalanced by consumer advocates, like women's organizations, who were too weak in Indonesia to have much influence in questioning the *safari* campaigns. International family-planning agencies operating in Indonesia might have intervened on behalf of the rights of women adopting Norplant, but the potentially most influential agency, the Population Council (a U.S.-based organization supported by the Rockefeller Foundation), had originally developed Norplant. The Population Council acted in Indonesia as an innovation champion, rather than as a change agency concerned with high-quality diffusion and adoption.

This case illustration demonstrates the tradeoff between the number of adopters of an innovation versus the quality of the adoption-decisions, a choice ultimately faced by every change agent and every change agency. The case of Norplant in Indonesia also suggests the need for microlevel investigations of change agent–client interaction at the time of adoption, a type of research discussed in a later section of this chapter.

Factors in Change Agent Success

Why are certain change agents relatively more successful than are others?

Change Agent Effort

One factor in change agent success is the amount of effort spent in communication activities with clients. Generalization 9-1 states: *Change agents' success in securing the adoption of innovations by clients is positively related to the extent of change agent effort in contacting clients.* The degree of success of change agents is usually measured in terms of the rate of adoption of innovations by members of the client system. This success measure is frequently used because the main objective of most change agencies is to secure the adoption of new ideas by their clients (although the case of Norplant in Indonesia raises the question of whether this measure is always most appropriate). Alternative measures of change agent success might be the degree to which the desired consequences of innovation adoption actually occur to clients (see Chapter 11), or the quality of innovation-decisions (as in the case of Norplant in Indonesia).

Evidence for Generalization 9-1 comes from an investigation of the influence of health providers' recommendations to their patients to stop smoking cigarettes. This study was conducted by Korhonen and others (1999) in North Karelia, a province in Finland that in the 1970s had the highest rates of heart disease in the world. The author remembers visiting a dairy farmer in North Karelia in the early 1970s, when the heart disease prevention intervention was getting under way. After a tour of the farmer's dairying operations, we were invited to his home for midmorning coffee, which consisted of an open-faced sandwich covered with butter, reindeer meat, and a thick slab of cheese, accompanied by shots of vodka and coffee. After this snack, the farmer smoked several cigarettes. This coffee break amounted to a ticking cardiac time bomb!

By the 1990s, however, a long-term campaign to decrease the risk of heart disease in North Karelia resulted in changed diets and smoking

behavior. Korhonen and others (1999) found that smoking cessation recommendations from medical doctors and nurses were very effective in
changing people's behavior. These health providers were highly credible,
as people perceived that doctors were expert in understanding the health
effects of smoking. Few of the health providers themselves smoked, and
most appeared to be quite healthy, so they were personal models for
healthy behavior. However, the influence potential of health providers as
change agents for smoking cessation in North Karelia was very limited
because they devoted little time or effort to changing smoking behavior.
The doctors saw their main job as seeing a large number of patients,
spending relatively little time with each, and thus maximizing their
income from client fees. Little profit could be made from such preventive
health activities as discouraging smoking by their clients, compared to
treating what the doctors considered more serious health problems.

The sheer amount of client contact is by no means the sole explanation of change agent success, however. For instance, the timing of the
client contact, relative to the stage of diffusion of an innovation, is also a
factor in success. Stone (1952) analyzed the amount of effort expended
by agricultural extension agents in promoting a new idea to Michigan
farmers. In the first years of a diffusion campaign, the rate of adoption
of the innovation roughly paralleled the amount of change agents'
effort, as measured by the number of agent days per year devoted to
the innovation. After about 30 percent adoption was reached, however,
the extension agents' efforts decreased, whereas farmers continued to
adopt the new idea at an almost constant rate. Once the opinion leaders
adopt and a critical mass is reached, the adoption curve shoots upward
in a self-generating fashion, and a change agent can begin to retire from
the scene (at least for that particular innovation). The S-curve of adoption will then continue to climb, largely independent of change agents'
efforts, under further impetus from opinion leaders.

Client Orientation

A change agent's social position is midway between the change agency
and the client system, and the change agent is necessarily subject to
role conflict. A change agent is often expected to engage in certain
behaviors by the change agency and at the same time may be expected
by clients to carry out quite different actions. How is this role conflict
best resolved, from a viewpoint of achieving change agents' success?

Generalization 9-2 states: *Change agents' success in securing the adoption of innovations by clients is positively related to a client orientation, rather than to a change agency orientation.* Client-oriented change agents are more feedback-minded, have closer rapport with their clients, enjoy higher credibility in the eyes of their clients, and base their diffusion activities primarily on clients' need.

Compatibility with Clients' Needs

An important and difficult role for the change agent is to diagnose clients' needs. We suggest Generalization 9-3: *Change agents' success in securing the adoption of innovations by clients is positively related to the degree to which a diffusion program is compatible with clients' needs.* *

Change projects that ignore clients' felt needs often go awry or produce unexpected consequences. For example, one Indian village was provided with development funds to construct an irrigation well that could double crop yields. But the villagers wanted a well for drinking because they had to carry water for household use several miles from a river. The peasants built the well in the village center, rather than in the fields, and drank the water instead of irrigating their crops. If a change agent based his or her program only upon the felt needs of the villagers, the well was located appropriately for drinking purposes. Perhaps the change agent should have developed a stronger need for crop irrigation by pointing out the financial payoffs of the choice.

A change agent can allow clients to pursue a solution to their needs so completely that they commit errors or misdirect priorities. An example is provided by an unsupervised self-help program in Southeast Asia that led to unexpected results (Niehoff, 1964). Leaders in each village were allowed to decide on their own development projects; then a change agency provided construction materials, such as cement, hardware, and roofing materials. Hundreds of village projects were carried out, including building schools, roads, markets, irrigation canals, and dams. But more than half of the construction projects were Buddhist temples, a result that had not been expected or desired by the government change agency.

Change agents should be aware of their clients' felt needs and adapt their change programs to them. They should not, however, relinquish their role in shaping these needs.

---

*This generalization is similar to Generalization 6-2: *The compatibility of an innovation, as perceived by members of a social system, is positively related to its rate of adoption.*

Sustainability: "Chicken" Davis in Nigeria

Sustainability is the degree to which a program of change is continued after the initial resources provided by a change agency are ended. In recent years, the sustainability of change agents' programs has received much more attention than previously, both in the United States and in the developing nations of Latin America, Africa, and Asia. Unless an innovation is highly compatible with clients' needs and resources, and unless clients feel so involved with the innovation that they regard it as "theirs," it will not be continued over the long term. The importance of sustainability is emphasized by the case of the introduction of American chickens in eastern Nigeria in the late 1960s by Dr. "Chicken" Davis, a U.S. poultry science expert.

When Davis arrived in Nigeria, he immediately saw the need for improved poultry raising. Chicken meat was considered a national delicacy, consumers liked eggs, and the protein in poultry products improved human nutrition. But there was a severe shortage of poultry products. Village chickens ran wild, eating whatever feed they might find, and did not provide much meat. Many of the eggs they laid could not be found. "Chicken" Davis introduced Western methods of poultry farming: caged chickens were fed imported grain, and high-producing, rapidly growing baby chickens were flown in from U.S. hatcheries. Western-style chicken raising became very popular, and the poultry-farming enterprises promoted by "Chicken" Davis spread rapidly throughout eastern Nigeria. During the three years of Davis's program, millions of baby chicks were imported to Nigeria. The people's protein consumption increased, and the small-scale poultry farmers reaped handsome profits. When Dr. Davis retired from the international development agency for whom he worked, at the end of his three-year assignment in Nigeria, he was awarded a hero's medal by the president of Nigeria.

A few weeks later, a poultry epidemic swept through eastern Nigeria, killing all the imported birds. The wild village chickens were immune to the disease. Within a year of "Chicken" Davis's departure, only an unpleasant memory remained of his work. Not one Western chicken survived.

What mistakes did "Chicken" Davis make regarding the sustainability of the innovation that he introduced? Should he have paid greater attention to the indigenous knowledge system of chicken raising?

Change Agent Empathy

Empathy is the degree to which an individual can put himself or herself into the role of another person. Change agent empathy with clients is especially difficult when the clients are extremely different from change agents. We suggest Generalization 9-4: *Change agents' success in securing the adoption of innovations by clients is positively related to empathy with clients.*

Change agents are generally oriented to achieving widespread client adoption of innovations. They might be more effective in the long run if they achieved higher-quality adoptions, that is, adoption by clients who were more satisfied, and who passed this positive attitude along to potential adopters. Those involved in family-planning programs recognized that if the quality of client services are improved, more adoption of contraceptives would occur, discontinuance rates would drop, and the rate of adoption would increase. One means of improving the quality of clinic services has been to train nurses and other clinic staff to greet clients when they enter a health clinic, listen to them as they describe their need for family planning, establish eye contact with the client, smile, and establish a rapport with the client. These interpersonal skills were taught to clinic staff in Nigeria in a three-day training course, which was then evaluated by means of data from clinic records and by "mystery clients" who visited clinics to determine if the trainees used what they had been taught. The results? The quality of adoption of family-planning methods increased, and this satisfaction with contraceptives on the part of adopters was passed on to others (Kim et al., 1992).

In a similar field experiment in Ghana, "mystery clients" were used to evaluate the effects of training clinic staff in how to treat their clients in a courteous manner. Mystery clients are specifically trained to act like ordinary clients when they enter a health clinic to seek family-planning services, where they serve as unobtrusive observers of how clients are treated. The results from the mystery clients study in Ghana showed that increased empathy with clients, and a more positive relationship of change agents with clients in general, contributed to greater change agent success in securing the adoption of innovations by clients (Huntington et al., 1990).

Compare the highly empathic approach to family planning in Nigeria and Ghana with the coercive approach to Norplant diffusion in Indonesia, discussed earlier in this chapter.

Communication Campaigns

A well-known early campaign failure concerned the Cincinnati Campaign for the United Nations, which was intended to build public support for the United Nations. At this time, soon after the founding of the United Nations, it was perceived as a new idea. The Cincinnati campaign distributed 60,000 pieces of literature, presented 2,800 speeches at various organizations, and broadcast sixty radio spots each week (Star and Hughes, 1950). The campaign was targeted at segments of the city's population known to be poorly informed about the United Nations, which, according to precampaign formative research surveys, included females, elderly, the poor, and the less educated.

The six months' campaign unfortunately reached the wrong audience (the younger and better educated) and had very minor effects on most people in Cincinnati. For instance, individuals who knew anything about the United Nations changed from 70 to 72 percent, an evaluation survey indicated. The campaign messages did not get through to the targeted audience because of *selective exposure*, the tendency of individuals to attend to messages that are consistent with their prior attitudes and experiences (Hyman and Sheatsley, 1974). The UN messages did not get through to individuals who did not already know about the United Nations.

Another reason why the Cincinnati campaign failed was due to its abstract nature. The campaign slogan, "Peace Begins with the United Nations – and the United Nations Begins with You," was not connected to any specific behavior on the part of audience members. A local resident remarked, "Why, yes. I heard it over and over again. . . . But I never did find out what it means."

After some years of believing that communication campaigns only have minimal effects, scholars began to realize that campaigns *could* succeed if they were carried out in a more effective manner (Mendelsohn, 1973). Successful campaign strategies consisted of (1) utilizing *formative research*, study of the campaign's intended audience and the campaign's messages in order to plan the campaign more effectively, (2) setting specific but reasonable campaign goals, (3) using *audience segmentation*, the strategy of dividing a heterogeneous mass audience into relatively homogeneous audience segments, and (4) designing the campaign's mass media messages to trigger interpersonal network communication among members of the intended audience. A campaign can succeed if it is carried out in a way that is based on communication strategies like those above.

What is a campaign? The term derives from military origins and from Latin, meaning "to go to the field." Military terminology, like "target," for example, still is utilized in describing campaigns. So a campaign is purposive, intended to bring about certain specific effects (the Cincinnati Campaign for the United Nations failed because its purpose was so ambiguous). Further, a campaign is usually aimed at a large audience, and carried out in a more or less specifically defined time period, say a few weeks or months. Finally, a campaign usually entails an organized set of activities and messages, such as posters, television spots, and so forth. Thus a *campaign* intends to generate specific outcomes or effects by a relatively large number of individuals, usually within a specified period of time and through an organized set of communication activities (Rogers and Storey, 1988).

One illustration of a successful campaign was a radio-centered project to promote family planning and HIV prevention in the island nation of St. Lucia, in the Caribbean (Vaughan, Regis, and St. Catherine, 2000). This campaign used the strategy of *entertainment-education*, putting an educational idea in an entertainment message in order to achieve behavior changes (Singhal and Rogers, 1999). Focus group interviews with members of the intended audience for the entertainment-education messages (fertile-aged men and women in St. Lucia) were carried out by the campaign planners, to be sure that the campaign messages were understood but did not offend. St. Lucian scriptwriters wrote the radio scripts for *Apwe Plezi* ("After the Pleasure Comes the Pain"), in order to ensure that they were culturally appropriate. The main characters in the soap opera included positive and negative role models for the educational issues of the campaign. For example, one male character, an operator of heavy construction equipment, refused to marry the mother of his child (85 percent of St. Lucian births occur out of wedlock).

The radio intervention encouraged marriage, the use of family-planning methods, and preservation of the St. Lucian parrot, which was an endangered species because people were taking parrot eggs from the nests (the eggs were believed to be an aphrodisiac). A new brand of condoms, called "Catapult," was introduced only through the radio program, and its sales were a tracer of the campaign's effects, as were before/after surveys of the audience. *Apwe Plezi* was very popular, reaching about one third of the nation's adult population, in part because it was perceived as dealing with real-life problems of people in St. Lucia. T-shirts, posters, bumper stickers, and other promotional activities were included in the St. Lucian campaign. Street theater performances using *Apwe Plezi* characters also supplemented the radio broadcasts of the entertainment-education soap opera.

Why was this campaign so effective? It was planned on the basis of formative research with the intended audience, the messages were pretested with the audience, and the entertainment-education messages were lively and relevant. Fourteen percent of those listening to *Apwe Plezi* adopted a family-planning method as a result of listening to the radio soap opera. Even nonlisteners knew about Catapult condoms, an indicator that listeners talked to nonlisteners about the radio program. *Apwe Plezi* stimulated audience individuals to discuss family planning, the importance of marriage, and survival of the St. Lucian parrot with their peers, especially their sexual partners. As in other entertainment-education interventions, such as in Tanzania (Rogers et al, 1999), this interpersonal peer communication was decisive in clinching innovation-decisions.

Experience with many communication campaigns in recent years shows they can be quite effective if change agents conduct them according to appropriate communication strategies.

The ORT Campaign in Egypt*

When the oral rehydration therapy (ORT) campaign was launched in Egypt in 1983, 130,000 infants were dying each year from diarrhea-related dehydration, a rate of 70 per 1,000 children under the age of two. The objective of the campaign was to reduce this rate by 25 percent over the next five years. The campaign, described by a leading medical journal as "one of the world's most successful health education campaigns," greatly exceeded these goals. The campaign cut the infant mortality rate in half within two years and in five years reduced the mortality rate by 70 percent! Awareness of oral rehydration therapy reached 100 percent, and the adoption of oral rehydration salts (ORS), a mixture of salt and sugar, reached 96 percent. Prior to the campaign, the use of ORS was only 1 percent, even though the foil packets were plentiful. However, they were piled up in warehouses. At that time, antibiotics and starvation, a completely ineffective treatment, were the prevailing "cure" for dehydration.

A national oral rehydration program was created and adequately funded in Eygpt in 1983. The target audience for the ORT campaign was rural women, 80 percent of whom were illiterate. Thus print media were ruled out. Prior to the ORT campaign, a highly successful entertainment-educa-

---

*This case illustration is based on Abdullah (2003).

tion strategy had been used for family planning, featuring humorous one-minute television spots in which a popular female actress appeared as a nagging mother-in-law. The ORT campaign decided to build on this approach with a series of fifteen one-minute television spots. Drama was very appealing to the target audience, and low-income rural people in Egypt had a high level of television exposure. Extensive formative research was conducted for planning the campaign. An initial problem was what to call "dehydration," as a word did not exist for this condition in Arabic in Egypt. *Gafaf* was chosen as the most appropriate word and was used throughout the ORT campaign. A campaign logo was also selected, featuring a mother holding a baby and spoon-feeding it the ORT mixture.

A veteran male actor and comedian was initially chosen to appear in each television spot, but pretesting showed that the audience perceived him as inappropriate. He was replaced by Karima Moktar, a well-known soap opera actress, who was perceived as highly credible for the topic of ORT. The television spots showed her as a wise, tender, and loving mother. Each spot showed a baby suffering from diarrhea and dehydration, with Moktar either caring for the baby or advising its mother how to do so. Each spot showed how to mix and administer the ORS solution and ended with a jingle, "To prevent dehydration, give the baby ORS." The expression *Edilo mahloul,* meaning "Don't worry, there is a solution," became part of everyday life in Egypt. The fifteen television spots were frequently repeated on the Egyptian national television network and were very popular. The audience did not tire of repeated showings of the message. Some 80 percent of survey respondents said that the television spots were their main source or channel of communication about ORT. The national ORT program carefully monitored the distribution of the ORS packets, which were sold by pharmacies for 6 cents each. The ORS packets were also available free from three thousand ORT depot holders, each the responsibility of a respected opinion leader.

The ORT campaign was relatively long term, from 1983 to 1991. It saved the lives of hundreds of thousands of Egyptian children. Why was this campaign so unusually successful? It was long term, based on formative research, and used a combination of the entertainment-education television spots and the opinion leaders/depot holders.

Homophily and Change Agent Contact

As previously defined (see Chapter 8), *homophily* is the degree to which pairs of individuals who interact are similar, and *heterophily* is the degree to which they differ. Change agents usually differ from their clients in many respects, and have the most contact with clients who are much like themselves.

There is strong support for the following generalizations about change agents' contact with clients.*

Generalization 9-5: *Contact with change agents is positively related to higher socioeconomic status among clients.*

Generalization 9-6: *Contact with change agents is positively related to greater social participation by clients.*

Generalization 9-7: *Contact with change agents is positively related to higher formal education among clients.*

Generalization 9-8: *Contact with change agents is positively related to cosmopoliteness among clients.*

These generalizations suggest that more effective communication between change agents and their clients occurs when they have a higher degree of homophily with each other. Such effective communication is rewarding, and encourages change agents to contact clients who are more like themselves. The number of agricultural change agent contacts per year in a sample of 1,307 Brazilian farmers (Rogers et al., 1970) was:

Average Number of Contacts with Change Agent per Year

Innovators	20
Early adopters	15
Early majority	12
Late majority	5
Laggards	3

These data are typical of a number of studies of client contact with change agents. Change agent contact is one of the variables most highly related to innovativeness. Rogers and others (1970, pp. 6–12) con-

---

*In addition, three generalizations about change agent contact were listed in previous chapters: Generalization 5-5: *Earlier knowers of an innovation have greater contact with change agents than later knowers;* Generalization 7-21: *Earlier adopters of innovations have more contact with change agents than later adopters;* and Generalization 8-5: *Opinion leaders have greater contact with change agents than their followers.*

cluded, on the basis of investigating fifteen independent variables related to innovativeness among some four thousand farmers in three developing nations, "The single variable that emerges as most highly related to change agent contact, even when the effect of other variables is controlled, is agricultural innovativeness." Socioeconomic status was highly related to change agent contact for these peasant farmers in Brazil, Nigeria, and India. The three variables were related as follows:

Socioeconomic Status → Change Agent Contact → Innovativeness

This circle of interrelated variables means that change agents help those clients least who are most in need of their help.

Change Agents' Contact with Lower-Status Clients

Less educated, lower-income clients need the assistance of change agents more than do more elite clients. Then why don't change agents concentrate their efforts on their most disadvantaged clients? The answer reflects the innovativeness/needs paradox discussed in Chapter 7. More elite clients are homophilous with change agents, and so communication between the two is easier and more effective. Lower-status clients are socioeconomically different from change agents, and this heterophily gap impedes effective communication. If the change agent is an employee of a government agency or some other establishment institution, lower-status clients may distrust the change agent. Further, less privileged clients often lack the necessary resources to adopt innovations that the change agent is promoting.

Finally, many change agents do not try to contact their needier, lower-status clients because of a self-fulfilling prophecy that change agents have developed from past experience. Change agents think that their lower-status clients are not responsive to change agents' efforts at diffusing innovations; this stereotype in the change agent's mind discourages the change agent from initiating contact with less advantaged clients.

What could be done to encourage the lower-status and least innovative clients to have more change agent contact? One answer is to select change agents who are as much like their clients as possible. If most clients possess only a few years of formal education, a university-trained change agent will likely face greater communication difficulties than if he or she has fewer years of education. This is one reason why many diffusion programs employ para-professional change agent aides. Generalization 9-9 states:

Change agents' success in securing the adoption of innovations by clients is positively related to their homophily with clients.

In the highly effective STOP AIDS prevention program in the early days of the AIDS epidemic in San Francisco (see Chapter 2), speakers at the small group meetings of gay men matched the characteristics of their audience. The presenters were young gay men who were respected opinion leaders in the gay community. Further, the speakers were usually HIV-positive, which meant they were perceived as highly credible by their audience. They knew what they were talking about concerning transmission of the virus. Their message, in part, was "Don't do what I did. Practice safer sex" (Singhal and Rogers, 2003).

Para-Professional Aides

An *aide* is a less than fully professional change agent who intensively contacts clients to influence their innovation-decisions. One of the important advantages of aides is their much lower cost per client contacted, compare to professional change agents. Health programs in Asian nations have found they can employ thirty aides for the same cost as one medical doctor. But the main advantage of para-professional aides over professional change agents is that the aides are more homophilous with the lower-status members of the user system that they serve.

Technical expertise may not be the most important quality of a change agent in the eyes of many clients. Personal acceptability of the change agent is as important as, or more important than, technical expertise. Para-professional aides are much less technically expert than professionals, but they often more than make up for their lower degree of technical expertise through their greater social expertness. For example, family-planning aides in most developing nations are female para-professionals, who are better able to discuss the culturally sensitive topic of contraception with female clients than are the predominantly male doctors.

Selection of change agent aides according to gender, formal education, and personal acquaintance with the client system minimizes the social distance between the change agent system and the client system. Aides halve the social distance between professionals and low-status clients.

Change Agent Credibility

Even though change agent aides have less *competence credibility,* defined as the degree to which a communication source or channel is perceived as knowledgeable and expert, they have the special advantage of *safety credibility*, the degree to which a communication source or channel is perceived as trustworthy. Because an aide is perceived as a near peer by clients, they are not likely to suspect the aide of having selfish motives or manipulative intentions.

Heterophilous sources or channels (such as professional change agents) are perceived as having competence credibility, while homophilous sources or channels (such as aides) are perceived as having safety credibility. An ideal change agent would have a balance of competence and safety credibility. A change agent might be homophilous with his or her clients in social characteristics (such as socioeconomic status, ethnicity, and the like) but heterophilous in regard to technical competence about the innovations being diffused.

A change agent aide who has previously adopted an innovation that he or she is promoting may have an ideal combination of homophily/ heterophily and of competence credibility/source credibility. An illustration is peer educators in HIV prevention programs who are selected because of their trustworthiness in the eyes of the intended audience members. Most peer educators in CSW HIV prevention interventions are former commercial sex workers, and some continue their sex work while working as peer educators. Program experience has shown that their experience as a commercial sex worker is essential to providing them with trustworthiness and credibility in the eyes of their target audience. Most sex workers are driven into their profession by poverty, and so both the peer educators and their audience members are homophilous in socioeconomic status (Singhal and Rogers, 2003).

When peer outreach workers begin their educational work, they often are given a brief training course about methods of HIV transmission, safer sex methods such as condom use, and how to approach their intended audience members. Peer educators may distribute free condoms or sell them at a subsidized price. The income from condom sales may constitute the peer educator's remuneration for her HIV prevention work. CSWs are often trained by peer educators in how to negotiate condom use with their customers.

Generalization 9-10 states: *Change agents' success in securing the adoption of innovations by clients is positively related to credibility in the clients' eyes.*

The adoption of a new idea often entails the purchase of a new product. Clients often regard commercial change agents as having low credibility. A commercial change agent's motives, as perceived by his or her clients, may be one reason for the low credibility placed on his or her recommendations. Clients feel that salespeople promote the overadoption of new ideas in order to secure higher sales commissions. Commercial change agents are relatively more important as a source or channel at the knowledge stage and again at the implementation stage than at other stages (such as persuasion) in the innovation-decision process for agricultural innovations (Ryan and Gross, 1943; Beal and Rogers, 1957; Copp et al., 1958), as a client may purchase a small amount of a new product for trial. At this point the individual relies heavily upon commercial change agents for information on how to use the innovation. Their credibility is limited to how-to information, and does not usually extend to an ability to persuade the individual to form a favorable attitude toward the innovation. Such persuasive credibility is accorded to near peers, noncommercial change agents, and other sources who have nothing to gain, at least not to the extent that a commercial salesman has, from the client's adoption.

Commercial channels or sources in some cases can create awareness-knowledge of an innovation. For instance, Coleman and colleagues' (1966) medical drug study found that drug detail men and the commercial publications of pharmaceutical companies were reported by about 80 percent of the medical doctors as their source or channel of knowledge about the new drug tetracycline. Detail men are employees of pharmaceutical firms who call on doctors to provide them with details about medical innovations and to give them free samples of new drugs. The drug detail men are not credible at the persuasion and decision stages in the innovation-decision process, when a doctor is deciding whether or not to adopt (Coleman et al., 1966).

Inauthentic Professionalization of Aides

Inauthentic professionalism is the process through which an aide takes on the dress, speech, or other identifying marks of a professional change agent. For instance, peer educators for HIV prevention among CSWs often demand uniforms, identification badges, and other symbols of professional change agents (Singhal and Rogers, 2003). Aides usually identify with the professional change agents who supervise them, and they want to become more like them. They cannot gain the university degree that the professional possesses, so they try to act like them or at least look like them.

Such inauthentic professionalization may destroy the very het-
erophily-bridging function for which the change agent aides are
employed. If aides are made aware of the problem of inauthentic professionalism, however, they will usually act in ways to correct this threat
to their effectiveness with clients.

The Baltimore Needle-Exchange Project

Interpersonal networks can be used in an intervention program, as the Baltimore Needle-Exchange Project demonstrates. Dr. Thomas Valente, a
communication network scholar, was a professor of public health at Johns
Hopkins University in 1994, when he began using bar codes to identify each
clean needle that was distributed free in the city's program for injection
drug users. Each month, 200,000 clean needles were distributed, and
almost as many were returned at various locations in the city's drug-infested
central core. Valente and others (1998) found that 5,369 different individuals participated in the needle-exchange project from 1995 to 1997.

Valente constructed a huge network matrix, composed of the 5,369 individuals to whom the clean needles were given versus the 5,369 people who
returned them (sometimes this was the same person). Opinion leaders in
the network were people who distributed clean needles to many others.
Some 64 percent of all the needles were distributed by only 9 percent of the
drug users, who were called "satellite exchangers" by Valente. The clean
needles, which were distributed by the intervention program at no cost to
the users, were then sold on the street by the satellite exchangers for about
one dollar each. The entrepreneurial satellite exchangers made a profit
from their sales work, while also promoting HIV prevention. About twenty
clean syringes were given to an individual on each contact with the project.
The average injection drug user utilized 149 syringes during the two years
of study. But the typical satellite exchanger handled 1,046 syringes (about
seven times as many). Clearly, the needle-exchange system in Baltimore
was a well-connected network in which certain individuals played key roles.

The network nature of needle exchange in Baltimore suggested entry
points for outreach workers to promote HIV prevention through the distribution of clean needles by identifying opinion leaders among individuals at
risk for HIV infection.

The Use of Opinion Leaders

Opinion leadership is the degree to which an individual is able to influence other individuals' attitudes or overt behavior in a desired way with a relatively high frequency (see Chapter 8). Diffusion campaigns are more likely to be successful if change agents identify and mobilize opinion leaders. Generalization 9-11 is: *Change agents' success in securing the adoption of innovations by clients is positively related to the extent that he or she works through opinion leaders.*

The time and energy of the change agent are scarce resources. By focusing communication activities upon opinion leaders in a social system, the change agent can leverage these scarce resources and hasten the rate of diffusion of an innovation among clients. An economy of effort is achieved because contacting opinion leaders takes far less of the change agent's resources than if each member of the client system were to be consulted. The opinion leader approach magnifies the change agent's efforts. An analysis in Latin America a few years ago found that each agricultural extension worker was responsible for reaching ten thousand farmers. This daunting task would be impossible unless extension agents utilized opinion leaders. Furthermore, by enlisting the aid of opinion leaders, a change agent provides the aegis of local sponsorship and sanction for the new ideas that are introduced. Network messages from near peers such as opinion leaders are regarded as credible in convincing an individual to adopt an innovation. After the opinion leaders in a system adopt an innovation, it may be impossible to stop its further spread.

Change agents sometimes mistake innovators for opinion leaders. Opinion leaders have followers, whereas innovators are the first to adopt new ideas and are often perceived as deviants from the system's norms. When the change agent concentrates communication efforts on innovators, rather than on opinion leaders, awareness-knowledge of the innovations may be increased, but few clients are persuaded to adopt. The innovators' behavior does not necessarily convince the average members of a system to follow suit. A change agent may correctly identify the opinion leaders in a system but then concentrate his or her attention so much on these few leaders that they become *too* innovative in the eyes of their followers or become perceived as overly identified with the change agent. Thus, a change agent can "wear out" the credibility of opinion leaders by making them too innovative.

The Role of Demonstrations

Potential adopters of a new idea are aided in evaluating an innovation if they are able to observe it in use under conditions similar to their own. Such observation often occurs naturally, when one individual views another's experience in using the innovation. Change agents may try to increase the observability of an innovation, and thus speed its rate of adoption, by organizing a demonstration of the innovation.

Since the early days of the U.S. agricultural extension service in the 1910s, extension agents have conducted demonstrations of agricultural innovations in farmers' fields. For example, a chemical fertilizer might be demonstrated by laying out plots of corn (or some other crop) with, and without, chemical fertilizer. At the end of the crop season, the extension agent would help the farmer harvest the plots, measure the yields on both plots, and invite neighboring farmers to observe the demonstration's results. The change agent might lead a discussion of how fertilizer affects plant growth, or of the cost-benefits of applying fertilizer. Evaluation of on-farm demonstrations by diffusion researchers show that they can be an effective strategy, especially for innovations that are easily observable and that are in the early stages of the diffusion process (prior to reaching critical mass, when the S-curve takes off under its own self-generated impetus). The demonstration method was so important in the early days of the agricultural extension service that county home economics agents were commonly referred to as "home demonstration agents." They conducted demonstrations of home canning, new recipes, and sewing techniques for farm housewives.

The demonstration strategy is widely utilized today, not only in agriculture but also in energy conservation, mass transportation, education, environmental protection, substance abuse prevention, and in many other fields. Demonstrations may account for as much as 10 percent of the federal government's R&D budget (Baer et al., 1977).

Demonstrations perform two quite different functions: (1) *experimental demonstrations,* which are conducted to evaluate the effectiveness of an innovation under field conditions, and (2) *exemplary demonstrations,* which are conducted to facilitate diffusion of the innovation to other units (Myers, 1978). Often these two types of demonstrations are confused or a single demonstration is expected to fulfill both functions. An experimental demonstration is successful if the innovation demonstrated is evaluated adequately, whether this evaluation is positive or negative. In either case, knowledge is advanced about the effectiveness of the innovation. An example of an experimental demonstration is the field trials currently underway in several countries for a new AIDS vaccine (Singhal and Rogers, 2003). An experimental demonstration usually has low public visibility. The attitude of the demonstration's managers should be one of healthy skepticism toward the innovation.

In contrast, an exemplary demonstration, whose purpose is to facilitate the diffusion of an innovation, is intended to persuade potential adopters. It should be conducted with high public visibility, and the demonstration's managers should have an attitude of optimistic assurance about the innovation's effectiveness.

The demonstration of an innovation under field conditions can be a useful strategy for change agents to diffuse an innovation. The demonstration is often effective because it combines the perceived competence credibility of the change agent with the perceived safety credibility of the demonstrator. A demonstration can be particularly effective if the demonstrator is a respected opinion leader in the system.

Turner, Martin, and Cunningham (1998) investigated the role of a demonstration in persuading addiction treatment agencies in Ontario, Canada, to adopt OPTIONS, an early intervention program for people with a low level of addiction to alcohol and drugs. This new program, which resulted from a research project, was demonstrated by one agency, and other addiction agencies in Ontario were encouraged to visit the demonstration site, which hosted training workshops on the new treatment approach. Representatives of thirty-four other addiction agencies visited the demonstration site, which was perceived as similar to them. While the demonstration did not convince any of the thirty-four site-visiting agencies to adopt OPTIONS, it did move them through the trial stage of the innovation-decision process.

Client's Evaluative Ability

One of the change agent's unique inputs to the diffusion process is technical competence. But if the change agent takes a long-range approach to the change process, he or she should seek to raise clients' technical competence and their ability to evaluate potential innovations themselves. Then the clients could eventually become their own change agents. This suggests Generalization 9-12: *Change agents' success in securing the adoption of innovations by clients is positively related to increasing clients' ability to evaluate innovations.*

Unfortunately, change agents are often primarily concerned with such short-range goals as increasing the rate of adoption of innovations. Instead, increasing the self-reliance of clients should be the goal of change agencies, leading to termination of client dependance upon the change agent. This goal, however, is seldom reached by most change agencies. They usually promote the adoption of innovations, rather than seek to teach clients the basic skills of how to evaluate innovations themselves. Previously in the chapter, we saw how the Indonesian family-planning program coerced women to adopt Norplant. Many of the adopters, especially those who adopted during the *safari* campaigns, did not even understand that Norplant could be discontinued. Clearly, nothing was being done to increase the women's ability to evaluate the contraceptive.

The Agricultural Extension Service*

The *agricultural extension model* is a set of assumptions, principles, and organizational structures for diffusing the results of agricultural research to farmers in the United States. The agricultural extension service is reported to be one of the world's most successful change agencies. Certainly it is the most admired and most widely copied (see Chapter 4). The main evidence for the success of the agricultural extension model is the dramatic increase in U.S. farm productivity in the decades after World War II. "It is impossible for anyone to speak 10 words about diffusion without two of them being 'agricultural extension.' . . . In many ways, it constitutes the defining metaphor for all technology transfer efforts" (Eveland, 1986).

Historical Development of the Extension Services

The first effective extension approach was pioneered in Broome County, New York, in 1911. The Binghamton Chamber of Commerce in Broome County was particularly concerned about the welfare of farmers, as agriculture was the main local industry. Accordingly, the Chamber's "Farm Bureau" (so named in accordance with such other divisions of the Chamber of Commerce as the Roads and Alleys Bureau, the Better Business Bureau, etc.) decided to employ

---

*This case illustration is based on Rogers, Eveland, and Bean (1982), Rogers (1986a), and Rogers (1988a).

a recent agricultural graduate from Cornell University to diffuse innovations to farmers in Broome County. Part of his first year's salary was donated by the Delaware and Lackawanna Railroad, so he was called a "county agent" (all railroad employees were termed "agents" in those days, as, for example, "ticket agents," "station agents," etc.). The Binghamton Chamber of Commerce Farm Bureau included several leading farmers, who solicited their neighbors for donations to help pay the county agent's salary. Soon these donations were institutionalized into annual memberships in the Broome County Farm Bureau.

The idea of a county extension agent, and of a local farm bureau, spread rapidly across the United States after 1911. This movement was spurred by (1) provision of federal financing through the Smith-Lever Act of 1914 and (2) the need for higher agricultural production during World War I. As the county agent movement spread, so did the county agents' sponsoring body, the farm bureaus. Soon the county farm bureaus federated into state organizations, and then in 1919 into the American Farm Bureau Federation (AFBF). This organization began to operate as a legislative pressure group, a function incompatible with its original purpose of being the local sponsor of county extension agents. The farm bureau and the extension services split in 1919, but the two organizations remain friendly until the present day. The legislative assistance of the AFBF, and of state farm bureaus, is one reason for the financial strength and stability of the extension services. The annual amount of money and personnel invested in the agricultural extension effort since 1920 has increased sharply. By 1920 there were three thousand extension employees, and today the total is seventeen thousand.

Funds for extension services in the United States come from federal (40 percent), state (40 percent), and county government (20 percent) sources, which is why the total extension system is often referred to as the *"cooperative* extension service." The extension service has maintained a high level of growth at a time when federal spending on agriculture has not kept pace with increases in the federal budget.

State Extension Specialists

About four thousand extension service employees in the United States are subject-matter "specialists" at the state level (17 percent of all extension employees). These specialists interpret current research findings in their specialized fields to county extension employees, and thus indirectly to clients. American farmers are increasingly specialized as cotton growers, milk producers, and so forth. Thus specialized knowledge is increasingly important. Consider an extension agronomy specialist whose office is in the

Department of Agronomy at a state agricultural university. This specialist travels over the state to address farmer meetings and to keep county extension agents abreast of new developments in agronomy. Other extension specialists are in farm management, marketing, animal husbandry, entomology, home economics, and other fields.

Essentially the state extension specialist links research-based knowledge to the county extension agents. He or she is "the county agent's extension agent." In order to effectively fulfill this linkage function, the extension specialist must bridge the scientific/intellectual world of the land-grant university with the pragmatic world of the farmer and his or her county extension agent. Usually, a state extension specialist has had previous experience as a county extension agent and then moved, through graduate study, into a specialized agricultural field.

Broadening the Extension Service Mission

In 1911, extension activities were solely concerned with biological agriculture: agronomy, animal husbandry, poultry, and so forth. County extension agents placed their main emphasis upon production-increasing innovations such as new seeds, fertilizers, improved livestock, and farm equipment. Then the farmers' wives began to demand that their information needs for better nutrition, child care, and home management also receive attention by the extension service. Accordingly, the county agricultural agent, usually with a college degree in technical agriculture, was paired with a colleague: a county home economics agent (originally called a "home demonstration agent"), usually with a bachelor's degree in home economics from a land-grant university.

The county extension staff then expanded further to include a county agent responsible for 4-H Club activities. This 4-H Club agent usually possesses a bachelor's degree in technical agriculture, and is considered a future county agricultural agent in training. After some years' experience as a 4-H agent, he or she might be promoted to be a country agricultural agent.

By the 1940s, state extension services began to turn some of their attention to problems of agricultural marketing and to consumer information programs. These changes shifted the extension services away from strictly an agricultural production focus. This change meant that the extension service appealed to new, nonfarm audiences. The Smith-Lever Act of 1914, which provided federal aid to the state extension services, did not specify that the extension services should work only with farm people. The number of farmers has dropped from 35 percent of the total U.S. population in 1910 to less than 2 percent in recent years.

Conclusions About the Agricultural Extension Model

What lessons have been learned from the agricultural extension model?

1. The agricultural extension model has changed in major ways since its origin in 1911, in response to shifts in its environment. This flexibility is a key reason for its relative success.
2. The agricultural extension model is based on client participation in identifying local needs, planning programs, and in performing evaluation and feedback.
3. Agricultural research activities are oriented toward the utilization of research results, and this pro-utilization orientation facilitates the effectiveness of the extension service.
4. State extension specialists work in close social and spatial contact with agricultural researchers and professors in their academic specialty, and this closeness facilitates their linking research-based knowledge to farmer problems.
5. The agricultural extension model has been more effective in diffusing agricultural production technology to farmers than in diffusing other subject-matter content to farm and nonfarm audiences.
6. The agricultural extension model includes not only a systematic procedure for the diffusion of innovations from researchers to farmers, but also institutionalized means of orienting research activities toward users' needs (thus the land-grant college/agricultural experiment station/extension service complex is a total innovation-development system).
7. The U.S. extension services are considered highly successful, if success is measured mainly by continued growth in funds and personnel, due to (1) their ability to adjust to environment changes, and (2) the strong support of the American Farm Bureau Federation and elite farm leaders.
8. The extension services are criticized for an overemphasis on production agriculture and for a lack of concern with rural social problems, some of which resulted from the extension services' success in diffusing technological innovations in agriculture.

Centralized and Decentralized Diffusion Systems

For several decades, the classical diffusion model dominated the thinking of scholars, policy makers, and change agencies. In this model, an innovation originates from some expert source (often an R&D organization). This source then diffuses the innovation as a uniform package

to potential adopters who accept or reject the innovation. The individ
ual adopter of the innovation is thought of as a relatively passive
accepter. This classical model owes much of its popularity to the success of the agricultural extension services and to the fact that the basic
paradigm for diffusion research grew out of the Ryan and Gross (1943)
hybrid corn study. Much agricultural diffusion in the United States is
relatively centralized, in that key decisions about which innovations to
diffuse, how to diffuse them, and to whom, are made by technically
expert officials near the top of the diffusion system.

The classical diffusion model was challenged by Schön (1971), who
noted that diffusion theories lagged behind the reality of emerging diffusion systems. He particularly criticized classical diffusion theory
because of its assumption that innovations should originate from a centralized, expert source and then diffuse to users. While recognizing that
this classical model may fit much of reality, Schön noted that it fails to
capture the complexity of relatively decentralized diffusion systems in
which innovations originate from numerous local sources and then
evolve as they diffuse via horizontal networks.

In recent decades, the author gradually became aware of diffusion
systems that did not operate at all like centralized diffusion systems.
Instead of coming out of formal R&D systems, innovations often bub-
bled up from the operational levels of a system, with the inventing done
by certain lead users. Then the new ideas spread horizontally via peer
networks, with a high degree of re-invention occurring as the innovations are modified by users to fit their particular conditions. Such
decentralized diffusion systems are usually not managed by technical
experts. Instead, decision making in the diffusion system is widely
shared, with adopters making many decisions. In many cases, adopters
served as their own change agents in diffusing their innovations to others. One example of such a decentralized diffusion system is the Association for the Expansion of Solar Energy in the Dominican Republic,
studied by Peggy Lesnick (2000) and described in Chapter 8.

How does a decentralized diffusion system differ from its centralized
counterpart? Table 9-1 and Figure 9-1 show the differences between
centralized and decentralized diffusion systems. Our distinction is
somewhat oversimplified because it suggests a dichotomy (rather than a
continuum) of centralized/decentralized diffusion systems. In reality,
an actual diffusion system is usually some hybrid combination of certain
elements of a centralized and of a decentralized system (Figure 9-2).

Table 9.1 Characteristics of Centralized and Decentralized Diffusion Systems

Characteristics of Diffusion Systems	Centralized Diffusion Systems	Decentralized Diffusion Systems
Degree of centralization in decision making and power	Overall control of decisions by national government administrators and technical subject-matter experts	Wide sharing of power and control among the members of the diffusion system; client control by local systems; much diffusion is spontaneous and unplanned
Direction of diffusion	Top-down diffusion from experts to local users of innovations	Peer diffusion of innovations through horizontal networks
Sources of innovations	Formal R&D conducted by technical subject-matter experts	Innovations come from experimentation by nonexperts, who often are users
Who decides which innovations to diffuse?	Top administrators and technical subject-matter experts	Local units decide which innovations should diffuse on the basis of their informal evaluations of the innovations
Importance of clients' needs in driving the diffusion process	An innovation-centered approach; technology-push, emphasizing needs created by the availability of the innovation	A problem-centered approach; technology pull, created by locally perceived needs and problems
Amount of re-invention	A low degree of local adaptation and re-invention of the innovations as they diffuse among adopters	A high degree of local adaptation as they diffuse among adopters

Figure 9-1. Centralized and Decentralized Diffusion Systems

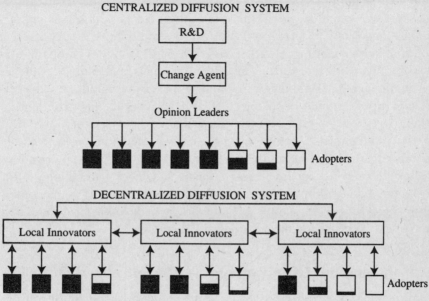

In decentralized diffusion systems, innovations spread by horizontal networks among near peers in a relatively spontaneous fashion. Innovations are created by certain local lead users and may be re-invented by other adopters.

Figure 9-2. The Continuum of Decentralized and Centralized Diffusion Systems

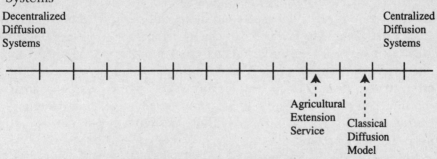

The classical diffusion model, based on the Ryan and Gross (1943) hybrid corn study, is relatively centralized. In recent years diffusion scholars began to realize that actual diffusion systems ranged on a continuum. The agricultural extension service in the United States is relatively centralized, as are many diffusion systems modeled loosely after it, but other diffusion systems are relatively decentralized.

Centralized diffusion systems are based on a more linear, one-way model of communication. Decentralized diffusion systems more closely follow a convergence model of communication, in which participants create and share information with one another in order to reach a mutual understanding (Rogers and Kincaid, 1981). A fundamental assumption of decentralized diffusion systems is that members of the user system have the ability to make sound decisions about how the diffusion process should be managed. This capacity of the users to manage their own diffusion system is greatest when (1) the users are highly educated and technically competent practitioners (for example, cardiovascular surgeons), so that all the users are experts, or (2) the innovations being diffused do not involve a sophisticated level of technology (for example, home energy conservation or organic gardening versus building a nuclear power plant), so that intelligent laymen have sufficient technical expertise to take advantage of them.

Advantages and Disadvantages of Decentralized Diffusion

Compared to centralized systems, innovations diffused by decentralized systems are likely to fit more closely with users' needs and problems. Users feel a sense of control over a decentralized diffusion system as they participate in making key decisions, such as which of their perceived problems most need attention, which innovations best meet these needs, how to seek information about an innovation and from what source, and how much to modify an innovation as they implement it in their particular setting. The high degree of user control over these key decisions means that a decentralized diffusion system is geared closely to local needs. Problems of change agent–client heterophily are greatly minimized. User motivations to seek innovations mainly drive a decentralized diffusion process, and this motivation may be more cost-efficient than situations in which professional change agents manage the diffusion process. User self-reliance is encouraged in a decentralized system. Finally, decentralized diffusion is publicly popular, as most users like such systems.

Several disadvantages, however, usually characterized decentralized diffusion systems (in comparison with centralized diffusion systems):

1. Technical expertise is difficult to bring to bear on decisions about which innovations to diffuse and to adopt, and it is possible for ineffective innovations to diffuse through a decentralized system

because of a lack of quality control. So when a diffusion system is disseminating innovations that involve a high level of technical expertise, a decentralized diffusion system is less appropriate than a more centralized diffusion system.

2. Furthermore, nonexperts in decentralized diffusion systems lack an understanding of diffusion strategies that should be utilized. As a result, site visits to observe an innovation in use by an adopter often are the main channels of diffusion. Such site visiting can be an effective means of diffusion, but it may create an overload problem for the site that is visited, as has occurred for certain individuals, organizations, or communities that have thousands of site visitors per year. Completely decentralized diffusion systems may suffer from the fact that local users, who control the system, lack adequate knowledge of users' problems and available innovations that could solve them.

3. Sometimes a national government wants an innovation diffused for which the people do not feel a need. In a highly decentralized system, such an innovation simply will not diffuse. An example is family planning in developing nations, which a government may regard as a high priority but which local couples may not want. Decentralized diffusion systems for contraceptive innovations do not exist in Latin America, Africa, and Asia. Similarly, environmental innovations such as recycling and carpooling may be a national priority but may not be popular with people. A decentralized diffusion approach would not work here.

This discussion suggests that:

1. Decentralized diffusion systems are most appropriate under certain conditions, such as for diffusing innovations that do not involve a high level of technical expertise among a set of users with relatively homogeneous needs and conditions.

2. Certain elements of centralized and decentralized diffusion systems can be combined to form a hybrid diffusion system that uniquely fits a particular situation. For example, a diffusion system may combine a central coordinating role, with decentralized decisions being made about which innovations should be diffused and which users should be site-visited. Technical evaluations of promising innovations by experts can be made in an otherwise decentralized diffusion system.

Summary

Change agents operate *interventions,* defined as actions with a coherent objective to bring about behavior change in order to produce identifiable outcomes. For example, an HIV prevention program such as STOP AIDS in San Francisco was designed to slow the rate of HIV infection. *Targeting* (defined as the process of customizing the design and delivery of a communication program on the basis of the characteristics of an intended audience segment) is one means of segmenting a heterogeneous audience so that customized messages that fit each individual's situation are delivered. Currently, the Internet is often utilized to deliver such targeted messages.

A *change agent* is an individual who influences clients' innovation-decisions in a direction deemed desirable by a change agency. Change agents face two main problems: (1) their social marginality, due to their position midway between a change agency and their client system, and (2) *information overload,* the state of an individual or a system in which excessive communication inputs cannot be processed and used, leading to breakdown. Seven roles of the change agent are: (1) to develop a need for change on the part of clients, (2) to establish an information-exchange relationship, (3) to diagnose problems, (4) to create an intent to change in the client, (5) to translate intentions into action, (6) to stabilize adoption and prevent discontinuance, and (7) to achieve a terminal relationship with clients.

Generalizations 9-1 through 9-4 and 9-9 through 9-12 suggest that a change agent's relative success in securing the adoption of innovations by clients is positively related to (1) the extent of the change agent's effort in contacting clients, (2) a client orientation, rather than a change agency orientation, (3) the degree to which the diffusion program is compatible with clients' needs, (4) the change agent's empathy with clients, (5) his or her homophily with clients, (6) credibility in the clients' eyes, (7) the extent to which he or she works through opinion leaders, and (8) increasing clients' ability to evaluate innovations.

Further, we propose that contact by change agents is positively related to (1) higher socioeconomic status among clients, (2) greater social participation, (3) higher formal education, and (4) cosmopoliteness (Generalizations 9-5 through 9-8).

An *aide* is a less than fully professional change agent who intensively contacts clients in order to influence their innovation-decisions. Not only do aides provide lower-cost contacts with clients than is possible with professional change agents, but they are also able to bridge the heterophily gap between professionals and clients, especially lower socioeconomic status clients. Aides have less *competence credibility,* the degree to which a communication source or channel is perceived as knowledgeable and expert, but they have greater *safety credibility,* the degree to which a communication source or channel is perceived as trustworthy. An aide's safety credibility is due to his or her homophily with the client system. *Inauthentic professionalism* is the process through which an aide takes on the dress, speech, or other identifying marks of a professional change agent.

In recent decades diffusion scholars have become aware that an alternative to the classical diffusion model exists in the form of decentralized diffusion systems. These diffusion programs have outrun the classical model (a relatively centralized approach). In *centralized* diffusion systems, such as the agricultural extension services in the United States, overall control of diffusion decisions (such as which innovations to diffuse, which diffusion channels to use, and to whom to diffuse innovations) is held by government officials and technical subject-matter experts. Diffusion in centralized systems flows from the top down, from experts to users.

In contrast, *decentralized* diffusion systems are client-controlled, with a wide sharing of power and control among the members of the diffusion system. Instead of coming out of R&D systems, innovations in decentralized systems bubble up from local experimentation by nonexpert users. Local units decide which innovations should diffuse through horizontal networks, allowing a high degree of re-invention. Decentralized diffusion systems are based upon convergence communication, in which participants create and share information with one another in order to reach a mutual understanding. Decentralized diffusion systems are (1) most appropriate for certain conditions and (2) can be combined with elements of centralized systems to form a hybrid diffusion system.

10

INNOVATION IN ORGANIZATIONS

Organizations are the ground on which innovations are scattered.

Comment by the president of a company in a research interview conducted by the author

Until this point, this book has been mainly concerned with the diffusion of innovations to *individuals*. Many innovations, however, are adopted by *organizations*. In many cases, an individual cannot adopt a new idea until an organization has previously adopted it. The present chapter deals mainly with collective and authority innovation-decisions, two types of decisions in which an organization is usually the system in which the innovation-decision occurs. We trace the important change from the early studies of organizational innovativeness, in which data were gathered typically from a large sample of organizations in order to determine the characteristics of more and less innovative organizations, to investigations of the innovation process *in* organizations using a stage model. The latter studies provide important insights into the nature of the innovation process and human behavior as organizations change.

Such innovation-process studies stress the implementation stage in putting an innovation into use in an organization. The innovation process studies improve upon most previous diffusion research, which generally stopped short of investigating implementation. Once an organization has made a decision to adopt, implementation does not always follow directly. Compared to the innovation-decision process by individuals, the innovation process in organizations is much more complex. Implementation typically involves a number of individuals, perhaps including both champions and opponents of the new idea, each of whom plays a role in the innovation-decision. Further, implementation amounts to mutual adaptation in which both the innovation and the organization change in important ways.

Types of Innovation-Decisions

Three types of innovation-decisions are:

1. *Optional innovation-decisions*, choices to adopt or reject an innovation that are made by an individual independent of the decisions by other members of a system. The Iowa farmers who adopted hybrid seed corn in the Ryan and Gross (1943) study made optional innovation-decisions. So did the medical doctors in Coleman and colleagues' (1966) investigation of the spread of a new drug.
2. *Collective innovation-decisions*, choices to adopt or reject an innovation that are made by consensus among the members of a system. A city's decision to adopt a no-smoking ordinance, made by a referendum or by a vote of the city council, is a collective innovation-decision. Once the decision is reached, each individual must act accordingly. For instance, individuals who smoke in a bar, restaurant, or other place (in a city with a no-smoking ordinance) are arrested and fined.
3. *Authority innovation-decisions*, choices to adopt or reject an innovation that are made by a relatively few individuals in a system who possess power, high social status, or technical expertise. The CEO of a company may decide, as did the chief executive of Nokia, the Finnish company dominant in manufacturing cellular telephones, that no company employees can send an e-mail attachment (out of concern for security). This authority innovation-decision is one with which the organization's employees must comply.

In addition, *contingent innovation-decisions* are choices to adopt or reject that can be made only after a prior innovation-decision. Thus, a doctor's decision to adopt a new medical procedure can be made only after the doctor's hospital has decided to purchase a necessary piece of medical equipment. Here an optional decision follows a collective decision. Other sequential combinations of two or more of the three types of innovation-decisions can also constitute a contingent decision.

Organizations

An *organization* is a stable system of individuals who work together to achieve common goals through a hierarchy of ranks and a division of labor. Organizations are created to handle large-scale routine tasks through a pattern of regularized human relationships. Their efficiency as a means of orchestrating human endeavors is in part due to this stability, which stems from the relatively high degree of structure that is imposed on communication patterns. A predictable organizational structure is obtained through:

1. *Predetermined goals.* Organizations are formally established for the explicit purpose of achieving certain goals. The objectives of an organization determine, to a large extent, the structure and function of the organization.
2. *Prescribed roles.* Organizational tasks are distributed among various positions as roles or duties. A role is a set of activities to be performed by an individual occupying a given position. Positions are the "boxes" on an organizational chart. Individuals may come and go in an organization, but the positions continue, as do the behaviors expected of individuals filling these positions.
3. *Authority structure.* In a formal organization, not all positions have equal authority. Instead, positions are organized in a hierarchical authority structure that specifies who is responsible to whom, and who can give orders to whom.
4. *Rules and regulations.* A formal, established system of written procedures governs decisions and actions by an organization's members. These rules prescribe procedures for hiring individuals, for promotion, for discharging unsatisfactory employees, and for coordinating the control of various activities so as to ensure uniform operations.
5. *Informal patterns.* Every formal organization is characterized by various kinds of informal practices, norms, and social relationships among its members. These informal practices emerge over time and fulfill an important function in any organization. Nevertheless, the intent of bureaucratic organizations is often to depersonalize human relationships as much as possible by standardizing and formalizing them.

Given the relative stability of organizations, one might expect that innovation would be rare. On the contrary, innovation goes on all the time in most organizations. Many barriers and resistances to change exist in an organization, but we should not forget that innovation is one of the fundamental processes under way in all organizations.

The great German sociologist Max Weber (1958) described bureaucratic organizations, like factories, armies, and government agencies, as characterized by a form of authoritarian control that he called the "iron cage." Rules are made and orders issued by individuals of authority and carried out by organizational members who accept the system of authority. At first, this control system operates in a rational and efficient manner, but the organizational effectiveness of the bureaucracy is often lost over time. Rules are enforced overzealously and applied to all cases in an impersonal and inappropriate way. Bureaucratic leaders become impersonal, and the rationality of the system disappears. Nevertheless, organization members, trapped in an iron cage of control, continue to support the bureaucratic authority system.

Virtual Organizations

During the 1990s, a new type of organization burst on the scene, the virtual organization, which radically changed many previous conceptions of organizational behavior. For example, Complexica is an entirely virtual organization with a dozen employees and several million dollars in annual sales. Established in 1999 by company president Dr. Roger Jones, Complexica is headquartered in an attractive office building in Santa Fe, New Mexico. Company headquarters consists of Jones and a desk with a powerful computer on it. Other Complexica employees are scattered around the world. One employee, who is something of a recluse, lives and works in his house trailer in the Sangre de Cristo Mountains, fifty miles from Santa Fe. Other employees are in London and Vienna. They work collaboratively, linked by the Internet, on software projects based on the theory of complex adaptive systems, a theory developed at nearby Los Alamos National Laboratory, where Jones previously was an employee, and at the Santa Fe Institute. Complexica's employees are in almost constant contact, perhaps every thirty minutes or so during the workday. Thanks to the Internet, the cost of communication across physical space has been practically eliminated. Virtual organizations would not be possible without the Internet.

A *virtual organization* is a network of geographically-distant employees who are linked by electronic communication. The employees may have occasional face-to-face meetings, but most of their daily work is carried out at a distance. Among the advantages of virtual organizations are the reduced costs of office and parking space, elimination of commuting time and expenses, and the possibility of locating employees closer to customers or suppliers. Many virtual employees work at home, in their car (a common practice in Bangkok, Thailand, where traffic congestion is terrible), or en route by other means. They may not have an office in a company building.

Communication is fundamental in any organization, but in virtual organizations communication is preeminent (DeSanctis and Monge, 1998). Roger Jones launched Complexica as a completely virtual organization because it meant that he did not need to obtain venture capital (he had had an unfortunate experience with venture capitalists in a previous start-up company). The work done by Complexica, an informatics company, can be carried out just as easily at distance locations as if all employees were in adjoining offices in the same building. The emerging informatics industry is agglomerated in Santa Fe, so Rogers Jones needs to be there, in order to interface with the some thirty other high-technology start-up companies in the industry. The other company employees can be located anywhere in the world, while connected electronically.

Employees who live in different time zones can be a problem for virtual companies such as Complexica (Santa Fe and Vienna are separated by eight hours), but its employees have learned to work around this problem. Some U.S.-based computer software companies hire virtual employees in India, twelve time zones away, so that the company's employees can accomplish two days' work every twenty-four hours (Singhal and Rogers, 2001). The company's U.S. employees in Silicon Valley, say, work on a software programming task from 9:00 A.M. to 7:00 P.M. California time and then send their completed code via the Internet to a virtual work team in Bangalore or Hyderabad, who carry forward the task for another work shift and then bounce their completed code halfway back around the world to their California counterparts. The software engineers employed in India are paid only about 10 percent of American salaries, which provides the company a considerable economic advantage.

Virtual organizations are more flexible (there is little organizational culture to overcome when making a change), have less hierarchy, and the organization has edgeless, permeable boundaries (Ahuja and Carley, 1998; DeSanctis and Monge, 1998). These are important benefits that can give a virtual organization a competitive advantage in the marketplace. For these reasons, the number of organizations that have at least some virtual employees has increased sharply in the past decade. Virtuality can be considered an innovation, one that is diffusing rapidly among business organizations, and this new idea has spawned a large number of scholarly publications (a recent review of literature includes seven hundred publications on this topic). Most research on virtual organizations is conducted by communication scholars and by organization/management scholars in business schools.

Virtual organizations also have a downside. For example, some investigations found that virtual employees have less organizational identification, lower satisfaction, and higher turnover rates. Virtual communication is often less inhibited than face-to-face exchanges and may lead to greater conflict and misunderstanding. Training employees in proper methods of virtual communication may help overcome these problems.

Organizations today are obviously quite different from the structures described by Max Weber when he was writing a hundred years ago.

Organizational Innovativeness

Diffusion research began with investigations of individual decision makers such as farmers. When this paradigm was extended to medical doctors and teachers, the early diffusion studies ignored the fact that teachers are school employees and that most doctors work in hospitals or in a group medical practice. Several decades later, diffusion studies were conducted in which the unit of adoption was the organization, rather than the individual. These early studies of organizational innovativeness were oversimplifications in that the data were obtained from a single individual (usually the top executive in the organization). In essence, each organization in these studies was reduced to the equivalent of an individual. The entire organization was treated as a single unit of analysis.

Much useful knowledge was gained from the organizational innovativeness studies, and a number are still being carried out today. For instance, an innovation spreads among the companies in an industry in a diffusion process that is similar to the way that an innovation diffuses among the individuals in a community or some other system.

Scholars simply transferred the models and methods of investigating innovativeness, developed earlier for individuals, to the study of organizations. Hundreds of studies of organizational innovativeness were completed by the 1970s. Then diffusion research in organizations began to be conducted by looking at the innovation process *within* an organization. Instead of determining the variables related to more innovative and less innovative organizations, the process of innovation was traced in an organization over time. Now the focus was increasingly on innovation as a process, with emphasis on a stage model (somewhat parallel to the stages in the individual innovation-decision process).

The early studies of organizational innovativeness helped illuminate the characteristics of innovative organizations. Many of these characteristics were equivalent to the characteristics of innovative individuals. For example, larger-sized organizations have generally been found to be more innovative, just as are individuals with larger incomes and higher socioeconomic status. But certain of the organizational characteristics do not have individual counterparts. For instance, organizational structural characteristics such as system *openness* (defined as the degree to which the members of a system are linked to other individuals who are external to the system) and *formalization* (defined as the degree to which an organization emphasizes following rules and procedures in the role performance of its members) were found to be related positively and negatively, respectively, to organizational innovativeness. A fair degree of conceptual originality took place in the organizational innovativeness studies, even though their research methodologies were directly copied from the individual-level innovativeness studies.

Why have studies of organizational innovativeness become somewhat passé?

1. The organizational innovativeness studies found rather low relationships between the independent variables (measuring qualities of the organization) that were investigated and the dependent variable of innovativeness. Often a hundred or more organizations were included in the sample that was studied, and the typical investigation was highly quantitative. The dependent variable of innovativeness was usually measured as a composite score composed of the adoption of ten to twenty innovations. The innovation process for each innovation in each organization of study was thus submerged through aggregation into an overall innovativeness score for each organization. This cross-sectional approach to data analysis meant that the "process" (that is, the over-time) aspects of the innovation process were ignored in favor of a variance research approach.

2. One vexing problem of the organizational innovativeness studies was how adequately the data provided by the chief executive officer represented the actual innovation behavior of the entire organ-

ization. Because the organizational innovativeness investigations typically gathered data only from the top executive of each organization in a sample of organizations, there was no way to determine how adequately these data truly represented the entire organization's behavior with regard to an innovation. For example, questionnaire data were gathered from eight city officials (the chief administrator, financial officer, police chief, etc.) in each of 276 U.S. cities about the adoption of three planning/budgeting innovations (Bingham and Frendreis, 1978). One would expect that the chief executive and the financial officer would agree about such a basic matter as to whether or not their city had adopted a budgeting innovation, but agreement on this subject between these two top officials occurred only about two thirds of the time. This troubling finding was a setback for diffusion scholars studying organizational innovativeness. Gathering data only from a few individuals at the top of a large sample of organizations did not seem to provide very valid measures of the concepts of study.

Size and Organizational Innovativeness

The size of an organization has consistently been found to be positively related to its innovativeness. Generalization 10-1 states: *Larger organizations are more innovative.*

Mytinger (1968, p. 7) asked, "Is [innovativeness due to] the man, the agency, or the place?" The innovativeness of forty local health departments in California was related to (1) their size, measured as the number of staff and the size of their budget, which in turn rested on (2) the size of the city they served and (3) the cosmopoliteness, accreditation, and prestige of the health director among his or her peer health officials. Overall, "This study suggests that *size*—size of community and size of [the health] department—is perhaps the most compelling concomitant to innovativeness" (Mytinger, 1968, p. 7).

Mahler and Rogers (1999) gathered data from 324 German banks about their adoption of twelve communication technology innovations, such as providing banking services to their customers by e-mail, electronic funds transfer for corporate customers, and toll-free telephone banking. An innovativeness scale was computed for each bank, based on the number of the twelve innovations adopted, and whether the bank adopted each innovation relatively earlier or later than other banks. The 324 banks were classified into the five adopter categories (see Figure 10-1). Innovativeness was

Figure 10-1. Adopter Categorization of 324 German Banks on the Basis of Their Innovativeness Scores

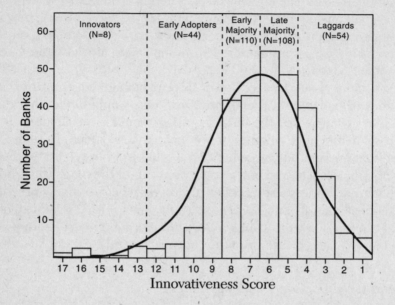

Studies of organizational innovativeness, once very popular, are illustrated by this investigation of the innovativeness of German banks in adopting twelve new communication technologies. The distribution of German banks in adopter categories is approximately similar to that of individuals (see Chapter 7). Large size was highly related to innovativeness. For example, each bank's total assets were correlated .75 with its innovativeness scores, and the number of bank employees was correlated .70 with innovativeness.

Source: Mahler and Rogers (1999, p. 732).

very highly related to size, whether measured by total bank assets, number of employees, number of branch banks, number of subsidiaries, or number of customers.

The finding that larger size is related to organizational innovativeness might seem surprising, given the conventional business wisdom that smaller companies can be more flexible in their operations and freer of stifling bureaucracy. In Chapter 4, we discussed the special advantages of skunkworks as a means of freeing an R&D unit from the larger corporation of which it is part. Nevertheless, the size-to-innovativeness relationship holds across a large number of investigations.

Why do researchers consistently find that size is one of the best predictors of organizational innovativeness? First, size is a variable that is easily measured, presumably with a relatively high degree of precision. So size is included for study in almost every organizational innovativeness investigation.

Second, size is probably a surrogate measure of several dimensions that lead to innovation: total resources, slack resources (defined as the degree to which an organization has more resources than those required for its ongoing operations), employees' technical expertise, organizational structure, and so on. These unidentified variables have not been clearly understood or adequately measured by most studies. These "lurking" variables may be a fundamental reason for the common finding that size and innovativeness are related. Few scholars have much theoretical interest in size as a variable, but it is a convenient stand-in for other variables that are of interest.

Structural Characteristics and Organizational Innovativeness

Innovativeness is related to such independent variables as (1) individual (leader) characteristics, (2) internal organizational structural characteristics, and (3) external characteristics of the organization (Figure 10-2).

Figure 10-2. Independent Variables Related to Organizational Innovativeness

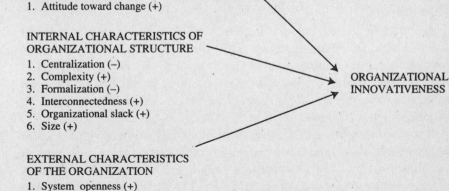

Independent Variables   *Dependent Variable*
INDIVIDUAL (LEADER) CHARACTERISTICS
1. Attitude toward change (+)

INTERNAL CHARACTERISTICS OF
ORGANIZATIONAL STRUCTURE

1. Centralization (−)
2. Complexity (+)   ORGANIZATIONAL
3. Formalization (−)   INNOVATIVENESS
4. Interconnectedness (+)
5. Organizational slack (+)
6. Size (+)

EXTERNAL CHARACTERISTICS
OF THE ORGANIZATION
1. System openness (+)

Here we look at organizational structure variables related to the innovativeness of organizations.

Centralization is the degree to which power and control in a system are concentrated in the hands of a relatively few individuals. Centralization has usually been found to be negatively associated with innovativeness. The more that power is concentrated in an organization, the less innovative the organization is. The range of new ideas considered by an organization is restricted when only a few strong leaders dominate the system. In a centralized organization, top leaders are poorly positioned to identify operational-level problems or to suggest relevant innovations to meet these needs. Although the initiation of innovations in a centralized organization is less frequent than in a decentralized organization, centralization can encourage the implementation of innovations once a decision is made to adopt.

Complexity is the degree to which an organization's members possess a relatively high level of knowledge and expertise, usually measured by the members' range of occupational specialties and their degree of professionalism (expressed by formal training). Complexity encourages organizational members to grasp the value of innovations, but it may make it difficult to achieve consensus about implementing them.

Formalization is the degree to which an organization emphasizes its members' following rules and procedures. The degree to which an organization is bureaucratic is measured by its formalization. Such formalization acts to inhibit the consideration of innovations by organization members but encourages the implementation of innovations.

Interconnectedness is the degree to which the units in a social system are linked by interpersonal networks. New ideas can flow more easily among an organization's members if it has a higher degree of network interconnectedness. This variable is positively related to organizational innovativeness.

Organizational slack is the degree to which uncommitted resources are available to an organization. This variable is positively related to organizational innovativeness, especially for innovations that are higher in cost. Perhaps one reason why organizational size is so highly related to innovativeness is that larger organizations have more slack resources, as mentioned previously.

The results of the several hundred studies of organizational innovativeness generally show relatively low correlations of each of these independent variables (in Figure 10-2) with the dependent variable of innovativeness of organizations. Generalization 10-2: *Each of the organizational struc-*

ture variables may be related to innovation in one direction during the initiation phases of the innovation process, and in the opposite direction during the implementation phases. Low centralization, high complexity, and low formalization facilitate initiation in the innovation process, but these structural characteristics make it difficult for an organization to implement an innovation (Zaltman et al., 1973). Thus, we see how bringing the initiation and implementation subprocesses of the innovation process into the analysis better explains the results of past research on variables related to organizational innovativeness.

While scholarly interest in organizational innovativeness studies has waned somewhat in recent years, such investigations continue to be conducted, often with interesting results. For example, Fennell (1984) studied the diffusion and adoption of two related innovations (alcoholism counseling programs for employees and the provision of insurance coverage for alcoholism treatment of employees) by 173 private companies employing at least 250 workers in Illinois. If a company adopted the alcoholism insurance coverage program, the adoption of alcoholism counseling was also facilitated. Larger size and greater complexity were related to adoption of the alcoholism insurance program, which in turn often led to the adoption of alcoholism counseling, despite the opposition of labor unions and the organizations' medical departments.

This investigation looked at two related innovations that were adopted by the same sample of organizations. As discussed in previous chapters, many diffusion studies focus on only one innovation, or at least they do not trace the interrelationships between the rates of adoption for two or more new ideas that are diffusing in the same system or systems. Needed is research that does not assume that the diffusion pathways of such innovations are necessarily independent.

A particularly interesting investigation representing a new type of organizational innovativeness study was reported by Alan D. Meyer and James B. Goes (1988). These scholars studied twelve medical innovations (CAT scanners, ultrasonic imaging, laser surgery, electronic fetal monitoring, fiberoptic endoscopy, and others) as they were adopted by the twenty-five hospitals in a midwestern city. These 300 innovation-decisions, each representing an innovation in an organization, were the units of analysis. Note this important departure from the usual organizational innovativeness study in which each of the twenty-five hospitals would have been scored on their relative innovativeness in adopting the twelve innovations. Instead, Meyer and Goes (1988) used a nine-point scale for each innovation-decision process, ranging from a hospital's staff being aware of the innovation (1 point) through adopting and using the innovation regularly (8 points) to expanding and upgrading the new technology (9 points). Essentially, this dependent variable is the degree to which a hospital has progressed through the stages in the innovation process for each of the twelve innovations of study.

Meyer and Goes (1988) found that the degree of progress of an innovation through the innovation process in a hospital (the dependent variable under study) was explained (1) by the perceived attributes of the innovations, with observability, low risk, and low complexity explaining 40 percent of the variance in the dependent variable), and (2) by hospital environmental, organizational, and leadership variables, which explained only 11 percent of the variance in the dependent variable. Large-sized hospitals with complex structures that used aggressive marketing strategies and were located in an urban environment were particularly innovative. Especially important in the progress of a medical technology through the innovation process was a hospital's chief executive officer, who often exerted substantial influence on the innovation's behalf. Thus, innovation champions were crucial in moving a medical innovation through the innovation process in a hospital.

The Role of Champions

A *champion* is a charismatic individual who throws his or her weight behind an innovation, thus overcoming indifference or resistance that the new idea may provoke in an organization. An innovation champion can play an important role in boosting a new idea in an organization. Of course, anti-innovation champions (that is, opponents) can prevent a new technology from reaching the routinization stage of the innovation process.

Past research shows that an innovation champion is often important in the innovation process in organizations. Generalization 10-3 states: *The presence of an innovation champion contributes to the success of an innovation in an organization.* Schön (1963, p. 84) stated: "The new idea either finds a champion or dies."

One may think of an innovation champion as a powerful individual with a high office in an organization, say a company president or vice president, or at least a top manager. Certainly it does no harm to have an administrative "patron saint" bless an innovation being considered by an organization (Smith, Redican, and Olsen, 1992). Day (1984) found that this picture of powerful innovation champions tended to be true for innovations that were costly, highly visible, or radical. There must be a champion of innovations that are highly uncertain, or else they may indeed die. But champions of less radical innovations are often middle managers. For example, Goodman and Steckler (1989) found in their study of how ten new research-based programs were adopted by health organizations in Virginia that the most effective champions were assistant directors or division directors of health agencies. They were not so senior in rank that they were inaccessible to their staff. The important qualities of champions were that they (1) occupied a key linking position in their organization, (2) possessed analytical and intuitive skills in understanding various individuals' aspirations, and (3) demonstrated well-honed interpersonal and negotiating skills in working with other people in their organization. Thus champions were brokers and arrangers for an innovation in an organization, helping fit it into the organizational context. Often the innovation was redefined and the organization was restructured by a coalition of individuals, with the champion orchestrating this informal coalition. Champions in an organization play a role something like that of an opinion leader in a community.

When a sample of twenty-five innovation champions was matched with twenty-five nonchampions, Howell and Higgins (1990) found that the champions were higher risk takers, more innovative, and more influential with others. So champions tend to be quite innovation-minded. But they are not necessarily distinctive from others in being more powerful. In many cases, people skills may be more important than power.

The general picture of an innovation champion emerges not as a particularly powerful individual in an organization, but rather as someone particularly adept at handling people, an individual skillful in persuasion and negotiation. An illustration of this type of innovation champion was a masters student in public health who played a key role in the innovation process through which the El Paso, Texas, City Council adopted a no-smoking ordinance in 2001 (Rogers, Peterson, and McOwiti, 2002). The graduate student enrolled in a required internship course and was assigned to do background research for a nongovernment organization, Community Voices, that was working for passage of the clean indoor air ordinance. He attended meetings of the no-smoking coalition in El Paso, taking notes and speaking when called upon. Often, organization leaders at these planning meetings would say, "We need to get the facts on that issue. Oh, Student Intern, could you help us?"

Soon the intern found himself spending more and more time on the no-smoking issue. He was working part-time as a waiter in a restaurant with a smoking section and had to purchase expensive antibiotic drugs for recurrent ear infections that he felt were due to second-hand smoke. The coalition's leaders, learning of his condition, asked him to testify at a hearing before the El Paso City Council about the health difficulties of individuals working in smoking sections of restaurants and bars. As he became personally acquainted with the eight members of the El Paso City Council, he began to spend several hours a day hanging out in city hall. One council member asked the student intern to determine how much the business volume of bowling alleys and bingo parlors in a neighboring city had been affected after that city had adopted a no-smoking ordinance. Then the student intern was asked to obtain copies of several no-smoking ordinances of the comprehensive type that El Paso's city government was considering. The intern contacted other cities for their ordinances. A Council member asked him to interview a sample of El Paso restaurant owners as to their attitudes toward the proposed no-smoking ordinance. Another council member requested data from San Diego, another border city that had previously adopted a no-smoking ordinance, as to how many restaurant customers drove across the border to Mexico to eat at restaurants where smoking was permitted.

The student intern became a kind of lobbyist for the no-smoking issue on a day-by-day basis, sensing whether each Council member was leaning for or against the proposed clean indoor air ordinance. In June, 2001, the El Paso City Council voted 7 to 1 in favor of the ordinance, and thereafter no smoking was allowed in any restaurant, bar, or other public place in the twenty-second largest city in the United States. The student intern, relieved, returned to his textbooks and courses with the satisfaction of knowing that he had served as an innovation champion.

El Paso had another champion for the no-smoking issue, a respected city council member who was elected mayor of the city, just before the vote in favor of the ordinance. The mayor played an important role in swaying the votes of the city council members, and in implementing the new law, once it was approved. The mayor was politically powerful and widely known. Very few citizens of El Paso ever heard of the student intern. His role became obvious only upon investigation of the innovation process for the no-smoking policy.

In other southwestern cities, the author and his research team found different types of champions for the no-smoking issue. For example, in Silver City, New Mexico, the most important champion was a fifteen-year old high school girl who was elected chairperson of the local anti-smoking coalition. She maintained daily contact with city officials until the issue was approved. Then, when her mother moved to Albuquerque,

New Mexico, the youthful champion became active in anti-smoking organizations there and was elected chairperson of the Albuquerque coalition that was seeking passage of a no-smoking policy. When the author interviewed this champion in 2002, she estimated that she spent forty hours per week in volunteer anti-smoking activities. In Lubbock, Texas, a ten-year-old boy with asthma became one of the main champions of that city's successful campaign to approve a no-smoking policy.

These examples suggest that innovation champions come in all ages, with varying degrees of formal power, and with different types of abilities. Perhaps their exact characteristics depend on the nature of the innovation and the organization. In any event, the champion's role is to initiate the innovation process and to guide the new idea through to approval and implementation.

The Innovation Process in Organizations

An important turning point in the history of research on innovation in organizations occurred with the publication of an influential book, *Innovations and Organizations,* by Professor Gerald Zaltman and colleagues (1973). These authors specified the distinctive aspects of innovation when it took place in an organization. In such studies, the main dependent variable of study often became implementation (that is, putting an innovation into use) rather than adoption (the decision to use an innovation). Up to this point, most studies of innovations and organizations had concerned organizational innovativeness, measured as the adoption or nonadoption of a set of innovations by a sample of organizations. After the early 1970s, research on innovations and organizations tended to center on investigations of a single innovation over time in an organization or organizations. Often the innovation of study was a new communication technology, such as an e-mail system, a management information system, or some other computer-based technological innovation. Certainly these new communication technologies have given new life to research on innovation in organizations.

The innovation process in organizations identifies the main sequence of decisions, actions, and events in this process. Data about the innovation process are obtained from the recallable perceptions of key actors in the innovation process, written records of the organization about the adoption decision, and other data sources.

An explosion occurred in the number of studies on innovation in organizations published since the 1980s. Why? One reason is that business school scholars, particularly in departments of management and organization, became fascinated with studying the innovation process. A large, well-funded research program on this topic was launched in the business school at the University of Minnesota in 1983. This program, led by Professor Andrew H. Van de Ven, consisted of thirty scholars who conducted fourteen in-depth case studies of technological innovations in a variety of fields: industry, education, agriculture, health, defense, and so on. Van de Ven and his colleagues pursued a common theoretical framework in gathering and analyzing their data on the innovation process (Van de Ven, Angle, and Poole, 1989; Van de Ven et al., 1999).

Another important reason for the increasing attention accorded to innovation in organizations is due to the widespread introduction of new communication technologies in organizations, as mentioned previously. The implementation of many of these innovations has failed, causing a great deal of interest in better understanding how to effectively introduce computer-related technologies. Innovation in organizations has become recognized as an important problem facing organization managers.

Such interactive innovations as e-mail have little functional advantage (and often a considerable disadvantage) for the very first users in an organization. Obviously, the very first adopter of electronic mail has no one with whom to communicate. Thus the rate of adoption for the new interactive technologies proceeds slowly at first in an organization, at least until a critical mass is reached (see Chapter 8). A distinctive intellectual advantage of studying new communication technologies is that such investigations provide new types of data and allow scholars to study new variables with new theories (Van de Ven and Rogers, 1988). For example, the adoption of such innovations can be measured by computer records of each individual's degree of use of e-mail, personal computers, and so forth (Astebro, 1995).

The general assumption of research on innovation in organizations is that organizational variables act on innovation behavior in a manner over and above that of the aggregate of individual members of the organization. Thus the organizational context of these innovation process studies adds a kind of intellectual "supercharger" to the analysis (see Chapter 8). "Organizations are often seen in this research as constraints or resistances to innovations, at least to the extent that many problems are usually encountered in attempts to implement an innovation in an organization. Alternatively, these difficulties can be seen as evidence that a particular innovation may not fit well with an organization's perceived problem, or that the innovation's expected consequences are perceived by the organization's members as more negative than positive" (Van de Ven and Rogers,

1988). So organizational structure is not necessarily a negative influence in the innovation process in organizations.

Adoption of New Communication Technologies

Insight into the innovation process in organizations can be gained from recent research on the diffusion and adoption of such new communication technologies as personal computers and e-mail in companies. One might expect that these innovations would be so obviously advantageous that their diffusion would be rapid and relatively effortless, but such is not the case. These new communication technologies represent a very major change in human behavior, and require a good deal of learning, and time.

Until about twenty years ago, most bosses had a secretary who took dictation or typed up letters and memos that the boss wrote by hand. Today, thanks to personal computers, the secretary and the typewriter are gone, and the boss does his own typing on a computer keyboard. Thanks to e-mail, many messages are conveyed electronically in something approaching a paperless office. Just how these important changes in office behavior came about in recent years has been the subject of a number of interesting investigations. For example, Heikkilä (1995) found in his study of a Finnish company that a great deal of time and effort were required for an employee to learn how to use a personal computer, once he or she had adopted the technology. Much of this learning occurred on a day-to-day basis as an individual asked coworkers for help. Months and months were needed before an employee became proficient in using a personal computer for word processing, e-mail, spreadsheets, and other functions. Often this learning process required up to 20 or 25 percent of employees' time at work, as well as considerable effort by their colleagues to help them learn. Much past writing about the innovation process for computers has seriously underestimated the amount of effort needed to master this technology.

A study of 471 managers in fifty-four U.S. companies found that computer anxiety was an important barrier to the adoption and use of personal computers (Igbaria et al., 1994). A typical comment was "I am afraid I might damage it [the computer] in some way." Such computer anxiety had a negative relationship to the fun of using computers, which in turn played an important role in helping employees get started in learning how to use their computer equipment. The perceived usefulness of computers was six times more influential than fun in explaining the degree of use of computers. Training can be designed to relieve computer anxiety, which in turn leads to fun and perceived usefulness, and thus to increased computer use. Simply providing computer equipment to employees is unlikely to result in increased computer use unless training is also provided. Allowing employees to play bridge and other games on their office computers may be a good use of their time and a step toward learning how to use their equipment, Igbaria and others (1994) suggest.

White-collar employees in the Volvo car plant in Gothenburg, Sweden, were not very computer-literate in the early 1980s, when the company's executives decided to push for the adoption of personal computers and e-mail as a means of speeding up internal communication flows, so that the company could react more rapidly when manufacturing a new model car. In 1985, the Volvo employees were provided with computers and ordered by management to adopt an e-mail system. The number of e-mail accounts quickly jumped from 18 percent to 40 percent, although the number of individuals actually using the e-mail system remained about the same. The employees had convenient and low-cost alternatives to e-mail, such as internal mail and telephones, and many resisted using e-mail. Gradually, the strong support of top leaders at Volvo helped jump-start the rate of adoption, as it passed the critical mass. Most influential in this innovation process was the role of department-level managers and each employee's peers. Also, a local support center was established in each department to assist employees in learning how to use computers and e-mail. This training and support unit encouraged use of the new communication technologies.

By the end of a five-year period, most of the 7,400 employees at Volvo were using e-mail on a regular basis. Again, as in the Ryan and Gross (1943) study of hybrid seed corn and thousands of other diffusion investigations conducted since, we see that the diffusion process requires a considerable period of time. The innovation process does not happen instantly, even when an organization's leaders are strongly in favor of a new communication technology.

Stages in the Innovation Process

The innovation process consists of a sequence of five stages (Figure 10-3), two in the initiation subprocess and three in the implementation subprocess. Later stages in the innovation process cannot be undertaken until earlier stages have been completed, either explicitly or implicitly. The first two of the five stages in the innovation process, agenda-setting and matching, together constitute *initiation,* defined as all of the information gathering, conceptualizing, and planning for the adoption of an innovation, leading up to the decision to adopt.

Figure 10-3. Five Stages in the Innovation Process in Organizations

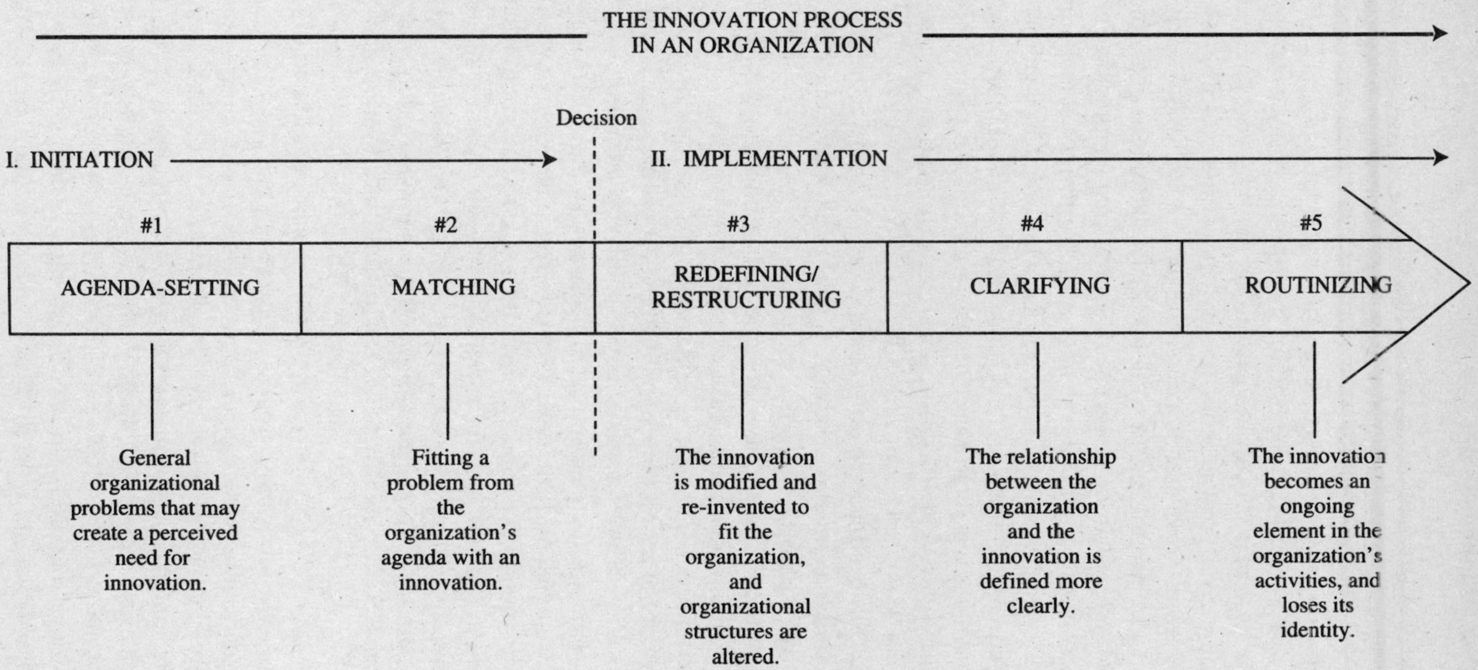

THE INNOVATION PROCESS
IN AN ORGANIZATION

I. INITIATION   II. IMPLEMENTATION

Decision

#1	#2	#3	#4	#5
AGENDA-SETTING	MATCHING	REDEFINING/ RESTRUCTURING	CLARIFYING	ROUTINIZING

General organizational problems that may create a perceived need for innovation.

Fitting a problem from the organization's agenda with an innovation.

The innovation is modified and re-invented to fit the organization, and organizational structures are altered.

The relationship between the organization and the innovation is defined more clearly.

The innovation becomes an ongoing element in the organization's activities, and loses its identity.

The innovation process in an organization consists of two broad activities: (1) *initiation*, consisting of all of the information gathering, conceptualization, and planning for the adoption of an innovation, leading up to the decision to adopt, and (2) *implementation*, consisting of all of the events, actions, and decisions involved in putting the innovation into use. The decision to adopt, shown as a dotted line, divides the two stages of initiation from the three stages of implementation.

1. Agenda-Setting

Agenda-setting occurs when a general organizational problem is defined that creates a perceived need for an innovation (Figure 10-3). The agenda-setting process is continuously under way in every system, determining what the system will work on first, next, and so forth. *Agenda-setting* is the way in which needs, problems, and issues bubble up through a system and are prioritized in a hierarchy for attention (Dearing and Rogers, 1996). The agenda-setting stage in the innovation process in an organization consists of (1) identifying and prioritizing needs and problems and (2) searching the organization's environment to locate innovations of potential usefulness to meet these organizational problems.

The agenda-setting stage may require an extended period of time, often several years. The case studies of the innovation process conducted by the Minnesota Innovation Research Program led to the conclusion that "Innovations are not initiated on the spur of the moment, nor by a single dramatic incident, nor by a single entrepreneur" (Schroeder et al., 1989).

Agenda-setting initiates the sequence of the innovation process, for it is here that the initial motivation is generated to impel later steps in the innovation process. At the agenda-setting stage, one or more individuals in an organization identify an important problem and then identify an innovation as one means of coping with the problem.

A *performance gap* is the discrepancy between an organization's expectations and its actual performance. This difference between how an organization's members perceive its performance, in comparison to what they feel it should be, can be a strong impetus to seek an innovation. Generalization 10-4 states: *A performance gap can trigger the innovation process.* The Minnesota Innovation Research Program showed that in most cases a shock to the organization reached a threshold of attention and led to action by the organization's participants. This shock, often caused by direct personal confrontations with needs or problems, led an organization to initiate the innovation process (Schroeder et al., 1989).

Most organizations engage in an opportunistic surveillance by scanning the environment for new ideas that might benefit the organization. As March (1981) noted, innovation in organizations "often seems to be driven less by problems than by solutions. Answers often precede questions." Most organizations face multiple problems, but possess knowledge of only a few innovations that offer solutions. So the chance of identifying an innovation to cope with a particular problem is relatively small. But if organizational members begin with a wanted solution, there is a good chance that the innovation will match some problem faced by the organization. Consequently, most organizations continuously scan for innovations and match a promising innovation with one of their relevant problems.

Sometimes knowledge of an innovation, rather than the recognition of a problem or need by an organization leading to search for a solution, launches the innovation process. For example, an investigation of forty-three adoptions of computer-related innovations in three large corporations by Wildemuth (1992) found a rational identification of organizational problems at the agenda-setting stage. A search for innovations to meet these needs (at the matching stage) did not occur. "Instead, participants took an opportunistic approach to the acquisition of computing resources. Prior to the purchase of hardware and software, there were no specific plans for its use" (Wildemuth, 1992). As we explained in Chapter 5 for the individual-level innovation-decision process, sometimes a perceived need sets off the innovation process in an organization, and sometimes knowledge of an innovation creates a need for it.

On the basis of his analysis of how new traffic safety laws were passed by the U.S. Senate, Jack Walker (1977) concluded, "Those who manage to shape the legislative agenda . . . are able to magnify their influence many times over by determining the focus of attention and energy in the entire political process." Setting the agenda for innovation in an organization is tremendously powerful.

2. Matching

Matching is defined as the stage in the innovation process at which a problem from the organization's agenda is fit with an innovation, and this match is planned and designed. At this second stage in the innovation process, conceptual matching of the problem with the innovation occurs in order to establish how well they fit. In this reality testing, the organization's members attempt to determine the feasibility of the innovation in solving the organization's problem. Such planning entails anticipating the benefits, and the problems, that the innovation will encounter when it is implemented. The organization's decision-makers may conclude that the innovation is mismatched with the problem. This decision leads to rejection, terminating the innovation process prior to the new idea's implementation.

Effectively matching an innovation with an organization's need is key to whether the new idea is sustained over time. This degree of fit is one particular type of compatibility of the innovation (see Chapter 6). Goodman and Steckler (1989) found that whether or not an innovation "found a home" by fitting with a need or an existing program in a health organization was crucial to its later sustainability.

The matching decision marks the watershed in the innovation process between initiation and *implementation,* all of the events, actions, and decisions involved in putting an innovation into use. The implementation subprocess consists of three stages: redefining/restructuring, clarifying, and routinizing.

3. Redefining/Restructuring

At this stage, the innovation imported from outside the organization gradually begins to lose its foreign character. *Redefining/restructuring* occurs when the innovation is re-invented so as to accommodate the organization's needs and structure more closely, and when the organization's structure is modified to fit with the innovation.

Both the innovation and the organization are expected to change, at least to some degree, during the redefining/restructuring stage of the innovation process. However, a study of several innovations in three organizations by Tyre and Orlikowski (1994) found that only a brief window of opportunity existed in an organization during which an innovation could be modified. Thereafter, the innovation was rapidly routinized and embedded in the organization's structure and was unlikely to change further.

INNOVATION AND ORGANIZATION STRUCTURE Not only is an innovation modified to fit the organization, the structure of the organization may be changed to accommodate the innovation. Sometimes a new organizational unit is created for the innovation, such as when an organization installs a new online training system for its employees and creates a new office to administer this new program. In some cases, an innovation may affect the structure of the entire organization, such as when an e-mail system is introduced in a company. Suddenly, every employee has direct communication access to the chief executive.

Implementation of a technological innovation in an organization amounts to a mutual adaptation of the innovation and the organization. Typically, both change during the subprocess of implementation. "Innovations not only adapt to existing organizational and industrial arrangements, but they also transform the structure and practice of these environments" (Van de Ven, 1986). This mutual adaptation occurs because the innovation almost never fits perfectly in the organization in which it is to become embedded. A fair degree of creative activity is required to avoid—or overcome—the misalignments that occur between the innovation and the organization adopting it. Often these organizational changes are initially underestimated by the organization. Generalization 10-5 states: *Both the innovation and the organization usually change in the innovation process in an organization.*

An illustration of this generalization is provided by a case study of implementation conducted by Professor Dorothy Leonard at the Harvard Business School. She studied an innovation called Solagen by the Eastman Kodak Company. The previous practice for obtaining gelatin, used by Kodak to make film, had consisted of a 150-year-old process of decomposing animal bones and hide in a lime oil for six weeks. Kodak Research Laboratories developed Solagen, a chemical process that reduced the decomposition process to forty-eight hours. The Solagen process was tested in a pilot plant, with positive results, and Kodak made plans for building a plant costing millions of dollars. Very precise calibration of the Solagen process was required because it occurred so rapidly. The plant operators were accustomed to thrusting a six-foot pole into the lime pit in order to determine if undecomposed bones remained at the bottom. In the new plant, operators had to determine the degree of decomposition by readings on a dial; decisions had to be made in a matter of minutes rather than days. The plant operators could not cope with this new need to make rapid decisions. Because of the complexity of the new technology, despite its obvious advantages, implementation of the Solagen process failed (Leonard-Barton, 1988a).

Note that in this case, the innovation came from within Eastman Kodak, rather than being imported from across the corporation's boundaries. Generally, such internally generated innovations are more likely to be successfully implemented, as the innovation more closely fits the organization's situation, and the organization's participants identify the innovation as "theirs." The case studies conducted by the Minnesota Innovation Research Program concluded: "Innovation receptiveness, learning, and adoption speed are facilitated when the innovation is initially developed within the user organization, and inhibited when end-users [adopters] are provided with no opportunities to re-invent innovations that were initially developed elsewhere. Organizational units not involved in the development or re-invention of an innovation tend to view it as an external mandate" (Schroeder et al., 1986).

The redefining/restructuring stage in the innovation process in an organization amounts to social constructionism, in which perceptions of the organization's problem and the innovation come together and each are modified in the process. If the innovation comes from inside the organization, individuals regard it as familiar and compatible and hence find it easier to give meaning to the new idea. When the innovation enters the organization from external sources but the exact form that it takes is flexible and a good deal of re-invention occurs, the organization's participants perceive the new idea as being theirs.

RADICAL INNOVATIONS Some innovations create a high degree of uncertainty in an organization, an uncomfortable state that may foster resistance to the technology. This uncertainty is one reason for the special difficulties that computer technologies often encounter in the implementation subprocess. A *radical innovation* (also called a "disruptive" or "discontinuous" innovation) is such a major change that it represents a new paradigm for carrying out some task. In some cases, an innovation can be so radical that it created a whole new industry, such as semiconductors, lasers, and e-commerce (Walsh and Linton, 2000).

The more radical an innovation, indexed by the amount of knowledge that organization members must acquire in order to adopt, the more uncertainty it creates and the more difficult its implementation. A study of six innovations by forty companies in the U.S. footwear industry found that large-sized firms were more likely to have technical specialists and thus to adopt more radical innovations (Dewar and Dutton, 1986). Incremental innovations did not create so much uncertainty and did not require so much technical expertise to implement; thus they were more equally adopted by both larger and smaller shoe manufacturers.

Some innovations are so radical and create such a high degree of uncertainty that they must be adopted through an innovation process that is relatively unstructured and almost completely unroutine. An unstructured decision process is one that has not been encountered previously in quite the same form and for which no predetermined set of ordered responses and routines exists (Mintzberg, Raisinghani, and Théorêt, 1976). Most past research on innovation in organizations has dealt with relatively routine innovation-decisions, for which customary and widely understood procedures exist. However, radical innovations represent a type of unstructured decision, and their adoption entails a much more difficult process.

For example, Gibson and Rogers (1994) investigated the first R&D consortium, the Microelectronics and Computer Technology Corporation (MCC), in the United States in the 1980s. An R&D consortium is a cooperative activity in which member corporations invest in order to conduct research for the benefit of each participating company. Twenty large U.S. electronics companies launched the MCC in 1982 in order to compete more successfully with their Japanese counterparts. The MCC was the first organization of its kind in the United States, and over a period of several years its member firms had to learn how to collaborate in the R&D consortium while still competing with one another in the marketplace. Gradually, with further experience, U.S. corporations became accustomed to the general idea of R&D consortia, which became less radical and could be adopted through more structured decisions. A decade later, by 1994, several hundred R&D consortia were established in the United States. So over time the once radical innovation became less radical and more routine.

4. Clarifying

Clarifying occurs as the innovation is put into more widespread use in an organization, so that the meaning of the new idea gradually becomes clearer to the organization's members. Too-rapid implementation of an innovation at the clarifying stage can lead to disastrous results. An illustration of undue haste in implementing an innovation is provided by the Santa Monica Freeway Diamond Lane experiment in Los Angeles, described later in this chapter.

A somewhat similar example of haste leading to rejection occurred with a no-smoking ordinance in Alamogordo, New Mexico, in 2002. The main champion of the issue, a member of the city council, pushed for an immediate vote on a proposed no-smoking ordinance. The man's wife, a strong anti-smoking advocate, had encouraged her husband to bring the proposed policy to a vote. Alamogordo is a relatively small town, and many of its people framed the issue not as a matter of public health (the health dangers of second-hand smoke have been soundly proven by extensive scientific research) but rather as the violation of individual rights. Conservatively minded individuals in Alamogordo demanded: "What right has the city government to order me not to smoke if I want to?" Further, the no-smoking coalition from a neighboring city, Las Cruces, collaborated with local no-smoking champions in Alamogordo in the public campaign. This activity was regarded as unwanted interference and was resented by members of the Alamogordo City Council. They promptly voted down the clean indoor air ordinance (Rogers, Peterson, and McOwiti, 2002).

Some months later, the issue was placed on the ballot in a referendum and failed in a close vote.

Misunderstandings or unwanted side effects of an innovation may occur. Corrective action can be taken to avoid such problems, but management of the innovation process, especially at the clarifying stage, is difficult and complicated. As the previously discussed examples of passage and nonpassage of no-smoking ordinances in cities illustrate, a particular policy innovation can be framed in various ways. This framing has important consequences for whether the policy is approved or rejected. In the case of a no-smoking ordinance, the policy can be framed as (1) a health issue, (2) an economic issue (will individual business volume and the amount of city taxes collected drop?), or (3) an individual rights issue. Health professionals, of course, cite the research evidence on second-hand smoking effects, but restaurant and bar owners frame the same issue as one of economic loss and of interference with individual rights.

Stable arrangements are being made for the innovation in the organization at the clarifying stage in the innovation process. The innovation is gradually becoming imbedded in the organizational structure. Once a city such as El Paso approved a no-smoking ordinance, its meaning for restaurant and bar owners had to be clarified. How much is the fine for smokers in a public place? Who is responsible for enforcement of the new law? Who must post no-smoking signs? These are the questions that must be worked out in order to clarify what the new policy actually means.

The clarifying stage in the innovation process in an organization consists of social construction. When a new idea is first implemented in an organization, it has little meaning to the organization's members and is surrounded by uncertainty. How does it work? What does it do? Who in the organization will be affected by it? Will it affect me? These are typical questions that individuals seek to answer at the clarifying stage. As the people in an organization talk about the innovation, they gradually gain a common understanding of it. Thus their meaning of the innovation in constructed over time through a social process of human interaction. As discussed previously, innovation champions uusally play an important role in this clarifying process.

5. Routinizing

Routinizing occurs when an innovation has become incorporated into the regular activities of the organization and has lost its separate identity. At that point, the innovation process is completed. Routinizing is not as simple and straightforward as it might seem at first glance.

Considerable research has been conducted in recent years on *sustainability*, a closely related concept to routinizing, defined as the degree to which an innovation continues to be used after initial efforts to secure adoption is completed. Consider a research intervention that is conducted in a health organization, in which a new program is introduced and evaluated. After the research project is completed and special funding and expertise end, will the innovative program continue, or will it be dropped? This decision regarding sustainability is also called "institutionalization" by some scholars (Goodman and Steckler, 1989).

One important factor in explaining the degree to which an innovation is sustained by an organization is *participation*, defined as the degree to which members of the organization are involved in the innovation process (Green, 1986). If many of an organization's members participate in designing, discussing, and implementing an innovation, its sustainability over time is more likely. If the innovation-decision is an authority decision, with only one or a few powerful individuals involved, and if these authorities happen to leave the organization, sustainability of the innovation is at risk. Collective innovation-decisions usually have greater sustainability than do authority innovation-decisions, due to the wider participation in them.

Further, the degree to which an innovation is *re-invented* (defined previously as the degree to which an innovation is modified by adopters as it diffuses) is positively related to the innovation's sustainability. When an organization's members change an innovation as they adopt it, they begin to regard it as their own, and are more likely to continue it over time, even when the initial special resources are withdrawn or diminish.

An illustration of the many studies of the sustainability of innovations in health organizations was conducted by O'Loughlin and colleagues (1998), who followed up on 189 heart disease prevention interventions that had been implemented by public health departments and other organizations in Canada. About 44 percent of the heart health interventions had been sustained over time, and another 35 percent were being continued but on shaky grounds. Sustainability of the innovation was related (1) to its degree of re-invention, (2) the fit between the intervention and the organization, and (3) the involvement of a local champion. Similar findings concerning the sustainability of health innovations were reported by Goodman and Steckler (1989) and by Smith, Redican, and Olsen (1992).

The research on sustainability indicates that an innovation in an organization may be vulnerable to discontinuance. Even if the innovation process goes smoothly, unexpected problems can arise when the routinizing stage is under way. Perhaps an innovation *should* be discontinued in some cases, such as when it does not effectively solve the problem that it was implemented to deal with. So sustainability is not universally a positive outcome of the innovation process.

Studying innovation as a process in an organization may suggest that respondents provide data at more than one point in time. For example, Bach (1989) gathered data from the sixty-seven physicians and physician assistants in a medical clinic (1) two weeks before the introduction of an innovation, (2) the day after the innovation was launched, and (3) fourteen weeks later. This three-point data gathering meant that data on the rate of adoption were determined by actual behavior, rather than depending entirely on recall. The innovation was a pocket-sized booklet containing daily log sheets on which a physician's clinic work was recorded, to facilitate more accurate charges and payments. Rather amazingly, one third of the respondents adopted the innovation within two weeks of its introduction at group meetings in which its advantages were explained. This rapid rate of adoption of the innovation may have occurred because the innovation met a specific need in the organization and because it originated from within the organization. The clarifying stage of the innovation process was almost unnecessary, with routinization occurring almost immediately for most adopters.

Discontinuance of an innovation can occur during the routinization stage and sometimes does, as the Santa Monica Freeway Diamond Lane experiment demonstrates.

The Santa Monica Freeway Diamond Lane Experiment: Implementation Failure*

In the mid-1970s, one lane in each direction of the four-lane, twelve-mile length of Interstate 10, which runs from the Pacific Ocean beaches of Santa Monica through downtown Los Angeles, was painted with large diamonds, and restricted to buses and cars carrying at least three passengers. The

---

*This case illustration draws on Aberg, Castillo, and Goldberg (1976) and on Schwalbe (1975).

objectives of the Santa Monica Freeway Diamond Lane project were to improve traffic flow, lower gasoline consumption, and lessen air pollution due to auto exhaust (a major problem in smoggy Los Angeles at the time).

Viewed in light of these objectives, the Diamond Lane experiment was a complete success. The Diamond Lane carried 90 percent as many people as it had before the lane was restricted, and it did so in only 30 percent as many vehicles. Travel time from Santa Monica to downtown Los Angeles on the Santa Monica Freeway's Diamond Lane was cut from twenty minutes to fifteen minutes, and even in the nonpreferential lanes, average travel time decreased by one minute. The vehicle occupancy rate increased from a preproject 1.20 persons per vehicle to 1.35 persons per vehicle. Bus ridership increased by 250 percent, and the number of car pools tripled. These were remarkable changes in commuting behavior, the kind that any city would love to achieve.

Despite these objective indicators of success, public reaction toward the Santa Monica Diamond Lane experiment was very negative. After five months of troubled existence, the Diamond Lane experiment was discontinued. How could such an objectively successful implementation of an innovation end in failure?

The answer lies in the subjective perceptions of the Los Angeles public and how they were formed. For example, although the Diamond Lane moved people at a much faster rate, this special lane appeared, especially to motorists stalled in bumper-to-bumper traffic on the other lanes of the Santa Monica Freeway, to have a vehicle on it only every quarter mile or so (this spacing was because the vehicles in the Diamond Lane moved at a much faster rate). Motorists in the slow-moving vehicles reacted against the Diamond Lane in a variety of ways. One driver threw a can of nails onto it. Another tried to paint out the diamonds. Some people rented themselves out as riders for a dollar a day to bring a car pool up to the required minimum of three passengers. Some drivers made cardboard cutout passengers or put stuffed dummies on the seat beside them. An organization, Citizens Against Diamond Lanes, was formed to lobby against the project. CALTRANS (the California Department of Transportation), the state agency implementing the project, received several thousand letters; 90 percent opposed the Diamond Lane experiment. Nevertheless, CALTRANS, an organization dominated by transportation engineers, felt that the public's negative reaction was just a temporary problem. Then the Los Angeles City Council voted against the project. Several lawsuits were filed, calling for an end to the Diamond Lane Project. After five months, one of these lawsuits was supported by the courts, and the Diamond Lane experiment ended.

The Santa Monica Freeway Diamond Lane experiment had been developed in haste as a result of several crises. For one, the 1974 OPEC oil shortage heightened concerns about reducing gas consumption. Further, the mid-1970s marked the end of freeway building in Los Angeles, due to a lack of federal highway funding and the increasing prominence of environmental issues. Yet the number of vehicles on the city's streets continued to increase by 3 percent a year. As traffic congestion worsened, auto pollutants contributed to the pall of smog over the city. One possible solution to these problems seemed to be the designation of diamond lanes on the Santa Monica Freeway, the world's busiest highway. A year or two previously, a high-occupancy-vehicle lane experiment had been highly successful on the Shirley Highway, south of Washington, D.C. The Urban Mass Transportation Administration provided CALTRANS with $800,000 in federal funds for the Santa Monica Freeway Project.

Mistakes in implementation were made from the beginning. A fundamental error was to overlook the fact that the Shirley Highway had *added* a high-occupancy-vehicle lane to existing lanes, while in Los Angeles, one lane in each direction was *taken away* from the eight existing lanes of traffic. The result was to throw traffic in the non-designated lanes into a bumper-to-bumper crawl. The Diamond Lane project began on a Monday, a day of the week character-ized by heavy traffic flow, causing the *Los Angeles Times* to call the day "Mad Monday." The experiment was termed "Chaos on the Freeway." The Los Ange-les media mounted a strong attack on the Diamond Lane Project, which the CALTRANS employees initially ignored as they were more concerned with technical aspects of the project. Traffic accidents on the Santa Monica Freeway increased: from eleven per week prior to the experiment, to fifty-nine during the first week of the project (this figure later dropped to twenty-five per week). Collaboration between CALTRANS and the California Highway Patrol (CHPs) was poor. Initially, CHPs issued citations to drivers with fewer than three passengers per vehicle. As public support for the project dwindled, CHPs became less willing to police these offenders. Finally, CHPs simply stopped giv-ing tickets, and all drivers immediately began using the Diamond Lane.

What lessons were learned from the failure of the Santa Monica Freeway Diamond Lane project? Perceptions of an innovation shape public acceptance, not objective indicators like the number of car pools or the number of vehicle passengers moving per hour in a high-occupancy-vehicle lane. Media coverage of an innovative project can shape public acceptance. Finally, constructing an extra lane for a high-occupancy-vehicle lane, rather than taking one away from existing traffic, is quite a different matter. This lesson has been utilized in hun-dreds of high-occupancy-vehicle lane projects in U.S. cities implemented since the unsuccessful Santa Monica Freeway experience. More generally, the Santa Monica Diamond Lane demonstrated the crucial importance of the imple-mentation subprocess in the innovation process.

New Communication Technologies in Organizations

The distinctive nature of virtual organizations, made possible by the Internet, was discussed in a previous section of this chapter. Further, Internet-related innovations have been a favorite topic of study in recent research on the innovation process in organizations. Finally, the new communication technologies are sometimes harnessed to record data about the diffusion of an Internet-related innovation in an organization.

An illustration is provided by Feeney (2002), who investigated the diffusion of the Blackboard digital course management system at Temple University. Since this innovation was launched in 1999, the Blackboard system has logged the adoption date and course title for each of the 2,800 course adoptions during a thirty-month period. The beauty of the Blackboard system was that each adoption was logged unobtrusively, twenty-four hours per day, removing the need to depend on respondent recall data. Undoubtedly, this pioneering use of the new communication technologies for recording diffusion data will become much more popular in future years.

Summary

An *organization* is a stable system of individuals who work together to achieve common goals through a hierarchy of ranks and a division of labor. Individual behavior in an organization is relatively stable and predictable because organizational structure is characterized by predetermined goals, prescribed roles, an authority structure, rules and regulations, and informal patterns. Although behavior in organizations is relatively stable, innovation is ongoing.

At first, innovation in organizations was mainly studied by correlating independent variables with organizational innovativeness in cross-sectional data analysis. A consistent finding in this organizational innovativeness research was that larger organizations are more innovative (Generalization 10-1). Rather low correlations of characteristics variables with organizational innovativeness were found, perhaps because the organizational structure variables that were studied were related to innovation in one direction during the initiation subprocess of the innovation process and in the opposite direction during the implementation subprocess (Generalization 10-2). For instance, low centralization, high organizational complexity, and low formalization facilitate innovation in the initiation subprocess, but impede implementation. Today, research on organizational innovativeness is much less likely to be conducted than is study of the innovation process in organizations.

The presence of an innovation champion contributes to the success of an innovation in an organization (Generalization 10-3). A *champion* is defined as a charismatic individual who throws his or her support behind an innovation, thus overcoming the indifference or resistance that the new idea may provoke. Research has shown that innovation champions may be powerful individuals in an organization, or they may be lower-level individuals who possess the ability to coordinate the actions of others. The degree to which champions are powerful seems to depend on the nature of the innovation and the organization in which it is gaining acceptance.

Studies of organizational innovativeness tended to be replaced by research on the innovation process in organizations. We divide the innovation process into two subprocesses: (1) *initiation,* all of the information gathering, conceptualizing, and planning for the adoption of an innovation, leading up to the decision to adopt and (2) *implementation,* all of the events, actions, and decisions involved in putting an innovation into use. The two initiation stages are (1) agenda-setting and (2) matching. The three implementation stages are (1) redefining/restructuring, (2) clarifying, and (3) routinizing.

Agenda-setting occurs in the innovation process when a general organizational problem that may create a perceived need for an innovation is defined. A *performance gap,* the discrepancy between an organization's expectations and its actual performance, can trigger the innovation process (Generalization 10-4). *Matching* is the stage in the innovation process at which a problem from the organization's agenda is fit with an innovation, and this match is planned and designed.

Redefining/restructuring occurs when the innovation is re-invented so as to accommodate the organization's needs and structure more closely and when the organization's structure is modified to fit with the innovation. Both the innovation and the organization usually change during the innovation process (Generalization 10-5).

Clarifying occurs as the innovation is put into more widespread use in an organization, so that the meaning of the new idea gradually becomes clearer to the organization's members. *Routinization* occurs when the innovation has become incorporated into the regular activities of the organization and loses its separate identity. Sustainability, a closely related concept to routinization, is defined as the degree to which an innovation continues to be used after the initial effort to secure adoption is completed. Sustainability is more likely if widespread participation has occurred in the innovation process, if re-invention took place, and if an innovation champion was involved. This fifth stage, routinization, marks the end of the innovation process in an organization.

11

CONSEQUENCES OF INNOVATIONS

Changing people's customs is an even more delicate responsibility than surgery.

Edward H. Spicer, *Human Problems in Technological Change* (1952), p. 13.

Consequences are the changes that occur an individual or a social system as a result of the adoption or rejection of an innovation. Invention and diffusion are but means to an ultimate end: the consequences that result from adoption of an innovation. In spite of the importance of consequences, they have received relatively little study by diffusion researchers. Furthermore, the data we have about consequences are rather "soft" in nature, based mainly on case studies, which makes it difficult to generalize about consequences. Here we establish categories for classifying consequences, but we cannot predict when and how these consequences will happen. The unpredictability of an innovation's consequences, at least in the long term, is one important type of uncertainty in the diffusion process.

Change agents generally give little attention to consequences. They often assume that adoption of a given innovation will produce mainly beneficial results for adopters. This assumption is one expression of the pro-innovation bias. Change agents should recognize their responsibility for the consequences of innovations that they introduce. Ideally, they should be able to predict the advantages and disadvantages of an innovation before introducing it to their clients. This is seldom done, and often it cannot be done.

The introduction of snowmobiles to Lapp reindeer herders in northern Finland illustrates how difficult it is to predict the effects of technology.

Snowmobile Revolution in the Arctic[*]

In the United States the snowmobile is used for winter recreation. Since the invention of the "Ski-Doo," a one-person snow vehicle, in 1958, the adoption of snowmobiles spread dramatically, and within a dozen years more than a million were in use in North America. Some outcry against the Ski-Doo (which quickly became a generic name for all makes of snowmobiles) was voiced, owing to the noise pollution they caused in previously peaceful outdoor areas of the United States and Canada.

But among the Skolt Lapps, a reindeer-herding people of northern Finland who live above the Arctic Circle, the rapid introduction of snowmobiles caused far-reaching consequences that were "disastrous" (Pelto, 1973). One method of investigating the consequences of technological innovation is for a scholar to intensively study a small community. Dr. Pertti Pelto, an anthropologist then at the University of Connecticut, lived among the Skolt Lapps in the Sevettijärvi region of northern Finland for several years, beginning in 1958, prior to the introduction of snowmobiles in 1962. Pelto returned to this community repeatedly over the next decade in order to assess the impacts of the snowmobile revolution through participant observation, personal interviews with the Lapps, and via collaboration with a research assistant/key informant (who was the first Skolt Lapp to buy a snowmobile). Pelto chose to concentrate on a single technological innovation because its consequences were so striking and hence relatively easier to identify. Many of the impacts of the Ski-Doo were very unfavorable. Pelto argued that the snowmobile represents a class of technological innovations that shifts energy sources from local and autonomous origins (reindeer-drawn sleds, in this case) to a dependence upon external sources (snowmobiles and gasoline).

Prior to the introduction of snowmobiles, the Skolt Lapps herded semi-domesticated reindeer for their livelihood. Reindeer meat was the main food, and reindeer sleds were the principal means of transportation. Rein-

---

[*]This case illustration is based on Pelto (1973), Pelto et al. (1969), and Pelto and Muller-White (1972).

deer hides were used for making clothing and shoes. Surplus meat was sold at trading stores for cash to buy flour, sugar, tea, and other staples. The Lapps saw themselves mainly as reindeer herders, and prestige was accorded to men who had a good string of draft reindeer. Lapp society was an egalitarian system in which each family had approximately equal numbers of animals. Skolt children received a "first tooth reindeer," a "nameday reindeer," and reindeer as gifts on various other occasions, including as wedding gifts, so that a new household began with a small herd of the beloved animals. The Lapps felt a special relationship with their reindeer and treated them with great care. The reindeer was the central object in Lapp culture.

In 1961, a Bombardier Ski-Doo from Canada was displayed in Rovaniemi, the capital city of Finnish Lapland. A schoolteacher purchased this snowmobile for recreational travel but soon found that it was useful for hauling wood and store-bought supplies. Snowmobiles soon began to be used for reindeer herding. Within a year, two Ski-Doos were purchased for reindeer herding in an area where the land was forested and rocky. The Lapp reindeer men had to drive their machines by standing up on the footboards or kneeling on the seat, instead of riding in the usual straddle position (as on a motorcycle). They drove standing erect so that they could spot reindeer at a greater distance and steer around rocks, trees, and other obstacles. But the erect riding style of the Lapps was dangerous when they hit an obstruction, as the driver was thrown forward. Breakdowns of the snowmobiles occurred often in the rough Lappish terrain.

Despite these problems, the rate of adoption of snowmobiles was very rapid. Three snowmobiles were adopted in the second year of diffusion, five more the next year, then eight more, and sixteen in 1966–1967, the fifth year. By 1971, almost every one of the seventy-two households in Sevettigärvi (the village studied by Professor Pelto) had at least one snowmobile. An improved model, the Motoski, was introduced from Sweden. It had a more powerful motor and was better suited to driving over rough terrain.

The main advantage of the snowmobile was faster travel. The round trip from Sevettigärvi to buy staple supplies in stores in Norway was reduced from three days by reindeer sled to five hours by snowmobile. Within a few years of their initial introduction, snowmobiles completely replaced skis and reindeer sleds as a means of herding reindeer. Unfortunately, the noise and smell of the machines drove the reindeer into a wild state. The friendly relationships between the Lapps and their animals were disrupted by the high-speed machines. Frightened running by the reindeer decreased the number of reindeer calves born each year. The average number of reindeer per household in Sevettigärvi dropped from fifty two in presnowmobile days to only twelve in 1971, a decade later. This average is misleading because about two thirds of the Lapp households completely dropped out of reindeer raising as a result of the snowmobile. Most could not find other work and became unemployed. On the other hand, one family, which was relatively early in purchasing a snowmobile, built up a large herd and by 1971 owned one third of all the reindeer in the community.

Not only did the frightened reindeer have fewer calves, but the precipitous drop in the number of reindeer also occurred because many of the animals had to be slaughtered for their meat in order to purchase the snowmobiles, gasoline for their operation, and spare parts and repairs. A new machine cost about $1,000, and gas and repairs typically cost about $425 per year. Despite this relatively high cost for the Skolt Lapps, who lived on a subsistence income, snowmobiles were considered a household necessity, and the motorized herding of reindeer was considered much more prestigious than herding by skis or with reindeer sleds. The snowmobile revolution pushed the Skolt Lapps into a tailspin of cash dependency, debt, and unemployment.

Why didn't the Lapps, given their love for the reindeer and the disastrous effects of snowmobiles, resist this technological innovation? Pelto (1973) suggests that the reason is that at no point in the diffusion of snowmobiles could they have predicted the possible future outcomes of the technology. An assessment of the technology's impacts could have been made in the 1960s, but it was not, because the Lapps were not technically able to anticipate the far-reaching consequences of the snowmobile. Further, Lapp society is very individualistic, and, given the technology's advantages for the first adopters (who were wealthier and younger than the average), initial adoption was impossible to prevent. Thereafter, the diffusion process quickly ran its course.

As a result, the reindeer-centered culture of the Skolt Lapps was severely disrupted. Most families today are unemployed and dependent on the Finnish government for subsistence payments. The snowmobile revolution in the Arctic led to disastrous consequences for the reindeer and for the Lapps who depended on the animals for their livelihood.

Since the anthropological study of the snowmobile revolution by Pertti Pelto, further technological developments have occurred in Lapland. During the summer months, the Lapps began using motorcycles to herd their reindeer. Certain affluent Lapps even began using helicopters. An increasing number of reindeer that are slaughtered for meat have been found to have stomach ulcers.

Technological innovation certainly has not been kind to the Skolt Lapps.

Studying Consequences

Instead of asking, as much past diffusion research has done—"What variables are related to innovativeness?"—future investigations need to ask, "What are the *effects* of adopting innovations?" Innovativeness, the main dependent variable in much past diffusion research, now becomes a predictor of a more ultimate dependent variable, the consequences of innovation. Most past diffusion research stopped with an analysis of the *decision* to adopt a new idea, ignoring how this choice is implemented and with what consequences.

Why have there been so few studies of consequences?

1. *Change agencies, which often sponsor diffusion research, overemphasize adoption per se, tacitly assuming that the consequences of innovation-decisions will be positive.* Change agencies assume that an innovation is needed by their clients, that its introduction will be desirable, and that adoption of the innovation represents "success." These pro-innovation assumptions are not always valid.

2. *The usual survey research methods are less appropriate for the investigation of innovation consequences than for studying innovativeness.* Extended observation over time, or an in-depth case study, are usually utilized to study consequences. Diffusion researchers have relied almost entirely upon survey methods of data gathering, ignoring the study of consequences, as the usual one-shot survey methods are inappropriate for investigating the effects of innovations. Unfortunately, case study approaches suffer in that they often yield idiosyncratic, descriptive data from which generalization to other innovations and other systems is difficult.

   The study of consequences is complicated by the fact that they usually occur over extended periods of time. An innovation's consequences cannot be understood simply by adding an additional question or two to a survey instrument, another hundred respondents to a sample population, or another few days of data gathering in the field. Instead, a long-range research approach must be taken in which consequences are analyzed as they unfold over a period of time, which may be several years. Professor Pelto, for example, returned to his Finnish village in Lapland for additional data gathering over many years.

   A panel study in which respondents are interviewed both before and after an innovation is introduced can thus yield infor-

mation about consequences. Data about consequences can also be
obtained from field experiments in which an innovation is introduced on a pilot basis and its results evaluated under realistic conditions, prior to its widespread diffusion. Panel studies and pilot
field experiments can provide quantitative data about an innovation's consequences which can lead to generalizations, rather than
mere description. Such generalizations can be predictive to a
future point in time, rather than being just a postmortem of consequences that have already occurred. We draw upon several
panel studies and field experiments in our following discussion of
the equality consequences of innovations. Many past studies of
consequences have been ethnographic analyses of a single community, often conducted by an anthropologist.

3. *Consequences are difficult to measure.* Individuals using an innovation are often not fully aware of all of the consequences of their
   adoption. Therefore, attempts to study consequences that rest on
   respondents' reports often lead to incomplete and misleading conclusions.

   Judgments concerning consequences are almost unavoidably
subjective and value-laden, regardless of who makes them. A
researcher from one culture may find it difficult to make completely objective judgments about the desirability of an innovation
in another country. *Cultural relativism* is the viewpoint that each
culture should be judged in light of its own specific circumstances
and needs. No culture is "best" in an absolute sense. Each culture
works out its own set of norms, values, beliefs, and attitudes that
function most effectively for its people. For instance, newcomers
to India are often puzzled by the millions of sacred cows that
roam the countryside freely, while many people suffer from
hunger. A foreigner is unlikely to understand that Indian cattle
provide manure, which is essential for fuel, fertilizer, and housing
construction. The holiness of cows in the Hindu religion is in fact
quite functional, rather than being just a cultural oddity.

   Cultural relativism poses problems for the measurement of
consequences. Data about the results of an externally introduced
innovation that are gathered from clients, change agents, or scientific observers, are subjectively flavored by their cultural beliefs.
Consequences should be judged as to their functionality in terms
of the user's culture, without imposing outsiders' normative
beliefs about the needs of the client system.

A further problem in measuring the consequences of an innovation is that they are often confounded with other effects. For example, in assessing the results of a new fertilizer or pesticide on crop yields, one cannot ignore the consequences caused by natural events such as droughts, floods, or volcanic eruptions. One problem in measuring the consequences of innovations is untangling cause-and-effect relationships. Ideally, we should only measure the consequences that are exclusively the outcome of the innovation, the changes that would not have occurred if the innovation had not been introduced. But many important consequences are unanticipated and indirect. These effects of an innovation are difficult to determine in a precise manner. For instance, the classification of unanticipated consequences relies on an investigator's ability to determine the original objectives for introducing an innovation in a system. These purposes may be partly concealed by subsequent rationalizations on the part of the members of the system.

Classification of Consequences

One step toward an improved understanding of the consequences of innovations is to classify them in a taxonomy. Consequences are not unidimensional. They can take many forms and are expressed in various ways. We find it useful to analyze three dimensions of consequences: (1) desirable versus undesirable, (2) direct versus indirect, and (3) anticipated versus unanticipated.

Desirable Versus Undesirable Consequences

Desirable consequences are the functional effects of an innovation for an individual or for a social system. *Undesirable consequences* are the dysfunctional effects of an innovation to an individual or to a social system. The determination of whether consequences are functional or dysfunctional depends on how the innovation affects the adopters. An innovation can cause consequences for individuals other than its adopters. For instance, rejecters of a new idea may be affected because an innovation benefits the other members of the system who adopt it, widening the socioeconomic gap between adopters and rejecters. Everyone in a system usually is touched by the consequences of a technological innovation, whether they are adopters or rejecters. An example is the Internet, which advantages certain individuals and disadvantages others through the digital divide, explained later in this chapter.

Certain innovations have undesirable impacts for almost everyone in a social system. The snowmobile in Lapland had ill consequences for almost everyone, although a few Lapps became very rich reindeer owners as a result of the innovation. Every social system has certain qualities that should not be destroyed if the system is to be maintained. These might include family bonds, respect for human life and property, maintenance of individual respect and dignity, and appreciation for others, including appreciation for contributions made by ancestors. Other sociocultural elements are more trivial and can be modified, discontinued, or supplanted with relatively less impact.

An innovation may be functional for a system but not functional for certain individuals in the system. The adoption of miracle varieties of rice and wheat in India and other nations in recent decades led to the Green Revolution. The resulting higher crop yields and farm incomes were important benefits for farmers, as were the lower consumer food prices for society. The Green Revolution also led to a reduction in the number of farmers, migration to urban slums, higher unemployment rates, and, in some countries, political instability. Although many individuals profited from the adoption of the new seeds, the Green Revolution led to unequal conditions for the system as a whole. So whether the consequences are desirable or undesirable depends on whether one takes certain individuals, or the entire system, as a point of reference.

WINDFALL PROFITS Positive consequences of an innovation may occur for certain members of a system at the expense of others. By the time laggards adopt a new idea, they are often forced to do so by economic pressures. By being the first in the field, innovators frequently secure a kind of economic gain called windfall profits.

Windfall profits are a special advantage earned by the first adopters of a new idea in a system. Their unit costs are usually lower, and their additions to total production have little effect on the selling price of the product. But when all members of a system adopt a new idea, total production increases, and the price of the product or service eventually drops.

An innovator must take risks in order to earn windfall profits. Not all new ideas turn out successfully, and occasionally the innovator gets his or her fingers burned. Adoption of a noneconomic or unsuccessful innovation can result in "windfall losses" for the first individuals to adopt. An example of windfall losses occurréd in the diffusion of pocket calculators. The first model, sold in 1971, measured three by five inches, cost $249 and could only add, subtract, multiply, and divide. Within a year, the price of a four-function calculator dropped to $100; in another year the price was only $50; and within a decade the calculator cost less than $10. Its size shrank to the thickness of a credit card. In this case, *later* adopters gained a windfall benefit by waiting to adopt.

Similarly, the author purchased a new VCR in 1980 for $2,000. Innovators who adopted so early suffered windfall losses when the selling price dropped to $100 for a VCR by 1990. Furthermore, the author's VCR was a Sony Betamax, which was replaced by another standard by the mid-1980s. It does not always pay to be an innovator!

Usually new ideas make the rich richer and the poor poorer, widening the socioeconomic gap between the earlier and later adopters of a new idea. Data from the Iowa hybrid seed corn study by Gross (1942) were reanalyzed by Rogers (1962). The innovators of this new idea, who adopted in the late 1920s, earned almost $2,500 more than the laggards, who adopted hybrid seed in 1941. The innovators earned windfall profits because of (1) a higher market price for corn that lasted only until most of the farmers adopted hybrid seed, thus increasing corn production, (2) their larger corn acreage (for example, the innovators who adopted in 1927, averaged 124 acres of corn while the typical laggard, who adopted in 1941, raised only 70 acres of corn), and (3) the greater number of years they received the higher yields from hybrid seed.

SEPARATION OF DESIRABLE AND UNDESIRABLE CONSEQUENCES Most innovations cause both desirable and undesirable consequences. Understandably, individuals generally want to obtain the functional effects of an innovation and to avoid the dysfunctional effects. Doing so assumes that certain of the desired consequences from a technological innovation can be separated from the consequences that are not wanted. Such an assumption of separation usually involves desired advantages of a new technology, such as increased effectiveness, efficiency, or convenience, versus such unwanted consequences as changes in social values and institutions. Previously, we discussed the desired advantage of the snowmobile among the Finnish Lapps (more rapid transportation), which unfortunately brought with it a steep decline in the reindeer population, widespread unemployment, and other social problems.

We conclude with Generalization 11-1: *The effects of an innovation usually cannot be managed so as to separate the desirable from the undesirable consequences.*

As discussed in Chapter 7, the Old Order Amish in the United States have maintained a distinctive culture for hundreds of years. The Amish do not adopt technological innovations such as cars and tractors, electricity, and household conveniences because the consequences of these innovations would contribute to the breakdown of their society. The Amish understand the principle of inseparability in managing technological innovations. They willingly forgo the advantages of tractors and modern farm equipment (such as larger farms, higher crop yields, and increased income) in order to avoid the undesirable consequences of increased dependence on non-Amish businesses (such as farm machinery dealers), lessened farm labor requirements, and the pressure for larger-sized farms.

The largest Amish community in the United States is located in Lancaster County, Pennsylvania, where this religious sect has survived for more than two hundred years by following the general rule of not adopting technological innovations. The fertile soil allows the Amish to succeed financially on small-sized farms of about 50 acres, which they operate on a labor-intensive basis. Their high fertility provides the workforce, so that mechanized equipment is not needed. Skyrocketing land prices, however, have made it difficult for Amish parents to set up their grown children in farming in recent years. When the young people enter urban occupations such as carpentry and construction work, they often drop out of Amish society. So the Old Order Amish in Lancaster County today face an uncertain future.

But the Amish adherence to the principle of inseparability has served them well. They forego most modern technological innovations in farming and household living because they fear the social consequences that would inevitably accompany them.

Direct Versus Indirect Consequences

The intricate and often invisible web of interrelationships among the elements of a culture means that a change in one part of a system often initiates a chain reaction of indirect consequences stemming from the direct consequences of an innovation. *Direct consequences* are the changes to an individual or a social system that occur in immediate response to adoption of an innovation. *Indirect consequences* are the changes to an individual or a social system that occur as a result of the direct consequences of an innovation. These are consequences of consequences.

An illustration of the direct and indirect consequences of an innovation is provided by an anthropological study of the adoption of wet rice farming by a tribe in Madagascar (Linton and Kardiner, 1952). The nomadic tribe had cultivated rice by dryland methods. After each harvest they would move to a different location in a kind of slash-and-burn agriculture. Then they changed to wetland (irrigated) rice farming. A pattern of land ownership developed, social status differences appeared, the nuclear family replaced the extended clan, and tribal government changed. The consequences of the technological innovation were both direct and far-reaching, in that several generations of indirect consequences from wet rice growing spread from the more direct results.

ORT: The Consequences of Consequences

Until the 1980s, an estimated 5 million young children died each year from diarrhea-related causes, representing about 30 percent of all infant deaths in the world. Diarrhea is often caused by contaminated water due to inadequate sanitation and personal hygiene. In babies, diarrhea can cause a 10 percent loss of body weight, which, in a matter of hours, can lead to the baby's death due to dehydration.

Powdered milk–based baby formulas such as Nestlé's Lactogen contributed to infant deaths due to diarrhea because the powdered formula was not used as directed. During the 1980s, widespread public alarm and the actions of the World Health Organization (WHO) helped to convince Nestlé and other powdered milk baby formula manufacturers to change their marketing practices. Social marketing campaigns were launched in Latin America, Africa, and Asia to promote breast-feeding, and to discourage the use of powdered formulas for babies (see Chapter 9).

The most promising breakthrough in the struggle to prevent deaths due to infant diarrhea occurred when a young medical doctor in Bangladesh invented oral rehydration therapy (ORT). Despite its elegant scientific name the recipe for ORT is remarkably simple: add one bottle cap of salt and eight bottle caps of sugar to three soft drink bottles of clean water. Salt and sugar are available in every peasant household in the Third World. In a pilot project in The Gambia in West Africa, parents were instructed to measure the salt and sugar with a bottle cap from an empty Coke bottle and then to mix the ingredients in the bottle. ORT is essentially Gatorade without the green color. It is also similar to the chicken soup given to sick children by Jewish mothers. ORT is an electrolyte mixture that functions to rehydrate the body (that is, to return water to the body so that a baby does not die from dehydration) and provide lost salt. The sugar provides quick energy to help the body recover from dehydration.

ORT is a lifesaver, but it can also be dangerous. If the ratio of salt to sugar is accidentally reversed, the baby may die. If clean water is not used, the baby gets diarrhea again. ORT does not cure the bacteria that cause diarrhea. ORT only prevents the progression from diarrhea to dehydration to death. Can the correct mixing of the ORT formula be taught through the mass media? In the first ORT campaigns, conducted in Honduras and The Gambia, a poster illustrating the correct mixing of the ORT formula was designed without words (because of widespread illiteracy on the part of the intended audience). Salt and sugar look alike, and formative research on the poster showed that misunderstanding sometimes occurred. Some national ORT programs decided that it was more effective to distribute small foil packets of the salt and sugar, which were then mixed with water and given to the sick baby. These ORT packets were sold for a few cents in groceries or distributed free in government health clinics.

The results of the early ORT campaigns in Honduras and The Gambia indicated that certain traditional beliefs about infant diarrhea would have to be considered if ORT were to diffuse widely and be used effectively. In Honduras, for example, the traditional "cure" for diarrhea was to administer a purge (similar to Ex-Lax). Furthermore, it was widely believed that a sack of worms exists in everyone's abdominal cavity, and that when the worms become agitated and leave the sack, diarrhea results. So the prevention of infant diarrhea depended on not disturbing the sack of worms. Many people in The Gambia believed that infant diarrhea was caused by supernatural forces or by the will of Allah. The concept of dehydration ran counter to these traditional beliefs. Pilot social marketing of ORT in The Gambia and Honduras indicated that a communication campaign could raise the levels of public knowledge and adoption of ORT, but it was much more difficult to convey the concept of dehydration effectively. Most people who used ORT did not have a scientifically correct understanding of how it worked, as such principles-knowledge rests on understanding the chemical process of electrolytes. Health officials asked the rhetorical question "Does one need to know how a motor works in order to drive a car?"

By the mid-l990s, almost every developing nation in Latin America, Africa, and Asia had launched an effective ORT campaign. Integrated child survival campaigns typically emphasize ORT along with breast-feeding, immunization of children, improving the quality of drinking water, and better personal sanitation (such as using latrines and washing one's hands regularly).

As ORT diffused widely in Third World countries during the late 1980s and early 1990s, the rate of infant mortality dropped and the populations of these nations climbed. How were schooling, housing, and jobs to be provided for the millions of infants whose lives were saved by ORT? One answer was a faster rate of adoption of family-planning methods. But in many of the poorest countries where the ORT campaigns had been highly successful, national family-planning programs were relatively ineffective. The beneficial consequences of the rapid adoption of one innovation led to the worsening of another social problem.

The diffusion of ORT suggests that the indirect consequences of an innovation are often especially difficult to plan for, and manage, as they are often unanticipated.

Anticipated Versus Unanticipated Consequences

Anticipated consequences are changes due to an innovation that are recognized and intended by the members of a social system. An example of such a manifest consequence is the snowmobiles' advantage to the Lapps of providing rapid transportation. The Lapps could not, however, anticipate such latent consequences of this innovation as its disastrous effects on their reindeer herds. Although they are less discernible to observers, the "subsurface" consequences of an innovation may be just as important as the anticipated consequences.

Unanticipated consequences are changes due to an innovation that are neither intended nor recognized by the members of a social system. The disintegration of respect for elders among the Yir Yoront, in the case study that follows, is an example of an unanticipated consequence of the adoption of steel axes by Australian aborigines. This change in family relationships was of tremendous importance to the tribe, even though such a consequence was not readily apparent when steel axes were first introduced by well-meaning missionaries.

No innovation comes without strings attached. The more technologically advanced an innovation, the more likely its introduction will produce many consequences, both anticipated and latent. A system is like a bowl of marbles: move any one of its elements, and the positions of all the others inevitably change also.

This interdependency of the elements in a system is poorly understood by the adopters of an innovation, and may not even be comprehended by the change agents who introduce a new idea in a system. Unanticipated consequences represent a lack of understanding of how an innovation functions, and of the internal and external forces at work in a social system. Awareness of a new idea creates uncertainly about how the innovation will actually function for an individual or other adopting unit in a system. This uncertainty motivates active information seeking about the innovation, especially through interpersonal peer networks. Individuals particularly seek to reduce uncertainty concerning an innovation's expected consequences. Such uncertainty can be decreased to the point where an individual feels well informed enough to adopt the new idea. But uncertainty about an innovation's consequences can never be completely removed.

An adopter is often able to obtain adequate information from peers about the desirable, direct, and anticipated consequences of an innovation. But the unanticipated consequences are, by definition, unknown by individuals at the time of adoption of the innovation. Such unforeseen impacts of a new idea represent innovation-evaluation information that cannot be obtained by an individual from other members of his or her system. Professional change agents often cannot know the unanticipated consequences of an innovation until after its widespread adoption has occurred (if then), as we see in the following case of the steel ax, introduced by missionaries to an isolated Australian tribe.

We conclude this discussion of the three classifications of consequences with Generalization 11-2: *The undesirable, indirect, and unanticipated consequences of an innovation usually go together, as do the desirable, direct, and anticipated consequences.*

---

*Steel Axes for Stone-Age Aborigines**

The consequences of the adoption of steel axes by a tribe of Australian aborigines vividly illustrate the need for consideration of the undesirable, indirect, and unanticipated consequences of an innovation (this case was mentioned previously, in Chapters 1 and 2). The Yir Yoront traveled in small nomadic groups over a vast territory in search of game and other food. The central tool in their

---

*This case illustration is adopted from Sharp (1952, pp. 69–92).

culture was the stone ax, which they found indispensable for food production, constructing shelter, and heating their homes. A complete revolution was precipitated by the replacement of the stone ax by the steel ax.

Anthropologist Lauriston Sharp (1952) conducted an investigation of the Yir Yoront by the method of participant observation. He studied Yir Yoront culture by taking part in its everyday activities. Because of its isolation, the tribe was relatively unaffected by Western civilization until the establishment of a nearby missionary post. The missionaries distributed many steel axes among the Yir Yoront as gifts and as payment for work performed.

Previously, the stone ax had been a symbol of masculinity and respect for elders. Only men owned stone axes, although women and children were the principal users of these tools. Axes were borrowed from fathers, husbands, or uncles according to a system of social relationships prescribed by custom. The Yir Yoront obtained their stone ax heads in exchange for spears through bartering with other tribes, a process that took place as part of elaborate rituals at seasonal fiestas.

When the missionaries distributed the steel axes to the Yir Yoront, they hoped that a rapid improvement in living conditions would result. There was no great resistance to using the steel axes, because the tribe was accustomed to securing their tools through trade. Steel axes were more efficient for most tasks, and stone axes rapidly disappeared.

However, to the disappointment of the missionaries, the steel ax contributed little to social progress. The Yir Yoront used their new-found leisure time for sleep, "an act they had thoroughly mastered." The missionaries distributed the steel axes equally to men, women, and children. Young men were more likely to adopt the new tools than were the elders, who did not trust the missionaries. The result was a disruption of status relationships among the Yir Yoront and a revolutionary confusion of age and sex roles. Elders, once highly respected, now became dependent upon women and younger men and were often forced to borrow steel axes from these social inferiors.

The trading rituals of the tribe also became disorganized. Friendship ties among traders broke down, and interest declined in the annual fiestas, where the barter of stone axes for spears had formerly taken place. The religious system and social organization of the Yir Yoront became disorganized as a result of the tribe's inability to adjust to the innovation. To the horror of the missionaries, the men began prostituting their daughters and wives in exchange for the use of other people's steel axes.

Many of the consequences of the innovation among the Yir Yoront were undesirable, indirect, and unanticipated. These three types of consequences often go together, just as desirable, direct, and anticipated consequences are often associated.

Form, Function, and Meaning of an Innovation

The case of the steel ax among the Yir Yoront also illustrates a common error made by change agents in regard to an innovation's consequences. They usually are able to anticipate the form and function of an innovation's consequences, but not its meaning for potential adopters. What are the form, function, and meaning of an innovation?

1. *Form* is the directly observable physical appearance and substance of an innovation. Both the missionaries and the Yir Yoront recognized the form of the new tool because of its similarity in appearance to the stone ax.
2. *Function* is the contribution made by an innovation to the way of life of members of a social system. The tribe immediately perceived the steel ax as a cutting tool, to be used in much the same way as the stone ax had been.
3. *Meaning* is the subjective and frequently unconscious perception of an innovation by members of a social system. A famous anthropologist, Ralph Linton (1936), explained, "Because of its subjective nature, meaning is much less susceptible to diffusion than either form or [function]. . . . A receiving culture attaches new meanings to the borrowed elements of complexes, and these may have little relation to the meanings which the same elements carried in their original setting."

What mistakes did the missionaries make in the introduction of the steel ax? These change agents understood the form and function of the steel ax. They believed the Yir Yoront would use the new tool in much the same way as they had the stone ax, such as for cutting brush. But the missionaries made an egregious error in not predicting the meaning of the new idea for the Yir Yoront. They did not anticipate that the steel ax would lead to more sleep, prostitution, and a breakdown of social relationships. Change agents frequently do not sense or understand the social meaning of the innovations that they introduce, especially the negative consequences that accrue when an apparently desirable innovation is used under different conditions. Change agents are especially likely to make this mistake if they do not empathize with the innovation's users, which is particularly likely when the change agents are heterophilous with their clients.

We conclude with Generalization 11-3: *Change agents more easily anticipate the form and function of an innovation for their clients than its meaning.*

The Irish Potato Famine*

One of the worst famines in history was the Irish potato famine of 1850, which left at least one million people dead of starvation, forced another 2 million to migrate to the United States, and left several million to live in abject poverty. What caused this famine?

The story begins a century earlier, when a new wonder food, the potato, was introduced from North America. Ireland's climate was perfect for potato growing, and Ireland was relatively free from potato diseases and insects. Potato yields were abundant. The population began to increase, from 2 million Irish in the 1700s to 4.5 million by 1800, and then to 8 million in 1845. Catholic priests blessed this increased human fertility, which gave them more souls to save. Thanks to the potato, the human population continued to expand. Absentee landlords who visited their estates were amazed at the hordes of dirty, wretched people living in absolute poverty. Even with the prospering potato, most Irish lived on the edge of hunger.

Then in 1845, a fungus, *Phytophthora infestans*, arrived from America and wiped out the entire potato crop. Previously, during the long Atlantic crossing, often requiring a month or more, infected potatoes being carried to feed passengers had rotted, and the fungus had died. But the new clipper ships made the transatlantic crossing so quickly, in twelve to fourteen days, that infected potatoes did not have time to rot and the fungus survived the trip. The weather in 1845 and 1846 was cool and rainy, perfect for rapid spread of the fungus.

Who or what was responsible for the devastating Irish potato famine in Ireland? Was it the unwitting do-gooder who first brought the potato to Ireland? Was it the fungus? Was it the improved sailing technology of the clipper ships, which shortened the trans-Atlantic crossing, allowing the fungus to arrive on Irish shores? Or was it the Catholic religion of the Irish, which favored large families?

---

*This case illustration is based on Paddock (1992).

Achieving a Dynamic Equilibrium

Perhaps the missionaries introduced too many steel axes to the Yir Yoront too rapidly. What rate of change allows a system to achieve the maximum benefits of an innovation and yet not produce disequilibrium in the social system?

Three types of equilibrium are possible in a system:

1. *Stable equilibrium,* which occurs when there is almost no change in the structure or functioning of a social system. An example of stable equilibrium is a completely isolated and traditional system in which the rate of change is almost zero, perhaps something like the Yir Yoront before the arrival of the missionaries.
2. *Dynamic equilibrium,* which occurs when the rate of change in a social system occurs at a rate that is commensurate with the system's ability to cope with it. Change occurs in a system in dynamic equilibrium, but it occurs at a rate that allows the system to adapt to it.
3. *Disequilibrium,* which occurs when the rate of change is too rapid to permit a social system to adjust. An analogy is a traffic circle with one too many cars on it; the circulation of vehicles slows down until eventually all movement stops. The social disorganization that accompanies disequilibrium makes it a painful and inefficient way for change to occur in a system.

The long-range goal of most change agents is to produce a condition of dynamic equilibrium in their client system. Innovations should be introduced into the system at a deliberate rate that allows for careful balancing of the system's ability to adjust to the changes. Gauging the optimum rate of change in a system is difficult. The missionaries among the Yir Yoront misjudged the rate at which the aborigines' system could absorb the consequences of the steel ax.

The Mosquito Killer*

Dichlorodiphenyltrichloroethane (DDT) was one of the important health innovations of the past century, saving the lives of millions of people by protecting them against malaria-carrying mosquitos. This chemical was discovered by a Swiss chemist, Paul Müller, in the late 1930s, while he was looking for a means to protect woolens against moths. Later, in 1948, Müller was awarded the Nobel Prize for his discovery. But for many years, practical uses for DDT were not found. Early in World War II in the Pacific, malaria transmitted by mosquitos was handicapping the fighting ability of U.S. military personnel. For example, 10,000 of the 17,000 men in the First Marine

---

*This case illustration is adapted from Gladwell (2001) and Speilman and D'Antonio (2001).

Division were incapacitated by malarial headaches, fevers, and chills and had to be withdrawn from island fighting against the Japanese.

Anyone who has ever had malaria will never forget the raging thirst, headaches, and bone-breaking pain. The word "malaria" comes from the Italian for "bad air." Only about a century ago, it was determined that the malaria parasite was carried by mosquitos, who infected humans by biting them to suck blood.

In 1943, DDT was being tested at an Army laboratory in Orlando, Florida. One of two duck ponds was doused with DDT, and all the mosquito larvae in this lake promptly died. But a week later, mysteriously, the larvae in the other duck pond, several miles distant, also died. Ducks from the treated pond had visited the second pond, and there was enough DDT residual on their feathers to kill the mosquito larvae. Clearly, here was a very powerful insecticide! DDT was rushed into use in the Pacific War. Dengue fever, borne by the *Aedes* mosquito, was sickening five hundred men a day in the invasion of Saipan. A DDT air strike was made on the island. The dengue fever promptly subsided, and the Marines were victorious. The capture of Saipan was important in the Pacific war, as this island provided the air base from which the *Enola Gay* dropped the atomic bomb on Hiroshima in 1945.

DDT also proved to be the perfect killer of the *Anopheles* mosquito, the main carrier of malaria. In the 1940s, malaria was a major public health problem worldwide. In India alone, 75 million people were infected with malaria, and the disease killed 800,000 people each year. Malaria was found throughout Europe, Asia, the Caribbean, and the American South. Leading the DDT attack on mosquitos was Dr. Fred Soper, who had his doctorate from the Johns Hopkins School of Public Health and worked for the Rockefeller Foundation, then leading efforts to improve health around the world. Soper was "the General Patton of entomology" (Gladwell, 2001, p. 44). His disciplined approach to mosquito eradication began with mapping the area to be cleared of mosquitos and then numbering each house. Each house was assigned to a sector, which in turn was assigned to an inspector with a spray pump filled with insecticide. The walls and ceiling of each house were sprayed, as the mosquitos would alight there before and after biting people living in the house. The DDT coating on the home's surface killed all mosquitos on contact for a period of six months or more.

Each inspector's daily work was checked by a supervisor, who was given a bonus if he found a mosquito that the spray man had missed. The spray man was docked a day's pay. Soper was a tough boss, completely devoted to eradicating the mosquito. On one occasion, a large ammunition dump near Rio de Janeiro exploded. Soper heard the explosion, checked his map, and noted that an inspector was spraying that area. Soper immediately sent condolences and a check to the widow. The next day, the inspector surprised everyone by showing up for work. Soper fired him on the spot—for being alive and having shirked his duties as a spray man.

The most dangerous of the sixty species of *Anopheles* mosquito in transmitting the malaria parasite to humans is the *gambiae,* which is native to Africa. Unfortunately, this species was carried across the Atlantic by ships, and soon 18,000 square miles of Brazilian coastal areas were infected. Soper and his army of 4,000 sprayer-inspectors eradicated the *gambiae* in one year. Initially, Soper's antimosquito army used a spray called Paris green (copper acetarsenite). When he learned of DDT in 1943, Soper wrote in his diary, "Malaria results (for DDT) ARE FANTASTIC" (quoted in Gladwell, 2001, p. 46). He soon launched an attack on malaria-carrying mosquitos on the large island of Sardinia in the Mediterranean, which had the most serious malaria epidemic in Italy. Soper trained a cadre of 25,000 inspectors and supervisors. At the end of a five-year spraying campaign, in which 256 tons of DDT were dusted onto the island, the number of malaria cases in Sardinia dropped from 10,000 annually to just four in 1950!

With this success behind him, Soper set out to eradicate malaria-carrying mosquitos worldwide. In league with other malariologists, he convinced the World Health Organization (WHO) to establish a Global Malaria Eradication Programme, with the goal of killing mosquitos in every nation. The enthusiastic goal of the WHO program was to eliminate the *Anopheles* mosquito, and hence malaria. In Taiwan, much of the South Pacific, North Africa, Sri Lanka, the Balkans, and Australia, the campaign was a success. In India, malaria fatalities dropped to zero by the early 1960s. Millions, perhaps tens of millions, of lives were saved by Soper's DDT sprayers. Perhaps no other man-made drug or chemical has saved more lives.

Soon, however, problems arose in Soper's war on the mosquito. In the late 1940s, a malariologist observed a healthy mosquito flying around a room that had been heavily sprayed with DDT. How could this incredible event have happened? DDT attacks a mosquito's nervous system, sending it into a lurching, twitching spasm before it dies. But due to random genetic mutation, a few mosquitos in every large population are resistant to DDT. Perhaps the insecticide does not bind to the mosquito's nerve endings because the mosquito has a thicker skin. Resistant mosquitos then continue to breed, while other mosquitos are killed by DDT, and soon entire new generations are DDT-resistant. Another type of protection from the DDT spraying of walls and ceilings occurred among a type of mosquitos in the Solomon Islands. These mosquitos did not alight on the walls or ceilings of homes; instead, they flew in through a window, bit a human, and then flew back out.

The development of DDT-resistant mosquitos came as a great shock to Soper and his fellow mosquito killers. After some years, countries that had been enthusiastic allies of Soper began to cancel their eradication campaigns. In 1969, WHO dropped its Global Eradication Programme. Soper toured Asia, and was appalled at what he observed. Everywhere mosquitos, and malaria, were on the increase. Soper blamed these defeats on a lack of discipline in the DDT-spraying campaigns. Some labeled him a "disease fascist." Soper advocated heavier and heavier doses of DDT, but in areas with the heaviest spraying, the resistant mosquitos especially flourished. Soper's dream of a world free of malaria was rapidly unraveling. Then Rachel Carson's bombshell book *Silent Spring* was published in 1962, arguing that DDT was being used without concern for its environmental consequences. Once the world set foot on the treadmill of DDT spraying, Carson claimed, it was unable to get off. The U.S. Environmental Protection Agency banned the general use of DDT in the United States in 1972. "DDT is a prisoner of politics and may never escape" (Spielman and D'Antonio, 2001, p. 204).

Fred Soper was an absolutist, a fanatic, who believed that DDT spraying was *the* way to prevent malaria. He scoffed at experts who argued that draining the breeding areas of the mosquitos should accompany the spraying and that DDT should be used sparingly and as only one of several tools in a malaria eradication campaign. Standing ramrod straight and always dressed in a suit, Fred Soper learned the hard way that even dramatically effective technological innovations can have perverse consequences. When Soper died in 1975, he was viewed as an enemy by environmentalists. But to the many millions of people whose lives had been saved by his actions, Soper was a hero.

Equality in the Consequences of Innovations

A specific mistake made by the missionaries among the Yir Yoront was their choice of people to whom they introduced the innovation. Unaware of the cultural emphasis on respect for elderly males, the change agents indiscriminately gave steel axes to women, children, and young men. One of the ways in which change agents shape the consequences of an innovation is who they work with most closely. If a change agent were to contact the poorer and less educated individuals in a social system, rather than the socioeconomic elites (as is usually the case), the benefits from the innovations that are so introduced would be more equal. Usually, however, change agents have most contact with the better-educated, higher-status individuals in a system, and thus tend to widen socioeconomic gaps through the innovations that they introduce.

In addition to the desirable/undesirable, direct/indirect, and antici-
pated/unanticipated aspects of the consequences of innovation (discussed earlier), one might classify consequences as to whether they
increase or decrease equality among the members of a social system.

The diffusion of innovations generally causes wider socioeconomic
gaps within an audience because:

1. Innovators and early adopters have favorable attitudes toward
   new ideas and more actively search for innovations. They also possess more resources and thus can adopt higher-cost innovations
   that later adopters cannot afford.
2. Professional change agents concentrate their client contacts on
   innovators and early adopters in hopes that the opinion leaders
   among these earlier adopting categories will then pass along the
   new ideas they have learned to their followers. But most interpersonal network links connect individuals who are similar in adopter
   category and socioeconomic status. So innovations generally
   trickle *across*, rather than *down*, in the interpersonal communication networks of a system.
3. By adopting innovations relatively sooner than others in their system,
   innovators and early adopters achieve windfall profits, thereby
   widening the socioeconomic gap between these earlier adopting categories versus later adopting categories. Thus the earlier adopters get
   richer, and the later adopters' economic gain is comparatively less.

The diffusion of innovations usually decreases the degree of equality in
a social system. But this tendency toward gap-widening need not occur, if
special strategies are followed to narrow gaps. The previous example of the
impact of the snowmobile on the Skolt Lapps, illustrated two dimensions
of consequences: (1) the first dimension of helping everyone travel more
rapidly (thus achieving a higher average *level* of "Good," some widely
desired objective) and (2) the second dimension of the *unequal distribution* of the "Good," the tendency for reindeer ownership to become concentrated in the hands of just a few Lapps (Figure 11-1).

The Communication Effects Gap

Most past diffusion studies attempted to determine the first dimension
of communication effects by pursuing the question "What are the
effects of a communication activity to diffuse an innovation?" These

Figure 11-1. The Two Dimensions of Consequences of an Innovation in a System: (1) the Level of Good (above), and (2) the Degree of Equality (below)

1. Before the Innovation

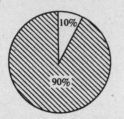

The total amount of income or other Good in the system is held by a wealthy minority (of, say, 10 percent)

2. After the Innovation

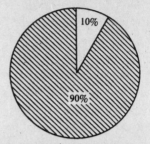

The total amount of Good is now larger, but the proportion held by the wealthy minority remains the same.

I.   The level of Good in a system increases, but its distribution remains at the same degree of equality-inequality.

1. Before the Innovation

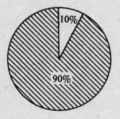

The prior conditions are the same as above.

2. After the Innovation

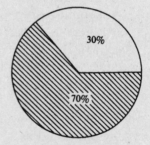

Both the total amount of Good in the system and the proportion of Good held by the wealthy increase as a consequence of the innovation. Hence there is less equality.

II. The level of Good in a system increases, and its distribution becomes more concentrated and hence less equal.

effects are measured as the average change in the knowledge, attitudes, or overt behavior (that is, adoption) regarding an innovation by a set of individuals (Figure 11-2*a*).

Research on the second dimension of communication effects is quite different (Figure 11-2*b*). Here one asks, "Has the communication

Figure 11-2a. The First Dimension of Communication Effects (for All Members of the System) Is an Average Increase of Four Units, Measured as the Difference from t_1 to t_2.

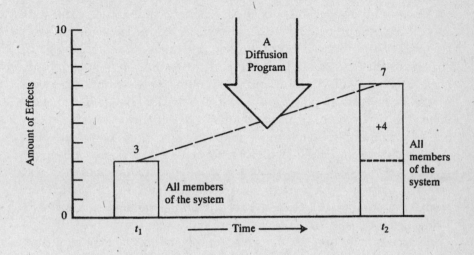

Figure 11-2b. The Second Dimension of Communication Effects (Which Analyzes Effects Separately for Downs and Ups) Indicates That the Effects Gap Is Widened by the Diffusion Program.

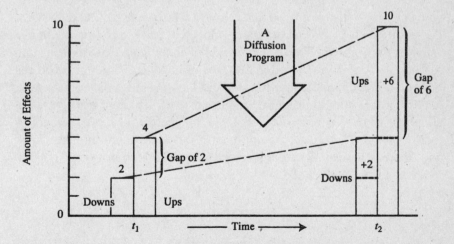

Note that the Downs are *absolutely* better off as a result of the diffusion intervention (+2), but *relatively* worse off (as the Ups gained +6). So the information-rich got richer, and the information-poor got less poor.

activity to diffuse an innovation had a greater, or different, effect on certain individuals, rather than on others?" The investigator seeks to ascertain the *equality* of effects of communication, not just how much effect occurred *on the average* (or in the aggregate).

About the time that diffusion researchers became interested in this second dimension, dealing with the equality issue, Tichenor and colleagues (1970) proposed a useful research paradigm for studying gaps, suggesting that data should be gathered at two or more points in time, both before and after a diffusion intervention. The measure of effects should be not just the average amount of behavior change in the audience (the first dimension) but whether gaps in socioeconomic status and/or in knowledge of information increased or decreased (this is the second dimension of effects). In essence, Tichenor and colleagues (1970) suggested that we should look at who in an audience was affected most and who least. Figures 11-2*a* and 11-2*b* depict this research paradigm, which was very influential on diffusion scholars studying the equality of consequences of innovation.

A main implication of the communication effects gap paradigm, inspired by Tichenor and colleagues (1970) and carried forward in numerous other studies (Viswanath and Finnegan, 1996), was to look *within* an audience to determine whether certain segments were more affected by an innovation's diffusion than were other segments. This analytic approach looked for differential effects, rather than just for average effects or aggregate effects on the entire audience. Scholars began to investigate the degree to which a diffusion program widened or narrowed gaps among the members of a system. The categorization of an audience into two or more segments (who might be called the "ups" and "downs") could be on the basis of socioeconomic status (for example, larger versus smaller businesses in an industry), adopter category (for instance, earlier adopters versus later adopters), or the level of information that individuals possessed (the information-rich versus the information-poor). Almost no matter how the "ups" and "downs" are classified, certain regularities about equality and inequality in the consequences of diffusion are found.

Gap-Widening Consequences of the Diffusion of Innovations

Generalization 11-4 states: *The consequences of the diffusion of innovations usually widen the socioeconomic gap between the earlier and later adopting categories in a system.* A second, related conclusion, Generalization 11-5, is: *The consequences of the diffusion of innovation usually widen the socioeconomic gap between the audience segments previously high and low in socioeconomic status.*

Havens and Flinn (1974) examined the consequences of new coffee varieties among Colombian farmers over the period from 1963 to 1970. The community of study, Támesis, is located high in the Andes Mountains in the Department of Antioquia (later to become famous as the base of operations of the Medellín drug cartel). At the time of the Havens and Flinn (1974) study, however, the main source of income in this region of Colombia was coffee growing. The quality of the aromatic beans, grown on bushes covering the steep slopes of Antioquia, was excellent, and the coffee, marketed in the United States and elsewhere by Cafeteros, the Colombian Coffee Growers Association (whose logo is Juan Valdez and his donkey), received a top price. Coffee growing was a very profitable enterprise.

Of the original sample of fifty-six coffee growers in the study, seventeen adopted the new varieties, which considerably increased their yields. They adopted chemical fertilizers and herbicides along with the new coffee varieties in order to achieve these high yields. As a result of adopting this package of innovations, the seventeen adopters raised their net income from 6,700 pesos in 1963 to 21,000 pesos in 1970, an increase of 14,300 pesos (213 percent). The thirty nonadopting coffee farmers (who did not use the new coffee varieties) raised their net income from 4,500 pesos to 12,000 pesos, an increase of only half as much (7,500 pesos, or 166 percent). One effect of the coffee variety innovations was to widen the income gap between the adopters and nonadopters from 2,200 pesos in 1963 to 9,000 pesos in 1970. The improved coffee varieties caused much greater income inequality among Colombian farmers.

How much of this increased inequality among the Colombian coffee growers was due to the adoption of the new coffee varieties and how much to other factors, such as initially larger farms, higher formal education, and other characteristics of the adopters? Havens and Flinn (1974) computed the net income per acre of coffee grown, thus removing the effect of the larger-sized farms of the adopters. The adopters and nonadopters both began at about the same level of income per acre in 1963: 290 pesos per acre and 222 pesos per acre, respectively. But by 1970, when the adopters were enjoying the higher yields that resulted from growing the new varieties, their income per acre shot up to 1,642 pesos per acre (an increase of 1,352 pesos), while the nonadopters' income per acre rose to 632 pesos (an increase of 415 pesos). Much of the increased income inequality between the adopters and nonadopters was due to the introduction of the coffee variety innovations. The results of the new coffee varieties in Colombia illustrates the communication effects gap (Generalization 11-4).

What did the adopters in Colombia do with their higher income? Some bought larger farms, often land sold by the unsuccessful non-adopters of the new coffee varieties. In 1963, the adopters averaged farms of 19 acres and the nonadopters 8 acres. By 1970, the adopters had increased the size of their farms to 33 acres, while the nonadopters' farms had shrunk to an average size of 6 acres. In addition, eleven of the nonadopters dropped out of farming and either became day laborers or else migrated to the city (presumably, their farms were purchased by adopters of the new coffee varieties).

If adoption of the new coffee varieties would have such important consequences, why didn't the thirty-nine nonadopters also start growing the new varieties? Adopting a new coffee variety is a major decision in Colombia because three years are required before the new trees produce. Many farmers needed credit to tide them over this period until their investment in the new variety began to pay off. Smaller *campesinos*, who did not have much land to put up as collateral, were generally unable to borrow funds to enable them to adopt the new coffee varieties. So Generalization 11-5, about widening the socioeconomic gap between those high and low in socioeconomic status, is also illustrated by the Colombian coffee varieties study.

This vicious circle explains how adoption of the coffee variety innovations widened the socioeconomic gaps between (1) adopters and nonadopters and (2) individuals originally high and low in socioeconomic status. The innovation was like a lever, widening the gap between the rich and the poor.

Social Structure and the Equality of Consequences

How an innovation is introduced determines, in part, the degree to which it causes unequal consequences. Evidence for this point comes from an investigation of the impacts of adopting irrigation wells by villagers in Bangladesh and in Pakistan (Gotsch, 1972). In each country, an irrigation well cost about the same amount and provided water for 50 to 80 acres of farmland. The introduction of Green Revolution wheat and rice varieties created a need for irrigation in both nations. But the equality of the consequences of an identical innovation was quite different in Pakistan from those in Bangladesh, mainly because of the different social organization that accompanied the new technology.

In Pakistan, 70 percent of the irrigation wells were purchased by farmers with 25 acres or more (considered very large farms). Only 4 percent of the villagers with farms of less than 13 acres adopted. When the irrigation water was accompanied by the use of fertilizers and other agricultural chemicals, a farmer typically could increase his net farm income by about 45 percent. So the irrigation wells in Pakistan made the rich richer and the poor farmers *relatively* poorer.

However in Bangladesh, average farm size was only 1 or 2 acres, not large enough to justify private ownership of an irrigation well. So village cooperatives typically purchased a pump and well and provided irrigation water to everyone who belonged to the co-op. Incomes were doubled because farmers could raise a winter crop of rice during the season when rainfall was scarce. In Bangladesh, the rate of adoption of the wells was slower than in Pakistan because the innovation-decision was collective rather than individual-optional in nature. But the consequences of the innovation were distributed much more equally than they were in Pakistan, where an initially high degree of social stratification concentrated the impacts of the irrigation wells on the richer farmers.

The social structure in which the innovation of pump-well irrigation was introduced in Bangladesh and Pakistan, rather than the innovation itself, determined the distribution of its socioeconomic impacts. This investigation, along with others, suggests Generalization 11-6: *A system's social structure partly determines the equality versus inequality of an innovation's consequences.* When a system's structure is already very inequal, it is likely that when an innovation is introduced (especially if it is a relatively high-cost innovation), its consequences will lead to even greater inequality in the form of wider socioeconomic gaps.

The irrigation consequences research in Bangladesh and Pakistan illustrates, as does the Colombian coffee study, that an innovation's adoption and its impacts are related to characteristics of the social system, as well as to variables at the individual level of analysis. The fact that village co-ops already existed in Bangladesh when irrigation wells were introduced and that small coffee growers in Colombia could not obtain credit to adopt the new coffee varieties largely determined who adopted and who could not. The determining factors were mainly at the system level, although their impacts occurred through individuals' actions, and there were consequences for both individuals and the system.

Social structural factors are not necessarily static barriers or facilitators of the adoption of innovations and their consequences. A rural development agency in Bangladesh had organized the village coopera-tives just before the introduction of irrigation wells, for exactly the pur-pose that they served: to enable small farmers, through banding together, to adopt relatively high-cost innovations such as tractors and irrigation wells. Here we see again the potential power of organizing for social change, that a set of individuals, once organized in groups, can express a collective efficacy in achieving group actions that they could not attain as relatively powerless individuals.

Strategies for Narrowing Gaps

As the previous studies suggest, innovations do not inevitably widen socioeconomic gaps within a system. But such gap-widening inequality will usually occur unless a change agency devotes special efforts to pre-vent it. What strategies can be used by change agencies for gap narrow-ing? We list possible strategies here, organized under the major reasons why socioeconomic gaps ordinarily widen as a consequence of innova-tions.

I. "Ups" Have Greater Access to Information, Creating Awareness of Innovations, Than Do "Downs."

1. Messages that are redundant or that are of less interest and/or benefit to the higher socioeconomic subaudience should be pro-vided. This strategy enables the lower-socioeconomic subaudi-ence to catch up. This "ceiling effect" strategy was used for nar-rowing the socioeconomic gap among Indian villagers through special television programming (Shingi and Mody, 1976).

2. Communication messages should be tailored especially for the lower-socioeconomic subaudience in terms of their particular characteristics, such as formal education, beliefs, communication habits, and the like. Communication messages are seldom espe-cially designed for this audience segment, and hence most messages are ineffective in closing gaps. Although the technical content of these messages may be the same as for the "ups," to be effective in reaching the lower socioeconomic audience, the design, treat-ment, and presentation of messages may have to be different. For example, more line drawings, photographs, and other visual aids are often needed because the "downs" have lower levels of formal

education. Formative research* may help produce effective messages for the "downs," such as by testing prototype messages before they are produced in large quantities. For instance, content analyses show that most health-related Web sites on the World Wide Web require at least a high school education to comprehend (Berland et al., 2001). However, an effective Web site about improved nutrition for low-income rural Hispanic people in New Mexico was produced, using extensive formative research (Buller et al., 2001).

3. Communication channels that get through to "downs" should be utilized so that access is not a barrier to gaining awareness-knowledge of innovations. In the United States, for example, lower-socioeconomic audiences are especially heavy television viewers but depend less on print media than do "ups." In developing nations, many "downs" are not literate, so print media are useless. In these countries, "downs" are much more likely to be exposed to radio than to watch television.

4. "Downs" should be organized into small groups in which they can learn about innovations and discuss them. The group context for listening, discussion, and action provides a basis for the "downs" to gain self-efficacy and collective efficacy, a belief that they have control over their environment. This strategy is organizing for social change, mentioned previously.

5. Change agent contact should be shifted from the innovators and early adopters to the late majority and laggards. Later adopting categories tend to place less credibility in professional change agents, and they seldom actively seek information from them, as they place greater trust in interpersonal peer networks. But when change agents directly contact late majority and laggards, and if the innovations are appropriate to their needs, the response has often been encouraging (Röling et al., 1976).

Consider the case of a change agent working in one village. One farmer owns 100 acres, while the remaining hundred farmers have an average of one acre each. If the change agent contacts the hundred smaller farmers, he or she may be able to persuade them

Formative research is investigation conducted while an activity, process, or system is ongoing, in order to improve its effectiveness. In contrast, *summative research* is investigation conducted in order to reach a decision about the effectiveness of an activity, process, or system after it has run its course.

to adopt new crop varieties and other agricultural innovations, so that their yields increase by an average of ten bushels per acre within five years. But with much less effort, the change agent can contact the farmer with the largest farm, who is already innovative and receptive to new ideas. The increase of ten bushels per acre on the elite individual's farm equals the consequences of the much greater efforts by the change agent with all one hundred smaller farmers. This illustration shows why change agent contact is generally concentrated on earlier adopters, and on individuals of higher social status.

II. *"Ups" Have Greater Access to Innovation Evaluation Information from Peers than Do "Downs."*

Trickle-down theory suggests that "downs" rapidly learn of the "ups'" personal experience with an innovation and follow suit. In many systems, however, "ups" talk primarily to "ups," and "downs" to "downs" (Röling et al., 1976). How can this problem be overcome?

1. Opinion leaders among the disadvantaged individuals in a system should be identified and change agent contact should be concentrated on them, to activate their peer networks about an innovation.
2. Change agent aides should be selected from among the "downs," who can contact their homophilous peers about innovations.
3. Groups should be formed among the "downs" to provide them with leadership and social reinforcement in their innovation decision making. Such small groups give the "downs" greater economic, political, and social strength (as in the example of the Bangladesh village cooperatives that adopted irrigation pump wells).

III. *"Ups" Possess Greater Slack Resources for Adopting Innovations Than "Downs."*

"Ups" can usually adopt innovations much more easily than "downs," particularly if these new ideas are expensive and technologically complex, and if they provide economies of scale. What strategies can overcome these gap-widening tendencies?

1. Appropriate innovations for "downs" should be recommended. R&D activities should be directed at the problems of the lower-socioeconomic members of a system to create these innovations.

2. A social organization should be created to allow "downs" to command the resources needed to adopt certain high-cost innovations. An illustration of this strategy of organizing for social change is the village co-ops in Bangladesh that facilitated the adoption of irrigation pump wells by small farmers.

3. A means through which "downs" can participate in the planning and execution of diffusion programs, including setting program priorities as to which innovations will be diffused, should be provided.

4. Special diffusion agencies should be established to work only with "downs," thus enabling change agents to meet the particular needs of the lower socioeconomic audience. If such an agency had existed among the Colombian coffee growers studied by Havens and Flinn (1974), it might have provided agricultural credit to the small farmers so that they could adopt the new coffee varieties.

Wider Gaps Are Not Inevitable

Field experiments by Shingi and Mody (1976) and by Röling and others (1976) suggest Generalization 11-7: *When special efforts are made by a diffusion agency, it is possible to narrow, or at least not to widen, socioeconomic gaps in a social system.*

The Shingi and Mody (1976) field experiment in India evaluated the ceiling effect strategy of providing messages that are redundant or of less interest and/or benefit to "ups" but appropriate to the lower socioeconomic subaudience. Two Indian communication scholars, Prakash M. Shingi and Bella Mody, content-analyzed agricultural television programs before they were broadcast in order to determine the twenty-one main items of information about wheat-growing and potato-raising innovations that they contained. The television programs were designed to provide useful information to smaller farmers in India, but to be redundant with much of the information already possessed by larger farmers.

Shingi and Mody (1976) found that larger-sized farmers with large properties watched only a few of the televised programs before they were "turned off" by viewing agricultural information that they already knew. Farmers with small properties eagerly watched the television series because the information it contained was new to them. All farmers had unlimited access to viewing the programs on a community television set that was provided to each village by the government of India.

Shingi and Mody measured the degree of agricultural knowledge before and after the television programs, in personal interviews. Gaps between "ups" and "downs" were narrowed by the television programs because of the ceiling effect: "By choosing program content that large farmers already understand, television producers can *close rather than widen* the communication effects gap" (emphasis in original). Shingi and Mody concluded that *"The communication effects gap is by no means inevitable.* It can be avoided if appropriate communication strategies are pursued in development efforts" (emphasis in original).

---

*The Digital Divide**

The *digital divide* is the gap that exists between individuals advantaged by the Internet and those individuals relatively disadvantaged by the Internet. A digital divide exists (1) within a nation such as the United States and (2) between European nations and the United States versus the developing nations of Latin America, Africa, and Asia. The numbers of Internet users per thousand population in various areas in 2001, when there were about 450 million Internet users worldwide, were:

North America	479 per 1,000
Western Europe	218 per 1,000
Latin America	21 per 1,000
Asia	17 per 1,000
Middle East/Africa	7 per 1,000
Worldwide	52 per 1,000

These wide gaps in Internet use result from a lack of economic resources, a lack of central-station electricity and telecommunications facilities, and government policies that discourage Internet use. For example, the government of China regulates all Internet traffic, which must pass through a government-controlled portal (this policy may be changing). At present, the considerable informational advantages of Internet access accrue only to certain individuals living in certain nations.

---

*This case illustration is adapted from Rogers (2002a).

In the United States, the digital divide separates individuals of higher and lower socioeconomic status, rural versus urban Americans, older versus younger individuals, and African Americans and Hispanics versus Euro-Americans. For example, a national survey by the National Technical Information Administration (NTIA) of 48,000 Americans in 2000 found that 34 percent of Hispanics and 33 percent of African Americans were using the Internet at home or at work, while the comparable figure for Euro-Americans was 56 percent. The characteristics of Internet users are similar to the characteristics of earlier adopters of most innovations. In order to use the Internet, an individual must have access to a computer (approximately half of U.S. households own a computer) and a telephone (owned by 94 percent of all Americans).

In 2002, about 71 percent of adult Americans were Internet users. Eventually, as the rate of diffusion of the Internet approaches saturation, the digital divide as we know it today will disappear. The inequality in access to Internet-provided information, however, may continue as the present access-divide is replaced by a learning-divide (in which certain individuals lack the skills of computer and/or Internet use), a content-divide (in which less educated individuals may not be able to comprehend the content of Web sites created by highly educated individuals), and other types of divides.

Several strategies can be utilized to bridge the digital divide. Public access to community computer centers such as cybercafés, which provide computer and Internet access, along with coffee and soft drinks, as a commercial service, or telecenters, which typically provide Internet access at no cost to the user. Such public access to the Internet is widespread in developing nations and in poor areas of the United States, where individuals and families cannot afford to buy computers and pay Internet access fees. Much could be done to bridge the digital divide by creating Web sites that are prepared especially for individuals with lower levels of formal education. For example, Web sites should be written at the eighth-grade level, as are newspapers in the United States, to reach the mass audience. However, as mentioned previously, a content analysis of health-related Web sites showed that they were written at a level requiring at least a high school education (Berland et al., 2001). The Internet allows individualized messages about an innovation to be sent to late adopters and laggards. To date, however, this potential for tailoring messages to the "downs" has been utilized only on a very limited scale.

Summary

Consequences are the changes that occur to an individual or to a social system as a result of the adoption or rejection of an innovation. Although obviously important, the consequences of innovations have received inadequate attention by change agents and by diffusion researchers. Consequences have not been studied adequately because (1) change agencies have overemphasized adoption per se, assuming that an innovation's consequences will be positive, (2) the usual survey research methods may be inappropriate for investigating consequences, and (3) consequences are often difficult to measure.

Consequences are classified as (1) desirable versus undesirable, (2) direct versus indirect, and (3) anticipated versus unanticipated. *Desirable consequences* are the functional effects of an innovation for an individual or for a social system. *Undesirable consequences* are the dysfunctional effects of an innovation for an individual or for a social system. Many innovations cause both positive and negative consequences, and it is thus erroneous to assume that the desirable impacts can be achieved without also experiencing undesirable effects. We conclude that the effects of an innovation usually cannot be managed so as to separate the desirable from the undesirable consequences (Generalization 11-1).

Direct consequences are the changes to an individual or a system that occur in immediate response to an innovation. *Indirect consequences* are the changes to an individual or a system that occur as a result of the direct consequences of an innovation. They are the consequences of the consequences of an innovation.

Anticipated consequences are changes due to an innovation that are recognized and intended by the members of a system. *Unanticipated consequences* are changes due to an innovation that are neither intended nor recognized by the members of a system.

The undesirable, indirect, and unanticipated consequences of an innovation usually go together, as do the desirable, direct, and anticipated consequences (Generalization 11-2). An illustration is provided by the introduction of the steel ax among Australian aborigines, which caused many undesirable, indirect, and unanticipated consequences, including breakdown of the family structure, the emergence of prostitution, and misuse of the innovation itself. The case of the steel ax illustrates three intrinsic elements of an innovation: (1) *form*, the directly observable physical appearance and substance of an innovation, (2) *function*, the contribution made by the innovation to the way of life of individuals or to the social system, and (3) *meaning,* the subjective and frequently subconscious perception of the innovation by members of the social system. Change agents more easily anticipate the form and function of an innovation for their clients than its meaning (Generalization 11-3).

Stable equilibrium occurs when almost no change is occurring in the structure or functioning of a social system. *Dynamic equilibrium* occurs when the rate of change in a social system is commensurate with the system's ability to cope with it. *Disequilibrium* occurs when the rate of change is too rapid to permit the system to adjust. Change agents generally wish to achieve a rate of change that leads to dynamic equilibrium, and to avoid disequilibrium.

One goal of diffusion programs is to raise the level of Good in a system. A second dimension of consequences is whether the *distribution* of Good among the members of a system becomes more or less equal. The consequences of the diffusion of innovations usually widen the socioeconomic gap between the earlier and later adopting categories in a system (Generalization 11-4). Further, the consequences of the diffusion of innovations usually widen the socioeconomic gap between the audience segments previously high and low in socioeconomic status (Generalization 11-5).

A system's social structure partly determines the equality versus the inequality of an innovation's consequences (Generalization 11-6). When a system's structure is already very unequal, the consequences of an innovation (especially if it is a relatively high-cost innovation) will lead to even greater inequality in the form of wider socioeconomic gaps.

What strategies could be followed in order to narrow gaps? The answer depends on three main reasons why socioeconomic gaps ordinarily widen as a consequence of diffusion: (1) "ups" have greater access to information that creates awareness of innovations; (2) they have greater access to innovation-evaluation information from peers; and (3) "ups" possess greater slack resources for adopting innovations than do "downs." When special efforts are made by a diffusion agency, it is possible to narrow, or at least not to widen, socioeconomic gaps in a social system (Generalization 11-7). In other words, widening gaps are not inevitable.

The *digital divide* is the gap that exists between individuals advantaged by the Internet and those individuals relatively disadvantaged by the Internet. This inequality exists both within the United States and between North America and Europe versus developing nations. Efforts to bridge the digital divide, such as providing public access to computers and the Internet in cybercafés and telecenters, are under way.

GLOSSARY

ADOPTER CATEGORIES Classifications of the members of a social system on the basis of their innovativeness.

ADOPTION A decision to make full use of an innovation as the best course of action available.

AIDE A less than fully professional change agent who intensively contacts clients to influence their innovation-decisions.

AUTHORITY INNOVATION-DECISION Choice to adopt or reject an innovation that is made by a relatively few individuals in a system who possess power, status, or technical expertise.

AWARENESS-KNOWLEDGE Information that an innovation exists.

CHAMPION A charismatic individual who throws his or her weight behind an innovation, thus overcoming indifference or resistance that the new idea may provoke in an organization.

CHANGE AGENT An individual who influences clients' innovation-decisions in a direction deemed desirable by a change agency.

COLLECTIVE INNOVATION-DECISION Choice to adopt or reject an innovation that is made by consensus of the members of a system.

COMMERCIALIZATION The production, manufacturing, packaging, marketing, and distribution of a product that embodies an innovation.

COMMUNICATION CAMPAIGN A campaign to generate specific effects, on the part of a relatively large number of individuals, within a specified period of time, and through an organized set of communication activities.

COMPATIBILITY The degree to which an innovation is perceived as being consistent with the existing values, past experiences, and needs of potential adopters.

COMPETENCE CREDIBILITY The degree to which a communication source or channel is perceived as knowledgeable or expert.

COMPLEXITY The degree to which an innovation is perceived as difficult to understand and use.

CONFIRMATION That which occurs when an individual seeks reinforcement of an innovation-decision that has already been made but may reverse this decision if exposed to conflicting messages about the innovation.

CONSEQUENCE A change that occurs to an individual or social system as a result of the adoption or rejection of an innovation.

CONTINGENT INNOVATION-DECISION Choice to adopt or reject that can be made only after a prior innovation-decision.

COSMOPOLITENESS The degree to which an individual is oriented outside of a social system.

CRITICAL MASS The point at which enough individuals in a system have adopted an innovation such that the innovation's further rate of adoption becomes self-sustaining.

DECISION That which occurs when an individual engages in activities that lead to a choice to adopt or reject an innovation.

DEVELOPMENT A widely participatory process of social change in a society intended to bring about both social and material advancement (including greater equality, freedom, and other valued qualities) for the majority of people through their gaining greater control over their environment.

DIGITAL DIVIDE The gap that exists between individuals advantaged by the Internet and those individuals relatively disadvantaged by the Internet.

DIFFUSION The process in which an innovation is communicated through certain channels over time among the members of a social system.

DISCONTINUANCE A decision to reject an innovation after it has previously been adopted.

HETEROPHILY The degree to which two or more individuals who interact are different in certain attributes.

HOMOPHILY The degree to which two or more individuals who interact are similar in certain attributes.

HOW-TO KNOWLEDGE The information necessary to use an innovation properly.

IMPLEMENTATION That which occurs when an individual puts an innovation into use.

INDIVIDUAL-BLAME The tendency to hold an individual responsible for his or her problems, rather than the system of which the individual is a part.

INFORMATION A difference in matter-energy that affects uncertainty in a situation where a choice among various alternatives exists.

INNOVATION An idea, practice, or object that is perceived as new by an individual or other unit of adoption.

INNOVATION-DECISION PROCESS The process through which an individual (or other decision-making unit) passes from first knowledge of an innovation to forming an attitude toward the innovation, to a decision to adopt or reject, to implementation and use of the new idea, and to confirmation of this decision.

INNOVATION-DEVELOPMENT PROCESS All the decisions, activities, and their impacts that occur from recognition of a need or problem, through research, development, and commercialization of an innovation, through diffusion and adoption of the innovation by users, to its consequences.

INNOVATIVENESS The degree to which an individual or other unit of adoption is relatively earlier in adopting new ideas than the other members of a system.

INVENTION The process by which a new idea is discovered or created.

KNOWLEDGE That which occurs when an individual learns of the innovation's existence and gains some understanding of how it functions.

OBSERVABILITY The degree to which the results of an innovation are visible to others.

OPINION LEADERSHIP The degree to which an individual is able to influence other individuals' attitudes or overt behavior informally in a desired way with relative frequency.

OPTIONAL INNOVATION-DECISION Choices to adopt or reject an innovation that is made by an individual independent of the decisions by other members of the system.

ORGANIZATION A stable system of individuals who work together to achieve common goals through a hierarchy of ranks and a division of labor.

PERSUASION That which takes place when an individual forms a favorable or unfavorable attitude toward an innovation.

PREVENTIVE INNOVATION An idea that an individual adopts in order to lower the probability that some future unwanted event will occur.

PRINCIPLES-KNOWLEDGE Information dealing with the functioning principles underlying how an innovation works.

PRO-INNOVATION BIAS The implication in diffusion research that an innovation should be diffused and adopted by all members of a social system, that it should be diffused more rapidly, and that the innovation should be neither re-invented nor rejected.

RATE OF ADOPTION The relative speed with which an innovation is adopted by members of a social system.

REJECTION A decision not to adopt an innovation.

RE-INVENTION The degree to which an innovation is changed or modified by a user in the process of its adoption and implementation.

RELATIVE ADVANTAGE The degree to which an innovation is perceived as better than the idea it supercedes.

RESEARCH TRADITION A series of investigations on a similar topic in which successive studies are influenced by preceding inquiries.

SAFETY CREDIBILITY The degree to which a communication source or channel is perceived as trustworthy.

SOCIAL CHANGE The process by which alteration occurs in the structure and function of a social system.

SOCIAL SYSTEM A set of interrelated units involved in joint problem solving to accomplish a common goal.

SUSTAINABILITY The degree to which an innovation is continued over time after a diffusion program ends.

TARGETING The process of customizing the design and delivery of a communication program on the basis of the characteristics of an intended audience segment.

THRESHOLD The number of other individuals who must be engaged in an activity before a given individual will join that activity.

TRIALABILITY The degree to which an innovation may be experimented with on a limited basis.

UNCERTAINTY The degree to which a number of alternatives are perceived with respect to the occurrence of an event and the relative probabilities of these alternatives.

BIBLIOGRAPHY

This bibliography includes (1) all of the publications cited in the text and (2) a number of other diffusion publications, especially those that did not appear in my fourth edition, plus several of the classics. This bibliography does not include all of the approximately 5,200+ diffusion publications (75 percent empirical and 25 percent nonempirical) currently available, as such a bibliography would itself constitute a large book. Most published work on the diffusion of innovations, however, is included either in this bibliography or in my four previous books on diffusion (Rogers, 1962, pp. 317–358; Rogers with Shoemaker, 1971, pp. 387–460; Rogers, 1983, pp. 414–439; Rogers, 1995, pp. 443–501). It is becoming increasingly difficult to locate every diffusion publication, due to the proliferating number of disciplines conducting diffusion research and to the increasing number of journals and other publication outlets in which diffusion research appears. Nondiffusion publications that are cited in this book are identified in this bibliography by the fact that they do not end with letters indicating a diffusion research tradition.

Each of the diffusion publications that follows is coded (1) as to the diffusion research tradition of the author, based on his or her institutional affiliation at the time of publication (see the list of codes below), and (2) as to whether the publication is empirical (E) or nonempirical (N). Nonempirical diffusion publications include bibliographies, theoretical writings, and summaries of diffusion findings reported in other, empirical publications.

DIFFUSION TRADITION	CODE FOR TRADITION
Anthropology	A
Agricultural economics	AE
Communication	C
Education	E
Early sociology	ES
Geography	G
General economics	GE
General sociology	GS
Industrial engineering	I
Marketing and management	MR
Public health and medical sociology	PH
Psychology	P
Public administration and political science	PS
Rural sociology	RS
Statistics	S
Other and unknown	O

Abbate, Janet (2001) "Government, Business, and the Making of the Internet." *Business History Review* 75:147–176. O(E)

Abbott, Jason P. (2001) "Democracy@internet.asia? The Challenges to the Emancipatory Potential of the Net: Lessons from China and Malaysia." *Third World Quarterly* 22(1):99–114. O(E)

Abdulla, Rasha A. (2003) "Entertainment-Education in the Middle East: Lessons from the Egyptian Oral Rehydration Therapy Campaign." In Arvind Singhal, Michael J. Cody, Everett M. Rogers, and Miguel Sabido. *Entertainment-Education Worldwide: History, Research, and Practice.* Mahwah, N.J.: Lawrence Erlbaum Associates. C(E)

Aberg, Leif, Greg Castillo, and Jay Goldberg (1976) "Restructuring of Transportation Patterns: A Study Centered About the Santa Monica Preferred

(Diamond) Lane." Unpublished paper, Annenberg School for Communication, University of Southern California, Los Angeles. C(E)

Abetti, Pier A. (1997) "The Birth and Growth of Toshiba's Laptop and Notebook Computers: A Case Study in Japanese Corporate Venturing." *Journal of Business Venturing* 12:507–529. MR(E)

Aboud, Abdillahi, Andrew J. Sofrank, and Serigne Ndiaye (1996) "The Effects of Gender on Adoption of Conservation Practices by Heads of Farm Households in Kenya." *Society and Natural Resources* 9:447–463. RS(E)

Abrahamson, Eric, and Lori Rosenkopf (1997) "Social Network Effects on the Extent of Innovation Diffusion: A Computer Simulation." *Organization Science* 8(3):289–309. MR(N)

Achilladelis, B., et al. (1971) *Project Sappho: A Study of Success and Failure in Innovation.* Report, Science Policy Research Unit, University of Sussex, Brighton, England. O(E)

Agarwal, Rita, and Joseph Prasad (1997) "The Role of Innovation Characteristics and Perceived Voluntariness in the Adoption of Information Technologies." *Decision Sciences* 28(3):557–582. MR(E)

Ahuja, M. K., and Kathleen M. Carley (1998) "Network Structure in Virtual Organizations," *Organizational Science* 10(6):704–713. MR(E)

Akinola, Amos A. (1986) "An Application of the Bass Model in the Analysis of Diffusion of Cocoa-Spraying Among Nigerian Cocoa Farmers." *Journal of Agricultural Economics* 37(3):395–404. AE(E)

Alange, Sverker, Staffan Jacobsson, and Annika Jarnehammar (1998) "Some Aspects of an Analytical Framework for Studying the Diffusion of Organizational Innovations." *Technology Analysis & Strategic Management* 10(1):3–21. MR(E)

Allen, David (1983) "New Telecommunication Services: Network Externalities and Critical Mass." *Telecommunication Policy* 12(3):257–271. GE(E)

Allen, Harley Earl (1956) *The Diffusion of Educational Practices in the Metropolitan School Study Council.* Ph.D. thesis, Teachers College, Columbia University, New York. E(E)

Altman, Lawrence (1997, November 4) "AIDS Surge Is Forecast in China, India, and Eastern Europe." *The New York Times,* p. A10.

Antonides, Gerit, H. Bas Amesz, and Ivo C. Hulscher (1999) "Adoption of Payment Systems in Ten Countries: A Case Study of Diffusion of Innovations." *European Journal of Marketing* 33:1123–1135. MR(E)

Arensberg, Conrad M., and Arthur H. Niehoff (1964) *Introducing Social Change.* Chicago: Aldine. A(N)

Armstrong, David, and Jerry Guidera (March 1, 2002) "Lobbying Campaign Could Determine Fate of a Hyped Scooter." *The Wall Street Journal,* A1, A6.

Armstrong, J. Scott, and J. Thomas Yokum (2001) "Potential Diffusion of Expert Systems in Forecasting." *Technological Forecasting and Social Change* 67:93–103. MR(E)

Arquette, Toby J. (1999) "Diffusion of Innovative Drug Treatments: An Experimental Analysis of Communication Channel Typology and the Effects of Clustering Innovations." Unpublished paper, Northwestern University, Evanston, Ill. C(E)

Asch, Susan M., and Charles Upton Lowe (1984) "The Consensus Development Program: Theory, Process, and Critique." *Knowledge* 5(3):369–385. GS(N)

Ashby, Jacquiline A., Jorge Alonso Beltrán, Maria del Pilar Guerrero, and Héctor Fabio Ramos (1996) "Improving the Acceptability to Farmers of Soil Conservation Practices." *Journal of Soil and Water Conservation* 51:309–312. RS(E)

Astebro, T. (1995) "The Effect of Management and Social Interaction on the Intra-Firm Diffusion of Electronic Mail Systems." *IEEE Transactions on Engineering Management* 42(4):319–331. MR(E)

Atkin, David J., Leo W. Jeffres, and Kimberly A. Neuendorf (1998) "Understanding Internet Adoption as Telecommunications Behavior." *Journal of Broadcasting & Electronic Media* 42(4):475–494. C(E)

Atkin, David J., and Robert LaRose (1994) "A Meta-Analysis of the Information Services Adoption Literature." *Advances in Telematics* 2:91–110. C(E)

Auwal, Mohammed A., and Arvind Singhal (1992) "The Diffusion of Grameen Bank in Bangladesh." *Knowledge* 14(1):7–28. C(E)

Ayres, Jeffrey M. (1999) "From the *Streets* to the Internet: The Cyber-Diffusion of Contention." *The Annals of the American Academy of Political Sciences* 566:132–143. PS(N)

Bach, Betsy Wackernagel (1989) "The Effect of Multiplex Relationships upon Innovation Adoption: A Reconsideration of Rogers' Model." *Communication Monographs* 56:133–149. C(E)

Backer, Thomas E. (2000) *Finding the Balance: Program Fidelity and Adaptation in Substance Abuse Prevention.* Report, Center for Substance Abuse Prevention, Washington, D.C. P(E)

Backer, Thomas E., and Everett M. Rogers (1998) "Diffusion of Innovations Theory and Worksite AIDS Programs." *Journal of Health Communication* 3(1):17–28. P(E)

Baer, Wally S., B. Johnson, and S. Merrow (1977) "Government-Sponsored Demonstrations of New Technologies." *Science* 196:950–957. O(E)

Bagehot, Walter (1873) *Physics and Politics.* New York: Appleton-Century.

Bailey, Norman T. J. (1957/1975) *The Mathematical Theory of Infectious Diseases and Its Applications.* London: Charles Griffin. PH(N)

Bandura, Albert (1977) *Social Learning Theory*. Englewood Cliffs, N.J.: Prentice-Hall.

Bandura, Albert (1986) *Social Foundations of Thought and Action*. Englewood Cliffs, N.J.: Prentice-Hall.

Bandura, Albert (1997) *Self-Efficacy: The Exercise of Control*. New York: Freeman.

Bardini, Thierry (1994) "A Translation Analysis of the Green Revolution in Bali." *Science, Technology, and Human Values* 19(2):152–168. C(E)

Bardini, Thierry (2000) *Bootstrapping: Douglas Engelbart, Coevolution, and the Origins of Personal Computing*. Stanford, Calif.: Stanford University Press.

Barton, Allen (1968) "Bringing Society Back In: Survey Research and Macro-Methodology." *American Behavioral Scientist* 12:1–9.

Bartosch, William J., and Gregory C. Pope (1999) "Local Restaurant Smoking Policy Enactment in Massachusetts." *Journal of Public Health Management Practice* 5(1):63–73. PS(E)

Bass, Frank M. (1969) "A New Product Growth Model for Consumer Durables." *Management Science* 13(5):215–227. MR(E)

Bass, Frank M., Trichy Krishnan, and Dipak C. Jain (1994) "Why the Bass Model Fits Without Decision Variables." *Marketing Science* 13:203–223. MR(E)

Bass, Frank M., Dipak C. Jain, and Trichy Krishnan (2000) "Modeling the Marketing-Mix Influence in New-Product Diffusion." In Vijay Mahajan, Eitan Muller, and Yoram Wind, eds., *New-Product Diffusion Models*. Dordrecht, Netherlands: Kluver Academic, 99–122. MR(E)

Battelle-Columbus Laboratories (1976) *Report of the President's Biomedical Research Panel: Analysis of Selected Biomedical Research Programs: Case Histories*. Report to the U.S. Public Health Service, Battelle-Columbus Laboratories, Columbus, Ohio. O(E)

Bayus, Barry L. (1994) "Are Product Life Cycles Really Getting Shorter?" *Journal of Product Innovation Management* 11(4):300–308. MR(E)

Bayus, Barry L., and A. Rao (1997) "Too Little and Too Early: Introduction Timing and New-Product Performance in the Personal Digital Assistant Industry." *Journal of Marketing Research* 34:50–63. MR(E)

Bayus, Barry L., Namwoon Kim, and Allan D. Shocker (2000) "Growth Models for Multiproduct Interactions: Current Status and New Directions." In Vijay Mahajan, Eitan Muller, and Yoram Wind, eds., *New-Product Diffusion Models*. Dordrecht, Netherlands, Kluver Academic, 141–163. MR(E)

Beal, George M., and Everett M. Rogers (1960) *The Adoption of Two Farm Practices in a Central Iowa Community*. Special Report 26, Agricultural and Home Economics Experiment Station, Ames, Iowa. RS(E)

Beal, George M., Everett M. Rogers, and Joe M. Bohlen (1957) "Validity of the Concept of Stages in the Adoption Process." *Rural Sociology* 22(2):166–168. RS(E)

Becker, Marshal H. (1970) "Factors Affecting Diffusion of Innovations Among Health Professionals." *American Journal of Public Health* 60:294–305. PH(E)

Becker, Marshall H. (1970b) "Sociometric Location and Innovativeness: Reformulation and Extension of the Diffusion Model." *American Sociological Review* 35:262–282. PH(E)

Belasco, David Berton (1989) "Adoption of Community Water Systems: An Area Study in Three Villages in Muhafzat Kofr-Shaykh, Egypt." Ph.D. diss., University of Denver. PS(E)

Bennett, Colin J. (1997) "Understanding Ripple Effects: The Cross-National Adoption of Policy Instruments for Bureaucratic Accountability." *Governance* 10:213–233. PS(E)

Berelson, Bernard, and Ronald Freedman (1964) "A Study in Fertility Control." *Scientific American* 210(5):29–37. PH(E)

Berland, Gretchen K., Marc N. Elliott, Leo S. Moreles, Jeffrey I. Algazy, Richard L. Kravitz, Michael S. Broder, David E. Knouse, Jorge A. Munoz, Juan-Antonio Puyol, Marielene Lara, Katherine E. Watkins, Hannah Yang, and Elizabeth A. McGlynn (2001) "Health Information on the Internet: Accessability, Quality, and Readability in English and Spanish." *JAMA* 285:2612–2621.

Berman, Paul, and Milbrey W. McLaughlin (1974) *Federal Programs Supporting Educational Change.* Vol. 1: *Model of Educational Change.* Report, Rand Corporation, Santa Monica, Calif. E(E)

Berman, Paul, and Milbrey W. McLaughlin (1975) *Federal Programs Supporting Educational Change.* Vol. 4: *The Findings in Review.* Report, Rand Corporation, Santa Monica, Calif. E(E)

Berman, Paul, and Milbrey W. McLaughlin (1978) *Federal Programs Supporting Educational Change.* Vol. 8: *Implementing and Sustaining Innovations.* Report, Rand Corporation, Santa Monica, Calif. E(E)

Berman, Paul, and Edward W. Pauly (1975) *Federal Programs Supporting Educational Change.* Vol. 2: *Factors Affecting Change Agents Projects.* Report, Rand Corporation, Santa Monica, Calif. E(E)

Berman, Paul, et al. (1975) *Federal Programs Supporting Educational Change.* Vol. 5: *Executive Summary.* Report, Rand Corporation, Santa Monica, Calif. E(E)

Berman, Paul, et al. (1977) *Federal Programs Supporting Educational Change.* Vol. 7: *Factors Affecting Implementation and Continuation.* Report, Rand Corporation, Santa Monica, Calif. E(E)

Berry, Frances Stokes (1994) "Sizing Up State Policy Innovation Research." *Policy Studies Journal* 22:442–456. PS(N)

Berry, Frances Stokes, and William D. Berry (1990) "State Lottery Adoptions as Policy Innovations: An Event History Analysis." *American Political Science Review* 84:395–415. PS(E)

Berry, Frances Stokes, and Geraldo Flowers (1999) "Public Entrepreneurs in the Policy Process: Performance-Based Budgeting Reform in Florida." *Journal of Public Budgeting, Accounting and Financial Management* 11(4):578–617. PS(E)

Bijker, W. E. (1999) *Of Bicycles, Bakelites, and Bulbs: Toward a Theory of Sociotechnical Change,* 3rd ed. Cambridge, Mass.: MIT Press. MR(E)

Bikhchandan, Sushil, David Hirschleifer, and Juo Welch (1998) "Learning from the Behavior of Others: Conformity, Fads, and Informational Cascades." *Journal of Economic Perspectives* 12(3):151–170. GE(E)

Bingham, Richard D., and John P. Frendreis (1978, May) "Innovation Characteristics and the Adoption of Zero-Based Budgeting: Agreement and Conflict in City Administration." Paper presented at the annual meeting of the Midwest Political Science Association, Chicago. PS(E)

Bishop, Rowland, and C. Milton Coughenour (1964) *Discontinuance of Farm Innovations.* Mimeo Bulletin AE 361, Department of Agricultural Economics and Rural Sociology, Ohio State University, Columbus. RS(E)

Blakely, Craig C., Jeffrey P. Mayer, Rand G. Gottschalk, Neal Schmitt, William S. Davidson, D. B. Roitman, and J. G. Emshoff (1987) "The Fidelity-Adaptation Debate: Implications for the Implementation of Public Sector Social Programs." *American Journal of Community Psychology* 15(3):253–268. P(E)

Boczkowski, Pablo J. (1999) "Mutual Shaping of Users and Technology in a National Virtual Community." *Journal of Communication* 49(2):86–108. C(E)

Bohlen, Joe M., C. Milton Coughenour, Herbert F. Lionberger, Edwin O. Moe, and Everett M. Rogers (1958) *Adopters of New Farm Ideas.* North Central Regional Extension Publication 13, Michigan State University, East Lansing, Mich. RS(N)

Bond, Katherine C., Thomas W. Valente, and Carl Kendall (1999) "Social Network Influences on Reproductive Health Behaviors in Urban Northern Thailand." *Social Science and Medicine* 49:1599–1614. PH(E)

Bongaarts, John, and Susan Cotts Watkins (1996) "Social Interactions and Contemporary Fertility Transitions." *Population and Development Review* 22(4):639–682. GS(E)

Bordenave, Juan Diaz (1976) "Communication of Agricultural Innovations in Latin America: The Need for New Models." *Communication Research* 3(2):135–154. C(N)

Bottomley, Paul A., and Robert Fildes (1998) "The Role of Prices in Models of Innovation Diffusion." *Journal of Forecasting* 17(7):539–555. MR(E)

Borich, Timothy O., and Peter F. Korsching (1990) "Community Image and Community Innovativeness." *Journal of the Community Development Society* 21(1):1–18. RS(E)

Bose, Santi Priya (1964) "The Diffusion of a Farm Practice in Indian Villages." *Rural Sociology* 29:53–66. RS(E)

Bower, Joseph L., and Clayton M. Christiansen (1995) "Disruptive Technologies: Catching the Wave." *Harvard Business Review* 73:43–53. MR(E)

Bowers, Raymond V. (1937) "The Direction of Intra-Societal Diffusion." *American Sociological Review* 2:826–836. ES(E)

Bowers, Raymond V. (1938) "Differential Intensity of Intra-Societal Diffusion." *American Sociological Review* 3:21–31. ES(E)

Braithwaite, John (1994) "A Sociology of Modelling and the Politics of Empowerment." *British Journal of Sociology* 45(3):445–479. GS(E)

Brandner, Lowell, and Murray A. Straus (1959) "Convergence Versus Profitability in the Diffusion of Hybrid Sorghum." *Rural Sociology* 24:381–383. RS(E)

Braun, Norman (1995) "Individual Thresholds and Social Diffusion." *Rationality and Society* 7:167–182. O(E)

Brewer, M. (1985) "Experimental Research and Social Policy: Must It Be Rigor Versus Relevance?" *Journal of Social Issues* 41(4):159–176.

Broadhead, R. S., D. D. Hechathorn, D. L. Weaklin, D. L. Anthony, H. Madray, R. J. Mills, and J. Hughes (1998) "Harnessing Peer Networks as an Instrument for AIDS Prevention: Results from a Peer-Driven Intervention." *Public Health Reports* 113(S1):42–57. PH(E)

Brown, Lawrence A. (1981) *Innovation Diffusion: A New Perspective.* New York: Methuen. G(N)

Brown, William J., Michael D. Basil, and M. C. Bocarner (1998, June) "Responding to the Death of Princess Diana: Audience Involvement with an International Celebrity." Paper presented at the annual meeting of the International Communication Association, Jerusalem. C(E)

Brownson, Ross C., and Edwardo J. Simoes (1999) "Measuring the Impact of Prevention Research on Public Health Practice." *American Journal of Preventive Medicine* 16(35):72–79. PH(E)

Bryant, H. (1996) "Breast Cancer Screening in Canada: Climbing the Diffusion Curve." *Canadian Journal of Public Health* 87(suppl. 2):S60–S62. PH(E)

Bucklin, Louis P., and Sanjit Sengupta (1993) "The Co-Diffusion of Complementary Innovations: Supermarket Scanners and UPC Symbols." *Journal of Product Innovation Management* 10:148–160. MR(E)

Buller, David B., W. Gill Woodall, Everett M. Rogers, Patricia Burris-Woodall, Donald Zimmerman, Michael Slater, Judith Pepper, K. Bartlett, Joan Hines, E. Unger, Barbara Hau, and Michelle M. LeBlanc (2001) "Formative Research Activities to Provide Web-Based Nutrition Information to Adults in the Upper Rio Grande Valley." *Family and Community Health* 24(3):1–12. C(E)

Burt, Ronald S. (1980) "Innovation as a Structural Interest: Rethinking the Impact of Network Position on Innovation Adoption." *Social Networks* 2:327–355. GS(N)

Burt, Ronald S. (1987) "Social Contagion and Innovation: Cohesion Versus Structural Equivalence." *American Journal of Sociology* 92:1287–1335. GS(E)

Burt, Ronald S. (1999) "The Social Capital of Opinion Leaders." *The Annals of the American Academy of Political Sciences* 566:37–54. GS(E)

Burt, Ronald S. (2000) "Decay Functions." *Social Networks* 22:1–28. GS(E)

Burt, Ronald S., and Gregory A. Janicik (1996) "Social Contagion and Social Structure." In Dawn Jacobucci, ed., *Networks in Marketing*. Thousand Oaks, Calif.: Sage. GS(E)

Cancian, Frank (1979) *The Innovator's Situation: Upper-Middle-Class Conservatism in Agricultural Communities*. Stanford, Calif.: Stanford University Press. A(E)

Caplan, Nathan, and Stephen D. Nelson (1973) "On Being Useful: The Nature and Consequences of Psychological Research on Social Problems." *American Psychologist* 28:199–211.

Carlson, Richard O. (1965) *Adoption of Educational Innovations*. Center for the Advanced Study of Educational Administration, University of Oregon, Eugene. E(E)

Carter, Anthony T. (2001) "Social Processes and Fertility Control." In John Casterline, ed., *Diffusion Processes and Fertility Transition*. Washington, D.C.: National Academy Press, 139–178. A(N)

Carter, Thomas (1994) *The Process of Change: Tools for the Change Agent*. Report, National Dairy Development Board, Anand, India. O(N)

Casterline, John (2001) "Diffusion Processes and Fertility Transition: Introduction." In John Casterline, ed., *Diffusion Processes and Fertility Transition*. Washington, D.C.: National Academy Press, 1–38. O(N)

Casterline, John, ed. (2001) *Diffusion Processes and Fertility Transition*. Washington, D.C.: National Academy Press. O(N)

Castro, Felipe G., John Elder, Kathyrn Coe, Helen M. Tafoya-Barraza, Santiago Moratto, Nadia Campbell, and Greg Talavera (1995) "Mobilizing Churches for Health Promotion in Latino Churches: *Compañeros en la Salud*." *Journal of the National Cancer Institute Monographs* 18:127–135. P(E)

Celentano, David C., Katherine C. Bond, Cynthia M. Lyles, Sakol Eiumtrakul, Vivian F.-L. Go, Chris Beyrer, Chianarong na Chiangmai, Kenrad E. Nelson, Chirasak Khamboonruang, and Chayan Vaddhanaphuti (2000) "Preventive Intervention to Reduce Sexually Transmitted Infections: A Field Trial in the Royal Thai Army." *Archives of Internal Medicine* 160:535–540. PH(E)

Cha, Jaemin (2002) "The Internet and Perceived Risk: Purchases of Online Airline Tickets." Unpublished paper, Michigan State University, East Lansing. C(E)

Charters, W. W., Jr., and Roland S. Pellegrin (1972) "Barriers to the Innovation Process: Four Case Studies of Differentiated Staffing." *Educational Quarterly* 9:3–4. E(E)

Chatterjee, Rabikar, Jehoshua Eliashberg, and Vithala R. Rao (2000) "Dynamic Models Incorporating Competition." In Vijay Mahajan, Eitan Muller, and Yoram Wind, eds., *New-Product Diffusion Models.* Dordrecht, Netherlands: Kluver Academic, 165–205. MR(E)

Chaves, Mark (1996) "Ordaining Women: The Diffusion of an Organizational Innovation." *American Journal of Sociology* 101:840–877. GS(E)

Christiansen, Clayton M. (1992) "Explaining the Limits of the Technology S-Curve. Part I: Component Technologies." *Production and Operations Management* 1(4):334–357. MR(E)

Christiansen, Clayton M. (1997) *The Innovator's Dilemma: When New Technologies Cause Great Firms to Fail.* Boston: Harvard Business School Press. MR(E)

Clark, G. (1984) *Innovation Diffusion: Contemporary Geographical Approaches.* Norwich, Conn.: Geo Books. G(E)

Clark, Judy, and Jonathan Murdoch (1997) "Local Knowledge and the Precarious Extension of Scientific Networks: A Reflection on Three Case Studies." *Sociologia Ruralis* 37(1):38–60. RS(E)

Clarke, Hillary, Michael P. Wilson, Michael Cummings, and Andrew Hyland (1999) "The Campaign to Enact New York City's Smoke-Free Air Act." *Journal of Public Health Management Practice* 5:1–13. PS (E)

Cleland, John (2001) "Potatoes and Pills: An Overview of Innovation/Diffusion Contributions to Explanations of Fertility Decline." In John Casterline, ed., *Diffusion Processes and Fertility Transition.* Washington, D.C.: National Academy Press, 39–65. O(N)

Cliff, A. D., P. Haggett, J. K. Ord, and G. R. Versey (1981) *Spatial Diffusion: An Historical Geography of Epidemics in an Island Community.* New York: Cambridge University Press. G(E)

Cohen, Morris A., Teck H. Ho, and Hirofumi Matsuo (2000) "Operations Planning in the Presence of Innovation-Diffusion Dynamics." In Vijay Mahajan, Eitan Muller, and Yoram Wind, eds., *New-Product Diffusion Models.* Dordrecht, Netherlands: Kluver Academic, 237–259. MR(E)

Coleman, James S., Elihu Katz, and Herbert Menzel (1957) "The Diffusion of an Innovation Among Physicians." *Sociometry* 20:253–270. PH(E)

Coleman, James S., Elihu Katz, and Herbert Menzel (1959) "Social Processes in Physicians' Adoption of a New Drug." *Journal of Chronic Diseases* 9:1–19. PH(E)

Coleman, James S., Elihu Katz, and Herbert Menzel (1966) *Medical Innovation: A Diffusion Study.* New York: Bobbs-Merrill. PH(E)

Comroe, Julius H., Jr. (1977) *Retrosprectoscope: Insights into Medical Discovery.* Menlo Park, Calif.: Von Gehr Press.

Conell, Carol, and Samuel Cohn (1995) "Learning from Other People's Actions: Environmental Variation and Diffusion of French Coal Mining Strikes, 1890–1935." *American Journal of Sociology* 101(2):366–403. GS(E)

Cool, Karel O., Ingemar Dierickx, and Gabriel Szulanski (1997) "Diffusion of Innovations within Organizations: Electronic Switching in the Bell System, 1971–1982." *Organization Science* 8(5):543–561. MR(E)

Cooper, Alvin, Corelia R. Scherer, Sylvain C. Boies, and Barry L. Gordon (1999) "Sexuality on the Internet: From Sexual Exploitation to Pathological Experience." *Professional Psychology: Research and Practice* 30(2):154–164. P(E)

Cooper, R., and Robert Zmud (1990) "Information Technology Implementation Research: A Technological Diffusion Approach." *Management Science* 36(2):123–139. MR(E)

Copp, James H., Maurice L. Sill, and Emory J. Brown (1958) "The Function of Information Sources in the Farm Practice Adoption Process." *Rural Sociology* 23:146–157. RS(E)

Coughenour, C. Milton, and Shankariah Chamala (2000) *Conservation Tillage and Cropping Innovations: Constructing the New Culture of Agriculture.* Ames, Iowa: Iowa State University Press. RS(E)

Cowan, Ruth Schwartz (1985) "How the Refrigerator Got Its Hum." In Donald Mackenzie and Judy Wajeman, eds., *The Social Shaping of Technology: How The Refrigerator Got Its Hum.* Philadelphia: Open University Press, 202–218. O(E)

Cramer, J. M., and F. A. Reijenga (1999) "The Role of Innovators in the Introduction of Preventive Policy in Local Governments." *Journal of Cleaner Production* 7:263–269. AE(E)

Crane, Diana (1972) *Invisible Colleges.* Chicago: University of Chicago Press. GS(E)

Crane, Diana (1999) "Diffusion Models and Fashion: A Reassessment." *The Annals* 566:13–24. GS(N)

Crystal, S., U. Sambamoorthi, and C. Menzel (1998) "The Diffusion of Innovations in AIDS Treatment: Zidovudine Use in Two New Jersey Cohorts." *Health Services Research* 23:311–321. PH(E)

Cunningham, John A., Garth W. Martin, Leslie Coates, Marilyn A. Herie, Bonnie J. Turner, and Joanne Cordingley (2000) "Disseminating a Treatment Program to Outpatient Addiction Treatment Agencies in Ontario." *Science Communication* 22(2):154–172. PH(E)

Cunningham-Sabo, Leslie D. (2000) "Nutrition Education for Navajo Elders: Use of Diffusion of Innovation Attributes." Ph.D. diss., University of New Mexico, Albuquerque. E(E)

Curry, Barbara K. (1992) *Instituting Enduring Innovations: Achieving Continuity of Change in Higher Education.* ASHE/ERIC Higher Education Report 7, School of Education and Human Development, George Washington University, Washington, D.C. E(E)

Danaher, P., B. Hardie, and William Putsis (2000) "Marketing Mix Variables and the Diffusion of Successive Generations of Technological Innovations." *Journal of Marketing Research* 37:60–73. MR(E)

D'Aunno, Thomas, Thomas E. Vaughan, and Peter McElroy (1999) "An Institutional Analysis of HIV Prevention Efforts by the Nation's Outpatient Drug Abuse Treatment Units." *Journal of Health and Social Behavior* 40:175–192. GS(E)

David, Paul A. (1986) "Clio and the Economy of QWERTY." *American Economic Review* 75(2):332–337. GE(E)

David, Soniia (1998) "Intra-Household Processes and the Adoption of Hedgerow Cropping." *Agriculture and Human Values* 15:31–42. RS(E)

Day, Diana L. (1994) "Raising Radicals: Different Processes for Championing Innovative Corporate Ventures." *Organization Science* 6:111–119. MR(E)

Dearing, James W. (1993) "Rethinking Technology Transfer." *International Journal of Technology Management* 8:1–8. C(N)

Dearing, James W. (1997) "Interorganizational Diffusion: Integrated Demonstrations and the U.S. Department of Energy." In Beverly Davenport Sypher, ed., *Case Studies in Organizational Communication.* New York: Guilford, 262–276. C(E)

Dearing, James W., and Gary Meyer (1994) "An Exploratory Tool for Predicting Adoption Decisions." *Science Communication* 16(1):43–57. C(E)

Dearing, James W., Gary Meyer, and Jeff Kazmierczak (1994) "Portraying the New: Communication Between University Innovators and Potential Users." *Science Communication* 16(1):11–42. C(E)

Dearing, James W., Gary Meyer, and Everett M. Rogers (1994) "Diffusion Theory and HIV Risk Bahavior." In Ralph J. DiClemente and John L. Peterson, eds., *Preventing AIDS: Theories and Models of Behavioral Interventions.* New York: Plenum Press, 79–93. C(N)

Dearing, James W., and Everett M. Rogers (1996) *Agenda-Setting.* Thousand Oaks, Calif.: Sage. C(E)

Dearing, James W., Everett M. Rogers, Gary Meyer, Mary K. Casey, Nagesh Rao, Shelly Campo, and Geoffrey M. Henderson (1996) "Social Marketing and Diffusion-Based Strategies for Communicating Health with Unique Populations: HIV Prevention in San Francisco." *Journal of Health Communication* 1:343–363. C(E)

DeFleur, Melvin (1987) "The Growth and Decline of Research on the Diffusion of News, 1945–1985." *Communication Research* 14(1):109–130. C(E)

Dekimpe, Marnik G., Philip M. Parker, and Myklos Sarvary (1998) "Staged Estimation of International Diffusion Models: An Application to Global Cellular Telephone Adoption." *Technological Forecasting and Social Change* 57:105–132. MR(E)

Dekimpe, Marnik G., Philip M. Parker, and Miklos Sarvary (2000a) "Global Diffusion of Technological Innovations: A Coupled-Hazard Approach." *Journal of Marketing Research* 37:47–59. MR(E)

Dekimpe, Marnik G., Philip M. Parker, and Miklos Sarvary (2000b) "Globalization: Modeling Technology Adoption Timing Across Countries." *Technological Forecasting and Social Change* 63:25–42. MR(E)

Dekimpe, Marnik G., Philip M. Parker, and Myklos Sarvary (2000c) "Multimarket and Global Diffusion." In Vijay Mahajan, Eitan Muller, and Yoram Wind, eds., *New-Product Diffusion Models*. Dordrecht, Netherlands: Kluwer Academic, 49–73. MR(E)

Derksen, Linda, and John Gartell (1993) "The Social Context of Recycling." *American Sociological Review* 58:434–442. GS(E)

DeSanctis, G., and Peter Monge (1998) "Communication Processes for Virtual Organizations." *Organization Science* 10(6):693–703. C(E)

Deutschmann, Paul J. (1963) "The Mass Media in an Underdeveloped Village." *Journalism Quarterly* 40(1):27–35. C(E)

Deutschmann, Paul J., and Wayne A. Danielson (1960) "Diffusion of Knowledge of the Major News Story." *Journalism Quarterly* 37:345–355. C(E)

Deutschmann, Paul J., and Orlando Fals Borda (1962a) *La Comunicacíon de las ideas entre los campesinos Colombianos*. Monografías Sociológicas 14, Universidad Nacional de Colombia, Bogotá. C(E)

Deutschmann, Paul J., and Orlando Fals Borda (1962b) *Communication and Adoption Patterns in an Andean Village*. Report, Programa Interamericano de Información Popular, San José, Costa Rica. C(E)

Deutschmann, Paul J., and A. Eugene Havens (1965) "Discontinuances: A Relatively Uninvestigated Aspect of Diffusion." Unpublished paper, Department of Rural Sociology, University of Wisconsin, Madison. C(E)

Dewees, Christopher M., and Glen R. Hawkins (1988) "Technical Innovation in the Pacific Coast Trawler Fishery: The Effects of Fishermen's Characteristics and Perceptions of Adoption Behavior." *Human Organization* 47(3):224–234. O(E)

Dewey, John (1896) "The Reflex Arc Concept in Psychology." *Psychological Review* 3:357–370.

DiFrancisco, Wayne, Jeffrey A. Kelly, Laura Otto-Salaj, Timothy L. McAuliffe, Anton M. Somlai, Kristin Hackl, Timothy G. Heckman, David R. Holtgrave, and David J. Rompa (1999) "Factors Influencing Attitudes within AIDS Service Organizations Toward the Use of Research-Based HIV Prevention Interventions." *AIDS Education and Prevention* 12(1):72–86. PH(E)

Dimit, Robert M. (1954) "Diffusion and Adoption of Approved Farm Practices in 11 Countries in Southwest Virginia." Ph.D. diss., Iowa State University, Ames. RS(E)

Dino, Geri A., Kimberly A. Horn, Fennifer Goldcamp, Laura Kemp-Rye, Shirley Westrate, and Karen Monaco (2001) "Teen Smoking Cessation: Making It Work Through School and Community Partnerships." *Journal of Public Health Management Practice* 7(2):71–80. PH(E)

Dooley, Kevin, Anand Subra, and John Anderson (2001) "Maturity and Its Impact on New Product Development Project Performance." Unpublished paper, Arizona State University, Tempe. MR(E)

Dooley, Kevin, Anand Subra, and John Anderson (2002) "Adoption Rates and Patterns of Best Practices in New Product Development." Unpublished paper, Arizona State University, Tempe. MR(E)

Dornblaser, B. M., T. Lin, and Andrew H. Van de Ven (1989) "Innovation Outcomes, Learning, and Action Loops." In Andrew H. Van de Ven, H. A. Angel, and M. Scott Poole, eds., *Research on the Management of Innovation: The Minnesota Studies.* New York: Ballinger/Harper and Row. MR(E)

Dougherty, D., and C. Hardy (1996) "Sustained Product Innovation in Larger, Mature Organizations: Overcoming Innovation-to-Organization Problems." *Academy of Management Journal* 39:1120–1153. MR(E)

Downs, George W., Jr., and Lawrence B. Mohr (1976) "Conceptual Issues in the Study of Innovations." *Administrative Science Quarterly* 21:700–714. PS(N)

Drazin, R., and C. Schoonhowern (1996) "Community, Population, and Organization Effects on Innovation: A Multilevel Perspective." *Academy of Management Journal* 39:1065–1083. MR(E)

Duff, Robert W., and William T. Liu (1975) "The Significance of Heterophilous Structure in Communication Flows." *Philippine Quarterly of Culture and Society* 3:159–175. PH(E)

Dugger, Celia W. (2001, April 22) "Abortion in India Is Tipping Scales Sharply Against Girls." *The New York Times,* 1, 10.

Dupagne, Michel (1999) "Exploring the Characteristics of Potential High-Definition Television Adopters." *Journal of Media Economics* 12(1):35–50. C(E)

Durfee, Mary (1999) "Diffusion of Pollution Prevention Policy." *The Annals* 566:108–119. O(N)

Dutton, William H., Everett M. Rogers, and Suk-Ho Jun (1987) "Diffusion and Social Impacts of Personal Computers." *Communication Research* 14(2):219–250. C(N)

Dvorak, August, et al. (1936) *Typewriting Behavior.* New York: American.

Dyck, B., and F. B. Starke (1999) "The Formation of Breakaway Organizations: Observations and a Process Model." *Administrative Science Quarterly* 44:792–822. MR(E)

Earp, Joanne L., E. Eng, M. S. O'Malley, M. Altpeter, G. Rauscher, L. Mayne, H. F. Matthews, K. S. Lynch, and B. Gaquish (2002) "Increasing Use of Mammography among Older, Rural African American Women: Results from a Community Trial." *American Journal of Public Health* 92(4):646–654. PH(E)

Earp, Joanne L., C. I. Viadro, A. Vincus, M. Altpeter, V. Flax, L. Mayne, and E. Eng (1997) "Lay Health Advisors: A Strategy for Getting the Word Out about Breast Cancer." *Health Education Behavior* 24:432–451. PH(E)

Edwards, Ruth W., Pamela Jumper-Thurman, Barbara A. Plested, Eugene R. Oetting, and Louis Swanson (2000) "Community Readiness: Research to Practice." *Journal of Community Psychology* 28(3):291–307. O(E)

Einsiedel, Edna F., and Deborah L. Eastlick (2000) "Consensus Conferences as Deliberative Democracy." *Science Communication* 21(4):323–343. C(E)

Elford, J., G. Bolding, and L. Sherr (2001) "Peer Education Has No Significant Impact on HIV Risk Behaviours Among Gay Men in London." *AIDS* 15:535–537. PH(E)

Elford, J., G. Hart, L. Sherr, L. Williamson, and G. Balding (2002) "Peer Led HIV Prevention Among Homosexual Men in Britain." *Sexually Transmitted Diseases* 78:158–159. PH(E)

Elwood, William N., and A.N. Ataabadi (1997) "Influence of Interpersonal and Mass-Mediated Interventions on Injection Drug and Crack Users: Diffusion of Innovations and HIV Risk Behaviors." *Substance Use Misuse* 32(5):635–651. C(E)

Emrick, John A., et al. (1977) *Evaluation of the National Diffusion Network.* Vol. 1: *Findings and Recommendations.* Report, Stanford Research Institute, Menlo Park, Calif. E(E)

Emshoff, James G., and Craig Blakely (1987) "Innovation in Education and Criminal Justice: Measuring Fidelity of Implementation and Program Effectiveness." *Educational Evaluation and Policy Analysis* 9:300–311. O(E)

Emshoff, James, Craig Blakely, Denis Gray, Susan Jakes, Paul Brownstein, and Judy Coulter (2002) "An ESID Case at the Federal Level." Unpublished paper, Georgia State University, Atlanta. O(E)

Ennett, Susan T., Nancy S. Tobler, Christopher Ringwalt, and Robert L. Flewellin (1994) "How Effective Is Drug Abuse Resistance Education? A

Meta-Analysis of Project D.A.R.E. Outcome Evaluations." *American Journal of Public Health* 84(9):1394–1401. PH(E)

Entwisle, Barbara, John B. Casterline, and Hussein A.-A. Syed (1989) "Villages as Context for Contraceptive Behavior in Rural Egypt." *American Sociological Review* 54:1019–1034. GS(E)

Entwisle, Barbara, R. D. Rindfuss, D. K. Guilkey, A. Chamratrithirong, S. R. Curran, and Y. Sawangdee (1996) "Community and Contraceptive Choice in Rural Thailand: A Case Study of Nang Rong." *Demography* 33:1–11. PH(E)

Estabrooks, Carole A. (1999) "Modeling the Individual Determinants of Research Utilization." *Western Journal of Nursing Research* 21(6):758–772. O(E)

Eveland, J. D. (1979, August) "Issues in Using the Concept of 'Adoption of Innovations.'" Paper presented at the annual meeting of the American Society for Public Administration, Baltimore. O(N)

Eveland, J. D. (1986) "Diffusion, Technology Transfer and Implications: Thinking and Talking About Change." *Knowledge* 8(2):303–322. O(N)

Eveland, J. D., et al. (1977) "The Innovative Process in Public Organizations." Mimeo report, Department of Journalism, University of Michigan, Ann Arbor. C(E)

Fairweather, George W., David H. Sanders, and Louis G. Tornatzky (1974) *Creating Change in Mental Health Organizations.* New York: Pergamon Press. P(E)

Fals Borda, Orlando (1960) *Facts and Theory of Socio-Cultural Change in a Rural System.* Monographías Sociológicas 2 bis, Universidad Nacional de Colombia, Bogotá. RS(E)

Farquhar, John W. (1996) "The Case for Dissemination Research in Health Promotion and Disease Prevention." *Canadian Journal of Public Health* 87(suppl. 2):S44-S49. PH(E)

Feeney, David (2002) "Rates of Adoption of a University Course Management System." Ph.D. diss., University of West Virginia, Morgantown. E(E)

Fennell, Mary L. (1984) "Synergy, Influence, and Information in the Adoption of Administrative Innovations." *Academy of Management Journal* 27(1):113–129. MR(E)

Ferrence, Roberta (1996) "Using Diffusion Theory in Health Promotion: The Case of Tobacco." *Canadian Journal of Public Health* 87 (suppl. 2):S24-S27. PH(E)

Ferrence, R. (2001) "Diffusion Theory and Drug Use." *Addictions* 96(1):165–173. PH(N)

Fershtman, Chaim, Vijay Mahajan, and Etlan Muller (1990) "Market Share and Pioneering Advantage: A Theoretical Approach." *Management Science,* 37:211–223. MR(E)

Festinger, Leon (1957) *A Theory of Cognitive Dissonance.* Stanford, Calif.: Stanford University Press.

Fichman, Robert G., and Chris F. Kemerer (1997) "The Assimilation of Software Process Innovations: An Organizational Learning Perspective." *Management Science* 43:1345–1363. MR(E)

Fiol, C. M. (1996) "Squeezing Harder Doesn't Always Work: Continuing the Search for Consistency in Innovation Research." *Academy of Management Journal* 21:1012–1021. MR(E)

Fischer, Claude S. (1992) *America Calling: A Social History of the Telephone to 1940.* Berkeley: University of California Press. GS(E)

Fischer, David Hackett (1994) *Paul Revere's Ride.* New York: Oxford University Press.

Fliegel, Frederick C., with Peter F. Korsching (2001) *Diffusion Research in Rural Sociology: The Record and Prospects for the Future.* Middleton, Wisc.: Social Ecology Press. RS(N)

Fliegel, Frederick C., and Joseph E. Kivlin (1966a) "Farmers' Perceptions of Farm Practice Attributes." *Rural Sociology* 31:197–206. RS(E)

Fliegel, Frederick C., and Joseph E. Kivlin (1966b) "Attributes of Innovations as Factors in Diffusion." *American Journal of Sociology* 72(3):235–248. RS(E)

Fliegel, Frederick C., Joseph E. Kivlin, and Gurmeet S. Sekhon (1968) "A Cross-National Comparison of Farmers' Perception of Innovation as Related to Adoption Behavior." *Rural Sociology* 33:437–499. RS(E)

Flora, June A., with Darius Jatilus, Chris Jackson, and Stephen P. Fortmann (1993) "The Stanford Five-City Heart Disease Prevention Project." In Thomas E. Becker and Everett M. Rogers, eds., *Organizational Aspects of Health Communication Campaigns: What Works?* Newbury Park, Calif.: Sage, 101–128. C(E)

Flowers, P., G. J. Hart, L. M. Williamson, J. S. Frankis, and G. J. Derr (2002) "Does Bar-Based, Peer-Led Health Promotion Have a Community-Level Effect Amongst Gay Men in Scotland?" *International Journal of STD and AIDS* 13:102–108. PH(E)

Flynn, Lelsa Reinecke, Ronald E. Goldsmith, and Jacqueline K. Eastman (1994) "The King and Sumers Opinion Leadership Scale: Revision and Refinement." *Journal of Business Research* 31:55–64. MR(E)

Foster, A. D., and M. R. Rosenzweig (1995) "Learning by Doing and Learning from Others: Human Capital and Technical Change in Agriculture." *Journal of Political Economy* 103(6):1176–1209. O(E)

Fox, Karen F. A., and Philip Kotler (1980) "The Marketing of Social Causes: The First Ten Years." *Journal of Marketing* 44:24–33. MR(E)

Foxall, Gordon R. (1994) "Consumer Initiators: Adaptors and Innovators." *British Journal of Management* 5 (special issue):S3-S12. MR(E)

Frank, Kenneth A., Andrew G. Topper, and Yong Zhao (2002) "Diffusion of Innovations, Social Capital, and Sense of Community." Unpublished paper, Michigan State University, East Lansing. E(E)

Frank, Lauri Dieter (2001, June) "Spatial Clusters of European Union Countries by the Diffusion of Mobile Communications." Paper presented at the annual meeting of the ISPIM, International Society for Professional Innovation Management, Lappeenranta, Finland. MR(E)

Frank, Lauri Dieter (2002) "Diffusion of Mobile Communications in Finland." Unpublished paper, Telecom Business Research Center, Lappeenranta University of Technology, Lappeenranta, Finland. MR(E)

Frank, Lauri Dieter, and Jukka Heikkila (2002) "Diffusion Models in Analysing Emerging Technology-Based Services." Unpublished paper, Telecom Business Research Center, Lappeenranta University of Technology, Lappeenranta, Finland. MR(E)

Frank, Lauri Dieter, Sanna Sundqvist, Kaisu Puumalainen, and Sanna Taalikka (2002) "Cross-Cultural Comparison of Innovators: Empirical Evidence from Wireless Services in Finland, Germany, and Greece." Unpublished paper, Telecom Business Research Center, Lappeenranta University of Technology, Lappeenranta, Finland. MR(E)

Freedman, Ronald, and John Y. Takeshita (1969) *Family Planning in Taiwan.* Princeton, N.J.: Princeton University Press. PH(E)

Friedland, William H., and Amy Barton (1975) *Destalking the Wily Tomato: A Case Study of Social Consequences in California Agricultural Research.* Research monograph 15, University of California at Santa Cruz. GS(E)

Fulk, Janet (1993) "Social Construction of Communication Technology." *Academy of Management Journal* 36(5):921–950. C(E)

Gagnon, Y.-C., and J.-M. Toulouse (1996) "The Behavior of Business Managers When Adopting New Technologies." *Technological Forecasting and Social Change* 52:59–74. MR(E)

Galavotti, Christine, R. Cabral, A. Lansky, Diane M. Grimley, G. E. Riley, and James Prochaska (1995) "Validation of Measures of Condom and Other Contraceptive Use Among Women at High Risk for HIV Infection and Unintended Pregnancies." *Health Psychology* 14(6):570–578. PH(E)

Gallagher, Scott, and Seung Ho Park (2002) "Innovation and Competition in Standard-Based Industries: A Historical Analysis of the U.S. Home Video Game Market." *IEEE Transactions on Engineering Management* 49(1):67–82. MR(E)

Ganesh, Jaishankar, and V. Kumar (1996) "Capturing the Cross-National Learning Effect: An Analysis of an Industrial Technology Diffusion." *Journal of the Academy of Marketing Science* 24:328–337. MR(E)

Ganesh, Jaishankar, V. Kumar, and Velavan Subramaniam (1997) "Learning Effect in Multinational Diffusion of Consumer Durables: An Exploratory Investigation." *Journal of the Academy of Management Science* 25:214–228. MR(E)

Garrison, Bruce (2001) "Diffusion of Online Information Technologies in Newspaper Newsrooms." *Journalism* 2(2):221–239. C(E)

Gatignon, Hubert, and Thomas S. Robertson (1991) "Diffusion of Innovations." In H. H. Kassarsian and Thomas S. Robertson, eds., *Handbook of Consumer Theory and Research*. Englewood Cliffs, N.J.: Prentice-Hall. MR(N)

Geroski, P. (2000) "Models of Technology Diffusion." *Research Policy* 29:603–625. MR(E)

Gibson, David V., and Everett M. Rogers (1994) *R&D Consortia on Trial*. Boston: Harvard Business School Press. MR(E)

Gielens, Katrijin, and Marnik G. Dekimpe (2001) "Do International Entry Decisions of Retail Chains Matter in the Long Run?" *International Journal of Research in Marketing* 18(3):235–259. MR(E)

Ginossar, Tamar (2002) "Information Seeking and Empowerment of Internet Cancer Support Members" Ph.D. diss., Albuquerque: University of New Mexico. C(E)

Givon, Moshe, Vijay Mahajan, and Eitan Muller (1995) "Software Piracy: Estimation of Lost Sales and the Impact on Software Diffusion." *Journal of Marketing* 59:29–37. MR(E)

Givon, Moshe, Vijay Mahajan, and Eitan Muller (1997) "Assessing the Relationship Between the User-Based Market Share and Unit Sales–Based Market Share for Pirated Software Brands in Competitive Markets." *Technological Forecasting and Social Change* 55(2):131–144. MR(E)

Gladwell, Malcolm (1996, June 3) "The Tipping Point." *The New Yorker*, 32–38. O(N)

Gladwell, Malcolm (1999, January 11) "Six Degrees of Lois Weisberg." *The New Yorker*, 52–62. O(N)

Gladwell, Malcolm (1999, October 4) "The Science of the Sleeper: How the Information Age Could Blow Away the Blockbuster." *The New Yorker*, 48–50, 52–55. O(N)

Gladwell, Malcolm (2000) *The Tipping Point: How Little Things Can Make a Big Difference*. Boston: Little, Brown. O(N)

Gladwell, Malcolm (2000, March 13) "John Rock's Error." *The New Yorker*, 52–63. O(N)

Gladwell, Malcolm (2001, March 5) "The Trouble with Fries." *The New Yorker,* 52–57. O(N)

Gladwell, Malcolm (2001, July 2) "The Mosquito Killer." *The New Yorker,* 42–51. O(N)

Glantz, Stanton (1999) "Smoke-Free Ordinances Do Not Affect Restaurant Business. Period." *Journal of Public Health Management Practice* 5(1):vi–x. PS (N)

Glasgow, Russell E., Elizabeth G. Eakin, Edwin B. Fisher, Stephen J. Bacak, and Ross C. Brownson (2001) "Physician Advice and Support for Physical Activity: Results from a National Survey." *American Journal of Preventive Medicine* 21(3):189–196. PH(E)

Glick, Henry R., and Scott P. Hays (1991) "Innovation and Reinvention in State Policymaking: Theory and Evolution in Living Will Laws." *Journal of Politics* 53:835–850. PS(E)

Globe, Samuel, et al. (1973) "The Interactions of Science and Technology in the Innovative Process: Some Case Studies." Report to the National Science Foundation, Battelle-Columbus Laboratories, Columbus, Ohio. O(E)

Goes, J. B., and S. H. Park (1997) "Interorganizational Links and Innovation: The Case of Hospital Services." *Academy of Management Journal* 40:673–696. MR(E)

Golder, Peter N., and Gerald J. Tellis (1997) "Will It Ever Fly? Modeling the Takeoff of Really New Consumer Durables." *Marketing Science* 16(3):256–270. MR(E)

Golder, Peter N., and Gerald J. Tellis (1998) "Beyond Diffusion: An Affordability Model of the Growth of New Consumer Durables." *Journal of Forecasting* 17:259–280. MR(E)

Goldman, Karen D. (1994) "Perceptions of Innovations as Predictors of Implementation Levels: The Diffusion of a Nationwide Health Education Campaign." *Health Education Quarterly* 21:433–444. E(E)

Goodman, Robert M., and Allan Steckler (1989) "A Model for the Institutionalization of Health Promotion Programs." *Family and Community Health* 11(4):63–78. PH(E)

Goodson, P., M. Murphy Smith, A. Evans, B. Meyers, and N. H. Gottlied (2001) "Maintaining Prevention in Practice: Survival of PPIP in Primary Care Settings." *American Journal of Preventive Medicine* 20(3):184–189. PH(E)

Gotsch, Carl H. (1972) "Technical Change and the Distribution of Income in Rural Areas." *American Journal of Agricultural Economics* 54:326–341. AE(E)

Granovetter, Mark S. (1973) "The Strength of Weak Ties." *American Journal of Sociology* 78:1360–1380. GS(N)

Granovetter, Mark S. (1978) "Threshold Models of Collective Behavior." *American Journal of Sociology* 83:1420–1443. GS(N)

Granovetter, Mark, and R. Soong (1983) "Threshold Models of Diffusion and Collective Behavior." *Journal of Mathematical Sociology* 9:165–179. GS(N)

Grattet, Ryken, Valerie Jenness, and Theodore R. Curry (1998) "The Homogenization and Differentiation of Hate Crime Law in the United States, 1978 to 1995: Innovation and Diffusion in the Criminalization of Bigotry." *American Sociological Review* 63:286–307. GS(E)

Gray, Virginia (1973) "Innovation in the States: A Diffusion Study." *American Political Science Review* 67:1174–1185. PS(E)

Gray, Virginia (1973b) "Rejoinder to 'Comment' by Jack L. Walker." *American Political Science Review* 4:1192–1193. PS(E)

Green, Lawrence W. (1986) "The Theory of Participation: A Qualitative Analysis of Its Expression in National and International Health Policies." *Advances in Health Education and Promotion* 1:211–236. PH(N)

Green, Lawrence W. (2001) "From Research to 'Best Practices' in Other Settings and Populations." *American Journal of Health Behavior* 25(3):165–178. PH(N)

Greenberg, Bradley S. (1964) "Diffusion of News about the Kennedy Assassination." *Public Opinion Quarterly* 28:225–232; and in Bradley S. Greenberg and Edwin B. Parker, eds., (1965) *The Kennedy Assassination and the American Public: Social Communication in Crisis.* Stanford, Calif.: Stanford University Press. C(E)

Greenberg, Steve (1992) "Misunderstanding Black Popular Music in White America." In *The New Global Culture.* Washington, D.C.: American Enterprise Institute. C(N)

Greve, Heinrich R. (1995) "Jumping Ship: The Diffusion of Strategy Abandonment." *Administrative Science Quarterly* 40:444–473. MR(E)

Griffin, Robert J., and Sharon Dunwoody (2000) "The Relation of Communication to Risk Judgement and Preventive Behavior Related to Lead in Tap Water." *Health Communication* 12(1):81–107. C(E)

Grilli, Roberto, Nicola Magrini, Angelo Penna, Giorgio Mura, and Alessandro Liberti (2000) "Practice Guidelines Development by Specialty Societies: The Need for a Critical Appraisal." *Lancet* 355:103–106. O(E)

Grindereng, Margaret P. (1967) "Fashion Diffusion." *Journal of Home Economics* 59(3):171–174. O(E)

Gronhaug, Kjell, and Geir Kaufmann (1988) *Innovation: A Cross-Disciplinary Perspective.* Oslo: Norwegian University Press. MR(N)

Gross, Neal C. (1942) "The Diffusion of a Culture Trait in Two Iowa Townships." M.S. thesis, Iowa State College, Ames. RS(E)

Grüber, Arnulf (1991) "Diffusion: Long-Term Patterns and Discontinuities." *Technological Forecasting and Social Change* 39:159–180. O(E)

Grüber, Arnulf (1996) "Time for a Change: On the Patterns of Diffusion of Innovations." *Daedalus* 125(3):19–42. O(E)

Grüber, Arnulf (1997) "Time for a Change: On the Patterns of Diffusion of Innovation." In Jesse H. Ausubel and H. Dale Langford, eds., *Technological Trajectories and the Human Environment*. Washington, D.C.: National Academy Press, 14–32. O(E)

Grüber, Harald (1998) "The Diffusion of Innovations in Protected Industries: The Textile Industry." *Applied Economics* 30(1):77–83. GE(E)

Grüber, Harald (2001) "Competition and Innovation: The Diffusion of Mobile Telecommunications in Central and Eastern Europe." *Information Economics and Policy* 13:19–34. GE(E)

Grüber, Harald, and Frank Verboven (2001) "The Diffusion of Mobile Telecommunications Innovations in the European Union." *European Economic Review* 45:577–588. GE(E)

Grüber, Harald, and Frank Verboven (2001b) "The Evolution of Markets under Entry and Standards Regulation: The Case of Global Modile Telecommunications." *International Journal of Industrial Organization* 19:1189–1212. GE(E)

Guerin, L. J., and Turlough F. Guerin (1994) "Constraints to the Adoption of Agricultural and Environmental Innovations and Technologies: A Review." *Australian Journal of Experimental Agriculture* 34:549–571. O(N)

Guerin, Turlough F. (1999) "An Australian Perspective on the Constraints to the Transfer and Adoption of Innovations in Land Management." *Environmental Conservation* 26(4):289–304. O(E)

Hägerstand, Torsten (1952) *The Propagation of Innovation Waves*. Lund, Sweden: Lund Studies in Geography 4. G(E)

Hägerstand, Torsten (1953/1968) "Innovation of Loppet ur Korologisk Synpunkt" (Innovation Diffusion as a Spatial Process). Department of Geography Bulletin 15, University of Lund, Lund, Sweden; and University of Chicago Press. G(E)

Hamblin, Robert L., R. B. Jacobson, and J. L. Miller (1973) *A Mathematical Theory of Social Change*. New York: Wiley. GS(E)

Hamblin, Robert L., et al. (1979) "Modeling Use Diffusion." *Social Forces* 57:799–811. GS(E)

Hansen, Lars Jorgen, Niels de Fine Olivarius, Anders Beich, and Sverre Barfod (1999) "Encouraging GPs to Undertake Screening and a Brief Intervention in Order to Reduce Problem Drinking: A Randomized Controlled Trial." *Family Practice* 16(6):551–557. PH(E)

Hardin, Garrett (1968) "The Tragedy of the Commons." *Science* 162:1243–1248.

Harding, Joe, et al. (1973) "Population Council Copper-T Study in Korea: Summary Report." Policy Research and Planning Group, The 21C Corporation, Berkeley, Calif. A(E)

Hassinger, Edward (1959) "Stages in the Adoption Process." *Rural Sociology* 24:52–53. RS(N)

Havelock, Ronald G. (1972, December) "The Role of Research Communities in National Problem Solving." Paper presented at the annual meeting of the Institute of Electrical and Electronic Engineers, New York. E(E)

Havelock, Ronald G. (1974) "Locals Say Innovation Is Local: A National Survey of School Superintendants." In Stanford Temkin and Mary V. Brown, eds., *What Do Research Findings Say About Getting Innovations into Schools? A Symposium.* Philadelphia, Research for Better Schools. E(E)

Havens, A. Eugene (1975) "Diffusion of New Seed Varieties and Its Consequences: A Colombian Case." In Raymond E. Dumett and Lawrence J. Brainard, eds., *Problems of Rural Development: Case Studies and Multidisciplinary Perspective.* Leiden, Netherlands: Brill, 94–111. RS(E)

Havens, A. Eugene, and William L. Finn (1974) "Green Revolution Technology and Community Development: The Limits of Action Programs." *Economic Development and Cultural Change* 23:469–481. RS(E)

Hawley, Florence (1946) "The Role of Pueblo Social Organization in the Dissemination of Catholicism." *American Anthropologist* 48:407–415. A(E)

Hays, Carol E., Scott P. Hays, John O. Deville, and Peter Mulhall (2000) "Capacity for Effectiveness: The Relationship Between Coalition Structure and Community Impact." *Evaluation and Program Planning* 23:373–379. PS(E)

Hays, Scott P. (1996a) "Patterns of Reinvention: The Nature of Evolution During Policy Diffusion." *Policy Studies Journal* 24(4):551–566. PS(E)

Hays, Scott P. (1996b) "Influences on Reinvention During the Diffusion of State Policy Innovations." *Political Research Quarterly* 49:613–632. PS(E)

Hays, Scott P. (1996c) "Policy Reinvention and Diffusion of Public Campaign Funding Laws." *Spectrum: The Journal of State Government* 69:23–31. PS(E)

Hays, Scott P. (1996d) "The States and Policy Innovation Research: Lessons from the Past and Directions for the Future." *Policy Studies Journal* 24:321–326. PS(E)

Hays, Scott P., Michael Esler, and Carol E. Hays (1996) "Environmental Commitment among the States: Integrating Alternative Approaches to State Environmental Policy." *Publius: The Journal of Federalism* 26(2):41–58. PS(E)

Hays, Scott P., and Henry R. Glick (1996) "The Role of Agenda-Setting in Policy Innovation: An Event History Analysis of Living Will Laws." *American Politics Quarterly* 24(4):497–516. PS(E)

Hays, Scott P., and Henry R. Glick (1997) "The Role of Agenda-Setting in Policy Innovation: An Event History Analysis." *American Politics Quarterly* 25(4):497–516. PS(E)

Hays, Scott P., Carol E. Hays, John Vinzant, and Kathleen Gary (2000, August) "Change Agents, Policy Entrepreneurs, Focusing Events, and the Adoption of Municipal Ordinances for Tobacco Control." Paper presented at the annual meeting of the American Political Science Association, Washington, D.C. PS(E)

He, Zhou (2001, May) "Adoption and Use of the Internet Among Adult Audiences in Mainland China: The Role of Perceived Popularity of the Internet, Perceived Characteristics of the Internet, and Perceived Need for the Internet." Paper presented at the annual meeting of the International Communication Association, Washington, D.C. C(E)

Hedstrom, Peter (1994) "Contagious Collectivities: On the Spatial Diffusion of Swedish Trade Unions, 1890–1940." *American Journal of Sociology* 99:1157–1179. GS(E)

Heikkilä, Jukka (1995) "The Diffusion of a Learning Intensive Technology into Organisations: The Case of Personal Computing." Ph.D. diss., Helsinki School of Economics and Business Administration, Helsinki, Finland. MR(E)

Helsen, Kristiaan, Kamel Jedidi, and Wayne DeSarbo (1993) "A New Approach to Country Segmentation Utilizing Multinational Diffusion Patterns." *Journal of Marketing* 57:60–71. MR(E)

Herbig, Paul A., and Fred Palumbo (1994) "The Effect of Culture on the Adoption Process: A Comparison of Japanese and American Behavior." *Technological Forecasting and Social Change* 46:71–101. MR(E)

Herzog, William A., J. David Stanfield, Gordon C. Whiting, and Lynne Svenning (1968) *Patterns of Diffusion in Rural Brazil.* Diffusion of Innovations Research Report 10, Department of Communication, Michigan State University, East Lansing. C(E)

Higgins, S. H., and P. T. Hogan (1999) "Internal Diffusion of High Technology Industrial Innovations: An Empirical Study." *Journal of Business and Industrial Marketing* 14(1):61–75. MR(E)

Hightower, James (1972) *Hard Tomatoes, Hard Times: The Failure of America's Land Grant Complex.* Cambridge, Mass.: Schenkman.

Hoffman, Paul (1998) *The Man Who Loved Only Numbers: The Story of Paul Erdős and the Search for Mathematical Truth.* New York: Hyperion.

Holden, Robert T. (1986) "The Contagiousness of Aircraft Hijacking." *American Journal of Sociology* 91(4):874–904. GS(E).

Holloway, Robert E. (1977) "Perceptions of an Innovation: Syracuse University's Project Advance." Ph.D. diss., Syracuse University, Syracuse, N.Y. E(E)

Holmlöv Kramer, P. G., and Karl-Eric Warneryd (1990) "Adoption and Use of Fax in Sweden." In M. Carnevale, M. Lucertini, and S. Nicosia, eds., *Modeling the Innovation: Communications, Automation and Information Systems.* Amsterdam: Elsevier Science, 95–108. MR(E)

Hölttä, Risto (1989) "Multidimensional Diffusion of Innovations." Ph.D. diss., Helsinki School of Economics and Business Administration, Helsinki, Finland. MR(E)

Hostetler, John A. (1980) *Amish Society.* Baltimore, Md.: Johns Hopkins University Press.

Hostetler, John A. (1987) "A New Look at the Old Order." *The Rural Sociologist* 7:278–292.

Howell, Jane M., and Christopher A. Higgins (1990) "Champions of Technological Innovations." *Administrative Science Quarterly* 35:317–341. MR(E)

Hu, P. J., P. Y. K. Chan, O. R. L. Sheng, and K. Y. Tam (1999) "Examining the Technology Acceptance Model Using Physician Acceptance of Telemedicine Technology." *Journal of Management Information Systems* 16(2):91–112. MR(E)

Hu, Q., C. Saunders, and M. Gebelt (1997) "Diffusion of Information Systems Outsourcing: A Re-Evaluation of Influence Sources." *Information Systems Research* 8(3):288–301. MR(E)

Huntington, Dale, Cheryl Lettenmaier, and Isaac Obéng-Quaidoo (1990) "User's Perspective of Counseling Training in Ghana: The 'Mystery Client' Trial." *Studies in Family Planning* 21(3):171–177. PH(E)

Hyman, Herbert H., and Paul B. Sheatsley (1974) "Some Reasons Why Information Campaigns Fail." *Public Opinion Quarterly* 11:412–423.

Igbaria, Magid, Stephen J. Schiffman, and Thomas J. Wieckowski (1994) "The Retrospective Roles of Perceived Usefulness and Perceived Fun in the Acceptance of Microcomputer Technology." *Behavior and Information Technology* 13:349–361. MR(E)

Isenson, Raymond S. (1969) "Project Hindsight: An Empirical Study of the Sources of Ideas Utilized in Operational Weapons System." In William Gruber and Donald G. Marquis, eds., *Factors in the Transfer of Technology.* Cambridge, Mass.: MIT Press. O(E)

Islam, Towhidul, and Nigel Meade (1997) "The Diffusion of Successive Generations of a Technology: A More General Model." *Technological Forecasting and Social Change* 56:49–60. MR(E)

Jain, Dipak, Vijay Mahajan, and Eitan Muller (1995) "An Approach for Determining Optimal Product Sampling for the Diffusion of a New Product." *Journal of Product Innovation Management* 12:124–135. MR(E)

James, Michael L., C. Edward Wotring, and Edward J. Forrest (1995) "An Exploratory Study of the Perceived Benefits of Electronic Bulletin Board Use and Their Impact on Other Communication Activities." *Journal of Braodcasting and Electronic Media* 39:30–50. C(E)

Jarrar, Yasar F., and Mohammed Zairi (2000) "Best Practice Transfer for Future Competitiveness: A Study of Best Practice." *Total Quality Management* 11(4/5 and 6):S734-S740. MR(E)

Jeffres, Leo W., and David Atkin (1996) "Predicting Use of Technologies for Communication and Consumer Needs." *Journal of Broadcasting and Electronic Media* 40:318–330. C(E)

Johnson, J. David (2000) "Levels of Success in Implementing Information Technologies." *Innovative Higher Education* 25:59–76. C(E)

Johnson, J. David (2001) "Success in Innovation Implementation." *Journal of Communication Management* 5(4):341–359. C(N)

Johnson, J. David, W. A. Donohue, Charles K. Atkin, and Sally H. Johnson (1995) "Differences Between Organizational and Communication Factors Related to Contrasting Innovations." *Journal of Business Communication* 32:65–80. C(E)

Johnson, J. D., M. Meyer, M. Woodworth, C. Etherington, and W. Stengle (1998) "Information Technologies within the Cancer Information Service: Factors Related to Innovation Adoption." *Preventive Medicine* 27(5):S71-S83. C(E)

Kalish, Shlomo, Vijay Mahajan, and Eitan Muller (1995) "Waterfall and Sprinkler New-Product Strategies in Competitive Global Markets." *International Journal of Research in Marketing* 12:105–119. MR(E)

Kalof, Linda, Thomas Dietz, Paul C. Stern, and Gregory A. Guagnano (1999) "Social Psychological and Structural Influences on Vegetarian Beliefs." *Rural Sociology* 64(3):500–511. GS(E)

Kaner, Eileen F. S., Catherine A. Lock, Brian R. McAvoy, Nick Heather, and Eilish Gilvarry (1999) "A RCT of Three Training and Support Strategies to Encourage Implementation of Screening and Brief Alcohol Intervention by General Practitioners." *British Journal of General Practice* 49:699–703. PH(E)

Kaplan, Abraham (1964) *The Conduct of Inquiry.* San Francisco: Chandler.

Kaplan, Abram W. (1999) "From Passive to Active About Solar Electricity: Innovation Decision Process and Photovoltaic Interest Generation." *Technovation* 19:467–481. O(E)

Katz, Elihu (1956) "Interpersonal Relations and Mass Communications: Studies in the Flow of Influence." Ph.D. diss., Columbia University, New York. GS(E)

Katz, Elihu (1957) "The Two-Step Flow of Communication: An Up-to-Date Report on an Hypothesis." *Public Opinion Quarterly* 21:61–78. GS(E)

Katz, Elihu (1961) "The Social Itinerary of Social Change: Two Studies on the Diffusion of Innovation." In Wilbur Schramm, ed., *Studies of Innovation and of Communication to the Public.* Stanford, Calif.: Stanford University, Institute for Communication Research; and (1962) *Human Organization* 20:70–82. GS(E)

Katz, Elihu (1962) "Notes on the Unit of Adoption in Diffusion Research." *Sociological Inquiry* 32:3–9. GS(N)

Katz, Elihu (1992) "On Parenting a Paradigm: Gabriel Tarde's Agenda for Opinion and Communication Research." *International Journal of Public Opinion Research* 4:80–86. C(N)

Katz, Elihu (1999) "Theorizing Diffusion: Tarde and Sorokin Revisited." *The Annals* 566:144–155. C(N)

Katz, Elihu, and Paul F. Lazarsfeld (1955) *Personal Influence: The Part Played by People in the Flow of Mass Communications.* New York: Free Press.

Katz, Elihu, Martin L. Levin, and Herbert Hamilton (1963) "Traditions of Research on the Diffusion of Innovations." *American Sociological Review* 28:237–253. GS(N)

Katz, James, and Philip Aspden (1998) "Internet Dropouts in the USA: The Invisible Group." *Telecommunications Policy* 4:327–339. C(E)

Kaufman, R. J., J. M. Andrews, and Y.-M. Wang (2000) "Opening the 'Black Box' of Network Externalities in Network Adoption." *Information Systems Research* 11(1):61–82. MR(E)

Kearns, Kelvin P. (1992) "Innovations in Local Government: A Sociocognitive Network Approach." *Knowledge and Policy* 5(2):45–67. PS(E)

Kegeles, S. M., R. B. Hays, and Thomas J. Coates (1996) "The Mpowerment Project: A Community-Level HIV Prevention Intervention for Young Gay Men." *American Journal of Public Health* 86:1129–1136. PH(E)

Keller, D. S., and M. Gebnter (1999) "Technology Transfer of Network Therapy to Community-Based Addictions Counselors." *Journal of Substance Abuse Treatment* 16(2):183–189. PH(E)

Kelly, Jeffrey A., Timothy G. Heckman, L. Yvonne Stevenson, Paul N. Williams, Thom Ertl, Robert B. Hays, Noelle A. Leonard, Lydia O'Donnell, Martha A. Terry, Ellen D. Sogolow, and Mary Spink Neumann (2000) "Transfer of Research-Based HIV Prevention Interventions to Community Service Providers: Fidelity and Adaptation." *AIDS Education and Prevention* 12 (suppl. A):87–98. PH(E)

Kelly, Jeffrey A., Debra A. Murphy, Kathleen J. Sikkema, Timothy L. McAuliffe, Roger A. Roffman, Laura J. Solomon, Richard A. Winett, and Seth C. Kalichman (1997) "Randomized, Controlled, Community-Level HIV-Prevention Intervention for Sexual-Risk Behaviour Among Homosexual Men in US Cities." *Lancet* 350:1500–1505. PH(E)

Kelly, Jeffrey A., Ellen D. Sogolow, and Mary Spink Neumann (2000) "Future Directions and Emerging Issues in Technology Transfer Between HIV Prevention Researchers and Community-Based Service Providers." *AIDS Education and Prevention* 12(suppl. A):126–141. PH(E)

Kelly, Jeffrey A., Anton M. Somlai, Wayne J. DiFranceisco, Laura L. Otto-Salaj, Timothy L. McAuliffe, Kristin L. Hackl, Timothy G. Heckman, David R. Holtgrave, and David Rompa (2000) "Bridging the Gap Between the Science and Service of HIV Prevention: Transferring Effective Research-Based HIV Prevention Interventions to Community AIDS Service Providers." *American Journal of Public Health* 90:1082–1088. PH(E)

Kelly, Jeffrey A., Janet S. St. Lawrence, Yolanda E. Diaz, L. Yvonne Stevenson, Allan C. Hauth, Ted L. Brasfield, Seth C. Kalichman, Joseph E. Smith, and Michael E. Andrew (1991) "HIV Risk Behavior Reduction Following Intervention with Key Opinion Leaders of Population: An Experimental Analysis." *American Journal of Public Health* 81(2):168–171. PH(E)

Kelly, Jeffrey A., Janet S. St. Lawrence, Yvonne Stevenson, Allan C. Hauth, Seth C. Kalichman, Yolanda E. Diaz, Ted L. Brasfield, Jeffrey J. Koob, and Michael G. Morgan (1992) "Community AIDS/HIV Risk Reduction: The Effects of Endorsements by Popular People in Three Cities." *American Journal of Public Health* 82(11):1483–1489. PH(E)

Kessler, Eric H., and Paul E. Bierly III (2002) "Is Faster Really Better? An Empirical Test of the Implications of Innovation Speed." *IEEE Transactions on Engineering Management* 49(1):2–12. MR(E)

Kettinger, W., and V. Grover (1997) "The Use of Computer-Mediated Communication in an Organizational Context." *Decision Sciences* 28(3):513–555. MR(E)

Kiiski, Sampsa, and Matti Pohjola (2002) "Cross-Country Diffusion of the Internet." *Information Economics and Policy* 14:297–310. MR(E)

Kim, Young-Mi, Jose Rimon, Kim Winnard, Carol Carso, I. V. Mako, Sebloniga Lawal, Stella Babalola, and Dale Huntington (1992) "Improving the Quality of Service Delivery in Nigeria." *Studies in Family Planning* 23(2):118–127. PH(E)

Kincaid, D. Lawrence (2000a) "Social Networks, Ideation, and Contraceptive Behavior in Bangladesh: A Longitudinal Analysis." *Social Science and Medicine* 50:215–231. PH(E)

Kincaid, D. Lawrence (2000b) "Mass Media, Ideation, and Behavior: A Longi tudinal Analysis of Contraceptive Change in the Philippines." *Communication Research* 27(6):723–763. PH(E)

Kinnunen, Jussi (1996) "Gabriel Tarde as a Founding Father of Innovation Diffusion Research." *Acta Sociologica* 39:431–441. GS(N)

Kirton, M. J. (ed.) (1989) *Adopters and Innnovators: Styles of Creativity and Problem-Solving*. London: Routledge. MR(N)

Kivlin, Joseph E., and Frederick C. Fliegel (1967) "Orientations to Agriculture: A Factor Analysis of New Practices." *Rural Sociology* 33:127–140. C(E)

Klein, K. J., and J. S. Sorra (1996) "The Challenge of Innovation Implementation." *Academy of Management Review* 21:1055–1080. MR(E)

Klovdahl, Alden S. (1985) "Social Networks and the Spread of Infectious Diseases: The AIDS Example." *Social Science Medicine* 21(11):1203–1216. GS(E)

Kohl, John W. (1966) "Adoption Stages and Perceptions of Characteristics of Educational Innovations." Ed.D. diss., University of Oregon, Eugene. E(E)

Kohler, Hans-Peter (1997) "Learning in Social Networks and Contraceptive Choice." *Demography* 34(3):369–383. GS(E)

Kohler, Hans-Peter, Jere R. Behrman, and Susan C. Watkins (1999) "The Structure of Social Networks and Fertility Decisions: Evidence from S. Nyanza District, Kenya." Working Paper 5, Max Planck Institute for Demographic Research, Rostock, Germany. GS(E)

Kohli, Rajiv, Donald R. Lehmann, and Jae Pae (1999) "Extent and Impact of Incubation Time in New Product Diffusion." *Journal of Product Innovation Management* 16:134–144. MR(E)

Korhonen, Tellervo, Antti Uutela, Heikki J. Korhonen, Eeva-Liisa Urjanheimo, and Pekka Puska (1999) "Smoking Cessation Advice from Health Professionals: Process Evaluation of a Community-Based Program." *Patient Education and Counseling* 36:13–21. PH(E)

Korsching, Peter F. (2001) "Preface to the Second Edition." In Frederich C. Fliegel with Peter F. Korsching, *Diffusion Research in Rural Sociology: The Record and Prospects for the Future*. Middleton, Wisc.: Social Ecology Press, vi–viii. RS(N)

Korsching, Peter F. (2001b) "Diffusion Research in the 1990s and Beyond." In Frederich C. Fliegel with Peter F. Korsching, *Diffusion Research in Rural Sociology: The Record and Prospects for the Future*. Middleton, Wisc.:, Social Ecology Press, 105–134. RS(N)

Kortelainen, Tertlu A. (1997) "Applying Concepts of Diffusion Research in an Informatics Study." *Scientometrics* 40(3):555–568. O(E)

Kraut, Robert E., Ronald E. Rice, Colleen Cool, and Robert S. Fish (1998) "Varieties of Social Influences: The Role of Utility and Norms in the Success of a New Communication Medium." *Organization Science* 9(4):437–453. C(E)

Kremer, Kathy S., Michael Crolan, Stephen Gaiteyer, S. Noor Tirmizi, Peter F. Korsching, Gregory Peter, and Pingsheng Tong (2000) "Evolution of an Agricultural Innovation: The N-Track Soil Nitrogen Test: Adopt, and Discontinuance, or Reject?" *Technology in Society* 23:93–108. RS(E)

Kroeber, A. L. (1937) "Diffusion." In Edwin R. A. Seligman and Alvin Johnson, eds., *The Encyclopedia of Social Science,* vol. 2. New York: Macmillan. A(N)

Kuester, Sabine, Huber Gatignon, and Thomas S. Robertson (2000) "Firm Strategy and Speed of Diffusion." In Vijay Mahajan, Eitan Muller, and Yorum Wind, eds., *New-Product Diffusion Models.* Dordrecht, Netherlands: Kluver Academic, 28–47. MR(E)

Kuhn, Thomas S. (1962/1970) *The Structure of Scientific Revolutions.* Chicago: University of Chicago Press.

Kumar, V., Jaishankar Ganesh, and Raj Echambadi (1998) "Cross-National Diffusion Research: What Do We Know and How Certain Are We?" *Journal of Product Innovation Management* 15:255–268. MR(E)

Kunkel, John H. (1977) "The Behavioral Perspective of Social Dynamics." In Robert L. Hamblin and John H. Kunkel, eds., *Behavioral Theory in Sociology.* New Brunswick, N.J.: Transaction. GS(E)

Kwon, HoCheon (2002) "The Global Internet Diffusion and Correlation among Factors: Cross-National Analysis," Ph.D. diss., State University of New York at Buffalo. C(E)

Kwon, Hyosun Stella, and Laku Chidambaram (1998) "A Cross-Cultural Study of Communication Technology Acceptance: Comparison of Cellular Phone Adoption in South Korea and the United States." *Journal of Global Information Technology Management* 1:43–58. MR(E)

Lamar, Ronald V. (1966) "In-Service Education Needs Related to Diffusion of an Innovation." Ph.D. diss., University of California, Berkeley. E(E)

Lanjouw, Jean Olson, and Ashok Mody (1996) "Innovation and the International Diffusion of Environmentally Responsive Technology." *Research Policy* 25:549–571. O(E)

Lansing, J. Stephen (1987) "Balinese 'Water Temples' and the Management of Irrigation." *American Anthropologist* 89:326–341. A(E)

Lansing, Stephen (1991) *Priests and Programmers: Engineering the Knowledge of Bali.* Princeton, N.J.: Princeton University Press. A(E)

LaRose, Robert, and David Atkin (1992) "Audiotext and the Re-Invention of the Telephone as a Mass Medium." *Journalism Quarterly* 69(2):413–421. C(E)

LaRose, Robert, and Anne Hoag (1997) "Organizational Adoptions of the Internet and the Clustering of Innovations." *Telematics and Informatics* 13(1):49–61. C(E)

Larsen, Judith K., and Rekha Agarwal-Rogers (1977) *Re-Invention of Innovation: A Study of Community Health Centers.* Report, American Institute for Research in the Behavioral Sciences, Palo Alto, Calif. P(E)

Larsen, Judith K., and Everett M. Rogers (1984) "Consensus Development Conferences." *Knowledge* 5:537–548. O(E)

Latkin, Carol A. (1998) "Outreach in Natural Settings: The Use of Peer Leaders for HIV Prevention Among Injecting Drug Users' Networks." *Public Health Reports* 113(S1):151–159. PH(E)

Lawton, Stephen B., and William H. Lawton (1979) "An Autocatalytic Model for the Diffusion of Educational Innovations." *Educational Administration Quarterly* 15(1):19–53. E(E)

Lazarsfeld, Paul F., Bernard Berelson, and Hazel Gaudet (1944/1948/1968) *The People's Choice: How the Voter Makes Up His Mind in a Presidential Election.* New York: Duell, Sloan, and Pearce; New York: Columbia University Press.

Lazarsfeld, Paul F., and Herbert Menzel (1963) "Mass Media and Personal Influence." In Wilbur Schramm, ed., *The Science of Human Communication.* New York: Basic Books.

Lazarsfeld, Paul F., and Robert K. Merton (1964) "Friendship as Social Process: A Substantive and Methodological Analysis." In Monroe Berger et al., eds., *Freedom and Control in Modern Society.* New York: Octagon.

Lee, Paul S. N., Louis Leung, and Clement Y. K. So, eds., (2003) *Impact and Issues in New Media: Toward Intelligent Societies.* Cresskill, N.J.: Hampton Press. C(N)

Leonard-Barton, Dorothy (1988a) "Implementation as Mutual Adoption of Technology and Organization." *Research Policy* 17:251–267. MR(E)

Leonard-Barton, Dorothy (1988b) "Implementation and Characteristics of Organizational Innovation: Limits and Opportunities for Managerial Strategies." *Communication Research* 15(5):603–631. MR(E)

Lesnick, Peggy C. (2000) "Technology Transfer in the Dominican Republic: A Case Study of the Diffusion of Photovoltaics." Ph.D. diss., Union Institute, Cincinnati, Ohio. C(E)

Lessley, Bradley J. (1980) *The Dvorak Keyboard.* Report. Dvorak International Federation, Salem, Oregon.

Leung, Louis (1998) "Lifestyles and the Use of New Media Technology in China." *Telecommunications Policy* 22(9):781–790. C(E)

Leung, Louis (2000) "Societal, Organizational, and Individual Perceptual Factors Influencing the Adoption of Telecommuting in Hong Kong." Unpublished paper, Chinese University of Hong Kong. C(E)

Leung, Louis, and Ran Wei (1998) "Factors Influencing the Adoption of Interactive TV in Hong Kong: Implications for Advertising." *Asian Journal of Communication* 8(2):124–147. C(E)

Leung, Louis, and Ran Wei (1999) "Who Are the Mobile Phone Have-Nots? Influences and Consequences." *New Media and Society* 1(2):209–226. C(E)

Leung, Louis, and Ran Wei (2000) "More than Just Talk on the Move: Uses and Gratifications of the Cellular Phone." *Journalism and Mass Communication* 77(2):308–320. C(E)

Leuthold, Frank O. (1965) *Communication and Diffusion of Improved Farm Practices in Two Northern Saskatchewan Communities.* Mimeo report, Centre for Community Studies, Saskatoon, Saskatchewan. RS(E)

Leuthold, Frank O. (1967) "Discontinuance of Improved Farm Innovations by Wisconsin Farm Operators." Ph.D. diss., University of Wisconsin, Madison. RS(E)

Lewis, Laurie K., and David R. Seibold (1993) "Innovation Modification During Interorganizational Adoption." *Academy of Management Review* 18(2):322–354. C(E)

Lewis, Laurie K., and David R. Siebold (1996) "Communication During Interorganizational Innovation Adoption: Predicting Users' Behavior Coping Responses to Innovations in Organizations." *Communication Monographs* 63:131–157. C(E)

Lievrouw, Leah A. (2002) "Determination and Contingency in New Media Development: Diffusion of Innovations and Social Shaping of Technology Perspectives." In Leah A. Lievrouw and Sonia Livingstone, eds., *Handbook of New Media: Social Shaping and Consequences of ICTs.* Thousand Oaks, Calif.: Sage, 183–199. C(N)

Lievrouw, Leah A., and Janice T. Pope (1994) "Contemporary Art as Aesthetic Innovation: Applying the Diffusion Model to the Art World." *Knowledge* 15(4):373–395. C(E)

Lilien, Gary L., Arvind Rangaswamy, and Christophe van den Bulte (2000) "Diffusion Models: Managerial Applications and Software." In Vijay Mahajan, Eitan Muller, and Yoram Wind, eds., *New-Product Diffusion Models.* Dordrecht, Netherlands: Kluver Academic, 295–311. MR(E)

Lin, Carolyn A. (1998) "Exploring Personal Computer Adoption Dynamics." *Journal of Broadcasting and Electronic Media* 42:95–112. C(E)

Lin, Carolyn A. (1999) "Online-Service Adoption Likelihood." *Journal of Advertising Research* 39:79–89. C(E)

Lin, Carolyn A. (2001) "Audience Attributes, Media Supplementation, and Likely Online Service Adoption." *Mass Communication and Society* 4(1):19–38. C(E)

Lin, Carolyn A. (2002) "A Paradigm for Communication and Information Technology Adoption Research." In Carolyn A. Lin and David J. Atkin, eds., *Communication Technology and Society: Audience Adoption, and Use.* Creskill, N.J.: Hampton Press, 447–475. C(N)

Lin, Carolyn A., and David J. Atkin, eds., (2002) *Communication Technology and Society: Audience Adoption and Use.* Creskill, N.J.: Hampton Press. C(N)

Lin, Carolyn A., and Leo W. Jeffres (1998) "Factors Influencing the Adoption of Multimedia Cable Technology." *Journalism and Mass Communication Quarterly* 75(2):341–352. C(E)

Lindscy, Timothy (1998) "Diffusion of P2 Innovations." *Pollution Prevention Review* 8:1–14. O(E)

Linton, Ralph (1936) *The Study of Man.* New York: Appleton-Century-Crofts. A(N)

Linton, Ralph, and Abram Kradiner (1952) "The Change from Dry to Wet Rice Cultivation in Tanala-Bertsileo." In Guy E. Swanson et al., eds., *Readings in Social Psychology.* New York: Henry Holt. A(E)

Liu, William T., and Robert W. Duff (1972) "The Strength of Weak Ties." *Public Opinion Quarterly* 36:361–366. GS(E)

Lock, Catherine A., Eileen F. S. Kaner (2000) "Use of Marketing to Disseminate Brief Alcohol Intervention to General Practitioners: Promoting Health Care Interventions to Health Promoters." *Journal of Evaluation of Clinical Practice* 6(4):345–357. PH(E)

Lock, Catherine A., Eileen F. S. Kaner, Nick Heather, and Eilish Gilvarry (1999) "A Randomized Trial of Three Marketing Strategies to Disseminate a Screening and Brief Alcohol Intervention Programme to General Practitioners." *British Journal of General Practice* 49:695–698. PH(E)

Lohr, Jeffrey M., Katherine A. Fowler, and S. O. Lilienfeld (2002) "The Dissemination and Promotion of Pseudoscience in Clinical Psychology: The Challenge to Legitimate Clinical Science." *The Clinical Psychologist* 55(3):4–10. P(N)

Lomas, Jonathan, Murray Enkin, Geoffrey M. Anderson, Walter J. Hannah, Eugene Vayda, and Joel Singer (1991) "Opinion Leaders vs. Audit and Feedback to Implement Practice Guidelines." *JAMA* 265(17):2202–2207. PH(E)

Lopes, Paul (1999) "Diffusion and Syncretism: The Modern Jazz Tradition." *The Annals* 566:25–36. GS(E)

Lopes, Paul, and Mary Durffee (1999) "Preface to the Social Diffusion of Ideas and Things." *The Annals* 566:8–12. GS(N)

Lowe, Charles U. (1980) "The Consensus Development Programme: Technology Assessment at the National Institute of Health." *British Medical Journal* 303:153–158. O(E)

Lowe, Charles U. (1981) *Biomedical Discoveries Adopted by Industry for Purposes Other than Health Services.* Report, Office of Medical Applications of Research, National Institutes of Health, Washington, D.C. O(E)

Luthra, Rashmi (1994) "A Case of Problematic Diffusion: The Use of Sex Determination Techniques in India." *Knowledge* 15(3):259–272. C(E)

Lynam, D. R., R. Zimmerman, S. P. Novak, T. K. Logan, C. Martin, C. Leukefeld, and Richard Clayton (1999) "Project DARE: No Effects at 10-Year Followup." *Journal of Consulting and Clinical Psychology* 67:590–593. O(E)

Lynn, Michael, and Betsey D. Gelb (1996) "Identifying Innovative National Markets for Technical Consumer Goods." *International Marketing Review* 13:43–57. MR(E)

MacDonald, Peter, and Michael Chow (1999) "'Just One Damn Machine After Another?' Technological Innovation and the Industrialization of Tree Harvesting Systems." *Technology in Society* 21:323–344. O(E)

Machiavelli, Niccolò (1513/1961) *The Prince,* trans. by George Bull. Baltimore: Penguin Books.

Magill, Kathleen P., and Everett M. Rogers (1981) "Federally Sponsored Demonstrations of Technological Innovations." *Knowledge* 3(1):23–42. C(E)

Magill, Kathleen P., Thomas E. Shanks, and Everett M. Rogers (1980) *The Innovation Process for Three Mass Transportation Innovations: Vanpooling, Auto-Restricted Zones, and Priority Highway Lanes for High Occupancy Vehicles.* Report to the Urban Mass Transportation Administration, Institute for Communication Research, Stanford University, Stanford, Calif. C(E)

Mahajan, Vijay, and Eitan Muller (1994) "Innovation Diffusion in a Borderless Global Market: Will the 1992 Unification of the European Community Accelerate Diffusion of New Ideas, Products, and Technologies?" *Technological Forecasting and Social Change* 45:221–235. MR(E)

Mahajan, Vijay, and Eitan Muller (1996) "Timing, Diffusion, and Substitution of Technological Innovations: The IBM Mainframe Case." *Technological Forecasting and Social Change* 51:109–132. MR(E)

Mahajan, Vijay, and Eitan Muller (1998) "When Is It Worthwhile Targeting the Majority Instead of the Innovators in a New-Product Launch?" *Journal of Marketing Research* 35:488–495. MR(E)

Mahajan, Vijay, Eitan Muller, and Frank M. Bass (1991) "New Product Diffusion Models in Marketing: A Review and Directions for Research." In Nebojsa Nakicenovic and Arnulf Grübler, eds., *Diffusion of Technologies and Social Behavior.* New York: Springer, 125–177. MR(N)

Mahajan, Vijay, Eitan Muller, and Yoram Wind, eds., (2000a) *New-Product Diffusion Models.* Dordrecht, Netherlands: Kluver Academic. MR(N)

Mahajan, Vijay, Eitan Muller, and Yoram Wind (2000b) "New-Product Diffusion Models: From Theory to Practice." In Vijay Mahajan, Eitan Muller, and Yoram Wind, eds., *New-Product Diffusion Models*. Dordrecht, Netherlands: Kluver Academic, 4–24. MR(N)

Mahajan, Vijay, and Yoram Wind, eds., (1986) *Innovation Diffusion Models of New Product Acceptance*. Cambridge, Mass.: Ballinger. MR(N)

Mahler, Alwin, and Everett M. Rogers (1999) "The Diffusion of Interactive Communication Innovations and the Critical Mass: The Adoption of Telecommunications Services by German Banks." *Telecommunications Policy* 23:719–740. GE(E)

Majchrzak, Ann, Ronald E. Rice, Arvind Malhotra, Nelson King, and Sulin Ba (2000) "Technology Adaption: The Case of Computer-Supported Inter-Organizational Virtual Teams." *MIS Quarterly* 24(4):569–600. C(E)

March, James G. (1981) "Footnotes to Organizational Change." *Administrative Science Quarterly* 26:563–577.

Markus, A., and M. Weber (1989) "Externally Induced Innovation." In Andrew H. Van den Ven, H. A. Angle, and M. Scott Poole, eds., *Research on the Management of Innovation: The Minnesota Studies*. New York: Ballinger/Harper and Row. MR(E)

Markus, M. Lynne (1987) "Toward a 'Critical Mass' Theory of Interactive Media: Universal Access, Interdependence and Diffusion." *Communication Research* 14:491–511. MR(N)

Markus, M. Lynne (1990) "Toward a 'Critical Mass' Theory of Interactive Media." In Janet Fulk and Charles Steinfield, eds., *Organizations and Communication Technology*. Newbury Park, Calif.: Sage, 194–218. MR(N)

Marsden, Peter V., and Joel Podolny (1990) "Dynamic Analysis of Network Diffusion Processes." In Jerver Wessie and Hank Flap, eds., *Social Networks Through Time*. Utrecht, Netherlands: ISOR, 197–214. GS(E)

Marshall, Roger (1995) "Variation in the Characteristics of Opinion Leaders Across Cultural Borders." *Journal of International Consumer Marketing* 8(1):5–22. MR(E)

Martin, Graeme, and Phil Beaumont (1998) "Diffusing 'Best Practice' in Multinational Firms: Prospects, Practice and Contestation." *International Journal of Human Resource Management* 9(4):671–695. MR(E)

Martin, G. W., M. A. Herie, B. J. Turner, and J. A. Cunningham (1998) "A Social Marketing Model for Disseminating Research-Based Treatments to Addictions Treatment Providers." *Addictions* 93(11):1703–1715. PH(E)

Mason, Robert G. (1962) "An Ordinal Scale for Measuring the Adoption Process." In Wilbur Schramm, ed., *Studies of Innovation and Communication to the Public*. Stanford, Calif.: Institute for Communication Research, Stanford University. C(E)

Mayer, Michael E., William B. Gudykunst, Norman K. Perrill, and Bruce D. Merrill (1990) "A Comparison of Competing Models of the News Diffusion Process." *Western Journal of Speech Communication* 54:113–123. C(E)

McAdam, Doug (1986) "Recruitment to High-Risk Activism: The Case of Freedom Summer." *American Journal of Sociology* 92(1):64–90. GS(E)

McAdam, Doug (1988) *Freedom Summer.* New York: Oxford University Press. GS(E)

McAdam, Doug, and Ronnelle Paulsen (1993) "Specifying the Relationship Between Social Ties and Activism." *American Journal of Sociology* 99(3):640–667. GS(E)

McAdam, Doug, and Dieter Rucht (1999) "The Cross-National Diffusion of Movement Ideas." *The Annals* 566:56–74. GS(E)

McFadden, Daniel L., and Kenneth E. Train (1995) "Consumers' Evaluation of New Products: Learning from Self and Others." *Journal of Political Economy* 104(4):683–703. O(E)

McGuire, William J. (1989) "Theoretical Foundations of Campaigns." In Ronald E. Rice and Charles K. Atkin, eds., *Public Communication Campaigns,* 2nd ed., Newbury Park, Calif.: Sage, 43–65.

McKee, M., N. Fulop, P. Bouvier, A. Hort, H. Brand, F. Rasmussen, L. Kohler, Z. Varasovszky, and N. Rosdahl (1996) "Preventing Sudden Infant Deaths: The Slow Diffusion of an Idea." *Health Policy* 37(2):117–135. PH(E)

McKinney, Martha M., Janet M. Barnsley, and Arnold D. Kaluznky (1992) "Organizing for Cancer Control: The Diffusion of a Dynamic Innovation in a Community Cancer Network." *International Journal of Technology Assessment in Health Care* 8(2):268–288. PH(E)

McLeod, Kari S. (2000) "Our Sense of Snow: The Myth of John Snow in Medical Geography." *Social Sciences and Medicine* 50:923–935. PH(E)

Mendelsohn, Harold (1973) "Some Reasons Why Information Campaigns Can Succeed." *Public Opinion Quarterly* 39:50–61. C(E)

Mensch, Barbara S., Daniel Bagah, Wesley H. Clark, and Fred Binka (1999) "The Changing Nature of Adolesence in the Kassina-Nankana District of Northern Ghana." *Studies in Family Planning* 30(2):95–111. O(E)

Menzel, Herbert (1957) "Public and Private Conformity Under Different Conditions of Acceptance in the Group." *Journal of Abnormal and Social Psychology* 55:398–402. PH(E)

Menzel, Herbert (1959) *Social Determinants of Physicians' Reaction to Innovation in Medical Practice.* Ph.D. diss., Madison, University of Wisconsin. PH(E)

Menzel, Herbert (1960) "Innovation, Integration, and Marginality: A Survey of Physicians." *American Sociological Review* 25(5):704–713. PH(E)

Menzel, Herbert, James S. Coleman, and Elihu Katz (1959) "Dimensions of Being 'Modern' in Medical Practice." *Journal of Chronic Diseases* 9(1):20–40. PH(E)

Menzel, Herbert, and Elihu Katz (1955) "Social Relations and Innovation in the Medical Profession: The Epidemiology of a New Drug." *Public Opinion Quarterly* 19:337–353. PH(E)

Meyer, Alan D., and James B. Goes (1998) "Organizational Assimilation of Innovations: A Multilevel Contextual Analysis." *Academy of Management Journal* 31(4):897–923. MR(E)

Meyer, Jeffrey P., and William S. Davidson II (2000) "Dissemination of Innovation as Social Change." In Julian Rappaport and Edward Seidman, eds., *Handbook of Community Psychology.* New York: Kluwer Academic/Plenum, 421–438. P(N)

Merton, Robert K. (1949/1968) *Social Theory and Social Structure.* New York: Free Press.

Miles, Mathew B. (ed.) (1964) *Innovation in Education.* New York: Teachers College, Columbia University. E(N)

Miller, Robin Lin, David Klotz, and Haftan M. Eckholdt (1998) "HIV Prevention with Male Prostitutes and Patrons of Hustler Bars: Replication of an HIV Prevention Intervention." *American Journal of Community Psychology* 26(1):97–131. P(E)

Mintrom, Michael (1997) "Policy Entrepreneurs and the Diffusion of Innovation." *American Journal of Political Science* 41:738–770. PS (E)

Mintrom, Michael (2000) *Policy Entrepreneurs and School Choice.* Washington, D.C.: Georgetown University Press. PS(E)

Mintrom, Michael, and Sandra Vergari (1996) "Advocacy Coalitions, Policy Entrepreneurs, and Policy Change." *Policy Studies Journal* 24:420–434. PS (E)

Mintzberg, Henry, Duru Raisinghani, and Andre Théorêt (1976) "The Structure of 'Unstructured' Decision Processes." *Administrative Science Quarterly* 21:246–275. MR(N)

Mitchell, B. R., J. D. Mitchell, and A. P. Disney (1996) "User Adoption Issues in Renal Telemedicine." *Journal of Telemedicine and Telecare* 2(2):81–86. O(E)

Mitchell, J. D. (1999) "The Uneven Diffusion of Telemedicine Services in Australia." *Journal of Telemedicine and Telecare* 5(suppl. 1):S45-S47. O(E)

Mitchell, K., S. Nakamanya, A. Kmali, and J. A. G. Whitworth (2001) "Community-Based HIV/AIDS Education in Rural Uganda: Which Channel Is Most Effective?" *Health Education Research* 16(4):411–423. PH(E)

Mitta, R., and Ruth Simmons (1995) "Diffusion of the Culture of Contraception: Program Effects on Young Women in Bangladesh." *Studies in Family Planning* 26(1):1–13. GE(E)

Mohammed, Shaheed (2001) "Personal Communication Networks and the Effects of an Entertainment-Education Radio Soap Opera in Tanzania." *Journal of Health Communication* 6(2):137–154. C(E)

Mohr, Lawrence B. (1966) "Determinants of Innovation in Organizations." Ph.D. diss., University of Michigan, Ann Arbor. PS(E)

Mohr, Lawrence B. (1969) "Determinants of Innovation in Organizations." *American Political Science Review* 63:111–126. PS(E)

Mohr, Lawrence B. (1978) "Process Theory and Variance Theory in Innovation Research." In Michael Radnor et al., eds., *The Diffusion of Innovations: An Assessment.* Report to the National Science Foundation, Center for Interdisciplinary Study of Science and Technology, Northwestern University, Evanston, Ill. PS(E)

Mohr, Lawrence B. (1982) *Explaining Organizational Behavior: The Limits and Possibilities of Theory and Research.* San Francisco: Jossey-Bass. PS(N)

Montgomery, Mark R., and John B. Casterline (1993) "The Diffusion of Fertility Control in Taiwan: Evidence from Pooled Cross-Section Time-Series Models." *Population Studies* 47:457–479. GS(E)

Montgomery, Mark R., and John B. Casterline (1996) "Social Learning, Social Influence, and New Models of Fertility." In John B. Casterline, R. D. Lee, and K. A. Foote, eds., *Fertility in the United States,* suppl. to *Population and Development Review* 22:609–638. GS(E)

Montgomery, Mark R., and W. Chung (1999) "Social Networks and the Diffusion of Fertility Control: The Republic of Korea." In R. Leete, ed., *Dynamics of Values of Fertility Change.* Oxford, England: Oxford University Press, 179–209. GS(E)

Moon, M. J., and S. Bretschneider (1997) "Can State Government Actions Affect Innovation and Its Diffusion? An Extended Communication Model and Empirical Test." *Technological Forecasting and Social Change* 54(1):57–77. MR(E)

Mooney, Christopher Z., and Mei-Hsien Lee (1999) "Morality Policy Reinvention: State Death Penalties." *The Annals* 566:80–92. O(E)

Moore, Gary C., and Izak Benbasat (1990) "An Examination of the Adoption of Information Technology by End-Users: A Diffusion of Innovations Perspective." Working paper 90-MIS-012, Department of Commerce and Business Administration, University of British Columbia, Vancouver, Canada. MR(E)

Moore, Gary C., and Izak Benbasat (1991) "Development of an Instrument to Measure the Perceptions of Adopting an Information Technology Innovation." *Information Systems Research* 2(3):192–220. MR(E)

Moore, Geoffrey K. (1991) *Crossing the Chasm: Marketing and Selling High-Tech Products to Mainstream Customers.* New York: HarperBusiness.

Morrill, Richard L., Gary L. Gale, and Grant Ian Thrall (1988) *Spatial Diffusion.* Newbury Park, Calif.: Sage. G(N)

Mort, Paul R. (1953) "Educational Adaptability." *School Executive* 71:1–23. E(E)

Mort, Paul R. (1957) *Principles of School Administration.* New York: McGraw-Hill. E(N)

Moses, Stephen, Francis A. Plummer, Elizabeth N. Ngugi, Nico J. D. Nagelkerke, Aggrey O. Anzala, and Jackonlah O. Ndinya-Achola (1991) "Controlling AIDS in Africa: Effectiveness and Cost of an Intervention in a High-Frequency STD Transmitter Core Group." *AIDS* 5:407–411. PH(E)

Mosteller, Frederick (1981) "Innovation and Evaluation." *Science* 211:881–886. S(N)

Mountjoy, Daniel C. (1996) "Ethnic Diversity and the Patterned Adoption of Soil Conservation in the Strawberry Hills of Monterey, California." *Society and Natural Resources* 9:339–357. O(E)

Myers, Daniel J. (2000) "The Diffusion of Collective Violence: Infectiousness, Susceptability, and Mass Media Networks." *American Journal of Sociology* 106(1):173–208. GS(E)

Myers, Summer (1978) *The Demonstration Project as a Procedure for Accelerating the Application of New Technology.* Report, Institute of Public Administration, Washington, D.C. O(N)

Mytinger, Robert E. (1968) *Innovation in Local Health Services: A Study of the Adoption of New Programs by Local Health Departments with Particular Reference to New Health Practices.* Division of Medical Care Administration, Public Health Service, U.S. Department of Health, Education, and Welfare, Washington, D.C. PH(E)

Nader, Ralph (1965) *Unsafe at Any Speed.* New York: Grossman.

National Research Council (2001) *Diffusion Processes and Fertility Transition: Selected Perspectives.* Washington, D.C.: National Academy Press. GS(N)

Neiagus, A., S. R. Freedman, B. J. Kottiri, and Donald C. des Jarlais (2001) "HIV Risk Networks and HIV Transmission Among Injecting Drug Users." *Evaluation and Program Planning* 24:221–226. PH(E)

Neuendorf, Kimberly, David Atkin, and Leo Jeffres (1998) "Understanding Adopters of Audio Information Services." *Journal of Braodcasting and Electronic Media* 42:80–94. C(E)

Newell, Sue, and Jacky Swan (1995) "Professional Associations as Important Mediators of the Innovation Process." *Science Communication* 16(4):371–387. O(E)

Nice, David C. (1994) *Policy Innovation in State Government.* Ames: Iowa State University Press. PS (E)

Niehoff, Arthur (1964) "Theravada Buddhism: A Vehicle for Technical Change." *Human Organization* 23:108–112. A(E)

Nielsen, Thomas S. (1999) "Using Adopter Categories in Marketing." *Nebraska Library Association Quarterly* 30(4):20–22. O(N)

Nohria, Nitin, and Ranjay Gulati (1996) "Is Slack Good or Bad for Innovation?" *Academy of Management Journal* 38(5):1245–1264. MR(E)

Noyce, Robert N., and Marcian E. Hoff, Jr. (1981) "A History of Microprocessor Development at Intel." *IEEE Micro* 7:8–21.

O'Brien, David J., Andrew Raedeke, and Edward W. Hassinger (1998) "The Social Networks of Leaders in More or Less Viable Communities Six Years Later: A Research Note." *Rural Sociology* 63(1):109–127. RS(E)

Oh, Jeongho (2000) "Structural Determinants and Causal Configuration of Successful Internet Diffusion: Cross-National Analysis." Ph.D. diss., Northwestern University, Evanston, Ill. C(E)

Oldenburg, B. F., J. F. Sallis, M. L. French, and N. Owen (1999) "Health Promotion Research and the Diffusion and Institutionalization of Interventions." *Health Education Research* 14(1):121–130. PH(E)

O'Loughlin, J., L. Renaud, L. Richard, L. S. Gomez, and G. Paradis (1998) "Correlates of the Sustainability of Community-Based Heart Health Promotion Interventions." *Preventive Medicine* 27:702–712. PH(E)

Olson, Mancur H. (1965) *The Logic of Collective Action: Public Goods and the Theory of Groups.* Cambridge, Mass.: Harvard University Press.

Orlandi, Mario A., C. Landers, R. Weston, and N. Haley (1991) "Diffusion of Health Promotion Innovations." In Karen Glanz, F. M. Lewis, and B. K. Rimer, eds., *Health Behavior and Health Education: Theory, Research, and Practice.* San Francisco: Jossey-Bass, 288–313. PH(E)

Ostrom, Elinor (1990) *Governing the Commons: The Evolution of Institutions for Collective Action.* New York: Cambridge University Press. PS(E)

Paddock, W. C. (1992) "Our Last Chance to Win the War on Hunger." *Advances in Plant Pathology* 8:197–222. O(E)

Palloni, Alberto (2001) "Diffusion in Sociological Analysis." In John Casterline, ed., *Diffusion Processes and Fertility Transition.* Washington, D.C.: National Academy Press, 66–114. GS(N)

Pankratz, Melinda M., Denise Halfours, and HanSan Cho (2000) "The Diffusion of a Federal Drug Prevention Policy." Unpublished paper, University of North Carolina, Chapel Hill. PH(E)

Parcel, Guy S., Michael R. Ericksen, Chris Y. Lovato, Nell H. Gottlieb, Susan G. Brink, and Lawrence W. Green (1989) "The Diffusion of School-Based Tobacco Use Prevention Programs: Project Description and Baseline Data." *Health Education Research* 4(1):111–124. PH(E)

Parcel, Guy S., Nancy M. O'Hara-Tompkins, Ronald B. Harrist, Karen M. Basen-Engquist, Laura K. McCormick, Nell H. Gottlieb, and Michael P. Eriksen (1995) "Diffusion of an Effective Tobacco Prevention Program. Part II: Evaluation of the Adoption Phase." *Health Education Research* 10(3):297–307. PH(E)

Parcel, Guy S., Cheryl L. Perry, and Wendell C. Taylor (1990) "Beyond Demonstration: Diffusion of Health Promotion Innovations." In Neil Bracht, ed., *Health Promotion at the Community Level.* Thousand Oaks, Calif.: Sage, 229–251. PH(E)

Parcel, Glenn S., Wendell C. Taylor, Susan G. Brink, Nell Gottlieb, Karen Engguist, Nancy M. O'Hara, and Michael P. Ericksen (1989) "Translating Theory into Practice: Intervention Strategies for the Diffusion of a Health Promotion Innovation." *Family and Community Health* 12(3):1–13. PH(E)

Parker, Philip M. (1993) "Choosing Among Diffusion Models: Some Empirical Evidence." *Marketing Letters* 4(1):81–94. MR(E)

Parker, Philip M. (1994) "Aggregate Diffusion Forecasting Models in Marketing: A Critical Review." *International Journal of Forecasting* 10:353–380. MR(E)

Parker, Philip M., and Hubert Gatignon (1996) "Order of Entry, Trial Diffusion, and Elasticity Dynamics: An Empirical Case." *Marketing Letters,* 7(1):95–109. MR(E)

Parkinson, Robert (1972) "The Dvorak Simplified Keyboard: Forty Years of Frustration." *Computers and Automation* 21:1–8.

Pelletier-Fleury, N., V. Fargeon, and J. L. Lanoe (1997) "Transaction Costs Economics as a Conceptual Framework for the Analysis of Barriers to the Diffusion of Telemedicine." *Health Policy* 42:1–14. PH(E)

Pelto, Pertti J. (1973) *The Snowmobile Revolution: Technology and Social Change in the Arctic.* Menlo Park, Calif.: Cummings. A(E)

Pelto, Pertti J., and Ludger Muller-Wille (1972) "The Snowmobile Revolution: Technology and Social Change in the Arctic." In H. Russel Bernard and Pertti Pelto, eds., *Technology and Social Change.* New York: Macmillan. A(E)

Pelto, Pertti J., et al. (1969) "The Snowmobile Revolution in Lapland." *Journal of the Finno-Ugrian Society* 69:1–42. A(E)

Pemberton, H. Earl (1936a) "The Curve of Culture Diffusion Rate." *American Sociological Review* 1:547–556. ES(E)

Pemberton, H. Earl (1936b) "Culture-Diffusion Gradients." *American Journal of Sociology* 42:226–233. ES(E)

Pemberton, H. Earl (1937) "The Effect of a Social Crisis on the Curve of Diffusion." *American Sociological Review* 1:547–556. ES(E)

Pemberton, H. Earl (1938) "The Spatial Order of Culture Diffusion." *Sociology and Social Research* 3:246–251. ES(E)

Perry, James L., and Kenneth L. Kraemer (1979) *Technological Innovation in American Local Governments: The Case of Computing.* New York: Pergamon Press. PS(E)

Perry, Tekla S., and Paul Wallich (1985, October) "Inside the PARC: The Information Architects." *IEEE Spectrum* 62–75.

Perse, Elizabeth M., and Debra Greenberg Dunn (1998) "The Utility of Home Computers and Media Use: Implications of Multimedia and Connectivity." *Journal of Broadcasting and Electronic Media* 42(4):435–456. C(E)

Piderit, Sandy Kristin (2000) "Rethinking Resistance and Recognizing Ambivalence: A Multidimensional View of Attitudes Toward an Organizational Change." *Academy of Management Journal* 25:783–794. MR(E)

Piotrow, Phyllis T., Jose G. Rimon II, Kim Winnard, D. Lawrence Kincaid, Dale Huntington, and Julie Convisser (1990) "Mass Media Family Planning Promotion in Three Nigerian Cities." *Studies in Family Planning* 21(5):265–274. PH(E)

Pitcher, Brian L., Robert L. Hamblin, and Jerry L.L. Miller (1978) "The Diffusion of Collective Violence." *American Sociological Review* 43:23–25. GS(E)

Polacsek, Michelle, Everett M. Rogers, W. Gill Woodall, Harold Delaney, Denise Wheeler, and Nagesh Rao (2001) "MADD Victim Impact Panels and Stages-of-Change in Drunk Driving Prevention." *Journal of Studies on Alcohol* 63:344–350. C(E)

Poole, Marshall Scott, and Andrew H. Van de Ven (1989) "Toward a General Theory of Innovation Process." In Andrew H. Van de Ven, H. A. Angle, and M. Scott Poole, eds., *Research on the Management of Innovation: The Minnesota Studies.* New York: Ballinger/Harper and Row. C(E)

Pope, Alexander (1711) *An Essay on Criticism,* part II.

Price, Derek J. de Solla (1963) *Little Science, Big Science.* New York: Columbia University Press.

Prochaska, James O., Carlo C. DiClemente, and John C. Norcross (1992) "In Search of How People Change: Applications to Addictive Behaviors." *American Psychologist* 47(9):1102–1114. P(E)

Puska, P., K. Koskela, A. McAlister, H. Mayranen, A. Smolander, L. Viri, V. Korpelainen, and E. M. Rogers (1986) "Use of Lay Opinion Leaders to Promote Diffusion of Health Innovations in a Community Programme: Lessons Learned from the North Karelia Project." *Bulletin of the World Health Organization* 64(3):437–446. PH(E)

Putnam, Robert D. (1993) *Making Democracy Work: Civic Traditions in Modern Italy.* Princeton, N.J.: Princeton University Press. PS(E)

Putsis, William P. J., Jr. (1998) "Parameter Variation and New Product Diffusion." *Journal of Forecasting* 17:231–257. MR(E)

Putsis, William P. J., Jr., Sridhar Balasubramanian, Edward H. Kaplan, and Subrata Sen (1997) "Mixing Behavior in Cross-Country Diffusion." *Marketing Science* 16(4):354–369. MR(E)

Putsis, William P., Jr., and V. Srinivasan (2000) "Estimation Techniques for Macro Diffusion Models." In Vijay Mahajan, Eitan Muller, and Yoram Wind, eds., *New-Product Diffusion Models.* Dordrecht, Netherlands: Kluver Academic, 263–291. MR(N)

Puumalainen, K. L., L. D. Frank, and S. K. Sundqvist (2002) "Modeling the Diffusion of Mobile Subscriptions in Finland: Effects of Data Aggregation." Unpublished paper, Telecom Business Research Center, Lappeenranta University of Technology, Lappeenranta, Finland. MR(E)

Puumalainen, Kaisu, and Sanna Sundqvist (2002) "Predicting and Managing the Diffusion of Innovations: The Challenge in Mobile Telecommunications Business." Unpublished paper, Telecom Business Research Center, Lappeenranta University of Technology, Lappeenranta, Finland. MR(E)

Rahim, S. A. (1961) *The Diffusion and Adoption of Agricultural Practices: A Study in a Village in East Pakistan.* Comilla, East Pakistan: Pakistan Academy for Village Development. C(E)

Rahim, S. A. (1965) *Communication and Personal Experience in an East Pakistan Village.* Comilla, East Pakistan: Pakistan Academy for Village Development. C(E)

Raisinghani, Makesh Sukhdev (1997) "Strategic Evaluation of Electronic Commerce Technologies (Internet, Innovation Diffusion)." Ph.D. Dissertation, University of Texas at Arlington. MR(E)

Rakowski, William, John P. Fulton, and Judith P. Feldman (1993) "Women's Decision Making About Mammography: A Replication of the Relationship Between Stages of Adoption and Decisional Balance." *Health Psychology* 12(3):209–214. P(E)

Ram, S., and Hyung-Shik Jung (1994) "Innovativeness in Product Usage: A Comparison of Early Adopters and Early Majority." *Psychology and Marketing* 11(1):57–67. MR(E)

Ramusen, Wayne D. (1968) "Advances in American Agriculture: The Mechanical Tomato Harvester as a Case Study." *Technology and Culture* 9:531–543. O(E)

Rangaswamy, Arvind, and Sunil Gupta (2000) "Innovation Adoption and Diffusion and the Digital Environment: Some Research Opportunities." In

Vijay Mahajan, Eitan Muller, and Yoram Wind, eds., *New-Product Diffusion Models.* Dordrecht, Netherlands: Kluver Academic, 75–96. MR(E)

Rao, G. Appa, Everett M. Rogers, and S. N. Singh (1980) "Interpersonal Relations in the Diffusion of an Innovation in Two Indian Villages." *Indian Journal of Extension Education* 16:(1 and 2):19–24. RS(E)

Ratchford, Brian T., Siva K. Balasubramanian, and Wagner A. Kamakura (2000) "Diffusion Models with Replacement and Multiple Purchases." In Vijay Mahajan, Eitan Muller, and Yoram Wind, eds., *New-Product Diffusion Models.* Dordrecht, Netherlands: Kluver Academic, 123–140. MR(E)

Ray, Michael L., A. G. Sawyer, M. L. Rothschild, R. M. Heeler, E. C. Strong, and J. B. Reed (1975) "Marketing Communication and the Hierarchy-of-Effects." In Peter Clarke, ed., *New Models for Mass Communication Research.* Thousand Oaks, Calif.: Sage. MR(E)

Ray-Couquard, I., T. Philip, M. Lehman, B. Fervers, F. Farsi, and F. Chauvin (1997) "Impact of a Clinical Guidelines Program for Breast and Colon Cancer in a French Cancer Center." *JAMA* 278(19):1591–1595. O(E)

Reagan, Joey (2002) "The Difficult World of Predicting Telecommunication Innovations: Factors Affecting Adoption." In Carolyn A. Lin and David J. Atkin, eds., *Communication Technology and Society: Audience Adoption and Uses.* Creskill, N.J.: Hampton Press, 65–87. C(N)

Redmond, W. H. (1994) "Diffusion at Sub-National Levels: A Regional Analysis of New Product Growth." *Journal of Product Innovation Management* 11:201–212. MR(E)

Rennie, J. (1995) "The Uncertainties of Technological Innovation." *Scientific American* 275:57–58. O(N)

Rhinehart, E., D. A. Goldman, and E. J. O'Rourke (1991) "Adaptation of the Centers for Disease Control Guidelines for the Prevention of Nosacomial Infection in a Pediatric Intensive Case Unit in Jakarta, Indonesia." *American Journal of Medicine* 91(suppl. 3B):213S-220S. PH(E)

Rice, Ronald E., and Everett M. Rogers (1980) "Re-Invention in the Innovation Process." *Knowledge* 1:499–514. C(E)

Rice, Ronald E., and J. Tyler (1995) "Individual and Organizational Influences on Voice Mail Use and Evaluation." *Behaviour and Information Technology* 14(6):329–341. C(E)

Rice, Ronald E., and Jane Webster (2002) "Adoption, Diffusion, and Use of New Media." In Carolyn A. Lin and David J. Atkin, eds., *Communication Technology and Society: Audience Adoption and Use.* Creskill, N.J.: Hampton Press, 191–277. C(N)

Roberts, John H., and James M. Lattin (2000) "Disaggregate-Level Diffusion Models." In Vijay Mahajan, Eitan Muller, and Yoram Wind, eds., *New-*

Product Diffusion Models. Dordrecht, Netherlands: Kluver Academic, 207–236. MR(E)

Robertson, Maxine, Jacky Swan, and Sue Newell (1996) "The Role of Networks in the Diffusion of Technological Innovation." *Journal of Management Studies* 33(3):333–359. MR(E)

Rogers, Everett M. (1958) "Categorizing the Adopters of Agricultural Practices." *Rural Sociology* 23(4):346–354. RS(E)

Rogers, Everett M. (1961) *Characteristics of Agricultural Innovators and Other Adopter Catagories.* Research Bulletin 882, Agricultural Experiment Station, Wooster, Ohio. RS(E)

Rogers, Everett M. (1962) *Diffusion of Innovation.* New York: Free Press. RS(N)

Rogers, Everett M. (1973) *Communication Strategies for Family Planning.* New York: Free Press. C(N)

Rogers, Everett M. (1976) "Communication and Development: The Passing of the Dominant Paradigm." *Communication Research* 3:121–148. C(N)

Rogers, Everett M. (1983) *Diffusion of Innovations,* 3rd ed. New York: Free Press. C(N)

Rogers, Everett M. (1986a) "Models of Knowledge Transfer: Critical Perspectives." In George M. Beal, Wimal Dissanayake, and Sumiye Konoshima, eds., *Knowledge Generation, Exchange, and Utilization.* Boulder, Colo.: Westview Press, 37–60. C(N)

Rogers, Everett M. (1986b) *Communication Technology: The New Media in Society.* New York: Free Press. C(N)

Rogers, Everett M. (1987) "Progress, Problems, and Prospects for Network Research: Investigating Relationships in the Age of Electronic Communication Technologies." *Social Networks* 9:285–310. C(N)

Rogers, Everett M. (1988) "The Intellectual Foundation and History of the Agricultural Extension Model." *Knowledge* 9:410–510. C(N)

Rogers, Everett M. (1991a) "Rise of the Classical Diffusion Model." *Current Contents* 13(15):16. C(N)

Rogers, Everett M. (1991b) "The 'Critical Mass' in the Diffusion of Interactive Technologies in Organizations." In Kenneth L. Kraemer, James I. Cash, Jr., and Jay F. Nunmaker, Jr., eds., *The Information System Research Challenges: Survey Research Methods.* Boston: Harvard Business School Press, 245–263. C(N)

Rogers, Everett M. (1993) "Diffusion and the Re-Invention of Project D.A.R.E." In Thomas E. Backer and Everett M. Rogers, eds., *Organizational Aspects of Health Communication Campaigns: What Works?* Newbury Park, Calif.: Sage, 139–162. C(E)

Rogers, Everett M. (1994) *A History of Communication Study: A Biographical Approach.* New York: Free Press.

Rogers, Everett M. (1995) *Diffusion of Innovations,* 4th ed., New York: Free Press.

Rogers, Everett M. (1999) "Georg Simmel and Intercultural Communication." *Communication Theory* 9(1):58–74.

Rogers, Everett M. (2000) "Reflections on News Event Diffusion Research." *Journalism and Mass Communication Quarterly* 77(3):561–576. C(N)

Rogers, Everett M. (2001) "The Department of Communication at Michigan State University as a Seed Institution for Communication Study." *Communication Studies* 52(3):234–248.

Rogers, Everett M. (2002a) "The Digital Divide." *Convergence* 7(4):96–111. C(N)

Rogers, Everett M. (2002b) "The Nature of Technology Transfer." *Science Communication* 23(3):323–341. C(N)

Rogers, Everett M., Joseph R. Ascroft, and Niels G. Roling (1970) *Diffusion of Innovations in Brazil, Nigeria, and India.* East Lansing, Michigan State University, Department of Communication, Diffusion of Innovations Research Report 24. C(E)

Rogers, Everett M., J. D. Eveland, and Alden Bean (1982) *Extending the Agricultural Extension Model.* Report, Institute for Communication Research, Stanford University, Stanford, Calif. C(N)

Rogers, Everett M., and Pi-Chao Chen (1980) "Diffusion of Health and Birth Planning Innovations in the People's Republic of China." In George I. Lythscott et al., eds., *Report on the Chinese Rural Health Delegation.* Report, Foggarty Center for International Health, U.S. Department of Health and Human Services, Washington, D.C. C(E)

Rogers, Everett M., Lori Collins-Jarvis, and Joseph Schmitz (1994) "The PEN Project in Santa Monica: Interactive Communication and Political Action." *Journal of the American Society for Information Sciences* 45(6):1–10. C(E)

Rogers, Everett M., James W. Dearing, Nagesh Rao, Michelle L. Campo, Gary Meyer, Gary J. B. Betts, and Mary K. Casey (1995) "Communication and Community in a City Under Siege: The AIDS Epidemic in San Francisco." *Communication Research* 22(6):664–678. C(E)

Rogers, Everett M., and D. Lawrence Kincaid (1981) *Communication Networks: Toward a New Paradigm for Research.* New York: Free Press. C(E)

Rogers, Everett M., and Udai Pareek (1982) *Acceptability of Fertility Regulating Mechanism: A Synthesis of Research Literature.* Report to the World Health Organization, Institute of Communication Research, Stanford University, Stanford, Calif. C(N)

Rogers, Everett M., Jeffrey C. Peterson, Leslie Cunningham-Sabo, and Sally M. Davis (in press), *Community Participation and the Utilization of Health Research*. Report, Prevention Research Center, University of New Mexico, Albuquerque. C(E)

Rogers, Everett M., Jeffrey C. Peterson, and Thomas McOwiti (2002) "Diffusion of a Policy Innovation: No-Smoking Ordinances in New Mexico." Unpublished paper, Department of Communication and Journalism, University of New Mexico, Albuquerque. C(E)

Rogers, Everett M., and L. Edna Rogers (1961) "A Methodological Analysis of Adoption Scales." *Rural Sociology* 26(4):325–336. RS(E)

Rogers, Everett M., and Nancy Seidel (2002) "Diffusion of News of the Terrorist Attacks of September 11, 2001." *Prometheus* 20(3):209–219. C(E)

Rogers, Everett M., with Floyd F. Shoemaker (1971) *Communication of Innovations: A Cross-Cultural Approach.* New York: Free Press. C(E)

Rogers, Everett M., and Thomas M. Steinfatt (1999) *Intercultural Communication.* Prospect Heights, Ill.: Waveland Press.

Rogers, Everett M., and J. Douglas Storey (1988) "Communication Campaigns." In Charles R. Berger and Steven H. Chaffee, eds., *Handbook of Communication Science.* Newbury Park, Calif.: Sage, 817–846. C(N)

Rogers, Everett M., with Lynne Svenning (1969) *Modernization Among Peasants: The Impact of Communication.* New York: Holt, Reinhart and Winston. C(E)

Rogers, Everett M., Shiro Takegami, and Jing Yin (2001) "Lessons Learned About Technology Transfer." *Technovation* 21:253–261. C(E)

Rogers, Everett M., Peter W. Vaughan, Ramadhan M. A. Swalehe, Nagesh Rao, Peer Svenkerud, and Suruchi Sood (1999) "Effects of an Entertainment-Education Radio Soap Opera on Family Planning Behavior in Tanzania." *Studies in Family Planning* 30(3):193–211. C(E)

Rogers, Everett M., Jing Yin, and Joern Hoffman (2000) "Technology Transfer from U.S. Research Universities." *Journal of the Association of University Technology Managers* 12:43–80. C(E)

Rohrbach, Louise Ann, Carol N. D'Onofrio, Thomas E. Backer, and Susanne B. Montgomery (1996) "Diffusion of School-Based Substance Abuse Prevention Programs." *American Behavioral Scientist* 39(7):919–934. PH(E)

Rolfs, J. (1974) "A Theory of Interdependent Demand for a Communication Service." *Bell Journal of Economics and Management Science* 5:16–37. MR(E)

Röling, Niels, Joseph Ascroft, and Fred Y. Chege (1976) "The Diffusion of Innovations and the Issue of Equity in Rural Development." *Communication Research* 3:155–170. C(E)

Rosen, Emmanuel (2000) *The Anatomy of Buzz: How to Create Word of Mouth Marketing.* New York: Doubleday/Currency. MR(E)

Ross, Donald H. (1958) *Administration for Adaptability.* New York: Metropolitan School Study Council. E(E)

Rubin, Alan M., and Keren Eyal (2002) "The Videocassette Recorder in the Home Media Environment." In Carolyn A. Lin and David J. Atkin, eds., *Communication Technology and Society: Audience Adoption and Uses.* Creskill, N.J.: Hampton Press, 329–349. C(N)

Rutenberg, Naomi, and Susan Cotts Watkins (1997) "The Buzz Outside the Clinics: Conversations and Contraception in Nyanza Province, Kenya." *Studies in Family Planning* 28(4):290–307. GS(E)

Ruttan, Vernon W. (1996) "What Happened to Technology Adoption Diffusion Research?" *Sociologia Ruralis* 36(1):51–73. AE(N)

Ryan, Bryce (1948) "A Study in Technological Diffusion." *Rural Sociology* 13:273–285. RS(E)

Ryan, Bryce, and Neal C. Gross (1943) "The Diffusion of Hybrid Seed Corn in Two Iowa Communities." *Rural Sociology* 8:15–24. RS(E)

Ryan, Bryce, and Neal C. Gross (1950) *Acceptance and Diffusion of Hybrid Corn Seed in Two Iowa Communities.* Research Bulletin 372, Agricultural Experiment Station, Ames, Iowa. RS(E)

Rychetnik, L., M. Frommer, P. Hawe, and A. Shiell (2002) "Criteria for Evaluating Evidence of Public Health Interventions." *Journal of Epidemiological Community Health* 56:119–127. PH(E)

Salamon, Sonya, Richard L. Farnsworth, Donald G. Bullock, and Raj Yusef (1997) "Family Factors Affecting Adoption of Sustainable Farming Systems." *Journal of Soil and Water Conservation* 52:265–271. RS(E)

Saloner, G., and A. Shepard (1995) "Adoption of Technologies with Network Effects: An Empirical Analysis of the Adoption of Automated Teller Machines." *RAND Journal of Economics* 26:479–501. GE(E)

Saltiel, John, James W. Bauder, and Sandy Palakovich (1994) "Adoption of Sustainable Agricultural Practices: Diffusion, Farm Structure, and Profitability." *Rural Sociology* 59:333–349. RS(E)

Samuels, Bruce, and Stanton A. Glantz (1991) "The Politics of Local Tobacco Control." JAMA 266(15):2110–2117. PS (E)

Sapp, Stephen G., and Helen H. Jensen (1997) "Socioeconomic Impacts on Implementation and Confirmation Decisions: Adoption of U.S. Beef in Japan." *Rural Sociology* 62:508–524. RS(E)

Sathye, Milind (1999) "Adoption of Internet Banking by Australian Consumers: An Empirical Investigation." *International Journal of Bank Marketing* 17(7):324–334. MR(E)

Sawai, Kiyoshi (1994) "A Study of How Coleman's Book on Diffusion of New Drugs Has Been Cited in Subsequent Published Articles." *Library and Information Science* 32:105–122. O(E)

Schauffler, Helen Halpin, Fennifer K. Mordavsky, and Sara McMenamin (2001) "Adoption of the APCPR Clinical Practice Guideline for Smoking Cessation: A Survey of California's HMOs." *American Journal of Preventive Medicine* 21(3):153–161. PH(E)

Schelling, Thomas C. (1978) *Micromotives and Macrobehavior.* New York: Norton.

Schmitz, Andrew, and David Seckler (1970) "Merchanized Agriculture and Social Welfare: The Case of the Tomato Harvester." *American Journal of Agricultural Economics* 52:569–577. AE(E)

Schmitz, Joseph, Everett M. Rogers, Ken Phillips, and Don Paschal (1995) "The Public Electronic Network (PEN) and the Homeless in Santa Monica." *Journal of Applied Communication Research* 23:26–43. C(E)

Schoder, Detlef (2000) "Forecasting the Success of Telecommunication Services in the Presence of Network Effects." *Information Economics and Policy* 12:181–200. O(E)

Schofield, Margot J., Kim Edwards, and Robert Pearce (1997) "Effectiveness of Two Strategies for Dissemination of Sun-Protection Policy in New South Wales Primary and Secondary Schools." *Australian and New Zealand Journal of Public Health* 21(7):743–750. PH(E)

Schön, Donald A. (1963) "Champions for Radical New Inventions." *Harvard Business Review* 41:77–86. MR(E)

Schön, Donald A. (1971) *Beyond the Stable State.* New York: Random House. MR(E)

Schooler, Carolyn, Steven H. Chaffee, June A. Flora, and Connie Roser (1998) "Health Campaign Channels: Tradeoffs Among Reach, Specificity, and Impact." *Human Communication Research* 24(3):410–432. C(E)

Schroeder, R. G. (1989) "The Development of Innovation Ideas." In Andrew H. Van de Ven, H. A. Angle, and M. Scott Poole, eds., *Research on the Management of Innovation:* The Minnesota Studies. New York: Ballinger/Harper and Row. MR(E)

Schumpeter, Joseph A. (1950) *Capitalism, Socialism, and Democracy.* New York: Harper and Row. GE(N)

Schwalbe, Ted (1976) "A Study in Public Policy: The Santa Monica Freeway Diamond Lane Experiment." Unpublished paper, Annenberg School for Communication, University of Southern California, Los Angeles. C(E)

Scott, S. G., and R. A. Bruce (1994) "Determinants of Innovative Behavior: A Path Model of Individual Innovation in the Workplace." *Academy of Management Journal* 37(3):580–607. MR(E)

Shaneyfette,. Terrence M., Michael F. Mayer, and Johann Rothwang (1999) "Are Guidelines Following Guidelines? The Methodological Quality of Clinical Practice Guidelines in the Peer-Reviewed Medical Literature." *JAMA* 281(20):1900–1905. O(E)

Shankar, Venkatesh, Gregory S. Carpenter, and Lakshman Krishnamurthi (1998) "Late Mover Advantage: How Innovative Late Entrants Outsell Pioneers." *Journal of Marketing Research* 35:54–70. MR(E)

Shannon, Claude E., and Warren Weaver (1949) *The Mathematical Theory of Communication.* Urbana: University of Illinois Press.

Shapeman, J., and Thomas E. Backer (1995) "The Role of Knowledge Utilization in Adopting Innovations from Academic Medical Centers." *Hospital & Health Services Administration* 40(3):401–423. PH(E)

Sharp, Lauriston (1952) "Steel Axes for Stone Age Australians." In Edward H. Spicer, ed., *Human Problems in Technological Change.* New York: Russell Sage Foundation. A(E)

Shefner-Rogers, Corinne L., Nagesh Rao, Everett M. Rogers, and Arun Wayangankar (1998) "The Empowerment of Women Dairy Farmers in India." *Journal of Applied Communication Research* 26(3):319–337. C(E)

Shen, O. R. L., R. L. Olivia, P. J. H. Hu, and C. P. We (1998) "Adoption and Diffusion of Telemedicine Technology in Health Care Organizations: A Comparative Case Study in Hong Kong." *Journal of Organizational Computing and Electronic Commerce* 8(4):247–277. O(E)

Shermesh, Stefan, and Gerald Tellis (2002) "The International Takeoff of New Products: The Role of Economics and Culture." Unpublished paper, University of Southern California, Los Angeles. MR(E)

Sherry, Lorraine, Shelley Billig, Fern Tavalin, and David Gibson (2000) "New Insights on Technology Adoption in Schools." *T.H.E. Journal* 27(7):43–48. E(E)

Sherry, Lorraine, D. Lawyer-Brook, and L. Black (1997) "Evaluation of the Boulder Valley Internet Project: A Theory-Based Approach." *Journal of Interactive Learning Research* 8(2):199–234. E(E)

Shingi, Prakash M., and Bella Mody (1976) "The Communication Effects Gap: A Field Experiment on Television and Agricultural Ignorance in India." *Communication Research* 3:171–193. MR(E)

Siegel, Michael, Julia Carol, Jerrie Jordan, Robin Hobart, Susan Schoenmarklin, Fran DuMelle, and Peter Fisher (1997) "Preemption in Tobacco Control: Review of an Emerging Public Health Problem." *JAMA* 278(10):858–863. PS (E)

Sikkema, K. L., Jeffrey A. Kelly, R. A. Winett, L. J. Solomon, V. A. Cargill, R. A. Rofferman, T. L. McAuliffe, T. G. Heckman, E. A. Anderson, D. A.

Wagstaff, A. D. Norman, M. J. Perry, D. A. Crumble, and M. B. Mercer (2000) "Outcomes of a Randomized Community-Level HIV-Prevention Intervention for Women Living in 16 Low-Income Housing Developments." *American Journal of Public Health* 19:57–63. PH(E)

Sill, Maurice L. (1958) "Personal, Situational, and Communicational Factors Associated with the Farm Practice Adoption Process." Ph.D. diss., Pennsylvania State University, University Park. RS(E)

Silverman, Leslie J., and Wilfrid C. Bailey (1961) *Trends in the Adoption of Recommended Farm Practices.* Bulletin 617, Agricultural Experiment Station, State College, Mississippi. RS(E)

Simmel, Georg (1908/1964) *The Sociology of Georg Simmel*, trans. by Kurt H. Wolf. New York: Free Press.

Simmel, Georg (1922/1955) *The Web of Group-Affiliations*, trans. by Reinhard Bendix. New York: Free Press.

Singhal, Arvind, and Everett M. Rogers (1999) *Entertainment-Education: A Communication Strategy for Social Change.* Mahwah, N.J.: Lawrence Erlbaum Associates.

Singhal, Arvind, and Everett M. Rogers (2001) *India's Communication Revolution: From Bullock Carts to Cyber Marts.* New Delhi: Sage/India.

Singhal, Arvind, and Everett M. Rogers (2003) *Combating AIDS: Communication Strategies in Action.* New Delhi: Sage/India.

Singhal, Arvind, Everett M. Rogers, and Meenakshi Mahajan (1999) "The Gods Are Drinking Milk! Word-of-Mouth Diffusion of a Major News Event in India." *Asian Journal of Communication* 9(1):86–107. C(E)

Smith, Dennis W., Kerry J. Redican, and Larry K. Olsen (1992) "The Longevity of Growing Healthy: An Analysis of the Eight Original Sites Implementing the School Health Curriculum Project." *Journal of School Health* 62(3):83–87. PH(E)

Smith, Douglas K., and Robert C. Alexander (1988) *Fumbling the Future: How Xerox Invented, and Then Ignored, the First Personal Computer.* New York: Morrow.

Smith, M. U., and Ralph J. DiClemente (2000) "STAND: A Peer Educator Training Curriculum for Sexual Risk Reduction in the Rural South." *Preventive Medicine* 30(6):441–449. PH(E)

Snyder-Halpern, Rita (1998) "Measuring Organizational Readiness for Nursing Research Programs." *Western Journal of Nursing Research* 20(2):223–237. O(E)

Sommers, David G., and Ted L. Napier (1993) "Comparison of Amish and Non-Amish Farmers: A Diffusion/Farm-Structure Perspective." *Rural Sociology* 58(1):130–145. RS(E)

Soule, Sarah A. (1997) "The Student Divestment Movement in the United States and the Shantytown: Diffusion of a Protest Tactic." *Social Forces* 75:855–883. GS(E)

Soule, Sarah A. (1999) "The Diffusion of an Unsuccessful Innovation." *The Annals* 566:120–131. GS(N)

Soumerai, Stephen B., et al. (1998) "Effect of Local Medical Opinion Leaders on Quality Care for Acute Myocardial Infarction: A Randomized Controlled Trial." *JAMA* 279(17):1358–1363. PH(E)

Specter, Michael (2001, November 26) "The Phone Guy." *The New Yorker,* 62–72. O(N)

Speece, Mark, and Douglas MacLachlan (1995) "Application of a Multi-Generation Diffusion Model to Milk Container Technology." *Technological Forecasting and Social Change* 49:281–295. MR(E)

Speicher, S. A. Renee (1997) "Intraorganizational Diffusion of Communication Technology (Technology Diffusion, Innovation, Structuration Theory)." Ph.D. diss., University of Kansas, Lawrence. C(E)

Speilman, Andrew, and Michael D'Antonio (2001) *Mosquito: A Natural History of Our Most Persistent and Deadly Foe.* New York: Hyperion. PH(E)

Spender, J. C., and E. H. Kessler (1995) "Managing the Uncertainties of Innovation: Extending Thompson." *Human Relations* 48(1):35–56. MR(E)

Spicer, Edward H., ed., (1952) *Human Problems in Technological Change.* New York: Russell Sage Foundation. A(E)

Star, Shirley A., and H. G. Hughes (1950) "Report on an Education Campaign: The Cincinnati Plan for the United Nations." *American Journal of Sociology* 55:389–400.

Stark, Rodney (1997) *The Rise of Christianity: How the Obscure, Marginal Jesus Movement Became the Dominant Religious Force in the Western World in a Few Centuries.* New York: HarperCollins. O(E)

Steckler, Allan, Robert M. Goodman, K. R. McLeroy, S. Davis, and G. Koch (1992) "Measuring the Diffusion of Innovative Health Promotion Programs." *American Journal of Health Promotion* 6(3):214–224. PH(E)

Steenkamp, Jan-Benedict E. M., Frenkel ter Hofstede, and Michel Wedel (1999),"A Cross-National Investigation into the Individual and National Cultural Antecedents of Consumer Innovativeness." *Journal of Marketing* 63:55–69. MR(E)

Steffens, Paul R. (2002) "A Diffusion Model for Consumer Durable Goods Incorporating a Varying Mean Replacement Age." *Journal of Forecasting* 9:197–205. MR(E)

Steffensen, F. H., H. T. Sorensen, and F. Olsen (1999) "Diffusion of New Drugs in Danish General Practice." *Family Practice* 16(4):407–413. O(E)

Stoetzer, M.-W., and Alwin Mahler, eds., (1995) *Die Diffusion von Innovationen in der Telecommunikation*. Berlin: Springer. MR(N)

Stone, John T. (1952) *How Country Agricultural Agents Teach*. Mimeo bulletin, Agricultural Extension Service, Michigan State University, East Lansing. RS(E)

Strang, David, and Sarah A. Soule (1998) "Diffusion in Organizations and Social Movements: From Hybrid Corn to Poison Pills." *Annual Review of Sociology* 24:265–290. GS(E)

Strang, David, and Nancy Brandon Tuma (1993) "Spatial and Temporal Heterogeneity in Diffusion." *American Journal of Sociology* 99(3):614–619. GS(E)

Studlar, Donley T. (1999) "Diffusion of Tobacco Control in North America." *The Annals* 566:68–79. PH(E)

Sundqvist, Sanna, Kaisu Puumalainen, Lauri Frank, and Seppo Pitkanen (2002) "Forecasting Capability of Diffusion Models for Wireless Telecommunications." Unpublished paper, Telecom Business Research Center, Lappeenranta University of Technology, Lappeenranta, Finland. MR(E)

Sung, John F., et al. (1997) "Effects of Cancer Screening Intervention Conducted by Lay Health Workers Among Inner-City Women." *American Journal of Preventive Medicine* 13(1):51–57. PH(E)

Svenkerud, Peer J., Arvind Singhal, and Michael J. Papa (1998) "Diffusion of Innovation Theory and Effective Targeting of HIV/AIDS Programmes in Thailand." *Asian Journal of Communication* 8:11–30. C(E)

Talukadar, Debu, Karunakaran Sudhir, and Andrew Ainslie (2001) "Identifying Similarities in Diffusion Patterns Across Countries and Products: A Bayesian Variance Components Approach." *Marketing Science* 20:319–327. MR

Tanriverdi, Huseyin, and C. Suzanne Iacono (1999) "Diffusion of Telemedicine: A Knowledge Barrier Perspective." *Telemedicine Journal* 5(3):223–244. MR(E)

Tarde, Gabriel (1903/1969) *The Laws of Imitation, trans. by Elsie Clews Parsons*. New York: Holt; Chicago: University of Chicago Press. GS(E)

Teng, James T. C., Varun Grover, and Wolfgang Güttler (2002) "Information Technology Innovations: General Diffusion Patterns and Its Relationships to Innovation Characteristics." *IEEE Transactions on Engineering Management* 49(1):13–27. MR(E)

Tessaro, I. A., S. Taylor, L. Belton, M. K. Campbell, S. Benedict, K. Kelsey, and B. DeVellis (2000) "Adopting a Natural (Lay) Helpers Model of Change for Worksite Health Promotion for Women." *Health Education Research* 15(5):603–614. PH(E)

Thomas, William I., and Florian Znaniecki (1927) *The Polish Peasant in Europe and America.* New York: Knopf.

Thorlindsson, Thoralfur (1994) "Skipper Science: A Note on the Epistemology of Practice and the Nature of Expertise." *Sociological Quarterly* 35(2):329–345. GS(E)

Thurow, Roger (2002, July 26–28) "Could Just 10 Horsepower Be Enough to Free All the Women of Mali?" *The Wall Street Journal,* A1, A8.

Tichenor, Philip J., George A. Donohue, and Clarence N. Olien (1970) "Mass Media Flow and Differential Growth in Knowledge." *Public Opinion Quarterly* 34:159–170. C(E)

Tierney, John (2001, August 5) "The Makers of a New Electronic Game Decided to Let Kids Do Their Marketing for Them." *The New York Times Magazine,* 1–7.

Tolney, Stewart E. (1995) "The Spatial Diffusion of Fertility: A Cross-Sectional Analysis of Countries in the American South, 1940." *American Sociological Review* 60:299–308. GS(E)

Tornatzky, Louis G., and Katherine J. Klein (1982) "Innovation Characteristics and Adoption-Implementation: A Meta-Analysis of Findings." *IEEE Transactions on Engineering Management* EM-29(1):28–45. P(N)

Trevino, Linda Klebe, Jane Webster, and Eric W. Stein (2000) "Making Connections: Complementary Influences on Communication Media Choices, Attitudes, and Uses." *Organizational Science* 11:163–182. MR(E)

Tuludhar, Jayanti, Peter J. Donaldson, and Jeanne Noble (1998) "The Introduction of Norplant Implants in Indonesia." *Studies in Family Planning* 29(3):291–299. O(E)

Turner, Bonnie J., Garth W. Martin, and John A. Cunningham (1998) "The Effectiveness of Demonstrations in Disseminating Research-Based Counseling Programs." *Science Communication* 19(4):349–365. O(E)

Tyre, Marcie J., and Wanda J. Orlikowski (1994) "Windows of Opportunity: Temporal Patterns of Technological Adaptation in Organizations." *Organization Science* 5(1):98–118. MR(E)

Urban, Glen L., and Eric Von Hippel (1988) "Lead User Analysis for the Development of New Industrial Products." *Management Science* 74(5):569–582. MR(E)

Urban, Glen L., Bruce D. Wenberg, and John R. Hauser (1996) "Premarket Forecasting of Really New Products." *Journal of Marketing* 60:47–60. MR(E)

Valente, Thomas W. (1993) "Diffusion of Innovation and Policy Decision-Making." *Journal of Communication* 43(1):30–41. PH(E)

Valente, Thomas W. (1995) *Network Models of the Diffusion of Innovations.* Creskill, N.J.: Hampton Press. PH(E)

Valente, Thomas W. (1996) "Social Network Thresholds in the Diffusion of Innovations." *Social Networks* 18:69–89. PH(E)

Valente, Thomas W. (2003, in press), "Models and Methods for Studying the Diffusion of Innovations." In P. Carrington, Stanley Wasserman, and J. Scott, eds., *Recent Advances in Network Analysis.* PH(E)

Valente, Thomas W., and Rebecca L. Davis (1999) "Accelerating the Diffusion of Innovations Using Opinion Leaders." *The Annals* 566:55–67. PH(E)

Valente, Thomas W., and Robert K. Foreman (1998) "Integration and Radiality: Measuring the Extent of an Individual's Connectedness and Reachability in a Network." *Social Networks* 20:89–109. PH(E)

Valente, Thomas W., Robert K. Foreman, Benjamin Junge, and David Vlahov (1998) "Satellite Exchange in the Baltimore Needle-Exchange Program." *Public Health Reports* 113(suppl. 1):90–96. PH(E)

Valente, Thomas W., Beth Hoffman, Annamara Ritt-Olson, Kara Lichtman, and C. Anderson Johnson (2002) "Use of Network Analysis to Structure Health Promotion Programs." Unpublished paper, Department of Preventive Medicine, University of Southern California, Alhambra. PH(E)

Valente, Thomas W., and Everett M. Rogers (1995) "The Origins and Development of the Diffusion of Innovations Paradigm as an Example of Scientific Growth." *Science Communication* 16(3):238–269. PH(N)

Valente, Thomas W., and Walter P. Saba (1998) "Mass Media and Interpersonal Influence in a Reproductive Health Communication Campaign in Bolivia." *Communication Research* 25:96–124. PH(E)

Valente, Thomas W., and Walter P. Saba (2001) "Campaign Exposure and Interpersonal Communication Factors in Contraceptive Use in Bolivia." *Journal of Health Communication* 6:303–322. PH(E)

Valente, Thomas W., and David Vlahov (2001) "Selective Risk Taking Among Needle Exchange Participants in Baltimore: Implications for Supplemental Interventions." *American Journal of Public Health* 91:406–411. PH(E)

Valente, Thomas W., Susan Watkins, Miriam N. Jato, Ariane Van Der Straten, and Louis-Philippe Tsitsol (1997) "Social Network Associations with Contraceptive Use among Cameroonian Women in Voluntary Associations." *Social Science and Medicine* 45:677–687. PH(E)

Van de Ven, Andrew H. (1986) "Central Problems in the Management of Innovation." *Management Science* 32(5):590–607. MR(E)

Van de Ven, Andrew H., H. A. Angle, and M. Scott Poole, eds., (1989) *Research on the Management of Innovation: The Minnesota Studies.* New York: Ballinger/Harper and Row. MR(E)

Van de Ven, Andrew H., D. E. Polley, R. Garud, and S. Venkataramam (1999) *The Innovation Journey.* New York: Oxford University Press. MR(E)

Van de Ven, Andrew H., and Everett M. Rogers (1988) "Innovations and Organizations: Critical Perspectives." *Communication Research* 15(5):632–651. MR(N)

Van den Ban, A. W. (1963) "Hoe Vinden Nieuee Landbouwmethodeningand" (How a New Practice Is Introduced). *Landbouwvoorlichting* 20:227–239. RS(E)

Van den Bulte, Christophe, and Gary L. Lilien (1997) "Bias and Systematic Change in the Parameter Estimates of Macro-Level Diffusion Models." *Marketing Science* 16:338–353. MR(E)

Van den Bulte, Christophe, and Gary L. Lilien (2001) "Medical Innovation Revisited: Social Contagion Versus Marketing Effort." *American Journal of Sociology* 106:1409–1435. GS(E)

Vaughan, Peter W., Alleyne Regis, and Edwin St. Catherine (2000) "Effects of an Entertainment-Education Radio Soap Opera on Family Planning and HIV Prevention in St. Lucia." *International Family Planning Perspectives* 26(4):148–157. O(E)

Vaughan, Peter W., and Everett M. Rogers (2000) "A Staged Model of Communication Effects: Evidence from an Entertainment-Education Radio Soap Opera in Tanzania." *Journal of Health Communication* 5(3):203–227. O(E)

Viswanath, K., and John R. Finnegan (1996) "The Knowledge Gap Hypothesis: Twenty-Five Years Later." In Burt Berelson, ed., *Communication Yearbook 19*. Thousand Oaks, Calif.: Sage, 187–227. C(N)

Von Hippel, Eric (1976) "The Dominant Role of Users in the Scientific Instrument Innovation Process." *Research Policy* 5(3):212–239. MR(E)

Von Hippel, Eric (1982) "Get New Products." *Harvard Business Review* 60:117–122. MR(E)

Von Hippel, Eric (1988) *The Sources of Innovation*. New York: Oxford University Press. MR(E)

Von Hippel, Eric, Stephan Thombe, and Mary Sonnack (1999) "Creating Breakthroughs at 3M." *Harvard Business Review* 77:3–9. MR(E)

Walker, Jack L. (1966) "The Diffusion of Innovations Among the American States." *American Political Science Review* 63:880–899. PS(E)

Walker, Jack L. (1971) "Innovation in State Policies." In Herbert Jacob and Kenneth N. Vines, eds., *Politics in the American States: A Comparative Analysis*. Boston: Little Brown. PS(E)

Walker, Jack L. (1973) "Comment: Problems in Research on the Diffusion Policy Innovations." *American Political Science Review* 67:1186–1191. PS(N)

Walker, Jack L. (1976) "Setting the Agenda in the U.S. Senate: A Theory of Problem Selection." Discussion Paper 94, Institute of Public Policy Studies, University of Michigan, Ann Arbor. PS(N)

Walker, Jack L. (1977) "Setting the Agenda in the U.S. Senate: A Theory of Problem Selection." *British Journal of Political Science* 7:423–445. PS(N)

Walsh, Steven T., and Jonathan D. Linton (2000) "Infrastructure for Emergent Industries Based on Discontinuous Innovations." *Engineering Management Journal* 12(2):23–31. MR(E)

Weber, Max (1958) *The Protestant Ethic and the Spirit of Capitalism.* New York: Scribner's.

Wei, Ran (2001) "From Luxury to Utility: A Longitudinal Analysis of Cell Phone Laggards." *Journalism & Mass Communication Quarterly* 78(4):702–719. C(E)

Wei, Ran, and Louis Leung (1998) "Owning and Using New Media Technology as Predictors of Quality of Life." *Telematics and Informatics* 15:237–251. C(E)

Weimann, Gabriel (1994) *The Influentials: People Who Influence People.* Albany, N.Y.: State University of New York Press. GS(E)

Weinstein, Neil D., and Peter M. Sandman (2002) "The Precaution Adoption Process Model and Its Application." In Ralph J. DiClemente, Richard A. Cosby, and Michelle C. Kepler, eds., *Emerging Theories in Health Promotion Practice and Research: Strategies for Improving Public Health.* San Francisco, Jossey-Bass, 16–39. P(E)

Wejnert, Barbara (2001) "Integrating Models of the Diffusion of Innovations." *Annual Review of Sociology* 28:261–292. GS(N)

Wellin, Edward (1955) "Water Boiling in a Peruvian Town." In Benjamin D. Paul, ed., *Health, Culture and Community.* New York: Russell Sage Foundation. A(E)

Wellman, Barry (1985) "Network Analysis: Some Basic Principles." In Randal Collins, ed., *Sociological Theory.* San Francisco, Jossey-Bass.

Wells, J. G., and D. K. Anderson (1997) "Learners in a Telecommunications Course: Adoption, Diffusion, and Stages of Concern." *Journal of Research on Computing in Education* 30(1):83–105. E(E)

Westphal, James D., Ranjay Gulati, and Stephen M. Shortell (1997) "Customization or Conformity? An Institutional and Network Perspective on the Content and Consequences of TOM Adoption." *Administrative Science Quarterly* 42:366–394. MR(E)

White, Marilyn Domas (2001) "Diffusion of an Innovation: Digital Reference Service in Carnegie Foundation Master's (Comprehensive) Academic Institution Libraries." *Journal of Academic Librarianship* 27(3):173–187. O(E)

Whyte, William H., Jr. (1954) "The Web of Word of Mouth." *Fortune* 50:140–143, 204–212.

Wiebe, Gerhard D. (1952) "Merchandising Commodities and Citizenship on Television." *Public Opinion Quarterly* 15:679–691.

Wiebe, R. (1992) *Diffusion von Telekommunikation: Problem der Kritischen Masse.* Weisbaden, Germany: Gabler. O(E)

Wiebe, R. (1995) "Systemguter und klassische Diffusiontheorie: Elemente einer Diffusiontheorie Kritische Masse-Systeme." In M.-W. Stoetzer and Alwin Mahler, eds., *Die Diffusion von Innovationen in der Telekommunikation.* Berlin: Springer. MR(E)

Wildemuth, Barbara M. (1992) "An Empirically Grounded Model of the Adoption of Intellectual Technologies." *Journal of the American Society for Information Science* 43(3):210–224. O(E)

Williams, Frederick R., Ronald E. Rice, and Everett M. Rogers (1988) *Research Methods and the New Media.* New York: Free Press. C(N)

Wiseman, Paul (2002, June 19) "China Thrown Off Balance as Boys Outnumber Girls." *USA Today* 1–2.

Wissler, Clark (1914) "The Influence of the Horse in the Development of Plains Culture." *American Anthropologist* 16:1–25. A(E)

Wissler, Clark,(1923) *Man and Culture.* New York: Thomas Y. Crowell. A(E)

Witt, U. (1997) "Lock-In vs. Critical Mass: Industrial Change under Network Externalities." *International Journal of Industrial Organization* 15:753–773. O(E)

Wolf, Steven A., and Spencer D. Wood (1997) "Precision Farming: Environmental Legitimation, Commodification of Information, and Industrial Coordination." *Rural Sociology* 62(2):180–206. RS(E)

Wolfe, R. A. (1994) "Organizational Innovation: Review, Critique, and Suggested Research Directions." *Journal of Management Studies* 31:405–431. MR(N)

Wolfeiler, Dan (1998) "Community Organizing and Community Building Among Gay and Bisexual Men: The STOP AIDS Project." In Meredith Minkler, ed., *Community Organizing and Community Building for Health.* New Brunswick, N.J.: Rutgers University Press, 230–240. PH(E)

Wollons, Roberta, ed., (2000) *Kindergartens and Cultures: The Global Diffusion of an Idea.* New Haven, Conn.: Yale University Press. O(E)

Wollons, Roberta (2000b) "On the International Diffusion, Politics, and Transformation of the Kindergarten." In Roberta Wollons, ed., *Kindergartens and Cultures: The Global Diffusion of an Idea,* New Haven, Conn.: Yale University Press, 1–15. O(E)

Wright, M., C. Upitchard, and T. Lewis (1997) "A Validation of the Bass New Product Diffusion Model in New Zealand." *Marketing Bulletin* 8:15–29. MR(E)

Zaltman, Gerald, Robert Duncan, and Jonny Holbek (1973) *Innovations and Organizations.* New York: John Wiley and Sons. MR(E)

Zekeri, Andrew (1994) "Adoption of Economic Development Strategies in

Small Towns and Rural Areas: Effects of Past Community Action." *Journal of Rural Studies* 10(2):185–195. RS(E)

Zhou, Jonathan, and Zhou He (2001) "Adoption and Use of the Internet Among Adult Audiences in Mainland China." Unpublished paper, City University of Hong Kong. C(E)

Zhou, Xueguang (1993) "Occupational Power, State Capacities, and Diffusion of Licensing in the American States, 1890 to 1950." *American Sociological Review* 58:536–552. GS(E)

NAME INDEX

SUBJECT INDEX

ABOUT THE AUTHOR

Dr. Everett M. Rogers is Distinguished Professor in the Department of Communication and Journalism at the University of New Mexico (UNM), where he teaches and conducts research on the diffusion of innovations. He also holds courtesy appointments in the UNM Center on Alcoholism and Substance Abuse Addictions, where he conducts research on preventing drunk driving, and in the UNM Center for Prevention Research, where he conducts research on the sustainability of public health innovations. Rogers also is currently involved in research projects on bridging the digital divide in New Mexico and on how Indian audiences give meaning to health content in Hollywood soap operas such as *The Bold and the Beautiful*. Currently in his forty-fifth year of university teaching, Rogers has taught at Ohio State University, Michigan State University, the University of Michigan, Stanford University, and the University of Southern California, and at the National University of Colombia (Bogotá), the University of Paris, the University of Bayreuth (Germany), and Nanyang Technological University (Singapore).

The four previous editions of *Diffusion of Innovations* have received various awards. In 1990, the Institute for Scientific Information designated *Diffusion of Innovations* as a "Citation Classic" on the basis of the large number of citations (approximately 7,000) that it received in articles published in social science journals. This book was selected by *Inc.* magazine in 1996 as one of the ten classic books in business and in 2000 was designated as a "Significant Journalism and Communication Book of the Twentieth Century" by *Journalism and Mass Communication Quarterly*. It was also awarded the first Fellows Book Award in the Field of Communication by the International Communication Association's fellows in 2000.